EXPERIMENTAL ECONOMICS

Experimental Economics

Douglas D. Davis

Charles A. Holt

PRINCETON UNIVERSITY PRESS

PRINCETON, NEW JERSEY

Copyright © 1993 by Princeton University Press
Published by Princeton University Press
41 William Street, Princeton, New Jersey 08540
In the United Kingdom: Princeton University Press,
Chichester, West Sussex

Library of Congress Cataloging-in-Publication Data

Davis, Douglas D., 1957–
    Experimental economics / Douglas D. Davis, Charles A. Holt.
      p.   cm.
    Includes bibliographical references and index.
    ISBN 0–691–04317–5
      1. Economics—Methodology.   I. Holt, Charles A., 1948–   .
II. Title.
HB131.D38   1992
330 ′ .072—dc20   92–27662
                                               CIP

This book has been composed in Times-Roman typeface.

The publisher would like to acknowledge Douglas D. Davis and
Charles A. Holt for providing the camera-ready copy from which this
book was printed.

Princeton University Press books are printed on acid-free paper, and
meet the guidelines for permanence and durability of the Committee on
Production Guidelines for Book Longevity of the Council on Library
Resources.

Printed in the United States of America

10 9 8 7 6 5 4 3 2 1

Contents

6   Public Goods, Externalities, and Voting   317

7   Asymmetric Information   381

Preface

This book provides a comprehensive treatment of the major areas of experimental economics. Although we present some new material, the emphasis is on organizing and evaluating existing results. The book can serve both as a teaching device and as an introduction to laboratory methods for professional economists who wish to find out about this relatively new area of research. Moreover, methodological and procedural issues are covered in detail, and there are a number of instructional appendices.

The book can be used as an anchoring device for a graduate course, which would be supplemented with journal articles, working papers, and detailed surveys. A topics course for advanced undergraduates can be structured around the first four chapters, selected readings from later chapters, and less technical published papers.

Acknowledgments

Much of what we understand about how people behave in experiments can be traced to our thesis advisers, Arlington Williams (for Davis) and the late Morris DeGroot (for Holt), and to our coauthors on related research: Jordi Brandts, Catherine Eckel, Glenn Harrison, Loren Langen, Roger Sherman, and Anne Villamil. Our views have been further refined by discussions with Charles Plott, Alvin Roth, and Vernon Smith, and with our current and former colleagues at the Autonomous University of Barcelona, University of Minnesota, University of Virginia, and Virginia Commonwealth University. In addition, we are indebted to Catherine Eckel, Robert Forsythe, Glenn Harrison, Ronald Harstad, Elizabeth Hoffman, John Kagel, Ed Olsen, Steve Peterson, Roger Sherman, Vernon Smith, and James Walker for detailed comments on one or more chapters. We received useful suggestions from participants in the Public Economics Workshop at the University of Virginia and from participants in seminars at Pompeu Fabra University in Barcelona, the Autonomous Technological Institute of Mexico (ITAM), the University of Alicante, the 1991 Economic Science Meetings in Tucson, Arizona, and the 1991 Symposium of Economic Analysis in Barcelona. We wish to thank Lisa Anderson, Leonce Bargeron, Kurt Fisher, Anne Gulati, and Maria Mabry for research assistance, and Mar Martinez Gongora and Zanne Macdonald for other suggestions. Finally, we should recognize that our fathers are both professors, and that we would not have finished this project without the support and encouragement of our families.

EXPERIMENTAL ECONOMICS

CHAPTER 1

INTRODUCTION AND OVERVIEW

1.1 Introduction

As with most science, economics is observational; economic theories are devised to explain market activity. Economists have developed an impressive and technically sophisticated array of models, but the capacity to evaluate their predictive content has lagged. Traditionally, economic theories have been evaluated with statistical data from existing "natural" markets. Although econometricians are sometimes able to untangle the effects of interrelated variables of interest, natural data often fail to allow "critical tests" of theoretical propositions, because distinguishing historical circumstances occur only by chance. Moreover, even when such circumstances occur, they are usually surrounded by a host of confounding extraneous factors. These problems have become more severe as models have become more precise and intricate. In game theory, for example, predictions are often based on very subtle behavioral assumptions for which there is little practical possibility of obtaining evidence from naturally occurring markets.

As a consequence of these data problems, economists have often been forced to evaluate theories on the basis of plausibility, or on intrinsic factors such as elegance and internal consistency. The contrast between the confidence economists place in precise economic models and the apparent chaos of natural data can be supremely frustrating to scientists in other fields. Biologist Paul Ehrlich, for example, comments: "The trouble is that economists are trained in ways that make them utterly clueless about the way the world works. Economists think that the world works by magic."[1]

Other observational sciences have overcome the obstacles inherent in the use of naturally occurring data by systematically collecting data in controlled, laboratory conditions. Fundamental propositions of astronomy, for example, are founded on propositions from particle physics, which have been painstakingly evaluated in the laboratory. Although the notion is somewhat novel in economics, there is no inherent reason why relevant economic data cannot also be obtained from laboratory experiments.[2]

The systematic evaluation of economic theories under controlled laboratory conditions is a relatively recent development. Although the theoretical analysis of market structures was initiated in the late 1700s and early 1800s by the path-breaking insights of Adam Smith and Augustine Cournot, the first market experiments did not occur until the mid-twentieth century. Despite this late start, the use of experimental methods to evaluate economic propositions has become increasingly widespread in the last twenty years and has come to provide an important foundation for bridging the gap between economic theory and observation. Although no panacea, laboratory techniques have the important advantages of imposing professional responsibility on data collection, and of allowing more direct tests of behavioral assumptions. Given the ever-growing intricacy of economic models, we believe that economics will increasingly become an experimental science.[3]

This monograph reviews the principal contributions of experimental research to economics. We also attempt to provide some perspective on the general usefulness of laboratory methods in economics. As with any new mode of analysis, experimental research in economics is surrounded by a series of methodological controversies. Therefore, procedural and design issues that are necessary for effective experimentation are covered in detail. Discussion of these issues also helps to frame some of the ongoing debates.

This first chapter is intended to serve as an introduction to the remainder of the book, and as such it covers a variety of preliminary issues. We begin the discussion with a brief history of economics experiments in section 1.2, followed by a

---

[1] Personal communication with the authors.

[2] The general perception is that economics is not an experimental science and, consequently, that it is somewhat speculative. The *Encyclopedia Britannica* (1991, p. 395) presents this view: "Economists are sometimes confronted with the charge that their discipline is not a science. Human behavior, it is said, cannot be analyzed with the same objectivity as the behavior of atoms and molecules. Value judgements, philosophical preconceptions, and ideological biases must interfere with the attempt to derive conclusions that are independent of the particular economist espousing them. Moreover, there is no laboratory in which economists can test their hypotheses." (This quotation was suggested to us by Hinkelmann, 1990.)

[3] Plott (1991) elaborates on this point.

description of a simple market experiment in section 1.3. The three subsequent sections address methodological and procedural issues: Section 1.4 discusses advantages and limitations of laboratory methods, section 1.5 considers various objectives of laboratory research, and section 1.6 reviews some desirable methods and procedures. The final two sections are written to give the reader a sense of this book's organization. One of the most prominent lessons of laboratory research is the importance of trading rules and institutions to market outcomes. Much of our discussion revolves around the details of alternative trading institutions. Consequently, section 1.7 categorizes some commonly used institutional arrangements. Section 1.8 previews the remaining chapters. The chapter also contains an appendix, which consists of two parts: The first part contains instructions for a simple "double-auction" market, while the second part contains a detailed list of tasks to be completed in setting up and administering a market experiment. This checklist serves as a primer on how to conduct an experiment; it provides a practical, step-by-step implementation of the general procedural recommendations that are discussed earlier in the chapter.

Prior to proceeding, we would like encourage both the new student and the experienced experimentalist to read this first chapter carefully. It introduces important procedural and design considerations, and it provides a structure for organizing subsequent insights.

1.2 A Brief History of Experimental Economics

In the late 1940s and early 1950s, a number of economists independently became interested in the notion that laboratory methods could be useful in economics. Early interests ranged widely, and the literature evolved in three distinct directions. At one extreme, Edward Chamberlin (1948) presented subjects with a streamlined version of a natural market. The ensuing literature on *market experiments* focused on the predictions of neoclassical price theory. A second strand of experimental literature grew out of interest in testing the behavioral implications of noncooperative game theory. These *game experiments* were conducted in environments that less closely resembled natural markets. Payoffs, for example, were often given in a tabular (normal) form that suppresses much of the cost and demand structure of an economic market but facilitates the calculation of game-theoretic equilibrium outcomes. A third series of *individual decision-making experiments* focused on yet simpler environments, where the only uncertainty is due to exogenous random events, as opposed to the decisions of other agents. Interest in individual decision-making experiments grew from a desire to examine the behavioral content of the axioms of expected utility theory. Although the lines separating these literatures have tended to fade somewhat over time, it is useful for purposes of perspective to consider them separately.

Market Experiments

Chamberlin's *The Theory of Monopolistic Competition (A Re-orientation of the Theory of Value)*, first published in 1933, was motivated by the apparent failure of markets to perform adequately during the Depression. Chamberlin believed that certain predictions of his theories could be tested (at least heuristically) in a simple market environment, using only graduate students as economic agents.

Chamberlin reported the first market experiment in 1948. He *induced* the demand and cost structure in this market by dealing a deck of cards, marked with values and costs, to student subjects. Through trading, sellers could earn the difference between the cost they were dealt and the contract price they negotiated. Similarly, buyers could earn the difference between the value they were dealt and their negotiated contract price. Earnings in Chamberlin's experiment were hypothetical, but to the extent his students were motivated by hypothetical earnings, this process creates a very specific market structure. A student receiving a seller card with a cost of $1.00, for example, would have a perfectly inelastic supply function with a "step" at $1.00. This student would be willing to supply one unit at any price over $1.00. Similarly, a student receiving a buyer card with a value of $2.00 would have a perfectly inelastic demand at any price below $2.00.

Sellers and buyers received different costs and values, so the individual supply and demand functions had the same rectangular shapes, but with steps at differing heights. Under these conditions a market supply function is generated by ranking individual costs from lowest to highest and then summing horizontally across the sellers. Similarly, a market demand function is generated by ranking individual valuations from highest to lowest and summing across the buyers. Competitive price and quantity predictions follow from the intersection of market supply and demand curves.

Trading in these markets was both unregulated and essentially unstructured. Students were permitted to circulate freely around the classroom to negotiate with others in a decentralized manner. Despite this "competitive" structure, Chamberlin concluded that outcomes systematically deviated from competitive predictions. In particular, he noted that the transactions quantity was greater than the quantity determined by the intersection of supply and demand.

Chamberlin's results were initially ignored in the literature. In fact, Chamberlin himself all but ignored them.[4] Given the novelty of the laboratory method, this is perhaps not surprising. But Vernon Smith, who had participated in Chamberlin's initial experiment as a Harvard graduate student, became intrigued by the method. He felt that Chamberlin's interpretations of the results were misleading in a way that could be demonstrated in a classroom market. Smith conjectured that

---

[4] The 1948 paper was mentioned only briefly in a short footnote in the eighth edition of *The Theory of Monopolistic Competition*.

the decentralized trading that occurred as students wandered around the room was not the appropriate institutional setting for testing the received theories of perfect competition. As an alternative, Smith (1962, 1964) devised a laboratory "double auction" institution in which all bids, offers, and transactions prices are public information. He demonstrated that such markets could converge to efficient, competitive outcomes, even with a small number of traders who initially knew nothing about market conditions.

Although Smith's support for the predictions of competitive price theory generated little more initial interest among economists than did Chamberlin's rejections, Smith began to study the effects of changes in trading institutions on market outcomes. Subsequent work along these lines has focused on the robustness of competitive price theory predictions to institutional and structural alterations.[5]

Game Experiments

A second sequence of experimental studies was produced in the 1950s and 1960s by psychologists, game-theorists, and business-school economists, most of whom were initially interested in behavior in the context of the well-known "prisoner's dilemma," apparently first articulated by Tucker (1950).[6] The problem is as follows: Suppose that two alleged partners in crime, prisoner A and prisoner B, are placed in private rooms and are given the opportunity to confess. If only one of them confesses and turns state's evidence, the other receives a seven-year sentence, and the prisoner who confesses only serves one year as an accessory. If both confess, however, they each serve five-year terms. If neither confesses, each receives a maximum two-year penalty for a lesser crime. In matrix form, these choices are represented in figure 1.1, where the sentences are shown as negative numbers since they represent time lost. All boldfaced entries in the figure pertain to prisoner B. The ordered pair of numbers in each box corresponds to the sentences for prisoners A and B, respectively. For example, when B confesses and A does not, the payoff entry (–7, **–1**) indicates that the sentences are seven years for A and one year for B.

This game presents an obvious problem. Both prisoners would be better off if neither confessed, but each, aware of each other's incentives to confess in any case, "should" confess. Sociologists and social psychologists, initially unconvinced

---

[5] A separate line of experimentation began in the mid-1970s when Charles Plott, who had previously been on the faculty with Vernon Smith at Purdue University, realized that Smith's procedures could be adapted to create public goods and committee voting processes in the laboratory. The subsequent political science and economics literature on voting experiments is surveyed in McKelvey and Ordeshook (1990).

[6] See Roth (1988) for a discussion of how Tucker came to publish his note on the prisoner's dilemma.

Prisoner B

		Confess	Don't Confess
	Confess	(–5, –5)	(–1, –7)
Prisoner A	Don't Confess	(–7, –1)	(–2, –2)

Figure 1.1 The Prisoner's Dilemma

that humans would reason themselves to a jointly undesirable outcome, initiated a voluminous literature examining the determinants of cooperation and defection when subjects make simultaneous decisions in prisoner's-dilemma experiments.[7]

The standard duopoly pricing problem is an immediate application of the prisoner's dilemma: although collusion would make each duopolist better off than competition, each seller has an incentive to defect from a cartel. For this reason, the psychologists' work on the prisoner's dilemma was paralleled by classic studies of cooperation and competition in oligopoly situations by Sauerman and Selten (1959), Siegel and Fouraker (1960), and Fouraker and Siegel (1963). As a consequence, economists became interested in oligopoly games that were motivated by more complex market environments (e.g., Dolbear et al., 1968, and Friedman, 1963, 1967, and 1969). In particular, the interdisciplinary approach at graduate business schools such as Carnegie-Mellon's Graduate School of Industrial Administration led to a series of experimental papers, including an early survey paper (Cyert and Lave, 1965) and an experimental thesis on various aspects of oligopoly behavior (Sherman, 1966). Much of the more recent literature pertains to the predictions of increasingly complex applications of game theory, but always in environments that are simple and well specified enough so that the implications of the theory can be derived explicitly.

Individual-Choice Experiments

A third branch of literature focused on individual behavior in simple situations in which strategic behavior is unnecessary and individuals need only optimize.

---

[7] Coleman (1983) lists some 1,500 experimental investigations of the prisoner's-dilemma game. Particularly insightful early studies include Rapoport and Chammah (1965) and Lave (1962, 1965).

These experiments were generally designed to evaluate tenets of the basic theory of choice under uncertainty, as formulated by von Neumann and Morgenstern (1947) and Savage (1954).

In experiments of this type, subjects must choose between uncertain prospects or "lotteries." A lottery is simply a probability distribution over prizes, for example, $2.00 if heads and $1.00 if tails. A subject who makes a choice between two lotteries decides which lottery will be used to determine (in a random manner) the subject's earnings. Many of these experiments are designed to produce clean counter-examples to basic axioms of expected utility theory. For example, consider the controversial "independence axiom." Informally, this axiom states that the choice between two lotteries, X and Y, is independent of the presence or absence of a common (and hence "irrelevant") lottery Z. This axiom could be tested by presenting participants with two lotteries, X and Y. If participants indicate a preference for X over Y, the experimenter could subsequently determine whether a 50/50 chance of X and some third lottery Z is preferred to a 50/50 chance of Y and Z. Numerous, consistent violations of this axiom have been observed through questioning of this sort.[8] This research has generated a lively debate and has led to efforts to devise a more general decision theory that is not contradicted by observed responses.

Not all individual decision-making problems involve expected-utility theory. May (1954), for example, systematically elicited intransitive choices over a series of riskless alternatives. Other prominent examples, to be discussed later in the text, include a series of experiments designed to evaluate the rationality of subjects' forecasts of market prices (Williams, 1987) and tests of the behavioral content of optimal stopping rules in sequential search problems (Schotter and Braunstein, 1981). Experiments testing Slutsky-Hicks consumption theory have been carried out with humans (Battalio et al., 1973) and rats (Kagel et al., 1975). Incentives for rats were denominated in terms of the number of food pellets they received for a given number of lever presses. Some rat subjects exhibited a backward-bending labor supply curve; an increase in the wage resulted in fewer lever presses.

1.3 A Simple Design for a Market Experiment

Before discussing procedures and different kinds of experiments, it is useful to present a concrete example of an experiment. For simplicity, we consider a market experiment. We first discuss a market design, or the supply and demand arrays induced in a specific market. Subsequently, we discuss the empirical consequences of a variety of theoretic predictions in this design and then report the

---

[8] These "Allais paradoxes" are discussed in chapter 8.

results of a short market session. The market involves six buyers, denoted B1 . . . B6, and six sellers, denoted S1 . . . S6. Each agent may make a maximum of two trades. In each trade, sellers earn an amount equal to the difference between the trading price and their cost for the unit. Conversely, buyers earn the difference between their unit value and the trading price. In this way, a unit value represents a maximum willingness to pay for a unit, and a unit cost is a minimum willingness to accept.

Table 1.1 Parameters for a Laboratory Market

Buyers' Values			Sellers' Costs		
Buyer	Unit 1	Unit 2	Seller	Unit 1	Unit 2
B1	1.40	1.40	S1	1.30	1.40
B2	1.50	1.30	S2	1.20	1.50
B3	1.60	1.20	S3	1.10	1.60
B4	1.70	1.10	S4	1.00	1.70
B5	1.80	1.00	S5	.90	1.80
B6	1.90	.90	S6	.80	1.30

Individual cost and valuation arrays for sellers and buyers are given in table 1.1. Each buyer has a high-value unit and a low-value unit (except for B1, who has constant values). Providing buyers with multiple units but restricting them to purchase the highest-valued unit first implements an assumption that individual demand is downward sloping. Horizontally summing across individual demands generates the downward-sloping market demand schedule illustrated in figure 1.2. Note, for example, that the highest value in table 1.1 is $1.90 for B6. This generates the highest step on the left side of the demand function in figure 1.2. The labels on the steps in the figure indicate the identity of the buyer with a value at that step. Symmetrically, sellers in table 1.1 each have a low-cost unit and a high-cost unit. Requiring sellers to sell the lower-cost unit first induces upward-sloping individual supply functions. Summing across individual supplies creates the market supply schedule illustrated in figure 1.2.

It is clear from figure 1.2 that the predicted *competitive price* is between $1.30 and $1.40, and the predicted *competitive quantity* is 7. A third measure of market performance, *surplus*, is generated via trading, as buyers and sellers execute contracts on mutually beneficial terms. If B3 and S6 strike a contract for their first

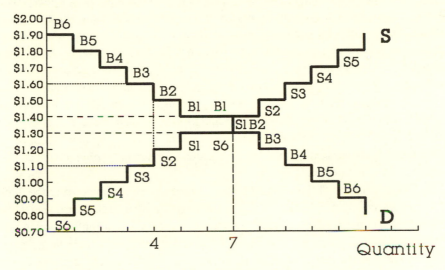

Figure 1.2 Supply and Demand Structure for a Market Experiment

units, then the surplus created is $.80 ($1.60 – $.80). The maximum possible surplus that can be extracted from trade is $3.70, which is the area between the supply and demand curves to the left of their intersection. These predictions are summarized in the left-most column of table 1.2.

Efficiency, measured as the percentage of the maximum possible surplus extracted, is shown in the fourth row of the table. Competitive price theory predicts (in the absence of externalities and other imperfections) that trading maximizes possible gains from exchange, and thus, predicted efficiency for the competitive theory is 100 percent.[9] Finally, the available surplus could be distributed in a variety of ways, depending on the contracts made in the sequence of trades. Suppose B3 and S6 strike the contract as just mentioned for a price of $1.30. At this price, $.30 of the created surplus goes to B3 ($1.60 – $1.30), while $.50 of the surplus goes to S6 ($1.30 – $.80). The distribution of this surplus would be just reversed if the contract was struck at a price of $1.10. Under competitive conditions, the surplus should be distributed roughly equally among buyers and sellers in this design. If prices were exactly in the middle of the competitive range, then 50 percent of the surplus would go to the buyers and 50 percent to the sellers. As indicated by the "~" marks in the bottom two entries in the Perfect Competition

---

[9] Some aspects of the efficiency concept are discussed in section 3.2 of chapter 3.

column, however, deviations from the 50/50 split are consistent with a competitive outcome, due to the range of competitive prices in this design.

To evaluate the results of an experiment, it is useful to consider some alternative theories. If students in an economics class are given the value and cost information in table 1.1 (but not the representation in figure 1.2) and are asked to provide a theory that predicts the price outcomes for double-auction trading, they commonly suggest procedures that involve calculating means or medians of values and costs. If students are then shown figure 1.2 and asked to suggest alternatives to the theory of perfect competition, the suggestions are often couched in terms of maximization of one form or another. Perhaps the three most frequently suggested theories are (a) maximization of combined sellers' profits, (b) maximization of combined buyers' earnings, and (c) maximization of the number of units that can be traded at no loss to either party.[10]

The predictions of these three alternative theories are summarized in the three columns on the right side of table 1.2. Consider the predictions listed under the Monopoly column in the table. Assuming that units sell at a uniform price, the profit-maximizing monopoly price is $1.60, and four units will trade in a period. This yields a total revenue of $6.40 (four times $1.60). The least expensive way of producing four units is to use the "first units" of sellers S3-S6, for a total cost of $3.80 ($0.80 + $0.90 + $1.00 + $1.10). The resulting profit is the difference between revenue and cost, which is $2.60.[11] Buyers' surplus at the monopoly price is only $0.60 ($0.30 for B6, $0.20 for B5, and $0.10 for B4). Total surplus is the sum of sellers' profits and buyers' surplus; this sum is $3.20, which is 87 percent of the maximum possible gains from trade ($3.70) that could be extracted from the market. Sellers will earn roughly 81 percent of that surplus (or the area between $1.60 and the supply curve for the first four units in figure 1.2).[12] The symmetric predictions of buyer surplus maximization are summarized in the monopsony column of table 1.2. Finally, consider quantity maximization as a predictor. From a reexamination of table 1.1 it is clear that this design has the interesting feature that a maximum of twelve profitable trades can be made in a period, if all trades take

---

[10] In our experience, economics students offer these theories more frequently than the (surplus-maximizing) model of perfect competition, which appears in all of their textbooks.

[11] It can be verified that this is the monopoly price by constructing a marginal revenue curve. Alternatively, consider profits at nearby prices: Raising the price to $1.70 decreases sales to three units and profits to $2.40. Lowering the price to $1.50 increases sales to five units, but profits fall to $2.50. Other prices are even less profitable.

[12] An even more profitable theory of seller profit maximization is that sellers perfectly price discriminate by selling one unit at $1.90, one unit at $1.80, etc. In this case, seven units trade, 100 percent efficiency is extracted, and all earnings go to sellers. A symmetric, cost-discrimination theory of buyer earnings maximization is also possible. These theories are left out of table 1.2 for ease of presentation.

place at different prices.[13] In each trade, a buyer and seller will negotiate over the ten-cent difference between supply and demand steps, so there is no point prediction about the price and surplus distribution. Each trade generates a ten-cent surplus, so the total surplus is only $1.20, or about 32 percent of the maximum possible surplus. In order for twelve units to be traded, prices will be about as dispersed as individuals' values and costs, as indicated by the range of ".80 to 1.90" in the right-hand column of the table.

Table 1.2 Properties of Alternative Market Outcomes

	Perfect Competition	Monopoly	Monopsony	Quantity Maximization
Price	1.30 to 1.40	1.60	1.10	.80 to 1.90
Quantity	7	4	4	12
Surplus	3.70	3.20	3.20	1.20
Efficiency	100%	87%	87%	32%
Buyers' Surplus	~50%	19%	81%	–
Sellers' Surplus	~50%	81%	19%	–

We conducted a short market session using twelve student participants and the parameters summarized in table 1.1.[14] The session consisted of two "trading periods." At the beginning of each period, the twelve participants were each privately assigned one of the cost or valuation schedules listed in table 1.1. Then they were given ten minutes to negotiate trades according to double-auction trading rules mentioned above: sellers could call out offer prices, which could be accepted by any buyer, and buyers could call out bid prices, which could be accepted by any seller. (The instructions used for this experiment are reproduced in appendix A1.1.) The transactions prices for the first period are listed below in temporal order, with prices in the competitive range underlined.

---

[13] Let S_{ij} denote the jth unit of seller S_i, etc. Then twelve profitable trades can occur if they take place in the following order: S_{11} trades with B_{11}, B_{21} with S_{12}, S_{21} with B_{22}, S_{22} with B_{31}, S_{31} with B_{32}, S_{32} with B_{41}, S_{41} with B_{42}, S_{42} with B_{51}, S_{51} with B_{52}, S_{52} with B_{61}, S_{61} with B_{62}, and finally S_{62} with B_{12}.

[14] Participants were fourth-year economics majors at the University of Virginia, and they were recruited from a small seminar class. None of the subjects had previously participated in a laboratory market. The session was conducted orally, with all prices recorded on the blackboard. Earnings were paid in cash at the end of two periods.

Period 1: $1.60, 1.50, 1.50, <u>1.35</u>, 1.25, <u>1.39</u>, <u>1.40</u>.

Participants calculated their earnings at the end of the first period, and then the market was opened for a second period of trading, which only lasted seven minutes. The transactions prices for the second period are:

Period 2: $<u>1.35</u>, <u>1.35</u>, <u>1.40</u>, <u>1.35</u>, <u>1.40</u>, <u>1.40</u>, <u>1.35</u>.

Thus, by the second period, outcomes are entirely consistent with competitive predictions: All transactions were in the competitive price range, and seven units sold. The market was 100 percent efficient in both periods. These competitive results are typical of those obtained with the parameterization in figure 1.2. Notice that the number of traders was relatively small, and that no trader initially knew anything about supply and demand conditions for the market as a whole.[15]

1.4 Experimental Methods: Advantages and Limitations

Each of the three literatures mentioned in section 1.2 has generated a body of findings using human subjects (usually college undergraduates) who make decisions in highly structured situations. The skeptical reader might question what can be learned about complex economic phenomena from behavior in these simple laboratory environments. Although this issue arises repeatedly in later chapters, it is useful to present a brief summary of the pros and cons of experimentation at this time.

The chief advantages offered by laboratory methods in any science are replicability and control. *Replicability* refers to the capacity of other researchers to reproduce the experiment, and thereby verify the findings independently.[16] To a degree, lack of replicability is a problem of any observational inquiry that is nonexperimental; data from naturally occurring processes are recorded in a unique and nonreplicated spatial and temporal background in which other unobserved factors are constantly changing.[17] The problem is complicated in economics because the

---

[15]   If the demand and supply functions are more asymmetric, convergence to a stationary pattern of behavior typically involves more than two periods. Chapter 3 considers some conditions under which convergence in double-auction markets is either slow or erratic.

[16]   This notion of replication should be distinguished from the conventional use of the term in econometrics. As Roth (1990) notes, the notion of replication in econometrics refers to the capacity to reproduce results with a given data set. In an experimental context, replication is the capacity to create an entirely new set of observations.

[17]   Laboratory observations, of course, also occur at spatially and temporally distinct locations, but laboratory procedures are implemented specifically to control for such effects. With careful attention, the experimenter can approximately duplicate a test environment in a subsequent trial.

collection and independent verification of economic data are very expensive. Moreover, the economics profession imposes little professional credibility on the data-collection process, so economic data are typically collected not by economists for scientific purposes, but by government employees or businessmen for other purposes. For this reason it is often difficult to verify the accuracy of field data.[18] Better data from naturally occurring markets could be collected, and there is certainly a strong case to be made for improvements in this area. But relatively inexpensive, independently conducted laboratory investigations allow replication, which in turn provides professional incentives to collect relevant data carefully.

Control is the capacity to manipulate laboratory conditions so that observed behavior can be used to evaluate alternative theories and policies. In natural markets, an absence of control is manifested in varying degrees. Distinguishing natural data may sometimes exist in principle, but the data are either not collected or collected too imprecisely to distinguish among alternative theories. In other instances, relevant data *cannot* be collected, because it is simply impossible to find economic situations that match the assumptions of the theory. An absence of control in natural contexts presents critical data problems in many areas of economic research. In individual decision theory, for example, one would be quite surprised to observe many instances outside the laboratory where individuals face questions that directly test the axioms of expected utility theory. The predictions of game theory are also frequently difficult to evaluate with natural data. Many game-theoretic models exhibit a multiplicity of equilibria. Game theorists frequently narrow the range of outcomes by dismissing some equilibria as being "unreasonable," often on very subtle bases, such as the nature of beliefs about what would happen in contingencies that are never realized during the equilibrium play of the game (beliefs "off of the equilibrium path"). There is little hope that such issues can be evaluated with nonexperimental data.

Perhaps more surprising is the lack of control over data from natural markets sufficient to test even basic predictions of neoclassical price theory. Consider, for example, the simple proposition that a market will generate efficient, competitive prices and quantities. Evaluation of this proposition requires price, quantity, and market efficiency data, given a particular set of market demand and supply curves. But neither supply nor demand may be directly observed with natural data. Sometimes cost data may be used to estimate supply, but the complexity of most markets forces some parameter measurements to be based on one or more convenient simplifications, such as log linearity or perfect product homogeneity,

---

[18] The *Washington Post* (July 5, 1990, p. D1) summarized this consensus: "In studying government data, everyone from the National Academy of Sciences to the National Association of Business Economists has reached the same conclusion — there are serious problems regarding the accuracy and usefulness of the statistics."

which are violated in nonlaboratory markets, often to an unknown extent.[19] Demand is even more difficult to observe, since there is nothing analogous to cost data for consumers.

Although econometric methods may be used to estimate market supply and demand curves from transactions-price data, this estimation process typically rests on an assumption that prices are constantly near the equilibrium. (Then shifts in supply, holding demand constant, may be used to identify demand, and conversely for supply estimates.) Alternatively it is possible to estimate supply and demand without assuming that the market is in equilibrium, but in this case it is necessary to make specific assumptions about the nature of the disequilibrium. In either case, it is a questionable exercise to attempt to evaluate equilibrium tendencies in a market where supply and demand are estimated on the basis of specific *assumptions* about whether or how markets equilibrate.

Thus, tests of market propositions with natural data are joint tests of a rather complicated set of primary and auxiliary hypotheses. Unless auxiliary hypotheses are valid, tests of primary hypotheses provide little indisputable information. On the one hand, negative results do not allow rejection of a theory. Evidence that seems to contradict the implications of a theory may arise when the theory is true, if a subsidiary hypothesis is false. On the other hand, even very supportive results may be misleading because a test may generate the "right" result, but for the wrong reason; the primary hypotheses may have no explanatory power, yet subsidiary hypotheses may be sufficiently incorrect to generate apparently supportive data.

Laboratory methods allow a dramatic reduction in the number of auxiliary hypotheses involved in examining a primary hypothesis. For example, using the cost and value inducement procedure introduced by Chamberlin and Smith, a test of the capacity of a market to generate competitive price and quantity predictions can be conducted without assumptions about functional forms and product homogeneity that are typically needed to estimate competitive price predictions in a naturally occurring market. By inducing a controlled environment that is fully understood by the investigator, laboratory methods can be used to provide a minimal test of a theory. If the theory does not work under the controlled "best-shot" conditions of the laboratory, the obvious question is whether it will work well under any circumstances.

Even given the shortcomings of nonexperimental data, critics are often skeptical about the value of laboratory methods in economics. Some immediate sources of skepticism are far less critical than they first appear. For example, one natural reservation is that relevant decision makers in the economy are more sophisticated

---

[19] Anyone who is familiar with predatory pricing cases, for example, knows the difficulties of measuring a concept as simple as average variable cost. Moreover, tests for predatory pricing (such as the Areeda/Turner test) are operationalized in average-cost rather than in more theoretically precise marginal-cost terms, because marginal-cost measures are too elusive.

than undergraduates or MBA students who comprise most subject pools. This critique is more relevant for some types of experiments (e.g., studies of trading in futures markets) than for others (e.g., studies of consumer shopping behavior), but in any event, it is an argument about the choice of subjects rather than about the usefulness of experimentation. If the economic agents in relevant markets think differently from undergraduates, then the selection of subjects should reflect this. Notably, the behavior of decision makers recruited from naturally occurring markets has been examined in a variety of contexts, for example, Dyer, Kagel, and Levin (1989), Smith, Suchanek, and Williams (1988), Mestelman and Feeny (1988), and DeJong et. al (1988). Behavior of these decision makers has typically not differed from that exhibited by more standard (and far less costly) student subject pools. For example, Smith, Suchanek, Williams (1988) observed price "bubbles" and "crashes" in laboratory asset markets, with both student subjects and business and professional people.[20]

A second immediate reservation concerning the use of experiments is that the markets of primary interest to economists are complicated, while laboratory environments are often relatively simple. This objection, however, is as much a criticism of the theories as of the experiments. Granted, performance of a theory in a simple laboratory setting may not carry over to a more complex natural setting. If this is the case, and if the experiment is structured in a manner that is consistent with the relevant economic theory, then perhaps the theory has omitted some potentially important feature of the economy. On the other hand, if the theory fails to work in a simple experiment, then there is little reason to expect it to work in a more complicated natural world.[21]

It is imperative to add that experimentation is no panacea. Important issues in experimental design, administration, and interpretation bear continued scrutiny. For instance, although concerns regarding subject pool and environmental simplicity are not grounds for dismissing experimental methods out of hand, these issues do present prominent concerns. While available evidence suggests that the use of relevant professionals does not invariably affect performance, a number of studies do indicate that performance can vary with proxies for the aptitude of participants, such as the undergraduate institution (e.g., Davis and Holt, 1991) or using graduate instead of undergraduate students.[22] For this reason, choosing a specific participant pool may be appropriate in some instances.

---

[20] In some instances the use of "relevant professionals" impedes laboratory performance. Dyer, Kagel, and Levin (1989) and Burns (1985) find that relevant professionals involved in laboratory markets sometimes attempt to apply rules of thumb, which, while valuable for dealing with uncertainty in the parallel natural market, are meaningless guides in the laboratory. DeJong et al. (1988) report that businessmen need more instruction on the use of a computer keyboard.

[21] This defense is well articulated by Plott (1982, 1989).

[22] Ball and Cech (1991) provide a very extensive survey of subject-pool effects.

Similarly, the relative simplicity of laboratory markets can be an important drawback if one's purpose is to make claims regarding the performance of natural markets. Economists in general are well acquainted with the pressures to "oversell" research results in an effort to attract funds from agencies interested in policy-relevant research. Experimental investigators are by no means immune to such temptations. It is all too easy, for instance, to give an investigation of a game-theoretic equilibrium concept the appearance of policy relevance by attaching catchy labels to the alternative decisions, and then interpreting the results in a broad policy context. But realistically, no variant of a prisoner's-dilemma experiment will provide much new information about industrial policy, regardless of how the decisions are labeled.

Technical difficulties in establishing and controlling the laboratory environment also present important impediments to effective experimentation. This is particularly true when the purpose of the experiment is to elicit information about individual preferences (as opposed to evaluating the outcomes of group interactions given a set of induced preferences). The effectiveness of many macroeconomic policies, for example, depends on the recognition of intertemporal tradeoffs. Do people anticipate that tax cuts today will necessitate increases later, perhaps decades later? Do agents care about what happens to future generations? Do agents have a bequest motive? Although these are clearly behavioral questions, they may be very difficult to address in the laboratory. Most people may only consider questions regarding bequests seriously in their later years, and responses regarding intended behavior at other times may be poor predictors. Although elaborate schemes have been devised to address elicitation issues, it is probably fair to say that experimentalists have been much less successful with the elicitation of preferences than with their inducement. In addition, there are some ongoing questions about whether it is technically possible to induce critical components of some economic environments in the laboratory, for example, infinite horizons or risk aversion. Some very clever approaches to these problems will be discussed in later chapters.

Overall, the advantages of experimentation are decisive. Experimental methods, however, complement rather than substitute for other empirical techniques. Moreover, in some contexts we can hope to learn relatively little from experimentation. It is important to keep the initial infatuation with the novelty of the technique from leading to the mindless application of experimental methods to every issue or model that appears in the journals.

1.5 Types of Experiments

The "stick" of replicability forces those who conduct experiments to consider in detail the appropriate procedures for designing and administering experiments, as well as standards for evaluating them. Laboratory investigations can have a variety of aims, however, and appropriate procedures depend on the kind of experiment being conducted. For this reason it is instructive to discuss several alternative objectives of experimentation: tests of behavioral hypotheses, sensitivity tests, and documentation of empirical regularities. This discussion is introductory. Chapter 9 contains a more thorough discussion of the relationship between economic experiments and tests of economic propositions.

Tests of Behavioral Hypotheses

Perhaps the most common use of experimental methods in economics is theory falsification. By constructing a laboratory environment that satisfies as many of the *structural* assumptions of a particular theory as possible, its *behavioral* implications can be given a best chance. Poor predictive power under such circumstances is particularly troubling for the theory's proponents.

It is rarely a trivial task to construct idealized environments, that is, environments consistent with the structural assumptions of the relevant model. Indeed, this task is not likely to be accomplished in one iteration of experimentation. Despite the glamour of the much heralded "critical experiment," such breakthroughs are rare. Rather, the process of empirical evaluation more often involves a continuing interaction between theorist and experimenter, and often addresses elements initially ignored in theory. For example, Chamberlin's demonstration that markets fail to generate competitive outcomes led Smith to consider the effects of trading rules on market performance, and ultimately led to the extensive consideration of important institutional factors that had been typically ignored by theorists. In this way, experiments foster development of a dialogue between the theorist and the empiricist, a dialogue that forces the theorist to specify models in terms of observable variables, and forces the data collector to be precise and clever in obtaining the desired control.

Theory Stress Tests

If the key behavioral assumptions of a theory are not rejected in a minimal laboratory environment, the logical next step is to begin bridging the gap between laboratory and naturally occurring markets. One approach to this problem involves examining the sensitivity of a theory to violations of "obviously unrealistic" simplifying assumptions. For example, even if theories of perfect competition and perfect contestability organize behavior in simple laboratory implementations, these theories would be of limited practical value if they were unable to accommodate finite numbers of agents or small, positive entry costs. By examining laboratory markets with progressively fewer sellers, or with positive (and increasing) entry costs, the robustness of each theory to its simplifying assumptions can be evaluated.

Systematic stress-testing a theory in this manner is usually not possible with an analysis of nonexperimental data.[23]

Another immediate application of a theory stress test involves information. Most game theories postulate complete information, or incomplete information in a carefully limited dimension. But in some applications (e.g., industrial organization) game theory is being used too simplistically if the accuracy of its predictions is sensitive to small amounts of uncertainty about parameters of the market structure. There is some evidence that this is not the case, that is, that the concept of a noncooperative (Nash) equilibrium sometimes has *more* predictive power when subjects are given no information about others' payoff functions (Fouraker and Siegel, 1963, and Dolbear et al., 1968). This is because subjects do not have to calculate the noncooperative equilibrium strategies in the way that a theorist would; all they have to do is respond optimally to the empirical distribution of others' decisions observed in previous plays of the game.

Searching for Empirical Regularities

A particularly valuable type of empirical research is the documentation of surprising regularities in relationships between observed economic variables. For example, the negative effect of cumulative production experience on unit costs has led to a large literature on "learning curves." Roth (1986) notes that experimentation can also be used to discover and document such "stylized facts." This search is facilitated in laboratory markets in which there is little or no measurement error and in which the basic underlying demand, supply, and informational conditions are known by the experimenter. It would be difficult to conclude that prices in a particular industry are above competitive levels, for example, if marginal costs or secret discounts cannot be measured very well, as is usually the case. Anyone who has followed an empirical debate in the economics literature (for example, the concentration-profits debate in industrial organization) can appreciate the attractiveness of learning *something* from market experiments, even if the issues considered are more limited in scope.

1.6 Some Procedural and Design Considerations

The diversity of research objectives and designs complicates identification of a single set of acceptable laboratory procedures. Consequently, both desirable and undesirable procedures will be discussed in various portions of the text, and specific examples and applications will be given in the chapter appendices. However, there

---

[23] This "stress test" terminology is due to Ledyard (1990).

are some general design and procedural considerations common to most laboratory investigations, and it is instructive to review them at this time. For clarity, this discussion will be presented primarily in terms of market experiments.

In general, the experimental design should enable the researcher to utilize the main advantages of experimentation that were discussed above: replicability and control. Although a classification of design considerations is, to some extent, a matter of taste, we find the following categories to be useful: procedural regularity, motivation, unbiasedness, calibration, and design parallelism. *Procedural regularity* involves following a routine that can be replicated. *Motivation, unbiasedness*, and *calibration* are important features of control that will be explained below. *Design parallelism* pertains to links between an experimental setting and a naturally occurring economic process. These design criteria will be discussed in a general manner here; specific practical implications of some of these criteria are incorporated into a detailed list of suggestions for conducting a market experiment in appendix A1.2.

Prior to proceeding, it is convenient to introduce some terminology. No standard conventions have yet arisen for referring to the components of an experiment, so for purposes of clarity we will adopt the following terminology:

session:	a sequence of periods, games, or other decision tasks involving the same group of subjects on the same day
cohort:	a group of subjects that participated in a session
treatment:	a unique environment or configuration of treatment variables, i.e., of information, experience, incentives, and rules
cell:	a set of sessions with the same experimental treatment conditions
experiment design:	a specification of sessions in one or more cells to evaluate the propositions of interest
experiment:	the collection of sessions in one or more related cells

The reader should be warned that some of these terms are often used differently in the literature. In particular, it is common to use the word "experiment" to indicate what we will call a "session." Our definition follows Roth (1990), who argues that the interaction of a group of subjects in a single meeting should be called a "session," and that the word "experiment" should be reserved for a collection of sessions designed to evaluate one or more related economic propositions. By this definition an experiment is usually, but not always, the evidence reported in a single paper.[24]

---

[24] We will, however, continue to use "experiment" in a loose manner in instructions for subjects.

Finally, most experimental sessions involve repeated decisions, and some terms are needed to identify separate decision units. Appropriate terminology depends on the type of experiment: A decision unit will be referred to as a *trial*, when discussing individual decision-making experiments, as a *game* when discussing games, and as a *trading period* when discussing market experiments.

Procedural Regularity

The professional credibility that an experimenter places on data collected is critical to the usefulness of experiments. It is imperative that others can and do replicate laboratory results, and that the researcher feel the pressure of potential replication when conducting and reporting results. To facilitate replication, it is important that the procedures and environment be standardized so that only the treatment variables are adjusted. Moreover, it is important that these procedures (and particularly instructions) be carefully documented. *In general, the guiding principle for standardizing and reporting procedures is to permit a replication that the researcher and outside observers would accept as being valid.* The researcher should adopt and report standard practices pertaining to the following:[25]

- instructions
- illustrative examples and tests of understanding (which should be included in the instructions)
- criteria for answering questions (e.g., no information beyond instructions)
- the nature of monetary or other rewards
- the presence of "trial" or practice periods with no rewards
- the subject pool and the method of recruiting subjects
- the number and experience levels of subjects
- procedures for matching subjects and roles
- the location, approximate dates, and duration of experimental sessions
- the physical environment, the use of laboratory assistants, special devices, and computerization
- any intentional deception of subjects
- procedural irregularities in specific sessions that require interpretation

Even if journal space requirements preclude the publication of instructions, work sheets, and data, the researcher should make this information available to journal referees and others who may wish to review and evaluate the research.

---

[25] This list approximately corresponds to Palfrey and Porter's (1991) list in "Guidelines for Submissions of Experimental Manuscripts."

The use of computers has done much to strengthen standards of replicability in economics.[26] The presentation of the instructions and the experimental environment via visually isolated computer terminals increases standardization and control within an experiment and decreases the effort involved in replication with different groups of subjects. Moreover, some procedural tasks that involve a lot of interaction or privacy are much easier to implement via computer, and computerization often enables the researcher to obtain more observations within a session by economizing on the time devoted to record keeping and message delivery.[27]

Importantly, however, computers are not *necessary* to conduct most experiments. Even with extensive access to computers, some noncomputerized procedures retain their usefulness. The physical act of throwing dice, for example, may more convincingly generate random numbers than computer routines if subjects suspect deception or if payoffs are unusually large. Similarly, even when instructions are presented via computer, we generally prefer to have an experimenter read instructions aloud as the subjects follow on their screens. This increases common knowledge, that is, everyone knows that everyone else knows certain aspects of the procedures and payoffs. Reading along also prevents some subjects from finishing ahead of others and becoming bored.

A final issue in procedural matters regards the creation and maintenance of a subject pool. Although rarely discussed, the manner in which subjects are recruited, instructed, and paid can importantly affect outcomes. Behavior in the laboratory may be colored by contacts the students have with each other outside the laboratory; for example, in experiments involving deception or cooperation, friends may behave differently from anonymous participants. Problems of this type may be particularly pronounced in some professional schools and European university systems, where all students in the same year take the same courses. Potential problems may be avoided by recruiting participants for a given session from multiple classes (years). For similar reasons, an experimenter may wish to avoid being present in sessions that involve subjects who are currently enrolled in one of his or her courses. Such students may alter their choices in light of what they think their professor wants to see.

The researcher should also be careful to avoid deceiving participants. Most economists are very concerned about developing and maintaining a reputation among the student population for honesty in order to ensure that subject actions are

---

[26] At present there are some two dozen computerized economics laboratories in the United States, as well as several in Europe.

[27] The effects of computerization in the context of the double auction are discussed in chapter 3, section 3.3. Also, one of the advantages of computerization lies in the way instructions can be presented. Instructions for a computerized implementation of a posted-offer auction are presented in appendix 4.2 to chapter 4.

motivated by the induced monetary rewards rather than by psychological reactions to suspected manipulation. Subjects may suspect deception if it is present. Moreover, even if subjects fail to detect deception within a session, it may jeopardize future experiments if the subjects ever find out that they were deceived and report this information to their friends.[28] Another important aspect of maintaining a subject pool is the development of a system for recording subjects' history of participation. This is particularly important at universities where experiments are done by a number of different researchers. A common record of names and participation dates allows each experimenter to be more certain that a new subject is really inexperienced with the institution being used. Similarly, in sessions where experience is desired, a good record-keeping system makes it possible to control the repeated use of the same subjects in multiple "experienced" sessions.

Motivation

In designing an experiment, it is critical that participants receive salient rewards that correspond to the incentives assumed in the relevant theory or application. *Saliency* simply means that changes in decisions have a prominent effect on rewards. Saliency requires (1) that the subjects perceive the relationship between decisions made and payoff outcomes, and (2) that the induced rewards are high enough to matter in the sense that they dominate subjective costs of making decisions and trades. For example, consider a competitive quantity prediction that requires the trade of a unit worth $1.40 to a buyer, but which costs a seller $1.30. This trade will not be completed, and the competitive quantity prediction will "fail," if the joint costs of negotiating the contract exceed $.10.

One can never be assured, a priori, that rewards are adequate without considering the context of a particular experiment. On the one hand, participants will try to "do well" in many instances by maximizing even purely hypothetical payment amounts. On the other hand, inconsistent or variable behavior is not necessarily a signal of insufficient monetary incentives. No amount of money can motivate subjects to perform a calculation beyond their intellectual capacities, any more than generous bonuses would transform most of us into professional athletes.[29] It has been fairly well established, however, that providing payments to

---

[28] Many economists believe that deception is highly undesirable in economics experiments, and for this reason, they argue that the results of experiments using deceptive procedures should not be published. Deceptive procedures are more common and perhaps less objectionable in other disciplines (e.g., psychology).

[29] Vernon Smith made a similar point in a different context in an oral presentation at the Economic Science Association Meetings, October 1988.

subjects tends to reduce performance variability.[30]   For this reason, economics experiments almost always involve nonhypothetical payments.

Also, as a general matter, rewards are monetary. Monetary payoffs minimize concerns regarding the effects of heterogeneous individual attitudes toward the reward medium. Denominating rewards in terms of physical commodities such as coffee cups or chocolate bars may come at the cost of some loss in control, since participants may privately value the physical commodities very differently. Monetary payoffs are also highly divisible and have the advantage of nonsatiation; it is somewhat less problematic to assume that participants do not become "full" of money than, say, chocolate bars.

In many contexts, inducing a sufficient motivation for marginal actions will require a substantial variation in earnings across participants, even if all participants make careful decisions. High-cost sellers in a market, for example, will tend to earn less than low-cost sellers, regardless of their decisions. If possible, average rewards should be set high enough to offset the opportunity cost of time for all participants. This opportunity cost will depend on the subject pool; it will be higher for professionals than for student subjects. If there are several alternative theories or hypotheses being considered, then the earnings levels should be adequate for motivational purposes at *each* of the alternative outcomes under consideration. For example, if sellers' earnings are zero at a competitive equilibrium, then competitive pricing behavior may not be observed, since zero earnings may result in erratic behavior.

In some experiments, subjects' earnings are denominated in a laboratory currency, for example, tokens or francs, and later converted into cash. A very low conversion rate (e.g., 100 laboratory "francs" per penny earned) can create a fine price grid to more nearly approximate theoretical results of continuous models. A coarse price grid in oligopoly games, for example, can introduce a number of additional, unwelcome equilibria.   A second advantage of using a laboratory currency "filter" arises in situations where the experimenter wishes to minimize interpersonal payoff comparisons by giving subjects different conversion ratios that are private information. Procedures of this sort have been used in bargaining experiments. A laboratory currency may also be used to control the location of focal payoff points when payoff levels are of some concern. The effects of earnings levels on the absolute payoff level could be controlled, for example, by conducting treatments in the same design, but under different franc/dollar conversion rates. The

---

[30]   In the absence of financial incentives, it is more common to observe occasional large and nonsystematic deviations in behavior from the norm. In addition, the relevant economic model often yields better predictions when sufficient financial motivation is provided. For example, Siegel and Goldstein (1959) showed that an increase in the reward level resulted in an increase in the proportion of rational, maximizing choices in a forecasting experiment. This experiment is discussed in chapter 2.

denomination of payoffs in lab dollars could also control for differences in focal points in sessions conducted in different countries with different currencies.

Some experimentalists further maintain that a currency filter can increase incentives; for example, subjects may make an effort to earn 100 francs, even if they would scoff at the monetary equivalent of, say, one penny. We find this money-illusion argument less persuasive. Many tourists in a foreign country for the first time return with stories about spending thousands of pesos, or whatever, and not worrying about the real cost of goods. It is possible that the use of a laboratory currency could similarly mask or even dilute financial incentives. Moreover, even if laboratory payoffs do create a monetary illusion, they could also create an artificial "game-board" sense of speculative competitiveness. For these reasons, it is probably prudent to denominate laboratory earnings in cash, unless the researcher has a specific design motivation for using a laboratory currency.

Three additional comments regarding motivation bear brief mention. First, it is a fairly standard practice to pay participants an appearance fee in addition to their earnings in the course of the experiment. Payment of a preannounced fee facilitates recruiting of subjects, establishes credibility, and perhaps provides some incentive for participants to pay attention to instructions. Second, it is usually important for the experimenter to be specific about all aspects of the experiment in order to control the motivation. For example, the failure to provide information about the duration or number of periods in a session may affect subjects' perceptions of the incentives to collude in an unknown and uncontrolled manner. The third point is a qualification of the second. There is a risk of losing control over incentives if subjects are given complete information about others' money payoffs. With complete information, envy and benevolence are more likely, which is a problem if the theoretical model stipulates that agents maximize their own payoffs. Smith (1982) includes *privacy* (only knowing one's own payoff function) in a list of sufficient conditions for a valid microeconomics experiment. Privacy is appropriate for some purposes, such as tests of theories that specify privacy or stress tests of those that do not. On the other hand, privacy may not be appropriate for experiments motivated by a game-theoretic model that specifies complete information about the game structure.[31]

Unbiasedness

Experiments should be conducted in a manner that does not lead participants to perceive any particular behavioral pattern as being correct or expected, unless explicit suggestion is a treatment variable. The possibility of replication should provide incentives sufficient to deter egregious attempts at distorting participant

---

[31] Smith (1982) contains a classic discussion of motivation, which is based on formal definitions of nonsatiation, saliency, and privacy.

behavior. We mention the issue of biasedness, however, not to warn researchers away from patently suggestive behavior, but rather to note how careful even the most well-intentioned researcher must be to avoid subtle behavioral suggestions. Unlike other observational laboratory data (say atomic particles), human participants can be eager to do what the researcher desires and can respond to surprisingly subtle indications that they are doing "well." If an experiment is conducted by hand, it is sometimes useful to have the experiment administrator be unaware of the theoretical predictions in a particular design. In a laboratory market session, for example, this can be done by adding a parameter-disguising constant to all values and costs, which shifts supply and demand vertically by the same distance, without changing the essential structure of the market. Altering the shift parameter with each session makes it possible for an experiment monitor to be unaware of the equilibrium price. These alterations also reduce the chance that *ex post* discussions among students will affect behavior in subsequent sessions.

Some researchers believe that sessions should be conducted by assistants who do not know the purpose of the experiment, that is, in a "double-blind" setting. Our own feeling is that the researcher has the strongest incentive and ability to spot procedural problems, and therefore we prefer to be present during a session. But subjects in some types of experiments, especially those involving fairness issues, may be influenced by the fact that they are being observed by third parties. In such situations, it may be best for the researcher to be unobtrusive or unobserved.

Another possible source of bias is the terminology used to explain the incentives. The trade of abstract commodities, as opposed to "pollution permits" or "failing firms," may prevent unobserved personal preferences or aversions for particular goods from influencing results. Certain economic or market terms may also suggest particular types of behavior, for example, "cartel" or "conspiracy." For these reasons, it is usually considered a good practice to avoid references to any particular good. There is, however, a tradeoff to be made here. Although simple tests of game-theoretic concepts can and should be conducted without giving economic names to the decision variables, the use of market terminology in other, more complicated trading institutions is valuable in communicating the payoff structure effectively. For example, although is possible to conduct one of Smith's double-auction market experiments without ever using words such as "buyer," "seller," or "price," it would be very difficult to explain the structure to the subjects. (If you are not convinced, try it! Revise the double-auction instructions in appendix A1.1 so that they are entirely neutral with respect to market terminology.)

One should use common sense in evaluating the tradeoff between providing enough of an economic context to explain the incentive structure and not providing suggestive terminology. It is worthwhile to spend a lot of time working on instructions; the safest procedure is to begin with standard, often-used instructions, and to modify them for the purpose at hand. Pilot experiments and individual "debriefing" sessions can be useful in spotting problems with the wording. For example, one of the authors once had a subject tell him that the word "oligopoly" on a receipt form "gave away" the purpose of the experiment, since the subject remembered from his introductory economics class that oligopolists are supposed to collude. This subject was unusually successful at colluding. As a result, all previously collected data were discarded, and the receipt form was changed.

Calibration

Experiments also need to be designed with an eye to the generated data. Calibration involves the establishment of a clear basis of comparison. Suppose, for example, that the hypothesis being investigated is that competitive behavior is altered by a treatment, say, the consolidation of market power in the hands of a few sellers. In this case, it is desirable to begin with a "baseline" condition in which competitive outcomes are generated in the absence of market power. A related aspect of calibration is the use of a design in which the predictions of alternative theories are cleanly separated. This aspect is important because the process of evaluating a behavioral theory comes through falsification rather than validation, and falsification is more convincing if there is a reasonable alternative that is not falsified.

To make this discussion concrete, consider an evaluation of data that could be generated with the experimental market design in figure 1.2. Suppose that nine independent sessions (with different cohorts of subjects) have been conducted, each lasting for the same number of trading periods. Suppose further that we are concerned about evaluating the tendency for this market to generate predicted competitive prices (between $1.30 and $1.40). One way to analyze the results would be to take a single price measure from each session, such as the average final-period price. Admittedly, such a procedure discards much of the relevant data, but its simplicity makes it a useful expositional device. Also, the consequent observations have the advantage of statistical independence, since each session is done with a different group of subjects.[32]

Consider now some possible mean-price outcomes. Suppose first that prices deviated rather substantially and uniformly from the competitive prediction. For example, assume that the average of the nine price observations is $1.60, with a standard deviation (of the final-period mean prices) of $0.20. In this case, the null hypothesis of the competitive price prediction could be rejected at normal levels of

---

[32] More sophisticated econometric techniques may be worthwhile if the results are not immediately apparent. Such techniques would involve the specification of the structure of the error terms in the process that generates transactions price data. The simple procedure used in the text is less powerful but avoids auxiliary assumptions.

significance.[33]   Now consider what happens when prices are closer to the competitive prediction. For example, suppose the mean of the nine observations was $1.45, with the same $.20 standard deviation. The null hypothesis of the competitive prediction could no longer be rejected at any conventional level of significance.[34] But neither could it be accepted.   In fact, we would be unable to make an affirmative statistical claim about the competitive prediction even if the mean price was closer to the competitive range.   Rather, affirmative claims are limited to nonquantitative observations that prices "appear" to conform to the competitive prediction.   This is the process (and problem) of falsification; we can sometimes determine when data do not support a theory, but it is far more difficult to conclude that evidence actually supports a theory.

We avoid the philosophical issue of what is ultimately necessary for empirical verification of a theory.   However, more convincing claims can be made if the data allow falsification of rival theories.   For example, consider what could be said if the mean of the nine price observations was $1.35, with a $.20 standard deviation, in light of the monopoly or monopsony predictions listed in table 1.2.   Although these observations cannot directly allow acceptance of the hypothesis that prices are competitive, the competitive-price hypothesis cannot be rejected, and the alternative hypotheses that prices are at the collusive level for either buyers or sellers can be rejected at standard significance levels.   This is the issue of calibration.   Theories are much more meaningfully evaluated in light of alternatives.   Rejection of reasonable alternatives strengthens a failure to reject the maintained hypothesis. Conversely, a theory that organizes some aspects of the data well should not be discarded until a better alternative is found.

Behavioral "noise" is inevitable.   For example, although prices clustered about the competitive prediction in the two periods of the market session discussed in section 1.3, they were not uniformly confined within the bounds of the competitive price range.   In fact, it is quite reasonable to suspect that some residual price variability would remain, even after a relatively large number of trading periods with the same traders.   In light of this behavioral noise, two points need to be made.   The first is a design issue.   Careful experimental design requires more than merely identifying alternative predictions.   The behavioral consequences of rival predictions should further be sufficiently distinct to be readily differentiated from inherent performance variability.   For example, an alteration in the figure 1.2 design that made the demand curve much more elastic would make the behavioral distinction between cooperative and competitive behavior much more difficult, since the price consequences of these two alternatives would be much closer.

---

[33]   For example, a t-test statistic for the null hypothesis that observed prices are not significantly different from the competitive prediction would be 3, or [$1.60 − $1.40] / [.20 / $\sqrt{9}$]. Nonparametric tests are discussed in chapter 9.

[34]   The t-test statistic for the null examined in the previous footnote would be .75.

The second issue has to do with anticipated performance variability that is outside the domain of the theory. Although some behavioral variability is effectively irreducible noise, there exist other theoretically irrelevant factors that quite regularly affect performance, such as experience with the experimental environment, group effects, and the order in which treatments are presented. To draw legitimate statistical claims, it is important to control for these anticipated sources of variability.

Blocking, or systematic pairing of observations, may be used to neutralize the effects of such nuisance variables. Consider, for example, a market experiment designed to evaluate the effects of communication among sellers on pricing. The experiment contains two treatments: A (no-communication) and B (communication). If it turns out that communication tends to produce higher, collusive prices, it would also not be surprising to observe a *sequencing*, or order-of-treatment, effect. In a given session, we might expect to see higher prices in no-communication treatment A when it follows communication treatment B than when it precedes B. Sometimes the economics of the problem suggests a particular sequence. For example, it is often reasonable for a status quo treatment to precede a treatment that implements a possible alternative policy. When the economics of the situation does not require a particular sequence, it may be advisable to reverse the order of the treatments in every other session to control for sequence effects.

Another way to avoid sequence effects would be to have only one treatment per session, but this necessitates a large number of sessions if there is considerable variability from one group of subjects to another. To clarify this point, suppose that six sessions using the A and B treatments are conducted, and that the sequence is alternated in every other session. Sessions in figure 1.3 are denoted as separate rows. In each row, the average price for each treatment is denoted with an A or a B, along a horizontal scale where prices increase with rightward movements. There is a clear treatment effect; in each session, price is higher for treatment B. But group effects are such that there is very little correlation between treatment and average price in the aggregate. Very little could have been concluded if the data in figure 1.3 had been generated from twelve independent sessions; both A and B observations tend to cluster about the vertical bar printed in the center of the graph. (Look in particular at the bottom row.) But consideration of the data in figure 1.3 as paired treatments allows one to reject the hypothesis of no treatment effect with a very high degree of confidence, with at least the same confidence that one can reject the hypothesis that a coin is fair after observing six heads in a row. In this context, blocking allows one to control for sequence and subject-group effects at the same time.[35] The example in figure 1.3 also illustrates the notion that the structure of the experimental design (treatment cells, blocking, and numbers of trails) should

---

[35] One potential disadvantage of using multiple treatments per session is that the amount of time available with each treatment is reduced. This can be a problem if adjustment to equilibrium is slow or erratic.

be planned with a consideration for the subsequent statistical analysis of the hypotheses of interest. This is rarely done by experimental economists, as noted by Hinkelmann (1990).

Session	Lower Prices			Higher Prices				
1		A	B					
2						A		B
3	A	B						
4			AB					
5				A	B			
6						A	B	
1-6	A	BA	BAB	A	B	A	AB	B

Figure 1.3   Hypothetical Data from a Blocked Design

Sometimes the number of things that can be systematically blocked is unreasonably large and the alternative configurations can be selected randomly, in a *randomized block*. For example, in an experiment with three buyers and one seller, there are twenty-four ways in which the order of subject arrival times can be related to the four role assignments. It would not be advisable to let the first person to arrive always have the monopoly role, since early arrival may be correlated with some unobserved characteristic of importance. A complete block would require twenty-four sessions, and a random assignment method is a simpler way to avoid systematic biases.[36]

Design Parallelism

As a final design issue, we consider the extent to which experiments should be constructed to resemble naturally occurring economic situations. The term *design parallelism* is used here to indicate closeness to natural situations rather than

---

[36] We will say more about the relationship between experimental design and statistical analysis of data in chapter 9.

closeness to the theories that economists have devised.[37]   Given the relative simplicity of laboratory environments, nonexperimentalists tend to be skeptical, and experimentalists should be cautious of claims about behavior in natural markets. Nevertheless, as a general matter, the experimenter should strive for parsimony. Recall that theory falsification is a prominent goal of experimental analysis. Such tests require specification of a laboratory environment that satisfies the conditions of the theory, rather than the conditions of a natural market. Increasing design parallelism by adding complexity to an experiment is seductively easy, but it often results in situations that are difficult to analyze in theory and difficult for subjects to comprehend quickly.

The process of theory falsification in an idealized environment is not devoid of policy relevance. Although simple experiments will not predict the effects of a particular theory or policy remedy in richer environments, such experiments can provide a reasonable amount of evidence about whether policy proposals will have desired effects. For example, Isaac and Smith (1985) conducted a series of sessions with a proposed antipredation rule that prohibits a temporary price reduction by a dominant firm in response to entry; these sessions exhibited higher prices and lower efficiencies than were observed in comparable "unprotected" markets, conducted without the rule. These results make the regulatory "cure" highly suspect, for it harms performance even under the best of circumstances.
In general, if the behavioral assumptions of a theory fail under simple conditions, the burden of explanation should be shifted to the advocates of the related policy.

Maximum parsimony is not always desirable, however. Adding complexity is justifiable when attempting to make positive claims about a theory as part of the stress-testing process. The likelihood that a theory works in the natural world increases as the theory outperforms rival theories in increasingly complex experimental environments. In fact, it would seem logical to follow a laboratory study with a *field experiment*, that is, a test in a restricted natural setting. Field experiments are usually expensive, and as a consequence they are rare.

One important issue in design parallelism is the appropriate amount of information to give subjects. For example, a minimal test of the behavioral assumptions of an oligopoly or game theory should reproduce the informational environment that is assumed in the theory, even though this may require much more precise information than is typically possessed by firms in industrial markets. On the other hand, experiments in which traders do not know each other's costs and values, such as Smith's (1962) initial market experiments, can be appropriately viewed both as sensitivity tests and as efforts to discover stylized facts in "realistic"

---

[37]   Smith (1982) used the term parallelism to mean transferability, i.e., that the results of the experiment will carry over to the corresponding nonexperimental setting. We use the term design parallelism to emphasize parallelism in the structure of the two settings, as opposed to parallelism in behavior.

environments. Therefore, the degree of design parallelism depends on the purpose of the experiment.

Summary

Although the discussion above may appear somewhat abstract, it is important to emphasize that it has is a very practical side. Those familiar with experimental methods simply will not take the results of an experiment seriously unless it satisfies some basic procedural standards. The most common "fatal errors" made by inexperienced researchers are:

- failure to use complete and unbiased instructions
- failure to use salient financial rewards
- failure to include a baseline control treatment that calibrates results
- failure to restrict focus on a few treatments of interest that do not change too many things at once
- failure to choose the degree of institutional complexity appropriate to the problem being investigated

Any one of these failures pretty much renders results meaningless, even if the experiment is otherwise carefully conceived and reported. Finally, although these mistakes are readily spotted by the critic after the experiment is conducted, they can only be corrected before collecting data. A little extra planning and reflection prior to conducting an experiment can save many headaches.

1.7 Laboratory Trading Institutions

Economists have traditionally viewed economic problems almost exclusively in terms of *structural* characteristics, such as the number of agents, their endowments, initial information, preferences, costs, and productive technologies. These structural characteristics, which must be induced in an experiment, are often referred to as the *environment*. The discovery of the behavioral importance of trading rules by Smith and others has led economists to reconsider the importance of *institutions*. In a loose sense, a market institution specifies the rules that govern the economic interaction: the nature and timing of messages and decisions, and the mapping from these messages and decisions to the traders' monetary earnings.

Adding a specification of a trading institution to the analysis of an economic problem is consistent with the analytic approach taken by game theorists: both the game theorist and the experimentalist will assert that a full articulation of the problem's institutional and environmental components is necessary. The game theorist, however, uses somewhat different terminology. The articulation of a problem for the game theorist requires identification of each of the components of an extensive-form game that maps vectors of feasible strategies into utility "payoffs" for each player. Relevant components are comprised of a series of factors, which include the number of players, their payoff functions, and their knowledge (information sets).[38] There is no simple correspondence between the game-theoretic and experimental terminology. For example, some payoff-relevant factors, such as commissions and transactions taxes, can be considered to be components of the trading institution. Other payoff-relevant factors, such as values or costs, define components of the environment. Each terminology has its benefits, and at various points each will be used.[39]

Regardless of the type of experiment or the focus of investigation, institutional rules and other environmental features must be specified. Most advanced theory texts do not pay much attention to institutional rules. For example, at the outset of a typical text, a tatonnement mechanism with its famous hypothetical auctioneer may be presented to justify price-taking competitive behavior. In a tatonnement mechanism, an auctioneer calls out a series of prices. Each agent responds to the announcements by truthfully indicating a quantity that the agent desires to purchase or sell at the price under consideration. In this sense, traders are "price takers." A competitive, binding allocation occurs when quantity supplied equals quantity demanded.[40] Competitive outcomes are assumed in the typical microeconomics text, at least until a chapter on imperfect competition that is likely to motivate noncompetitive outcomes with other institutions, such as the Cournot quantity-choice model, which (strictly speaking) rarely exists in naturally occurring markets.[41] This neglect of institutional detail is unfortunate, since seemingly small alterations in the laboratory trading rules can have large effects, both on game-theoretic predictions and on observed behavior. Therefore, issues of institutional design are central in experimental economics.

Experimentalists tend to classify experiments by both the institution and the subfield of economics that provides the research hypotheses. These two dimensions are closely related in practice. For example, Smith's double auctions are commonly used in the study of financial markets. Institutions with publicly posted list prices are commonly used in the analysis of retail markets with many small buyers. The organization of this book, therefore, is largely determined by the sequence of institutions considered. For this reason, a description of the commonly used

---

[38] These terms are discussed in detail in chapter 2.

[39] The terminology of the experimentalist has the advantage of forcing consideration of the manipulable components of an economic process even in instances where the structure of the game is too complicated to allow game-theoretic equilibrium analysis.

[40] Price vectors, rather than single prices, are called out by the auctioneer in a multimarket setting.

[41] The Cournot institution is discussed below.

laboratory institutions will provide a useful overview of the remainder of the book. It is also important to see how different institutions are related, since the intuition gained by observing trading in one institution can help one understand behavior in closely related contexts.

The essential differences between the initially bewildering array of laboratory institutions to be encountered are listed in tables 1.3 and 1.4. The tables are distinguished by the timing of decisions. Simpler environments, where decisions are made independently (and in this sense simultaneously), are summarized in table 1.3. Table 1.4 summarizes more complex institutions where decisions are made sequentially, and in real time. In each table, the name of the institution is listed in the left column. The second column indicates the numbers of sellers and buyers, where a dash corresponds to any integer, and the special cases of one seller or one buyer are indicated with the number 1. The parenthetical notation in the second column indicates the number of units to be sold in auctions with an exogenously fixed supply. The third column shows whether buyers or sellers send price messages, which are called "bids" for buyers or "offers" or "asking prices" for sellers. The fourth column indicates whether messages are made simultaneously or sequentially. The final column, on the right side of the table, shows who responds to price proposals and how contracts are confirmed.

The remainder of this section summarizes principal characteristics of these trading institutions. The discussion is divided into two subsections; simultaneous-decision institutions are considered first, followed by discussion of sequential-decision institutions.

Institutions Involving Simultaneous Decisions

It is natural to begin this discussion with the simple quantity-choice framework first articulated by Cournot (1838), because much of oligopoly theory is formulated in terms of this institution. In the *Cournot institution*, seller subjects select quantities simultaneously, and then each seller is told the aggregate quantity selected by all sellers. This market quantity determines price according to a simulated-buyer inverse demand schedule, which can be given to subjects in tabular form. Subjects use their own cost information to calculate their money profits. Subjects may or may not have complete information about other sellers' costs. As summarized in the first row of table 1.3, there can be any number of buyers and sellers, and no one sends price messages, since price is endogenous.[42] An important disadvantage of this Cournot (posted quantity) institution is that critical behavioral assumptions are built into it; the implicit assumption is that, after output quantities are produced,

---

[42] The Cournot institution has been used in experiments by Carlson (1967), Holt (1985), Holt and Villamil (1986), Welford (1990), and others.

competition will drive price down (up) to the level at which there is no excess supply (demand).

Table 1.3 Trading Institutions with Simultaneous Decisions

	#Sellers/# Buyers (# units)	Who Proposes Prices	Decisions and Timing	How Contracts Confirmed
Cournot (quantity choice)	- / -	price is endogenous	quantities posted simultaneously	simulated buyers
Posted Offer Auction	- / -	sellers	offers posted simultaneously	buyers shop in sequence
Ultimatum Bargaining (offer version)	1/1	seller	seller makes single offer on 1 unit	buyer accepts or rejects
Posted Bid Auction	- / -	buyers	bids posted simultaneously	sellers shop in sequence
Discriminative Auction	1 / - (N units)	buyers	bids posted simultaneously	highest N bidders pay own bids
1st Price Sealed-Bid Auction	1 / - (1 unit)	buyers	bids posted simultaneously	high bidder pays own "1st" price
Competitive Sealed-Bid Auction	1 / - (N units)	buyers	bids posted simultaneously	highest N bidders pay N+1st price
Second Price Sealed-Bid Auction	1 / - (1 unit)	buyers	bids posted simultaneously	highest bidder pays 2nd price
Clearinghouse Auction	- / -	buyers and sellers	bids and offers posted simultaneously	intersection of bid and offer arrays

The most prominent alternative to the Cournot model of quantity competition is the Bertrand (1883) model of price competition. An important implication of the Bertrand model is that price competition can lead to competitive outcomes, even in highly concentrated markets. Given a homogeneous product, excess capacity, and simultaneous price postings, this result follows, since each seller always has an incentive to undercut any common supracompetitive price. The extremity of this prediction has led some commentators to defend the Cournot model as a more reasonable predictor of the outcome of *price* competition in markets with few sellers. For example, Spence (1976, p. 235) notes that "the quantity version captures a part of the tacit coordination to avoid all-out price competition, that I believe characterizes most industries." Hart (1979, p. 28) makes a similar argument: "We reject the Bertrand approach because it has the implausible implication that perfect competition is established even under duopoly." These arguments, however, cannot be used to justify the exogenous imposition of the Cournot institution in laboratory markets. Indeed the arguments suggest the opposite: that is, the use of a price-choice institution to see whether the resulting prices approximate the level determined by the equilibrium in a Cournot quantity-choice game.

The Cournot institution is reasonably used in experimental analysis to test the predictions of theories built on a Cournot model. However, both theories and tests of theories that more explicitly address the mechanics of price determination will allow more direct insights into the dynamics of naturally occurring processes. For this reason, it is desirable to implement an institution where fewer behavioral assumptions are "hard wired" into the trading mechanism. Bertrand models with price-setting firms have the distinct advantage of having a direct analogue in those natural markets where sellers independently post and advertise a price.

Instances where sellers publicly post "list" prices are common: sellers quote prices on a take-it-or-leave-it basis in many retail and mail-order situations, for example. Laboratory implementations of this price-setting activity are typically operationalized in the form of a *posted-offer auction*. In this institution, sellers independently select a price and a maximum quantity limit. After prices and quantity limits have been selected, the prices are displayed on the blackboard or on all traders' computer screens. Then buyers are chosen randomly from a waiting mode. The first buyer selected makes purchases from sellers at their posted prices. When a buyer has purchased all desired units, another buyer is selected randomly and is given the same opportunity. The trading period ends when all buyers have had an opportunity to shop or when all sellers are out of stock. Then earnings are calculated, and a new period typically follows. The characteristics of the posted-offer auction are summarized in the second row of table 1.3.

Allowing one side of the market to post terms of trade on a nonnegotiable basis represents an important behavioral asymmetry. To anticipate these effects, imagine a bilateral monopoly situation in which a single unit may be traded. The seller has a cost of $1.00, and the buyer has a value of $2.00. With unstructured bilateral bargaining, one would expect the traders to reach a price agreement somewhere in the middle. But if the trading institution enables the seller to post a take-it-or-leave-it price offer, one would expect the seller to extract the bulk of the available surplus. In theory, the seller could sell the unit at any price below $2.00. But extreme price demands are somewhat tempered in this context, as agents sometimes refuse to complete contracts proposed on very inequitable terms (see chapter 5). A posted-offer institution with one seller and one buyer, and where only a single unit is exchanged, is referred to as an *ultimatum bargaining game*. The characteristics of this game are summarized in row 3 of table 1.3. The intuition provided by the ultimatum game carries over somewhat to posted-offer oligopoly cases: in laboratory experiments, the overall effect of allowing sellers to post offers is to raise prices and reduce market efficiency (Plott and Smith, 1978, and Plott, 1986a).[43] The effects of posted-pricing are considered in detail in chapter 4.

There are a number of closely related institutions in which some agents post terms of agreement on a nonnegotiable basis. Characteristics of these related institutions are listed in the remaining rows of table 1.3. Reversing the roles of buyers and sellers in a posted offer (i.e., allowing buyers to post bids and subsequently selecting sellers in random order to make sales decisions) implements the *posted-bid auction*, which is characterized in the fourth row. The case where buyers submit posted bids to a single seller, who offers some fixed number of units, N, to the highest bidders, generates a *discriminative auction*, summarized in the fifth row of the table. For example, if two units are offered for sale and four bidders submit bids of 15, 17, 10, and 9, then the first two bidders obtain the units at prices of 15 and 17 respectively. This auction is called discriminative since winners must pay their own bid prices, and in this sense the seller engages in "price discrimination." The U.S. Treasury uses a variation of a discriminatory auction to sell Treasury bills to major buyers each week. When there is only one unit or "prize," the high bidder in a discriminative auction wins the auction and purchases it at his/her bid price, which is the highest, or "first" price. Therefore, a discriminative auction with a single unit is sometimes called a *first-price sealed-bid auction*. In contrast to the discriminative case, it is possible to design a mechanism for selling multiple units in which all of the N highest (winning) bidders pay a uniform price. When the uniform price is specified to be the highest rejected bid, the institution is known as a *competitive auction*. In the previous example, with two units and bids of 15, 17, 10, and 9, the first two bidders obtain the units, but they pay the same price, 10. Since all winning bidders pay the same market-clearing price, this institution can create an impression of fairness. A *second-price auction* is a special case of a competitive sealed-bid auction with only one prize; the highest rejected bid is the second highest price, which is what the winning bidder must pay. One issue to be considered in chapter 5 is whether sales revenues are higher with a discriminative or a competitive auction.

---

[43] Since the posted-price institution is similar to the rate-posting procedures that have been imposed by government regulators in several industries, the relative inefficiency of the posted price institution has important policy implications (Hong and Plott, 1982).

As a final simultaneous-choice institution, we mention the *clearinghouse auction,* summarized in the bottom row of table 1.3. This auction is two-sided; buyers submit bids and sellers submit offers. Once submitted, bids are arrayed in descending order, from highest to lowest, while offers are arrayed in ascending order, from lowest to highest. A price is then determined by a crossing of the bid and offer arrays. This two-sided institution eliminates the performance asymmetries associated with allowing only one side of the market to submit price quotes. Variants of the clearinghouse auction are used in stock exchanges. For example, the New York Stock Exchange opens each day with a clearinghouse auction, prior to commencing trades on a continuous basis. Several European stock exchanges are organized exclusively on clearinghouse rules (Van Boening, 1990). Experiments regarding some variants of the clearinghouse auction, which are either currently being used or proposed, are reviewed in chapter 5.

Institutions Involving Sequential Decisions

We turn our attention now to markets where agents make key decisions sequentially and in real time. These institutions, summarized in table 1.4, are much more difficult to analyze theoretically than those presented in table 1.3, but they are closer to institutional rules in many financial, commodities, and producer goods markets. We proceed from the most complex institution, Chamberlin's *decentralized negotiations* listed at the bottom of table 1.4, and work up the table.

As noted earlier, Chamberlin's subjects were allowed to roam freely around the room and negotiate contracts. Each seller (buyer) had one unit that could be sold (purchased) with a cost (reservation value) listed on a card. After a contract was completed, the buyer and seller would report the price to the professor's desk, and the price was usually written on the blackboard at the time it was reported. The most striking departure from the competitive outcome predicted by the intersection of the induced supply and demand curves was the tendency for quantity exchanged to be too high.

Chamberlin attributed the high sales quantity to the decentralized nature of the bargaining process. He supported this conjecture with a *simulation* in which he first constructed a series of submarkets by randomly drawing three buyer cards and three seller cards drawn from a deck of cost and value cards, and enacting all trades that would occur in a competitive equilibrium for the submarket. Cards for units that were not traded were returned to the deck, and the process was repeated many times. This simulation generated transaction quantities that exceeded the competitive level, and the excess quantity declined as the size of the simulated submarkets was increased. (Note the difference between an experiment with human traders and a simulation with artificial agents that follow exogenously specified decision rules.)

To understand how decentralized negotiations can result in high trading volume, recall the quantity-maximization hypothesis for the market illustrated in

Table 1.4 Trading Institutions with Sequential Decisions

	#Sellers/ #Buyers	Who Proposes Prices	Decisions and Timing	How Contracts Confirmed
Dutch Auction	1 / - (1 unit)	seller clock	price lowered sequentially	buyer who stops clock
English Auction	1 / - (1 unit)	auctioneer	prices raised sequentially	sale to high bidder
Bid Auction	- / -	buyers	prices raised sequentially	sellers
Offer Auction	- / -	sellers	prices lowered sequentially	buyers
Double Auction	- / -	both types	bids raised and offers lowered sequentially	both types
Decentralized Negotiation	- / -	both types	sequential but decentralized	both types

figure 1.2 and summarized in the rightmost column of table 1.1. Note that up to twelve units can trade in this market (five more than the competitive quantity), but prices must be quite variable to generate (inefficient) trades of extra-marginal units with high costs or low values. While centralized bid and offer information would tend to eliminate trades involving extra-marginal units, the absence of information on the bid-ask spread in decentralized markets would facilitate the consummation of these inefficient contracts.

Subsequent experimental results are largely consistent with Chamberlin's explanation of excess-quantity with decentralized trading. Although the earnings in Chamberlin's experiment were hypothetical, Hong and Plott (1982) observed excess trading volume in decentralized trading among financially motivated subjects who communicated with each other bilaterally by telephone.[44]

---

[44] One apparent exception to this excess-quantity result is Joyce (1983), who observed only small quantity increases in "Chamberlin" markets (with decentralized trading among subjects walking around a room) over symmetric double-auction markets of the type used by Smith (1962). A closer examination of Joyce's structure, however, suggests that, if anything, the relatively small quantity increases observed by Joyce actually support the excess-quantity hypothesis. Joyce's supply and demand arrays allowed for the possible trade of only one extra-marginal unit; his design is quite similar to the design in figure 1.2 if one were to remove the second, high-cost units for sellers S2-S5 and the second, low-value units for

Smith (1962, 1964) induced more price uniformity and fewer extra-marginal trades with his *double auction*. Under double-auction rules, any buyer who makes a bid must raise his/her hand and be recognized. The bid is then publicly announced to the market. Sellers' offers are also publicly announced. All bids and offers are written on the blackboard as they are made. Only the most attractive bid or offer has "standing" or can be accepted. Any buyer is free at any time to accept a standing offer, and any seller can accept a standing bid. It is a common practice to add an "improvement rule," that is, that a new bid be greater than the standing bid and that a new offer be lower than the standing offer. This is a double auction in the sense that bids rise, as in a typical auction for antiques, and offers fall at the same time. The acceptance of a bid or offer constitutes a binding contract that typically invalidates all previous bids and offers, but new bids or offers can be tendered. After time allotted to the market period is over, the market closes, and subjects calculate their earnings.[45] Then the market reopens, usually with the same initial endowments of unit values or costs for each buyer or seller, and with no inventory carryover. Under these stationary market conditions, the aggregate demand and supply functions are the same at the beginning of each period. Traders are normally given no information about the values and costs of other traders.

Smith (1976) recalls that he "did not seriously expect competitive price theory to be supported," but that the double auction would give the theory its best chance. Smith's experiments generally produced prices and quantities that were surprisingly near competitive levels, although some marginally profitable units did not always trade, for example, the units of traders B1 and S1 in figure 1.2.

Due to its impressively robust performance, the double auction is probably the most commonly used laboratory trading mechanism. Such auctions are often conducted on either a mainframe computer network, such as the University of Illinois' NovaNet computer system (formerly PLATO), or on a network of personal computers. Williams (1980) and Smith and Williams (1981, 1983) describe other details of the NovaNet (PLATO) implementation. In particular, there is an improvement rule and a "rank queue," which stores ranked bids that are below the highest outstanding bid (or inversely ranked offers that are above the lowest outstanding offer).[46] An improvement rule with a rank-ordered queue (an electronic "specialist's book") provides the least variability in observed prices, and this is the rule that implements the prominent features of trading on the New York Stock Exchange.

---

buyers B3-B6. Then, at most, the excess quantity could be one unit, and the resulting efficiency loss would be small if the difference between cost and value of the extra-marginal units were small, as was the case in his experiment.

[45] A market period lasts from three to ten minutes, depending on the numbers of traders and units being traded.

[46] The effects of these rules are discussed in chapter 3.

The striking competitive tendency of the double-auction institution, which has been confirmed by hundreds of sessions in a variety of designs, indicates that neither complete information nor large numbers of traders is a necessary condition for convergence to competitive equilibrium outcomes. Smith (1976, p. 57) concludes:

> There are no experimental results more important or more significant than that the information specifications of traditional competitive price theory are grossly overstated. The experimental facts are that no double auction trader needs to know *anything* about the valuation conditions of other traders, or have *any* understanding or knowledge of market supply and demand conditions, or have *any* trading experience (although experience may speed convergence) or satisfy the quaint and irrelevant requirement of being a price "taker" (every trader is a price *maker* in the double auction).

The third and fourth rows of table 1.4 describe two simple variations on the double auction where only sellers or only buyers make price quotes: An *offer auction* is an institution in which sellers can make offers sequentially, and buyers are able to accept any offer, but not to make bids. This institution may approximate the way consumers use travel agents to purchase tickets via computerized airline reservations networks. Conversely, a *bid auction* refers to the opposite case in which buyers can make bids sequentially, but sellers can only indicate that a bid is accepted. In markets with at least four buyers and four sellers, the effects of differences between these three institutions are apparently minor, at least for some supply and demand parameterizations.[47] Finally, note that a bid auction with a single seller is essentially an *English auction* (but with no auctioneer) in which the seller waits while bids rise until only one active bidder remains. This is the familiar type of auction used for antiques and art, and its characteristics are shown in the second row of table 1.4. The top row of the table pertains to a *Dutch auction*, in which a single selling agent lowers the price sequentially until a buyer agrees to pay the seller's price. Often the prices are indicated by a mechanical pointer, like the hand of a clock, which falls over a price scale until a buyer presses a button to stop the clock. The first buyer to do this obtains a unit at the price in effect at the time that the clock was stopped. The Dutch auction derives its name from its extensive use in wholesale flower markets in Holland.

---

[47] Smith (1964) initially observed a consistent ranking: bid-auction prices > double-auction prices > offer-auction prices. But there is no theoretical basis for expecting such a ranking to occur generally, and this pattern did not appear in a subsequent experiment conducted under a different parameterization (Walker and Williams, 1988).

Other Institutions

There are many ways to alter the institutions described in this section. These alternatives deserve serious consideration. In particular, the double auction and the posted-offer auction are relied on too extensively, the double auction because it yields predictable competitive results in most contexts, and the posted-offer auction because it is simple to implement.

Consider, for example, two recent modifications of the posted offer. First, recall the standard restriction that sellers may not make sales at prices below the posted price in either a Bertrand game or the posted-offer auction that implements it. Buyers solicit and obtain price concessions from sellers in a wide variety of natural markets, particularly markets for producer goods and consumer durables. In contrast to the double auction, where price reductions are public and nonselective in the sense that any price reduction is offered to all buyers, price concessions in many decentralized markets are private and selective. Indeed, the apparent absence of secret discounts from list prices was one of the factors that triggered the Federal Trade Commission investigation of contractual practices of lead-based gasoline additive producers (the *Ethyl* case).[48]

Experiments with discounts from posted list prices are relatively rare. Grether and Plott (1984), motivated by the *Ethyl* case, conducted experiments in which sellers' list prices were communicated electronically to buyers and sellers in individual rooms. Then buyers could contact sellers by telephone to seek discounts, subject to contractual constraints that were the target of the FTC litigation.

More recently, Davis and Holt (1991) have implemented a *list/discount institution* in which sellers post prices at their computer terminals, as in a posted-offer auction, and buyers are selected from a waiting queue in a random sequence. Once selected, a buyer can request a discount, and the seller may or may not respond with a price reduction for that buyer. Davis and Holt report that sellers do discount if permitted, but that discounting opportunities do not necessarily make the pricing situation more competitive. Although this research is preliminary, one important result is that sellers will offer discounts if given the opportunity. Therefore, the posting of a single, nonnegotiable price in the standard posted-offer institution is an important restriction, and data from posted-offer markets should be interpreted with care.

A second and quite interesting variation of the posted offer is the introduction of continuous trading in a real-time context. Millner, Pratt, and Reilly (1990a and 1990b) have developed a *flow-market* version of the posted-offer institution. Sellers can alter prices at any instant, and the simulated demand determines sales flows per

---

[48]   *Ethyl Corporation, E.I. du Pont de Nemours and Company, PPG Corporation and Nalco Chemical Corporation*, Docket no. 9128. Federal Trade Commission.

unit of time as a function of the prices. Although flow markets are difficult to analyze theoretically, they introduce an element of realism that, as we shall see, is especially useful in the analysis of "hit-and-run" entry.

1.8 Conclusion and Overview

Laboratory methods have provided economists with a level of replicability and control that was not previously available. Moreover, as illustrated by the effects of changes in trading rules on market performance, it is clear that experiments can be used to demonstrate the importance of variables typically thought to be unimportant in explaining behavior. Thus, experimentation holds out the promise of a new, symbiotic relationship between economic theory and evidence.

Experiments also provide an inexpensive way to examine various economic policy proposals, and while the results of policy experiments are seldom definitive, the presumption is that what does not work in simple situations should not work in more complex natural environments. Thus, experimentation may allow identification of proposals that are unlikely to be effective, and this can shift the burden of proof for policy proposals that do exhibit predicted results in the laboratory.

Experiments have been used to evaluate performance in a wide variety of trading institutions. It is easiest to derive the implications of relevant theories in more structured institutions. More complicated institutions, especially those that allow discounting and active buyer shopping for discounts, are difficult to analyze but generate environments that are appropriate for the study of markets with large buyers. Posted-offer and double-auction markets represent the most thoroughly investigated institutions. The posted-offer institution is easy to implement and is a good approximation of the pricing process in retail situations in which the seller prices on a take-it-or-leave-it basis. Informationally rich double-auction markets correspond to the open trading that occurs in many centralized stock markets. Extensions of posted-offer and double-auction institutions deserve serious consideration.

The remainder of this text is devoted to the techniques and lessons of experimental investigation in economics. The discussion begins, in chapter 2, with an introduction to topics in individual decision theory and game theory. This chapter has a dual purpose: first, it reviews (or perhaps introduces) some essential theoretical assumptions and tools used in the remainder of the manuscript. Second, it introduces some useful experimental techniques for evaluating these elements. Given this foundation, we turn our attention to the behavioral consequences of a variety of trading institutions. Double-auction markets are the subject of chapter 3, while posted-offer markets are the subject in chapter 4. The fifth chapter then considers a variety of additional institutions, ranging from very simple trading mechanisms, such as bilateral bargaining and uniform price auctions, to more sophisticated mechanisms, such as variants of the clearinghouse auction. Some prominent areas where experiments have been used are considered in the next two chapters. Chapter 6 discusses experiments involving public goods and externalities, and chapter 7 discusses experiments designed to investigate problems of asymmetric information. Chapter 8 contains a somewhat more technically demanding discussion of individual choice experiments. We conclude the book by returning to a discussion of experimental methodology. Chapter 9 discusses the relationship between research objectives, experimental design, and statistical analysis of data. This final chapter is essential for readers who wish to make the transition from reviewing prior experimental results to doing their own original research.[49]

---

[49] A teacher using this material as a course reference may wish to deviate from this order of presentation. In a one-semester undergraduate course, one could truncate the discussion of chapter 2, and then follow chapters 3 and 4 with the applications discussions in chapters 6 and 7. Topics in chapters 5, 8 and 9 could be presented as time permits, at the end of the semester.

APPENDIX A1

This appendix contains instructions for administering an oral double auction. The instructions are based on those widely used in experimental economics, but they are written for demonstration rather than research purposes.[50] It is assumed that neither the experiment administrator nor the participants have experience with double auctions. Additional examples and explanations have been added to anticipate many common mistakes and questions. Some of the explanations may consequently seem rather tedious to an experimentalist, and some of the sequences of bids and offers in the Trading Rules section may be a little too suggestive of actual trading strategies for research purposes. To adapt these instructions for use as a research tool, we suggest removing the material marked with brackets.

This appendix is divided into two parts. The first part contains instructions for participants, while the second part presents a detailed list of administrative tasks associated with conducting a laboratory market session. Although many of these tasks also apply to other types of experiments, the discussion here is in terms of a double auction, since lists of procedural guidelines are both clearer and more interesting when they are presented in the context of a specific experiment. Tasks necessary for a classroom demonstration are marked with an asterisk to distinguish them from those that are only necessary for research purposes.[51] Most of the lists are also relevant if the experiment is computerized, but fewer assistants and less paper and preparation materials are required.

---

[50] There are a variety of instances where one might use a laboratory trading session for purposes of demonstration. In particular, it is useful to conduct a double auction in an initial meeting of an experimental economics course, before students have done any reading in chapter 1. An exercise of this type not only demonstrates the robust convergence of the double auction, but it also directs the attention of students to the links between theoretical predictions and evidence. The authors often have participants record data from the classroom session, as well as the underlying cost and value parameters for the market. Students are then asked to consider theories explaining why the (typically rather stable) series of prices was observed. A subsequent class discussion would focus on the empirical consequences of theories, and on how the predictions of rival theories may be behaviorally distinguished.

[51] For an alternative, somewhat more detailed list, see Plott (1986b).

A1.1 Oral Double-Auction Instructions [*for demonstration*]

Today we are going to set up a market in which some of you will be buyers and others will be sellers. The commodity to be traded is divided into distinct items or "units." We will not specify a name for the commodity; we will simply refer to units.

Trading will occur in a sequence of trading periods. The prices that you negotiate in each trading period will determine your earnings, in dollars and cents. You will keep track of these earnings on the forms provided. [*These earnings are hypothetical; nobody will make or receive actual cash payments.*][52]

We will proceed in the following way. First I will explain how buyers and sellers compute their earnings, and then I will explain how sales and purchases are arranged in the market. Importantly, these instructions explain how *both* sellers and buyers calculate earnings and negotiate contracts. In today's market, however, you will be *either* a buyer or a seller. Information specific to your role in today's market will be presented to you at the end of the instructions. After reading the instructions and reviewing your specific information, I will give you a chance to ask any questions you might have. Then we will begin the first trading period.

Instructions for Sellers

Seller decisions and earnings will be recorded on a sheet similar to the Seller Decision Sheet, shown below. Trading periods are designated by separate columns. In each trading period, a seller may sell up to two units. For the first unit that may be sold during a period, the seller incurs a cost of the amount listed in row 2, marked "cost of 1st unit." If a second unit is sold during the same period, the seller incurs the cost listed in row 5, marked "cost of 2nd unit." A seller may sell one or both units in a period and may sell to either a single buyer or different buyers.

Sellers earn money by selling units at prices that are above their costs. Earnings from the sale of each unit are computed by taking the difference between the sales price and the unit cost. Total earnings for the period are computed by adding up the earnings on all units sold.

Consider, for example, trades in period 0 of the Seller Decision Sheet. In this practice period, the cost for the first unit is $130, and the cost for the second unit is $140, as shown in rows 2 and 5. Suppose a seller negotiates sales of both units in period 0; the first unit for a price of $190 and the second unit for a price of $160. To record these sales, please enter $190 in row 1 and $160 in row 4 of the Seller

---

[52] If cash earnings are to be paid, substitute the following: All money that you earn during the trading will be yours to keep and will be paid to you, privately, in cash at the end of the session today. These earnings are in addition to the $_.__ initial payment that the assistant will give to each of you at this time.

unit	row		0	1	2	3

SELLER DECISION SHEET for SELLER _____

			trading period			
unit	row		0	1	2	3
1st unit	1	selling price				
	2	cost of 1st unit	$130			
	3	earnings				
2nd unit	4	selling price				
	5	cost of 2nd unit	$140			
	6	earnings				
	7	total earnings for the period	(not paid)			
	8	cumulative earnings	$0.00			

A Sample Seller Decision Sheet

Decision Sheet. Remember to stay in the shaded column for period 0.

Earnings on the sale of the first unit are obtained by subtracting the cost in row 2, which is $130, from the selling price in row 1, which is $190. The difference of $60 should be entered in row 3 at this time. Similarly, everyone should compute the earnings from the sale of the second unit and enter it in row 6. Total earnings for the period would be the sum of $60 (on the first unit sold) and $20 (on the second unit sold). If this were not a practice period, this sum of $80 would now be entered in row 7. Earnings in this example are for illustrative purposes only; actual earnings will be lower.

Subsequent periods are represented by numbered columns: period 1, period 2, etc. The blanks in each column of the Seller Decision Sheet will help sellers to keep track of their earnings in a period. But please remember: all calculations for each period should be reflected in the column *for that period*.

Importantly, a seller does not incur the cost for a unit unless the unit is sold. Thus, earnings for each unsold unit in a period are zero. If you are a seller, the first unit you sell during a trading period is *your* "1st unit," regardless of whether or not other sellers have previously sold units in the period. The sale price for your first unit should be recorded in row 1 immediately after the sale, and the earnings should be recorded in row 3. If you sell a second unit, record its sale price in row 4 immediately. You cannot sell your second unit before your first unit, and therefore you will move *down a column* during a period. Units listed on adjacent columns are unavailable until subsequent trading periods. At the end of the period, record your total earnings in row 7 of your decision sheet. Earnings for subsequent periods will be calculated similarly, and you should keep track of your cumulative earnings in the bottom row of the decision sheet.

Instructions for Buyers

Buyer decisions and earnings will be recorded on a sheet similar to the Buyer Decision Sheet, shown below. This sheet is formatted in a manner parallel to the Seller Decision sheet, with trading periods designated by separate columns. In each trading period, a buyer may purchase up to two units. For the first unit that may be bought during a period, the buyer receives the amount listed in row 1, marked "value of 1st unit." If a second unit is purchased during the same period, the buyer receives the additional amount listed in row 4, marked "value of 2nd unit." A buyer may purchase one or both units in a period and may buy from either a single seller or different sellers.

Buyers earn money by purchasing units at prices that are below their values. Earnings from the purchase of each unit are computed by taking the difference between the value of the unit and the purchase price. Total earnings for the period are computed by adding up the earnings on all units purchased.

Consider, for example, purchases in period 0 of the Buyer Decision Sheet. In this practice period, the value of the first unit is $210 and the value of the second unit is $170, as shown in rows 1 and 4. Suppose a buyer negotiates the purchase of two units in period 0; the first unit for a price of $160 and the second unit for a price of $150. To record these purchases, please enter $160 in row 2 and $150 in row 5 of the Buyer Decision Sheet. Remember to stay in the shaded column for period 0.

Earnings on the purchase of the first unit are obtained by subtracting the purchase price in row 2, which is $160, from the value in row 1, which is $210. The difference of $50 should be entered in row 3 at this time. Next, everyone should compute the earnings from the purchase of the second unit and enter it in row 6. Total earnings for the period would be the sum of $50 (on the first unit purchased) and $20 (on second unit purchased). If this were not a practice period, this sum of $70 would now be entered in row 7. Earnings in this example are for illustrative purposes only; actual earnings will be lower.

			trading period			
unit	row		0	1	2	3
1st unit	1	value of 1st unit	$210			
	2	purchase price				
	3	earnings				
2nd unit	4	value of 2nd unit	$170			
	5	purchase price				
	6	earnings				
	7	total earnings for the period	(not paid)			
	8	cumulative earnings	$0.00			

BUYER DECISION SHEET for BUYER _____

A Sample Buyer Decision Sheet

Subsequent periods are represented by separate columns; period 1, period 2, etc. The blanks in each column of the Buyer Decision Sheet will help buyers to keep track of their earnings in a period. But please remember; all calculations for each period should be reflected in the column *for that period.*

Importantly, a buyer does not receive the value for a unit unless the unit is purchased. Thus, earnings for each unpurchased unit in a period are zero. If you are a buyer, the first unit that you purchase during a period is *your* "1st unit," regardless of whether or not other buyers have previously bought units in the period. The purchase price for your 1st unit should be recorded in row 2 immediately after the purchase, and the earnings should be recorded in row 3. If you buy a second unit, record its purchase price in row 5 immediately. You cannot buy your second unit before your first unit. Therefore, you will move *down a column* during a period. Units listed in subsequent columns are not available until subsequent trading periods. At the end of the period, record your total earnings in row 7 of your decision sheet. Earnings for subsequent periods will be calculated similarly, and you should keep track of your cumulative earnings in the bottom row of the decision sheet.

Trading Rules

I will begin each five-minute trading period with an announcement that the market is open. At any time during the period, any buyer is free to raise his/her hand and, when called on, to make a verbal bid to buy a unit at a price specified in the bid. Similarly, any seller is free to raise his/her hand and, when called on, to make a verbal offer to sell a unit at the price specified in the offer. All bids and offers pertain to one unit, it is not possible to sell two units as a package.

All buyers and sellers have identification numbers; your number is given in the upper part of a Decision Sheet that is in your folder. These numbers should be used when making a bid or offer. Buyers should use the word "bid," and sellers should use the word "ask." For example, if Buyer 1 wants to make a bid of $120, then this person would raise his/her hand and, when recognized, say "Buyer 1 bids $120." I will repeat the buyer number and the bid to give the person at the blackboard time to record it. Similarly, if Seller 5 decides to offer a unit for sale at $250, this seller should raise his/her hand and, when recognized, say "Seller 5 asks $250." I will repeat this information while it is recorded, and the blackboard will appear

Bids	Asks
B1 120	S5 250

We ask you to help us enforce a bid/ask improvement rule: All bids must be higher than the highest outstanding bid, should one exist, and asking prices must be lower than the lowest outstanding offer, should one exist. In the example above, the next bid must be above $120, and the next ask must be below $250.

[For example, suppose that Buyer 1, the next person recognized, raises his/her own bid from $120 to $130, and then Seller 4 is called on and asks $165. I would repeat the bid and ask as they are recorded on the blackboard:

Bids	Asks
B1 120	*S5 250*
B1 130	*S4 165*

]

To save space, the bids and asks will be written in small numbers, without the dollar signs and decimals. Please tell us if you cannot read the numbers recorded or if you think that a bid or ask was not recorded correctly.

Any seller is free at any time to accept or not accept the bid of any buyer, and any buyer is free to accept or not accept the asking price of any seller. To accept a bid or ask, simply raise your hand. After you are recognized, announce your identity and indicate acceptance, e.g., Buyer 2 accepts Seller 3's ask.

[*Suppose that Buyer 3 bids $160, and that the next person recognized is Seller 5 who accepts this bid. I would repeat this acceptance, while the person at the blackboard circles the buyer number, seller number, and transactions price. To see how this will look, please draw a flat circle around the boldfaced row in the following chart.*]

Bids		Asks	
B1	120	S5	250
B1	130	S4	165
B3	**160**	**S5 accepts**	

Instead of accepting the bid of $160, Seller 5 could have stated an asking price that is below the highest outstanding bid, say at $150, but to do so would result in a lower sale price than could have been obtained by accepting the bid of $160.]

If a bid or ask is accepted, a binding contract has been closed for a single unit, and the buyer and seller involved will immediately record the contract price and earnings for the unit. After each contract is closed, all previous bids and asks will be automatically withdrawn before any new ones can be made.

[*Following the acceptance of Buyer 3's bid of $160, a horizontal line would have been drawn below the circled contract. Subsequent bids need not be above $160 and in fact could be below any of the earlier bids. The horizontal line is to remind you that the contract invalidates previous bids and asks.*

If Seller 4 wished to ask $165 again, this seller would raise his/her hand and be recognized. Suppose that Buyer 1 bids $140 and Buyer 3 is then recognized and accepts Seller 4's asking price. The blackboard will appear as below, except that the parties to a contract will be circled instead of boldfaced.]

Bids		Asks	
B1	120	S5	250
B1	130	S4	165
B3	**160**	**S5 accepts**	
B1	140	S4	165
B3 accepts			

Notice that Buyer 3 has just purchased his/her second unit. Instead of accepting the lowest standing offer of $165, this buyer could have made a higher bid, say $170, but to do so would have resulted in a higher purchase price than could have been obtained by accepting the offer of $165.]

Except for bids, asks, and their acceptances, you are expected not to speak to any other person, even if there are many bids and offers that are not accepted.

Procedural Details and Review

In your folder, you will find a sheet, labeled "Buyer Decision Sheet" or "Seller Decision Sheet." This sheet is separate from these instructions. It identifies your role as a buyer or seller and will be used to calculate your earnings. THE INFORMATION ON THIS SHEET IS PRIVATE, PLEASE DO NOT REVEAL IT TO ANYONE. Others may or may not have the same cost or value numbers that you have. You should now look at your decision sheet to see whether you are a buyer or a seller. Has everyone done this? Also, please note your identification number at the top of this sheet; this is how you will identify yourself during the trading process.

Now is the time for questions. You may ask questions about any aspect of the market of which you are unsure. However, be careful not to reveal the private cost or value information that appears on your decision sheet. Are there any questions?

(Questions)

We are about to begin trading period 1. Buyers should check the redemption values in rows 1 and 4 of the column for period 1. Recall, the only way for a buyer to earn money on a unit is to purchase it for a price that is below its redemption

value.[53] Similarly, sellers should check the cost numbers in the column for period
1. Recall, the only way for a seller to earn money on a unit is to sell it for a price
that exceeds its cost.[54] Barring any further questions, we will begin trading period
1. Are there any remaining questions?

(Questions)

Beginning the Session

The market is now open for bids and offers. If you raise your hand, please do
not speak until I call on you. I will do my best to call on people in the order in
which the hands went up, but if many hands go up at the same time I will have to
choose between people in a nonsystematic way. The period will last for ___
minutes and will end at _____. Are there any bids or asks?

(After the first contract is made, but not after subsequent contracts, read the
paragraph that follows.)

At this time the buyer and seller involved in this contract should record the
price and calculate their earnings. This buyer and seller now have finished with
their first units, and the relevant value or cost for them is that of their second unit
for period 1. The rest of you are still considering the sale or purchase of your first
unit in the period 1 column. Remember that when you make a contract, you move
down the column for the current period to your second unit; you do not move across
a row until the beginning of the next period. At this time, the recorder should draw
a horizontal line below the final bids and asks. There are ___ minutes remaining
in period 1, and the market is open for bids and asks.

(At the appropriate times, the one-minute and 30-second warnings are given.
At the end of the period, read:)

Period 1 has ended, and you should add up the earnings on units traded and
enter the total in row 7 of the column for this period. If you did not buy or sell a
unit, the earnings for that unit are zero. We will erase the blackboard as soon as all
transaction prices are recorded. At this time, one of us will come around to your
desk to check your calculations. Please do not talk with each other; if you have a
question, raise your hand.

---

[53] If trades at a loss are not permitted, insert: Buyers will not be permitted to make a purchase at
a price that exceeds their redemption value for the unit.

[54] If trades at a loss are not permitted, insert: Sellers will not be permitted to make a sale at a price
that is less than their cost for the unit.

Ending the Session (The following statement is to be read at the end of a research session.)

The final period has ended. Please refrain from talking while you finish adding up your cumulative earnings across periods in row 8. One of us will come around to assist you with this if necessary. Then add the $_.__ participation fee (paid previously) to the total and round the result up to the nearest 25-cent increment (e.g., $5.35 becomes $5.50). Enter the total on the receipt form that you will find in your folder. Please fill out the rest of the receipt form, making sure that you include the date, your signature, and your social security number. Then remain seated without talking until you are asked to take your receipt form to be paid. Please leave all other materials in the folder on your desk. Thank you for your participation.

A1.2 Suggestions for Conducting an Oral Double Auction

This section contains practical considerations that may help in the administration of an experiment. Our suggestions are organized into a series of lists that address concerns in approximately chronological order. The categories include experimental design, advance arrangements, preparation of folders and materials, recruiting, room preparation, starting the session, controlling the market trading, and ending the session.

Much more detailed planning is required for conducting a market for research than for demonstration purposes. In the latter case, attention may be confined to comments marked with an asterisk. Finally, although our listed considerations apply fairly generally to experimental sessions other than double-auction markets, they are not intended to be definitive in any application. In designing and conducting an experiment, the researcher should keep in mind the general principles of replicability, motivation, calibration, control, and unbiasedness discussed in the text.

Experimental Design

*1. Decide on the numbers of buyers and sellers. These numbers depend on the purpose and design of the experiment, but it is unwieldy to conduct an oral double auction with more than fifteen to twenty traders. In addition, it is useful to have four extra people to help:

i.   an *auctioneer* to read instructions and recognize buyers and sellers (this would be the instructor in a classroom demonstration)

ii.   a *first recorder* to record bids, asks, and contracts on the blackboard

iii.   a *second recorder* to record data on paper and keep time

iv.   a *monitor* to check for illegal trades (e.g., trades at a loss if they are not
       permitted)

If there are extra students present in a classroom demonstration, you can distribute
decision sheets to every second or third person and let students who are not
participating assist those who are.

*2. Decide on value and cost parameters. The participant decision sheets in
the instructions given above contain space for two units per person for a maximum
of three trading periods. Increases in the numbers of units or periods would require
straightforward changes in the instructions and decision sheets. No modification is
necessary if you use variants of the design discussed in section 1.3 (summarized in
table 1.1).[55]

3. Decide whether to permit trades at a loss (sales below cost or purchases
above value). In our experience, there will sometimes be trades at a loss in the first
period with inexperienced subjects. If trades at a loss are not permitted, extra
monitoring will be required; see item 1.iv in this list. Even if such trades are
permitted in a demonstration experiment, you may wish to explain (privately) why
the trade will result in a loss.

4. Decide on parameter shifts. For research sessions, it is essential to avoid
the possibility that prior expectations will affect behavior. After a session ends and
participants have left the room, they may talk with other potential participants. In
oral auctions, there is also the possibility that the auctioneer can affect outcomes,
perhaps inadvertently, through facial expressions. One solution is to add a
parameter-disguising constant to all values and costs, and to keep the auctioneer
uninformed of the equilibrium price. Decide on the length of the periods. Trading
will go more quickly after the first period or two, so shorter periods may be used
in a research experiment if trading volume is not too large. As a rough guide, count
on about forty-five seconds per unit that is expected to trade. Changes in the time
limits will require obvious changes in the instructions.

---

[55] This design has a number of features that are desirable for purposes of demonstration, including
symmetry (which tends to speed convergence), and clean separation between the competitive prediction
and rival predictions such as monopoly, monopsony, and quantity maximization. The numbers of buyers
and sellers may be easily modified in a way that retains the design's desirable features. For example, an
additional buyer and seller pair may be added to table 1.1 as follows. Key new buyer B7's values off
of those for B6: Make B7's first unit worth .10 more than B6's first unit, and B7's second unit should
be worth .10 less than B6's second unit. The new seller S7 should be given a first unit that costs .10 less
than S6's first unit, and then given the second unit previously held by S6 as a second unit. Then set the
cost of S6's second unit to .10 more than the cost of S5's second unit. The addition of trader pairs in
this manner preserves the difference between quantity maximization and competitive predictions.

Advance Arrangements

1. Hire four assistants to cover the roles described above, and stress the need to arrive on time.

2. Instruct assistants not to talk unnecessarily during the experiment and not to provide suggestive or colorful answers to questions.

3. Reserve the room for the time needed, plus about fifteen minutes before the starting time and about thirty minutes afterward, to reduce "end-effects" and to prevent a situation in which students for an incoming class are crowding around the doorway.

4. When paying earnings in cash, obtain sufficient change, usually a roll of quarters and the rest in $1, $5, and $10 bills. Note that the maximum earnings may be calculated in advance as the product of the number of periods and the sum of buyers' and sellers' surplus. To facilitate the making of change, bills should be primarily in small denominations.

Preparation of Folders and Materials

*1. Photocopy instructions for all participants, assistants, and observers. (For research sessions, remove "T" chart examples from the Trading Rules section of the instructions, as indicated by the square brackets.)

*2. Photocopy enough buyer and seller decision sheets, excerpted from the above instructions.

*3. Write the buyer or seller identification numbers at the top of each decision sheet. Unlike the example in section 1.3, there is probably less chance of mistaken identity if you use low numbers for buyers and high numbers for sellers, with no overlap.

*4. Write the buyers' values and sellers' costs, *for each unit and for each period*, on the appropriate decision sheets.

*5. Check to be sure that values and costs are recorded correctly and in the appropriate rows: 1 and 4 for buyers' values and 2 and 5 for sellers' costs. For a more thorough check, use the subjects' own decision sheets to reconstruct the market supply and demand functions.

*6. Make a folder for each participant with the identification number written on the folder and the following included: instructions, decision sheet marked with participant's identification number and cost or value parameters, and receipt form (if you are paying earnings in cash and will be reimbursed).

*7. Make a folder for yourself, with a copy of the instructions to be read and extra copies of receipt forms for alternates.

*8. Make a folder for each assistant, with instructions for all, a pad of paper for the person who records contracts, and, if relevant, a list of demand and cost parameters for the person who is to check for illegal trades (sales below cost or purchases above value). An example of such a list is given in section 1.3. It is most convenient to have multiple copies of the parameter list (one for each period) so the assistant can mark off units as they are traded.

*9. Bring extra pens for participants.

Recruiting

1. Prior to the day of the session, go to classes just at the beginning of class, with the instructor's prior approval, and use a prepared announcement to obtain a list of potential subjects. Ask the instructor not to make a speech about experimentation after you finish.

2. Use an announcement that is not suggestive about the type of behavior expected in the experiment, for example:

> You are invited to participate in one or more economics experiments that will be conducted in the next several months at the _____ (name of college or university) under the supervision of Professor _____.
>
> The experiment involves an economic decision-making situation, and if you participate, you will be paid $_.__ for appearing promptly at your scheduled appointment time. In addition, you will be able to earn money during the session, which will last about two hours. These earnings will be determined by your decisions and by the decisions of other participants. We cannot say in advance exactly what your earnings will be, but they will typically exceed the compensation that you would receive for working a comparable number of hours. All earnings will be paid in cash immediately after the session.
>
> There will be a number of sessions, each of which will last for about two hours. If you are interested in participating in one or more sessions, please supply the information requested below and return this sheet. If you do so, someone from the Economics Department will call you later to arrange a specific time and place. Thank you.
>
> Your Name_____
> Phone (day)_____
>   (evening, if different)_____

Please indicate which times are most likely to be convenient this semester; feel free to indicate more than one time:

> _____1530–1730 on a Tuesday
> _____1530–1730 on a Wednesday
> _____1530–1730 on a Thursday

3. When calling individuals who have expressed in interest in participation, identify yourself, be polite, and do not oversell, since a reluctant subject is unlikely to show up. A possible approach:

> Hello, this is _____ calling from the Economics Department about the experiment in which you expressed an interest. We're organizing a session tomorrow from __:__ to about __:__ in the afternoon (morning). Are you able to come? (If not, thank them and ask if they would like to be called again.) Do you have a pen to record the time and place? (Record the person's name on the participant list while they are going to get a pen.) The experiment will be held in room ___ of _____ (building) at __:__ p.m. (a.m.) tomorrow. There is no need to arrive early, but we cannot start until everyone is present, so please come on time. We need to have an exact number of people, so if you must cancel *for any reason*, please call us at _____ and leave a message saying that you will not come. We always recruit a couple of extras in case someone cancels at the last minute. As mentioned in the class announcement, we will pay everyone $__.__ for showing up, and therefore if all of the positions are taken when you arrive, we will pay you this amount and call you back another day. If you participate, all money that you earn in the session (plus the participation payment) will be paid to you in cash immediately afterward. You do not need to bring anything.

4. In some situations, on-the-spot recruiting is preferred to telephone recruiting.[56] To do this, divide the above recruiting announcement that is read in class into two parts. There should be a place for the student's name and phone number on the top part (names are needed so that unexpected substitutes can be turned away at the time of the experiment). The bottom part should be a tear-off part containing the time and place of the session. Instruct participants that returning the top part with their name and phone number written in the blanks indicates their intention to show up on time. It helps to confirm the details by phone with subjects who can be reached.

5. With either method of recruiting, you should be able to answer questions in a manner that reassures prospective subjects and arouses interest, without introducing biased expectations. Some useful comments: "This is not a test or an exam, it is not stressful." "I cannot be more precise about how much you may earn, since earnings differ from person to person and from experiment to experiment. I can say that most people volunteer to participate again." "I do not have time to describe the experiment in detail, and the nature of the experiment may change from

---

[56] In Spain, for example, it is very difficult to reach students by phone.

day to day. Some experiments involve students taking the roles of buyers and sellers in a market-like situation, for example."

6. Recruit subjects in a manner that minimizes the chances of getting friends or roommates. This is most easily accomplished via telephone recruiting, by calling individual subjects the night before the session, and using a list of phone numbers and names of people who had earlier expressed a general interest in participating on particular weekdays or time periods. This point is probably not important for individual decision-making experiments in which there is no interaction among subjects.

7. Make a list of participants' names so that you can check them off at the door when they arrive. In our experience, you will need to over-recruit by about 25 percent of the number of participants needed for a session when participants are inexperienced. Fewer alternates are needed if participants have had experience in a previous session. More alternates may be needed if you are recruiting directly from a class, for a session that is to take place several days later.

Room Preparation

*1.   Reorganize the seats in the room, if necessary, so that it is not possible for participants to read numbers off of others' decision sheets.

*2.   Check to be sure that the blackboard is clean or prepared with the T charts for recording bids and asks, and check for chalk and erasers. The T charts should be large enough to be read, but small enough so that lots of data can fit on the same blackboard.

*3. When the session is being conducted for research, arrange for one of the experimenters to arrive about twenty minutes early to ensure that subjects who come early do not talk with one another.

Starting the Session

1. Devise a random device (e.g., a bowl with marked, folded pieces of paper) to be used to assign subjects to roles as buyer or seller. This is particularly important in markets with large cost and value asymmetries.

2. Ask each subject who has been assigned a position to be seated and remain quiet until the session begins; proscribing talking facilitates replication and minimizes the effects of personal relationships.

3. Have an assistant show subjects to their seats while you stay at the door to meet subjects. This is a good time to distribute pens and any "consent form" that may be required by your university (such forms must typically be approved by a human subjects committee).

4. Keep subjects from opening their folders before you begin to read the instructions. This minimizes the possibility that subjects see the private information on each others' decision sheets.

5. If subjects have not participated previously, begin the experiment by making the initial payment and by showing them the cash that you will use to make payments after the session (otherwise some may have doubts about cash payments).

*6. Read the instructions aloud to the students; this creates common knowledge, and it will prevent boredom by ensuring that all finish at the same time. The instructions should not be read too quickly. Read the instructions exactly as they are written. Pause at appropriate times, for example, when subjects are asked to look at a different page or to write responses to questions based on an example. To facilitate replication, do not insert clarifying comments or examples. The urge to interject explanations is a sure sign that the instructions are too brief.

*7. Repeat questions clearly before answering them. Answers should only clarify the instructions. Do not provide new information; feel free to reread the relevant part of the instruction or say that you cannot answer that question. *Never* discuss the goals or anticipated outcomes.

Controlling the Market Trading

*1. The bids and asking prices should be written in relatively small letters and numbers so that the blackboard does not fill up too quickly. Be consistent and keep bids on the left and asking prices on the right. To save time, omit dollar signs and decimals. Insist that participants give their role and identification number (e.g., Buyer 1) before submitting bids and asks. Do not let people speak without being recognized, otherwise you will lose control. To keep roles clear, you should insist that buyers use the word "bid" and sellers use the word "ask," as in "Buyer 1 bids 140" or "Seller 5 asks 180."[57]

*2. The auctioneer should be prompted to give warnings when one minute and thirty seconds remain in the trading period. The period should be stopped exactly on time; to do otherwise will encourage traders to delay.

*3. The time between periods should be brief, say a couple of minutes. There should be no talking. If talking is a problem, explain that the instructions specify that participants should remain quiet at all times, as if you are just carrying out orders from above.

4. Have an assistant in the room with subjects at all times to maintain quiet, especially while subjects are being paid after the session in a separate location.

---

[57] Alternatively you could let sellers use the word "offer" instead of "ask."

5. To facilitate replication, be consistent about what remains on the chalkboard from one period to the next, either clean it every time or leave the same amount of data up from previous periods.

*6. Have an assistant check earning calculations after the first period. The assistant should also spot check major earning calculations throughout the session. Subjects are typically very honest, but it is necessary to avoid major calculation errors that dilute incentives.

7. In the event of a major error such as trading units from the wrong period, remember that such errors are equivalent to undesired shifts in supply or demand, and therefore that the session is probably useless for any purpose other than training subjects for later sessions. (It is often useful to replicate sessions using subjects who all have previous experience with the trading institution.)

Ending the Session

1. Ensure that subjects leave all instructions, decision sheets, etc. in their folders before being paid.

2. Pay subjects individually in a separate location, hallway, or visually isolated part of the room. Even though the session has ended, privacy in the payment process is important to avoid conditions in which feelings of envy, guilt, or benevolence after one session may affect a subject's behavior in a subsequent session. An assistant should send the subjects to you one at a time to avoid crowding around the payment area.

3. Ensure that subjects write their names, social security numbers, and signatures on receipt forms that you will need for records and to grant reimbursements. Receipt forms should then be placed face down so that other subjects will not be able to see the payment amounts.

4. Subjects should be able to leave the room individually without having to discuss earnings with others, even though you have no control over later hallway discussions.

5. Write a brief report after the session with the date, names of persons present, earnings, experimental design or treatment variables, significant procedural errors, and any salient pattern of the data. One of the least confusing ways to identify experiments is by date, unless you run more than one session on the same day.

REFERENCES

Ball, Sheryl B., and Paula A. Cech (1991) "The What, When and Why of Picking a Subject Pool," working paper, Indiana University.

Battalio, Raymond, John Kagel, R. Winkler, E. Fisher, R. Basmann, and L. Krasner (1973) "A Test of Consumer Demand Theory Using Observations of Individual Consumer Purchases," *Western Economic Journal, 11*, 411–428.

Bertrand, J. (1883) "Review of *Theorie Mathematique de la Richesse Sociale and Recherches sur les Principes Mathematicque de la Theoire des Richesse,*" *Journal des Savants*, 499–508.

Burns, Penny (1985) "Experience and Decision Making: A Comparison of Students and Businessmen in a Simulated Progressive Auction," in V. L. Smith, ed., *Research in Experimental Economics*, vol. 3. Greenwich, Conn.: JAI Press, 139–157.

Carlson, John (1967) "The Stability of an Experimental Market with a Supply-Response Lag," *Southern Economic Journal, 33*, 305–321.

Chamberlin, Edward H. (1948) "An Experimental Imperfect Market," *Journal of Political Economy, 56*, 95–108.

———— (1962) *The Theory of Monopolistic Competition (A Re-orientation of the Theory of Value)*, 8th edition. Cambridge: Harvard University Press.

Coleman, Andrew (1983) *Game Theory and Experimental Work*. London: Pergamon Press.

Cournot, Augustine (1838) *Researches into the Mathematical Principles of the Theory of Wealth*, trans. N. Bacon. New York: Kelly, 1960.

Cyert, Richard M., and Lester B. Lave (1965) "Collusion, Conflit et Science Economique," *Economie Appliquee, 18*, 385–406.

Davis, Douglas D., and Charles A. Holt (1991) "List Prices and Discounts," working paper, University of Virginia.

DeJong, Douglas V., Robert Forsythe, and Wilfred C. Uecker (1988) "A Note on the Use of Businessmen as Subjects in Sealed Offer Markets," *Journal of Economic Behavior and Organization, 9*, 87–100.

Dolbear, F. T., L. B. Lave, G. Bowman, A. Lieberman, E. Prescott, F. Rueter, and R. Sherman (1968) "Collusion in Oligopoly: An Experiment on the Effect of Numbers and Information," *Quarterly Journal of Economics, 82*, 240–259.

Dyer, Douglas, John Kagel, and Dan Levin (1989) "A Comparison of Naive and Experienced Bidders in Common Value Offer Auctions: A Laboratory Analysis," *Economic Journal, 99*, 108–115.

Encyclopedia Britannica, Macropaedia: Knowledge in Depth, 27, (1991) 15th edition. Chicago: University of Chicago Press.

Fouraker, Lawrence E., and Sidney Siegel (1963) *Bargaining Behavior*. New York: McGraw Hill.

Friedman, James W. (1963) "Individual Behavior in Oligopolistic Markets: An Experimental Study," *Yale Economic Essays*, *3*, 359–417.

——— (1967) "An Experimental Study of Cooperative Duopoly," *Econometrica*, *35*, 379–397.

——— (1969) "On Experimental Research in Oligopoly," *Review of Economic Studies*, *36*, 399–415.

Grether, David M., and Charles R. Plott (1984) "The Effects of Market Practices in Oligopolistic Markets: An Experimental Examination of the *Ethyl* Case," *Economic Inquiry*, *22*, 479–507.

Hart, Oliver D. (1979) "Monopolistic Competition in a Large Economy with Differentiated Commodities," *Review of Economic Studies*, *46*, 1–30.

Hinkelmann, Klaus (1990) "Experimental Design: The Perspective of a Statistician," working paper, Virginia Polytechnic Institute.

Holt, Charles A. (1985) "An Experimental Test of the Consistent-Conjectures Hypothesis," *American Economic Review*, *75*, 314–325.

Holt, Charles A., and Anne Villamil (1986) "A Laboratory Experiment with a Single-Person Cobweb," *Atlantic Economic Journal*, *14*, 51–54.

Hong, James T., and Charles R. Plott (1982) "Rate Filing Policies for Inland Water Transportation: An Experimental Approach," *The Bell Journal of Economics*, *13*, 1–19.

Isaac, R. Mark, and Vernon L. Smith (1985) "In Search of Predatory Pricing," *Journal of Political Economy*, *93*, 320–345.

Joyce, Patrick (1983) "Information and Behavior in Experimental Markets," *Journal of Economic Behavior and Organization*, *4*, 411–424.

Kagel, John H., Raymond C. Battalio, Howard Rachlin, Leonard Green, Robert L. Basmann, and W. R. Klemm (1975) "Experimental Studies of Consumer Behavior Using Laboratory Animals," *Economic Inquiry*, *13*, 22–38.

Lave, Lester B. (1962) "An Empirical Approach to the Prisoner's Dilemma," *Quarterly Journal of Economics*, *76*, 424–436.

——— (1965) "Factors Affecting Cooperation in the Prisoner's Dilemma," *Behavioral Science*, *10*, 26–38.

Ledyard, John (1990) "Is There a Problem with Public Good Provision?" forthcoming in A. Roth and J. Kagel, eds., *A Handbook of Experimental Economics*. Princeton: Princeton University Press.

May, Kenneth O. (1954) "Intransitivity, Utility and the Aggregation of Preference Patterns," *Econometrica*, *22*, 1–13.

McKelvey, Richard D., and Peter C. Ordeshook (1990) "A Decade of Experimental Research on Spatial Models of Elections and Committees," in J. M. Enlow and M. J. Hinich, eds., *Readings in the Spatial Theory of Voting*. Cambridge: Cambridge University Press.

Mestelman, Stuart, and D. H. Feeny (1988) "Does Ideology Matter?: Anecdotal Experimental Evidence on the Voluntary Provision of Public Goods," *Public Choice*, 57, 281–286.

Millner, Edward L., Michael D. Pratt, and Robert J. Reilly (1990a) "Contestability in Real-Time Experimental Flow Markets," *Rand Journal of Economics*, 21, 584–599.

———— (1990b) "An Experimental Investigation of Real-Time Posted-Offer Markets for Flows," working paper, Virginia Commonwealth University.

Palfrey, Thomas, and Robert Porter (1991) "Guidelines for Submission of Manuscripts on Experimental Economics," *Econometrica*, 59, 1197–1198.

Plott, Charles R. (1982) "Industrial Organization Theory and Experimental Economics," *Journal of Economic Literature*, 20, 1485–1527.

———— (1986a) "Laboratory Experiments in Economics: The Implications of Posted-Price Institutions," *Science*, 232, 732–738.

———— (1986b) "An Introduction to Some Experimental Procedures," working paper, California Institute of Technology.

———— (1989) "An Updated Review of Industrial Organization: Applications of Experimental Methods," in R. Schmalensee and R. D. Willig, eds., *Handbook of Industrial Organization*, vol. 2. Amsterdam: North-Holland, 1109–1176.

———— (1991) "Will Economics Become an Experimental Science?" *Southern Economic Journal*, 57, 901–919.

Plott, Charles R., and Vernon L. Smith (1978) "An Experimental Examination of Two Exchange Institutions," *Review of Economic Studies*, 45, 133–153.

Rapoport, Anatol, and Albert M. Chammah (1965) *Prisoner's Dilemma: A Study in Conflict and Cooperation.* Ann Arbor: University of Michigan Press.

Roth, Alvin E. (1986) "Laboratory Experimentation in Economics," in T. Bewley, ed., *Advances in Economic Theory, Fifth World Congress.* Cambridge: Cambridge University Press, 269–299.

———— (1988) "Laboratory Experimentation in Economics: A Methodological Overview," *Economic Journal*, 98, 974–1031.

———— (1990) "Lets Keep the Con out of Experimental Economics: A Methodological Note," working paper, University of Pittsburgh.

Sauerman, Heinz, and Reinhard Selten (1959) "Ein Oligopolexperiment," *Zeitschrift fur die Gesamte Staatswissenschaft*, 115, 427–471.

Savage, Leonard J. (1954) *The Foundations of Statistics.* New York: Wiley.

Schotter, Andrew, and Yale M. Braunstein (1981) "Economic Search: An Experimental Study," *Economic Inquiry*, 19, 1–25.

Sherman, Roger (1966) "Capacity Choice in Duopoly," doctoral dissertation, Carnegie-Mellon University.

Siegel, Sidney, and Lawrence E. Fouraker (1960) *Bargaining and Group Decision Making.* New York: McGraw Hill.

Siegel, Sidney and D. A. Goldstein (1959) "Decision-making Behavior in a Two-Choice Uncertain Outcome Situation," *Journal of Experimental Psychology, 57*, 37–42.

Smith, Vernon L. (1962) "An Experimental Study of Competitive Market Behavior," *Journal of Political Economy, 70*, 111–137.

——— (1964) "The Effect of Market Organization on Competitive Equilibrium," *Quarterly Journal of Economics, 78*, 181–201.

——— (1976) "Experimental Economics: Induced Value Theory," *American Economic Review Papers and Proceedings, 66*, 274–279.

——— (1982) "Microeconomic Systems as an Experimental Science," *American Economic Review, 72*, 923–955.

Smith, Vernon L., Gerry L. Suchanek, and Arlington W. Williams (1988) "Bubbles, Crashes, and Endogenous Expectations in Experimental Spot Asset Markets," *Econometrica, 56*, 1119–1151.

Smith, Vernon L., and Arlington W. Williams (1981) "On Nonbinding Price Controls in a Competitive Market," *American Economic Review, 71*, 467–474.

——— (1983) "An Experimental Comparison of Alternative Rules for Competitive Market Exchange," in Englebrecht-Wiggins et al., eds., *Auctions, Bidding and Contracting: Uses and Theory*. New York: New York University Press, 307-334.

Spence, A. Michael (1976) "Product Selection, Fixed Costs, and Monopolistic Competition," *Review of Economic Studies, 43*, 217–235.

Tucker, A. W. (1950) "A Two-Person Dilemma," working paper, Stanford University, published as "On Jargon: The Prisoner's Dilemma," *UMSP Journal, 1*, 1980, 101.

Van Boening, Mark V. (1990) "Call Versus Continuous Auctions: A Comparison of Experimental Spot Asset Markets," working paper, University of Arizona.

von Neumann, J., and O. Morgenstern (1944) *Theory of Games and Economic Behavior*. Princeton: Princeton University Press.

Walker, James, and Arlington Williams (1988) "Market Behavior in Bid, Offer, and Double Auctions: A Reexamination," *Journal of Economic Behavior and Organization, 9*, 301–314.

Welford, Charissa P. (1990) "Horizontal Mergers: Concentration and Performance," in *Takeovers and Horizontal Mergers: Policy and Performance*, doctoral dissertation, University of Arizona.

Williams, Arlington W. (1980) "Computerized Double-Auction Markets: Some Initial Experimental Results," *Journal of Business, 53*, 235–258.

——— (1987) "The Formation of Price Forecasts in Experimental Markets," *The Journal of Money, Credit and Banking, 19*, 1–18.

CHAPTER 2

DECISIONS AND GAMES

2.1 Introduction

Most of the laboratory experiments discussed in this book can be classified either as individual decision-making problems or as "games" in which maximizing individuals interact. To understand these experiments, some familiarity with the relevant theories is necessary, and for this reason we introduce in this chapter a variety of topics in decision theory and game theory. The treatment here is "applied" in the sense that most theoretical results are not derived. Rather, useful concepts are presented in the context of issues that arise in experimental design, and they are evaluated in light of experimental evidence. Moreover, the discussion is not comprehensive, even for the purposes of this manuscript. Some special issues in game theory and decision theory, for example, are covered in much more detail in later chapters. Our intention here is to enable a reader with a limited (or rusty) background to proceed directly to some of the more applied topics in the chapters that follow: posted-offer auctions, public goods, bilateral bargaining, and so forth.[1]

The chapter is organized as follows. First, we consider some issues in individual decision theory: Section 2.2 contains a discussion of lotteries and expected values, section 2.3 discusses a simple sequential search experiment, and section 2.4 pertains to expected utility maximization and risk aversion. Next, we turn our attention to some basic elements of noncooperative game theory: Section 2.5 considers normal-form games and the notion of a noncooperative equilibrium, while section 2.6 considers extensive-form games and backward-induction rationality.

---

[1] This material is no substitute for a systematic treatment of these topics, and anyone with a serious interest in experimental economics should sooner or later master the material in an up-to-date course with an appropriate emphasis on decision and game theories (e.g., Kreps, 1990).

A brief final section discusses the relationship between competitive price theory and the decision-theoretic and game-theoretic tools discussed here. We argue that although there is some overlap, each set of tools has a fairly distinct area of application. Game theory, for example, can be cumbersome and unnecessary in some contexts, for example, in "thick" markets with clear price signals. In these instances the predictions of standard price theory often suffice.

2.2 Lotteries and Expected Values

Representations of Probability Distributions

Many individual-choice experiments involve situations in which a subject must choose between probability distributions of payoffs, that is, between lotteries. Such experiments may be used to evaluate assumptions and theories about how decisions are made under uncertainty. Consider, for example, the choice between the following lotteries:

$S1$: $3 with certainty, or

$R1$: $4 with a probability of .8, and $0 with a probability of .2.

The effective presentation of the "risky" alternative $R1$ raises a number of procedural issues. Although it is unnecessary and perhaps undesirable to try to explain the concept of probability, it is important for subjects to have a clear idea of the likelihood of the relevant events. One way to explain these concepts to participants is to link them to some concrete randomizing device, such as dice or a roulette wheel. For example, the probabilities .8 and .2 in lottery $R1$ may be induced by telling a subject that the payment is $4 if the throw of a ten-sided die yields 3, 4, . . . 10, and that the payment is $0 if the die yields 1 or 2. This information can sometimes be even more clearly conveyed with the use of a visual device, such as table 2.1. In this table the relative frequency of the numbers 0 and 4 in the lottery $R1$ row indicates the probabilities of .2 and .8. Notably, the placement of the zeros on the left side of the $R1$ payoff row could be a source of bias.[2] The researcher could control for potential biases of this sort by varying the

---

[2] Davis and Holt (1991) noticed some tendency for subjects to choose decisions located at the top and left side of payoff tables in simple matrix games with no economic incentives, i.e., with flat payoffs that were independent of the decision made. In animal experiments, this is called "lever bias." It is not always practical to eliminate or control for all possible sources of such bias; added control may be too costly. The researcher must make a judgment about the advisability of such controls, given the psychological context and the magnitudes of the economic incentives.

placement of the zeros in the table of lottery representations used by different groups of subjects.

Table 2.1 Representation of Lottery Payoff Structure

Throw of Die	1	2	3	4	5	6	7	8	9	10
$ Payoffs for Lottery *S1*:	3	3	3	3	3	3	3	3	3	3
$ Payoffs for Lottery *R1*:	0	0	4	4	4	4	4	4	4	4

Dice, particularly specialized dice, are a very useful means of inducing probability distributions. For example, to generate a distribution that makes each integer between 1 and 200 equally likely, one might use a twenty-sided die for the first two digits (hundreds and tens) and a ten-sided die for the third (units) digit. Since the probabilities sum to 1, the probability of each integer outcome is 1/200, as indicated by the rectangular density labeled as "uniform case" on the left side of figure 2.1. This discrete analogue of the uniform distribution is probably the most commonly used distribution in experiments, because it is easy to induce with dice, it is easy to explain to the subjects, and it often facilitates the calculation of the optimal or equilibrium decisions.[3] The probability of outcome x is the *density* at x, and it will be denoted by $f(x)$. All 200 outcomes are equally likely for the uniform case on the left side of figure 2.1, so $f(x) = 1/200 = .005$. The probability that an outcome is less than or equal to x is the *distribution function*, denoted as $F(x)$. The distribution function for the uniform case is the sum of the densities from the lower limit, 1, up to the value of x, and therefore $F(x) = x/200$, which is plotted as a straight line with slope 1/200 on the right side of figure 2.1. For example, the area under the uniform density to the left of $x = 50$ is one-fourth of the total density, so $F(50) = .25$, which is the probability that x is less than or equal to 50.

Dice may also be used to induce a discrete variant of a "triangular" distribution, another probability distribution sometimes used in experiments. A triangular distribution results from summing two variables with uniform distributions. This is most easily seen by considering a binary coin toss: If heads is a 1 and tails is a 0, then a single toss of a fair coin yields uniform, equal probabilities of .5 for 0 and .5 for 1. The sum of two tosses yields a peaked, triangular density in which the probability of the middle outcome of 1 is twice as great as the probabilities of

---

[3] The uniform distribution is a continuous distribution, but we will refer to the distribution with equal (i.e., uniform) densities on a discrete set of points as being uniform.

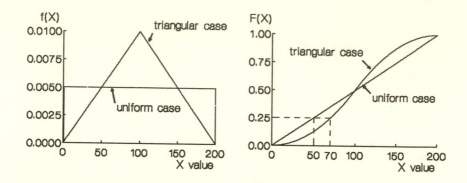

Figure 2.1 Density and Distribution Functions for Two Distributions

the extreme outcomes of 0 or 2. To verify this, note that an outcome of 0 results from 2 consecutive tails, an outcome of 2 results from two consecutive heads, and each of these events occurs with probability $(.5)(.5) = .25$. An outcome of 1 results from a head and a tail (a head first and tail second, or vice versa), which occurs with probability $(.5)(.5) + (.5)(.5) = .5$. A triangular distribution with a much larger set of discrete outcomes may be generated via the use of a more sophisticated randomizing device. For example, the sum of the outcomes of two spins of a roulette wheel with 100 stops is a triangular distribution for the integers between 0 and 200, as shown on the left side of figure 2.1.

One advantage of using a triangular distribution instead of a uniform distribution is a reduced likelihood of extreme outcomes. This is evident from a comparison of the uniform and triangular densities in the figure: Even though both distributions are symmetric around a common expected value of 100, the uniform distribution is more risky since it has more density in the tails of the distribution, that is, below 50 and above 150.[4] Thus the uniform distribution represents a "mean-preserving increase in risk" over the triangular distribution.

The strong central tendency reflected by the peak in the triangular density function is also illustrated by the "S" shape of the triangular distribution function on the right side of figure 2.1. The relationship between the density and distribution functions for the triangular case is easily seen from comparison with the

---

[4] The expected value of a distribution that is uniform between 1 and 200 is actually 100.5, but this will be ignored in the discussion. The comparison between the triangular and uniform cases would be more accurate if the uniform case were defined at .5, 1.5, 2.5, . . . 199.5, which is symmetric around 100. The density for the triangular case in figure 2.1 is symmetric around 100 and is zero at the endpoints of 0 and 200. This is obtained by summing the outcomes of two spins of a roulette wheel with 100 stops marked .5, 1.5, . . . 99.5.

corresponding functions for the uniform case. Consider the density functions on the left side of the figure. The area under the flat uniform density to the left of $x = 50$ is twice as great as the area under the triangular density to the left of $x = 50$. Since the distribution function at a point is the density to the left of that point, $F(50)$ is twice as high for the uniform case as for the triangular case (compare the points where these distributions cross the vertical dashed line at $x = 50$ on the right side of figure 2.1). Similarly, the higher density in the center for the triangular case causes the distribution function for the triangular case to be steeper in this region.

Many economic models are based on other, more complicated distributions. An important disadvantage of using distributions other than the uniform and triangular distributions in the laboratory is that other distributions are rather difficult to motivate.[5] One possible way to present more complicated distributions is to provide a graph of the density, along with lots of practice draws from a computer-generated distribution. An alternative approach is to use a table to transform draws from a uniform distribution on [0, 1] into draws from some desired alternative distribution. For example, the triangular distribution in figure 2.1 could be generated by this method by rolling two 10-sided dice to determine a random number (proportion) between 0 and 1.0, which represents the value of $F(x)$ on the vertical axis of the distribution function. Then the graph of $F(x)$ for the triangular distribution could be used to determine a corresponding value of x. For example, if the throw yields .50 for $F(x)$, then the corresponding value of x is 100. If the throw yields .25 for $F(x)$, then moving horizontally across from .25 on the vertical axis to the curved $F(x)$ line for the triangular case, and then down to the horizontal axis, we get an x value of about 70, as shown in figure 2.1. This approach is quite general and can be used to induce any distribution.

Density functions are usually easier for participants to understand than distribution functions, especially if the density is segmented into areas of equal probability by dashed vertical lines. Therefore, the two-step method (of using the uniform distribution to generate a probability $F(x)$ and using the distribution function to generate a value of x) should be complemented with a graph of the density. Taken with a lot of practice draws, this graphical approach may be effective.

The possibility that subjects suspect deception is a potential impediment to inducing even the simplest distribution. A researcher may alleviate this problem to some extent through the public display of the randomizing method. If dice are used, for example, the researcher may want to throw them in the presence of the subjects, letting one of them verify the result. When an experiment is computerized, probabilistic outcomes are commonly generated with a programmed random number generator. In this case, it may be advisable to conduct some pilot sessions in which subjects are asked open-ended questions about whether procedures were thought to

---

[5] Some standard distributions, such as the normal distribution, have the additional problem of being unbounded.

be biased or inconsistent with the description given in the instructions. It is possible, and sometimes desirable, to have the program pause for the throw of the dice, which can then be entered manually at the keyboard. Our own preference is to use dice if time is not a constraint and if each throw is very important, as would be the case in a session with very high payoffs. If the session requires that a large number of random numbers be generated, and if the stakes are not too high, it is probably fine to use computer-generated random numbers. Using uniform distributions, Holt and Sherman (1991) observed no systematic behavioral differences between sessions with computer-generated random numbers and numbers generated by dice.

Expected Values and Risk Neutrality

A subject who chooses one lottery over another reveals that the second is not strictly preferred to the first. Economists who study such choices are often concerned with representing these preferences mathematically. The simplest such representation is constructed from the probability-weighted likelihood of each outcome in a lottery, or from a lottery's *expected value*. In table 2.1, for example, the safe lottery *S1* yields $3 with certainty, and so it has an expected value of $3. The expected value of the risky lottery *R1* is obtained by weighing each money outcome by the corresponding probability of that outcome: .8($4) + .2($0) = $3.20. A subject who always chooses the lottery with the highest expected monetary value would choose *R1*, since its expected value of $3.20 exceeds the expected value of $3 for *S1*. If this pattern held up for all choices of all possible lotteries, including those with many more possible outcomes, then we would say that the person is an "expected-value maximizer."

For reasons that will be clear later in this book, many lottery-choice experiments involve choices between lotteries with three outcomes, and it is useful to introduce some general notation for this family of lotteries. Consider a lottery *Li* with three outcomes, x_1, x_2, and x_3, where $x_1 < x_2 < x_3$. If x_1 occurs with probability p_1, x_2 occurs with probability p_2, and x_3 occurs with probability p_3, the expected value of the lottery *Li* is

(2.1) $$Li = p_1 x_1 + p_2 x_2 + p_3 x_3 .$$

This expression represents the preferences of a risk-neutral subject in the sense that one lottery, say *L1*, is preferred to another lottery, *L2*, if and only if the value of (2.1) is higher for lottery *L1* than for *L2*. Importantly, it is not necessary for the subject to know anything about expected values or probabilities for this representation to be useful as a predictive device. For some subjects, this expression may provide accurate predictions even if they do not formally calculate expected values.

The term *risk neutrality* comes from the fact that a risk-neutral person would, by definition, be indifferent between two lotteries with the same expected value, even though one of the lotteries may be much riskier in terms of payoff variability. For example, a risk-neutral person would be indifferent between a certain $3.20 and a 4/5 chance of $4.00 (zero otherwise). A risk-averse person would prefer the certain alternative, while a risk-preferring participant would select the 4/5 chance of $4.00. Although participants rarely appear to be risk preferring, some participants are risk neutral and others appear to be risk averse.

Care must also be taken in designing and interpreting the results of individual decision-making experiments, since the value a participant places on a lottery depends critically on the participant's risk attitudes. Although participants are not always risk-neutral, it is generally advisable to begin analyzing an experimental situation in terms of risk neutrality. In most contexts, the implications of a model are more precise and easier to derive under risk neutrality than under risk aversion. Moreover, if behavior deviates systematically from predictions based on risk neutrality, then the size and direction of the deviations may allow us to determine whether and to what extent subjects are risk averse. Risk-neutral predictions are also useful when risk-neutral preferences are imposed on subjects. Risk neutrality may be imposed in a number of ways, one of which is reviewed in section 2.4. As a prior matter, it is useful to consider an experiment in which the choices between lotteries are relatively well organized by the predictions of a model based on risk neutrality.

2.3 A Sequential Search Experiment

Economists often begin analyzing a situation by studying a very simple model and then adding complexity after the intuition of the simple case is well understood. Consider the most basic model of optimal search: a worker can seek wage offers, but with each offer the worker incurs a search cost of c. At any given stage in the search process, the worker must decide whether to search again or to stop and accept the best wage offer encountered thus far. This may be viewed as a choice between lotteries: One lottery consists of the sure return of stopping with the best offer thus far, while another, riskier lottery results from continued search.

For simplicity, assume that the worker is risk neutral, there is no limit to the number of searches, and wage offers are independent draws from a known distribution with a density function $f(x)$. Also, the worker has "perfect recall" in the sense that any offer rejected in an earlier stage may be accepted later, and the future is not discounted (the worker does not grow impatient while searching). This is a classic sequential search problem, with lots of possible variations and economic applications (e.g., DeGroot, 1970; Lippman and McCall, 1976). The combination of no time discounting and a constant underlying wage distribution implies that at the start of each stage, the future always looks the same. This invariance is an unusual property of the classic search problem and leads to several implications, which are summarized in the following three statements

(i) *No desire to recall*: Since the decision problem facing a searcher is unchanged at the beginning of each stage, a wage that should be rejected at some stage should also be rejected if it is ever encountered in any subsequent stage. Similarly, a wage that should be accepted at some stage should be accepted at any stage.

(ii) *Reservation wage property*: The implication of (i) is that the optimal search strategy is to have a "reservation wage" and to search until an offer that exceeds this reservation wage is encountered.

(iii) *Reservation wage = expected payoff of optimal search*: By definition of the reservation wage, the searcher is just indifferent between accepting that wage and searching again. Any offer above the reservation wage would be preferred to undertaking an optimal search, but the search process would be preferred to any offer that is below the reservation wage. Therefore, the reservation wage precisely equals the expected payoff of searching optimally.

The implication of (iii) is that if one were to elicit the least amount of money that a subject would accept for giving up the right to search, then the value elicited could be interpreted as the reservation wage.

Since search is costly, intuition suggests that the expected payoff from optimal search, and hence the reservation wage, will be a decreasing function of the marginal cost of search. Below, we show that this intuition is correct by deriving the optimal reservation wage for the case of a risk-neutral searcher. In a subsequent subsection we compare optimal search predictions with the results of a search experiment.

The Optimal Reservation Wage

It is instructive to develop the optimal reservation wage in the context of a specific example. Suppose that searches for a worker (or subject in an experiment) are random draws from a distribution with uniform probabilities of 1/200 for each number from 1 to 200, and that the cost, c, of each "search" or draw is 5. The decision problem for the searcher is whether to accept the best offer obtained thus far, w, or to pay the cost c to search again. For extreme values of w, the choice between accepting and searching is obvious. The expected value of a single draw is $1(1/200) + 2(1/200) + \ldots 200(1/200) = 100.5$. Thus, if $w = 0$, it pays to draw again since the gain that may be expected from searching vastly exceeds the cost.

Similarly, if $w = 200$, further search would be fruitless, since no better outcome is possible.

More generally, the expected benefits of search increase as w diminishes. If $w = 199$, there is a 1/200 chance of obtaining a better draw, so the expected gain is 1/200 of a cent $= (200 - 199)/200$. If $w = 198$, the possible draws of 199 and 200 would represent improvements, so the expected gain from searching once increases to 3/200 of a cent, for example, $(200 - 198)/200 + (199 - 198)/200$. With still lower w values, the number of possible better draws increases, generating a longer string of probability-weighted improvements: $(200 - w)/200 + (199 - w)/200 + (198 - w)/200 + \ldots$. This same reasoning applies when the distribution is not uniform. Let $f(x)$ denote the probability of any possible improving offer, x. Then the formula for the expected gain (over the current level of w) is given on the left side of equation (2.2)

$$(2.2) \qquad \sum_{x = w+1}^{200} (x-w)f(x) \;=\; c.$$

Obviously, the expected gain on the left side of (2.2) is a decreasing function of the best standing alternative, w, and if w is 200, the expected gain is 0.

To optimize, the searcher must compare the expected gains from search with the search costs. One obvious decision rule would be to search again whenever the best standing offer is sufficiently low that the expected gain from an additional search is greater than the cost of search. When the search cost just equals the expected gain from additional search, the individual would be indifferent between continuing or stopping. Therefore, equation (2.2) determines the reservation wage. The expected-gain function for the uniform case is plotted in figure 2.2 for values of w between 100 and 200. The expected gain crosses the horizontal, search-cost line (with a height of 5) at about 155. When the distribution is triangular, there is less probability weight in the upper tail of the distribution, so the gains from additional search fall. As indicated in figure 2.2, the optimal reservation wage falls to 133 with a triangular distribution.

Two features of the optimal reservation wage bear emphasis. First, the result is rather unusual: An optimal strategy in this *dynamic*, multistage setting involves the *myopic* comparison of the gains and costs of search in the present stage. This follows from the fact that the future always looks the same to the searcher; there is never any change in the search cost, the distribution of offers, or the number of periods remaining.[6] Second, even in the very simple case considered, the explicit calculation of the reservation wage is a rather formidable task. No one believes that individuals explicitly perform the calculations in (2.2). But whether or not the

---

[6] Appendix 2.1 contains an intuitive proof that the optimal dynamic policy reduces to (2.2).

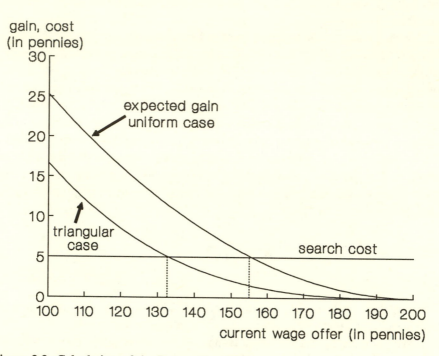

Figure 2.2 Calculation of the Reservation Wage

reservation wage derived from (2.2) is a better predictor of individual behavior than alternative theories is an empirical question.

Data from a Search Experiment

Schotter and Braunstein (1981) conducted a search experiment by bringing subjects, one at a time, into a room with an interactive computer terminal. Each subject participated in twelve search sequences under a variety of treatment conditions. We will only summarize the results of sequences that match the conditions considered in the previous subsection, that is, in which there was no limit on the number of searches and in which the subjects could go back and recall a previously rejected offer. The instructions explained that the purpose of the experiment was to study how people search in situations in which they do not know all of the alternative wages or prices.[7] At each stage in a search sequence, the

---

[7] The instructions to a search experiment by Cox and Oaxaca (1989) avoided both reference to an economic context and to the word "search." Although Cox and Oaxaca also used a somewhat different design than Schotter and Braunstein, results in both papers were roughly consistent with the predictions of optimal search theory. Our guess is that these variations in terminology do not affect outcomes in this

computer generated a random number from a probability distribution and displayed it. The subject then either pressed SEARCH to see another draw or STOP to receive the maximum wage offer obtained up to that point. Each draw reduced the subject's earnings by the search cost, which in all but one treatment was 5 cents. After some practice sequences, but before the twelve sequences involving financial incentives, each subject was asked to state the minimum amount that he/she would accept to not search. As explained above, this selling price should equal the reservation wage. This was an informal question, not an elicitation procedure with financial incentives of the type that will be discussed in chapter 8.

Table 2.2 Schotter and Braunstein Search Experiment Results

Sequence	Treatment: Distribution (c, sequence)	Optimal R.W.	Mean Reported Sell Price	Mean Highest Rejection	Mean Accepted Wage
1	triangular (c=5, random)	133	135	123	146
2	triangular (c=5, fixed)	133	136	*	*
12	triangular (c=5, fixed)	133	136	*	*
3	uniform (c=5, random)	155	157	125	170
4	triangular (c=10, random)	115	128	93	147

* The data for the fixed (nonrandom) offer sequences are not comparable.

Relevant results are summarized in table 2.2. In sequences 1, 2, and 12, the subjects drew samples from the triangular distribution shown in figure 2.1, with a search cost of 5 cents. In each of these three cases, the optimal reservation wage (R.W.) calculated from figure 2.2 is 133, as shown in the third column of the table. The sequences differed slightly in the way the draws were generated: Draws in sequence 1 were truly random, but (unknown to subjects) draws in sequences 2 and 12 were predetermined series, in which the first draw to exceed 133 was the fifth draw (for stage 2) or the sixth draw (for stage 12). The means of the reported

context. The search experiment instructions in appendix 2.2 present an intermediate case: We use the word "search," but we avoid reference to an economic context.

selling prices for sequences 1, 2, and 12 are the top three entries in the fourth column. As predicted by the theory, these were strikingly close to the theoretical reservation wage level of 133. In another sequence (3) the authors used the more risky uniform distribution, which raises the theoretical reservation wage to 155. As shown in the fourth row of the table, this alteration raised the reported mean selling price to 157, and it also raised both the mean accepted wage and the mean highest rejected wage somewhat. A switch to a higher search cost lowered the mean selling price, the highest rejected wage, and the mean accepted wage, as shown in the bottom row of the table.

Overall, the results are surprisingly consistent with optimal search theory. It is worth noting, however, that the average accepted wages in the right-hand column are a little low. For example, when the optimal reservation wage is 155, the first wage that exceeds this should be accepted. With a uniform distribution this accepted wage would be equally likely to be anywhere in the range from 155 to 200, with an average of 177.5, which is about 7 cents above the average accepted wage in the third row. Cox and Oaxaca (1989) observed similar results in a finite horizon environment:[8] In 600 sequences conducted under a variety of treatment conditions, subjects terminated search exactly as predicted by optimal risk-neutral behavior 77 percent of the time. But when participants deviated from the optimal rule, they almost universally stopped too soon, that is, at too low a wage.

Observed behavior is not entirely consistent with optimal search theory. In particular, subjects exhibit some tendency to return to accept an offer that they passed over at an earlier stage, in violation of the no-recall property (i). Recalls of this type occurred about 25 percent of the time in the Schotter and Braunstein experiment (p. 19).[9]

Summary

The simple model of sequential search is one instance where participant choices appear to correspond closely to the theory of optimal sequential search. Participants appear to shop with a reservation wage in mind (e.g., without recall) and, despite the complexity of actually calculating the optimal reservation wage, they generally cease

---

[8] In addition to alterations in instructions discussed in footnote 7, Cox and Oaxaca differ from both Schotter and Braunstein (1981) and Hey (1982) by using a physical (bingo-cage) device to generate random numbers.

[9] Kogut (1990) observed recall about 33 percent of the time in a search experiment with parameters that differed from those of Schotter and Braunstein. Kogut attributed recall to the effect of the "sunk costs", that is, search costs incurred for offers that were previously rejected. Hey (1987) reports that prohibiting the opportunity to recall generates decisions that correspond more closely to those predicted for a risk-neutral optimizer.

searching when an offer in excess of the optimal reservation wage is drawn.[10] Most of the observed deviations from optimal risk-neutral behavior involved early termination, that is, acceptance of an offer that is lower than the optimal reservation offer for that period.[11] This early termination is consistent with aversion to risk, to be discussed in the following section.[12]

2.4 Expected-Utility Maximization and Risk Aversion

Consider again the lottery choice problem illustrated in table 2.1. Recall that a risk-neutral participant would select "risky" lottery *R1* over "safe" lottery *S1*, since the expected value of *R1* is higher than that of *S1*. Yet participants appear to select the safe lottery frequently. Kahneman and Tversky (1979), for example, posed a variant of the problem in table 2.1 to ninety-five student subjects, and 80 percent selected S1. Payoffs in the Kahneman and Tversky experiment were hypothetical (in thousands of Israeli pounds), so the declared preferences are suspect. Nevertheless, this pattern of risk-averse behavior has been observed in many experiments, under conditions with both real and hypothetical incentives. To evaluate such results, it is imperative to have a basic understanding of expected-utility theory, which is the topic of this section.

Expected-Utility Maximization

If a subject is risk averse, then their preferences cannot be represented solely in terms of monetary payoffs. Rather, such preferences must be represented in terms of the utility of a lottery. Under a set of assumptions, known as the *von Neumann-Morgenstern axioms* (discussed in appendix A2.3), preferences can be represented by an expected-utility expression: $\Sigma_i\, p_i\, U(x_i)$, where the x_i are monetary payoffs, the p_i are the probabilities, and the $U(x_i)$ is a von Neumann-Morgenstern utility function. For the family of three-prize lotteries, the generalization of (2.1) becomes

---

[10] Of course, this does not necessarily imply that humans make the optimizing calculations. Hey (1982), for example, observes that there are a number of crude rules of thumb that motivate decisions and generate payoffs similar those predicted under the optimal stopping rule.

[11] Most of the deviations reported in the paper by Cox and Oaxaca (1989) were consistent with risk aversion. Similarly, Kogut (1990) reports that subjects stopped earlier than predicted under risk neutrality in 37.8 percent of the cases, subjects stopped as predicted under risk neutrality in 58.6 percent of the cases, and subjects stopped later in only 3.6 percent of the cases.

[12] Harrison and Morgan (1990) report an experiment in which subjects are allowed to purchase more than one offer in each period, that is, the search intensity is variable.

(2.3) $p_1 U(x_1) + p_2 U(x_2) + p_3 U(x_3)$.

Each utility expression in (2.3) is weighted by a corresponding probability, and therefore (2.3) is the expected value of utility, or alternatively, the *expected utility* of a lottery. Obviously, when utility is linear, $U(x) = x$, and the expected utility in (2.3) reduces to the expected money value in (2.1).

It is worth noting that a utility function of this type represents qualitative and not quantitative information about preferences. In particular, it follows from the linearity of (2.3) in the probabilities that the utility of a lottery is unique only up to an additive or multiplicative transformation. In other words, if A and B are constants with $B > 0$, then the von Neumann-Morgenstern utility functions $U(x)$ and $A + B[U(x)]$ represent the same preferences, since A and B will factor out of any comparison.[13] The intuition of this result is clear from a physical example: if this book weighs less than your dictionary, then two copies of this book plus today's newspaper weigh less than two copies of the dictionary plus the newspaper.

The independence of utility to additive and multiplicative transformations allows, without loss of generality, the normalization of the utility function at any two points. In particular, the normalizations $U(x_1) = 0$ and $U(x_3) = 1$ will provide useful simplifications in many instances. For example, these normalizations simplify the theoretical analysis of laboratory auctions of a prize; if the low bidders obtain no earnings, then a bidder's expected utility can be written as the probability of winning the prize times the utility of winning, without a second term that pertains to a loss, since the utility of losing is normalized to be zero.

Appendix A2.3 contains a simple proof that a von Neumann-Morgenstern utility function actually represents a person's preferences under a simple set of assumptions or "axioms." This appendix may be skipped by readers who are familiar with the concept of expected-utility maximization, but readers who are unfamiliar with this concept should review it carefully before proceeding to the discussion of individual-choice experiments in chapter 8. Although the proof is standard, it is included because it suggests a direct way in which a subject's utility function can be constructed by the experimenter. Moreover, the proof facilitates an understanding of the axioms. This is useful, for when contradictions and paradoxes are observed, it is natural to ask which axiom is violated.

Nonlinear Utility and Risk Aversion

The original impetus to the development of expected-utility theory resulted from a hypothetical experiment proposed by Daniel Bernoulli in 1738. Consider the

---

[13] In the jargon of mathematics, both the additive and multiplicative transformations are "linear transformations," since neither introduces nonlinearities.

following game: A coin is flipped repeatedly. The initial potential payoff is $2 and is doubled each time a tails occurs. The game continues until the first heads occurs, when the potential payoff becomes the actual payoff. Thus, if the first flip is a heads, the payoff is $2 and the game ends. If a tails occurs first, the potential payoff doubles to $4 and the coin is flipped again. If a second tails occurs, the potential payoff again doubles to $8 and so on, until the first heads is encountered. Before proceeding to the next paragraph, the reader should consider the largest amount of money that he or she would be willing to pay for the chance to play this game.

Although it is rare for anyone to say that they would pay very much, the expected value of the payoff from this game is infinite: ($2 × 1/2) + ($4 × 1/4) + ($8 × 1/8) + . . . = 1 + 1 + 1 + ... Initially, the refusal to pay large amounts of money to play this coin-flipping game was regarded as a paradox, known as the St. Petersburg Paradox. But refusal seems completely rational; if *you* had $10,000 in a savings account, would you be willing to give up the certain $10,000 in exchange for the gamble that has a 7/8 probability of giving you less than $10 in return? The game represents a very risky lottery, with extremely small and decreasing probabilities of extremely large and increasing payoffs. Although a risk-neutral person would be willing to make this exchange, the natural explanation for observed behavior is aversion to such extreme risk. On the basis of this observation, Bernoulli concluded that utility is not linear in monetary payoffs.

Nonlinear, risk-averse preferences can be illustrated in money/utility-of-money space. Consider the piece-wise linear utility function defined over equally spaced monetary payoffs, x_1 through x_6, shown in figure 2.3. Since $U(x_2)$ lies above the line connecting $U(x_1)$ and $U(x_3)$, the subject would prefer to have x_2 with certainty, yielding $U(x_2)$, to a 50/50 chance of x_1 and x_3, which has an expected value of $[x_1 + x_3]/2$ and an expected utility of $[U(x_1) + U(x_3)]/2$. Since the x_i values are equally spaced, it follows that $x_2 = [x_1 + x_3]/2$, and therefore the two lotteries have the same expected values. Obviously, raising $U(x_2)$ above the line connecting $U(x_1)$ and $U(x_3)$ is what makes the subject risk averse in the sense of preferring the less risky lottery, even though both have the same expected value.

Now let us return to the St. Petersburg Paradox, and consider the effect of a subject's doubts about whether large money payoffs really will be made as promised by the experimenter. If the experimenter only has $8 with which to pay the subject, then the expected value of the gamble would only be $2(.5) + $4(.25) + $8(1 − .5 − .25) = $4. A risk-neutral subject would surely expect that the experimenter has more than $8 in resources from which to make payments, so such a subject would be willing to pay more than $4 to play the game. But it is straightforward to show that even a relatively large reserve for payments has little effect on the expected value of playing the game. For example, a reserve of $16,284 raises the expected value to only $15.

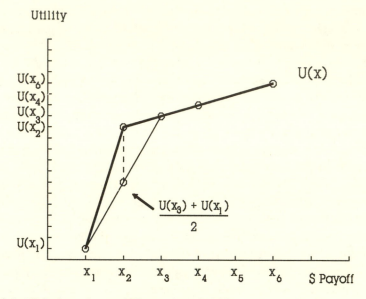

Figure 2.3 Risk Aversion and Concavity of Utility

A maximum payment has the effect of introducing a flat segment in the utility function. In figure 2.3, a maximum payment of x_6 would make the utility function horizontal to the right of x_6. The budget constraint for the experimenter introduces a nonlinearity that creates risk aversion for the subject. This discussion suggests an alternative resolution of the St. Petersburg Paradox that is not based purely on the concavity of a utility function with respect to income; the reasonable expectations about the resources of the experimenter create a concavity in the utility function of even a risk-neutral person.

Conversely, a minimum payment of x_1 would create a flat segment on the left side of figure 2.3. In most experimental settings, the experimenter is unable to take money away from the subject, so a minimum payment of zero is in effect, at least implicitly. The minimum payment has the opposite effect as the maximum payment, that is, preferences for risk can be increased. For example, suppose that the minimum payment is zero and that a subject's wealth falls to $1 by the beginning of the final stage of some game. In this stage, the subject would probably prefer to accept a risky bet that involves the possibility of large losses and gains, since the losses cannot be collected. This is an important procedural issue, and researchers often provide subjects with large initial balances or secondary earnings sources to mitigate the possibility of bankruptcy and the resulting preference for risk if the subject's wealth falls too close to zero.

It follows from this discussion that risk preferences may be affected by the size of the gamble relative to a subject's wealth. This observation has consequences both for theoretical work and for experiments, as will be made clear in the following two subsections.

Measures of Risk Aversion

Consider figure 2.3 further. An increase in $U(x_2)$, holding $U(x_1)$ and $U(x_3)$ constant, would result in more risk aversion for gambles with payoffs between x_1 and x_3. This type of increase in $U(x_2)$ makes the utility function less linear, and in a loose sense, more concave in the range between x_1 and x_3. This illustrates the general proposition of Pratt (1964) that increases in the concavity of the utility function increase risk aversion in a natural manner.

For the class of functions that are differentiable, there are two commonly used measures of this concavity. The first, denoted $R(x) = -U''(x)/U'(x)$ is called the *coefficient of absolute risk aversion*. A second measure is a *coefficient of relative risk aversion, $RR(x)$*, obtained by weighing $R(x)$ by income x: $RR(x) = -xU''(x)/U'(x)$. Both $R(x) = 0$ and $RR(x) = 0$ when $U''(x) = 0$, as occurs over a range where utility is linear. Both measures equal 0, for example, over the range from x_2 to x_6 in figure 2.3.

In theoretical work, it is often convenient to specify utility functions that hold one of the above risk-aversion measures constant. For example, a utility function of the form $U(x) = e^{-rx}$ (with $r > 0$) has the property that $R(x) = r$ for any x, and thus it exhibits constant absolute risk aversion. Notably, for any constant increment in wealth w,

$$(2.4) \qquad U(w + x) \;=\; e^{-r(w+x)} \;=\; e^{-rw}e^{-rx} \;=\; e^{-rw}U(x),$$

where e^{-rw} is a multiplicative constant that does not alter the concavity of $U(x)$ and that factors out of all expected-utility expressions. Utility specifications of this sort have important behavioral implications. For example, an additive change in wealth, such as an increase in money earned in a laboratory session, would not affect risk attitudes for a constant absolute risk-averse individual. But decisions for such an individual would be affected by a multiplicative payoff transformation, such as a doubling of payoffs to increase the financial motivation. Thus, depending on subject's risk preferences, changes in behavior brought about by a multiplicative payoff transformation could be attributable either to a change in motivation or to a change in risk attitudes.

Constant relative risk-averse individuals exhibit just the opposite characteristics. These individuals are insensitive to multiplicative transformations of a lottery with a given expected value, but they are sensitive to additive wealth changes. One class of functions exhibiting constant relative risk aversion is of the form $U(x) = x^{1-r}$, where $0 < r \neq 1$, since for any x, $RR(x) = r$. For this function it is straightforward to show that a multiplicative increase of all earnings by a factor of m produces a constant that factors out, and therefore does not affect choices: $U(mx) = (mx)^{1-\tau} = m^{1-\tau}U(x)$. But an additive change, w, does not factor out, since $U(x + w) = (x + w)^{1-\tau}$ which is not multiplicatively separable in x and w. Notably, the utility function in figure 2.3 does not exhibit constant relative risk aversion, since the subject would be risk averse in a choice between x_2 with certainty and a 50/50 lottery between x_1 and x_3, but risk neutral (with doubled payoffs) in a choice between x_4 and a 50/50 lottery between x_2 and x_6.

The possible sensitivity of the utility of income to additive wealth changes also has potentially important behavioral implications, since changes in behavior observed during the course of a session are potentially attributable either to wealth-induced changes in risk attitudes or to other possible motivations, such as learning. We consider this issue in more detail below.

Wealth Effects

If a subject does not exhibit constant absolute risk aversion, then both the risk attitudes and the decisions made by the subject during a session will change as wealth (actual or anticipated) changes. For example, consider a two-stage treatment where the participant makes choices in each stage between receiving x_2 (money) units with certainty, or receiving either x_1 or x_3 units with a 50/50 probability. An individual with the utility function shown in figure 2.3 would be risk averse in the first stage, as the relevant choice would be between x_2 and a 50/50 chance of x_1 and x_3. Suppose, however, that this individual selects x_2 in the first stage. Given current wealth of x_2, the same pair of lotteries in the second stage corresponds to a choice between a final wealth position of x_4 and a 50/50 chance of x_3 and x_5. Thus, the amount earned in the first stage makes the person risk neutral in the second stage. These observations indicate why it is irrational for an expected-utility maximizing subject to ignore the wealth that has accumulated in earlier stages of a session.[14]

It is also irrational, however, to ignore wealth that is anticipated to be obtained in subsequent stages. More precisely, consider the relationship between (1) starting with an initial receipt of x_2 and then making the lottery choice (between x_2 and a 50/50 chance of x_1 and x_3) and (2) making the lottery choice with the knowledge that x_2 will be earned subsequently. These two situations are equivalent in the sense that each decision produces the same probability distribution of final (post session) wealth levels: In terms of final wealth, the decision is between x_4 and a 50/50 chance of x_3 and x_5.

---

[14] A statement of what is rational is not a claim about how subjects will actually behave in any particular context. Even if subjects are coherent expected-utility maximizers, rationality requires that they have enough experience to comprehend the probabilities and payoffs in an intuitive manner. It is useful for the researcher to calculate the optimal decisions even when these conditions are not satisfied, as such calculations can provide benchmarks for evaluating the observed data.

This point may be clarified with some additional notation. Let w_{t-1} denote the wealth that has already been earned in the initial $t-1$ stages of a laboratory session, and let w^*_{t+1} denote a random variable that represents the subject's uncertain perception about earnings in stages subsequent to stage t. Finally, let $I^*_t(A)$ represent the random variable that determines earnings in the current stage, t, as a function of some decision variable A. Then an expected-utility maximizer would choose A to maximize

$$(2.5) \qquad E \{ U[w_{t-1} + I^*_t(A) + w^*_{t+1}] \},$$

where the expectation in (2.5) is taken over the joint distribution of the random variables representing current and future earnings in the session.

The presence of the random-future-earnings term in (2.5) is perhaps controversial; at least we are not aware of any explicit discussion of such a term in an experimental context. This term, however, may be quite important. For example, suppose that a laboratory session is conducted in a series of periods, and the subject earns money in each period. One common method of checking for wealth effects is to regress cumulative earnings at each stage on decisions in that stage. This approach may reveal no systematic correlation between the decisions and wealth accumulated in previous periods, but this does not indicate that risk attitudes are independent of wealth. Instead, what could be happening is that, as the subject's earnings rise from period to period, this increase in accumulated wealth is approximately matched by a reduction in anticipated earnings in subsequent periods as the number of such periods declines over time. This discussion indicates that, in theory, the relevant distinction is between actual and anticipated earnings; a less-than-anticipated level of earnings not only affects current wealth but may also reduce the anticipated level of future earnings, and vice versa, and such changes may affect on risk attitudes. But earnings that are more or less at the anticipated level may have little effect on the subject's assessment of the relevant wealth position.

Many, perhaps most, experimentalists do not accept our argument. As they correctly note, there is nothing in the basic axioms of expected-utility theory that requires the relevant payoffs to be in terms of final wealth at the end of the session rather than in terms of earnings at a given stage in the session. We view this observation as an empirical issue of subject perceptions rather than a theoretic problem. The question to be answered is whether subjects view the relevant decision problem as being the current stage in the session or the session as a whole.

Controlling for Risk Aversion with Lottery-Ticket Payoffs

Although ascertaining individual risk attitudes is an important research question, some predictions in economics are contingent on specific risk preferences. Risk neutrality is perhaps the most conventional assumption, but this assumption will yield biased predictions if subjects are risk averse. Eliciting information about a decision maker's preferences and risk attitudes, and then conducting experiments with the subset of appropriate participants, can be both expensive and ephemeral. Laboratory time is limited, and the monetary payments that must be made to encourage careful responses to such elicitations may alter the subject's wealth position enough to require further inferences about risk attitudes at the new wealth levels. Specific elicitation schemes are discussed in chapter 8.

An alternative to eliciting preferences is to attempt to induce risk attitudes directly, just as experimentalists induce values and costs. One popular way to induce risk neutrality is to conduct a session in two stages. In the first stage, earnings are denominated in terms of points instead of money. These points then essentially serve as tickets to a second-stage lottery. Specifically, let n be the number of points out of a theoretical maximum of N points earned in a first stage. Then the second stage is a lottery in which the subject earns a high monetary prize, W_H, with probability n/N and a low prize, W_L, otherwise. The subject's expected utility in the second stage is

$$(2.6) \qquad\qquad [\frac{n}{N}] U(W_H) \;+\; [1 - \frac{n}{N}] U(W_L).$$

Without loss of generality, the utilities $U(W_H)$ and $U(W_L)$ may be normalized at 1 and 0, respectively. Thus, the expected utility expression in equation (2.6) reduces to $[n/N]$, which is *linear* in the number of points, n. Consequently, even a risk-averse subject should be risk neutral in decisions regarding the earning of points in the first stage.

An example may be instructive. Consider a first-stage choice between a decision that yields a certain payoff of 50 of 100 possible points and a second decision in which payoffs of 25 or 75 points are equally likely. The former option results in a .5 chance of winning the high prize. The second option yields the high prize with a probability that is determined: .5[25/100] + .5[75/100], which also equals .5. Since both options result in exactly the same probability distribution over final monetary earnings, an expected-utility maximizer who only cares about the monetary outcomes would be indifferent between the two options. But this indifference is exactly what is implied by risk neutrality in the first stage, since both options yield the same expected number of points. Although this method is both convenient and popular, there is some question regarding its effectiveness, at least in particular contexts. This procedure is further discussed in chapter 8.

Dodging the Issue of Risk Preferences: A Probability-Matching Example

In some situations it is possible to avoid the problems of measuring or inducing utility functions by choosing an experimental design for which the predictions of the relevant theories are independent of risk attitudes. For example, suppose that at each stage in an experiment, a subject must choose between two alternatives, under the condition that the payoffs for these choices are determined by an unknown event, E_1 or E_2. Payoffs for each event are summarized in table 2.3. Suppose further that the probabilities of the two events are fixed, sum to one, and that the outcome at each stage is independent of previous outcomes. (Such events are called independent Bernoulli trials.) The specific problem for the subject, then, is to choose either the top decision D_1 or the bottom decision D_2, given a reward R for guessing correctly, and a penalty $-$L$ for guessing incorrectly. Payoffs are set so that R exceeds $-$L$.

Table 2.3 A Simple Elicitation Problem

	Event E_1	Event E_2
Decision D_1	$R	$-$L
Decision D_2	$-$L	$R

From the symmetry of the payoffs, it follows that the optimal decision is D_1 when E_1 is more likely, regardless of the decision maker's attitudes toward risk. To verify this formally (and to practice a bit with expected utility expressions), let the subject's beliefs about the probabilities of E_1 and E_2 be represented by p and $1 - p$, respectively, and calculate the expected utility of each decision in terms of $U(-L)$ and $U(R)$. It is straightforward to show that the optimal decision is D_1 when $p > .5$, regardless of concavity or convexity of the utility function.[15] Therefore, this decision problem is one way of using financial incentives to elicit information about which state is the one that a subject thinks is more likely.

A classic experiment by Siegel and Goldstein (1959) was patterned along the lines of table 2.3. During the twenty years prior to this paper, psychologists had been doing experiments in which subjects were asked to predict which of two events had occurred, without financial incentives of the type present in table 2.3. Subjects, instead, were told to "do your best to predict correctly." In a typical setup, one of the events would be more likely, for example, the probability p of event D_1 could be .75. Although subjects were not given the probabilities, the more likely event would quickly become apparent. Despite the fact that it is optimal to predict the more likely event D_1 at every stage, psychologists had observed that the proportion

---

[15] Without loss of generality, let $U(-L) = 0$ and $U(R) = 1$. Then decision D_1 has an expected utility of p, decision D_2 has an expected utility of $1-p$, and D_1 is preferred to D_2 if $p > 1/2$.

of times that the more likely event is predicted approximately *matched* the probability of this event. Like other psychologists, Siegel and Goldstein also observed probability matching under a no-incentive treatment. Twelve subjects each made a series of 100 predictions without financial rewards for correct guesses or penalties for errors (e.g., $R = $L = 0$). The proportion of times that the more likely outcome was predicted by individual subjects ranged from .60 to .80, with an average across subjects of .70 (in trials 80–100). When four of the twelve subjects were brought back a week later and allowed to continue for 200 additional trials, the average across subjects ended up being exactly equal to .75, the probability of the more likely event.

Siegel was an experimental psychologist who had seen the literature on probability matching. He suspected that the curious matching behavior was caused by boredom; participants might try to overcome the tedium of making repeated binary decisions by trying to out-guess the randomizing device. Absent financial incentives, guessing of this type is costless. Siegel reasoned that the effects of boredom could be decreased by providing subjects with financial rewards and/or penalties for their decisions. This hypothesis was evaluated by comparing results of the above "no-incentive" treatment with results in "reward-only" and "reward/loss" treatments. In the reward-only treatment, participants were paid 5 cents for each correct choice, but suffered no loss for any mistake ($R = 5$ and $L = 0$). In the reward/loss treatment, participants both received 5-cent rewards and suffered 5-cent penalties for errors ($R = 5$ and $L = 5$). Procedures for these latter treatments paralleled those used in the no-reward treatment: In each case, twelve subjects made predictions in a series of 100 trials, then a subsample of four subjects were brought back for an additional 200 trials in the subsequent week.

Figure 2.4 presents the temporal pattern of data for each of the three treatments. Each line illustrates the average proportion of D_1 responses made by participants in a given treatment. The lines are broken by a space after trial 100, to distinguish the average-response data generated by twelve participants, from the average-response data generated by the four-participant subsample in the last 200 trials. The prediction proportions start at about .5 for all three treatments, which is not surprising since subjects were not given the probabilities of the two events. By the end of the first 100 trials, however, there is a rather pronounced separation in responses: In trials 80–100, the boldfaced line for the reward/loss data reaches .93, the dashed line for the no-reward data reaches .7, and the solid line for the reward-only data is intermediate. These response patterns stabilized in the last 200 sessions. By the final block (trials 280–300), the average prediction proportion for the reward/loss treatment reached .95, the proportion for the reward-only treatment reached .85, and the proportion for the no-reward treatment stabilized at the exact level of probability matching, as noted previously.

One may not conclude from these results that participants always behave differently when provided with financial incentives. The matching behavior may

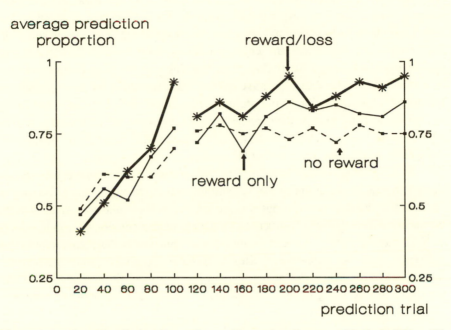

Figure 2.4 Mean Prediction Rates for an Event that Occurs with Probability .75, Averaged Across Subjects and Over Twenty-Trial Blocks (Source: Siegel, Siegel, and Andrews, 1964, figure 5)

have been prompted by a variety of elements in the design and administration of the experiment, and an experiment can be designed in which optimal behavior would be observed without the payment of financial incentives.[16]   As a rule, however, economists are rather uninterested in sorting out the potential biases of these effects. What we may conclude from this experiment is that financial incentives can sometimes eliminate subtle and unintended biases. For this reason, the payment of financial incentives is a critical element in the administration of economics experiments.[17]

Summary

Risk aversion is consistent with utility maximization if utility is concave in monetary payoffs. In theoretical work it is often convenient to specify utility

---

[16]   See the probability-matching experiment reported in Holt (1992).

[17]   See Smith (1990) and Harrison (1989) for further discussion of the importance of incentives in experiments.

functions so that expected-utility-maximizing decisions are invariant to either additive or multiplicative payoff transformations. These limiting specifications are also helpful because they help us categorize the effects of risk aversion on behavior. For example, if risk attitudes are sensitive to multiplicative wealth transformations, then changes in behavior that follow from doubling payoffs in an experiment may be caused either by the direct incentive effect of the transformation or by the indirect effect of this transformation on risk attitudes. Similarly, if risk attitudes are sensitive to additive wealth changes, then changes in decisions over the course of a session may be either a consequence of learning or a consequence of (actual or anticipated) changes in wealth that occur during the session.

As an alternative to measuring risk preferences, it is possible (at least in theory) to induce risk attitudes, but (as will be seen in chapter 8) the effectiveness of these risk-inducement procedures is the subject of some debate. Also, in some instances, models can be constructed in a manner that predictions are independent of risk attitudes. One relevant example of this situation is the theory motivating probability-matching experiments. Results of these experiments illustrate both the importance of psychological factors with no incentives or with low incentives and the importance of using financial incentives when evaluating economic theories.

2.5 Game Theory: Normal-Form Games

Game theory is the term used to describe a class of mathematical models of the interaction of rational agents. Since each agent's utility can be affected by all agents' decisions, game theory involves the study of conflict, coordination, and/or cooperation. In some sense, game theory is a generalization of decision theory; one can think of decision theory as a two-person game in which one of the players is "nature," a fictitious player who makes decisions based on a random device that determines the "state of nature." The utility of the other (active) player is determined jointly by that player's decision(s) and by the state of nature. Similarly, one can think of game theory as decision theory generalized to allow for multiple decision makers: each agent desires to maximize expected utility, where the expectation is based on the probability distribution that represents the agent's uncertainty about the other players' decisions.

The essential difference between decision theory and (noncooperative) game theory is that players' beliefs are exogenous in the former and endogenous in the latter. In decision theory, individuals optimize against a series of exogenously specified uncertain events. The only issue is to characterize optimal decisions for the given beliefs. In contrast, players' beliefs in a game can be affected by the payoff structure. This endogeneity of beliefs is captured by the standard *Nash equilibrium* condition: In equilibrium, each player makes decisions that are optimal, given the equilibrium decisions of others. In this sense, each player has correct or rational expectations about others' decisions. (More precise definitions of game-theoretic equilibria will be discussed below.)

Decision theorists sometimes characterize their work as *normative*; that is, as describing how rational individuals should make decisions and as helping such individuals discover the correct action. Therefore, it is not surprising that some of the more mathematically oriented game theorists also think of their work as providing a normative criterion for the behavior of rational individuals who know that the other players are also rational.[18] This perspective (which we find bizarre) provides little role for experimentation. Most economists are primarily interested in the *positive*, or descriptive, content of theories. In decision theory, for example, economists and psychologists have searched for inconsistencies between the axioms of expected-utility theory and observed behavior. The subsequent findings, such as the well-known Allais Paradox, have stimulated considerable interest in relaxing one or more of the expected-utility axioms enough to create a theory that accommodates the observed inconsistencies, but not so much that the theory has no empirical content. Similarly, there is little interest in a game theory, however elegant, that does not have positive predictive power. Indeed, the use of game theory in the analysis of industrial organization issues, for example, is clearly based on the implicit assumption that the theory has predictive value, and it is this assumption that is the motivation for experimentation.

The techniques of game theory have become pervasive in economic research. For example, almost all of the recent theoretical analysis of industrial organization and bargaining issues with small numbers of agents is game theoretic. Yet, as evidenced by the paucity of game theory in most microeconomics textbooks, the economics profession at large has been somewhat reluctant to include game theory in the canon of techniques used to explain observed behavior. This skepticism is not without justification. There are many alternative equilibria in most economic games with any degree of complexity. While a lively theoretical literature has generated a variety of devices for determining which equilibria are "reasonable," the devices are often inconsistent with each other. In general, this theoretical literature does not seem to be converging to a consensus position.

The combination of the widespread use of game theory and the unsettled nature of equilibrium selection criteria makes it a very fruitful area for experimental economics. Even if experiments are not designed for the purpose of evaluating game-theoretic issues, the predictions of game theory provide a useful point of reference in experimental contexts, since laboratory performance is best evaluated in light of alternative theories.

---

[18] For example, Rubinstein (1991, p. 909) remarks that "Game theory is viewed as an abstract inquiry into the concepts used in social reasoning when dealing with situations of conflict and not as an attempt to predict behavior."

Noncooperative Equilibria in Normal-Form Games

In this section, we consider a series of simple games that illustrate the relationships and differences between optimal behavior in a decision problem and equilibrium behavior in a game. It will be necessary to begin with some terminology that pertains to the simplest representation of a game: the *normal form*. The basic elements of a game are the *players*, or decision-making agents, their possible actions, or *feasible decision sets*, and their preferences. Players may have the opportunity to make decisions on more than one occasion and under varying information conditions. Consequently, it is useful to work with *strategies*, or complete plans of action that specify a feasible decision that a player will make at each stage of the game under each possible information condition. In other words, once a strategy is selected, the player could then hand the strategy over to an agent who would never have to request additional guidance from the player. Strategies can specify random decisions. In a game where players must decide whether or not to enter a market, for example, they might choose to enter with a probability of one-half. The interaction of a collection of strategies, one for each player, leads to a game *outcome*. In the absence of randomization, outcomes are uniquely determined by the strategies.

Each player's preferences over outcomes is represented by a von Neumann-Morgenstern utility function. The outcome of an experimental game typically determines each subject's earnings in terms of money instead of some other commodity, and utility is usually specified solely as a function of the subject's monetary earnings. In the event of jealousy or altruism, however, the utility of an outcome could also depend on another player's monetary earnings. A *payoff function* for the game specifies the players' utilities for each outcome; that is, it specifies a vector of utility numbers, one for each player, for each outcome. Therefore, a vector of strategies leads to an outcome, and an outcome leads to a vector of utilities.

A normal form of a game is the mapping from vectors of strategies to vectors of utility payoffs; that is, outcomes are suppressed in the normal-form representation, and the normal form may be very convenient for this reason. With only two players and a finite number of (nonrandomized) strategies for each, the normal form is essentially a table, with the strategies of one player (Row) listed on the left, and the strategies of the other player (Column) listed across the top. Each entry is a pair of utility payoffs, with Row's payoff listed first. For example, suppose that the two players are potential entrants into a new market and that each must decide whether to enter (E) or not (N). For simplicity, assume that each seller is risk neutral, so that the utility payoffs are the monetary earnings. In this game, each player has two strategies, and there are four outcomes (four ordered combinations of E and N). The normal-form representation is shown in table 2.4, where entries for the column player are bolded. If both players choose N, they each earn a "normal" profit of 0 from sales in their current market, as shown in the upper-left corner of the payoff table. Now look at the lower-right corner, which is reached when both enter. An entrant always incurs a fixed cost of F, and if both enter, they split the new profit of R and each earn $.5R - F$. If one enters and the other does not, the entrant earns a profit, $R - F$, and the other player earns $- L$, which is a loss that occurs as customers switch to the new market.

Table 2.4 An Entry Game in Normal Form

		Column player	
		N	E
Row player	N	0 , 0	$- L$, $R - F$
	E	$R - F$, $- L$	$.5R - F$, $.5R - F$

If $R - F > 0$ and $.5R - F > - L$, then decision E *dominates* decision N, in the sense that entry is best, regardless of what the other player may do. In this case, simple decision theory can be used to analyze the game; for *any* probability distribution that represents a player's beliefs about the other's decision, it is always optimal to enter. Therefore, the equilibrium outcome will be for both to enter.

Now suppose that $R - F > 0$ as before, but that $.5R - F < -L$. In this case, simultaneous entry is no longer an equilibrium outcome. For example, if Row knew that Column would enter, then Row would want to deviate and not enter. Therefore, strategy E is not a *best response* for either player to the other's use of strategy E. An example is instructive. Let $L = 0$, $F = 3$, and $R = 4$, which yields the normal form in table 2.5. If Row thinks that Column plans to enter, then the best response would be for Row not to enter, and if Column thinks that Row will not enter, then the best response is for Column to enter. Notice that the optimal decision now depends on a player's beliefs about the other's decision. If each thinks that the other will not enter, then decision theory indicates that both will enter. Game theory essentially uses an equilibrium condition to rule out beliefs such as these that are inconsistent with the actual decisions; that is, game theory rules out expectations that are irrational in this manner.

There are various definitions of an equilibrium for a game, the simplest of which was formalized by Nash (1950). A *Nash equilibrium* is a vector of strategies with the property that each player's equilibrium strategy is a *best response* to the others' strategies. In other words, if all others use their equilibrium strategies specified in the vector, then there is no unilateral deviation by one player that would

Table 2.5 A Game with Multiple Equilibria ($L=0$, $F=3$, $R=4$)

Column player

		N	E
	N	0 , 0	0 , 1
Row player	E	1 , 0	–1 , –1

raise that player's utility. The no-unilateral-deviation condition applies to all players, so that if all players were to announce their strategies, no player would regret having chosen the strategy that he/she announced. This hypothetical "announcement test" reveals the sense in which irrational beliefs are ruled out in a Nash equilibrium.

Example: A Prisoner's-Dilemma Experiment

In many simple games, there is a unique Nash equilibrium that yields lower payoffs for both players than some other, more cooperative outcome. For example, it is easy to imagine a situation in which neighboring shopkeepers each have a unilateral incentive to seek after-hours business, but they are both better off if they agree to restrict hours.[19] Think of "entry" for the game in table 2.4 as simply hiring an extra employee and extending the business hours; that is, the new market is the market for after-hours customers. In this case, F is the cost of staying open, R is the revenue from the new business, and L is the revenue from business that switches from normal hours to extended hours. Let the cost of extending service be large, $F = 1,100$, and let the transfer business be a significant fraction of the new business: $L = 800$ and $R = 1,300$. Using these parameters and adding a constant 800 (representing normal profit) to all payoff entries, the structure in table 2.4 yields the payoffs on the left side of table 2.6. Notice that the cooperative outcome, which maximizes the sellers' combined profits, involves no extension of hours, but that each can increase profits from 800 to 1,000 by unilaterally extending the hours (decision E). If both extend hours, however, their payoffs are only 350. This symmetric, low-payoff outcome is a Nash equilibrium since if either decides unilaterally to restrict hours (decision N), that seller's payoff falls from 350 to 0.

---

[19] Recently in Spain, shopkeepers have tried to organize resistance to the decisions of department stores to stay open during traditional lunch hours (2 – 5 p.m.). The department stores are probably better able to resist the social pressures to maintain traditional hours.

This low-payoff outcome is *Pareto dominated*; that is, the payoffs for each player are lower than the corresponding payoffs for another outcome. This type of game, with a Pareto-dominated Nash equilibrium, is a "prisoner's dilemma," which was discussed in chapter 1.

Table 2.6 A Prisoner's Dilemma Game

		Column player		Matchings	Percentage of cooperative choices (N)
		N	E	1 – 5	43%
Row player	N	800, **800**	0, **1,000**	6 – 10	33%
	E	1,000, **0**	350, **350**	11 – 15	25%
				16 – 20	20%

Source: Payoffs and data from Cooper et al., (1991).

The game shown on the left side of table 2.6 was used by Cooper et al. (1991) in an experiment in which subjects were paired with each other in a sequence of matchings. Each subject only encountered each other subject once, to induce a sequence of twenty single-stage games.[20] The payoffs in the figure were in terms of lottery tickets, which were subsequently used to determine whether a subject would earn a monetary prize of $1.00 after each matching. The purpose of this procedure was to induce risk neutrality, as discussed in the previous section. The data for this experiment are summarized on the right side of table 2.6. The cooperative decision, N, was made much more frequently in the early matchings: the rate of (disequilibrium) cooperative decisions decreased from 43 percent in the first five matchings to 20 percent in the final five matchings. We see that there is a strong tendency to cooperate, but that the Nash equilibrium has some drawing power as subjects gain experience. This cooperation is tacit, since subjects are unable to discuss the issues and make agreements during the experiment.

There have been hundreds of prisoner's-dilemma experiments conducted by economists and psychologists, but they typically involve multiperiod repetition of the same game with the same partner. This repeated prisoner's-dilemma structure is

---

[20] In addition, there was no "contagion" in the sense that there were no indirect feedback effects, such as would occur if subject A were paired with subject B, who was then paired with subject C, who in turn was paired subsequently with A. These and all higher-order feedback effects were eliminated by the design of the rotation schedule.

often motivated by an analogy with two duopolists, who interact in a series of market periods. In the one-period game, the equilibrium involves both duopolists setting low prices. The Pareto-dominant, high-price outcome is typically not a Nash equilibrium, since each seller has a unilateral incentive to cut price. In a repeated game, higher rates of cooperation may be observed. Repetition provides a medium for a type of communication, as the use of the noncooperative decision can be interpreted as a punishment. In particular, players may be hesitant to deviate from the (N, N) outcome, since a unilateral deviation only increases payoffs by 200 and may have the effect of triggering a punishment outcome (E, E) in subsequent periods. Since payoffs in the punishment outcome are 450 less than payoffs in the cooperative outcome, the threat of punishment would deter defection if there was even a 50 percent chance that the game would continue for a single additional period. In this way cooperative behavior can be part of a noncooperative equilibrium strategy, if there is no definite final period, and if the probability of repetition is sufficiently high. Trigger strategies of this sort, as well as other factors that facilitate tacit cooperation in repeated games, are discussed at length in subsequent chapters.

A Coordination Game

The prisoner's-dilemma game consists of a single Nash equilibrium, which is Pareto-dominated by a disequilibrium outcome. Other games of interest are characterized by multiple Nash equilibria, and although it is not necessarily the case that one equilibrium Pareto dominates the others, when such a situation arises, it is not uncommon to assume that economic agents coordinate on the Pareto-dominant equilibrium. This assumption represents a strengthening, or "refinement" of the notion of a Nash equilibrium, and it is precisely the type of assumption that can and should be evaluated in the laboratory.

A particularly severe coordination problem arises when the payoffs to each person in a group are affected by the minimum effort level of anyone in the group. A late-afternoon committee meeting presents a classic example. Suppose a meeting is scheduled for 4:00 p.m. and will take two hours. Suppose further that the meeting cannot begin until all committee members are present. Under these circumstances, everyone would clearly be better off if the meeting started promptly at 4:00. However, since the entire committee must be present in order for the meeting to start, no one should show up on time if it is likely that anyone else will be late.

A game with this structure is presented in table 2.7. This table determines each subject's payoff in pennies (rather than time) as a function of his/her own "choice of X" and the minimum of all subjects' choices of X. Notice the highest payoff of 130 in the lower right-hand corner of the table. This outcome occurs when all subjects choose 7. This is a Nash equilibrium, because if all others choose 7, you get 130 by choosing 7, and if you choose something less than 7 you reduce the

Table 2.7 A Coordination Game with Multiple, Pareto-Ranked Nash Equilibria: Your Payoff in Pennies

		Smallest value of X chosen						
		1	2	3	4	5	6	7
	1	70	-	-	-	-	-	-
Your	2	60	80	-	-	-	-	-
choice	3	50	70	90	-	-	-	-
of X	4	40	60	80	100	-	-	-
	5	30	50	70	90	110	-	-
	6	20	40	60	80	100	120	-
	7	10	30	50	70	90	110	130

Source: Van Huyck, Battalio, and Beil (1990).

minimum of the X choices, which moves you to the left in the table to a lower payoff. But any other symmetric configuration is also a Nash equilibrium. For example, if all subjects choose 1, then each gets 70, and no subject has an incentive to increase the X choice unilaterally, as this will not change the relevant column, but will lower the subject's payoff. The intuition is that if others are going to be late, then you should also be late, since your payoff depends on the minimum effort level, or the last person to arrive. In fact, all of the symmetric outcomes on the diagonal of table 2.7 are Nash equilibria, and they are all Pareto ranked by the common effort level. The relevant empirical issue is whether Pareto dominance is a criterion that can allow us to select one of these equilibria as being the likely outcome.

Van Huyck, Battalio, and Beil (1990) conducted a number of sessions using fourteen to sixteen subjects and the parameters in table 2.7. In a each session, the same group of subjects made X decisions independently in a ten-stage game, where each stage involves a repetition of the *stage game* in table 2.7. After decisions were made in each stage, they were collected and the minimum value of X was announced publicly. Figure 2.5 illustrates the results of one session reported by Van Huyck et. al. In the figure, the ten stages are enumerated along the horizontal axis, while X decisions, 1 through 7, extend out from the page, from lowest to highest. The vertical dimension illustrates the frequency of each choice. In stage 1, for example, 40 percent of the participants (six of fifteen) chose option 7, and another 54 percent (eight of fifteen) chose 5. Payoffs in this stage, however, were determined by the single participant who chose option 4. In subsequent stages, the incidence of low-numbered choices quickly increased, as indicated by the increasing size of the vertical bars in the back of the chart. These results are representative of the other sessions in the experiment. The minimum decision was never above 4 in the first

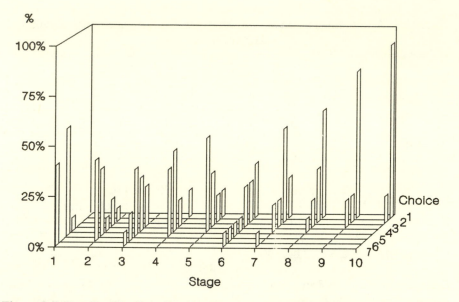

Figure 2.5 Results of a Coordination Game Session (Source: Van Huyck, Battalio, and Beil, 1990, Session 4)

stage in any of the sessions, and the minimum decision reached the lowest level of 1 by the fourth stage in all sessions. Decision 1 was overwhelmingly selected in the final stage. Even though the symmetric choice of 7 by all is a Pareto-dominant Nash equilibrium, the choice of 7 is very risky and can yield a payoff as low as 10 cents. In contrast, the choice of 1 yields a sure payoff of 70 cents, and this Nash equilibrium has the most drawing power, even though it is Pareto dominated. The riskiness of the Pareto-dominant equilibrium is magnified by the large number of subjects, each of whom can lower the minimum X level. When pairs of subjects played the same game, most were able to coordinate on the 7/7 outcome. Other coordination problems involving the provision of public goods will be considered in chapter 6.

Equilibria in Mixed Strategies

Now reconsider the game in table 2.5. Notice that there are multiple Nash equilibria, one in which Row enters and Column does not, and one in which Column enters and Row does not. Neither equilibrium is better than the other for both players; that is, neither Pareto dominates the other. The Nash concept does not select one of these two equilibria over the other. Indeed, this nonuniqueness is desirable since the symmetry of the situation suggests on an intuitive level that neither outcome is more likely. This type of game is usually called a "battle-of-the-sexes" game, since each of the two equilibria involves one of the players dominating the other, but each player prefers to give in to the other's wishes rather than to have open conflict in which both choose E and receive a payoff of -1.

Now imagine an experiment in which each subject is matched with a series of other subjects in a sequence of symmetric battle-of-the-sexes games. Given the symmetry of the situation, it might not be surprising if players sometimes choose E and sometimes do not. In addition to the two equilibria discussed above, there is another Nash equilibrium that is consistent with this variability. Suppose that each Column player flips a coin to determine the decision. Then Row's choice of E yields a 50/50 chance of either $+1$ or -1, and a choice of N yields 0 with certainty. These two decisions have the same expected utility, 0, and therefore Row is indifferent between them. Since Row is indifferent, Row would be willing to use a coin flip to determine the decision, thereby making Column indifferent between the two decisions. This is an equilibrium because if each flips a coin, then neither can increase expected utility by doing something other than flipping a coin.

Formally, a *pure strategy* is one that involves no randomization, and a *mixed strategy* or randomized strategy is a probability distribution over the set of a player's pure strategies. A *mixed equilibrium* is a Nash equilibrium in which one or more of the equilibrium strategies is mixed.

An important issue is whether the notion of a mixed equilibrium has any empirical value. In fact, subjects in experiments are rarely (if ever) observed flipping coins, and when told *ex post* that the equilibrium involves randomization, subjects have expressed surprise and skepticism. This observation does not necessarily mean that the concept of a mixed equilibrium has no empirical relevance. Recall the sequential rematching of Row and Column players described above. If half of the players choose E all of the time and the other half choose N all of the time then the random rematching process performs the necessary randomization; each player would encounter the E decision about half of the time, and hence would be indifferent between the two decisions. In this case, the aggregate frequency of E choices would correspond to the prediction of the equilibrium mixing probabilities.

Example: A Battle-of-the-Sexes Experiment

Cooper, DeJong, Forsythe, and Ross (1989) report the results of an experiment using the battle-of-the-sexes game with payoffs given on the left side of table 2.8. It is clear that there are two Nash equilibria in pure strategies: the Row player prefers the equilibrium in the lower-left corner, and the Column player prefers the equilibrium in the upper-right corner. As with the game in table 2.5, there is a third Nash equilibrium that involves mixing. In order for Row to be willing to randomize, it must be the case that each of Row's decisions yield the same expected payoff. (Otherwise, Row would prefer the decision with the higher payoff.) Let p denote the probability that Column chooses decision $C1$. Given this probability, Row's expected payoff is $200(1 - p)$ for decision $R1$ and $600p$ for decision $R2$. These expected payoffs are equal if $p = 1/4$. To summarize, when Column chooses $C1$ with probability 1/4, Row is indifferent between the two decisions and would be willing to randomize. By symmetry, the same arguments can be used to show that if Row randomizes, choosing $R1$ with probability 1/4, then Column is indifferent between the two decisions and would be willing to randomize.[21] For this reason, the "Nash theory" prediction for the percent of $R2$ or $C2$ choices is listed as 75 percent the right side of table 2.8.

Obviously, the multiplicity of non-Pareto-ranked equilibria in the battle-of-the-sexes game presents the players with a coordination problem. If players could coordinate their actions in a cooperative manner in a repeated game, they would alternate between the preferred corners. In a single-stage game with no possibility of coordination, the choice of strategy 2 with probability .5 maximizes the joint payoff, since it maximizes the chances of a "hit," that is, a combination of decisions in the upper-right or lower-left corners. To see this, let p_2 denote the probability that each player chooses strategy 2. Then the probability of a hit is $p_2(1 - p_2)$ + $(1 - p_2)p_2$, which is a symmetric quadratic expression that is maximized by setting $p_2 = .50$. Therefore, the entry in the "cooperation" Row on the right side of table 2.8 is 50 percent. Note that all four outcomes are equally likely if players randomize with probabilities of .5, so the probability of a hit is $.25 + .25 = .50$. This cooperation results in an expected payoff of 200 for each subject, which exceeds the expected payoff of 150 in a Nash equilibrium.

The procedures for the experiment were similar to those used in the Cooper et al. (1991) prisoner's-dilemma game discussed above: A group of subjects were matched in a sequence of twenty single-period games with different partners, and payoffs were in terms of tickets for a lottery with a prize of $1, to induce risk neutrality. As shown in the third row on the right side of table 2.8, strategy 2 ($R2$ or $C2$) was used less frequently than predicted by the mixed-strategy equilibrium; strategy 2 was used 63 percent of the time, as compared with the Nash prediction of 75 percent. Since the cooperative arrangement is to use strategy 2 half of the time, the authors suggest that the tendency to use strategy 1 more frequently than predicted is a type of tacit cooperation.

---

[21]   A rather curious feature of the mixed-strategy equilibrium concept bears emphasis. In constructing a mixed equilibrium, the modeler has a degree of freedom in selecting the proportion of time that a strategy is actually played, because by definition, each player must be indifferent between a number of alternative strategies. In a two-person game, these proportions are set to make one player just indifferent between the pure strategies over which the other player is randomizing. Construction of the equilibrium in this fashion raises questions regarding the dynamic properties of mixed equilibrium when subjects are rematched with a series of other players; there is often no general reason why a subject, being indifferent, would select a particular strategy with the precise frequency that would make other players indifferent over their strategies. This is an interesting area for theoretical and experimental research.

Table 2.8 A Battle-of-the-Sexes Game

		Column player			% R2 or C2 choices
				Nash theory	75%
		C1	C2	cooperation	50%
Row player	R1	0, 0	200, 600	data	63%
	R2	600, 200	0, 0	data with uncoordinated announcements	71%

Source: Payoffs and data from Cooper et al., (1989).

One way to resolve a coordination problem is to permit nonbinding preplay communications. Cooper et al. (1989) investigate a number of possibilities. With "two-way communications," each subject could independently communicate a single, nonbinding intended choice to the other. After seeing the other player's intention, players would choose decisions independently as in other single-stage games discussed previously. When the intended decisions corresponded to a hit, the actual decisions matched the communications in 80 percent of the cases, which indicates the usefulness of communication in overcoming coordination problems. When the intended decisions did not correspond to a hit, strategy 2 was subsequently used 71 percent of the time, as shown on the right side of table 2.8. The authors suggest that the failure to coordinate at the communication stage makes the second stage more noncooperative.[22]

Summary

Game theory is used to describe the interaction of rational agents under precisely specified information and action conditions. Most game-theory results are based on the notion of a Nash equilibrium, a condition under which no agent finds unilateral deviation from a given outcome profitable. In the laboratory, the Nash

[22] Prisbrey (1991) explores behavior in "reciprocity games," which in some cases resemble a repeated version of the battle-of-the-sexes game. With an indefinite horizon and symmetric payoffs, Prisbrey finds that participants appear to "reciprocate" or alternate between pure-strategy equilibria.

equilibrium appears to explain behavior fairly well when it is unique (but some important exceptions are discussed in later chapters). Data from one-stage prisoner's-dilemma games are consistent with the Nash equilibrium most of the time, even though this equilibrium conflicts with obvious notions of fairness and cooperation.

Many games contain multiple Nash equilibria. In this case, the selection of a particular equilibrium requires a refinement of the Nash equilibrium concept. One very standard refinement is the notion of Pareto dominance: Participants will tend to coordinate on the Nash equilibrium that provides the highest payoffs to everyone, if such an equilibrium exists. Despite the obvious appeal of this concept, data from a coordination game do not support the Pareto-dominance refinement.

When none of the Nash equilibria involving nonstochastic choices are Pareto dominant, additional Nash equilibria arise if players randomize, or play various strategies according to a probability distribution. Subjects in a battle-of-the-sexes game do not coordinate on either of the non-Pareto-ranked, pure-strategy equilibria. The resulting failure to coordinate generates a sizable number of *ex post* disequilibrium outcomes, in which both players would select an alternative strategy, given the choice that their opponent actually made. Coordinating devices, such as two-sided, nonbinding communications, reduce, but do not eliminate coordination problems in the battle-of-the-sexes game.[23]

2.6 Extensive Forms and Backward-Induction Rationality

As seen in the previous section, an important problem with the Nash equilibrium concept is that there are often multiple equilibria, even in simple games. This problem becomes markedly more pronounced as the number of stages in the game is expanded. In multistage games, theorists have most typically restricted or "refined" the Nash equilibrium concept by imposing a type of backward-induction rationality that rules out some of the equilibria. The trick with backward induction is to analyze the optimal decisions in the final stage first, then to consider the second-to-last stage, knowing how decisions will be made optimally in the final stage, and so forth backward in time until the initial decision node is reached. This principle can be applied to any game with a fixed number of stages; the equilibria for the final "stage-game" are computed before considering equilibrium decisions in the second-to-last stage, and so forth.

The process of backward induction can be illustrated in terms of a simple bargaining game in which one player proposes one of two possible ways to split a

---

[23] One-sided communication, where only one of the players submits a nonbinding preplay message, avoids the possibility of crossed intentions. One-sided communications of this type largely eliminated the coordination failures in the Cooper et al. (1989) experiment.

pie, and the other must either accept the proposed split or reject, which results in a zero payoff to both. This simplified version of an ultimatum bargaining game is represented in the tree-like structure on the left side of figure 2.6. In the first stage of the game, player 1 must make a decision at point I_1 between making a generous offer, G, and a stingy offer, S, as indicated by the two branches from point or node I_1. The generous offer takes the play to node I_{2G}, at which point the second player can reject, RG, which yields each agent a return of 0, or accept, AG, which determines a payoff of 1 for the first player and 2 for the second player, that is, outcome (1,2). Similarly, a stingy offer leads to node I_{2S}, where player 2's acceptance, AS, will yield (2,1), and player 2's rejection will yield (0,0).

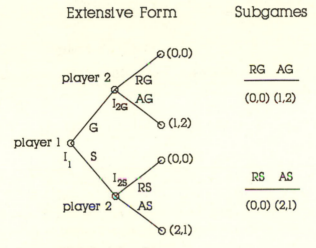

Figure 2.6 A Sequential Bargaining Game

One equilibrium outcome for the game on the left side of figure 2.6 is for player 1 to make the stingy offer and for player 2 to accept. Since the stingy offer provides player 2 with a positive payoff, player 2 cannot increase his/her payoff by rejecting. Nor is a unilateral deviation attractive for player 1, since no other decision could conceivably increase this player's payoff. There is a second equilibrium outcome in which player 1 makes a generous offer and player 2 only accepts if the offer is generous: decision G for the first player and decisions AG and RS for the second player. In this case, a unilateral deviation by the first player would lead to a rejection, and hence would be unattractive. Similarly, there is no unilateral deviation for player 2 that would increase this player's payoff.

Note that player 2 has two possible responses to each of the two offers, so player 2 has four strategies: (AS, AG), (AS, RG), (RS, AG), and (RS, RG). The fact that player 2's "tough" strategy (only accept a generous offer) is an equilibrium can be seen from the normal form of this game, which is shown in table 2.9. Recall that the normal form of a game is a listing of the players' payoffs that result from each possible vector of pure strategies, so the payoff matrix in table 2.9 has one row for each of player 1's offers and one column for each of the four response patterns available to player 2. The underlined (1, 2) outcome in the $(G; RS, AG)$ box is an equilibrium, since there is no unilateral deviation for either player that will increase the player's payoff. In particular, a deviation by player 1, that is, a stingy offer, would result in a payoff of 0. It is clear from the normal form that there are two other pure-strategy equilibria involving stingy offers that are accepted: $(S; AS, AG)$ and $(S; AS, RG)$.

Table 2.9   A Normal-Form Representation of the Simple Bargaining Game
(payoff for player 1, payoff for player 2)

		Player 2's strategies			
		(AS, AG)	*(AS, RG)*	*(RS, AG)*	*(RS, RG)*
Player 1's	*S*	(2 , 1)	(2 , 1)	(0 , 0)	(0 , 0)
strategies	*G*	(1 , 2)	(0 , 0)	<u>(1 , 2)</u>	(0 , 0)

The three pure-strategy equilibria are distinguishable, however, in that equilibrium $(G; RS, AG)$ relies on a threat by player 2 to reject a stingy offer. Even though this threat is never carried out in equilibrium, the threat is not credible in the sense that, if player 1 were to choose S, then player 2 would be put in a position of choosing between a positive payoff from acceptance and a zero payoff from rejection. This type of threat is ruled out by imposing a backward-induction rationality condition.

Before considering backward induction in a game-theoretic context, consider what backward induction would imply if this were a single-person decision problem. In particular, suppose that player 1 has the power to make player 2's choice for him/her. Then player 1 would choose to accept in the second stage, so we could replace the I_{2G} node and all that follows with the outcome (1,2), and we could replace the I_{2S} node and all that follows with (2,1). Then the first-stage decision is between G, which yields a payoff of 1 for the first player, and S, which yields a payoff of 2. Although backward induction is trivial in this simple example, it can be a very powerful device in dynamic decision-making situations involving more than two stages.

Now return to the two-person-game interpretation of figure 2.6. Backward induction in this context essentially requires that one analyze the "subgames" in the final stage before analyzing the game as a whole. The subgame for the I_{2G} node is shown by the payoff box in the upper-right part of figure 2.6. This is a trivial game in the sense that the only decision to be made is made by player 2, and the Nash equilibrium for this subgame involves AG because a unilateral deviation to RG would decrease player 2's payoff from 2 to 0. Similarly, the equilibrium for the other subgame also involves acceptance, AS, which precludes the noncredible threat to reject a stingy offer.

The preceding discussion was informal; to describe the application of this logic more formally, it is first necessary to review some terminology. The game representation on the left side of figure 2.6 is called an *extensive form*. The extensive form is a tree in which each of the nonterminal *nodes* corresponds to a decision that must be made by one of the players, and hence, each node is labeled accordingly. Each branch that emanates from a node represents a *feasible action* for the player that corresponds to that node. The label on each branch corresponds to the action. For example, at node I_1, player 1 has two feasible actions, S or G. There is a beginning node, in this case I_1. Starting from this beginning node, a sequence of actions determines a unique path through the tree, leading to an endpoint or *terminal node*. There are four terminal nodes in figure 2.6. All terminal nodes are labeled with a *payoff vector* that lists each player's payoffs if that node is reached.

In many games, a player may be uninformed about the previous or simultaneous decisions of another player, and this type of ignorance is represented by the specification of an *information set* that contains all nodes among which a player is unable to distinguish. An information set is represented by a dashed line that connects all nodes in the set. For example, if the player 2 had to make the accept-or-reject decision before finding out the first player's offer, then the nodes I_{2G} and I_{2S} would have been connected by a dashed line in figure 2.6. A player's *strategy* specifies an action to be taken in each of the player's information sets, so a strategy is a complete plan of action that covers all contingencies. For example, a strategy for player 2 could be (AG, RS), or to accept a generous offer and reject a stingy offer. Player 1's strategies consist of S or G. A *Nash equilibrium* is a vector of strategies, one for each player, with the property that no player can increase his/her own payoff through a unilateral deviation from the equilibrium strategy.

An important refinement of the Nash equilibrium concept in multistage games, due to Selten (1965), is defined in terms of parts of the game, or *subgames*. Essentially, a subgame is any part of the original game that, taken by itself, could constitute a game; that is, a subgame must have a well-defined initial node and must contain all parts of the original game that can be reached as a result of actions taken at and following this node in the original game. For example, there is one subgame that begins at node I_{2S}, and consists of the decisions made by player 2 following a stingy offer. In addition, the whole game is a subgame of itself, just as in mathematics a set is a subset of itself.

With this terminology, Selten's refinement of *subgame perfection* can be explained. A strategy in the original game specifies a complete plan of action in each subgame. An equilibrium is subgame perfect if the equilibrium strategies for the game as a whole also determine a Nash equilibrium for every possible subgame. The equilibrium strategy vector (*G*: *RS*, *AG*) in the above bargaining game, for example, fails subgame perfection, since player 2's strategy of rejecting a stingy offer, *RS*, is not an equilibrium for the subgame following the node I_{2S} (the submission of a stingy offer). Importantly, (*G*: *RS*, *AG*) fails subgame perfection because an action off the equilibrium path (*RS*) is not an equilibrium for the subgame beginning at I_{2S}. It is not uncommon to be able to eliminate equilibria in this manner. Some actions off the equilibrium path represent "threats" that support the equilibrium outcome. The notion of subgame perfection is used to eliminate equilibria supported by threats that are not credible in the sense that they are not equilibria for some subgames.

In many games, particularly those with exogenous uncertainty, the notion of subgame perfection is thought to be too weak in the sense that it does not rule out equilibria that seem to be unreasonable in an intuitive sense. An important instance where subgame perfection fails to eliminate unreasonable equilibria occurs when an unobserved random event makes it impossible to split the game as a whole into subgames. The problem arises because the uncertainty creates information sets with multiple nodes, and the initial node of a subgame cannot be one element of several elements in an information set. Loosely speaking, it is not possible to break information sets while creating subgames. When the game cannot be split into subgames, the notion of subgame perfection is not useful, and an alternative refinement must be developed. Appendix 2.4 illustrates this problem in the context of a modification of this section's pie-splitting example, and then presents the notion of a *sequential equilibrium*, which was devised to address this problem.[24]

A Centipede Game

As will become apparent in later chapters, subjects in many experiments do not begin to use backward induction reasoning immediately, and if they do, it is only after sufficient experience in the subgames in earlier matchings with different groups of other players. To generate some insight regarding why backward induction arguments fail to predict subjects' behavior, it is instructive to consider the following simple game.

Suppose two students are chosen from a classroom; one, player Red, happens to be wearing something red, while the other, player Blue, is wearing something

---

[24] The analysis of sequential equilibria is primarily used in the sections on games with asymmetric information in chapter 7, and therefore, the appendix on sequential equilibria can be skipped on a first reading.

blue. The players make a series of alternating decisions regarding whether to pass on a monetary prize that increases with the total number of decisions made in the game, or to take the prize and end the game. More specifically, at the outset of the game, Red is presented with two trays, a large tray, which contains 40 cents, and a small tray, which contains 10 cents. Red may either end the game with a take of the prize in the large tray (giving the small tray to Blue) or may pass both trays to Blue. In the event of a pass, Blue faces the same choices presented to Red, except that the prizes in the large and small trays are doubled; for example, the large tray contains 80 cents and the small tray contains 20 cents. A pass by Blue returns the pass-or-take choice to Red, with the prizes on the trays again doubled. Absent a take, the game ends after a doubling of prizes following the fourth round. In this case Red gets the large tray, worth $6.40, and Blue gets the small tray, worth $1.60.

Figure 2.7 contains the extensive form for this "centipede game,"[25] which derives its name from the multi-leg structure.[26] The game starts in the upper left-hand corner of the figure, with Red making the first take-or-pass decision, and it ends with Blue making the final decision. To apply backward induction, consider the subgame involving Blue's final decision, on the right side of the figure. A take gives Blue $3.20, and a pass gives Blue only $1.60, so Blue should take if the play ever reaches the final node. Now consider the decision that Red must make in the second-to-last stage. If Red foresees that Blue will take at the final stage (giving Red .80), then Red should take at the second-to-last stage and get 1.60. By reasoning backward through the game tree, we see that Blue should take in the second stage (because Red would take in the third), and Red should take in the first stage (because Blue would take in the second). The implication of backward-induction logic in this context is that the game ends in the first stage, with Red taking .40 and Blue getting .10. Even though this outcome is subgame perfect, it would be frustrating for the participants, since they could each earn much more if they both pass at each stage.

McKelvey and Palfrey (1991) report results of three sessions with these parameters. In each session, there were ten subjects who had the Red role and ten subjects who had the Blue role. Each subject was matched ten times with different subjects of the other color. The proportions of outcomes in each terminal node for matchings six to ten, are reflected by the thickness of the legs dropping vertically from the horizontal stem running across the top of figure 2.7. As indicated by the relatively thin left-most leg, only a small proportion of Reds took the .40 payoff in the first stage (8 percent), and most of the games end in the second and third stages. Obviously, behavior does not conform to the predictions of backward induction, even

---

[25] Appendix 2.5 contains instructions for a classroom implementation of a similar centipede game. An instructor using this book as a text might find it useful to present this game to students prior to assigning this section.

[26] This game was first discussed in Rosenthal (1982), and the original version contained 100 legs.

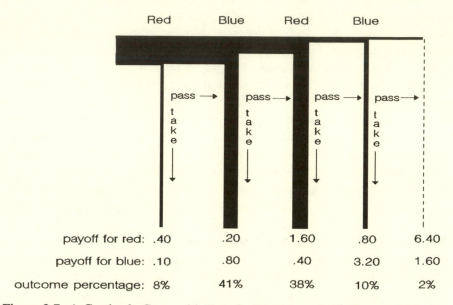

Figure 2.7 A Centipede Game with Data for Matchings 6–10 (Source: McKelvey and Palfrey, 1991, table 3b)

after some experience in earlier matchings.[27] The explanation offered by McKelvey and Palfrey is that some subjects are altruists who prefer to pass in early stages, and though these altruists are rare (say 1 in 20), the best response of the others is to pass with high probability in early stages.[28]

Summary

When games have multiple stages, the set of equilibria is often quite large. Economists have suggested a number of criteria for eliminating certain "unappealing" Nash equilibria. Many such equilibria can be eliminated by backward-induction arguments, or by first determining equilibrium strategies in the terminal subgames. Then the restrictions imposed by equilibria in the terminal subgames can be used to identify equilibria in larger subgames that include the terminal subgames, and so forth. The resulting refinement, known as subgame perfection, essentially requires that threats off the equilibrium path be credible.

---

[27] But subjects do tend to make the take decision somewhat more often in the final five matchings than was the case in the initial five matchings.

[28] This brief explanation does not capture the richness of the theoretical and econometric analysis in the McKelvey and Palfrey paper.

Despite the theoretical elegance of backward-induction rationality, it often fails to predict the behavior of subjects. Subjects appear to apply backward induction rationality somewhat more frequently when they repeatedly play a multiple-stage game, each time with a different partner.

2.7 Decision Theory, Game Theory, and Price Theory

In this chapter we have introduced a variety of topics in decision theory and game theory. These tools comprise much of the foundation of modern economic analysis. We will consider these tools and their behavioral analogues much more carefully in later chapters. In the next two chapters, however, our discussion is largely confined to competitive price theory, for example, where price and quantity predictions are determined from the intersection of market supply and demand. One important issue that must be addressed at this point is the relationship between simple competitive market predictions and the comparatively sophisticated tools of decision and game theories. In part, this question is easy to answer. The tools of decision theory apply to individual responses to particular kinds of uncertainty. Price theory, in contrast, deals with agents acting in groups.

The relationship between game theory and price theory, however, is less exclusive. As a general matter, game theory and price theory have rather distinct areas of application. Game-theoretic analyses are based on highly specific assumptions regarding the opportunities, actions, and information available to participants. Perhaps the most standard informational assumption is *complete information*; that is, players know all features of the structure of the game. In particular, each player knows the payoff functions of all players. In contrast, many economic situations of interest are characterized by private information. Agents often know very little about others' preferences, information sets, sets of feasible decisions, or any of the other essential elements of a game. A common practice in many experiments designed to address industrial organization issues is to provide each player with only the relevant aspects of his/her own payoff function. For example, in some of their duopoly experiments Fouraker and Siegel (1963) gave subjects only a table showing their own monetary earnings as a function of their quantity decision and of the other seller's quantity decision. They were given no information about the other's payoff table. Game-theoretic predictions provide only a point of reference in such experiments, since subjects do not know the structure of the game.

In many contexts, agents make decisions on the basis of observed indicators or market signals such as the price of a good. In this case, the predictions of competitive price theory may provide a more useful reference than the results of an attempt to analyze the situation as a game with considerable incompleteness of information. In competitive price theory, it is assumed that agents take price as given, rather than considering the effects of their decisions on price. This price-taking assumption is especially useful if it is difficult for agents to perceive the effects of their decisions on price, perhaps because the effect is in fact small, or perhaps because the presence of random shocks makes it difficult to observe such effects.

Further, analysis of the game underlying a given market situation is sometimes difficult. Identification of the set of all equilibria frequently becomes impossible, and there are well-known trading institutions that are sufficiently complex to preclude identification of any subgame-perfect Nash equilibria. As is apparent in the next chapter, competitive price theory may be especially useful in this category of situations.

Finally, when it is the case that market may be analyzed both from the perspective of price theory and from that of game theory, the alternative equilibrium predictions provide useful points of reference. These predictions coincide in some situations. For example, if sellers with constant average costs and no capacity constraints choose prices simultaneously, then each seller has a unilateral incentive to shade on any common price above the competitive level. Therefore, the Nash equilibrium is the competitive, zero-profit outcome. In other circumstances, game theory and price theory yield competing predictions. For example, it will be shown in chapter 4 that capacity constraints can provide unilateral incentives for sellers to raise prices above the competitive level. This is because a price increase need not reduce sales if rivals' capacities are limited. The existence of this type of "market power" can cause the Nash equilibrium prices to exceed the perfectly competitive price. The relative predictive powers of the alternative equilibria in such circumstances is an empirical issue, perhaps best examined in the laboratory.

APPENDIX A2

A2.1 Derivation of the Reservation Wage

A standard method of solving dynamic problems is to begin with an expression for the expected value of continuing optimally, which will be called a *value function*. Let $v(w)$ denote the expected value of continuing with a procedure that calls for search until a wage that exceeds w is encountered. Since nothing in the decision problem changes when an offer is passed over, $v(w)$ is independent of time. This expected value from continuing to search is composed of the three parts on the right side of equation (2.7).

$$(2.7) \qquad v(w) \; = \; \sum_{x=w+1}^{200} x f(x) \;\; + \;\; F(w)v(w) \;\; - \;\; c \; .$$

The left-hand term on the right side of the equation represents the case in which an acceptable value of x is encountered and accepted, so we sum over values of x that exceed the reservation wage w, that is, from $w+1$ to 200. Each of these x values is weighted by the density $f(x)$, which is the probability of encountering that value of x. Next, consider the second term, $F(w)v(w)$. The probability that the next draw is less than or equal to w is $F(w)$, in which case the draw is rejected and the search begins again with an expected value that is, by definition, $v(w)$. The third term is the cost of search, which is paid whether or not the draw is accepted. It is the presence of $v(w)$ on the right side of (2.7) that makes this a dynamic problem, since this $v(w)$ term represents what happens in future periods.

The problem is to use (2.7) to determine the optimal reservation wage w. Recall from statement (iii) in section 2.3 that the reservation wage equals the expected payoff from searching optimally; that is, that $w = v(w)$ at the optimal level of w. By making this substitution into (2.7) and rearranging terms, we obtain an equation that must be satisfied by the optimal reservation wage:

$$(2.8) \qquad c \; = \; \sum_{x=w+1}^{200} x f(x) \;\; - \;\; w[1 - F(w)] .$$

Since $1-F(w)$ is the probability that the offer is greater than w, (2.8) becomes

(2.9)
$$c = \sum_{x=w+1}^{200} xf(x) - w \sum_{x=w+1}^{200} f(x),$$

which reduces to the equation in (2.2) that equates marginal gain and marginal cost of additional search. Therefore, the optimal search strategy in this dynamic context is myopic. A calculus-based derivation of the reservation-wage equation for the case of continuous probability distributions is obtained by writing the continuous analogue of equation (2.7), solving for $v(w)$, and maximizing the resulting expression for $v(w)$ with respect to w.

A2.2 Instructions for a Sequential Search Experiment

This is an experiment in the economics of decision making.[29] Your decisions will determine your earnings, which will be paid to you privately, in cash, immediately after the experiment. At this time, we will give you an initial money balance of $7.00. This payment is to compensate you for showing up, and it will offset any initial expenses that you may incur.

Overview

This experiment consists of a fixed number of *search sequences*. In each search sequence you will be given the opportunity to purchase draws from a random distribution. The draws cost 10 cents each and are purchased in sequential order; that is, you see the outcome of one draw prior to deciding whether or not to purchase an additional draw or draws.

Each draw is a potential prize. Your problem is to decide when to stop purchasing draws and convert one of the potential prizes into a money prize. In a given search sequence, you can choose *only one* of the numbers that is drawn to be your money prize for that search sequence. In each sequence, you earn the difference between the money prize and the total amount you spend purchasing draws.

---

[29] These instructions are written for the case where an experimenter elicits decisions from a single participant. To use these instructions for educational purposes in a classroom, references to monetary payoffs should be deleted. Some procedural additions are necessary to conduct a simultaneous, multiperson version of this experiment for research purposes. In particular, care must be taken to ensure that record keeping is honest, and that search/stop decisions are not colored by the choices of others. However, for instructional purposes it may be sufficient for the instructor to allow all class members to indicate "search" or "stop" decisions simultaneously.

Each "potential prize" draw will be a number between 0 and 199 pennies, as determined by the throw of dice. Each number between and including 0 and 199 is equally likely (the twenty-sided die will determine the dollar and dime digits, 0, 1, 2, . . . 19, and the ten-sided die will determine the penny digit, 0, 1, . . . 9.[30]

The Search Process

Each search sequence proceeds as follows. At the beginning of the sequence, the experimenter will ask you to indicate whether or not you would like to search. If you decide not to search, the sequence ends, and your earnings for that search sequence are 0. If you search, the experimenter throws the dice to determine a potential prize (between 0 and 199), which we will call X_1. You should record X_1 on the attached piece of scrap paper. The experimenter will then ask you to decide whether to search or stop. If you say "search," the dice will be thrown again, yielding a second potential prize X_2, which you will record next to X_1 on your scrap paper. This process is repeated until you tell the experimenter that you wish to stop searching.

Earnings

Earnings are the difference between the draw that you choose for your money prize and the total costs of search. If, for example, you stop after drawing potential prize X_1 on the first search, your money prize is X_1 and you earn $X_1 - 10$ cents. If you stop after searching twice and obtaining potential prizes X_1 and X_2, you will earn either $X_1 - 20$ or $X_2 - 20$ cents, depending on whether you choose to convert X_1 or X_2 into your monetary prize. In general, you will search some number of times, n, generating a series of potential prizes $X_1 \ldots X_n$ that you record on a piece of scrap paper. After you stop, you will select one of these prizes, say X_i, to be your money prize. Your earnings, then, are $X_i - 10(n)$ cents.

Your earnings will be recorded on the attached Decision Sheet. There is a different row for each search sequence. Earnings in each sequence are calculated as follows. First, enter the number of throws of the dice, *including the final throw*, in column (2). Second, multiply this number by $.10 to obtain the total search cost. Write this number in column (3). Third, select one of the potential prizes from the search sequence for your money prize. Enter this value in column (4). Fourth, subtract the total search cost in column (3) from your prize in column (4) to obtain your earnings. Enter this amount in column (5). If this number is less than zero,

---

[30] If the twenty-sided die is numbered from 1 to 20, count the 20 as a 0, and if the ten-sided die is numbered from 1 to 10, count the 10 as a 0. This yields numbers from 0 to 199. To make the example consistent with section 2.3, simply add 1 to all outcomes, and change the instructions accordingly.

		DECISION SHEET FOR SEARCH EXPERIMENT			
(1) Search sequence	(2) Number of searches (including final one)	(3) Total search cost $(2) \times (.10)$	(4) Value of accepted draw	(5) Search sequence earnings $(4) - (3)$	(6) Cumula- tive earnings
practice					***
practice					***
practice					$7.00
1					
2					
3					
4					
5					
6					
7					
8					
9					
10					

Round your cumulative earnings up to the nearest 25-cent increment, and complete: I received the amount of $_____ as payment for participating in a laboratory experiment. Please write the amount out in words as you would in writing a check:

AMOUNT:_____

YOUR NAME (please print):_____

DATE:_____ SOCIAL SECURITY NUMBER:_____

SIGNATURE:_____

be certain to precede the entry with a minus sign.

Cumulative earnings are maintained in column (6) by adding (or subtracting) the earnings for a current search sequence to the previous total. Remember to include the initial $7.00 payment in the cumulative earnings.

Final Comments

Notice from the left-hand column (1) of your Decision Sheet that today's experiment will consist of three practice sequences (in which no money is earned) and exactly ten search sequences for which earnings will be paid. After the tenth sequence, please complete the receipt form at the bottom of the Decision Sheet. I will pay you your earnings after verifying your calculations, and you will be free to leave.

Are there any questions?

A2.3 Constructing a von Neumann-Morgenstern Utility Function[*]

Von Neumann-Morgenstern utility functions for monetary prizes can be constructed on the basis of four assumptions: continuity, monotonicity, reduction of compound lotteries, and substitution.[31]   These assumptions are explained in more detail elsewhere (e.g., DeGroot, 1970; Kreps, 1990), but an admittedly informal description here will indicate how a subject's utility function could be constructed. In a loose sense, *continuity* is a requirement that for any lottery, there is some probability such that a subject is indifferent between the lottery and a probability-weighted combination of the subject's most-preferred and least-preferred lotteries. *Monotonicity* requires that a subject would always prefer to increase the probability of a more-preferred prize if the probability of a less-preferred prize is reduced. Compound lotteries have prizes that are themselves lotteries, and *reduction of compound lotteries* requires that the probabilities of the ultimate money payoffs be calculated in the standard (multiplicative) manner. *Substitution* is an assumption that the preference for a lottery is unchanged if one of the prizes in the lottery is replaced with another lottery that is equally preferred as the prize being replaced.

The axioms will be used to construct a representation of preferences over lotteries with three prizes, but the generalization to any finite number of prizes is straightforward. Let the utility of the lowest monetary reward, x_1, be normalized to 0, and let the utility of the most preferred payoff, x_3, be normalized to 1. A subject

---

[*]   The material in this section is somewhat more advanced.

[31]   Since the prizes are monetary payoffs, and since subjects are assumed to prefer more money to less, it is not necessary to add assumptions that the preferences over prizes are complete and transitive.

should prefer the intermediate monetary payoff of x_2 with certainty to a probability mix of x_1 and x_3 when the probability of x_1 is sufficiently close to 0, and the subject should prefer the mix over x_2 when the probability of x_3 in the mix is sufficiently close to 1. By *continuity*, there exists a probability, v, such that the subject is just indifferent between receiving x_2 with certainty and receiving a mix of x_1 with probability $1 - v$ and x_3 with probability v.

An experimenter could elicit values of v from subjects in a variety of ways. Experimenters frequently attempt to elicit v values, for example, via a series of questions regarding preferences over various lotteries.[32] Given v, consider the utility function

(2.10) $U(x_1) = 0,   U(x_2) = v,   U(x_3) = 1.$

This utility function represents the subject's preferences if, for any two lotteries, the first lottery is preferred to the second if and only if the expected value of (2.10) for the first exceeds the expected value of (2.10) for the second. To verify this property, we use the three remaining assumptions: substitution, reduction of compound lotteries, and monotonicity.

Consider two lotteries with the three monetary prizes x_1, x_2, and x_3, where the money amounts are ranked in the same order as the subscripts: $x_1 < x_2 < x_3$. There is a "p" lottery with probabilities (p_1, p_2, p_3) and a "q" lottery with probabilities (q_1, q_2, q_3). The p lottery can be represented as (probability p_1 of x_1, probability p_2 of x_2, probability p_3 of x_3). The q lottery can be similarly represented. For simplicity, the word "probability" will be omitted in such representations.

Recall that x_2 with certainty is equally preferred to a mix: ($[1-v]$ of x_1, v of x_3). By *substitution*, we can replace x_2 in the original p lottery with this equally preferred mix:

(2.11)
$(p_1$ *of* x_1, p_2 *of* x_2, p_3 *of* $x_3)$

$\sim$ $(p_1$ *of* x_1, p_2 *of* $[(1-v)$ *of* x_1, v *of* $x_3]$, p_3 *of* $x_3)$,

where "$\sim$" indicates indifference. The lottery on the right side of (2.11) is a compound lottery involving only x_1 and x_3. By *reduction of compound lotteries*, the probabilities associated with these two monetary payoffs can be calculated in the normal multiplicative manner, and therefore, the lottery in (2.11) can be expressed as

---

[32] These questions are typically hypothetical. Hypothetical questions are problematic, however, because they may not provide sufficient incentives for the decision maker to make careful choices. As discussed in section 2.4, even salient questions may present problems in assessing risk attitudes, because a person's attitudes toward risk may be altered by wealth (in the form of either previous or expected earnings). Laboratory utility-elicitation procedures are discussed in chapter 8.

(2.12) $([p_1 + p_2 - p_2 v]$ of $x_1,$ $[p_2 v + p_3]$ of $x_3)$.

Similarly, the q lottery can be reduced to a lottery involving x_1 and x_3, with a probability of $[q_2 v + q_3]$ of the high payoff x_3. Since both the p lottery and the q lottery have been expressed as mixes of x_1 and x_3, by *monotonicity*, the subject prefers the lottery that yields the highest probability of the highest payoff x_3. In other words, the p lottery is preferred if and only if

(2.13) $p_2 v + p_3 \; > \; q_2 v + q_3.$

But the inequality in (2.13) is just a comparison of the expected utilities: For the utility function in (2.10), the utility of the p lottery is

$$(2.14) \quad p_1[U(x_1)] + p_2[U(x_2)] + p_3[U(x_3)] \; = \; p_1[0] + p_2 v + p_3[1]$$
$$= \; p_2 v + p_3.$$

A similar expression can be derived for the expected utility of the q lottery. It follows from (2.13) that the subject prefers the lottery with the highest expected value of the utility function in (2.10).

A2.4 Sequential Equilibria[*]

One of the most widely used special cases of the Nash equilibrium is the notion of a sequential equilibrium, which will be motivated here by an example. Consider a modification of the bargaining game in figure 2.6 in which nature first determines the size of the pie being split, and neither player knows the pie size at the time offers are made and considered. With a probability .5, the size of the pie will be 3, as it was in figure 2.6, and otherwise the size is doubled to 6. When the pie is large, the generous offer results in a (2, 4) payoff instead of a (1, 2) payoff, and a stingy offer with a large pie results in a (4, 2) split. The extensive form for this new game is shown in figure 2.8. The first move is made by nature, and the [.5] notation under each pie size indicates the exogenous probabilities that determine this move. Following the initial (unobserved) move by nature, player 1 makes a decision in information set I_1, a nondegenerate set that indicates player 1's uncertainty about the state of nature: As in the simple game with a pie of known size, player 1 makes either a generous offer, G, or a stingy offer, S. However, since the pie may be either large or small, there are two possible consequences for each

---

[*]   The material in this section is somewhat more advanced.

of the player 1's choices. Player 2 then makes a decision. subsequent to player 1's choice. Since player 2 sees the offer but does not know the state, player 2's relevant set is either I_{2G} or I_{2S}, depending on whether player 1's offer is G or S. Each node in an information set has the same number and labeling of decisions as all other nodes in that information set.

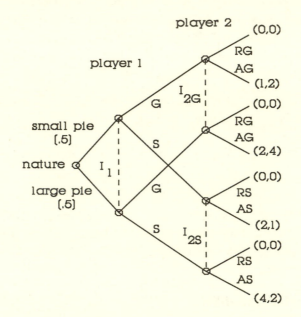

Figure 2.8   A Sequential Bargaining Game with an Unknown Pie Size

     In many respects, this game is very similar to the bargaining game without uncertainty, discussed in section 2.6.   There are still three information sets (I_1, I_{2G}, and I_{2S}), so the uncertainty does not change the number of strategies.   As illustrated by table 2.10, the uncertainty does not importantly affect the normal-form representation of the game.   The representation in table 2.10 is the same as table 2.9, except that the payoffs are averages of those for the small and the large pie sizes. The (2, 1) payoff vectors in the top row of table 2.9, for example, are replaced by the average of (2, 1) and (4, 2), or by (3, 1.5) in table 2.10.   Similarly, nonzero payoffs in the bottom row of table 2.10 are (1.5, 3) rather than (1, 2) as in table 2.9. The change in payoffs does not alter any of the qualitative relationships in the normal-form payoff table, so there are still three Nash equilibria in pure strategies: (S; AS, AG), (S; AS, RG), and (G; RS, AG).   Finally, the underlined (G; RS, AG) equilibrium is still unreasonable, since it requires the second player to make a threat to reject a stingy offer, which, once made, should be accepted regardless of the size of the pie.

Unlike before, however, *(G; RS, AG)* cannot be eliminated via subgame perfection. Due to the uncertainty regarding the size of the pie, there are no decisions or combinations of decisions with consequences independent of (nature's) initial action. In other words, there are no subgames smaller than the game as a whole. For this reason, the notion of subgame perfection has no cutting power in this context: Any equilibrium strategy vector for the game as a whole vacuously consists of an equilibrium for the only subgame.

Kreps and Wilson (1982) developed the notion of a *sequential equilibrium*, to eliminate "unreasonable" equilibria like *(G; RS, AG)* in games with exogenous uncertainty. The concept discriminates among equilibria through the specification of players' beliefs about the unknown events. These beliefs are restricted to be both rational and consistent with the information that is available to the players.

Characterizing a sequential equilibrium for the game in the above figure, for example, requires the specification of rational and consistent beliefs for each node of the three information sets. Consistency with nature's moves requires that each node have a probability of .5 in information set I_1. Similarly, consistency with nature's moves requires that player 2 must assign a probability of .5 to each node in his/her information sets I_{2G} and I_{2S}. (More generally, beliefs for player 2 must be consistent both with the actions of nature and player 1. In this simple example, however, the actions of player 1 do not affect the set of consistent beliefs for player

Table 2.10 A Normal-Form Representation of the Sequential Bargaining Game with an Unknown Pie Size

		Player 2's strategies			
		(AS, AG)	*(AS, RG)*	*(RS, AG)*	*(RS, RG)*
Player 1's	*S*	(3 , **1.5**)	(3 , **1.5**)	(0 , **0**)	(0 , **0**)
strategies	*G*	(1.5 , **3**)	(0 , **0**)	(1.5 , **3**)	(0 , **0**)

2, since player 1 makes a choice prior to learning anything about the relevant uncertainty.) Knowing this, it is apparent that it is never rational to reject a stingy offer in the information set I_{2S}, so *(G; RS, AG)* cannot be a sequential equilibrium for this game.

Although a subgame-perfect outcome may not be sequential (as just shown), Kreps and Wilson (1982) showed that the reverse is true: every sequential equilibrium outcome is subgame perfect. Therefore, sequentiality is a strengthening or "refinement" of subgame perfectness, just as subgame perfectness is a refinement of the Nash equilibrium concept. In theoretical work, the notion of a sequential equilibrium is probably the most widely used refinement of the Nash equilibrium concept. Other, stronger refinements have been proposed, e.g., van Damme (1987) and Cho and Kreps (1987). Chapter 7 contains a discussion of the experimental evidence pertaining to some of these refinements.

Importantly, our development of the sequential equilibrium notion is very informal. This presentation is offered only as a motivation of the manner in which additional refinements of the Nash equilibrium concept have been developed. The interested reader is encouraged to seek a more rigorous development. In any event, a more rigorous development is necessary for purposes of application.

A2.5 Instructions for the Centipede Game [for *classroom use*][33]

Today we are going to play a simple game that involves only two people. My choice of participants will be arbitrary, except that one of them must be wearing something red, and the other must be wearing something blue. I will refer to these participants as Red and Blue respectively.

[Select "Red" and "Blue" participants.]

The game proceeds as a series of decisions, to be made by Red and Blue in an alternating sequence. Notice the two trays in front of you. They will each contain different amounts of money. The tray on the left will always contain a larger prize, so we will refer to it as the "large" tray. We will refer to the tray on the right as the "small" tray. Each decision involves a choice of whether to "take" the money prize in the large tray, or to "pass" the trays along to the other participant. A "take" ends the game, with the "taker" getting the prize in the large tray, and the other participant getting the prize in the small tray. With a "pass" both prizes double in size, and the other participant makes a "pass" or "take" decision.

More specifically, notice that I have placed a quarter in the large tray, and a dime in the small tray. I will first give Red the opportunity to take the quarter in the large tray, or pass the trays to Blue. If Red takes the quarter, Blue gets the dime in the small tray and the game ends. Otherwise, I will double the prizes in each tray, and pass them to Blue, who is given the same choices. If Blue takes the prize in the large tray (now 50 cents), Red gets the 20 cents in the small tray, and the game ends. Otherwise, I once again double the amounts in each tray (to $1.00 and $.40), and return the decision to Red. This entire procedure will be repeated a

---

[33]   These procedures would be inappropriate for research purposes, for several reasons. For example, participants in a research experiment should be visually isolated and should not be allowed to speak with each other.

maximum of two times: If Red passes a second time, I will place $2.00 in the large tray and 40 cents in the small tray. If Blue passes a second time, I will double the prizes again and give the contents of the large tray ($4.00) to Red, and the contents of the small tray (80 cents) to Blue. This procedure is summarized:

	large tray	small tray
1) Red takes or passes	$.25	$.10
2) Blue takes or passes	$.50	$.20
3) Red takes or passes	$1.00	$.40
4) Blue takes or passes	$2.00	$.80

(if Blue passes in (4), then Red gets $4.00 and Blue gets $1.60)

While making decisions, the two participants may consult quietly with nearby students in the room, but they cannot talk with each other. Remember, I am putting real money in the trays, and what each person gets from the tray is theirs to keep. Are there any questions?

REFERENCES

Bernoulli, Daniel (1738) "Specimen Theoriae Novae de Mensura Sortis," *Comentarii Academiae Scientiarum Imperialis Petropolitanae*, 5, 175–192, translated by L. Sommer in *Econometrica*, 1954, 22, 23–36.

Cho, I. K., and David M. Kreps (1987) "Signaling Games and Stable Equilibria," *Quarterly Journal of Economics*, 102, 179-221.

Cooper, Russell, Douglas V. DeJong, Robert Forsythe, and Thomas W. Ross (1989) "Communication in the Battle of the Sexes Game: Some Experimental Results," *Rand Journal of Economics*, 20, 568–587.

———— (1991) "Cooperation without Reputation," working paper, University of Iowa.

Cox, James C., and Ronald L. Oaxaca (1989) "Laboratory Experiments with a Finite Horizon Job Search Model," *Journal of Risk and Uncertainty*, 2, 301–329.

Davis, Douglas D., and Charles A. Holt (1991) "Equilibrium Cooperation in Two-Stage Games: Experimental Evidence," working paper, Virginia Commonwealth University.

DeGroot, Morris H. (1970) *Optimal Statistical Decisions*. New York: McGraw Hill.

Fouraker, Lawrence E., and Sidney Siegel (1963) *Bargaining Behavior*. New York: McGraw Hill.

Harrison, Glenn W. (1989) "Theory and Misbehavior of First-Price Auctions," *American Economic Review*, 79, 749–762.

Harrison, Glenn W., and Peter Morgan (1990) "Search Intensity in Experiments," *The Economic Journal*, 100, 478–486.

Hey, John D. (1982) "Search for Rules of Search," *Journal of Economic Behavior and Organization*, 3, 65–81.

———— (1987) "Still Searching," *Journal of Economic Behavior and Organization*, 8, 137–144.

Holt, Charles A. (1992) "ISO Probability Matching," working paper, University of Virginia.

Holt, Charles A., and Roger Sherman (1991) "The Loser's Curse," working paper, University of Virginia.

Kahneman, Daniel, and Amos Tversky (1979) "Prospect Theory: An Analysis of Decision Under Risk," *Econometrica*, 47, 263–291.

Kogut, Carl A. (1990) "Consumer Search Behavior and Sunk Costs," *Journal of Economic Behavior and Organization*, 14, 381–392.

Kreps, David M. (1990) *A Course in Microeconomic Theory*. Princeton: Princeton University Press.

Kreps, David M., and Robert B. Wilson (1982) "Sequential Equilibrium," *Econometrica*, 50, 863-894.

Lippman, Steven A., and John J. McCall (1976) "The Economics of Job Search: A Survey," *Economic Inquiry*, 14, part I: 155–189, part II: 347–368.

McKelvey, Richard D., and Thomas R. Palfrey (1991) "An Experimental Study of the Centipede Game," Social Science Working Paper 732, California Institute of Technology.

Nash, John (1950) "Equilibrium Points in N-Person Games," *Proceedings of the National Academy of Sciences, U.S.A.*, 36, 48-49.

Pratt, John W. (1964) "Risk Aversion in the Small and in the Large," *Econometrica*, 32, 122-136.

Prisbrey, Jeffrey (1991) "An Experimental Analysis of the Two-Person Reciprocity Game," working paper, California Institute of Technology.

Rosenthal, Robert (1982) "Games of Perfect Information, Predatory Pricing, and the Chain Store Paradox," *Journal of Economic Theory*, 25, 92–100.

Rubinstein, Ariel (1991) "Comments on the Interpretation of Game Theory," *Econometrica*, 59, 909–924.

Schotter, Andrew and Yale M. Braunstein (1981) "Economic Search: An Experimental Study," *Economic Inquiry, 19*, 1–25.

Selten, Reinhard (1965) "Spieltheoretische Behandlung eines Oligopolmodells mit Nachfragetragheit," parts I - II, *Zeitschrift für die Gesamte Staatswissenschaft, 121*, 301-324 and 667-689.

Siegel, Sidney, and D. A. Goldstein (1959) "Decision-making Behavior in a Two-Choice Uncertain Outcome Situation," *Journal of Experimental Psychology, 57*, 37–42.

Siegel, Sidney, Alberta Siegel, and Julia Andrews (1964) *Choice, Strategy, and Utility*. New York: McGraw-Hill.

Smith, Vernon (1990) "Experimental Economics: Behavioral Lessons for Microeconomic Theory and Policy," Discussion Paper 90–14, Department of Economics, University of Arizona.

van Damme, Eric (1987) *Stability and Perfection of Nash Equilibria*. Berlin: Springer-Verlag.

Van Huyck, John B., Raymond C. Battalio, and Richard O. Beil (1990) "Tacit Coordination Games, Strategic Uncertainty, and Coordination Failure," *American Economic Review, 80*, 234–248.

CHAPTER 3

DOUBLE-AUCTION MARKETS

3.1 Introduction

Vernon Smith was drawn to Chamberlin's classroom auctions because they provided direct evidence regarding specific propositions of neoclassical price theory. As noted in the first chapter, Smith thought that there was a clear explanation of why the observed volume of trades exceeded the competitive equilibrium quantity. The problem with Chamberlin's decentralized auctions, Smith conjectured, was an insufficiency of public information about available bids and offers. Smith (1962, 1964) investigated this hypothesis by conducting a series of laboratory markets similar to Chamberlin's auctions, except that instead of allowing traders to mill about the room and haggle over prices in small clusters, all bids and offers were centrally and publicly recorded.[1] This modified set of trading rules has come to be known as a double auction, to contrast it with the one-sided nature of standard auctions in which a single seller receives bids from a number of buyers. In a one-sided, ascending-bid auction for a single "prize," buyers raise price bids until only one interested bidder remains. With multiple prizes (commodity units), buyers raise bids until the number of units demanded is reduced to a level that equals the number of commodity units offered for sale. The situation is reversed when there are multiple sellers competing for the sale of a fixed number of units or "contracts" sought by a single buyer. In this case, sellers compete by reducing price offers until there is no excess supply. In a double auction, both processes occur simultaneously, and trades occur somewhere in the midst of the initial bids and offers.

---

[1] A second major difference was that Chamberlin's markets only lasted for one period. In contrast, Smith allowed the same group of subjects to trade in a sequence of market periods, each with identical supply-and-demand structures.

Smith's double-auction markets generated competitive prices and quantities, and they did so under a remarkably robust set of circumstances. In fact, markets organized under double-auction trading rules appear to generate competitive outcomes more quickly and reliably than markets organized under any alternative set of trading rules. For this reason, double-auction markets have been frequently investigated as a standard against which the performance of other institutions is evaluated.

Interest in the double auction was further enhanced by the similarity of its trading rules with those used in major securities markets. Continuing developments in communications technology make electronic stock exchanges imminent, and analysis of market performance in computerized laboratories allows some insight into the possible effects of alternative forms of automation. As a result of their efficiency and applicability, double-auction markets have been more extensively analyzed than markets organized under any other set of trading rules.

This chapter introduces the procedures, performance properties, and some applications of the double auction. Laboratory procedures and performance measures are explained in detail in section 3.2. The role and effects of computerization are discussed in section 3.3. Sections 3.4 and 3.5 survey evidence on the resilience of price convergence properties to structural and environmental factors, such as changes in supply-and-demand conditions. The results of double auctions in multiple, related markets are surveyed in section 3.6. Section 3.7 pertains to double auctions for multiperiod assets that pay periodic dividends. The final section contains a brief summary.

3.2 Double-Auction Procedures and Performance

Regardless of whether bids and offers flash across a computer screen or are called out by aggressive traders in a "pit," trading is intense in a double auction. The volume of bid and offer messages also makes this institution informationally rich. Before discussing experimental results, it is instructive to give the reader some insight into how a laboratory double auction works, and how traders make decisions. Therefore, the first part of this section pertains to the mechanics of double-auction trading. The second part pertains to standard measures of market performance that are used by experimentalists.

A Double-Auction Trading Period

Double-auction markets are divided into a sequence of trading intervals, or periods. Each period lasts a preset amount of time. Usually three to five minutes are sufficient when five to ten units are being traded, although more time is needed in markets with a high volume. At the beginning of a period, buyers are endowed with unit valuations, and sellers with unit costs. This value and cost information is presented to participants in the form of record sheets like those shown in table 3.1 for a representative buyer, B4, and a representative seller, S1.

Table 3.1 Buyer and Seller Record Sheets

Record Sheet — Buyer B4				Record Sheet — Seller S1			
U n i t 1	(1)	Unit Value	4.60	U n i t 1	(1)	Sales Price	4.30
	(2)	Purchase Price	4.30		(2)	Unit Cost	3.70
	(3)	Unit Profit (1) − (2)	.30		(3)	Unit Profit (1) − (2)	.60
U n i t 2	(4)	Unit Value	4.40	U n i t 2	(4)	Sales Price	
	(5)	Purchase Price			(5)	Unit Cost	4.40
	(6)	Unit Profit (4) − (5)			(6)	Unit Profit (4) − (5)	
	(7)	Period Profit (3) + (6)			(7)	Period Profit (3) + (6)	

First look at the buyer record sheet on the left side of table 3.1. Buyer B4 may potentially purchase two units in this trading period, one valued at $4.60, and a second at $4.40. Typically, buyers are required to purchase higher-valued units before lower-valued units. Buyers' profits are calculated as the difference between the unit value and the purchase price. Earnings are zero on units not purchased. For example, if B4 agreed to purchase a first unit for a price of $4.30 (listed in entry (2)), B4 would earn $.30, as listed in entry (3). Similarly, seller S1's record sheet on the right side of the table shows two units, one with a cost of $3.70 and the other with a cost of $4.40. Sellers must sell lowest-cost units first (except in the case of a decreasing-cost producer, where the reverse rule is enforced). Sellers earn profits as the residual of the contract price over unit costs. If, for example, S1 agreed to sell a first unit for $4.30, then S1 would earn $.60, as shown in entry (3). Production is typically to fulfill orders, so there is no cost incurred on unsold units.

Often the researcher may wish to prohibit unprofitable actions, such as bids above unit values or offers below unit costs. Trades at a loss are usually the result of misunderstanding or keystroke errors, and such trades send noisy signals to the market. On the other hand, trades at a loss may be the result of deliberate efforts to punish one's competitors by taking business away from them, for example, with predatory pricing. Even if this behavior is extremely unlikely, experimentalists are hesitant to rule out particular trading strategies, and an intermediate path is to provide a warning and give subjects a chance to confirm a trade at a loss.

In a double auction, buyers call out bids as they compete to make the highest bid, and at the same time, sellers call out offers as they compete to make the lowest offer. Any seller may accept a standing bid at any time, and any buyer may accept a standing offer. Table 3.2 illustrates the manner in which negotiations might be recorded. As indicated in the first line on the left side of the table, seller S2 opens negotiations by raising a hand and announcing his/her identity (S2), and the offer ($5.00). In the following line, B4 opens bidding by announcing an identity (B4) and a bid ($4.10). These opening propositions form the initial bid/ask spread; they "stand" as most favorable contract terms until accepted or improved upon by other traders. In most double auctions that are done orally, nonimproving bids and offers are not permitted, so the next offer would have to be below $5.00, and the next bid would have to be above $4.10. As indicated in the subsequent rows of the table, seller S2's opening offer is improved by the remaining three sellers, while buyers B1 and B2 join B4 in improving (raising) the standing bid. Negotiations for the first unit end when one trader accepts the terms proposed by another, as illustrated by the underlined row where B4 accepts S1's offer of $4.30.

When a contract is struck, the experimenter circles it on the board, and the contracting parties (in this case B4 and S1) record the price on their record sheets and calculate profits, as shown in table 3.1. One common procedure is for a contract acceptance to invalidate all outstanding bids and offers, and therefore, an improvement rule does not constrain the initial bid or offer on the next unit, which would be the second unit for B4 and S1, and the first unit for the others. Negotiations continue until time expires or, in some implementations, until there is a unanimous vote to terminate the period.[2]

The negotiations summarized in table 3.2 constitute the entire set of bids and offers in a five-minute (300 second) trading period.[3] The shaded columns show the time at which each acceptance was made, where time is measured as the number of seconds remaining in the period. It is worth noting that buyers and sellers typically

---

[2] In particular, the unanimity stopping rule is a feature of the popular NovaNet (formerly PLATO) computerized double-auction mechanism, discussed below. In the NovaNet environment, voting to close a period does not impair a trader's ability to make or accept contracts. Trading periods are rarely stopped by vote.

[3] The data in table 3.2 are from records of experiment 15, an initial NovaNet computerized session reported by Williams (1980). Much of the experimental data presented in this chapter are generated by NovaNet sessions, due to the ease of accessing information from this large, public database.

Table 3.2 Sequence of Contracts for Period 5

Time	Bid	Offer	Time	Bid	Offer
296		S2 5.00	198	B4 4.20	
294	B4 4.10		194	B1 4.22	
293		S3 4.50	190		S3 4.40
291	B1 4.20		188	B4 4.25	
285	B2 4.21		180		S4 4.35
284		S1 4.40	176	B3 accepts	
279		S3 4.39	171		S1 4.45
276		S4 4.35	167	B4 4.20	
271	B4 4.25		165	B1 4.22	
267	B2 4.26		164		S2 4.40
265		S3 4.34	161	B4 4.25	
261		S1 4.30	160		S4 4.35
254	B4 accepts		151		S2 4.34
249	B2 4.20		143		S4 4.32
245		S3 4.39	135		S2 4.31
244	B1 4.22		131		S3 4.30
241	B2 4.23		121		S4 4.29
237		S4 4.35	118	B1 4.26	
230		S3 4.34	112		S3 accepts
209	B1 4.25		64		S3 4.28
208		S4 4.31	15	B4 4.25	
205	B2 4.26		13		S4 accepts
203		S2 accepts	10		S2 4.30

see nothing other than their own values or costs and a "ticker tape" list of bids, asks, and transactions. Prior to continuing, you may find it instructive to consider what inferences about the structure of this market are obvious from either the B4 or the S1 record sheet in table 3.1, and from table 3.2. As discussed in chapter 1, it is not often clear to participants that there is any reason why a particular price and quantity combination is generated.

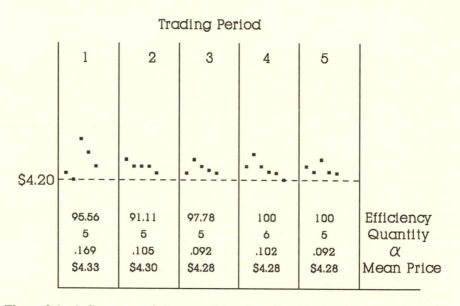

Figure 3.1 A Sequence of Contract Prices in a Double-Auction Market (Source: Williams, 1980)

The contract prices for a series of trading periods are plotted in chronological order as a sequence of dots in figure 3.1. The prices for each period are separated by vertical lines, and the period number is shown at the top of the figure. In period 1 the contract prices are scattered above the dashed line at $4.20, but the range of contract prices narrows in subsequent periods. By period 5 (listed in table 3.2), all contracts fall in the range between $4.25 and $4.35.

Evaluating Market Performance

Market supply-and-demand functions for the session in figure 3.1 are generated by combining individuals' cost and valuation information. There are four buyers and four sellers, and the market supply-and-demand curves are shown in figure 3.2. The identification numbers at each step indicate buyer and seller identities for each unit.

Demand and supply intersect at a price of $4.20, and the quantity traded in a competitive equilibrium will be 5 or 6.

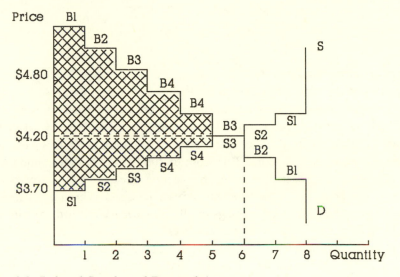

Figure 3.2 Induced Supply and Demand Arrays

The ambiguity of the quantity prediction is noteworthy. The discrete nature of supply-and-demand step functions often results in a horizontal overlap (a quantity tunnel) or a vertical overlap (a price tunnel). These tunnels can be avoided by having either demand or supply cross a flat segment of the other curve.[4]

Several aggregate measures of market performance in each period are shown at the bottom of figure 3.1. The market quantity and mean price measures are quite close to the competitive predictions. One useful measure of closeness is the market efficiency measure introduced in chapter 1. It is instructive to discuss this measure in more detail.

Of all the combinations of trades that could take place, competitive price theory predicts the combination that maximizes the surplus generated in exchange (the

---

[4] In early experiments, many designs employed a horizontal overlap in combination with trading "commissions," which ranged from $.05 to $.15 and were paid to both the buyer and seller for each contract. These commissions were used to induce the trade of marginally profitable units, such as the second units for B3 and S3 in figure 3.2. When commissions are used, buyers are not permitted to pay more than the valuation of a unit, even though the buyer would be willing to pay value plus commission. Similarly, sellers are not permitted to sell below cost. Without such restrictions, commissions would simply shift the demand curve up and the supply curve down by the commission amount, thus eliminating the quantity tunnel by creating a price tunnel. Commissions of this type are now used infrequently, mostly because commissions in naturally occurring markets do not generate the same incentives as those created by per-unit commissions in the laboratory.

shaded area in figure 3.2). This maximum surplus will be denoted by ε_c. Efficiency, E, is simply the proportion of this maximum surplus that is extracted:

$$E \; = \; \frac{\Sigma(MV_i - P_i) + \Sigma(P_i - MC_i)}{\varepsilon_c} \times 100,$$

where the summation is over the indices of units actually traded. Table 3.3 presents a summary of the surplus extracted in the trading period 5 of the session in figure 3.1. Note that since $\varepsilon_c = \$4.50$, and since total buyer and seller surpluses are $2.58 and $1.92, respectively, the market is 100 percent efficient. Efficiency calculations for each of the five trading periods in this session are printed in figure 3.1 below the sequence of contracts. Note that E is close to 100 percent in every period. This high efficiency is characteristic of double-auction markets. Many students and others are surprised that a market with private cost and value information can effectively maximize the total earnings of all participants combined, without them being able to conspire against the experimenter![5]

It is far from necessary that the act of profitable trading alone generates E values close to 100 percent for the market design in figure 3.2. Consider first an efficient sequence of contracts, where the buyer with the highest unit value (B1) trades with the lowest-cost producer (S1), the buyer with the second highest unit value (B2) trades with the second-to-lowest-cost producer (S2), and so on, until B3 and S3 strike the sixth contract in the market period by trading their second units and earning only the sales commission. All of these contracts could be consummated at a single price of $4.20. Now consider a second possible sequence of trades, identical to the first, except that B4's second purchase is S2's high-cost unit (costing $4.30) rather than S4's high-cost unit (costing $4.10), at a price of $4.35. Excluding S4 from the market in this way lowers the total surplus by $.20, which is the cost increase resulting from the inclusion of an inefficient extra-marginal unit that costs $4.30 instead of $4.10. Efficiency losses would be larger if the sale of S2's second unit precluded the sale of a unit with an even lower cost. Still larger surplus losses can arise from more volatile price swings. For example, if S1 makes a contract at $3.75 to sell his/her low-cost unit (cost $3.70) to B1, who is purchasing a low-value unit (value $3.80), then some buyer will be precluded from striking an efficient contract. If B2 were precluded from trading, then $1.20 (or the difference between the value of B2's first, high-value unit and B1's second, low-value unit) would be lost.

---

[5] In fact, even sophisticated individual behavior may not be an important prerequisite for obtaining efficient competitive outcomes in a double-auction market. Using simulated buyers and sellers, Gode and Sunder (1989) observe that very crude strategies (involving "zero intelligence") extract nearly all of the possible gains from exchange.

Table 3.3 Efficiency Calculations for Trading Period 5

		BUYERS				SELLERS		
Unit	ID	Unit Value	Price	Profit	ID	Price	Unit Cost	Profit
1	B4	4.60	4.30	.30	S1	4.30	3.70	.60
2	B2	5.00	4.26	.74	S2	4.26	3.80	.46
3	B3	4.80	4.35	.45	S4	4.35	4.00	.35
4	B1	5.20	4.26	.94	S3	4.26	3.90	.36
5	B4	4.40	4.25	.15	S4	4.25	4.10	.15
	Total Buyer Surplus			2.58	Total Seller Surplus			1.92

The efficiency index E can be quite sensitive to market structure and should therefore be interpreted with care. For example, increasing the value of B1's first unit from \$5.20 to \$10.20 in figure 3.2 would raise the maximum market surplus by the same amount, from \$4.50 to \$9.50. Nearly two-thirds of that surplus is extracted (\$6.00/9.50), however, if B1 manages to complete a single contract at the competitive price. Moreover, a failure to trade a marginal unit provides a much lower efficiency loss as a percentage of \$9.50 than as a percentage of \$4.50. The likelihood of efficiency losses is increased by the presence of extra-marginal units close to the competitive price. This may be seen by counterexample in figure 3.2. By raising the costs of the second units for S1 and S2 by \$6.00 and lowering the values of the second units for B1 and B2 by \$3.00, extra-marginal units could never trade. Efficiency losses caused by extra-marginal trades are impossible under these circumstances.

Even if a market is 100 percent efficient, the proportion of the available surplus going to buyers and sellers may vary widely in the process of adjustment. A measure of the distribution of surplus is often useful, particularly in discussions of dynamics. In the market example being discussed, sellers receive \$1.50 and buyers \$3.00 if all contracts are made at the equilibrium price. In trading period 5, buyers extracted .86 (\$2.58/\$3.00) of the surplus that would go to them at the competitive price, while sellers extracted 1.28 (\$1.92/\$1.50).

In some contexts, it is desirable to measure the extent to which sellers are able to profit from increases in prices over the competitive level. The standard basis of comparison is the profit level that results from a monopoly (joint-profit-maximizing) price. The index of monopoly effectiveness, M, first used by Smith (1980), is simply the ratio of the excess (supracompetitive) profits actually earned by sellers in a trading period to excess (supracompetitive) profits earned by sellers at the monopoly price, or

$$M \quad = \quad \frac{\pi \quad - \quad \pi_c}{\pi_m \quad - \quad \pi_c},$$

where π = actual sellers' profits in a trading period, π_c = sellers' profits in a competitive equilibrium, and π_m = sellers' profits under the hypothesis of joint profit maximization.

For the market structure shown in figure 3.2, sellers would earn \$3.70 if three units were traded at the profit-maximizing price of \$4.80. Since sellers earn \$1.50 if all contracts are made at the competitive price, the index of monopoly effectiveness for the trading period 5 in table 3.3 is [\$1.82 – \$1.50] /[\$3.70 – \$1.50], or .26. Notice that $M = 100$ if all contracts are struck at the profit-maximizing price, and $M = 0$ if all contracts occur at the competitive price. Unlike E, which is bounded between 0 and 100, M may exceed 100 if a seller successfully price discriminates, and M may fall below 0 if buyers earn more than predicted under the competitive hypothesis.

A final performance measure to be considered is the coefficient of convergence. It is often useful to have some measure of pricing behavior that captures both price variability and the deviation of prices from the competitive level. The most common measure, α, is the square root of the variance of prices around the predicted equilibrium price. This variance is calculated

$$\alpha^2 \quad = \quad \frac{\sum_{k=1}^{Q} (P_k - P_e)^2}{Q},$$

where Q = the number of contracts in a trading period, P_k = the kth contract price, and P_e = the competitive equilibrium price. By letting m and s^2 denote the mean and variance of observed prices in a period, and decomposing, we obtain[6]

$$\alpha^2 \quad = \quad s^2 \quad + \quad (m - P_e)^2.$$

Thus α^2 equals the variance in prices plus the squared deviation of mean price from the competitive equilibrium. If all contracts are made at the competitive price

---

[6] This decomposition can be verified by adding and subtracting the mean price, m, to each of the $P_k - P_e$ terms, and using the fact that the sum of the deviations from the mean is zero: $\Sigma(P_k - m) = 0$.

prediction, then $\alpha^2 = 0$. Note that α is unbounded from above and increases with price volatility and with deviations of the mean price from the competitive prediction. Values of α for each trading period of the session summarized in figure 3.1 are listed below the prices for that period. Observe that α drops substantially after the first period.

Performance in Standard Environments

Hundreds of laboratory double auctions are reported in the literature. The performance measures discussed above can be used to compare outcomes of these auctions with competitive predictions. Table 3.4 presents summary performance measures for double-auction sessions from seven selected studies. In every instance but one (Smith and Williams, 1982), the sessions summarized are control sessions, against which a variety of treatments were subsequently evaluated. The set of studies included in table 3.4 is by no means comprehensive. Rather, these studies are chosen for the comparability of data and the diversity of environments. The experiments were conducted in five locations, in either computerized (NovaNet) or oral environments, by four different sets of authors, using various combinations of experienced, inexperienced, and mixed-experience participants. Studies included between two and twelve sessions; the number of sessions is listed in parentheses below the site code. Sessions varied from three to fifteen periods in length (not shown in the table), with computerized sessions generally having more periods.

The three columns on the far right of table 3.4 present the average price deviation, $P - P_e$, the average efficiency, and the average quantity deviation, expressed as a proportion of the competitive quantity: $(Q - Q_e)/Q_e$. These double-auction markets clearly tend to generate competitive predictions. Price deviations never exceed five cents, at least 94 percent of predicted trades took place, and mean efficiency fell below 97 percent in only one NovaNet study using inexperienced participants (Smith and Williams, 1982).

3.3 Computers and the Double Auction

As should be clear from table 3.2, the double auction generates a large amount of data in a fairly short time. Accurately recording these data presents a formidable task. In addition, a researcher conducting an double auction orally must ensure that participants do not record profits incorrectly or make contracts that violate instructions, for example, trade at a loss. These burdensome record-keeping and monitoring requirements suggest clear benefits of computerization. Moreover, computerization standardizes the presentation of instructions and restricts subtle verbal and visual communications between participants during a trading period, allowing clearer isolation of treatment variables. A third advantage of

Table 3.4 Performance in Selected Double Auctions

Study	Site (# mkts.)	Exper-ience	Environ-ment	$P-P_e$ ($)	Effic-iency	$\frac{Q-Q_e}{Q}$
Smith and Williams (1981)	IU/UA (4)	X	NovaNet	−.01	99.4	.02
Smith and Williams (1982)	IU/UA (12)	NX	NovaNet	−.03	95.8	.05
Smith and Williams (1983)	UA (6)	M	NovaNet	.01	97.8	.06
Isaac and Plott (1981b)	CIT/PCC (3)	X	Oral	−.05	99.9	.04
Mestelman and Welland (1988)	MMU (5)	NX	Oral	.02	97.3	.04
Mestelman and Welland (1991)	MMU (5)	NX	Oral	.02	98.0	.02
Joyce (1983)	MT (2)	NX	Oral	.04	98.7	.04

Site Key:
IU   Indiana University
UA   University of Arizona
CIT   California Institute of Technology
PCC   Pasadena City College
MMU   McMaster University
MT   Michigan Tech

Experience Key:
NX   inexperienced
X   experienced
M   mixed

computerization derives from the recent interest in creating electronic stock exchanges.[7] A computerized laboratory market allows field-testing of some aspects of an electronic stock exchange.

---

[7] The Securities and Exchange Commission received a congressional mandate to move toward the creation of a national stock trading system in 1975, and electronic automation was a key motivation for the mandate. Automation is also becoming more important as some stock exchanges begin to allow after-hours trades. See, for example, George Anders and Craig Torres, "Computers Bypass Wall Street Middlemen and Stir Controversy," in *The Wall Street Journal*, August 28, 1991, p. A1.

The first computerized double-auction program was written by Arlington Williams in 1977, for use on the NovaNet (formerly PLATO) computer network. This program provides self-paced interactive instructions, complete control of the decision-making process, and complete data recording. Other versions of a computerized double-auction are now available.[8]

Effects of Computerization

A quick comparison of the computerized double auctions at the top of table 3.4 with the oral double auctions at the bottom does not reveal any clear difference; and convergence to the competitive equilibrium is obvious in both cases. But these comparisons are a little messy, because the table contains no pair of computerized and noncomputerized markets that use the same supply-and-demand structure. In initial NovaNet double auctions, Williams (1980) found increased price variability in the computerized markets relative to comparable oral markets. This higher variability probably reflects additional control over nonverbal, nonprice communications, since both the information and negotiating rules are identical in computerized and oral environments. Therefore, the added "noise" in the price sequence is probably a desirable feature of computerization.

Williams also conducted computerized sessions with subjects who had previously participated in a NovaNet double auction. Prices in these sessions were much less volatile; they were similar to prices observed in comparable noncomputerized (oral) double auctions with inexperienced subjects. Consider the price sequences in figure 3.3, where prices are plotted as deviations from the competitive level, which is indicated by the horizontal line at 0.[9] Although prices eventually cluster about the predicted level, both with inexperienced subjects (top panel) and with experienced subjects (bottom panel), there is less price variability in the latter case. This difference is representative of many computerized sessions, and for this reason experience has come to be regarded as an important treatment. Efficiencies in figure 3.3 are very high, regardless of experience. With inexperienced subjects, efficiencies exceed 94 percent in all but the first two periods, and efficiencies exceed 97 percent in all periods with experienced subjects.

---

[8] The task of programming a "real-time" environment is still far from trivial, and was an impressive technical feat in the mid 1970s. Williams's NovaNet double auction was the only computerized double auction available for most of a decade. Additional versions of the computerized double auction have been created, both for mainframe computers (e.g., Hackett, Battalio, and Wiggins, 1988; Friedman and Ostroy, 1989) and for networked personal computers (e.g., Johnson, Lee, and Plott, 1988; Gode and Sunder, 1989; Forsythe, et al., 1992).

[9] These data are from a symmetric four-seller, four-buyer design reported by Smith and Williams (1983): an inexperienced session (IIpda30) and an experienced session (IIpda04).

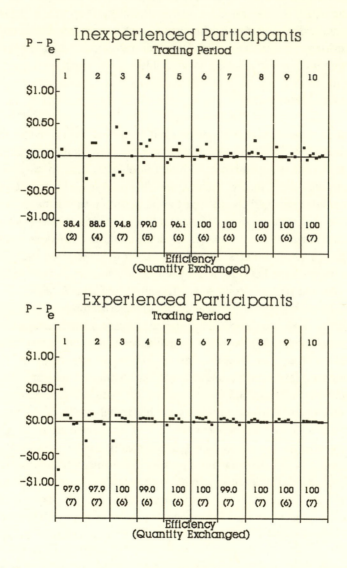

Figure 3.3 Representative Contract Price Series for Experienced and Inexperienced Double-Auction Sessions (Source: Smith and Williams, 1983)

Bid/Offer Acceptance Procedures

Computerization facilitates the use of more sophisticated trading rules. In particular, consider the rules that determine which bids and offers are permitted.

Smith and Williams (1983) evaluated the effects of four alternative rules. Under Rule 1, the most recent quote is displayed, whether or not it represents an improvement, that is, a bid that exceeds the highest outstanding bid or an offer that is below the lowest outstanding offer. Under this rule, a nonimproving quote bumps the better quote off of the display. Bidding Rule 1Q appends a temporal queue to Bidding Rule 1; all bids and offers are displayed to the market for a minimum of three seconds. Any bids or offers that arrive prior to expiration of the three-second minimum are queued by time of arrival and are displayed in subsequent three-second increments. In contrast, Rule 2 specifies a bid/ask spread-reduction rule that allows only bids and offers that improve the standing bid/ask spread. Bidding Rule 2Q appends a rank-order queue to Bidding Rule 2. Under Bidding Rule 2Q, the highest bid and the lowest offer are publicly displayed to the market, as in Bidding Rule 2, but buyers and sellers may also submit non-spread-reducing bids and offers, which are queued in rank order. These stored bids and offers become the standing quotes in the event that contracts remove the more attractive quotes. Also, while participants may not invalidate a standing bid or offer, they may pull out of the rank-order queue at any time.

The variation of experience and the four bidding rules generates an eight-cell (2×4) matrix of treatments. Smith and Williams investigated these effects in a four-buyer, four-seller market with symmetric supply-and-demand schedules. The authors conducted a total of twenty one sessions, with three sessions in each inexperienced cell and two sessions in each experienced cell, except for the cell with experience and Bidding Rule 2Q, which had three sessions. Using as data points the coefficient of convergence, $\alpha_i(t)$, for trading period t of session i, Smith and Williams estimated the parameters of an exponential decay function:

$$\ln \alpha_i(t) = a + bt + cx_s,$$

where $x_s = 1$ if participants were experienced, 0 otherwise.[10] Figure 3.4 illustrates the exponential decay function estimated for each bidding rule, with experienced subjects. In the absence of queues, varying the bid/offer acceptance procedures makes little difference in performance, as suggested by the near overlap of estimated equations for Bidding Rules 1 and 2. Smith and Williams conjecture that Bidding

---

[10] Contract prices in one period are unlikely to be independent of those in preceding periods. For this reason, the pooling of $\alpha_i(t)$ observations across trading periods in session i violates the independence assumptions of classical statistical inference. This use of nonindependent observations raises an important methodological issue. Statistical techniques for autocorrelated data generally require much longer time series than the eight to fifteen trading-period sequences that comprise most sessions. Thus, strict use of only truly independent observations in a cross-sectional analysis often implies that only one data point is generated per session, severely restricting use of the rich information set. Some researchers insist on tests that satisfy independence. Others provide results based on interrelated data, along with the caveat that statistical results should be interpreted as being descriptive rather than as true tests. As discussed in chapter 9, we have some reservations about this latter approach.

Rules 1 and 2 are behaviorally similar because participants tend to submit quotes that reduce the bid/ask spread, regardless of whether such behavior is required by the trading rules.

The addition of queues, however, has a clear effect on the convergence measure. As illustrated in figure 3.4, the temporal queue in Bidding Rule 1Q impedes convergence, while the rank-order queue in Bidding Rule 2Q facilitates convergence. Smith and Williams conjecture that the rank-order queue (or specialist's book) facilitates convergence because it adds competition away from the margin, as people jockey for position in the queue. In contrast, a temporal queue raises negotiation costs, so agents agree to inferior contracts more easily.

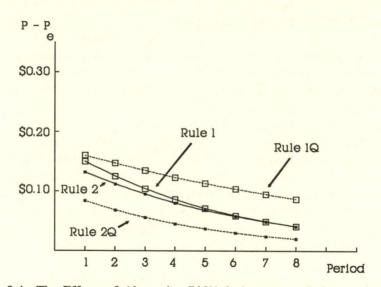

Figure 3.4   The Effects of Alternative Bid/Ask Acceptance Rules on the Price-Convergence Path   (Source: Smith and Williams, 1983)

Due to its strong convergence properties, Bidding Rule 2Q is commonly used as a default in the computerized double-auction markets discussed below. Bidding Rule 2, however, is most frequently employed in noncomputerized (oral) double auctions because of the difficulty of manually maintaining a rank-order queue. It is worth noting that Bidding Rules 2 and 2Q replicate bid/offer acceptance procedures in many modern stock and securities exchanges.[11]   Therefore, the

---

[11]   For example, the bid/offer spread reduction rule corresponds to Rules 71 and 72 of the NYSE (Leffler and Loring, 1963).

superior performance of Bidding Rule 2Q suggests some natural selection of efficient contracting rules in markets.[12]

3.4 Double-Auction Results: Design Effects

Once a theory receives support in a baseline environment, the next step is one of "stress testing," or conducting boundary experiments to discover the limitations of the theory's application. This section surveys a series of design boundaries: the effects of variations on the shapes and stability of supply-and-demand arrays.

A Design with Extreme Earnings Inequities

The first boundary to be considered involves rectangular demand and supply functions that have only a single step and intersect to form a "box." This box design results when all sellers' units have the same cost, and all buyers' units have the same value. These designs are not realistic in the sense that they do not conform to standard assumptions of diminishing marginal utility or increasing costs. But extreme or limiting variations in the shapes of supply-and-demand curves provide evidence relevant to the limits of application of competitive price theory. Design extremes may also provide some insight into the price adjustment process.

Before proceeding, the reader should reconsider the asymmetry of the design in figure 3.2 above. If all trades take place at the competitive price, buyers receive two thirds of the possible surplus, while sellers only receive one third of the surplus. As the sequence of contract prices in figure 3.1 suggests, this earnings disparity does not interrupt the ultimate convergence to the competitive price, although the convergence is from above. The most extreme earnings inequity results when traders on one side earn all of the surplus in equilibrium. For example, consider the double lines labeled as D_1 and S_1 on the left side of figure 3.5. In this case, each of four buyers is given four units at a constant per unit valuation of $6.80, resulting in a market demand of 16 units at prices up to $6.80, and zero at any higher price. Three of the four sellers in this design are endowed with three units, and a fourth

---

[12] Computerization has also stimulated institutional change. For example, it is now possible to design electronic markets in which traders in different locations can contact each other without going through the brokers that handle trades on large stock exchanges. One alternative is to have buyers and sellers send in bids and offers, which are arrayed into demand-and-supply functions. Since such messages can originate in different locations at all hours of the day or night, it is convenient to have all trades be consummated at a preannounced time at a common price determined by the crossing of supply and demand. At any previous time, traders can observe the tentative price determined by bids and offers received to date, but the price is not final until the market is "called." These call markets, which are used in several securities exchanges, raise a number of interesting design issues that are considered in the discussion of auctions in chapter 5.

seller is endowed with two units, all at a constant per-unit cost of $5.70, generating a market supply of 11 units at prices down to $5.70, and zero at any lower price. An excess demand of five units remains at every price between $6.80 and $5.70. The double-lined supply-and-demand curves determine a unique competitive equilibrium E1, with a price of $6.80 and a quantity of 11.[13] Sellers earn all surplus if all trades occur at the equilibrium price.

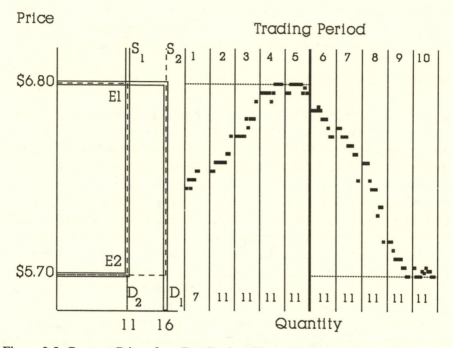

Figure 3.5 Contract Prices for a Box Design: First with Excess Demand, then with Excess Supply (Source: Holt, Langan, and Villamil, 1986)

This excess demand design was used in the first five periods of the session shown on the right side of figure 3.5.[14] Notice that prices in period 1 begin about midway between the costs and values. Prices climb in response to excess demand and reach the competitive prediction of $6.80 by period 5. Prior to each period, record sheets with the values and costs were passed out without comment, so the

---

[13] This allocation satisfies the formal definition of a competitive equilibrium: There is an allocation resulting from eleven trades at a price of $6.80 with the property that (1) no buyer or seller can increase his/her utility by changing the amount produced or purchased, taking the price of $6.80 as given, and (2) the market clears in the sense that eleven units are supplied and demanded.

[14] The data are from Holt, Langan, and Villamil (1986), who used experienced participants and paid buyers and sellers a nickel trading commission.

demand-and-supply shifts in period 6 were privately implemented. Buyers, who were probably quite frustrated after period 5, would notice that they had fewer units on their record sheets for the sixth period. Sellers, who had been making over $1.00 on each unit in period 5, were probably delighted to see that they had extra units in period 6. These changes resulted in the dashed-line demand-and-supply curves, D_2 and S_2, on the left side of figure 3.5, which generate a new equilibrium, E2, characterized by excess supply. Notice that the new equilibrium prediction was created solely by reducing the number of buyers' units (to 11) and increasing the number of sellers' units (to 16). This excess supply immediately affected the market: In period 6 the initial contract price was lower than any in the previous two periods. Prices decayed further in subsequent periods and dropped almost completely to the equilibrium prediction by periods 9 and 10. Very similar results have been reported earlier on variants of this design.[15] This tendency for severe excess demand or excess supply to push prices to extreme, "inequitable" levels has been observed with subjects in the United States, Canada, and China.[16]

Finally, notice that the transaction quantities are given at the bottom of figure 3.5, and that each of the 11 units at the predicted quantity sold in every trading period but the first. Therefore, efficiency was 100 percent in every period but the first, since efficiency and trading quantity are directly related in this constant-cost/constant-value design. The interesting point is that *any* price between $5.70 and $6.80 would yield a surplus-maximizing outcome; but only one of these prices is a competitive equilibrium. In this sense, competitive price theory provides a more precise description of the equilibrium data than is provided by a theory based on surplus maximization.

A Box Design with Multiple Price Equilibria

Even if competitive price theory predicts well in this context, there is the issue of what prices will result when there is a range of competitive equilibria. The typical assumption seen in theoretical models is that prices will stabilize near the midpoint of the equilibrium range. On the other hand, it is common to observe a sequence of laboratory prices at the same level during an adjustment process, as in figure 3.5. Such flat steps in the price sequences occur too frequently to be caused by chance; they seem to be the result of a tacit consensus reached during the

---

[15] See Smith (1964), Smith (1981), and Smith and Williams (1989). In one session with a box design in Smith and Williams (1989), participants were paid no trading commission. Prices tended to stabilize between $.05 and $.10 away from the equilibrium. Smith and Williams cite this result as evidence that a $.10 commission is necessary to induce marginal trades.

[16] See Kachelmeier and Shehata (1990), who found no evidence of a significant cultural effect in this box design.

negotiations. The empirical question is whether such a consensus could cause prices to stabilize at a point that is far from the midpoint of a range of competitive prices.

Consider the design on the left side of figure 3.6; any price between $5.50 and $6.60 is a competitive, market-clearing price, and a horizontal line is drawn at the midpoint of equal surplus division, for purposes of reference. Smith and Williams (1988) conducted a series of five NovaNet double-auction markets with this design, using four buyers and four sellers in each session. All participants had institution experience and were paid a $.10 per unit trading commission. The sequence of contracts for the first four trading periods of one of these sessions, labeled B2x, is shown immediately to the right of the supply-and-demand arrays in figure 3.6. Notice that only ten units are traded in each of these initial periods, and that prices tend to favor sellers.[17] The sequence of *mean* contract prices for all fifteen periods of session B2x is presented in the enlarged middle box on the far right side of the figure. For example, the first dot in the mean contract price chart, shown on the right hand side of figure 3.6, is the average of the ten first-period contract prices for session B2x shown in the middle of the figure. The sequence of mean contracts for the remaining four sessions (B1x, B3x, B4x, and B5x) is arrayed above and below the mean contract price chart for B2x. For purposes of comparison, the vertical height of each of the right-hand mean-price charts corresponds to the $1.10 difference between seller costs and buyer values. It is clear from these charts that prices do not tend to the equal rent split. But there is little reason a priori to expect an equal rent split. Unit value and unit cost information is private, and it would indeed be surprising if buyer and seller bargaining strategies were so universally similar that they regularly split an unknown difference!

Another interesting implication of the mean contract price charts is that the double-auction institution tends to produce a certain behavioral stability. Although the mean price shows some propensity to drift up or down from period to period within a session, there is a clear inertia. Moreover, it is not only the mean prices that exhibit stability, as indicated by the low variability of contract prices for the first four trading periods of session B2x.

Supply-and-Demand Instabilities

Most double auctions are conducted with repeated stationary designs, where the same agents are given the same induced costs and valuations in a sequence of repeated trading periods. A limiting stability boundary would involve random underlying shifts in supply and demand. However, rather than starting with results of this chaotic design, consider first the effects of simple repeated nonstationarities, in the form of simple demand and/or supply cycles.

---

[17] However, efficiency tends to be high with this design. Even in session B2x, all 11 possible units traded in 8 of the final 11 trading periods (not shown).

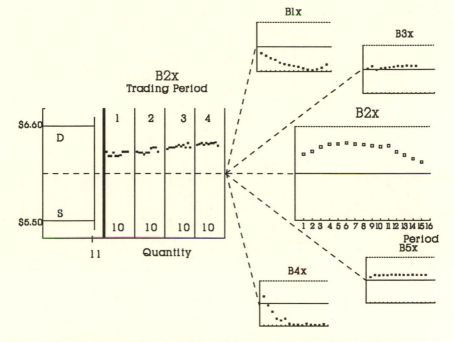

Figure 3.6 The Box Design and Mean Prices for Five Box Design Sessions
(Source: Smith and Williams, 1989)

The supply-and-demand arrays on the left side of figure 3.7 illustrate a cyclical design used by Williams and Smith (1984). Market supply and demand alternate between S_l and D_l (drawn with heavy lines) in odd-numbered periods, and S_h and D_h (drawn with the light lines) in even-numbered periods. This cycle shifts the competitive price prediction by \$1.60, from \$3.00 in odd periods to \$4.60 in even periods, while the competitive quantity prediction remains constant at 7 units. Traders respond quickly to this nonstationarity. The data on the right side of figure 3.7 show a clear tendency to gravitate to the competitive prediction in each period.

The results in figure 3.7 were replicated by Davis, Harrison, and Williams (1991), who also investigated markets in which either demand or supply cycled, while the other curve stayed stationary. The two left-hand vertical bars in figure 3.8 pertain to the four sessions in which both demand and supply cycle between high-price and low-price phases.[18] All summary data are plotted as deviations from the

---

[18] The sessions summarized in figure 3.8 involved four buyers and four sellers, all with experience. Participants were paid a \$.05 commission per trade in every design except for the cycling supply-and-demand design (where the intersection of supply-and-demand schedules generated a price tunnel).

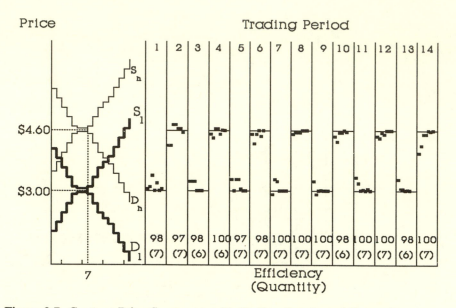

Figure 3.7 Contract Price Sequences with Cycling Supply and Demand
(Source: Williams and Smith, 1984)

equilibrium price for the relevant phase, high or low. In the low phase of the cycling-supply-and-demand design, the closing price "*" overlaps the "·" that denotes the mean price, and both of these are just below the equilibrium price for this low phase. The two "—" symbols indicate the upper and lower limits of a price band that contains 95 percent of the data.[19] The second bar from the left shows the summary price data for the high-price phase of this design; notice that the mean closing price is quite close to the equilibrium, but that mean prices lag below when both demand and supply shift up together.

The two vertical bars in the center of the figure summarize price data from three sessions in a second design, where demand remains stationary and supply shifts outward in the low-price phase and inward in the high-price phase. The competitive price prediction varies by $.80 in this design, while the competitive quantity prediction varies by 4 (from five to nine units). Notice that mean prices are above the equilibrium in the low phase and below the equilibrium in the high phase, although closing prices are at the equilibrium level. This same pattern is observed for the case of cycling demand, shown on the two vertical bars on the right side of the figure. The market response to nonstationarities worsens when either supply or demand shifts. This difference indicates something about the nature of bargaining

---

[19] This band has no other statistical interpretation, since the observations are not independent.

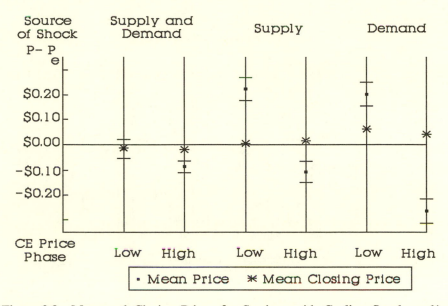

Figure 3.8   Mean and Closing Prices for Sessions with Cycling Supply and/or Cycling Demand (Source: Davis, Harrison, and Williams, 1991)

in the double auction. When both supply and demand cycle, both buyers and sellers are given incentive adjustments that signal a change in the equilibrium price. In contrast, when only supply or only demand cycles, the side of the market enjoying (suffering from) the change each period tries to maintain the old price (or convince the other side that less favorable price quotes are reasonable). Although prices in the previous period affect the initial prices in the subsequent period, the prices are driven toward the competitive price near the end of each trading period as the distance between the unit value and the unit cost for remaining untraded units shrinks.

The role of the closing price in a trading period as an indicator of the underlying competitive price is further illustrated in figure 3.9. The top part of this figure presents the sequence of contract prices for one of the cycling-demand sessions summarized on the right side of figure 3.8, with closing prices indicated by asterisks. Notice the tendency for prices to adjust more slowly than was the case with cycling supply and demand in figure 3.7. The bottom part of figure 3.9 presents the price sequence for a session where supply and demand are subject to random (i.e. noncyclical) shocks between trading periods, with the equilibrium price indicated by a horizontal dashed line. The volatility of prices is increased, but the proximity of the closing price to the competitive prediction in each trading period is remarkable.

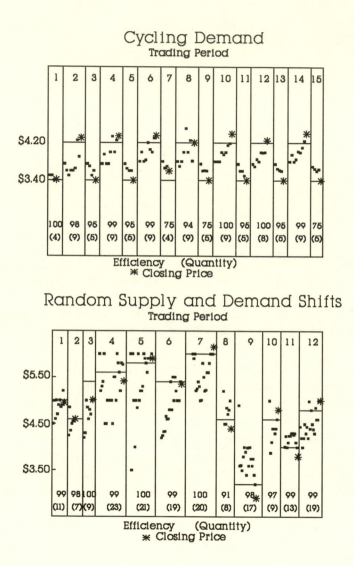

Figure 3.9 A Session with Regular Cycling Demand, and a Session with Random Demand and Supply Shocks (Sources: Williams and Smith, 1984, and Cox and Oaxaca, 1990)

The slower price adjustment for the random-shift design does not have much of an effect on efficiency, as can be seen by comparing the efficiency numbers in the bottom part of figures 3.7–3.9. Efficiency comparisons here are a little tentative, as the market structure in the random-shift treatment differs from the structures of the other treatments.[20]

Summary

Competitive price, quantity, and efficiency predictions are resilient to each of the design boundaries discussed in this section. Competitive price levels are eventually reached, even in the presence of severe earnings inequities, for example. The competitive price prediction begins to break down only when supply-and-demand nonstationarities become sufficiently complex. The boundary experiments reviewed here provide considerable insight into the process by which a behavioral equilibrium is generated in double auctions: First, even under conditions of severe earnings inequities and conditions of random supply-and-demand adjustments, traders manage to extract the bulk of possible gains from exchange, at least for the market structures that have been investigated to date. Second, and as a consequence of traders extracting maximal surplus, the closing price represents an unbiased signal regarding the underlying equilibrium, as marginal units that are near the intersection of supply and demand tend to be traded at the end of a period, and contracts for these units must be struck at near-competitive prices. Third, there is some price inertia, in both experiments with box and nonstationary designs; traders have a tendency to negotiate initial prices that are close to those realized at the end of the previous period. Thus, in a repeated stationary design, equilibration probably occurs as a consequence of participants striking contracts near the competitive prices forced by the sale of marginal units in preceding period(s).

3.5 Double-Auction Results: Structural Boundaries

The design boundaries considered in the previous section have not been of much interest to economists in general. In contrast, industrial organization economists are primarily concerned with a variety of market characteristics and trade practices that may generate noncompetitive outcomes. How do laboratory double-auction markets respond to variations in these more standard structural variables?

---

[20] The sequence of contract prices shown at the bottom of figure 3.9 is one of twenty-five sessions reported by Cox and Oaxaca (1990), who were interested in generating laboratory data to evaluate the performance of standard econometric techniques for the estimation of supply-and-demand functions. These markets each used ten experienced participants. At the beginning of each trading period, a participant drew a role assignment as one of five buyers or five sellers, and a valuation or cost schedule. Costs and valuations were drawn from a discrete version of linear supply and demand arrays. The additive random shocks to supply-and-demand were drawn from a uniform distribution on [-.4, .4]. A definite price prediction was essential to the Cox and Oaxaca study, so shocks were constrained in a way that supply and demand intersected with horizontal overlap.

This section reviews the results of experiments designed to assess the effects of alterations along the environmental and structural boundaries that are the focus of antitrust analysis. This literature is quite limited, as the drawing power of competitive predictions remains high in all but the most extreme alterations.[21] We begin by considering the effects of limitations on the number of sellers, and particularly the problem faced by the double-auction monopolist. The effects of market power and opportunities for conspiracy are examined subsequently.

Limitations on the Number of Sellers

Many of the experiments reviewed above involved as few as four sellers, so it is clear that a very large number of sellers is not necessary to generate competitive outcomes. The question remains: what is the minimum number of sellers sufficient for competitive outcomes? Smith and Williams (1989) addressed this numbers boundary in an experiment composed of five monopoly markets and four duopoly markets.[22] Each of the duopoly markets generated prices much closer to the competitive level than to the joint-profit-maximizing price, and the competitive quantity was consistently exchanged in most trading periods. Moreover, sellers did not extract a supracompetitive portion of the surplus; the index of monopoly effectiveness was negative for the last three trading periods in three of the four duopolies.

The temptation of duopolists to price below each other is not an issue in a monopoly, but the monopolist has another dilemma caused by the sequential nature of double-auction price negotiations. At first blush, the ability to negotiate prices individually would appear to be an advantage. Since no Robinson-Patman laws discourage price discrimination in the laboratory, the monopolist may substantially increase profits by charging each buyer a price just equal to the buyer's unit valuation. In practice, however, negotiating prices for individual units often becomes more of a handicap than an asset. Although perfect price discrimination maximizes profits in a static monopoly, the act of selling units at different prices informs buyers that the monopolist can make profitable sales at lower prices.

Consider figure 3.10, where the monopoly price is determined on the left by the point on the demand curve that is above the intersection of marginal revenue

---

[21] Markets organized under other trading rules appear much more susceptible to variations in standard environmental parameters. See, in particular, the next chapter on posted-offer markets.

[22] Supply-and-demand arrays for the monopoly design were configured in a manner very similar to the market illustrated in figure 3.2. Duopoly experiments were conducted with variants of the monopoly design. In two of the four duopolies, cost steps on the supply array for the monopoly design were split between the sellers. In the remaining duopoly sessions, each seller had the same cost structure as the monopolists, and demand was doubled to preserve the competitive price prediction. Participants were paid either a $.05 or $.10 trading commission in all but one duopoly session. Also, participants were institution-experienced in all but one (duopoly) session.

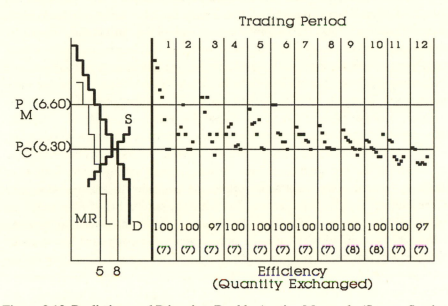

Figure 3.10 Predictions and Prices in a Double-Auction Monopoly (Source: Session M4xs from Smith and Williams, 1989)

(labeled MR) and marginal cost (labeled S). In the first period of this session, the seller starts with high prices, which price discriminate against buyers with units on the upper part of the demand curve. The final prices in this period are at the competitive level, and efficiency is 100 percent, as would be expected with price discrimination. This strategy is not as successful in subsequent periods, as buyers resist high prices after learning that the seller can sell units at lower, competitive prices. By periods 7 and 8, the monopolist is unable to obtain any contracts within twenty cents of the monopoly price, and mean prices fall below even the competitive level in periods 11 and 12. This tendency for prices to fall *below* the competitive levels was observed in the final periods of three of the five monopoly markets, yielding a negative index of monopoly effectiveness in these final periods.[23]

Conspiracies

Given the failure of double-auction monopolists to extract monopoly rents, it would seem unlikely that implicit or even explicit conspiratorial opportunities would

---

[23] Failed efforts at price discrimination were a predominant characteristic of all monopoly sessions reported by Smith and Williams (1989), although the monopolist managed to keep the mean price above the competitive level in two sessions. Smith (1981) reported similar results.

generate substantial price increases. This conjecture is supported by Isaac and Plott (1981a), who report an experiment with opportunities for sellers to conspire. Each of their (oral) double-auction sessions was composed of four buyers and four sellers. Buyers and sellers were in separate rooms; bids and offers were transmitted from room to room via telephone. Unknown to buyers, the sellers were given the chance to discuss prices between trading periods. Each seller meeting lasted for three minutes, and discussion was unregulated, except that cost information could not be disclosed, and side payments as well as physical threats were prohibited. Although sellers regularly tried to implement price-fixing agreements, given the opportunity, they were unable to maintain collusive prices. The four sellers encountered the same problem as double-auction monopolists. Although they could agree on a method of allocating reduced quantities at higher prices, the temptation to sell low-value units in the closing moments of a period was enticing, particularly if all sellers had completed the trades agreed upon by the cartel. Once again, buyers, upon seeing that sellers could afford to sell at lower prices, would refuse to accept higher prices in subsequent periods.[24]

Price Controls

The allocative inefficiencies of binding price regulations are well known; if regulation prevents price from separating high-value consumers from low-value consumers, then an inefficient amount of the good will be produced, and less efficient forms of allocation, such as queues or discrimination, may arise. Some industrial organization economists have further argued that even *nonbinding* price regulations cause inefficiencies, because they represent focal prices about which tacit conspiracies may form.

Isaac and Plott (1981b) report a series of sessions where both binding and nonbinding controls are variously imposed and/or removed from a double-auction market. Price controls prompted efficiency losses, but not exactly in the manner expected. Binding price ceilings indeed reduced market prices, but they generated even larger efficiency losses than might initially be expected. The price ceilings cause efficiency losses by inhibiting the formation of some contracts that would take place at the competitive price. Moreover, market efficiency falls because buyers with unit values below the competitive price are sometimes able to displace buyers with higher unit values. Finally, the removal of price controls, regardless of whether they were binding or not, caused a large increase in price volatility, as buyers and sellers searched for a market price free of the restraint.

Nonbinding price controls, however, do not appear to serve as the focal point for tacit conspiracies. To the contrary, not only do markets with nonbinding controls

---

[24] Isaac and Plott's results were replicated in the NovaNet environment by Isaac, Ramey, and Williams (1984). For a related result, see Clauser and Plott (1991).

appear to converge to the competitive price prediction, the prices appear to approach the competitive price in a way that makes potential conspirators worse off. With a nonbinding price ceiling slightly above the competitive price, for example, prices converge to the equilibrium from below.

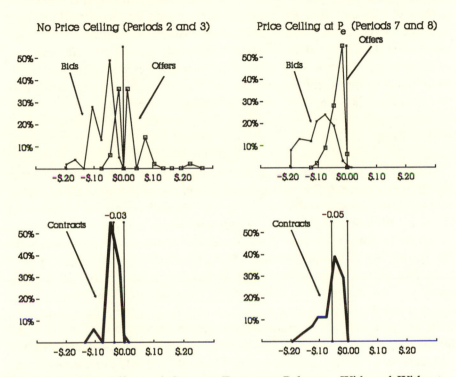

Figure 3.11   Bid, Offer, and Contract Frequency Polygons, With and Without a Nonbinding Price Ceiling   (Source: Session 2pda26, Smith and Williams, 1981)

Smith and Williams (1981) conducted an experiment composed of sixteen double-auction markets to examine more carefully the effects of nonbinding price controls.[25] Each session was composed of three five-period "weeks." At the end of each week, supply-and-demand arrays were shifted by a competitive-price-disguising constant. In the second and third weeks, a price ceiling or floor was imposed at one end of the competitive price range (the design included a vertical overlap at the competitive quantity). Smith and Williams found that nonbinding controls affected the price-convergence path by truncating the range of acceptable bids and offers. Figure 3.11 illustrates the effect of a nonbinding price ceiling on

---

[25] Each session used four buyers and four sellers. All participants had institution experience and were paid a $.10 per trade commission.

bids, offers, and contracts in the second and third periods of an unregulated week (shown in the left panels), and in the second and third periods of a regulated week (shown in the right panels). Bid and offer distributions are illustrated in the upper panels as dotted and thin solid lines, respectively. Contract price distributions are illustrated in the lower panels as thick solid lines. All distributions are illustrated in terms of deviations from the competitive prediction. In comparing the left and right sides of the figure, note the change in the distribution of offers. While many offers are well above the $0.00 deviation in the upper left panel, they are truncated by the ceiling in the upper right panel. This asymmetry causes prices to be lower: As indicated by the vertical dashed lines in the lower panels, average prices were two cents lower in the presence of the nonbinding price ceiling.

Market Power

Are there *any* conditions under which double-auction markets do not generate competitive outcomes? The only known exception is an experiment with a "market-power design" reported by Holt, Langan, and Villamil (1986) and replicated by Davis and Williams (1991). Market supply-and-demand arrays for this design are shown on the left side of figure 3.12. The market is composed of five sellers and five buyers. All participants received a $.05 per-unit trading commission. Two of the sellers, S1 and S2, are each endowed with a large portion of total market sales capacity in this design. Units that pertain to these two sellers are identified with lines extending from the seller identifier to cost steps in figure 3.12. It is apparent from the figure that 16 units trade at the competitive price in this design. Note also that S1 and S2 each have a single low-cost unit, two intermediate-cost units, and two high-cost units. At the competitive price, S1 and S2 will only earn the nickel sales commission by trading the high-cost units. Moreover, there is a horizontal overlap of only one unit at the competitive price.

Both S1 and S2 possess market power in this design in the following sense: If either of these sellers withhold their two high-cost units, market supply shifts two units to the left and intersects market demand at a price deviation of $.25. If prices were to rise by $.25 as a result, then this withholding would be unilaterally profitable for either seller, as the extra $.25 earned on the sale of each of the three lower-cost units more than makes up for the $.05 commission lost on each of the unsold high-cost units.

The sequence of contracts for a representative market is shown on the right side of figure 3.12. Prices stabilize nearly $.20 above the competitive level. Holt, Langan, and Villamil observed prices consistent with market power exercise in four of their seven sessions, but outcomes were competitive in the other three sessions. Davis and Williams (1991) generated similar results in a series of eight NovaNet double-auction sessions, although price deviations were somewhat smaller (on the order of $.10 to $.15) and more homogenous (with fewer competitive outcomes).

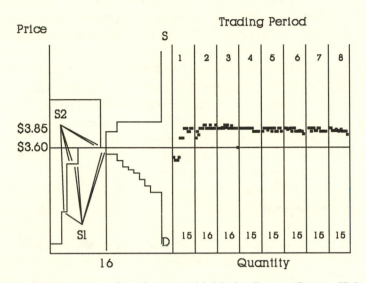

Figure 3.12 Contract Prices for a Session with Market Power (Source: Holt, Langan and Villamil, 1986)

There is some disagreement as to the source and importance of the observed deviations, since excess supply at supracompetitive prices is only one unit in this design (e.g., Plott, 1989, p. 1125). In any event, it is not the case that price increases were caused by withholding. Note in figure 3.12 that at least fifteen units traded in each period.

Summary

Behavior in the double auction appears as resilient to structural boundaries as it is to design boundaries. Competitive predictions are somewhat weakened when the market is reduced to only two sellers, but competitive price, quantity, and efficiency levels are often observed, even in monopolies. The only exception seems to be in an extreme market power design with excess supply of only one unit at supracompetitive prices. Markets organized under double-auction rules also appear to generate competitive outcomes in the face of opportunities for implicit, and even explicit conspiracy.

3.6 Multiple, Interrelated Double-Auction Markets

The combination of robust convergence properties and the similarity with securities markets has resulted in a wide range of experimental applications of the double-auction institution. These applications are primarily motivated by issues in finance and are the subject of the next section. A limited number of studies, however, have focused directly on the effects of generalizations of standard laboratory procedures. For example, Plott and Gray (1990) report that allowing traders the option of trading multiple-unit blocks has little effect on the performance of double-auction markets. Similarly, Mestelman and Welland (1987, 1988) find that performance is unaffected by permitting interperiod inventory carryovers or by requiring sellers to make production decisions at the beginning of each trading period. The remainder of this section pertains to two other modifications: (a) allowing middlemen traders to buy, sell, and inventory units across periods, and (b) allowing simultaneous trading in two related markets.

Middlemen and Seasonal Adjustments

The role of middlemen as efficiency-enhancing agents represents a natural extension of the study of cyclical price adjustments, which was considered in the previous section. Middlemen, who make profits by purchasing inventories of nonperishable goods in low-demand periods and selling inventories in high-demand periods, are often perceived as being nonproductive. Intertemporal arbitrage, however, can create surplus, just as the act of trading creates surplus.

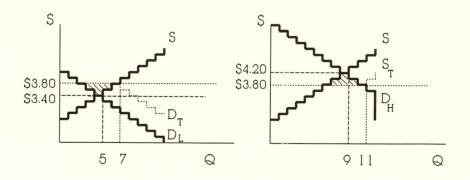

Figure 3.13 Efficiency Gains from Middlemen in an Intertemporal Equilibrium

The efficiency-enhancing role of the middleman is illustrated in figure 3.13. In a low-demand period, shown on the left side of figure 3.13, the demand (D_L) intersects supply (S) at a price of $3.40 and a quantity of 5 units. Efficient trading would generate a total surplus of $4.00. In a high-demand period, shown on the right side of figure 3.13, D_H intersects S at a price of $4.20, and a quantity of 9.

Maximum surplus is $14.40 in a high-demand period.   Now consider the introduction of a class of traders who can buy, sell, and inventory units across periods.   These middlemen could earn profits by buying units in a low-demand period at a price of about $3.40 and then selling them in the high-demand period for something slightly less than $4.20.

Competition between traders would reduce the profits from carrying inventories; trader costs rise as they vie with buyers and each other for units in low-demand periods. Similarly, trader revenues fall as they compete to sell units in high-demand periods.   Absent storage costs, the inventory/sales role of traders creates a single-price, intertemporal equilibrium represented by the horizontal dotted line at $3.80, as demand shifts out to the dotted line D_T in low periods and supply shifts out to the dotted line S_T in high periods.   In effect, trader purchases increase demand and raise the market price to $3.80 in periods of low demand, and the carryover increases supply and lowers price to $3.80 in periods of high demand.   As a consequence, 7 units trade in low-demand periods, and 11 units trade in high-demand periods (if participants are paid a trading commission to induce the sale of zero-surplus units).

Two features of this intertemporal equilibrium are notable.   First, as the difference between the acquisition cost and the sales price of inventoried units goes to zero, middlemen earnings are reduced to only trading commissions. Second, the middlemen create surplus. Purchasing units in periods of low demand generates an extra $.80 of surplus, shown by the shaded area on the left side of figure 3.13, so maximum surplus is 120 percent of that available in the market without middlemen ($4.80/$4.00).   Selling units out of inventory in periods of high demand also generates an extra $.80 of surplus, shown by the shaded area on the right of figure 3.13, and maximum surplus is roughly 106 percent of that available in high-demand periods without middlemen ($15.20/$14.40).

Figure 3.14 shows a sequence of contract prices for a session conducted in this design reported by Williams and Smith (1984).   There were four buyers, four sellers, and two traders.   All participants had institution experience, and they were paid a $.05 trading commission on each transaction.   Traders were given a $5.00 endowment at the outset of the experiment to finance initial purchases.   Units purchased by traders had a maximum life of two periods, and a scrap value to traders of $1.00.[26]   The odd-numbered periods were those with low demand.

As figure 3.14 suggests, middlemen do enhance efficiency in these markets. Except for the (preannounced) final period, efficiency exceeds the 100 percent level that is attainable without traders in all but one period (period 5).[27]   The stability of

---

[26]   The practical effect of the $1.00 scrap value is that it places a nonzero lower bound on prices for decaying inventoried units.

[27]   Knowing that period 15 is the final period, traders would be irrational to purchase inventories for future sale.

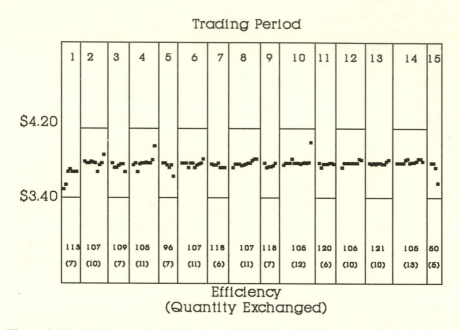

Figure 3.14   A Sequence of Contract Prices for a Nonstationary Market with Middlemen (Source: Session It-1, Williams and Smith, 1984)

prices across periods is also notable. Compare figure 3.14 with the sequence of contracts generated in this same cycling demand design, shown in the top of figure 3.9.[28]

A slight change in the interpretation of the middlemen experiment suggests a broader application. Think of middlemen as "producers" who buy a commodity (an input) in one market and sell it (as an output) in another. In most situations, the transformation from input to output is not 1 to 1, but is subject to diminishing returns. Goodfellow and Plott (1990) conducted an experiment where the production process involved a nonlinear transformation from input to output. There were three types of traders: input sellers, producers, and output buyers. The producers were buyers in the input market and sellers in the output market. Both markets were double auctions. The competitive equilibrium involved an input price and an output price that simultaneously equate supply and demand in both markets. It is much

---

[28]   The results shown in figure 3.14 are representative of those reported by Williams and Smith (1984); Williams (1979); and Miller, Plott, and Smith (1977). However, convergence to an intertemporal price was somewhat less pronounced in sessions using a design where both supply and demand shift (Williams and Smith, 1984). Plott and Uhl (1981) report similar (uniform-price) results for a single session of a market composed of middlemen who purchased and sold in locationally distinct markets.

harder to calculate the competitive equilibrium for this market than for case of linear transformations between inputs and outputs: The anticipated output price affects the demand for the input, the input price affects the supply of output, and none of these effects are linear. The simultaneous determination of these two market-clearing prices would probably take most economists longer than the fifteen to twenty minutes that it took for the laboratory sessions to reach the competitive equilibrium.

Multiple commodities

One reason it is useful to review performance of the double auction in more complicated environments is to demonstrate the role of a market as a *decentralized optimizing device*. In the Williams, Smith, and Ledyard (1986) design, to be discussed next, participants trade for two commodities that are related in consumption.

Supply for commodities x and y was induced in the usual manner, with an integer-valued version of a linear cost function. Unlike the experiments reviewed above, however, sellers were able to sell each of the two commodities simultaneously in a trading period.

Moreover, the induced valuations of buyers were interdependent. Rather than providing a single-dimensional unit value array, an integer-valued version of a two-commodity utility function was induced by paying a dollar amount $V_i(x_i, y_i)$ to subject i for the purchase of a bundle of commodities (x_i, y_i). For example, table 3.5 provides the valuation schedule for an individual facing an integer-valued version of a C.E.S. utility function: $V = c(ax^r + by^r)^{1-r}$, with $a = .77$, $b = .23$, $c = .606$ and $r = .25$. This individual was endowed with \$40.20 in "tokens" that could be used to purchase units of x and y. These tokens retained their value only within a trading period.

The complexity of purchase decisions in this context is clear from table 3.5. In making purchases, participants must evaluate the increased payoff of purchasing an extra unit of x or y, given past purchases and current prices. For example, suppose that at current prices and token income, the buyer can purchase two units of x and four units of y, which yields a total earnings of \$2.10 (see the shaded entry in the table). If the price of x equals the price of y, the person could increase earnings from \$2.10 to \$2.23 by purchasing one more unit of y and one less unit of x. But if the price of y were twice as large as the price of x, then purchasing one more unit of y would mean giving up all x and only earning \$1.11. The relative prices determine the slope of the discrete analogue of the budget line, and absolute price and income levels determine its intercepts. These experimental procedures provide an incentive for subjects to maximize the function $V_i(x_i,y_i)$ subject to the token constraint: $T \geq x_i P_x + y_i P_y$, where T is the endowment of tokens and P_x and P_y denote the prices of x and y, respectively. Induced utility maximization yields the

Table 3.5 Payoff Table for a Two-Commodity Double Auction

		\multicolumn{9}{c}{Units of X}
		0	1	2	3	4	5	6	7	8
	0	0.00	0.00	0.00	0.00	0.01	0.01	0.01	0.01	0.01
	1	0.22	0.61	0.72	0.80	0.86	0.92	0.97	1.02	1.07
U n i t s	2	0.44	1.05	1.21	1.33	1.43	1.52	1.59	1.66	1.73
	3	0.66	1.46	1.67	1.82	1.94	2.05	2.15	2.23	2.31
	4	0.89	1.85	2.10	2.28	2.43	2.55	2.66	2.77	2.86
	5	1.11	2.23	2.52	2.72	2.89	3.03	3.16	3.28	3.38
o f	6	1.33	2.60	2.92	3.15	3.34	3.50	3.64	3.77	3.89
	7	1.55	2.97	3.32	3.57	3.77	3.95	4.10	4.24	4.37
Y	8	1.77	3.32	3.70	3.98	4.20	4.39	4.56	4.71	4.85

individual demand functions:

$$x_i = d_{ix}(P_x, P_y) , \qquad y_i = d_{iy}(P_x, P_y).$$

Market demand functions, denoted by capital letters, are obtained by summing the individual demands of each subject index i:

$$X = D_x(P_x, P_y) = \Sigma d_{ix} , \qquad Y = D_y(P_y, P_x) = \Sigma d_{iy}.$$

The market supply function is obtained in a similar manner by summing individual sellers' marginal cost functions:

$$S_x(P_x) = \Sigma s_{ix} , \qquad S_y(P_y) = \Sigma s_{iy}.$$

The market clearing conditions

$$X = D_x(P_x, P_y) = S_x(P_x) , \qquad Y = D_y(P_x, P_y) = S_y(P_y)$$

are then used to calculate the two equilibrium prices and the two equilibrium quantities. For the parameters used in the experiment, these turn out to be $3.90 and 12 for market x, and $8.10 and 12 for market y. Given these prices and the token income of $40.20, the buyer could afford to purchase two units of x and four units of y, which results in earnings of $2.10 (recall that the token dollars are worthless after the experiment). Since the price of y is about double the price of x, it is straightforward to verify that there is no other feasible commodity bundle in table 3.5 that yields higher earnings. Other buyers had different incentives.

The attainment of equilibrium in this market is analogous to the solution of a set of simultaneous nonlinear equations, although subjects are unaware that this is the market consequence of their behavior. Figure 3.15 displays the price sequences for one session using this design; prices in both markets are within a nickel of the competitive price prediction in the last three periods.[29] This same convergence standard was satisfied in ten of the fifteen sessions reported in this study. Figure 3.15 also lists the exchange quantities under the price sequence for each market. In each of the last three periods, at least eleven of twelve predicted units traded in each market.

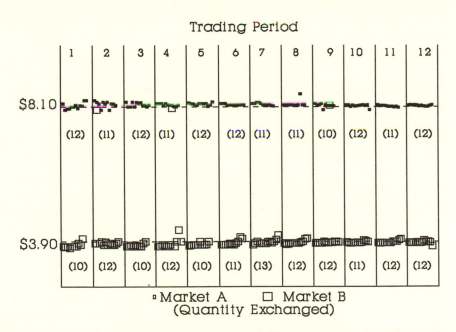

Figure 3.15   The Price Sequence for a Multiple-Commodity Double Auction (Source: Session 4pda009, Williams, Smith, and Ledyard, 1986)

---

[29] Participants in this session had both role and environment experience.

3.7 Double-Auction Asset Markets

When Smith designed the oral double-auction institution, his intention was to create an environment that paralleled organized stock and security exchanges, such as the New York Stock Exchange. These exchanges are, of course, much more complex than the simple commodity markets studied thus far. One important difference between standard double auctions and markets for financial assets regards the nature of the traded good: Rather than having value for a single period, financial assets are typically long-lived. Thus, assets derive their value not just from current sales or valuation, but from a stream of dividends that accrue over time. Uncertainty becomes a problem when goods are long-lived, because the current value of an asset depends on expectations regarding future dividend streams and resale prices. Heterogenous attitudes toward risk and time can alter expectations and affect the value of an asset.

This section introduces the experimental literature regarding asset markets. The presentation is divided into two parts. First we describe how to set up a laboratory market for trading a single asset, and then we review some of the general findings relevant to this particular design. Of special interest is the concept of a *rational expectations equilibrium*, fundamental to much macroeconomic and financial theory. In general, this equilibrium is just a requirement that beliefs and expectations be consistent with rational actions based on these expectations. The specific example that follows will help clarify this general notion.

A Laboratory Asset Market

This section describes a laboratory asset market devised by Smith, Suchanek, and Williams (1988). The design involves nine participants, who engage in trading under double-auction rules for fifteen periods. Unlike a market for a single-period asset, the number of trading periods is important for determining the value of the asset. This information is publicly announced at the beginning of the session. Also, unlike a market for single-period goods, there is no distinction between buyers or sellers. Rather, all agents are *traders*, who each possess a portfolio consisting of cash and units of the asset. During the session, traders may buy and sell asset units, subject to the limitations of their portfolio. Trader portfolios are summarized in table 3.6. As is clear from the table, the initial portfolios need not necessarily be identical. In this case, there are three different cash/asset portfolio combinations, ranging from three asset units and an initial cash balance of $2.25, to one asset unit and an initial cash balance of $9.45.

The multiperiod nature of an asset changes the way that values are induced. Rather than determining buyer valuation through redemption values, or seller valuation through sales costs, the value of each asset unit is derived from a stream of dividends that it generates throughout the session. This dividend stream is not

Table 3.6 Endowment Portfolios in a Nine-Trader Asset Market

Trader Identities	Asset Units	Initial Cash Balance	Expected Value of Portfolio
Traders 1 – 3	3	$2.25	$13.05
Traders 4 – 6	2	$5.85	$13.05
Traders 7 – 9	1	$9.45	$13.05

certain. At the end of each trading period, the experiment monitor draws and publicly announces a common dividend for all asset units. Prior to the start of the next trading period, each trader's cash holdings are augmented by the product of the dividend and the number of units held. The dividend draw is from one of four equally likely alternatives: $.60, $.28, $.08, and $.00. Since the alternatives are equally likely, the expected per-period dividend draw is $.24.

Asset units retain no residual, "buyout" value at the end of the fifteenth period in this design. Thus, the intrinsic value of the asset is derived entirely from its dividend stream. At any point during the session, the value of an asset may be calculated from the number of remaining dividend draws. For example, during the fifteenth period of a session, only a single dividend draw remains, so the expected value of the asset is $.24. Similarly, two dividend draws remain during the fourteenth period, so the expected value of the asset is $.48. Reasoning backward, it follows that each asset unit has an expected value of $.24(15) = $3.60 at the outset of the session. By adding each trader's initial cash balance to the product of $3.60 and the number of asset units, one can show that the expected value of each portfolio in table 3.6 is $13.05.

In addition to dividend payments, capital gains or losses may be realized by traders through the purchase and sale of assets. Each trader may buy and sell asset units as often as desired, subject to two limitations. First, traders may not sell units that they do not own at present (no short sales), and they must pay for asset units with current cash balances (no margin purchases). Second, "churning" is prohibited, for example, traders may not create a false sense of market activity by buying and selling asset units from themselves. At the end of the session, participants are paid the accumulated cash balance in their portfolio.

In this design, units have the same intrinsic value for all participants. Thus, trade should occur only if traders have divergent attitudes toward risk or different expectations regarding asset values. Although a scattering of differences in risk and time preferences would motivate some trading, most economists would probably expect low trading volume, at prices close to the intrinsic value. In particular, rational expectations rules out bubbles via a backward induction argument, which for simplicity is presented under the assumption of risk neutrality: At the end of the final period, there is no future, so expectations are irrelevant and units should be traded at the expected dividend value of $.24. Therefore, the only rational expectation for the last period's price is $.24, so units will trade for $.48 in the second-to-last period, and so forth. Given the known, finite horizon, no general speculative price increase should be observed.

Some Central Results

The three panels of figure 3.16 illustrate the mean contract prices and underlying values for a representative series of three sessions reported by Peterson (1991).[30] In each panel, the expected underlying value is shown as a dashed line. The kinks in the dashed line illustrate the discrete decline in intrinsic value following the payment of each period's dividend. The solid line connects the observed mean contract price in each trading period. Trading volume for these same three sessions is illustrated in the three panels of figure 3.17.

The left-most panel in each of the figures illustrates the results of an initial session in which participants had no previous experience with the asset market. (All participants, however, had participated previously in a standard double auction.) The mean price series in figure 3.16 reveals a large speculative "bubble" in contract prices, followed by a crash in the latter periods of the session. The quantity data in figure 3.17 show that the bubble arose under active trading in this initial session.

Predictions of the rational expectations equilibrium are much more nearly approximated when participants have experience with the institution. Seven of the nine participants who generated the "inexperienced" data series in figures 3.16 and 3.17 were subsequently brought back for a second session, along with two other participants who had previously participated in a single asset market session. Results of this "once-experienced" session are illustrated in the middle panels of figures 3.16 and 3.17. All nine of the participants in the once-experienced session were brought back for the "twice-experienced" session illustrated in the right-hand panels of the figures. Behavior in these second and third sessions is much more rational; the size of the speculative bubble diminishes and trading volume drops in each subsequent session. By the time participants are twice-experienced, a very low volume of trade is sustained, at prices very close to intrinsic value.

Consider some measures of the magnitude of speculative price increases and trading volume. Define R (Reach) as the normalized absolute price deviation from intrinsic value, or the ratio of price minus intrinsic value to intrinsic value. If all

---

[30] Even though the original design is due to Smith, Suchanek, and Williams, we present Peterson's results at this point because they clearly illustrate experience effects that turn out to be critical in this asset market context.

Price

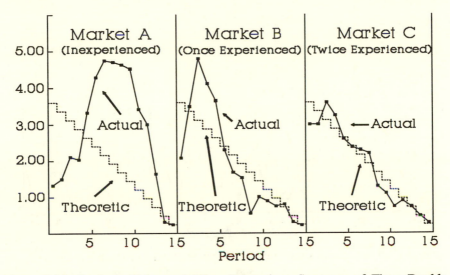

Figure 3.16   Intrinsic Value and Mean Prices in a Sequence of Three Double-Auction Asset Markets with the Same Participants   (Source: Sessions 3pd295, 3pd296, and 3pd297, Peterson, 1991)

trades took place at intrinsic value, on average, this ratio would equal 0. Similarly, define *TO* (Turnover) as the average number of times each asset unit traded in a session. The higher *TO*, the greater the trading volume. In a rational expectations equilibrium with identical traders, both $R = 0$ and $TO = 0$.

Large bubbles were observed under conditions of active trading in ten sessions with inexperienced participants reported by Smith, Suchanek, and Williams (1988). On average, $R = 5.68$, and $TO = 4.55$ for these sessions.   Speculative behavior diminished in three comparable sessions with once-experienced participants; *R* fell to 2.77 and *TO* fell to 3.2.   Rational-expectations predictions are nearly met in two comparable sessions with twice-experienced participants. In these sessions, $R = .28$, and $TO = 1.7$.[31]

Given the high volatility of stock prices in the late 1980s, the speculative bubbles observed in laboratory sessions attracted considerable attention. Subsequent investigations have indicated that bubbles are not simply an artifact of the simple laboratory environment.   King et al. (1991), for example, report that bubbles are

---

[31]   Smith, Suchanek, and Williams (1988) report the results of twenty-six asset market sessions. A number of these sessions, however, involved special treatments designed to assess the nature of price bubbles. Summary statistics in this paragraph pertain to a subset of these sessions that were identified by King et al. (1991) as suitable for examination of experience effects.

Trading
Volume

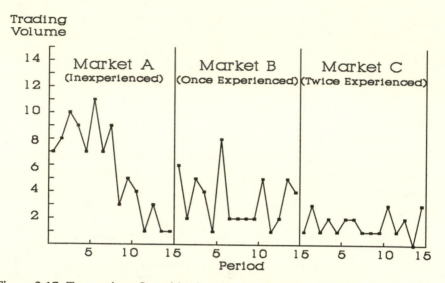

Figure 3.17 Transactions Quantities in a Repeated Series of Double-Auction Asset Markets (Source: Sessions 3pd295, 3pd296, and 3pd297, Peterson, 1991)

resilient to a number of institutional variations, including modifications that allow for short sales, margin buying, and brokerage fees. As might be expected, short sales and margin buying appear to exacerbate speculative behavior, since they give more latitude to aggressive, risk-taking agents. These authors also report that speculative behavior is resilient to portfolio variations and even to the injection of "insiders" who were informed of the persistence of speculative bubbles in the laboratory markets. Moreover, several rules intended to mitigate price volatility in the laboratory are not effective. In particular, limit-price-change rules appear to exaggerate speculative behavior, as such rules limit the maximum loss participants can sustain in any trading period.

Nor are the bubbles merely a consequence of an unsophisticated subject pool. Both the size and duration of speculative bubbles were undiminished in sessions conducted with business professionals (Smith, Suchanek, and Williams, 1988; Van Boening, 1990; King et al., 1991). Rather, it appears that the critical determinant of speculative behavior is common expectations that derive from common experience.

Although investigations of speculative bubbles suggest that they are remarkably robust, inferences regarding behavior of natural markets nevertheless remain precarious. This said, speculative behavior *may* play an important role in natural markets. In fact, Vernon Smith conjectured that the boom-and-bust behavior observed in natural markets is an inevitable consequence of divergent expectations and novice traders: "People panic. . . . They do it in our laboratory markets until they learn that trading away from fundamentals doesn't yield sustainable, continuing profits. . . . [In the real world,] these bubbles and crashes would be a lot less likely if the same traders were in the market all the time. [But novices are always entering the market.]"[32] One important task for laboratory research is to evaluate institutional devices that are intended to reduce the likelihood and intensity of speculative bubbles.

3.8 Conclusion

In markets organized under double-auction trading rules, the predictions of the competitive model appear to be robust to a wide variety of supply-and-demand configurations, to very harsh restrictions on the number of agents, and to conditions regulating communications between sellers. Competitive price theory also does a good job of organizing data in some enriched double-auction market structures, for example, where participants purchase multiple commodities, and where middlemen can enhance efficiency via speculation in an intertemporal setting. Although the loss of control in markets where traders buy and sell multiperiod assets has important behavioral consequences when participants are inexperienced, even these markets generate rational expectations equilibria with experience, as participants come to share common expectations.

But exactly *why* does the double auction perform so impressively? When will it fail? Answers to these questions require articulation of a testable model of the underlying double-auction game. No generally accepted theoretical model of the double auction exists, though admirable efforts have been made by Easley and Ledyard (1986) and Friedman (1984). It is easy to see why theorists have had such difficulties with the double auction; the rich message and action spaces characterizing the double auction hopelessly swamp game-theoretic analyses, unless major simplifying assumptions are introduced. Rather than starting from first principles, tractable models of the double auction will likely have to be based on some set of behavioral assumptions, justified on the basis of observed responses, that clearly generate convergence in simplified variants of the double auction. As an effort to provide some bases for such assumptions, we close this chapter by summarizing the effects of the various treatments discussed above on the convergence path, or on the adjustment process of double-auction markets to the competitive price prediction. We offer four observations.

First, *complete information regarding supply and demand arrays is not only unnecessary, but it may impede the convergence process.* The very fact that markets

---

[32] Jerry Bishop, "Stock Market Experiment Suggests Inevitability of Booms and Busts," *Wall Street Journal*, sec. 2, p. 1, November 17, 1987. Bracketed parts were attributed to Smith but are not direct quotes.

generate competitive predictions when participants are provided only with private information about costs or values (and public information about prices) challenges standard assumptions about conditions necessary for convergence.[33] Furthermore, limited available evidence suggests that the addition of complete information may retard rather than facilitate convergence. Smith (1980) reports results of an eight-session experiment conducted in a "box" design with severe earnings inequities in equilibrium. Complete information regarding costs and valuations slowed but did not interrupt the ultimate convergence in these markets.

Second, *even though cost and value information is private, the negotiating process is sufficiently symmetric that participants tend to split the available surplus in initial contracts.* This effect was cleanly documented by Smith and Williams (1982), who report an experiment designed to evaluate the effects of such rent asymmetries. Six sessions were conducted in a design where two-thirds of the surplus went to buyers and one-third went to sellers, if all contracts were struck at the competitive price prediction. Another six sessions were conducted in a symmetric design where the rent distribution was reversed. Smith and Williams conclude that the distribution of the actual surplus is affected by the relative theoretical magnitudes of consumers' and producers' surplus; when producer surplus exceeds consumer surplus, the price path tends to the competitive equilibrium price from below. When consumer surplus exceeds producer surplus, the convergence path tends to the competitive price prediction from above.[34]

Third, *the closing price in a trading period tends to provide remarkably precise information about the underlying competitive price.* This was noted in experiments in nonstationary environments. The relationship between the closing price and the competitive price prediction was also important in monopoly experiments. Monopolists were unable to extract monopoly prices consistently because they attempted to exercise their market power through price discrimination rather than quantity restriction. In the double auction, price discrimination often results in competitive prices because buyers will not repeatedly accept less favorable contract terms than those extended to other buyers.

Finally, *early contracts appear to have an important influence on the terms of trade for later contracts.* This was observed in "box" design experiments with vertically overlapping supply and demand. The role of past prices on the range of contract terms is also illustrated by price inertia from period to period in nonstationary environments.

---

[33] This point is elaborated by Smith (1982).

[34] Curiously, however, Smith and Williams find that the effects of changes in the distribution of the surplus are not symmetric. Perhaps because of the experience of subject pool members as buyers rather than sellers in natural markets, laboratory buyers tend to do better than sellers, and the contract path for markets characterized by relatively high buyer surplus tends to be closer to the competitive prediction than the contract path for a market with relatively high seller surplus.

REFERENCES

Clauser, Laura, and Charles R. Plott (1991) "On the Anatomy of the 'Nonfacilitating' Features of the Double Auction Institution in Conspiratorial Markets," Social Science Working Paper 771, California Institute of Technology.

Cox, James C., and Ronald L. Oaxaca (1990) "Using Laboratory Market Experiments to Evaluate Econometric Estimators of Structural Models," working paper, University of Arizona.

Davis, Douglas D., Glenn W. Harrison, and Arlington W. Williams (1991) "Convergence to Nonstationary Competitive Equilibria: An Experimental Analysis," working paper, Virginia Commonwealth University, a shorter version of which is forthcoming in *Journal of Economic Behavior and Organization*.

Davis, Douglas D., and Arlington W. Williams (1991) "The Hayek Hypothesis in Experimental Auctions: Institutional Effects and Market Power," *Economic Inquiry*, 29, 261–274.

Easley, David, and John O. Ledyard (1986) "Theories of Price Formation and Exchange in Double Oral Auctions," Social Science Working Paper 611, California Institute of Technology.

Forsythe, Robert, Forrest Nelson, George Neumann, and Jack Wright (1992) "Forecasting the 1988 Presidential Election: A Field Experiment," forthcoming in R. M. Isaac, ed., *Research In Experimental Economics*, vol. 4. Greenwich, Conn.: JAI Press.

Friedman, Daniel (1984) "On the Efficiency of Experimental Double Auction Markets," *American Economic Review*, 74, 60–72.

Friedman, Daniel, and Joseph Ostroy (1989) "Competitivity in Auction Markets: An Experimental and Theoretical Investigation," working paper, University of California, Santa Cruz.

Gode, Dhananjay K., and Shyam Sunder (1989) "Human and Artificially Intelligent Traders in Computer Double Auctions," working paper, Carnegie-Mellon University, GSIA.

Goodfellow, Jessica, and Charles R. Plott (1990) "An Experimental Examination of the Simultaneous Determination of Input Prices and Output Prices," *Southern Economic Journal*, 56, 969–983.

Hackett, Steven C., Raymond C. Battalio, and Steven Wiggins (1988) "The Endogenous Choice of Contractual Form in an Experimental Market," working paper, Texas A&M University.

Holt, Charles A., Loren Langan, and Anne P. Villamil (1986) "Market Power in Oral Double Auctions," *Economic Inquiry*, 24, 107–123.

Isaac, R. Mark, and Charles R. Plott (1981a) "The Opportunity for Conspiracy in Restraint of Trade," *Journal of Economic Behavior and Organization*, 2, 1–30.

——— (1981b) "Price Controls and the Behavior of Auction Markets: An Experimental Evaluation," *American Economic Review*, 71, 448–459.

Isaac, R. Mark, Valerie Ramey, and Arlington W. Williams (1984) "The Effects of Market Organization on Conspiracies in Restraint of Trade," *Journal of Economic Behavior and Organization*, 5, 191–222.

Johnson, Alonzo, Hsing-Yang Lee, and Charles R. Plott (1988) "Multiple Unit Double Auction User's Manual," Social Science Working Paper 676, California Institute of Technology.

Joyce, Patrick (1983) "Information and Behavior in Experimental Markets," *Journal of Economic Behavior and Organization*, 4, 411–424.

Kachelmeier, Steven J., and Mohamed Shehata (1990) "The Cultural and Informational Boundaries of Economic Competition: Laboratory Markets in the People's Republic of China, Canada, and the United States," working paper presented at the March 1990 Public Choice Meetings in Tucson, Arizona.

King, Ronald R., Vernon L. Smith, Arlington W. Williams, and Mark Van Boening (1991) "The Robustness of Bubbles and Crashes in Experimental Stock Markets," working paper, University of Arizona.

Leffler, George L., and C. Farwell Loring (1963) *The Stock Market*. New York: Ronald.

Mestelman, Stuart, and Douglas Welland (1987) "Advance Production in Oral Double Auction Markets," *Economics Letters*, 23, 43–48.

——— (1988) "Advance Production in Experimental Markets," *Review of Economic Studies*, 55, 641–654.

——— (1991) "The Effects of Rent Asymmetries in Markets Characterized by Advance Production: A Comparison of Trading Institutions," *Journal of Economic Behavior and Organization*, 15, 387–405.

Miller, Ross M., Charles R. Plott, and Vernon L. Smith (1977) "Intertemporal Competitive Equilibrium: An Empirical Study of Speculation," *Quarterly Journal of Economics*, 91, 599–624.

Peterson, Steven (1991) "Forecasting Dynamics and Convergence to Market Fundamentals: Evidence from Experimental Asset Markets," working paper, Virginia Commonwealth University, forthcoming in *Journal of Economic Behavior and Organization*.

Plott, Charles R. (1989) "An Updated Review of Industrial Organization: Applications of Experimental Methods," in R. Schmalensee and R. D. Willig, eds., *Handbook of Industrial Organization*, vol. 2. Amsterdam: North-Holland, 1109–1176.

Plott, Charles R., and Peter Gray (1990) "Multiple Unit Double Auction," *Journal of Economic Behavior and Organization*, 13, 245–258.

Plott, Charles R., and Vernon L. Smith (1978) "An Experimental Examination of Two Exchange Institutions," *Review of Economic Studies, 45*, 113–153.

Plott, Charles R., and Jonathan T. Uhl (1981) "Competitive Equilibrium with Middlemen: An Empirical Study," *Southern Economic Journal, 47*, 1063–1071.

Smith, Vernon L. (1962) "An Experimental Study of Competitive Market Behavior," *Journal of Political Economy, 70*, 111–137.

———— (1964) "The Effect of Market Organization on Competitive Equilibrium," *Quarterly Journal of Economics, 78*, 181–201.

———— (1976) "Bidding and Auctioning Institutions: Experimental Results," in Y. Amihud, ed., *Bidding and Auctioning for Procurement and Allocation.* New York: New York University Press, 43–64.

———— (1980) "Relevance of Laboratory Experiments to Testing Resource Allocation Theory," in J. Kmenta and J. B. Ramsey, eds., *Evaluation of Econometric Models.* New York: Academic Press, 345–377.

———— (1981) "An Empirical Study of Decentralized Institutions of Monopoly Restraint," in J. Quirk and G. Horwich, eds., *Essays in Contemporary Fields of Economics in Honor of E.T. Weiler (1914-1979).* West Lafayette: Purdue University Press, 83-106.

———— (1982) "Markets as Economizers of Information: Experimental Examination of the 'Hayek Hypothesis'," *Economic Inquiry, 20*, 165–179.

Smith, Vernon L., Gerry L. Suchanek, and Arlington W. Williams (1988) "Bubbles, Crashes and Endogenous Expectations in Experimental Spot Asset Markets," *Econometrica, 56*, 1119–1151.

Smith, Vernon L., and Arlington W. Williams (1981) "On Nonbinding Price Controls in a Competitive Market," *American Economic Review, 71*, 467–474.

———— (1982) "The Effects of Rent Asymmetries in Experimental Auction Markets," *Journal of Economic Behavior and Organization, 3*, 99–116.

———— (1983) "An Experimental Comparison of Alternative Rules for Competitive Market Exchange," in R. Englebrech-Wiggans et al., eds., *Auctions, Bidding, and Contracting: Uses and Theory.* New York: New York University Press, 307–334.

———— (1989) "The Boundaries of Competitive Price Theory: Convergence, Expectations, and Transactions Costs," in L. Green and J. Kagel, eds., *Advances in Behavioral Economics*, vol. 2. Norwood, N.J.: Ablex Publishing.

Van Boening, Mark V. (1990) "Call Versus Continuous Auctions: A Comparison of Experimental Spot Asset Markets," working paper, University of Arizona.

Williams, Arlington W. (1979) "Intertemporal Competitive Equilibrium: On Further Experimental Results," in V. L. Smith, ed., *Research in Experimental Economics*, vol. 1. Greenwich, Conn.: JAI Press, 255–278.

———— (1980) "Computerized Double-Auction Markets: Some Initial Experimental Results," *Journal of Business, 53*, 235–258.

Williams, Arlington W., and Vernon L. Smith (1984) "Cyclical Double-Auction Markets With and Without Speculators," *Journal of Business*, 57, 1–33.

Williams, Arlington W., Vernon L. Smith, and John O. Ledyard (1986) "Simultaneous Trading in Two Competitive Markets: An Experimental Examination," working paper, Indiana University.

CHAPTER 4

POSTED-OFFER MARKETS

4.1 Introduction

There are many markets in which firms will only sell at publicly posted "list" prices. Such posted pricing became common in retail markets in the last century, when store owner/managers were forced to rely on numerous sales clerks in order to exploit economies of scale in operation. Posted pricing is also a consequence of government regulation. In industries such as shipping and alcoholic beverages, regulatory agencies sometimes require that prices be filed with the agency and that discounts not be granted.[1] Theoretical models of these markets are usually built on the assumption that sellers choose prices or other decisions simultaneously at discrete points in time.

The first oligopoly experiments with sellers making simultaneous and binding decisions were conducted in the 1960s (e.g., Fouraker and Siegel, 1963; Friedman, 1963, 1967, 1969; Dolbear et al., 1968; and Sherman, 1972). These early studies were designed to test predictions of alternative theories in Bertrand (price-setting) or Cournot (quantity-setting) environments. To approximate the assumed conditions of oligopoly theory, subjects with seller roles were typically presented with the payoff consequences of their own and others' decisions in tabular form, and the decisions of simulated buyers were subsumed in the construction of the tables.

---

[1] Ketcham, Smith, and Williams (1984) discuss the origins of posted pricing in the United States, and Eckel and Goldberg (1984) describe a regulatory price-posting process in the Canadian brewing industry.

Given the early work on double-auction markets with human buyers and private value and cost information, it is not surprising that some economists became interested posted-price markets with these characteristics. In what has come to be known as a *posted-offer auction*, Williams (1973) had sellers choose prices independently, which were publicly posted on a take-it-or-leave-it basis. Subjects with buyer roles were then selected randomly, one by one, and were given the opportunity to make desired purchases at the posted prices. Williams also conducted *posted-bid auctions*, with sellers being chosen randomly to make desired sales at the bids posted by buyers.

As was the case for double auctions, the early posted-offer markets generated outcomes that were roughly consistent with competitive predictions. Williams, however, noticed some clear differences between his posted-price markets and Smith's auction markets. In particular, prices tended to be above the competitive level when sellers posted offers, and prices tended to be below the competitive level when buyers posted bids. And there was some evidence that convergence to the competitive price was slower than in Smith's (1964) one-sided auctions and double auctions in which price bids and offers could be revised during a trading period.[2] Therefore, the ability to post prices on a take-it-or-leave-it basis provided an advantage to the traders on the side of the market who posted prices. "Rigid commitment to a quotation for a specified period appears to exert significantly less pressure on the price leaders [posters] than continuous bid [price] revision" (Williams, 1973, p. 110, bracketed words added).

One unresolved aspect of Williams's study was that he only used a posted-bid or posted-offer treatment; he did not provide a clear control, which would have consisted of parallel one-sided auctions with the *same* demand-and-supply structure. In particular, Williams's experimental design differed from Smith's one-sided auctions in that agents could buy or sell more than a single unit per period, resulting in individual demand-and-supply curves with multiple steps. (Smith only allowed agents to trade a single unit per period in initial one-sided auctions). In a classic study, Plott and Smith (1978) conducted parallel sessions with different trading institutions and the same (multiunit) individual demand-and-supply curves. In particular, they compared posted-bid markets (buyers post bids simultaneously on a take-it-or-leave-it basis) with one-sided, oral bid auctions (buyers make and revise bids sequentially, and sellers only indicate willingness to purchase). Plott and Smith also found that buyers benefit when they post bids on a take-it-or-leave it basis (prices are lower). In addition, they observed slower convergence and lower efficiencies in posted-bid markets than in oral-bid markets. Plott and Smith concluded that these differences were due to the change in trading rules, not the change in the number of units per trader.

---

[2] By "one-sided auction," we mean a sequential bid or offer institution discussed in section 1.7.

The sorting out of relationships between trading institutions and market performance is one of the most important contributions of experimental economics. Because of parallels with pricing in retail and financial markets, the most commonly investigated simultaneous-choice auction is the posted offer, and the most commonly investigated sequential-choice auction is the double auction. The shift between these two laboratory institutions is the best-documented institutional adjustment. This chapter surveys the performance properties of the posted-offer auction and some of its applications to industrial organization issues. To highlight similarities and differences between posted-offer and double auctions, the following three sections parallel the early sections of the chapter 3: Section 4.2 introduces posted-offer procedures and basic performance characteristics, section 4.3 surveys the resilience of posted-offer outcomes to design boundaries (e.g., variations in supply and demand), and section 4.4 examines factors and imperfections that tend to generate supracompetitive prices. Posted-offer results are calibrated against comparable double-auction data in these sections. The simultaneous nature of price decisions in a posted-offer auction makes it possible to calculate noncooperative equilibria for simple designs (unlike the case of double auctions). When the noncooperative equilibrium for the seller pricing game yields prices above the competitive level, we will say that market power exists (in theory). Section 4.5 explores the behavioral consequences of market power. When Nash and competitive predictions differ, posted prices are often drawn away from the competitive prediction, toward or beyond a static Nash equilibrium. Section 4.6 summarizes the results of posted-offer experiments designed to evaluate three major issues in industrial organization: monopoly regulation, contestability, and predatory pricing. The final section contains some conclusions and comments on ways to modify posted-offer trading rules in a manner that corresponds to some commonly observed pricing practices.

4.2 Posted-Offer Procedures and Performance

The standard posted-offer auction consists of an indefinitely repeated series of periods. In each period, trading occurs as a two-step sequence. First, each seller privately selects a price for the period and indicates the maximum number of units to be offered that price. Each seller's price (but not the quantity limit) is displayed to buyers and to the other sellers, once they have completed their own posting decisions. After all sellers have posted prices, a shopping sequence begins. Buyers are randomly drawn, one at a time, and are given the opportunity to make as many purchases as desired from sellers, at the posted prices. Buyers may make purchases from any seller who has not sold his or her maximum specified sales quantity. When a buyer finishes shopping, another is randomly selected. This process continues until all buyers have shopped, or until all offered units have been purchased.[3]

Some insight into the dynamics of posted-offer markets may be gained by considering the information available to both sellers and buyers as they make decisions in a trading period. Figures 4.1 and 4.2 present buyer and seller screen displays adapted from posted offer software used by Davis and Holt (1991).[4] As indicated by the box at the bottom of figure 4.1, seller S3 has chosen a price of $5.75 for period 4 and is about to select a quantity limit. Notice the striking paucity of information available to the seller. Guided only by the history of units S3 sold in previous periods, previous prices, and the marginal cost information shown in the third column of figure 4.1, the seller must make a price/quantity-limit commitment at the outset of the period.

The information available to a buyer B1 is formatted similarly, with unit valuations listed on the left side of figure 4.2. As indicated by the price listings across the top of the figure, prices (but not limit quantities) are publicly displayed to buyers. Buyer B1's unit valuations are printed in the second column from the left. When viewed as a single-period game, buyers have a very simple, dominant strategy: to maximize earnings in a trading period, a buyer should simply purchase all profitable units at the lowest available price.[5] The decisions of Buyer B1 in figure 4.2 are consistent with this strategy. The buyer first made a purchase from S4 at a price of $5.72 and earned $.23. Seller S4 then stocked out, and S4's identifier was replaced with a NO UNITS message on all buyers' screens, indicating that no more purchases could be made from S4 in this period.[6] Buyer B1 then switched to the next lowest pricing seller, S3, and earned $.10 by purchasing a unit for $5.75, as indicated by the row extending across the screen for unit 2. The bolded box at the bottom of the marginal valuation table reveals that B1 is at present considering the purchase of a third unit, which would be unprofitable if purchased from any of the sellers with units remaining. As the other buyers wait for a chance

---

[3] To conduct a posted-offer auction in class, use the "trading rules" section in appendix A4.1 after reading the "instructions to buyers" and "instructions to sellers" from the double-auction instructions in A1.1.

[4] Appendix A4.2 contains the instructions from this program. Since many experiments are currently conducted with networked computers, it is important for the reader who wishes to appreciate the subjects' decision problem to look at these instructions. The format of figures 4.1 and 4.2 follows the Davis and Holt implementation, but the data are from a NovaNet posted-offer session reported by Davis and Williams (1986). NovaNet posted-offer screen displays are formatted differently but present the same information as in figures 4.1 and 4.2.

[5] Since most laboratory posted-offer markets are multiple-period games, other strategies may sometimes generate higher earnings. In particular, buyers may find that forgoing the purchase of marginal, low-value units in early periods enhances earnings in later periods. As noted below, this behavior is rare.

[6] Sellers are typically not given stock-out information of other sellers.

Unit	Price	Unit Cost	Profit	
1		5.05		
2		5.25		
3		5.80		

S3 Period 4
Posting Prices. Please select a List Price and press ENTER.   List Price: **$5.75**   Quantity :   Press *r* to rechoose or *c* to continue.

Figure 4.1 The Pricing Decision for a Posted-Offer Seller

to shop, they are likely to be anxious to be selected before sellers with lower prices stock out.

Except for some instances where earnings are unreasonably low or unequal, posted-offer buyers nearly always engage in the simple, "fully-demand-revealing" strategy of purchasing all potentially profitable units.[7] Thus, myopically optimal buying behavior is a fairly typical feature of trading under posted-offer rules, and for this reason, buyer behavior is often simulated in computerized posted-offer implementations. In fact, B3 in figure 4.2 was a simulated buyer.

Basic Performance Properties

Table 4.1 presents a complete list of the sequence of contracts for the sample trading period illustrated in figures 4.1 and 4.2. Notice that B1 was the third of six buyers selected from the waiting mode to shop. Low-price units sold first in the sample period, and so seller S2, for example, sold units only after S4 and S3 were

---

[7] For example, buyers consummated 1,634 of 1,655 possible contracts (that were individually profitable) in twelve posted-offer sessions reported by Ketcham, Smith, and Williams (1984). Similarly, Davis and Williams (1991) report that buyers failed to purchase even marginally profitable units in only 10 out of 521 possible instances.

				Seller	S1	S2	S3	No UNITS	S5	S6
				Price	5.80	5.78	5.75	5.72	5.85	5.80
Unit	Unit Value	Price	Earn-ings							
1	5.95	5.72	0.23					5.72		
2	5.85	5.75	0.10				5.75			
3	5.50									

B1 Period 4
Make a purchase by picking seller 1, 2, 3, , or 5, or Press *q* to quit.

Figure 4.2 A Shopping Sequence for a Posted-Offer Buyer

out of stock. High-priced sellers S1, S5, and S6 sold no units in the sample trading period, and therefore, they incurred no costs and had earnings of zero. Many fewer messages are sent in a posted-offer trading period than in a double-auction period, as can be seen by comparing the information in tables 4.1 and 3.2. To the extent that communications are costly, the posted-offer institution economizes on transactions costs and may represent a desirable set of institutional rules in markets where transactions costs are high relative to the value of transacted goods. As will be seen presently, this economy of information comes at some cost in the ability of markets to generate competitive prices and quantities.

Table 4.1 The Sequence of Contracts in a Posted-Offer Trading Period

Contract	1st	2nd	3rd	4th	5th	6th	7th	8th
Buyer ID	B3	B5	B1	B1	B4	B4	B6	B2
Seller ID	S4	S4	S4	S3	S3	S2	S2	S2
Price	5.72	5.72	5.72	5.75	5.75	5.78	5.78	5.78

Figure 4.3 is a plot of the price sequence for the first nine trading periods of a sample posted-offer market. Trading periods are separated by vertical bars in the figure, and the competitive price prediction is denoted by the dotted horizontal line extending across periods. The solid dots represent contracts, while the larger empty boxes represent prices where units that were offered did not result in contracts. Prices are arrayed in order of transaction. Consider period 4, for example, which was summarized above in table 4.1. There are three dots at $5.72, two dots at $5.75, three dots at $5.78, and empty boxes at prices chosen by sellers S1, S5, and S6.

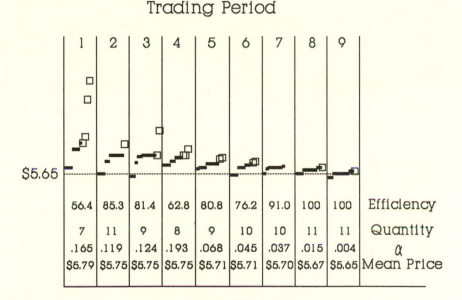

Figure 4.3 Price Sequence for a Posted-Offer Market

Several features of this session are worth noting. In particular, contract prices appear to fall toward the competitive equilibrium price from above. Also, the efficiencies, printed below the price sequence, are low, at least relative to the efficiencies for most double auctions.

Price convergence from above and low early-period efficiencies are predominant features of posted-offer markets, and it is useful to document them more carefully. We do this by comparing the results of the Smith and Williams (1982) "rent-asymmetries" double-auction experiment with a parallel posted-offer experiment reported by Davis and Williams (1986). Supply-and-demand arrays for the two designs are illustrated in the left half of figure 4.4. Each design uses six buyers and six sellers, and units are evenly allocated among participants. In design 1, shown in the top left corner of the figure, two-thirds of the surplus would go to buyers, and one-third of the surplus would go sellers, if all trades were conducted at the competitive price. The distribution of the surplus is reversed in design 2, shown at the bottom-left corner of the figure.

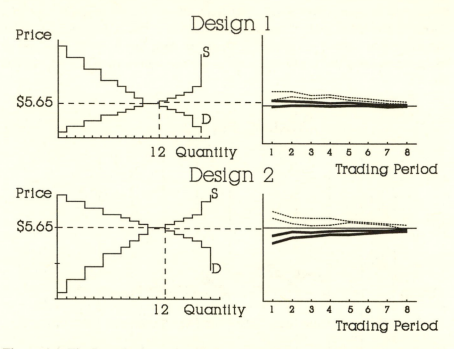

Figure 4.4 The Rent Asymmetries Designs, and 95 percent Price Bands for Double Auctions (bolded lines) and for Posted-Offer Auctions (dotted lines) (Sources: Smith and Williams, 1982, and Davis and Williams, 1986)

As discussed in the conclusion to chapter 3, these changes in the distribution of surplus tend to affect the convergence path in double-auction markets. Due to the symmetry of double-auction buying and selling rules, one might expect buyers and sellers to split the gains from trade more or less evenly, even in the absence of information regarding underlying supply and demand conditions. This surplus splitting occurs to some extent, and therefore, prices usually tend to the competitive prediction from below when seller surplus exceeds buyer surplus, and from above when the reverse is true. But double-auction buyers and sellers often do not behave in an entirely symmetric manner, perhaps because most laboratory participants have more experience as buyers rather than sellers outside of the laboratory. In particular, when the surplus split favors sellers, buyers tend to extract more of the rents than do sellers under converse conditions.[8] These results are succinctly summarized by the bolded "price bands" on the right side of figure 4.4. The band is constructed by finding the symmetric range above and below the mean price that contains 95 percent of the transactions prices in each period. The bolded price bands for double-auction data are slightly above the competitive price in design 1, but bands are well below the competitive price in design 2 markets.

Consider now the posted-offer markets, for which the 95 percent price bands are represented by the dotted lines in the upper and lower panels on the right side of figure 4.4. These price bands are based on observations from three sessions in each design. There is little apparent difference in the dotted-line price bands under the two surplus splits in designs 1 and 2. Comparison across institutions reveals a trading-institution effect that dominates the surplus-asymmetry effect. The dotted bands in the posted-offer markets lie above the corresponding (bolded) double-auction price bands in every period. Since the largely passive buyers in a posted-offer auction will tend to make all profitable purchases, the price-posting sellers will try to set high prices. To the extent this is true, prices start above the competitive level, and it is only the competition among sellers that forces prices down. This asymmetry of buyers' and sellers' roles in posted-offer markets is a likely explanation for the tendency of prices to be higher than in the more symmetric double-auction markets.

Table 4.2 lists the average efficiencies, by period, for each of the four treatments in figure 4.2. Note in the table that the posted-offer markets also tend to extract less surplus than comparable double-action markets, which extract the bulk of gains from exchange even in the first trading period. For either design conducted under posted-offer rules, first-period mean efficiencies are below 77 percent, and efficiencies average less than 85 percent for the eight trading periods common to each treatment cell. The inability of sellers to revise prices during a trading period may explain some of the efficiency differences between these institutions. Mistakes, in the form of overly high prices posted in one trading period, cannot be corrected until the following period. Units priced too high remain unsold, and sellers may even prefer to sell fewer units at high prices than to sell more units at low prices.

Despite the low early-period efficiencies for the posted-offer markets summarized in table 4.2, the markets in each design do eventually extract the bulk of possible gains from exchange. In either design, mean efficiency rates exceed 95 percent by the eighth trading period. Similarly, despite the comparatively slow convergence from above, these posted-offer markets do tend toward the competitive price prediction, if at a somewhat slower rate than for the comparable double auctions. These convergence characteristics are typical of many posted-offer markets, but some exceptions will be discussed below.

---

[8]   This behavioral asymmetry was first noticed by Chamberlin (1948), who suggest the buyer-experience explanation in the text.

Table 4.2 Mean Efficiency Comparisons between Posted-Offer and Double-
Auction Institutions

| | Mean Efficiency | | | |
| | Design 1 | | Design 2 | |
Trading Period	PO	DA	PO	DA
1	76.5	89.9	65.4	92.4
2	76.7	96.8	84.2	95.6
3	74.1	97.8	82.3	97.8
4	72.0	99.6	77.4	98.6
5	80.8	98.4	84.4	97.4
6	82.3	99.4	84.2	98.3
7	87.2	98.4	87.2	99.5
8	97.0	99.7	96.2	99.3
Average	80.8	97.5	82.6	97.4

Source: Davis and Williams (1986).

Table 4.3 provides further evidence regarding the general tendency of posted-offer markets eventually to extract the bulk of possible gains from exchange. The table summarizes results of four posted-offer experiments. The experiments were not chosen randomly, but instead were selected because they illustrate performance under "standard" conditions: for example, there are at least four sellers in every market, supply is upward sloping, demand is downward sloping, supply-and-demand arrays do not change across trading periods, and agents are presented with no opportunities for explicit conspiracy. Background information on the authors, sites, and number of market sessions is summarized in the first two columns of the table. Each study consisted of at least three market sessions, which each lasted for at least fifteen trading periods, and all participants were inexperienced, except as noted. As indicated in the table, the two studies conducted at McMaster University (MMU) were conducted orally, while the other studies used the NovaNet computerized implementation. The buyers column indicates that human buyers were used in three of the four studies.

The final three columns on the right side of table 4.3 list summary price, efficiency, and quantity information. In each column, overall performance measures for all periods common to each session in an experiment are listed above the corresponding (bolded) performance measures for the last five periods common to each session in the experiment. Although design differences muddy performance

Table 4.3 Mean Performance in Selected Posted-Offer Experiments:
Overall and **(Final 5 Periods)**

Study	Site (# mkts)	Environ- ment	Buyers	$P - P_e$	Effic- iency	$\dfrac{Q-Q_e}{Q}$
Ketcham, Smith, & Williams (1984)*	IU, AU (6 mkts)	Nova- Net	human	.05 **(.02)**	89.5 **(94.1)**	.16 **(.07)**
Mestelman & Welland (1988, design 1)	MMU (5 mkts)	Oral	human	.08 **(.03)**	88.4 **(97.2)**	.18 **(.08)**
Davis & Williams (1986, design 2)	IU (3 mkts)	Nova- Net	simu- lated	.04 **(-.01)**	87.9 **(93.3)**	.19 **(.09)**
Mestelman & Welland (1991, design 2)	MMU (5 mkts)	Oral	human	.04 **(.03)**	84.8 **(91.4)**	.21 **(.15)**

* Data are for their "Design I." Three of the six sessions involved experienced subjects. The other studies used inexperienced subjects.
Site Key: Indiana University (IU), University of Arizona (UA), McMaster University (MMU).

comparisons between the experiments summarized above and the similarly summarized double-auction markets listed in table 3.4 of chapter 3, such comparisons are clearly suggestive. Most prominently, the posted-offer markets appear, on average, to be drawn less completely toward competitive predictions than the double auctions. In particular, note that mean efficiency is below 90 percent in each of the posted-offer experiments summarized in table 4.3. In contrast, more than 96 percent of possible surplus was extracted in six of the seven double-auction studies reported in table 3.4. Comparisons between posted-offer markets and double-auction markets conducted in parallel designs will be discussed below.

Inspection of the bolded numbers summarizing performance for the last five common periods, however, indicates that inferior average performance is primarily a consequence of a slower convergence rate toward competitive predictions, at least in these "standard" posted-offer environments: Over the last five periods of each experiment, price deviations are $.03 or smaller, more than 91 percent of possible gains from exchange are extracted, and at least 91 percent of the potentially traded units are exchanged.

In contrast to double-auction markets, there has been no formal examination of the effects of computerization on laboratory posted-offer markets. The two bottom rows of table 4.3 allow some insight into the effects of computerization, as the design 2 for the Mestelman and Welland (1991b) oral auctions (bottom row) is similar to the design 2 used in the Davis and Williams (1986) computerized auctions. The virtually identical performance measures in the bottom two rows of table 4.3 suggests why discussion of the effects of computerization has been minimal in this context.[9] Computerization facilitates administration and data recording in posted-offer markets, and can increase experimental control, but computerization does not noticeably affect posted-offer market performance.

Given the general tendency of standard posted-offer markets to generate competitive price, quantity, and efficiency predictions, it is natural to examine performance in other situations, to circumscribe the limits of application for competitive predictions. The following three sections undertake this discussion. Section 4.3 examines design effects, or the consequences of manipulations in the shape and stationarity of market supply and demand arrays. Section 4.4 pertains to environmental effects, such as limits on the number of sellers, and the presence of opportunities for conspiracy. The more complicated design issue of "market power," which arises when some sellers are able to profit by unilaterally deviating from the competitive price, is the subject of section 4.5.

4.3 Posted-Offer Results: Design Effects

This section evaluates experiments designed to assess the robustness of competitive price predictions to alterations in supply-and-demand arrays. Specifically we consider three manipulations. A first design consists of a pair of supply-and-demand arrays where both unit costs and unit valuations are constant for all units. In these "box" arrays, the total number of units supplied and demanded are unequal, and therefore, 100 percent of the surplus goes to the "short side" of the market (either buyers or sellers), at the competitive price. This design allows assessment of the effects of severe earnings inequities on behavior. A second design manipulation consists of a variation of the box array, where supply and demand vertically overlap, yielding a range of competitive equilibrium prices. As will be seen presently, despite the multiplicity of prices consistent with a competitive equilibrium, there is a unique Nash equilibrium price for the single stage posted-offer market "game." Therefore, this version of the box design allows some insight

---

[9] These comparisons of computerized and oral posted-offer sessions are admittedly speculative. Supply-and-demand arrays for the oral and computerized experiments differ in two respects. First, the vertical distance between marginal cost and marginal valuation steps in the Mestelman and Welland design is roughly one-half that in the Davis and Williams design. Second, to induce the sale of marginal units and still avoid using trading commissions, Mestelman and Welland shifted marginal valuation schedules up and marginal cost schedules down by $.02, to create a $.04 competitive price tunnel in the oral sessions. Price deviations in each oral session are reported as deviations from the center of the equilibrium price range. Finally, marginal valuation and marginal cost steps for two buyers and two sellers were eliminated in the oral sessions, so four sellers and four buyers exchanged eight rather than twelve units at the competitive prediction.

into the drawing power of the Nash equilibrium prediction. The third design manipulation examined in this section is the effect of unannounced adjustments in demand, which allows assessment of the capacity of posted-offer markets to transmit information regarding changes in the structural conditions.

Extreme Earnings Inequities

Recall from chapter 3 that while the theoretic distribution of consumer and producer surplus affected the price convergence path in double-auction markets, the tendency of markets to gravitate toward competitive price and quantity predictions was robust to even the most inequitable rent distributions, for example, where all available surplus goes to either buyers or sellers at the competitive price. Boundary conditions of this type are created by inducing constant costs and valuations, and making quantity supplied differ from quantity demanded. For example, consider the double-lined supply-and-demand arrays labelled S1 and D1 on the left side of figure 4.5. There, 16 units are demanded at a constant marginal valuation of $5.80 per unit, and 11 units are supplied at a constant cost of $5.25 per unit. The market supply curve S1 intersects the market demand D1 at the point E1. The excess demand, combined with constant unit valuations, implies that all surplus goes to sellers at a price equal to the demand intercept. This equilibrium surplus distribution is reversed by reducing demand to 11 units and increasing supply to 16 units, as illustrated by the dashed lines labeled D2 and S2 in figure 4.5. The market demand curve D2 intersects the market supply curve S2 at sellers' costs, which implies that all surplus should go to buyers.

Cason and Williams (1990) report the results of an experiment designed to evaluate the effects of these severe earnings inequities in posted-offer markets. The experiment involved five sessions and was structured in a manner parallel to five double-auction sessions reported by Smith and Williams (1989). Each market consisted of four sellers and four buyers. In three of the sessions, supply-and-demand arrays S1 and D1 were initially imposed for a fixed number of periods, followed by conditions S2 and D2 for the remainder of each session. In the remaining two sessions, the order of treatments was reversed, to control for possible sequencing effects. Units were distributed among buyers and sellers as evenly as possible in every instance.[10]

---

[10] In addition to gains from trade, buyers and sellers received a $.10 per-unit trading commission. The procedures used by Cason and Williams in their posted-offer markets are not identical to those used by Smith and Williams in their double auctions. First, rather than lasting only ten trading periods, each posted-offer session lasted between nineteen and twenty-five periods. Second, the vertical distance between supply-and-demand arrays was cut from $1.10 to $.55 in four of the five posted-offer sessions. Third, buyers' decisions were simulated in four of the five posted-offer sessions (the sequence of contracts illustrated in the text was the session using the real buyers). Finally, no posted-offer sellers had prior experience. Participants were experienced in four of the five double-auctions.

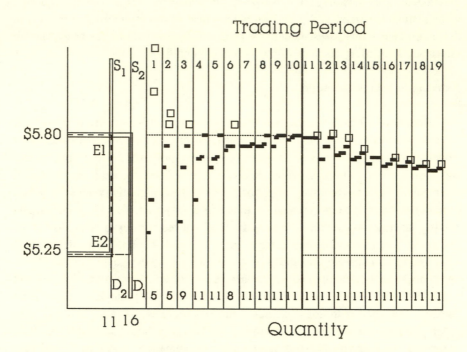

Figure 4.5 Supply-and-Demand Arrays, and Prices for a Posted-Offer Session with Severe Earnings Inequities (Source: Cason and Williams, 1990)

The sequence of prices shown on the right side of figure 4.5 illustrates the results from one of the five sessions. As before, trading periods are separated by vertical bars, and dots represent contracts. Price postings that did not result in sales contracts are represented by unfilled boxes. The dotted line, extending horizontally across the top of figure 4.5 for trading periods 1 to 10, denotes the price prediction under the excess demand equilibrium *E1*, and the dotted line running across the bottom of figure 4.5 represents the competitive price prediction under the excess supply equilibrium *E2*.

It is clear from the data in figure 4.5 that competitive price predictions have some drawing power in posted-offer markets. Contract prices converge to the upper dotted line predicted by *E1* in periods 1 to 10, and prices decay toward the lower dotted line predicted by *E2* in periods 11 to 19. Performance, however, is very different than in comparable double auctions (see figure 3.5 in chapter 3). Although prices rise to the demand intercept under conditions of excess demand, they do not decay nearly as quickly to marginal costs under conditions of excess supply.[11]

The slow convergence in periods of excess supply may be an artifact of this design. At any price up to $5.80, only the highest-pricing seller is left out of the market, and the second-to-highest-pricing seller sells three of four available units. Given these conditions, sellers realize that they need not post the lowest price, but rather, they must strive not to post the highest price. Thus, prices slowly decay, as the high-priced seller attempts to shade only below the next highest price posting. Conversely, prices rise quickly under conditions of excess demand, as each seller is certain to sell all units offered at any price up to $5.80, regardless of the others' prices.

The absence of opportunities to haggle over prices within posted-offer trading periods, combined with extremely low earnings for one side of the market, suggests that agents might attempt to manipulate prices by engaging in multiperiod strategic behavior. For buyers, strategic behavior can occur only in the form of "strategic withholding," or forgoing profitable transactions in one period in an effort to influence price postings in subsequent periods. Sellers, on the other hand, might either limit their offer quantities or withhold units by posting prices above the going level.

The very inequitable terms of trade created by the box design would seemingly provide a good environment for stimulating strategic buyer and/or seller behavior. But buyers and sellers were not equally successful at strategic manipulations in the Cason and Williams experiment. Consider first the behavior of buyers. The sequence of contracts shown in figure 4.5 was chosen for illustration because it is the only session where buying decisions were not simulated. The very high prices in the first ten periods did in fact stimulate three separate attempts at withholding (periods 3, 9, and 10). Shopping is done privately, so units passed over by one buyer tended to be taken by buyers who shopped subsequently. Thus, the withholding had no visible effect on the market transactions quantity. On the other hand, price-signaling by sellers was both more public and more successful. For example, in a second session (not shown), a single seller repeatedly posted a price well above the prices of others in the latter periods of an excess-supply treatment. This behavior generated higher, if not particularly stable, prices.

The excess-supply design used in the final 10 periods in figure 4.5 is useful for examining the effects of strategic seller behavior, but not ideal. In particular, no seller has market power to raise the price once it falls to competitive levels, as the

---

[11] Prices were more nearly drawn to the competitive prediction $E2$ in the other four sessions reported by Cason and Williams, which is surprising since these sessions involve simulated buyers. The illustrated sequence of contracts is representative, however, in that the convergence process toward excess supply equilibrium, $E2$, is slower and less complete than convergence toward excess demand equilibrium, $E1$.

following argument shows. The excess supply of five units in this design exceeds the capacity of any one seller, so when all but one of the sellers charge the competitive price of $5.25, the seller with the highest price will sell no units and earn nothing. Therefore, when all sellers charge the competitive price (and earn zero), no seller can increase earnings by unilaterally raising his or her price. In this sense, sellers have no market power in the excess-supply condition. Market power is discussed in more detail in section 4.5.

Multiple Price Equilibria

An interesting variation of the box designs involves giving buyers and sellers equal numbers of units, as shown on the left hand side of figure 4.6. Three sellers may offer two units each at a constant per unit cost of $5.00 per unit, for a market supply of six units. Symmetrically, three buyers may each purchase up to two units, at a constant marginal valuation of $6.10. Any price between $5.00 and $6.10 is a competitive equilibrium price.

Davis and Williams (1989) report the results of three posted-offer markets conducted under the supply-and-demand conditions illustrated on the left side of figure 4.6. Each market consisted of ten trading periods.[12] The sequence of contracts for the first four trading periods in one of these sessions, PO1, is displayed immediately to the right of the supply-and-demand arrays. The series of six dots in periods 1, 2, and 3 of PO1 indicate that all possible units were traded in these periods (and, in this design, that all possible gains from trade were extracted). One seller posted a price above buyers' unit valuations in the fourth trading period, generating an efficiency loss, as only four of the six units traded. Despite this efficiency loss, note that contract prices edge up in periods 3 and 4.

Prices continued to increase throughout the remainder of PO1, as is seen in the chart of mean contract prices for this session, shown in the middle panel on the right side of figure 4.6. In this panel, the upper and lower borders are drawn at the buyers' unit valuations, and at the sellers' unit costs, respectively, while the line running horizontally through the center of the panel represents the price where the surplus is divided equally between a buyer and a seller. The ten dots represent the mean contract prices in each of the ten trading periods of the session. Notice that contracts cluster about the buyers' limit price in the final three trading periods of session PO1.

Mean contract prices for the two other sessions conducted in this design are shown above and below PO1. Although prices are not as uniformly near the limit price in these sessions, they end up being well above the equal-rent-split price.

---

[12] Market data summarized in figure 4.6 were control periods in longer sessions. In each case, a new treatment condition was initiated after period 10. Sessions are archived in the NovaNet database under session numbers p267, iu08, and iu09.

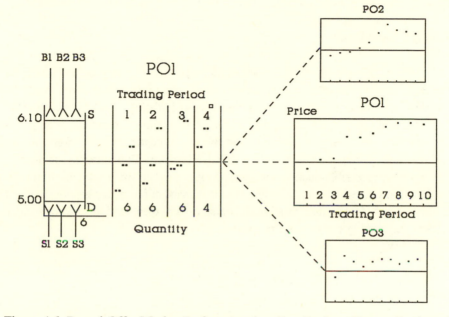

Figure 4.6 Posted-Offer Market Performance in a Box Design (Source: Davis and Williams, 1989)

Period 10 mean prices for PO2 and PO3, for example, were $.29 and $.22 above the equal-rent-split price, respectively. The tendency for prices to rise toward the limit price stands in stark contrast to comparable double auctions shown in figure 3.6, where prices exhibited no general tendency to converge to any particular price. This difference is another consequence of the asymmetry in bargaining positions of buyers relative to sellers in a posted-offer market.

It is worth pointing out that the limit price is a Nash equilibrium for the single-stage version of this posted-offer game. To see this, note that buyer-withholding would be irrational in a single-stage game, since a buyer would forgo a positive profit by withholding and would have no effect on prices (already posted). Given full revelation by buyers, sellers unilaterally maximize earnings by posting prices just below the limit price; a higher price results in no sales, and a lower price results in no increase in sales. The tendency for prices to rise in this design suggests that the Nash equilibrium has some drawing power.

Buyers were somewhat more successful at strategic behavior in this vertical overlap box design than was the case with excess demand. At the end of session PO2, for example, buyers apparently engaged in strategic withholding, collectively forgoing the purchase of at least one profitable unit in each of the periods 7, 8, 9, and 10. Mean prices fell from $.45 above the equal-rent-split price in period 7 to

$.29 above in period 10. But this behavior was not a resounding success: sellers still earned nearly three-fourths of the total realized surplus in these final periods.

Demand Instabilities

The restricted message space available to posted-offer buyers has additional consequences in markets where demand does not remain stationary throughout the course of a session. Buyers have no way of communicating a willingness either to purchase additional units at higher prices or to continue purchasing at prices acceptable in the preceding period, and therefore, posted-offer markets do not respond well to demand side shocks. This is succinctly illustrated by comparing performance of double-auction and posted-offer markets in a design where the market supply curve remains constant, but the demand curve shifts; first outward for a series of periods, creating inflationary pressures, and then back inward for a series of periods, creating deflationary pressures.

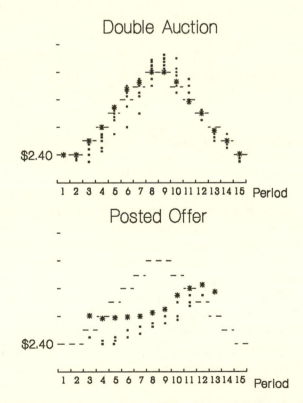

Figure 4.7   Double-Auction and Posted-Offer Contract Prices in a Design with Regular Demand Shifts (Source: Davis, Harrison and Williams, 1991)   Key: contract prices: ·, Final contract prices: *, Equilibrium Price: --.

The upper and lower panels of figure 4.7 summarize the results of a match pair of double-auction and posted-offer sessions using such a "trend-demand" design.[13] In each panel, periods are enumerated across the horizontal axis, and the dashed lines indicate the competitive equilibrium price prediction in each trading period. Notice that demand remained constant after period 1, generating an equilibrium price prediction of $2.40 in periods 1 and 2, as indicated by the flat, dashed-line step at $2.40. Demand then increased after periods 2 through 7, increasing the competitive price prediction by $.20 each period. Demand again remained fixed after period 8 but decreased after periods 9 through 14 in a way that made the competitive price prediction diminish by $.20 per period. The equilibrium quantity prediction (not shown) varies directly with demand, ranging from 5 in the periods of lowest demand (periods 1, 2, and 15) to 17 in periods of highest demand (periods 8 and 9). Contract prices are denoted by the dots listed vertically above each trading period number, while the asterisk indicates the final contract price in each trading period.

The sequence of prices for the double-auction session at the top of figure 4.7 illustrates several interesting patterns. First, the double-auction market does not respond flawlessly to these inflationary/deflationary demand shifts. Prices lag below the competitive prediction in early periods of inflation and then hang above the competitive prediction in early periods of deflation. Two features of market performance, however, suggest a resilience to the demand changes. First, note that the closing price in each trading period provides very accurate information regarding the equilibrium price. Second, and not shown, nearly all possible gains from trade were exhausted in each trading period. Efficiency never fell below 93 percent in any period, and on average, 98 percent of the possible gains from trade were extracted.

Performance in the posted-offer session, shown at the bottom of figure 4.7, is quite different: The contract-price series bears no direct relation to the underlying equilibria. Rather, the price dots look more like a string of lights strung across a Christmas tree: Prices gradually rise throughout the session, until the equilibrium price falls below the posted prices, and sales drop to zero in periods 14 and 15. The poor price-tracking capacity in the posted-offer session also generates very low efficiency. Overall average efficiency for the session is less than 50 percent, and more than 80 percent of the possible gains from exchange were extracted in only three of the fifteen periods. Also unlike the double auction, closing prices in each trading period in the posted-offer session provide no information regarding the underlying equilibrium. Rather, they merely reflect the tendency of posted-offer buyers to purchase the highest-price units last.

---

[13] The sessions were conducted using NovaNet software, and they used institution-experienced (but not design-experienced) participants. To induce the sale of marginal units, participants were paid a $.05 trading commission. The illustrated sessions are archived on NovaNet as 3pda281 and p214.

The same study reports additional evidence from posted-offer and double-auction markets in related designs with supply and/or demand nonstationarities. Results support the finding that competitive predictions are seriously impeded by demand-side adjustments in posted-offer markets. In contrast, posted-offer markets respond with surprising fluidity to supply-side shocks. The intuition for this difference is straightforward: Unlike demand-side adjustments, sellers individually perceive changes in aggregate supply via changes in their private cost schedules.

Summary

Both the structure and the stability of supply-and-demand arrays can affect the tendency of posted-offer markets to generate competitive outcomes. In a box design, where unit valuations are constant and where market supply and demand vertically overlap, sellers generally extract the bulk of available surplus. Moreover, variants of the box design without a vertical overlap indicate that posted-offer prices respond only slowly to conditions of excess supply. Finally, performance in designs where demand arrays do not remain constant throughout a session reveal a dynamic consequence of posted-offer trading rules: Since buyers have a very limited ability to indicate changes in reservation values, posted-offer markets respond very poorly to demand-side adjustments. Posted-offer prices are more sensitive to supply-side shocks.

4.4 Factors That Generate Supracompetitive Prices

In contrast to the double auction, posted-offer markets can be quite sensitive to changes in the number of sellers and to other environmental effects. This section reviews some of the variations that have been shown to generate price increases. We begin with a discussion of posted-offer monopolies, where supracompetitive prices are regularly observed, and then increase the size and complexity of markets, to identify the limits of market-power effects.

Monopoly

Figure 4.8 presents the results of a posted-offer monopoly, which consisted of five buyers and a single seller. The monopolist's marginal cost (S) and the marginal revenue (MR) curves cross at a quantity of 5 units, yielding a monopoly price, p_m, of 110 (shown as a horizontal dashed line). The "competitive" price $p_c = 80$ (shown as a solid line) occurs where marginal cost (S) and demand (D) intersect, at a quantity of $7 - 8$ units.

The seller was clearly successful at finding and maintaining a monopoly price; the profit-maximizing price of 110 was posted in each of the final five periods.

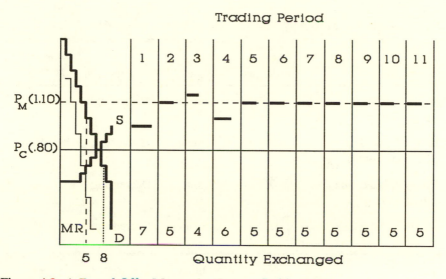

Figure 4.8 A Posted-Offer Monopoly (Source: Smith, 1981)

Buyers also fully revealed demand in these periods, so the index of monopoly effectiveness, M, was 1. The results of this posted-offer session are quite different from the near-competitive prices frequently observed in double-auction monopolies (see, e.g., figure 3.10). In fact, although posted-offer monopolists frequently succeed in extracting some portion of available monopoly rents, they are generally less successful than the seller in figure 4.8. Table 4.4 contains summary results for five posted-offer monopoly experiments. The M values in the right-hand column reveal a wide variability across designs, ranging from less than .10 to the perfect 1.0 observed in the single session reported by Smith (1981) and summarized in figure 4.8.

A variety of factors affect the exercise of monopoly power in the posted-offer markets, including buyer withholding, information, experience, and the monopolist's cost structure. Consider first the effects of buyer withholding. As discussed in the previous section, buyers may fail to reveal demand passively under conditions of severe earnings inequities, as part of an effort to bring prices down. Since posted-offer monopolies generate earnings inequities, it is not surprising that buyers frequently forgo some purchases that would increase their (short-run) earnings. For example, both Coursey, Isaac, and Smith (1984) and Isaac, Ramey, and Williams (1984) observed under-revelation in at least half of their monopoly sessions. Consider the decreasing-cost monopolies reported by Coursey et al. (1984), which are summarized in the third row of table 4.4. Decreasing costs imply that the final units sold in a period have the highest marginal profits, and thus, both seller profits and M values can be prominently affected when even only one buyer forgoes the

Table 4.4 Monopoly Effectiveness in Posted-Offer Monopolies

Author(s)	Subject Experience	Buyers	Cost Function	Monopoly M Value
Smith (1981) (1 session)	?	human	Increasing	1.00
Isaac, Ramey and Williams (1984)[a]	NX	human	Increasing	.45
Coursey, Isaac, and Smith (1984)	X	human	Decreasing	.56
Harrison and McKee (1985)[b]	DX	simulated	Decreasing	.72
Harrison, McKee and Rutström (1989)[b]	NX	simulated	Decreasing	.44
	DX	simulated	Increasing	.09
	DX	simulated	Constant	.77
	DX	simulated	Decreasing	.78

Key: NX = inexperienced subjects, X = experienced subjects, DX = design experience. Reported values are the average for the final period common to all sessions in an experiment.

[a] Data from market sessions with complete demand information were omitted.

[b] Subjects were preselected on the basis of a test for risk neutrality.

purchase of a single, marginally profitable unit. Roughly 9 percent of total demand was withheld, generating a final period $M = .56$. Despite the loss in profitability, this withholding had little effect on pricing. The final-period mean price was only $.07 below the monopoly prediction in these markets (and $.93 above the highest price consistent with the competitive prediction).

In any event, simulated buyers are frequently used to eliminate buyer withholding. Simulated-buyer treatments may be justified on the grounds that buyers are small and dispersed in many natural monopoly markets (e.g., telephones), and it is difficult to take the possibility of buyer under-revelation very seriously. Buyer simulation also has added advantages of administrative ease and low costs. As might be expected from the above discussion of buyer withholding, there is some evidence that higher monopoly effectiveness indices are generated with simulated buyers that are programmed not to withhold. For example, Coursey, Isaac, and

Smith (1984) used human buyers, and Harrison and McKee (1985) used simulated buyers in a very similar design. As can be seen by comparing the third and fourth rows of table 4.4, the M value of .72 with simulated buyers was well above the M value of .56 with human buyers.[14]

Incomplete information is another factor that may impede the extraction of monopoly profits. The laboratory monopolist is typically not told market demand parameters, and the process of searching for the profit-maximizing price can be far from trivial. Granted, in a world of continuous demand and cost curves, the search problem is fairly straightforward, because profits respond directly to incremental deviations toward or away from the optimal price. For example, the zero-cost monopoly facing the linear demand curve represented by the straight, dashed line on the left side of figure 4.9 would enjoy increases in incremental profits for any deviation toward the profit-maximizing price of $2.00, regardless of the initial price, as indicated by the convex (dashed line) profit curve on the right side of figure 4.9.

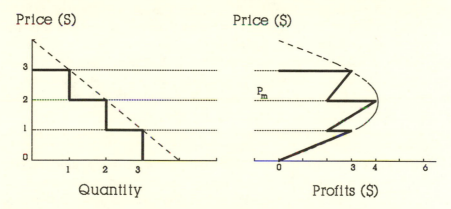

Figure 4.9 Discrete Demand Steps and the Monopolist's Price-Search Problem

This search problem becomes much more complicated, however, when demand is discrete (as is typically the case in market experiments), because the incremental returns to price adjustments toward the profit-maximizing level are discontinuous. To see this, suppose that instead of linear demand, consumers are divided into three distinct classes: a high-value group, who will pay up to $3.00 for a unit; an intermediate-value group, with a maximum value of $2.00 per unit; and a low-value group, who will pay a maximum of only $1.00 per unit. The case of one consumer in each group is illustrated by the step function on the left side of figure 4.9. Consider the problem of searching for the profit-maximizing price under this

---

[14] This comparison is not ideal, since monopoly pricing is facilitated by the design experience that sellers had in the Harrison and McKee study.

scenario. At prices between $0.00 and $1.00, the monopolist will earn $.03 for every penny price increase, and therefore, $3.00 is earned at a price of $1.00. The low-value consumer group drops from the market, however, if the price is raised to $1.01, and profits drop to $2.02. Observing the sizable negative marginal revenue, the monopolist might conclude that $1.00 is the profit-maximizing price. The situation is illustrated by the kinked, solid-line profit function shown on the right side of figure 4.9; while $1.00 is a local maximum, $2.00 remains the profit-maximizing price. Notice also the local profit spike at $3.00. Therefore, the monopolist would face a similar problem while searching for the optimal price from above.

Experience may help the monopolist in this price-search process. Consider the Harrison, McKee, and Rutström (1989) experiment summarized in the bottom four rows of table 4.4. The effects of experience are suggested by comparison of the fourth row from the bottom with the bottom row: In a design using simulated buyers and decreasing costs, monopolists with design experience averaged a monopoly effectiveness value of .78, compared to an M value of .44 for inexperienced, but otherwise similar, participants. Experienced monopolists also performed more homogeneously than inexperienced participants, and for this reason the authors conclude: "This suggests that small sample observations with inexperienced subjects be viewed with some skepticism" (p. 90). Interestingly, the *kind* of experience participants have affects their learning: "Experience in the form of more periods in the initial session is not equivalent to coming back and participating a second time despite having to face new cost and demand conditions in the latter situation" (p. 89).

Harrison, McKee, and Rutström (1989) also evaluate the effects of altering the shape of the cost function on monopoly pricing. A comparison of the data in the bottom three rows of table 4.4 reveals that monopolists are more successful at raising profits toward the monopoly level when costs are constant or decreasing: Monopoly M values are .09 with increasing costs, .78 with decreasing costs, and .77 with constant costs.

To summarize, the posted-offer trading institution appears to favor the exercise of monopoly power, although strategic buyer withholding and the discrete nature of cost steps often impede full exploitation of this power. The exercise of monopoly power also appears to be facilitated by design experience, and by constant or decreasing cost conditions.

Duopoly

Thin markets, particularly duopolies, have also been shown to generate collusive prices if the duration of the market is sufficiently long. Alger (1987), for example, observed cooperation in a series of extraordinarily long markets, some lasting as long as 150 trading periods. Buyer behavior was simulated. Price patterns in these long duopolies tend to be U-shaped, with prices initially falling toward the competitive level but then increasing, often toward the joint maximizing level after many periods. Alger concludes that data from sessions of short duration may misrepresent equilibrium market performance.

Benson and Faminow (1988) replicated Alger's U-shaped pricing patterns in markets of much shorter duration (33 to 40 periods), with a price space restricted to five options, and with design-experienced participants. Although there is a fair amount of variability in the data, prices were much closer to the competitive (and Nash) equilibrium with inexperienced subjects than was the case when they were experienced. Stable collusive profits were observed in six of the twelve sessions using experienced participants, with another two sessions breaking upward from the competitive prediction toward the collusive prediction at the end of the session. Thus, experience, both across sessions (in the form of familiarity with a market institution) and within sessions (in the form of repetition) appears to generate supracompetitive prices in duopolies.

Oligopoly

Most research on the effects of experience in posted-offer markets has involved duopolies. One might suspect that the U-shaped pricing patterns observed in duopolies would not persist in markets with more sellers, as the addition of sellers complicates both the implementation and maintenance of tacit collusion. It is certainly true that reasonably competitive outcomes are typical in relatively short posted-offer oligopolies. For example, all the studies summarized in table 4.3 involved only four to six sellers and yielded fairly high efficiencies after ten or fifteen periods. Evidence from long, multiperiod oligopolies also suggests that an increase in the number of price-setting sellers reduces the incidence of cooperative pricing. For example, when Alger (1987) increased the number of sellers from two to three or four, only about a third of the sessions generated collusive outcomes. Even less collusive results were reported by Kruse et al. (1990). These authors conducted a series of fifteen sixty-period posted-offer markets with four sellers and simulated demand, in a purposely unstable design (seller profits were 0 at the competitive price). Although prices did not stabilize at the competitive level, the average price was close to the competitive prediction in each case. Importantly, performance was often relatively competitive in both of these studies, even though seller profits were very low at the theoretical competitive price.[15] It is natural to conjecture that pricing would be even more competitive in long posted-offer sessions

---

[15] Alger's designs were similar to that used by Kruse et al. (1990) in the sense that earnings were either 0 or very low ($.05 per period) under the competitive prediction. Notably, the potential gains from collusion were (relatively) large in Alger's designs. Per-period profits at the joint maximizing price ranged from $.41 to $.78 per period.

that provide sellers with reasonable levels of earnings at the competitive equilibrium. As will be seen in the next section, this is not always true. Before turning to this issue, we review results of experiments with communications opportunities.

As should not be surprising, direct and explicit communications between participants represents one environmental characteristic that has been shown to increase the incidence of supracompetitive prices, even in relatively thick markets of short duration. Isaac, Ramey, and Williams (1984) conducted an experiment where sellers were given the opportunity to engage in unstructured price discussions at the conclusion of each trading period. In seven of the eight markets, prices substantially exceeded the competitive level. It is worth noting, however, that it is more difficult for multiple sellers to find and maintain a joint maximizing price than for a single seller, even when the multiple sellers can explicitly collude. The difficulty faced by conspirators may be seen by considering again the stepped demand function on the left side of figure 4.9. Instead of a single seller, suppose that there are three sellers, each with a capacity of a single unit and a cost of 0. Moreover, suppose that there are three buyers, each with a single unit. Despite a joint profit-maximizing price of $2.00, one might expect that three sellers would find it difficult to implement and maintain a scheme to raise prices above $1.00, since one of them would be left out of the market each period. Isaac, Ramey, and Williams (1984) found that colluding sellers clustered about a price with this "all-sellers-make-sales" characteristic in six of seven instances.

Friedman (1967, 1969) reports experiments with more structured opportunities for communication. Sellers were given complete cost information and were allowed to communicate via written pieces of paper. Each seller sent two messages, in sequential order, and then posted prices. Collusive outcomes were observed in about three-fourths of the cases.

Antitrust scholars have also been interested in less direct forms of communication. For example, there has been some concern about the anticompetitive effects of seller communications that result from public announcements to the trade press. Holt and Davis (1990) report an experiment designed to assess such announcements. Prior to the outset of each period, one seller was selected to make a price recommendation, which was publicly displayed to the other sellers (buyers were simulated). The other sellers could then agree with the recommended price, or disagree and indicate that the market price should be either higher or lower. Introducing the opportunity for sellers to make nonbinding public price announcements increased market prices. The effect, however, was transitory. In each of the four markets reported by Holt and Davis, sellers initially recommended posting prices near the limit price, and other sellers agreed. But at least one seller inevitably posted a price slightly below the suggested price. Other sellers responded in subsequent periods by similarly shading on the going price.

Price recommendations remained high but became meaningless predictors of the market price, as shading became pervasive.[16]

4.5 Market Power

A growing body of laboratory evidence suggests that the competitive predictions arising from the intersection of supply-and-demand curves are poor predictors of behavior in posted-offer markets, when one or more sellers possess *market power*, or can unilaterally manipulate the market price.[17] Posted-offer monopolists, for example, nearly always have market power.[18] As just seen, monopolists do not always fully exercise their power, especially when they are inexperienced, when they face human buyers, and when they have increasing costs. Moreover, supracompetitive prices can be observed in the absence of market power: Posted-offer duopolists frequently manage to collude tacitly, particularly in long sessions. These observations indicate that market power is not the only determinant of supracompetitive pricing. The issue is whether market power has an effect that is independent of other determinants.

Recall from chapter 3 that supracompetitive prices were sometimes observed in double auctions when sellers were given market power. Davis and Williams (1991) ran a parallel series of double and posted-offer auctions for the market-power design discussed in section 3.5. This design, which is reproduced on the left side of figure 4.10, has the property that either seller S1 or seller S2 can profitably manipulate the price by withholding marginally profitable, high-cost units from the market.[19] This withholding would shift the supply curve to the left and would raise price from the competitive level P_c to a higher price P_p.

The mean contract price paths for four posted-offer sessions using simulated buyers are illustrated in the upper panel on the right side of figure 4.10.[20] For

---

[16] A similar phenomenon has been observed in the job market for economics professors. Every fall there is a survey in which department chairpersons report the starting salary that they intend to offer during the upcoming recruiting season. Many chairs have come to realize that actual salary offers are several thousand dollars above the announced levels.

[17] This literature is surveyed in Holt (1989, 1992).

[18] Market power can also arise as a consequence of regulation. For example, Kujal (1992) shows that firm-specific output quotas can give sellers unilateral incentives to raise prices.

[19] There are five buyers and five sellers in this design. The units for small sellers S3, S4, and S5 are not highlighted in figure 4.10, but these units occupy the blank spaces on the aggregate supply curve.

[20] Buyer withholding, or fear of withholding, can affect performance in this design. Davis and Williams (1991) report an additional four posted-offer markets with human buyers. In two of these markets, considerably lower price paths were observed. In the session with the most competitive prices, a single buyer very successfully engaged in counter-withholding. In a second session, price cycled down but then rose again. Although there was no evidence of strategic buyer behavior in this session, this

comparison, the results of four double-auction sessions with human buyers are
illustrated in the bottom right panel. In each case, sessions using experienced
participants are denoted by bolded lines, while the unbolded lines denote sessions
with inexperienced participants. From inspection of the figure, the supracompetitive
prices for double-auction markets in the market power design are clear (as noted in
chapter 3). Supracompetitive prices are also generated in posted-offer markets, but
market power appears to have a much larger effect in this case: Mean contract
prices are well below P_p in each of the double-auction sessions, and at or above P_p
in the closing periods of each posted-offer session.

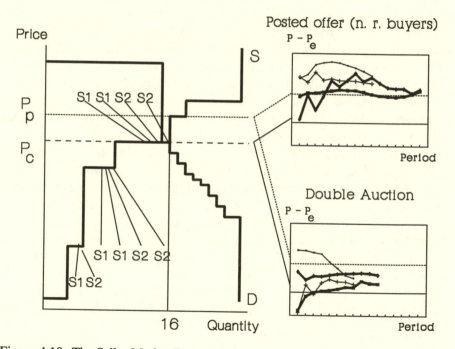

Figure 4.10 The Seller-Market-Power Design, and Mean Contract Prices for Four
Posted-Offer and Four Double-Auction Sessions (Source: Davis and Williams,
1991). Bolded lines denote sessions using experienced participants.

Why are such high posted prices observed in this design? A theorist looking
for an explanation would analyze this situation as a "Bertrand" game, by calculating
the Nash equilibrium prices. The Nash equilibrium may or may not coincide with
the competitive equilibrium. One possible interpretation of market power is that

---

outcome is consistent with results by Brown-Kruse (1991), who concludes that concerns about the
possibility of strategic buyer behavior may generally induce conservative pricing. In particular, Brown-
Kruse finds that markets with human buyers converge to competitive levels more quickly.

sellers are drawn to the game-theoretic Nash equilibrium prediction, when the two equilibria differ. With a few notable exceptions, however, people have done posted-offer experiments for years without identifying Nash equilibria. The calculation of Nash equilibria is useful both for the analysis of market power effects and for designing and evaluating other types of experiments. For these reasons, we discuss the analysis of Nash equilibria in posted-offer markets in the next subsection.

A More Precise Test

A subsequent experiment by Davis and Holt (1991) allows more direct evaluation of the effects of market power on posted prices. We simplify the above market-power design to make possible the calculation of the Nash equilibrium. Moreover, to distinguish the effects of market power from other factors that might increase prices (such as the number of sellers, or the shapes of aggregate supply-and-demand arrays), it is important to control for these alternative factors. We control for possible "numbers" and "supply and demand" effects, by constructing an alternative design that holds these factors constant, but where market power is not present.

Supply-and-demand arrays for "no-power" and "power" designs are illustrated in the upper and lower panels on the left side of figure 4.11. Note that aggregate supply-and-demand arrays are the same in each case: As a group, sellers may offer eleven units for sale. Five of the units cost $1.05 each, while the six remaining units cost $2.59 each. A simulated, price-taking buyer was programmed to reveal demand fully; that is, to purchase eight units at prices at or below $5.39, and to purchase three additional units at any price at or below the competitive equilibrium price of $3.09. Each design also has the same number of sellers (five), and seller identities are printed below each unit on the aggregate supply curves.

The designs differ in the way that units are allocated among the sellers. In the no-power design, illustrated in the upper panel, sellers S1, S2, and S3 are each endowed with three units, while sellers S4 and S5 each have one unit. Due to the excess supply of three units at any price above $3.09, there is no market power in this design. At any price above $3.09, only eight of the eleven units are demanded. A unilateral price increase by one of the large sellers will reduce profits for that seller to 0, because the buyer will first purchase the eight lower-priced units available from the other sellers and will be unwilling to buy a ninth unit at a price above the competitive price level. For the same reason, a price increase by a small seller will also result in no sales.

The highest competitive price turns out to be a Nash equilibrium in this design, since unilateral price decreases are also unprofitable: The entire market capacity is

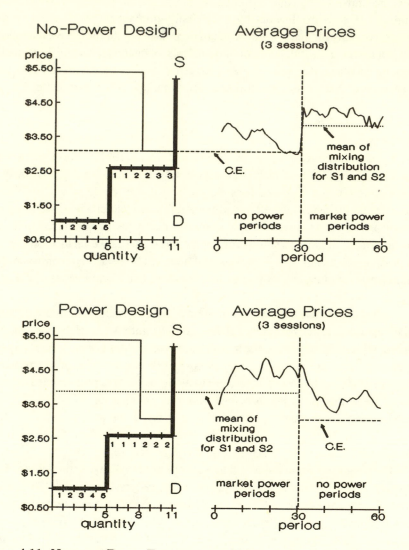

Figure 4.11 No-power/Power Treatments, and Mean Price Series (Source: Davis and Holt, 1991)

purchased at $3.09 or any lower price, so a price decrease will only have the effect of decreasing earnings on units that would sell anyway at $3.09. At this Nash-equilibrium price, sellers S1, S2, and S3 each earn $3.04; $2.04 from the sale of their first unit ($3.09 – $1.05), plus $1.00 from the sale of the second and third units ($3.09 – $2.59 for each unit). Sellers S4 and S5 each earn $2.04.[21]

Market power is introduced in the bottom panel of the figure by reallocating S3's two high-cost units to S1 and S2. With this reallocation, S1 and S2 each have a capacity of four units, and they earn $3.54 ($2.04 + $.50 + $.50 + $.50) at the competitive price of $3.09. The additional capacity, however, makes unilateral price deviations profitable for these sellers. For example, since the buyer will purchase eight units at prices up to $5.39, and since sellers S2, S3, S4 and S5 can supply at most seven units, seller S1 is certain to sell one (low-cost) unit by posting a price of $5.39. Profits from the sale of this single unit are $4.34 ($5.39 – $1.05), which exceed the earnings at the competitive price level. Thus, the competitive equilibrium is not a Nash equilibrium in this power design.

It is tedious but straightforward to verify that no equilibrium involving pure strategies exists in the power design. This can be seen as follows. First, note that small sellers S3, S4, and S5 have no power, and each of these sellers will try to price below S1 and S2 to insure the sale of their single unit. Thus, the large sellers will compete for the residual five units at prices in some range below the demand intercept at $5.39 but above the small sellers' prices. The upper limit of this range, $5.39, cannot be a Nash equilibrium, since either large seller has an incentive to "shade" or slightly undercut the other and sell four of the five residual units. The incentive to price shade remains at any price above a lower bound price p_{min}, where profits from the sale of all four units are no greater than the certain or "security" profits of $4.34 that can be earned by selling a single unit at the limit price. The resulting equation that determines p_{min} is

$$3(p_{min} - \$2.59) + (p_{min} - \$1.05) = \$4.34.$$

It follows from simple algebra that $p_{min} = \$3.29$. Neither is p_{min} a Nash equilibrium, since there is excess supply at a common price of p_{min}, and therefore, neither S1 nor S2 would expect to sell the four units necessary for earnings at p_{min} to equal the security earnings.

The unique Nash equilibrium for the power design involves randomization over the range between p_{min} and the demand intercept of $5.39. This equilibrium involves different pricing distributions for the large and the small sellers. The calculation of this equilibrium is discussed in appendix A4.3. For the present purpose, it is

---

[21] It follows from this discussion that the competitive equilibrium is a "strong" Nash equilibrium; i.e., a seller's profits actually fall when price is either increased or decreased unilaterally from a common competitive price. To increase further the drawing power of the competitive equilibrium, Davis and Holt included the low-cost units at $1.05 to ensure a reasonable level of earnings for sellers at the competitive price. These features were thought to be necessary, since the prices in pilot sessions with simpler designs were not regularly drawn to the competitive price, especially when this price was a weak Nash equilibrium or when it generated very low earnings.

sufficient to note that, for all sellers, most of the weight of the price density function is in the lower portion of range of randomization. The mean of the randomizing distribution for the large sellers is $3.88.

We conducted six sessions in these power and no-power designs. Participants were all experienced.[22] Each session consisted of two thirty-period sequences, one sequence conducted under the power treatment and the other conducted under the no-power treatment. To control for possible sequencing effects, the no-power treatment was presented first in three sessions and last in the remaining three sessions.

The two panels on the right side of figure 4.11 summarize results of this experiment. In each panel, the dashed vertical line indicates the treatment change. The dashed horizontal line indicates the competitive price (a Nash equilibrium in the no-power design). The dotted horizontal line represents the mean of the mixing distribution for the large sellers (in the power design). The upper panel illustrates average prices for the three sessions where the no-power treatment was presented first, while the lower right panel presents average prices for the three sessions where the power treatment was presented first. The addition of market power clearly increases prices. Regardless of the treatment sequencing order, average prices are substantially higher when power is present. Importantly, it is also evident from the right panels in figure 4.11 that participants do not use the equilibrium randomizing distribution in the power treatment. Rather, average prices rather uniformly exceed the mean of the mixed distribution, suggesting that tacit collusion may be one consequence of market power.

Experiments by Davis, Holt, and Villamil (1990) and, in a very different design, by Kruse et al. (1990), yield a similar conclusion: Static Nash equilibrium predictions appear to have more drawing power than competitive predictions in posted-offer markets. The presence of market power represents one important reason that Nash and competitive predictions can differ, and supracompetitive prices are persistently generated even in relatively thick posted-offer markets when such power is present. Although static Nash equilibrium predictions outperform alternatives, Nash equilibria are not perfect predictors of behavior when the predictions involve randomization.[23] In particular, sellers are sometimes able to collude tacitly and raise prices above the average levels that are generated by a Nash (noncooperative) equilibrium. Moreover, the multiplicity of cost and valuation steps often impedes calculation of Nash equilibria in many "normal" market designs.

---

[22] Procedures deviated slightly from those standard to posted-offer markets to better match the informational assumptions underlying the game-theoretic equilibrium predictions. In particular, sellers were provided complete information regarding cost and demand conditions, and they were also told the number of periods. All sessions were computerized.

[23] A general approach to calculating Nash equilibria in posted-offer markets is developed by Holt and Solis-Soberon (1990b).

4.6 Regulation and Restraint of Monopoly Power

Given that prices can rise above competitive levels in concentrated or monopolized posted-offer markets, it is natural to consider mechanisms that may constrain market power. Direct regulatory control is the traditional response to monopoly, but there is a recent interest in more decentralized alternatives. The first subsection that follows reviews experiments that implement some of these decentralized regulatory schemes. The second subsection reviews experiments designed to evaluate the argument that potential competition is as effective as actual competition in regulating monopoly power. The final subsection considers the reverse proposition, that is, whether an aggressive seller can price in a predatory manner to secure a monopoly position, despite the presence of potential competition. Since predatory pricing is difficult to document in antitrust cases, there is considerable interest in whether it can be observed in the laboratory.

Decentralized Regulatory Proposals

Rate-of-return regulation is the most standard response to monopoly pricing. Typically, a regulatory agency reviews a monopolist's operating costs and then establishes a price that is high enough to provide a reasonable rate of return on capital investment. Regulation of this type creates obvious incentive problems: A rational monopolist should try to inflate both costs and the rate base. But even aside from these incentive problems, rate-of-return regulation is at best average-cost pricing, since no subsidies are involved and the firm is not forced to produce at a loss. In "natural" (decreasing-cost) monopolies, this creates additional inefficiencies, because it fails to induce the sale of marginal, low-cost units.

The problem facing the regulator of a decreasing-cost monopolist is illustrated in the left panel in figure 4.12. The lowest regulated price that will not result in losses is p_c, since average cost exceeds average revenue at any lower price. But the resulting quantity, q_c, is inefficient because price exceeds marginal cost at this quantity. The efficient quantity, q_e, is determined by the intersection of demand and marginal cost. The efficiency loss associated with q_c is illustrated in figure 4.12 as the triangle (filled in with crossed lines) bounded by q_c, marginal cost, and demand.

Given the heavy informational requirements and the inherent inefficiency of rate-of-return regulation, there is considerable interest in alternative regulatory schemes. Loeb and Magat (1979) proposed a mechanism in which the regulator induces efficient outcomes by promising to pay a subsidy equal to the Marshallian consumer surplus available at the monopolist's selected price. In terms of the left panel of figure 4.12, the regulator pays a subsidy equal to the area below the demand curve and above the selected price. For example, given a selected price of p_m, the regulator will pay a subsidy equal to the area of the triangle bounded by p_m,

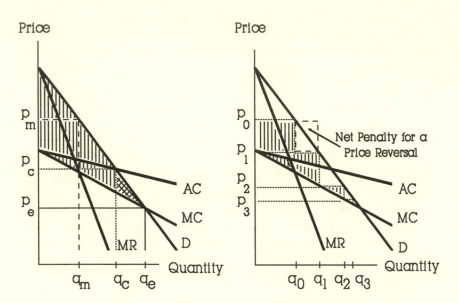

Figure 4.12 Loeb-Magat and Finsinger-Vogelsang Regulatory Mechanisms

the demand curve, and the vertical axis. Therefore, the total revenue (subsidy plus sales revenue) for each quantity is the area under the demand curve to the left of that quantity. This payment forces the profit-maximizing monopolist to consider consumer welfare. For each unit produced, the monopolist incurs the additional cost determined by the MC curve, and therefore, total cost for any quantity is just the area below the MC curve to the left of that quantity.[24] It follows from these observations that the profit for any quantity is the area between the demand curve and the marginal cost curve to the left of that quantity. This profit is maximized by picking price p_e and producing quantity q_e. At any price above p_e, less than q_e will be produced, and some portion of the shaded profit area will be forgone. Thus, the subsidy has the effect of making the monopolist's postsubsidy marginal revenue curve correspond to the market demand curve. In essence, the Loeb-Magat procedure eliminates welfare loss by allowing the monopolist to engage in perfect price discrimination.

Harrison and McKee (1985) show that when participants are provided full demand information, the Loeb-Magat mechanism works nicely in the laboratory; prices are driven down to efficient levels. This can be seen in table 4.5, which summarizes observed M values for unregulated monopolies, for monopolies regulated under the Loeb-Magat procedure, and for contested natural monopolies (to be

---

[24] For simplicity, fixed costs will be ignored in this discussion.

discussed in the next subsection). The column entitled Loeb-Magat Regulation in table 4.5 reveals that this mechanism generates negative M values, indicating that monopolists are nearly efficient. In particular, they extract an even lower proportion of the rents than would be extracted by a "competitive" producer (e.g., a producer who sets price equal average cost).[25] Harrison and McKee (1985) also found that the large subsidies generated by this mechanism could be eliminated by having prospective monopolists bid for the right to be a monopolist.[26]

Table 4.5 Effects of Monopoly Restraint Mechanisms on Monopoly Effectiveness in Decreasing-Cost Monopolies

	M Values		
	Monopoly	Loeb-Magat Regulation	Contested Market
Coursey, Isaac, and Smith (1984)	.56*		.02*
Harrison and McKee (1985)	.72	−.36	.09
Harrison, McKee, and Rutström (1989)	.78	−.24	.06

Key: * Denotes human buyers. Experienced sellers were used in all sessions.

Although an auction for the right to be a monopolist may mitigate the surplus transferred to a monopolist under the Loeb-Magat mechanism, the mechanism is impractical in its assumption that the regulatory agency possesses information sufficient to calculate the surplus-based subsidies accurately. Finsinger and Vogelsang (1981) proposed a modification designed to reduce this informational burden. In this modified mechanism, the subsidy is an approximation of Marshallian surplus that is calculated on the basis of *observed* prices and quantities. Let p_0 and q_0 denote the initial (supracompetitive) price and quantity charged by a monopolist before the rule is implemented, and let p_t and q_t denote the prices and quantities demanded in period $t = 1, 2 \ldots$. First consider the case of price decreases. The subsidy in period 1 is $q_0[p_0 - p_1]$, which is a reward that is proportional to the price reduction. This is a permanent reward that is paid in all subsequent periods. The

---

[25] In a natural monopoly, price competition would not be expected to lead to marginal cost prices (that would generate losses). The average-cost price, which is the lowest uniform price that does not generate losses, is commonly used as a point of reference. For the case of decreasing costs, the average-cost price is used to calculate "competitive" profits in the formula for monopoly M values.

[26] They used a second-price auction designed to induce demand revelation with risk-neutral subjects, and they preselected their subjects on the basis of a test for risk neutrality. Incentive properties of the second-price auction are discussed in chapter 5.

subsidy in each subsequent period is the sum of rewards for previous price cuts, plus the quantity-weighted value of the current price reduction. With a price decrease from p_1 to p_2, for example, the period 2 subsidy increases to $q_0[p_0 - p_1] + q_1[p_1 - p_2]$.

The effects of providing subsidies according to observed price/quantity combinations are illustrated on the right side of figure 4.12. The temporal sequence of selecting progressively lower prices generates a step-wise approximation to the demand curve. As in the Loeb-Magat mechanism, profits are the difference between the marginal cost curve and the (step-wise approximation to) the demand curve. This difference is represented by the shaded areas on the right side of figure 4.12. The mechanism elicits efficient quantities, since for any price above p_e, a sequential price reduction creates an additional small profit triangle. Importantly, the mechanism has the added feature that it requires no knowledge of the demand curve. Moreover, depending on the size of the price "steps," both the subsidies and profits can be considerably lower than under the Loeb-Magat mechanism, as can be seen by comparing the shaded areas on the left and right sides of figure 4.12.

A potential problem associated with implementing this mechanism is that a price *increase* results in a penalty that must be paid in all future periods. This effect can be seen by considering a price decrease followed by an equal price increase. In figure 4.12, for example, a price decrease from p_0 to p_1 generates a subsidy payment of $(p_0 - p_1)q_0$. This subsidy is lost if the monopolist reverses the price reduction. But the loss is more than complete: An increase from p_1 back to p_0 reduces the subsidy by $(p_1 - p_0)q_1$. The difference of benefits from a price decrease and penalties from a price increase generates a net penalty of $(p_1 - p_0)(q_1 - q_0)$, or the area in the figure identified as the "net penalty for a price cycle." In general terms, when prices are uniformly decreased, the Finsinger-Vogelsang mechanism has the effect of generating a step-wise approximation of demand from below. When prices are increased, however, the rule generates a step-wise approximation of demand from above. The difference between these approximations represents the permanent revenue losses from price cycles.

This unforgiving aspect of the mechanism caused bankruptcies in three of the four markets in which it was used in Cox and Isaac (1986). Bankruptcies occurred whether or not the monopolist was given complete information about the demand curve. More recently, Cox and Isaac (1987) developed a modification of the Finsinger-Vogelsang subsidy calculation for the case of a price increase. This modification avoids the penalties generated by price cycles; that is, there is a permanent penalty for permanent price increases, but not for reversed price increases. All ten markets using this new mechanism converged to the optimal (marginal-cost) price outcome.

In summary, decentralized regulatory schemes show considerable promise as a means of alleviating the monopoly-pricing problem in posted-offer markets, at least in the specific environments considered thus far in the laboratory. With demand information, the Loeb-Magat mechanism works very well, and an auction can be used to reduce subsidy payments. In the absence of demand information, the Cox-Isaac modification of the Finsinger-Vogelsang mechanism yields good results, at least in one decreasing-cost environment. Future examinations of this modified regulatory mechanism will likely take place in more sophisticated environments. For example, given the very poor response of posted-offer sellers to demand-side adjustments, it would be worthwhile to assess the performance of regulatory schemes in environments with nonstationary demand.

Potential Competition as a Regulator: Market Contestability

It has been about a hundred years since Clark (1887) emphasized the role of latent competition and raised the question of whether it would be as effective as actual competition in restraining monopoly pricing. More recently, the theory of contestable markets has formalized the effects of potential entry in a way that highlights the importance of sunk costs. To evaluate the design conditions of alternative experimental studies of market contestability, it is necessary to review the requirements of the theory for the special case of single-product markets used in laboratory tests to date.

Baumol, Panzar, and Willig (1982, p. 6) characterize a *contestable market* as one in which (1) there is at least one potential rival, (2) "potential entrants evaluate the profitability of entry at the incumbent firm's prices," and (3) there are no barriers to entry or exit, and in particular, there is a possibility of hit-and-run entry: "Such entrants need not fear changes in prices by the incumbent firms for, if and when such reactions do occur, . . . that firm need only exit." Therefore, there can be no sunk costs, and costs return to zero following exit. The fundamental result is that a contestable market can only be in equilibrium if the prices and quantities of the incumbent firm are *sustainable*, which in turn requires that no new firm with the same cost function as the incumbent can earn a profit by charging a lower price and serving all or part of the demand at that lower price. For the decreasing-cost, natural-monopoly environment considered in the laboratory, any equilibrium must involve the incumbent choosing the price and quantity for which demand equals average cost. For the special case of the single market, the price-equals-average-cost outcome is said to be the Ramsey-optimal outcome. As discussed above, this outcome cannot be fully efficient, since efficiency involves marginal-cost pricing, and subsidies to cover losses. But reliance on contestability has the advantage that it does not require demand information or subsidies.

The formal statement of the contestable markets theory does not predict that the average-cost pricing outcome will be always observed, but this seems to be the position taken by the theory's proponents: "Even if it is run by a monopoly, a contestable market will yield only zero profits and offer inducements for the adoption of Ramsey-optimal prices" (Baumol, Panzar, and Willig, 1982, p. 292). In particular, the assertion is that, in the absence of sunk costs, potential competition is as good as actual competition, and that even horizontal mergers among potential entrants that do not alter contestability will not have harmful effects.

Coursey, Isaac, and Smith (1984) conducted an experiment designed to evaluate the effects of contestability. It is instructive to examine their supply-and-demand configuration, because minor variations of this design were used in all of the experiments summarized below. In figure 4.13, marginal cost and demand are represented by bolded lines, marginal revenue by an unbolded line, and average cost by a dotted line. Given the discrete cost and valuation steps, marginal cost and marginal revenue intersect twice, as shown by the x's on the marginal-cost curve. The dashed horizontal line at P_m represents the lowest monopoly price. In this context, a "competitive price" is the Ramsey-optimal price, that is, the incumbent's average-cost price, which occurs over the range bounded by the parallel dashed lines labeled P_c.[27] Coursey, Isaac, and Smith evaluate the drawing power of P_c in a contested market, by adding a second seller with costs identical to those for the seller shown in figure 4.13. Note in the figure that, barring a conspiracy to restrict quantity, a single seller will exhaust demand at P_c. Thus, only one noncooperative seller earns profits in any period.

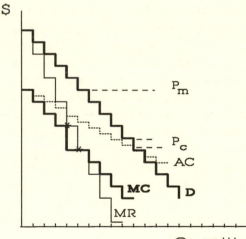

Figure 4.13 Pricing Predictions for a Natural Monopolist (Source: Coursey, Isaac, and Smith, 1984)

Ramsey-optimal outcomes predominated in the contested markets reported by Coursey, Isaac, and Smith: Four of their duopolies resulted in competitive price outcomes, and the other two exhibited downward price trends, with final period

---

[27] Of course, the fully efficient outcome, where the marginal cost and demand curves intersect, is not sustainable in this design since these curves do not cross at a positive price.

prices being closer to competitive than to monopoly prices. Average final-period market efficiency increased from 49 percent in the monopoly markets to 86 percent in the contested markets. Also, as shown in the first row of table 4.5, the final-period value of the monopoly effectiveness parameter, averaged across experiments, was .02, which is significantly lower than the M value of .56 for the benchmark monopoly markets. Similar low values of the monopoly effectiveness parameter were observed by Harrison and McKee (1985), and by Harrison, McKee, and Rutström (1989), as summarized in the second and third rows of table 4.5, even though the buyers in both experiments were simulated.

Contestable market theory would have little practical value for policy makers if the theory were sensitive to "small" sunk cost imperfections. Coursey et al. (1984) take the same decreasing-cost structure shown in figure 4.13 and introduce a sunk cost in the nature of a five-period operating license. This license had a price of $2.00, which is less than the theoretical monopoly profit. The "incumbent" was initially required to purchase this license, while the other seller stayed out and earned a "normal rate of return." After a specified number of periods, either or both firms could purchase the license; purchase decisions were made independently. (This is a sunk cost, because it cannot be recovered following exit.) The prices supported the "weak contestable markets hypothesis," in the sense that prices were closer to the competitive (Ramsey-optimal) level than to the natural monopoly level in all twelve sessions, six with simulated buyers and six with human buyers. But prices actually converged to the competitive level in only about half of the sessions, as compared with the two-thirds that had converged without sunk costs in Coursey, Isaac, and Smith (1984). Moreover, no single-seller, competitive natural monopoly was observed; the entrant entered in all twelve sessions in period 6, and all exiting sellers later reentered the market if given the chance, that is, if the market did not terminate. Despite the uniformly low prices, Gilbert (1989) argues that the observed entry in the sunk-cost environment is inconsistent with contestable markets theory because of the inefficient duplication of the license fees. (License fees used in the laboratory can correspond to real sunk costs in industrial markets.)

One prominent criticism of these experiments is that requiring sellers to post prices that remain in effect throughout a trading period deviates from the "hit-and-run entry" assumptions in contestability. Millner, Pratt, and Reilly (1990) surmounted this difficulty by implementing a continuous-time variant of the standard posted offer. In this "flow-market" institution, sellers provide units at a posted, per-second rate. There are no time periods, so sellers may change prices, and buyers may switch between sellers at any time. At any moment, sellers also have the option of withdrawing from the market and earning a constant per-second return in a "safe haven." The flow market much more nearly corresponds to "hit-and-run entry" than the standard posted-offer implementation: In their design, the seller with the lowest price at any instant generally makes all sales, and in this sense is the incumbent. The other seller can observe the price and decide whether to price below it. Since the probability of an incumbent's price change is essentially zero on a sufficiently short time interval, the entrant can be very sure that a price cut will initially capture the market. In addition, exit can be almost instantaneous.

The flow-market sessions were conducted in a decreasing-cost design similar to that used by Coursey et al. and used simulated, continuous-time buyers. Data from a representative session are shown in figure 4.14. The mean transactions price series for the last twenty-seven minutes of the thirty-minute session is shown in the upper panel of the figure. Notice that prices cycled from a minimum sustainable price, P_c, to levels that exceed the monopoly price, P_m. The lower panel illustrates price-posting behavior for the duopolists over the time segment between minutes 10 and 15. The dashed and solid lines represent prices posted by two sellers, S1 and S2, respectively. The lines are broken when a seller exits the market. As the lower panel suggests, sellers readily exercise their capacity to "hit and run." At the beginning of minute 10, for example, S1 (indicated by the solid line) is in the market alone, at a price near P_c. Seller S1 raises his price above P_m, inducing S2 (denoted by the dotted lines) to enter. In response to S2's entry, S1 lowers his price below P_m, setting off a series of price-cutting moves that eventually drive both sellers from the market. The cycle starts again prior to minute 12, when S2 enters again, posting a price so high that no units can sell.[28]

As figure 4.14 suggests, Millner, Pratt and Reilly observed no apparent tendency for pricing to be competitive. In the illustrated market, for example, the frequency of the cycle slowed toward the end of the session, and prices decayed very slowly toward P_m. In other sessions, the price cycles became even more unstable, perhaps approximating a continuous-time analogue of noncooperative randomization in the presence of small adjustment costs or perceptual delays.[29] In any event, the minimum stable price exhibited little drawing power.

This price cycling caused market performance to deteriorate. Compare, for example, mean efficiencies for monopoly and contested-duopoly sessions in the two Coursey et. al. experiments with those observed by Millner, Pratt, and Reilly, as summarized in table 4.6. From the first two rows of the table, it is seen that contestability unambiguously improves efficiency in the posted-offer markets.[30] In contrast, efficiencies in the flow markets, summarized in the third and fourth rows, were quite low, with mean efficiencies for experienced subjects not much different

---

[28] Notice in the upper panel of figure 4.14 that the transactions price series remains broken until prices are bid down to P_m, after minute 12.

[29] In a very narrow and uninteresting sense, this unstable behavior is consistent with the formal "fundamental result" of contestability theory, that is, that any equilibrium must be sustainable, at least as long as the concept of equilibrium precludes unstable behavior.

[30] Efficiencies in Coursey et al. (1985) are averages from the sessions using human buyers, and the reported E values for their sessions exclude losses from inefficient entry, and thus overstate efficiency.

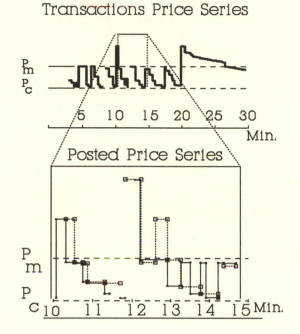

Figure 4.14 Mean Transactions Price Series (top) and Representative Pricing Behavior (bottom) for Decreasing-Cost Duopolists in a Flow Market

from the theoretical efficiency in a monopoly.[31]

Considering the results from both the standard discrete-time and the continuous-time flow market experiments, we believe that modifications in contestability theory are warranted. Results from discrete-time posted-offer experiments show that there exists a class of environments where the addition of an equally efficient potential competitor can reduce monopoly effectiveness to competitive levels. The erratic pricing and low efficiencies observed in the continuous-time flow markets, however, suggest that the environment articulated in the theory may not be a member of that class. In particular, sellers' commitment to posting prices that remain in effect for an entire trading period in the standard posted-offer environment indicates that certain inflexibilities, such as menu adjustment costs, may be critical to generating sustained competitive outcomes in contested markets with decreasing-cost sellers.

---

[31] As in the case of all contestable markets experiments, the competitive equilibrium benchmark used in efficiency calculations is the allocation that maximizes total surplus, subject to the constraint that no firm earn a loss. Therefore, the competitive equilibrium in this context involves a price-equals-average-cost condition for the incumbent.

Table 4.6   Effects of Contestability on Market Efficiency in Posted-Offer Markets
with Decreasing Costs

	Experience	Efficiency = (Realized Surplus/CE Surplus)		
		Predicted under Monopoly	Observed under Monopoly	Observed in Contested Market
Coursey, Isaac, and Smith (1984)	RX	60	49	86
Coursey, Isaac, Luke, and Smith (1985)	RX	60	--	82
Millner, Pratt, and Reilly (1990)	NX	50–60	55*	67*
Millner, Pratt, and Reilly (1990)	DX, RX	50–60	--	62*

Key: * - Simulated Buyers, NX - Inexperienced Participants, RX - Role Experience,
DX - Design Experience.

Additional experimentation in this area could answer questions about the importance of assumptions implicit in most designs examined to date, for example, that exit from the market generates zero earnings. In contrast, Millner, Pratt, and Reilly (1990) and Brown-Kruse (1991) report designs in which potential entrants could earn a positive rate of return by remaining in a "safe-haven." But the availability of even a sizable, but deterministic, fixed payment for staying out of the market may fail to discourage inefficient entry, because subjects probably feel a desire to be "in" rather than "out." The construction of an interesting, market-like alternative to entry may discourage inefficient entry. Experiments that deal directly with the policy implications of contestable markets theory would also be valuable. For example, is it really irrelevant that a horizontal merger wave among potential entrants will have no effect on performance in a contestable market?

Predatory Pricing

The existence of predatory pricing is one of the more controversial issues in industrial organization. Most, but not all, would agree that companies such as Standard Oil of New Jersey had engaged in predatory pricing behavior that reduces the predator's current profits in a manner that can only be justified by the prospect of subsequent monopoly profits. Nevertheless, barring barriers to entry, it is difficult to believe that a seller will sustain losses to inhibit entry. For this reason, and predatory behavior is thought to be rare. Since it is usually difficult to document predatory intent, and since even a perfectly competitive firm would never price below marginal cost, antitrust scholars have proposed the use of cost-based tests. Consequently, the arguments in predation cases often center on cost and profit/loss measurements. Laboratory experiments simply cannot address many of the issues concerning nonpredatory incentives to cut prices, such as the incentive to expand market share in order to reduce costs by moving down the experience curve, since the critical issue is the existence of learning-curve effects in naturally occurring markets.[32] On the other hand, costs do not have to be measured in the laboratory, so it is possible to spot behavior that cannot be optimal except as an attempt to exclude competitors.

Recall that the contestable-markets experiments involved sellers with identical technologies, and that even though profits were driven down to low levels, market dominance by one seller was not observed. Isaac and Smith (1985) conducted a series of posted-offer experiments in which they modified earlier contestable-markets designs so that two firms would efficiently exist in the market at competitive prices. The firms were asymmetric, with one firm, the incumbent, enjoying significant advantages in higher capacity, lower costs, and a larger initial cash endowment to cover any losses. Further, although an efficient competitive outcome would involve both sellers, there was a range of prices and quantity limits for which the incumbent, by selling some units below marginal cost, could prevent the other seller from being able to sell any units at a profit.[33] Predatory pricing of this nature was not observed in any of the markets, even after introducing several other design variations (e.g., sunk costs) intended to be progressively more favorable to such pricing, and hence the title "In Search of Predatory Pricing."[34] The most common outcome appeared to be a dominant-firm outcome, which is the price that maximizes the incumbent's profit along its residual demand function, obtained by subtracting the entrant's supply from market demand. This configuration is apparently not a Nash equilibrium for the single-period market game, and such an equilibrium was not provided.

---

[32] But it is possible to structure laboratory incentives so that sellers' costs are reduced by cumulated production experience, and in this manner, the effects (but not the existence) of a learning-curve can be evaluated experimentally.

[33] These sessions were conduced using the NovaNet implementation of the posted offer. Importantly, this implementation was altered to permit price and quantity choices that yielded losses.

[34] Isaac and Smith do not rule out the possibility of predation in other contexts, and they mention asymmetric information situations in which the incumbent may wish to predate in early periods to build a reputation.

A subsequent series of sessions implemented two restrictions on predatory pricing that had been proposed in the antitrust literature: a prohibition of quantity expansion by the incumbent for two periods after entry, and a prohibition of temporary price cuts, that is, price cuts by the incumbent after entry had to be maintained for five periods. The effect of this policy was to raise prices dramatically and to reduce efficiency.[35] These experimental results are important since the implementation of anti-predation policies with side effects would be unfortunate if predatory pricing is rare.

Harrison (1988) cleverly modified the Isaac and Smith (1985) design; he conducted a single posted-offer session with five separate markets. There were eleven sellers, each of whom could only enter one market at a time. Seven of the sellers were given the same cost function for each market; these firms would have the cost function of a small (low-capacity/high-cost) firm in the Isaac and Smith design, regardless of the market that they entered. The other four sellers could be a large firm in one market or a small firm in any one of the other four markets. The high-capacity, low-cost structure matched that of the large firm in the Isaac and Smith design, and there was only one potential large firm in each of four markets; in this sense, each potential large firm had its own market. Demand in each market was simulated and corresponded to the demand in Isaac and Smith. Harrison observed numerous instances of predatory pricing. In some cases, the price and quantity limits of the large seller in a market were such that this seller would make a loss. Harrison even reports cases of the small seller pricing below the average cost of the larger, more efficient seller. Probably due to financial constraints, Harrison's procedures were rather unusual: All participants were students in Harrison's class, who had participated in three different but related decreasing-cost posted-offer markets. The incidence of predatory outcomes might be affected by classroom interactions. Given the novelty of these predatory pricing results, it would be worthwhile to replicate this multimarket session under more standard conditions.[36]

To summarize, predatory pricing is not observed in simple posted-offer market environments that, in some respects, are quite favorable to predatory behavior. Moreover, some prominent antipredation proposals for limiting the price and quantity responses of an incumbent can have perverse effects in laboratory markets. But the provision of an interesting alternative market to serve as the home base for the prey does sometimes yield predatory outcomes.

---

[35] Holt and Solis-Soberon (1990a) analyze the theoretical effects of quantity and price-based antipredation policies in posted-offer environments.

[36] Jung, Kagel, and Levin (1991) observe behavior that can be interpreted as predatory in the context of a noncooperative game. "Signaling" games of this type are discussed in chapter 7.

Summary

Available laboratory evidence certainly does not provide definitive answers to any of the three issues reviewed in this section. The research, however, raises a number of important questions in each area. Contestability appears to control monopoly rather effectively in discrete-time, single-goods environments. But modification of the posted-offer environment to more nearly meet the "hit-and-run entry" assumption appears to weaken market performance. Certainly, this result raises questions about the range of application of contestability. On the other hand, decentralized mechanisms for monopoly restraint appear to show some promise. Future efforts in this regard should address performance in more complicated environments. Finally, predation appears to be rare. Predatory pricing was not observed in standard, single-good posted-offer markets. It has been observed, however, in a more complicated context, where sellers may offer goods in several markets. Further exploration of predation in multiple-market contexts is clearly needed.

4.7 Conclusions

The experiments summarized in this chapter illustrate the prominent effects that alterations in the trading institution can exert on market outcomes. The posted-offer auction allows much less interaction between buyers and sellers than is the case for the double auction. The reduced interaction cuts negotiation costs. This savings, however, comes at some cost in terms of performance. Posted-offer markets tend to competitive predictions more slowly than comparable double auctions, and they tend to converge to the competitive price prediction from above (if at all), implying a transfer of surplus from consumers to producers in the adjustment process. Moreover, even relatively thick posted-offer markets respond slowly to conditions of excess supply, and to unanticipated demand shocks.

Unlike the preceding discussion of the double auction in chapter 3, a substantial portion of this chapter has focused on traditional industrial organization and antitrust issues. Monopoly clearly represents a behavioral problem in posted-offer markets; monopolists are able to raise prices above competitive levels, although they are usually unable to exploit their monopoly power fully. In posted-offer duopolies, tacit collusion frequently arises when participants interact for a sufficiently long time period. Posted-offer oligopolies are more competitive, but supracompetitive prices have been observed when sellers are given significant market power or explicit opportunities to communicate and conspire.

Economists are well aware of the inefficiencies of direct regulation of natural monopolies, and a number of decentralized (automatic) regulatory mechanisms have been proposed. These proposals involve ways of subsidizing output increases, and several of these proposals seem to work well in laboratory environments. Theorists have argued that potential entry can also serve as a substitute for monopoly regulation. Experiments with contestable market structures provide significant support for this view, although it does not appear that hit-and-run entry by a single contestant will sustain a stable, competitive outcome.

In closing, we offer a cautionary note regarding the policy implications of these results. There is a broad and diverse array of markets that operate under trading rules that parallel the laboratory posted offer. However, there are many other markets with more complex institutional features.[37] When the production process involves delays, for example, sellers usually make some production decisions in advance of sale. Mestelman and Welland (1988) found that advance, binding production decisions severely damp the "convergence-from-above" characteristic of posted-offer markets.[38] In further research, Mestelman and Welland (1991a) find that inventory possibilities do not eliminate the tendency for posted-offer markets with advance production to be more competitive than those with production to demand.

A second complexity that distinguishes many markets from the standard posted-offer auction is the possibility of secret, buyer-specific discounts. Sellers, for example, frequently offer private, selective price discounts for producer goods and consumer durables. Grether and Plott (1984) report near-competitive prices in markets in which prices are posted but discounts are privately negotiated by telephone. But transactions prices were significantly higher when a discount given to one buyer was required to be given to all others (a "most-favored-customer" clause).[39] Davis and Holt (1990) initiate an investigation of the effects of discounting possibilities and find that discounting opportunities dramatically increase the variability of price outcomes, in a design with few sellers and high shopping costs. In some instances, sellers competed on the basis of both posted prices and discounts, and prices were even lower than those obtained in comparable posted-offer sessions with no discount opportunities. In other instances, sellers did not compete on the basis of the posted prices, and they essentially used the discounting opportunities to price discriminate. These markets generated considerably higher and

---

[37] Charles Plott has probably done more experiments with direct policy applications than any other economist, and has frequently done a commendable job of focusing on the relevant institutional features of a particular natural market. See, e.g., Grether and Plott (1984), Hong and Plott (1982), and Guler and Plott (1988).

[38] The observation that advance production makes these laboratory markets more competitive is a little surprising, since theoretical (Cournot) models with quantity-setting firms yield higher prices than models with price-setting firms and production to demand.

[39] This interpretation is based on a comparison of the Grether and Plott ABNN and LAYY treatments. See Holt (1992) for further discussion.

more variable prices than were observed in posted-offer control sessions with no discounting.[40]

Given the rich and fascinating complexity of markets that evolve naturally in developed economies, there is much interesting research to be done along these lines. The point is that the posted-offer institution provides a very useful basis of comparison with the double auction, but that the standard posted-offer procedure is perhaps too simple for some policy applications. In these cases, the use of experimentation to increase our understanding of market processes will require incorporation of additional features of the naturally occurring markets.

---

[40] Another interesting variation of the posted offer involves the introduction of a research and development stage. This modification allows examination of issues that determine the evolution of market structures in the long run. See Isaac and Reynolds (1992).

APPENDIX A4

A4.1 Instructions for a Posted-Offer Auction[41]

The following paragraphs are to be preceded by the first part of the Double-Auction Instructions in appendix A1.1: the introductory paragraph, "Instructions for Sellers," and "Instructions for Buyers." Posted-offer auction procedures are somewhat different from those of a double auction, so some additional considerations are important. First, the posted-offer period requires less time, but there may be more noise in initial price postings. Therefore, it is useful to modify the buyer and seller decision sheets from appendix A1.2 to allow for ten to fifteen periods. Second, in each period you will be collecting and returning seller decision sheets, so subjects who are given seller role assignments should be seated in an easily accessible place, for example, along aisles. Errors in returning decision sheets to the right sellers can be minimized by seating sellers in an order that corresponds to their identification numbers. Third, buyers are selected for shopping in a random order. For this reason, each buyer must be assigned the color of a marble in the bowl mentioned below. Finally, note that the italicized material in the instructions below is probably too suggestive of specific trading behavior to be used for a research experiment, but this material will eliminate questions in a classroom demonstration.

Trading Rules

All buyers and sellers have identification numbers; your number is given in the upper part of a Decision Sheet that is in your folder. I will begin each trading period with an announcement that each seller has two minutes in which to choose a price, which he or she will write on a Seller Decision Sheet, just above the period number in the column for the current period. Each seller only chooses a single price, so all sales that a seller makes in a period will be at the same price (unlike the example in the Instructions for Sellers above). After all sellers have chosen prices, the decision sheets will be collected and the prices will be written on the blackboard. Sellers' identification numbers will be used to label their prices on the blackboard.

After prices are posted, buyers will be given the opportunity to make whatever purchases they desire. Buyers' bids will be made as follows. Each buyer has a color written after the identification number at the top of his or her Buyer Decision

---

[41] These instructions are adapted from those commonly found in the literature; see Holt (1992) for a discussion of the wording.

Sheet. I have a bowl of colored marbles, which I will hold above my head and use to draw colors in sequence (without replacement). The first buyer selected in this way will be asked to indicate a seller and a desired purchase quantity. The designated seller will then accept any part of the buyer's bid by stating the quantity he or she wishes to sell. If the first seller selected will not sell all units that the buyer wants to purchase, the buyer is free to choose a second seller, and so on.

When the first buyer has made all desired purchases, another marble will be drawn from the bowl, and the buyer indicated by the color of the second draw will make bids in the same manner. The process will continue until all buyers have had a chance to make purchases. This completes the trading period. We will reopen the market for a new trading period by having sellers submit new prices, and the process will be repeated.

[*For example, suppose that there are two buyers, B1 and B2, and two sellers, S1 and S2, who chose prices of 165 and 250 respectively. Then these prices would be written on the blackboard as follows.*

Seller	S1	S2
Price	165	250
Buyer		
Buyer		

Suppose that B2 is the first buyer selected to shop, and that this buyer indicates a desire to purchase two units from seller S1, but that seller S1 only agrees to sell a single unit. Then B2 can request a purchase from another seller. If S2 agrees to sell a unit, the blackboard would appear as follows:

Seller	S1	S2
Price	165	250
Buyer	B2	B2
Buyer		

When B2 has finished making all desired purchases, another buyer is selected. Suppose that the next buyer, B1, requests to buy 2 units from seller S1, who declines. Then B2 can request units from seller S2. If S2 agrees to sell only a single unit, the blackboard will appear:

Seller	S1	S2
Price	165	250
Buyer	B2	B2
Buyer		B1

Since there are only two buyers in this example, the period ends when B1 finishes shopping, and sellers are then given 2 minutes in which to choose prices for the next period.]

Except for bids and their acceptance, you are expected not to speak to any other person.

(Next read the "Procedural Details and Review" from A1.1, followed by:)

Beginning the Session

Each seller should now select a price for the first period. Write this price in the period 1 column, in the space just above the period number and below the phrase "trading period." Do not write in any column other than the column for period 1 at this time. Price choices for each subsequent period will be made at the start of that period.

(After all sellers have made price choices, the seller decision sheets are collected. The experimenter will check to ensure that each seller has properly recorded a single price above the period number. Once all prices have been checked, the sellers' prices are written below their identification numbers on the blackboard. Then a buyer is selected randomly and given a chance to make purchases. The buyer is prompted for a bid as follows.)

The buyer selected is ____. If you wish to make a purchase, please tell me the seller number and the number of units that you would like to purchase. Seller ____, how many units are you willing to sell?

(After the first contract is made, but not after subsequent contracts, read the paragraph that follows.)

At this time both the buyer and seller involved in this contract should calculate their earnings.

— If one unit is sold, read: This buyer and seller have now finished with their 1st units, and the relevant value or cost for them is that of their 2nd unit for period 1.

— If two units are sold, read: The buyer and seller have finished trading for the period.

The rest of you are still considering the sale or purchase of your 1st unit in the period 1 column. Remember that when you make a contract you move down the column for the current period to your 2nd unit; you do not move across a row until the beginning of the next period.

(After the first buyer has finished making all desired purchases, another is selected, and the process is repeated. After all buyers have had an opportunity to make purchases, read:)

Period 1 has ended, and you should add up the earnings on units traded and enter the total in row (7) of the column for this period. If you did not buy or sell a unit, the earnings for that unit are zero. We will erase the blackboard as soon as all transactions prices are recorded. At this time, one of us will come around to your desk to check your calculations. Please do not talk with each other; if you have a question, raise your hand.

(After the final period, read the "Ending the Session" section from A1.1 in chapter 1.)

A4.2 Posted-Offer Instructions for Computer Implementation

These posted-offer instructions are taken from a Turbo-Pascal program for networked personal computers, written by Davis. The value and cost parameters and some hypothetical prices used in the examples are randomly drawn from the interval [$0.00, $9.99]. Details of the distributions and constraints used in generating these random numbers are available on request. The random parameters will typically differ from subject to subject and from session to session. In the instructions that follow, randomly generated parameters are underlined. While working through the instructions, subjects are asked to make price and quantity decisions. In the text that follows, we sometimes selected a decision to generate typical warning messages. Decisions that would be made by a subject appear in parentheses and are boldfaced, for example, (DECISION: **$3.44**).

The instructions are presented to the subjects in windows that are superimposed over the screen displays that have the same structure as those used in the market. Each paragraph in the instructions below corresponds to a new text window on the screen; sentences within a paragraph are generally presented only after the subject presses <ENTER>.

This appendix is intended to convey an appreciation for the benefits of interactive computerized instructions. Some of these benefits cannot be illustrated in printed text, since it is difficult to indicate many of the color cues, cursor movements, and other graphics features that facilitate understanding of the screen displays.

Instructions

This is an experiment in the economics of market decision making. Funding for this project has been provided by the National Science Foundation. In this experiment, your earnings will be determined by your own decisions and the decisions of others, as described in the following instructions. SO IT IS VERY IMPORTANT THAT YOU READ THESE INSTRUCTIONS CAREFULLY.

All of the money that you earn will be paid to you privately IN CASH immediately following the end of the experiment.

In this experiment some of you are sellers and some of you are buyers of a commodity. Sellers initially have the ability to produce one or more units of the commodity.

Sellers

Price	Unit Cost	Profit (Price − Unit Cost)
3.06	2.31	0.75
	3.99	

For example, the seller in the box [above] has the ability to produce two units. Sellers pay a production cost for each unit they sell. In this case the production costs are $2.31 for the first unit, and $3.99 for the second. EACH SELLER'S COST INFORMATION IS PRIVATE AND WILL BE REVEALED TO NO ONE.

Sellers' earnings are determined by the difference between the price of the commodity and the production cost. Suppose that the market price for the first unit is $3.06. Then earnings from the sale of the first unit would be $0.75. Earnings for the other unit(s) are determined in the same way.

Now consider earnings for buyers [below, top of next page]. Buyers initially have the ability to purchase one or more units of the commodity, and they receive a monetary payment for each unit they purchase.

For example, the buyer in the above box has the ability to purchase two units. The first unit is worth $5.54 and the second is worth $4.08. EACH BUYER'S VALUE INFORMATION IS PRIVATE AND WILL BE REVEALED TO NO ONE. Buyers' earnings are

Buyers

Unit Value	Price	Profit (Unit Value – Price)
5.54	3.06	2.48
4.08		

determined by the difference between their value for the unit and the price. Suppose that the market price for the first unit is $3.06. Then earnings from the purchase of the first unit would be $2.48. Earnings for the other unit(s) are determined in the same way.

Importantly, the COSTS, VALUATIONS and PRICE used in the preceding example were RANDOMLY GENERATED. All other costs and valuations used in these instructions will also be randomly generated. Aside from the fact that all numbers are between $0.00 and $9.99, any similarity between the costs and valuations you see here and the costs or valuations that you or anyone else faces in the experiment is entirely coincidental.

Now consider the buyer and seller screen displays in today's experiment. The seller's screen is very similar to this display [below]. In the experiment, however, sellers may be able to offer more than the two units shown here.

Unit	Price	Unit Cost	Profit	
1		2.74		
2		4.80		

S1 Period 1

Waiting for a New Trading Period.

Note the message space at the bottom of your screen. The message indicates that the seller is waiting for a new TRADING PERIOD to begin.

Notice also the red [shaded] margin in the message space. The first two characters printed there indicate that the seller in this example is identified as seller

S1. This experiment is divided into a series of trading periods. You've now seen the seller's screen display at the beginning of trading period 1.

Unit	Unit Value	Price	Unit Earnings	
1	<u>6.30</u>			
2	<u>4.57</u>			

B2 Period 1
Waiting for a New Trading Period to Begin.

Now we switch to the screen display [above] for the buyer at the beginning of trading period 1. The buyer's screen at the beginning of a trading period is very similar to this display. Like sellers, buyers may have the opportunity to purchase more than the two units shown. Notice the message in the space at the bottom of the screen. It indicates that a new trading period is about to begin. Note also the purple [shaded] margin above the message. The first two characters in that margin indicate that the buyer in this example is identified as buyer B2.

Consider now the way that prices are determined and trades take place in today's experiment. In the following explanation, you will be given the opportunity to make the decisions faced by both buyers and sellers. In the experiment, however, you will be EITHER a buyer or a seller.

First, sellers post prices. To demonstrate this, we go back and look at the screen display for seller S1 [below, top of next page]. Notice the POSTING PRICES message at the bottom of the screen. This indicates that the price posting sequence has started. Sellers are asked to post a LIST PRICE. Sellers may post any price between $0.00 and $9.99. As explained above, however, sellers make money by selling units at prices greater than costs. Sellers also select a QUANTITY LIMIT. This limit represents the maximum number of units the seller is willing to sell AT THE SELLER'S LIST PRICE. Sellers may offer as many units as they have available. However, if the list price does not exceed the cost of all offered units, the seller may lose earnings.

Now we'll practice actually posting a list price and quantity. You will notice a message at the bottom of the screen asking sellers to "Please select a list price for

Unit	Price	Unit Cost	Profit	
1	4.50	2.74		
2		4.80		

S1   Period 1
Posting Prices. Please select a List Price   List Price: **$4.50**
and press ENTER.   Quantity :
Press r to rechoose or c to continue

this period and press ENTER." DO THIS NOW. (DECISION: **$4.50**)[42]

Press r to rechoose, or c to continue. (DECISION: **c**)

You may profitably offer 1 unit at a price $4.50. Type the number of units you want to offer, and press ENTER. (DECISION: **1**)[43]

After making price and quantity decisions, sellers receive the waiting message at the bottom of the screen [below, top of next page]. In the experiment, sellers wait until all sellers have posted prices. To continue with these instructions, press <ENTER>.

You will see a variety of "waiting" messages at the bottom of your screen in various parts of these instructions. Although a buyer or seller would wait at these points in the experiment, do not wait in these instructions. To continue through the instructions, always press ENTER.

---

[42] Warnings are given for unprofitable prices. For example, a posting of $2.00 would generate the following response: WARNING: You cannot profitably sell any units for **$2.00**. You must charge at least $2.74 to make any profit.

[43] The participant is free to offer unprofitable units but will receive a warning. For example, if seller S1 in the instructions had selected a quantity of 2 after picking a price of $4.50, then the following message would appear on the screen:

WARNING: AT YOUR POSTED LIST PRICE YOU WILL LOSE MONEY ON SALES AFTER UNIT

1. Press c to confirm your selection, or r to rechoose.

Also, regardless of the initial price selection, in these instructions it was useful to have sellers offer only a single unit (so that a stock-out could be observed). Thus, the following message was printed every time that either 0 or 2 units was offered: You have selected to offer up to **0 [2]** units. In the experiment, you are free to offer this or any other admissible quantity. For these instructions, however, ASSUME YOU OFFERED ONLY 1 UNIT.

Seller		S1	S2	S3	S4	S5	You offered to sell up to 1
Price		**4.50**	*.**			*.**	unit(s) for $4.50

Unit	Price	Unit Cost	Profit				
1	4.50	2.74					
2		4.80					

S1 Period 1
Waiting for Other Sellers to Complete Posting Decisions.

A reminder of the seller's list price and quantity decision appears at the upper left hand corner of the seller's screen. Information from the seller's decision that is available to other sellers is displayed in the upper right part of the seller's screen.

We switch now back for a moment to buyer B2's display [not shown here, but similar to S1's display above]. Notice the price posted by seller S1 in buyer B2's screen display. Buyers see the list prices of all sellers as they are posted. There will be between one and five sellers in today's experiment (and between one and five buyers). In this example, there are five sellers and five buyers.

We now switch back to the screen display for seller S1 [above] to see the information S1 receives as other sellers complete posting decisions.

Other seller's prices are listed in gray. As you can see above, sellers S2 and S5 have finished making price/quantity decisions. Sellers see the list prices of other sellers AFTER making their own price/quantity listing. In the experiment actual prices rather than $*.**'s will appear.[44] Also, seller quantity decisions are PRIVATE and are revealed to neither BUYERS nor OTHER SELLERS.

We switch now to the screen display for buyer B2 [not shown]. Buyer B2 can now see the prices chosen by S1, S2 and S5. B2 is waiting for S3 and S4 to finish posting. We switch back again to seller S1's screen [above].

When all sellers have finished posting prices, buyers begin a SHOPPING SEQUENCE. Sellers receive the message in the blue space at the bottom of the screen

---

[44] The $*.** notation was used to avoid suggesting that a seller should choose a price that is greater or less than the anticipated prices of others.

[that says: "Shopping Sequence, Please be Patient"]. In the experiment, sellers wait until being selected by a buyer. To continue with these instructions, press <ENTER>.

Note also that buyer identities B1 through B5 are listed on the seller's screen [not shown]. In the shopping sequence, buyer purchases will appear below these ID numbers.

Buyers are placed in a waiting mode. Then they are randomly selected, one at a time, to shop for units. While buyers not selected are waiting they receive the message at the bottom of the screen. [Not shown, the message reads: Another randomly selected buyer is shopping. Please be patient.] To continue with these instructions, press <ENTER>.

				Seller:	S1	S2	S3	S4	S5
				Price:	4.50	*.**	*.**	*.**	*.**
Unit	Unit Value	Price	Unit Earnings						
1	6.30			4.50					
2	4.57								

B2 Period 1

Make a purchase by picking seller 1, 2, 3, 4, or 5,
or Press q to quit.

When a buyer is taken from the waiting mode to shop, the buyer screen changes in the manner shown [above]. The horizontal red bar [outlined with dark lines] passing through the first unit and running across the screen indicates that buyer B2 is shopping for a first unit.

As indicated by the message at the bottom of the screen, the buyer shops by selecting a seller 1, 2, 3, 4, or 5, by pressing an appropriate key. Although in the experiment, a buyer may choose to make a purchase from any eligible seller, for the purposes of these instructions, shop from seller 1 by pressing 1 on your keyboard. DO THIS NOW. (DECISION: **1**)

Notice that unit earnings are calculated for the buyer, and the buyer makes a decision about whether to shop for the next unit, the unit number 2 in this example, illustrated by the red box [outlined with dark lines in the table above] running through the second unit in the buyer's screen.

We switch back now to seller S3's screen [not shown] to illustrate the way a negotiation sequence that ended in a contract appears for a seller. Parallel to buyers, the transaction is recorded, and profits are calculated for the seller. The seller now awaits the sale of a second unit.

				Seller:	No Units	S2	S3	S4	S5
				Price:	4.50	*.**	4.50	*.**	*.**
Unit	Unit Value	Price	Unit Earnings						
1	6.30	4.50	1.80	4.50					
2	4.57								

B2   Period 1
Make a purchase by picking seller   , 2, 3, 4, or 5, or Press q to quit.

We now return to the buyer's screen [above]. The buyer may stop at any time. If the buyer has purchased all possible units or has shopped with all eligible sellers, then another buyer is selected from the waiting mode to begin shopping. Suppose B2 decides to continue shopping. Then B2 is asked to pick from among the available sellers (in this case, 2, 3, 4, or 5). Look at the last line of the screen and notice that Seller S1 is no longer available.

Suppose, coincidentally, that seller 3 happened to post the same price as seller S1. Although in the experiment, a buyer may choose to shop from any eligible seller, for the purposes of these instructions, make a purchase from seller 3 by pressing 3 on your keyboard. DO THIS NOW. [The instructions now return to a Seller screen and proceed back through to this point.]

Summary of Instructions

EARNINGS. Buyers and sellers earn money in a symmetric manner.

— BUYERS: Each BUYER has private redemption values for units. NO ONE but the buyer sees that buyer's particular values. BUYERS earn the difference between their unit value and the price.

— SELLERS: Each SELLER has private unit costs for units. NO ONE but the seller sees that seller's particular costs. SELLERS earn the difference between the price and their unit cost.

INSTITUTIONAL DETAILS. The experiment is divided into a series of trading periods. Each period proceeds as follows:

1. Price Posting: Sellers post list prices and quantities while buyers are in a waiting mode. In making a price/quantity posting, the seller indicates a willingness to sell the posted number of units at the list price. Units, however, may sell for less than the list price. Also, NO ONE KNOWS THE POSTED QUANTITY BUT THE POSTING SELLER.

2. Shopping: Buyers are randomly drawn from the waiting mode, one at a time, and are given the opportunity to make purchases. Buyers continue shopping until they are out of available units, out of eligible sellers, or wish to stop. As each buyer finishes shopping, another is randomly selected from the waiting mode. A period ends when all buyers have had an opportunity to shop, or when all sellers are out of units.

THIS COMPLETES THE INSTRUCTIONS. Choose a letter:
  a. Review the way EARNINGS are determined for buyers and sellers.
  b. Review the way sellers POST PRICES.
  c. Review the shopping sequence.
  d. See a summary of the instructions.
  e. EXIT the instructions and start the experiment. (DECISION: **e**)

REVIEW QUESTIONS: Prior to beginning the experiment we ask you to answer the following questions. Your answers are NOT recorded. Following your response, the correct answer, along with an explanation, will be provided. Please raise your hand if any explanation is unclear.

1. Suppose that you are a seller about to choose your price. Will you be able to see any other sellers' price before you choose your price? Press 'y' for yes or 'n' for no. (DECISION: **y**)

INCORRECT: Sellers see the prices posted by other sellers only after they have made a pricing decision.

2. Suppose you are a seller, and you have sold all but one of the units you made available by your quantity limit choice. Does a buyer know that you only have one unit left? Press 'y' for yes or 'n' for no. (DECISION: **n**)

CORRECT: Neither buyers nor other sellers ever see either your quantity limit or the number of units you have remaining. If you sell all your units, however, a "NO UNITS" message replaces your seller ID number on the buyers' (but not on the other sellers') screens. [Note: Both correct and incorrect answers prompted the same explanatory sentence for each question above.]

Verbal Instructions Delivered Prior to Period 1

Now we are about to begin the first period. Before we begin, it is natural for you to wonder how long the experiment will last. There will be fifteen periods, and at the end of period fifteen we will ask one of you to throw this six-sided die to determine whether to continue with a sixteenth period. A throw of a 5 or a 6 will cause the experiment to end, and a throw of 1, 2, 3, or 4 will cause the experiment to continue for a sixteenth period. If there is a sixteenth period, then the die will be thrown again at the end of the sixteenth period to determine whether the experiment will stop (with a throw of 5 or 6) or whether the experiment will continue for period 17 (with a throw of 1, 2, 3, or 4). The throw of the die will be used in this way at the end of each period to decide whether the experiment ends or continues for at least one more period.

Please do not talk or look on others' screens during the experiment.

Are there any questions? PRESS ENTER TO BEGIN.

A4.3 Calculation of a Mixed-Strategy Equilibrium*

A distinct advantage of the power and no-power designs illustrated in figure 4.11 is that the Nash equilibrium can be explicitly calculated for both cases. As explained in the text, it is easily verified that the competitive equilibrium is a Nash equilibrium for a single-stage version of the no-power design. The creation of market power by reallocating units from S3 to S1 and S2, so that capacity for S1 and S2 exceeds excess supply, is also easily understood. The derivation of the Nash equilibrium with randomized pricing strategies in the power design, however, is more complicated. This derivation is useful, since mixed-strategy equilibria are common when capacity-constrained sellers choose prices simultaneously as in a posted-offer auction. To clarify the way that an equilibrium with randomized pricing is determined, we first analyze a simplified, two-seller version of the market-power design. Equilibrium mixed-strategies for the more complex, five-seller case are discussed subsequently.

The Two-Seller Case

Consider the two-seller design illustrated in the left panel of figure 4.15. In this figure, each of two symmetric sellers, S1 and S2, may offer a total of 4 units: 1 unit at a cost of 0, and 3 units at a per unit cost of c. A total of 8 units are demanded by a single, fully revealing consumer: 5 units at a constant marginal value

---

* The material in this section is somewhat more advanced.

r, and another 3 units at a per unit marginal valuation of p_c. Given the excess supply of 3 units at any price above p_c, the highest competitive equilibrium price is p_c. Sellers each earn $4p_c - 3c$ in this competitive equilibrium. But if it is the case that $r > 4p_c - 3c$, then the competitive equilibrium is not a Nash equilibrium for the market period, because either S1 or S2 may unilaterally increase earnings from $4p_c - 3c$ to r by raising their price to r, where a single, zero-cost unit will be sold.

It is worth observing that this two-seller design is a variant of the five-seller design discussed in the text (and illustrated on the right side of figure 4.15), where S1 and S2 compete for a residual 8 units, given that S3, S4, and S5 price below any price that the large sellers might post. In fact, it will turn out to be the case that this is not an irrelevant exercise, since over a range of prices, S1 and S2 will face the same incentives in the five-seller case as in this two-seller case.

For reasons identical to those for the five-seller case discussed in the text, the existence of a pure-strategy Nash equilibrium in the two-seller market power design is precluded by incentives for S1 and S2 to shade on any common price down to a minimum price p_{min}. This minimum price p_{min} is the price such that earnings from selling all 4 units (as the low-price seller) equal the certain, or "security," earnings from selling 1 unit at the limit price r (as the high-price seller). Recall that when 4 units are sold, a large seller's cost is $3c$, since the first unit has a cost of zero. Therefore, p_{min} is the price for which $4p_{min} - 3c = r$, or equivalently, $p_{min} = (r - 3c)/4$.

The Nash equilibrium in this design involves randomization over the price range from p_{min} to r. For a seller to be willing to choose price randomly in some range, it must be the case that all prices in that range offer the same expected profit. Therefore, the pricing distributions for the mixed-strategy equilibrium are calculated by considering for each seller the price distribution that the *other* seller must follow in order for expected profits to equal a constant.

Consider first the conditions under which S1 will randomize. Recall that regardless of S2's actions, S1 is assured a security profit r, by posting the limit price r. For seller S1 to be indifferent between posting some arbitrary price p and the limit price r, it must be the case that S2 prices according to a distribution $G(p)$ that makes S1's expected earnings at p equal to security earnings.[45] Assuming continuous price alternatives, ties can be ignored. When S1 chooses a price of p, *S1* has the highest price with probability $G(p)$ and the lowest price with probability $1 - G(p)$. Therefore, S1 sells 1 unit with probability $G(p)$ and 4 units with probability $1 - G(p)$, for an expected profit $pG(p) + (4p - 3c)[1 - G(p)]$. It follows that seller S1 will be indifferent between posting p and posting r if

---

[45] This statement is only true if there is no mass of probability at the top of the distribution. But no equilibrium that is symmetric for S1 and S2 can have a mass at the top, or anywhere else, since each seller would strictly prefer to price just below the mass point, which is inconsistent with the constant-expected-profit condition for randomization.

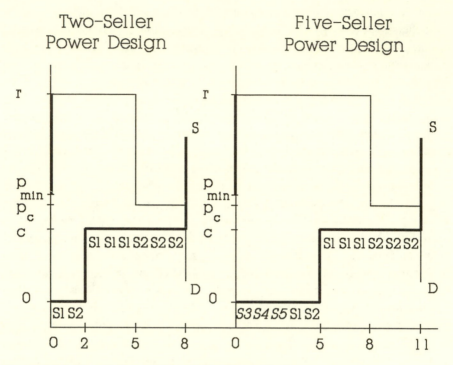

Figure 4.15 Two-Seller and Five-Seller Power Designs

$pG(p) + (4p - 3c)[1 - G(p)] = r$. Solving for $G(p)$, it follows that S2 must price so that

(4.1) $$G(p) = \frac{(4p - 3c - r)}{3(p - c)}.$$

    To summarize, (4.1) specifies the mixed distribution that seller S2 must use in order for S1 to be willing to choose randomly in a range of prices (which, by construction, yield equal expected profits). Since S2 is symmetric to S1, S1 must also use the price distribution in (4.1) for S2 to randomize. In equilibrium, both S1 and S2 randomize according to (4.1). Finally, it is easily verified that the equilibrium distribution is bounded between $p_{min} = (r + 3c)/4$ and r, since $G((r + 3c)/4) = 0$ and $G(r) = 1$.

The Five-Seller Case

Although the calculation of the Nash equilibrium price distributions is more complex with more sellers and cost asymmetries, the same procedures apply. Consider the five-seller power design illustrated in the right panel of figure 4.15. (This is just the power design shown earlier in the lower-left part of figure 4.11, except that general rather than specific parameters are printed along the vertical axis.) From inspection of the seller identities printed below the supply curve in figure 4.15, it is seen that the five-seller design is obtained from the two-seller design by adding sellers S3, S4, and S5, each with a single low-cost unit, and expanding demand from 8 to 11 units.

A mixed-strategy equilibrium in this context requires the identification of two price distributions; $G(p)$ for the large sellers, and $F(p)$ for the small sellers. These distributions are not symmetric; for example, large and small sellers will randomize differently. The method of calculation parallels the previous analysis except the two distributions must be simultaneously determined. The approach is to identify a level of security earnings for each type of seller, and a range of possible prices. Then the price distribution must be such that expected profit equals security earnings over the range of possible prices.

First consider the large sellers. For the same reasons given above, each large seller is assured of selling a single unit at the limit price r. Therefore, the expected profit for a large seller in a mixed equilibrium must equal r. A large seller's expected profits depend on the price distributions used by both types of sellers. Therefore, the constant-expected-profit condition provides one equation that must be satisfied by $F(p)$ and $G(p)$. A second condition is obtained by equating the expected profit for the small sellers to their security earnings level. Small sellers are different from the large sellers in that they are not assured of selling a unit at price r. Rather, a "secure" price for the small sellers must be determined by the minimum price used by the large sellers, since each small seller is assured of selling a single unit only if they price below the lowest price charged by large sellers. The analysis of the mixed equilibrium involves the simultaneous determination of the two distributions and of this security earnings level. For details, see Davis and Holt (1991).

REFERENCES

Alger, Dan (1987) "Laboratory Tests of Equilibrium Predictions with Disequilibrium Data," *Review of Economic Studies, 54,* 105–145.

Baumol, William J., John C. Panzar, and Robert D. Willig (1982) *Contestable Markets and the Theory of Industry Structure.* New York: Harcourt Brace Jovanovich.

Baumol, William J., and Robert D. Willig (1986) "Contestability: Developments Since the Book," *Oxford Economic Papers, 38,* 9–36.

Benson, Bruce L., and M. D. Faminow (1988) "The Impact of Experience on Prices and Profits in Experimental Duopoly Markets," *Journal of Economic Behavior and Organization, 9,* 345–365.

Brown-Kruse, Jamie L. (1991) "Contestability in the Presence of an Alternate Market: an Experimental Examination," *Rand Journal of Economics, 22,* 136–147.

Cason, Timothy N., and Arlington W. Williams (1990) "Competitive Equilibrium Convergence in a Posted-Offer Market with Extreme Earnings Inequities," *Journal of Economic Behavior and Organization, 14,* 331–352.

Chamberlin, Edward H. (1948) "An Experimental Imperfect Market," *Journal of Political Economy, 56,* 95–108.

Clark, John Bates (1887) "The Limits of Competition," *Political Science Quarterly,* 2, 45–61.

Coursey, Don, R. Mark Isaac, and Vernon L. Smith (1984) "Natural Monopoly and the Contested Markets: Some Experimental Results," *Journal of Law and Economics, 27,* 91–113.

Coursey, Don, R. Mark Isaac, Margaret Luke, and Vernon L. Smith (1984) "Market Contestability in the Presence of Sunk (Entry) Costs," *Rand Journal of Economics, 15,* 69–84.

Cox, James C., and R. Mark Isaac (1986) "Incentive Regulation: A Case Study in the Use of Laboratory Experimental Analysis in Economics," in S. Moriarity, ed., *Laboratory Market Research*, Norman Oklahoma: University of Oklahoma Center for Economic and Management Research, 121–145.

———— (1987) "Mechanisms for Incentive Regulation: Theory and Experiment," *Rand Journal of Economics, 18,* 348–359.

Davis, Douglas D., Glenn W. Harrison, and Arlington W. Williams (1991) "Convergence to Nonstationary Competitive Equilibria: An Experimental Analysis," working paper, Virginia Commonwealth University, a shorter version of which is forthcoming in *Journal of Economic Behavior and Organization.*

Davis, Douglas D., and Charles A. Holt (1990) "List Prices and Discounts," working paper, University of Virginia.

——— (1991) "Capacity Asymmetries, Market Power, and Mergers in Laboratory Markets with Posted Prices," working paper, Virginia Commonwealth University.

Davis, Douglas D., Charles A. Holt, and Anne P. Villamil (1990) "Supracompetitive Prices and Market Power in Posted-Offer Experiments," University of Illinois BBER Faculty Working Paper no. 90–1648.

Davis, Douglas D., and Arlington W. Williams (1986) "The Effects of Rent Asymmetries in Posted Offer Markets," *Journal of Economic Behavior and Organization, 7,* 303–316.

——— (1989) "The Effects of Market Information on a Pure Bargaining Equilibrium," working paper, Virginia Commonwealth University.

——— (1991) "The Hayek Hypothesis in Experimental Auctions: Institutional Effects and Market Power," *Economic Inquiry, 29,* 261–274.

Dolbear, F. T., L. B. Lave, G. Bowman, A. Lieberman, E. Prescott, F. Rueter, and R. Sherman (1968) "Collusion in Oligopoly: An Experiment on the Effect of Numbers and Information," *Quarterly Journal of Economics, 82,* 240–259.

Eckel, Catherine C., and Michael A. Goldberg (1984) "Regulation and Deregulation in the Brewing Industry: The British Columbia Example," *Canadian Public Policy, 10,* 316–327.

Finsinger, Jörg, and Igno Vogelsang (1981) "Alternative Institutional Frameworks for Price Incentive Mechanisms," *Kyklos, 34,* 388–404.

Fouraker, Lawrence E., and Sidney Siegel (1963) *Bargaining Behavior.* New York: McGraw-Hill.

Friedman, James W. (1963) "Individual Behavior in Oligopolistic Markets: An Experimental Study," *Yale Economic Essays, 3,* 359–417.

——— (1967) "An Experimental Study of Cooperative Duopoly," *Econometrica, 35,* 379–397.

——— (1969) "On Experimental Research in Oligopoly," *Review of Economic Studies, 36,* 399–415.

Gilbert, Richard J. (1989) "The Role of Potential Competition in Industrial Organization," *The Journal of Economic Perspectives, 3*(3), 107–127.

Grether, David M., and Charles R. Plott (1984) "The Effects of Market Practices in Oligopolistic Markets: An Experimental Examination of the *Ethyl* Case," *Economic Inquiry, 22,* 479–507.

Guler, Kemal, and Charles R. Plott (1988) "Private R&D and Second Sourcing in Procurement: An Experimental Study," California Institute of Technology, Social Science Working Paper no. 684.

Harrison, Glenn W. (1986) "Experimental Evaluation of the Contestable Markets Hypothesis," in E. Bailey, ed., *Public Regulation.* Cambridge, Mass.: MIT Press.

———— (1988) "Predatory Pricing in a Multiple Market Experiment: A Note," *Journal of Economic Behavior and Organization, 9*, 405–417.

Harrison, Glenn W., and Michael McKee (1985) "Monopoly Behavior, Decentralized Regulation, and Contestable Markets: An Experimental Evaluation," *Rand Journal of Economics, 16*, 51–69.

Harrison, Glenn W., Michael McKee, and E. E. Rutström (1989) "Experimental Evaluation of Institutions of Monopoly Restraint," chapter 3 in L. Green and J. Kagel, eds., *Advances in Behavioral Economics*, vol. 2. Norwood, N.J.: Ablex Press, 54–94.

Holt, Charles A. (1989) "The Exercise of Market Power in Laboratory Experiments," *Journal of Law and Economics, 32* (pt. 2), S107–S130.

———— (1992) "Industrial Organization: A Survey of Laboratory Research," forthcoming in A. Roth and J. Kagel, eds., *Handbook of Experimental Economics*. Princeton: Princeton University Press.

Holt, Charles A., and Douglas D. Davis (1990) "The Effects of Non-Binding Price Announcements in Posted-Offer Markets," *Economics Letters, 34*, 307–310.

Holt, Charles A., and Fernando Solis-Soberon (1990a) "Antitrust Restrictions on Predatory Pricing: Possible Side Effects," working paper, University of Virginia.

———— (1990b) "The Calculation of Equilibrium Mixed Strategies in Posted-Offer Auctions," forthcoming in R. M. Isaac, ed., *Research in Experimental Economics*. Greenwich: JAI Press.

Hong, James T., and Charles R. Plott (1982) "Rate Filing Policies for Inland Water Transportation: An Experimental Approach," *The Bell Journal of Economics, 13*, 1–19.

Isaac, R. Mark, Valerie Ramey, and Arlington Williams (1984) "The Effects of Market Organization on Conspiracies in Restraint of Trade," *Journal of Economic Behavior and Organization, 5*, 191–222.

Isaac, R. Mark, and Stanley S. Reynolds (1992) "Schumpeterian Competition in Experimental Markets," *Journal of Economic Behavior and Organization, 17*, 59–100.

Isaac, R. Mark, and Vernon L. Smith (1985) "In Search of Predatory Pricing," *Journal of Political Economy, 93*, 320–345.

Jung, Yun Joo, John H. Kagel, and Dan Levin (1991) "An Experimental Study of Reputation Effects in a Chain-Store Game," working paper, University of Houston.

Ketcham, Jon, Vernon L. Smith, and Arlington W. Williams (1984) "A Comparison of Posted-Offer and Double-Auction Pricing Institutions," *Review of Economic Studies, 51*, 595–614.

Kruse, Jamie, Steven Rassenti, Stanley S. Reynolds, and Vernon L. Smith (1990) "Bertrand-Edgeworth Competition in Experimental Markets," working paper, University of Arizona.

Kujal, Praveen (1992) "Firm-Specific Output Limits in Posted-Offer Markets: Distributive and Efficiency Effects," working paper, University of Arizona.

Loeb, M., and W. Magat (1979) "A Decentralized Method for Utility Regulation," *Journal of Law and Economics, 22*, 399–404.

Mestelman, Stuart, and Douglas Welland (1988) "Advance Production in Experimental Markets," *Review of Economic Studies, 55*, 641–654.

——— (1991a) "Inventory Carryover and the Performance of Alternative Economic Institutions," *Southern Economic Journal, 57*, 1024–1042.

——— (1991b) "The Effects of Rent Asymmetries in Markets Characterized by Advance Production: A Comparison of Trading Institutions," *Journal of Economic Behavior and Organization, 15*, 387–405.

Millner, Edward L., Michael D. Pratt, and Robert J. Reilly (1990) "Contestability in Real-Time Experimental Flow Markets," *Rand Journal of Economics, 21*, 584–599.

Plott, Charles R., and Vernon L. Smith (1978) "An Experimental Examination of Two Exchange Institutions," *Review of Economic Studies, 45*, 133–153.

Sherman, Roger (1972) *Oligopoly, An Empirical Approach.* Lexington, Mass.: Lexington Books.

Smith, Vernon L. (1964) "The Effect of Market Organization on Competitive Equilibrium," *Quarterly Journal of Economics, 78*, 181–201.

——— (1981) "An Empirical Study of Decentralized Institutions of Monopoly Restraint," in J. Quirk and G. Horwich, eds., *Essays in Contemporary Fields of Economics in Honor of E. T. Weiler (1914-1979).* West Lafayette: Purdue University Press, 83-106.

Smith, Vernon L., and Arlington W. Williams (1982) "The Effects of Rent Asymmetries in Experimental Auction Markets," *Journal of Economic Behavior and Organization, 3*, 99–116.

——— (1989) "The Boundaries of Competitive Price Theory: Convergence, Expectations, and Transactions Costs," in Leonard Green and John Kagel, eds., *Advances in Behavioral Economics*, vol. 2. Norwood, N. J.: Ablex Press.

Williams, Fred E. (1973) "The Effect of Market Organization on Competitive Equilibrium: The Multi-unit Case," *Review of Economic Studies, 40*, 97–113.

CHAPTER 5

BARGAINING AND AUCTIONS

5.1 Introduction

Almost all of the laboratory markets considered in previous chapters fall into two categories: the double-auction structure of many centralized stock exchanges and the posted-offer structure of many retail markets. Given the major differences in the outcomes generated by these institutions, it is natural to implement other laboratory trading arrangements that correspond to some of the other unique and diverse institutions found in market economies.

Perhaps the most primitive trading institution is *bilateral bargaining*. This arrangement is primitive in the sense that haggling by two parties is a sort of default social institution, one that arises naturally in the absence of social and economic conventions that allow more sophisticated institutional structures. Bargaining is also pervasive in highly developed market economies, for example, when two agents are linked in a continuing relationship, as with labor or international trade negotiations. Despite its simplicity, unstructured bilateral bargaining is difficult to analyze, since a wide range of outcomes can be consistent with a noncooperative Nash equilibrium. As a consequence, generations of economists have described bargaining outcomes as being "indeterminate." By identifying patterns in bargaining outcomes, experiments can be used to narrow the range of indeterminacy in bargaining situations.

A second class of institutions arises when a trader on one side of a market can bargain simultaneously with a number of traders on the other side through an *auction* process. As indicated in chapter 1, there is a rich variety of alternative auction structures. For example, bids can be tendered simultaneously or sequentially, and in the latter case, the auctioneer can either raise or lower the proposed sale price.

In choosing between alternative auction rules, a seller may seek to enhance revenues or reduce the likelihood of collusive bidding. Public agencies may also be concerned with the properties of auctions; they are typically concerned with rules that enhance allocative efficiency and minimize transactions costs. These kinds of performance issues can be evaluated in the laboratory by comparing bidding in alternative auction institutions under the same structural conditions.

The intuition gained in the study of simple auctions can be useful in the design of a third class of trading arrangements: *two-sided auctions* with multiple buyers and sellers. Many of these two-sided auctions are variants of "call market" mechanisms that are used in some stock exchanges. For example, daily opening prices are sometimes set by collecting opening bids and arraying them from high to low, and collecting opening asks and arraying them from low to high. The opening price is the intersection of these bid-and-ask arrays, and all successful opening bids and asks result in contracts at this uniform price. Advances in communications and computer technology have made it possible for large numbers of dispersed traders to do business through electronic call markets. The design and refinement of these new institutions is an ideal situation for the use of laboratory techniques.

This chapter is organized as follows. The first half contains a review of bargaining experiments: Sections 5.2 and 5.3 present the theory and results of bargaining in a free-form or unstructured context. Sections 5.4 and 5.5 pertain to bargaining situations in which the sequence of each person's offers and responses is precisely specified in the negotiation process. This added structure permits the identification and laboratory evaluation of game-theoretic equilibria. Auction experiments are reviewed in the second half of the chapter: Sections 5.6 and 5.7 pertain to four standard auction institutions, under conditions in which each bidder knows his or her own *private value* for an auctioned good, but does not know others' values. Section 5.8 then considers *common value* auctions, that is, situations in which the prize has the same value for all bidders, but bidders may have different estimates of this common value. Section 5.9 summarizes the results of experiments that implement two-sided, uniform-price auctions. The final section contains a brief conclusion.

5.2 Unstructured Bargaining without Side Payments

Although the status quo in many bilateral bargaining situations may be predetermined by a dealer's list price or by a previous contract, the negotiations are likely to occur in a free-form context, with no restriction on which party makes the first or any subsequent offer. Either party can terminate the negotiations by accepting the current proposal of the other. The simplest laboratory implementation of this type of bargaining involves the split of a fixed amount of money, say $1, by two participants, with the stipulation that both parties receive zero payoffs if there is no agreement within a specified amount of time. Of course, this divide-the-dollar game could be implemented as a double auction in which the buyer's value is $1.00 and the seller's cost is zero. The main difference is that subjects in typical bilateral bargaining experiments are not constrained to send only bids and offers; they may discuss nonprice aspects of the encounter, such as fairness issues.[1]

As may not be surprising, 50/50 splits are common; such splits are both "focal" and "fair" in the sense that payoffs are divided equally, and they are "efficient" in the sense that total earnings are maximized. The importance of these considerations can be clarified by considering how you would react if your bargaining partner were to demand a 60/40 payoff advantage.

Although the notions of focalness, fairness, and efficiency overlap in a divide-the-dollar game, they diverge in only slightly more complicated settings. Suppose, for example, that an item being divided is worth much more to one of the bargaining agents. Such a situation would be created in a divide-the-dollar game if the experimenter publicly announced that one of the players (player X) must pay a tax of 50 percent on earnings, while the other (player Y) can keep all money obtained during the negotiations. In this case, the focal 50/50 split would be unfair in the sense that player X earns only $.25 after the tax, while player Y receives $.50. The focal 50/50 split would also be inefficient, since the maximum total surplus (of $1.00) is realized when player Y receives the entire dollar. Other factors might also affect outcomes. For example, what would happen if X could transfer earnings to Y in an *ex post* side payment? What if one person was demanding more than half of the dollar to be split, and the time limit was approaching?[2]

In the remainder of this section, we develop the predictions of a theory of unstructured bargaining that is based on a series of behavioral axioms. Then we review some experiments designed to examine the empirical validity of these underlying axioms. The subsequent section considers bargaining experiments in which the activity of one party produces an externality that reduces the other's earnings, and the bargainers can agree on *ex post* side payments to share the gains from choosing the efficient, joint-payoff-maximizing level of the activity.

---

[1] Some additional structure is usually imposed in bargaining experiments for purposes of control. In particular, participants are almost always prohibited from making threats. Agreements to make *ex post* side payments are also generally prohibited. Side payments are permitted in bargaining experiments in which the ability to negotiate such payments is a desired treatment variable.

[2] The presence of a fixed time limit may seem artificial, but it may be desirable in the laboratory for several reasons. First, bargaining in naturally occurring markets often takes place under time pressures due to the imminent expiration of a contract, the threat of a strike, or the prospect of compulsory arbitration. In addition, Harrison and McKee (1985, p. 658) noted that a fixed time period ensures that neither party can gain an advantage by stalling if he or she senses that the other has a pressing appointment just after the scheduled laboratory session. Finally, extended bargaining reduces subjects' earnings per hour, and therefore, a fixed time period makes it easier to ensure that rewards are high enough to be salient on an hourly basis.

Nash Bargaining: Theory

For reasons similar to those encountered in analyzing the double auction, it is difficult to generate complete equilibrium predictions about unstructured bargaining outcomes using the tools of standard noncooperative game theory. The rich message-space and the real-time nature of unstructured bargaining create an unmanageably large set of strategies. One approach to this problem, to be deferred until a later section, is to impose some structure on the sequence of offers and counteroffers. With sufficient restrictions, a unique subgame-perfect equilibrium can be calculated.

An alternative to noncooperative game theory, considered here, is to specify a set of assumptions or *axioms* that the outcome of a bargaining process must satisfy. This is the approach of *cooperative game theory*, where the word "cooperative" is used because the theory is thought to be applicable to situations in which the players can making binding agreements about their strategies, and hence about the outcomes of the game.[3]

The most commonly used cooperative solution concept for bargaining games is the *Nash solution*, proposed by Nash (1950).[4] It is useful to begin with an informal discussion of the properties of this concept. When a fair 50/50 split is also efficient, this outcome is specified by the Nash solution. In a divide-the-dollar game, for example, fairness involves maximizing the *minimum* of the two player's payoffs, and efficiency involves maximizing the *sum* of the payoffs. Both of these objectives are achieved at the 50/50 split. When the fair outcome is not efficient, the Nash solution essentially provides a compromise. Loosely speaking, Nash specified assumptions about the bargaining outcome that, if satisfied, imply that the outcome must maximize the *product* of the two players' utility gains (over the disagreement outcome). Note that in a divide-the-dollar game, the product of the payoffs is maximized by giving 50 cents to each bargainer.

For a more formal statement of the properties of the Nash solution, some notation is necessary. The bargainers will be referred to as player X and player Y. Players are expected utility maximizers, and the utility functions U_x and U_y are increasing functions of the player's own money payoffs that are determined by bargaining. A failure to agree in the bargaining process results in disagreement

---

[3] The term "cooperative" in this context does not necessarily imply that outcomes will be more cooperative than would be predicted under noncooperative game theory. Recall that cooperative outcomes can be supported by "punishment strategies" in infinite-horizon noncooperative games. Instead, cooperative game theory is a method of analyzing games in terms of axioms or assumptions about outcomes, rather than in terms of moves or strategies (as is the case in noncooperative game theory). The term "axiomatic game theory" would have been a less confusing choice of terms.

[4] The Nash solution is not to be confused with the Nash equilibrium of noncooperative game theory. The Nash solution is nicely explained in many places, such as Nydegger and Owen (1975).

(utility) payoffs, d_x for player X and d_y for player Y. The game is characterized by these disagreement payoffs and by the set, S, of possible utility payoffs that can be reached by agreement. A *solution* to the game (S, d_x, d_y) is a function that specifies the utility pair (U_x, U_y) that will be the outcome of the bargaining process. The Nash solution is a particular outcome in S that satisfies the axioms to be discussed below.

Figure 5.1 illustrates this notation for the divide-the-dollar game. For simplicity, the figure is drawn under the assumption that both players are risk neutral (so utility is linear), and therefore, the von Neumann-Morgenstern utilities are equal to their monetary earnings. The set of possible allocations, S, is bounded by a payoff frontier, denoted by a boldfaced line with a slope of –1 (ignore the parenthetical remarks for now). For example, if the players agree that player Y gets all of the pennies, the outcome is (0, 100), the upper-left point on this frontier. The set S of possible utility outcomes is the set of points on and below the payoff frontier. The disagreement payoff outcome is the origin (0, 0) in this example.

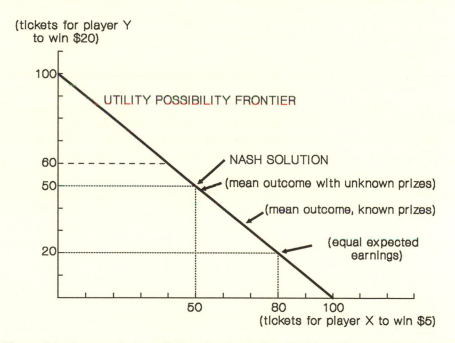

Figure 5.1   Symmetric Payoff Frontier for Dollar Division Game (parenthetical remarks pertain to a binary lottery game reported by Roth and Murnighan, 1982)

The Nash solution uniquely satisfies four axioms: Pareto optimality, symmetry, independence of irrelevant alternatives, and invariance to linear transformations of utility.[5] We will discuss these axioms in an informal manner and relate them to the example in figure 5.1.

1. *Pareto optimality* implies that it is impossible to increase the utility of one of the players without decreasing that of the other. When the utility possibility frontier has a negative slope, as in figure 5.1, Pareto optimality requires that the solution be a point on the frontier.

2. *Symmetry* requires that a symmetric bargaining game yield a symmetric outcome. More precisely, when the disagreement payoffs are equal and the set S of possible pairs of utility outcomes is symmetric around the 45 degree line, the bargaining outcome must be on this equal-utility line.[6] In figure 5.1, the condition of symmetry restricts the solution to a 45 degree line (not shown) drawn through the origin, so the Nash solution is a 50/50 split.

These two axioms are all that is needed to generate a unique solution in symmetric games; Pareto optimality and symmetry uniquely predict the 50/50 split determined by the intersection of the 45 degree line and the Pareto frontier. But many bargaining games are not symmetric. Disagreement payoffs may be unequal, and the set of possible utility outcomes may be asymmetric. The remaining two axioms are useful in situations where symmetry does not apply. Each of these axioms can sometimes be used to transform an asymmetric game into a symmetric one that is easier to analyze.

3. *Independence of irrelevant alternatives* is an assumption that the solution of a bargaining game is unaffected if a truncation of the set of possible utility outcomes does not remove the solution to the original (untruncated) game.[7] In terms of figure 5.1, for example, suppose that the rules of the divide-the-dollar game are altered to prohibit player Y from receiving more than 60 cents. In this case, the upper corner of the set S is truncated at the horizontal dashed line in figure 5.1, and the symmetry axiom can no longer be used to determine the outcome. Under the independence-of-irrelevant-alternatives axiom, the solution to this truncated game remains the 50/50 split.

4. *Invariance to linear transformations of utility* is a requirement that the solution be invariant to linear transformations of either or both bargainers' utility

---

[5] Nash (1950) also made a number of additional technical assumptions (the set of feasible utility payoffs is compact, convex, and contains at least one point that is strictly preferred to the disagreement outcome by both players).

[6] A set S is symmetric if the point (x, y) is in S whenever the point (y, x) is in S.

[7] Formally, let (S, d) and (T, d) be bargaining games with a common disagreement point, d, but different sets of possible utility payoffs, denoted by S and T respectively. If T is a subset of S and if T contains the solution (U_x, U_y) to (S, d), then this outcome (U_x, U_y) is also the solution to the game (T, d).

payoffs.[8] A linear transformation involves adding a constant and/or multiplying the utility function by a positive constant. Invariance to linear transformations implicitly applies to every bargaining theory that uses von Neumann-Morgenstern utility, since this utility representation is only unique up to a linear transformation.[9]

These four axioms restrict the possible outcomes in bargaining games. In fact, Nash (1950) proved the remarkable result that jointly, these axioms specify a bargaining outcome that maximizes the product of gains over the disagreement point. In terms of our notation, the Nash solution is the point in S that maximizes $(U_x - d_x)(U_y - d_y)$. For the example in figure 5.1 the origin is the disagreement point, and the product of utility gains is $U_x U_y$, which is the area of the rectangle with a diagonal from the origin to the point that represents the utility outcome. This rectangle is largest when the utilities for players X and Y are equal to 50.

Nash Bargaining: Initial Experimental Evidence

Considering the generality of its assumptions, the Nash solution provides a remarkably precise prediction. Systematic deviations from the Nash solution would imply that one or more of the Nash axioms are violated, at least in specific contexts. In natural bargaining situations, it is difficult to isolate the implications of a single axiom, such as invariance to linear transformations of utility. Experiments that attempt to isolate the predictive power of individual axioms will be discussed below. First we describe baseline conditions under which the Nash solution predicts well; then we discuss a series of more complex situations that provide some insight into the conditions under which the solution has less predictive power.

An early laboratory examination of axiomatic bargaining theory was reported by Nydegger and Owen (1975). The experiment consisted of negotiations between paired participants who bargained over the division of a known prize. Subjects were paid $1 for showing up, in addition to what they could earn by bargaining. They were paired and seated face to face at tables. After a single bargaining encounter, they were paid and dismissed. In the simplest baseline treatment, the ten participant pairs negotiated over a dollar, as illustrated in figure 5.1 (ignore the parenthetical remarks). The disagreement outcome generated payoffs of zero for each player. The Nash solution involves an equal division of payoffs. As mentioned above, equal division is appealing since it is "focal" and "fair" (the dollar is split evenly), and "efficient" (the maximum available earnings are realized). Not surprisingly, outcomes were consistent with the Nash solution: all ten pairs of subjects agreed to a 50/50 split.

---

[8] In particular, consider a game (S, d) with a solution (U_x, U_y). If the set S is altered by a linear transformation of utilities, then the solution to the new game is obtained by applying the same transformation to the utilities (U_x, U_y) at the solution to the original game.

[9] The invariance of utility functions to linear transformations was discussed in chapter 2.

Recall that when the game is symmetric, only the axioms of Pareto optimality and symmetry are needed to determine the Nash solution. The baseline treatment provides data consistent with these axioms. To evaluate the two remaining axioms, the authors also implemented two asymmetric treatments. The first asymmetric treatment involves a test of the independence-of-irrelevant-alternatives axiom. In this treatment, ten pairs of participants again bargained over the division of a dollar, but one of the players in each pair was constrained to earn no more than 60 cents. Using the independence-of-irrelevant-alternatives axiom, the 50/50 split remains the Nash solution, since it was not eliminated by the truncation. However, truncating "irrelevant" payoff possibilities in an asymmetric manner makes an equal division of payoffs less focal. Even though the points in the truncated portion of an outcome space may be irrelevant in the sense of not being outcomes in a symmetric divide-the-dollar game, these points may matter in the bargaining process. In particular, points with extreme payoff inequities may be important if both players initially demand favorable, unequal splits and later move toward a compromise in the center. Raiffa (1953) and others have proposed solutions that incorporate this intuition about the bargaining process. These solutions are thus sensitive to the maximum payoff that each player can obtain in the set S. Such solutions imply that the truncation of the points with high payoffs for player Y in figure 5.1 will increase the payoff obtained by player X.[10]   Despite these considerations, the independence-of-irrelevant-alternatives axiom performed well: all ten pairs of bargainers divided the dollar equally in the pairings with truncated payoff possibilities. These data provide a clear rejection of the Raiffa solution in this laboratory environment, since the observed outcomes are not affected by a reduction in one of the players' maximum payoff. This rejection indicates the importance of using experimental methods to evaluate cooperative game theories, no matter how intuitive these theories may seem.

The final Nydegger and Owen treatment provides a test of the invariance-to-linear-transformations-of-utility axiom. This treatment involved manipulations of the outcome space in a way that allows distinction of the Nash solution from the rival behavioral considerations of fairness and efficiency.   As before, ten pairs of participants engaged in face-to-face negotiations. In this treatment, however, they negotiated over the division of 60 poker chips, with the common knowledge that each chip would be worth one cent to player 2, and two cents to player 1. The

---

[10]   The Raiffa solution is found by considering the subset S' of points in S that are "individually rational," that is, that yield payoffs that are at least as high as the disagreement utility payoff for each player. The Raiffa solution is the intersection of (1) the utility frontier and (2) a straight line connecting the disagreement point and a point whose x coordinate is the maximum possible payoff for player X in S' and whose y coordinate is the maximum payoff for player Y in S'. In figure 5.1 after the truncation, the latter line is drawn from the origin to the point (100, 60), and it crosses the payoff frontier at (62.5, 37.5), which is the Raiffa solution. The Raiffa solution was characterized axiomatically by Kalai and Smorodinsky (1975), and therefore, this solution is sometimes called the Raiffa/Kalai/Smorodinsky solution.

payoff frontier for this game is illustrated in figure 5.2. Fair division differs from the efficient outcome in this treatment, since player 1 receives twice the payoff per chip as player 2. Thus, joint income is maximized when player 1 receives all the chips. As shown in figure 5.2, this efficient outcome involves a payoff of 120 for player 1 and nothing for player 2. A "fair" or equal-money-payoff condition occurs when each player earns 40 cents, as illustrated by the intersection of the dashed 45 degree line and the payoff frontier. In this outcome, player 1 takes 20 chips and player 2 takes 40 chips.

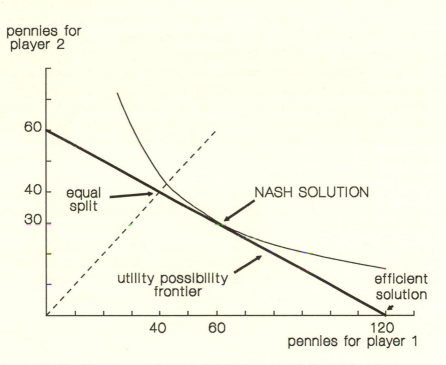

Figure 5.2 The Nydegger and Owen (1975) Asymmetric Bargaining Game (each of 60 poker chips is worth two cents to player 1 and one cent to player 2)

The Nash solution is a distinct, intermediate allocation that is somewhere between the fair and efficient outcomes in this example. As before, we assume that players are risk neutral, so utility can equal earnings, and therefore, the payoff possibilities in figure 5.2 correspond to the utility possibilities.[11] The Nash solution is derived by invoking the invariance-to-linear-transformations-of-utility axiom, and

---

[11] Tests that do not depend on an assumption of risk neutrality will be discussed below.

then adjusting the participants' utility functions in a way that makes the game symmetric. The easiest way to do this is to transform utilities so that each player has the same utility per chip. Multiply player 1's utility by .5 so that each chip, which yields two cents, will increase utility by 1. Leave player 2's utility to be equal to earnings in pennies. With utilities normalized in this way, each player has a minimum utility of zero (no chips), and a maximum utility of 60 (all chips). The set of feasible utility outcomes is a symmetric triangle with coordinates of (0, 0), (60, 0), and (0, 60). By the symmetry axiom, the solution in (transformed) utilities is (30, 30), so participants split the 60 chips equally. Importantly, this solution involves unequal money payoffs: Player 1 receives 60 cents, while player 2 receives 30 cents. In terms of the *untransformed* utilities, this prediction is indicated by the point marked NASH SOLUTION in figure 5.2.[12]

Results of sessions conducted under this asymmetric-payoff treatment were striking. All ten pairs split money payoffs rather than chips; in every case, player 1 received 20 chips, and player 2 received 40 chips. Recall that the other treatments using the same procedures had been consistent with symmetry, Pareto optimality, and independence of irrelevant alternatives. Therefore, the authors interpreted the failure to observe the Nash solution as a rejection of the invariance-to-linear-transformations-of-utility axiom.[13]

Rejection of the utility-invariance axiom presents a major flaw in axiomatic bargaining theory. The utility-invariance axiom allows predictions based on ordinal rather than cardinal utility (e.g., predictions denominated solely in terms of portions of the negotiated "pie," rather than in terms of the absolute utility derived from possible divisions to the negotiating parties). Since cardinal utilities are inherently unobservable, axiomatic game theory has much less empirical content without utility invariance. For this reason, further investigations of the Nash solution focused more closely on the utility-invariance axiom.

Evidence from Binary Lottery Games

Perhaps the most natural reason to question the apparent failure of the utility-invariance axiom is the assumption of risk neutrality implicit in the Nydegger and

---

[12]   An alternative and more direct way to find the Nash solution in figure 5.2 is to use Nash's theorem, that is, to find the point (U_x, U_y) in S that maximizes the product: $(U_x - d_x)(U_y - d_y)$. Since the disagreement outcome is zero for each, the Nash solution in this case maximizes the product of the utilities, $U_x U_y$. A locus of points with a constant product of the utilities is a rectangular hyperbola that is symmetric around a 45 degree line from the origin. In the untransformed game in figure 5.2, the Nash solution of (60, 30) is determined by the tangency of the payoff frontier and one such rectangular hyperbola.

[13]   Rapoport, Frenkel, and Perner (1977) also report the results of a face-to-face bargaining experiment, which the authors interpret as being inconsistent with the invariance-to-linear-transformations-of-utility axiom.

Owen test. (Recall that the linearity of the utility payoff frontier in figures 5.1 and 5.2 follows from an assumption that both bargainers are risk neutral and hence have linear utility functions.) Roth and Malouf (1979) avoided the controversial risk-neutrality assumption by using the two-stage lottery ticket payoff procedure described in chapter 2. In the first stage, two parties bargain over the division of 100 lottery tickets. In the second stage, each subject is given a chance to win a relatively high money prize, where the probability of winning the high prize equals the share of lottery tickets obtained. For example, a subject who obtains 75 out of the 100 tickets in the first stage would have a 3/4 chance of winning the high money prize. This two-stage procedure is called a *binary lottery game*. As indicated in chapter 2, an expected utility maximizer will be risk neutral in decisions involving lottery ticket earnings; the intuition is that expected utility is linear in the probabilities and hence is linear in terms of lottery tickets that determine the probability of winning a high monetary prize. By normalizing the utility of the high money prize to be 100 for each player (and the utility of the alternative, low prize to be 0), the utility frontier is as shown in figure 5.1, *regardless of the actual prize amounts*. By symmetry, the Nash solution is a 50/50 split *of the lottery tickets*, which can result in highly unequal expected monetary earnings when the two players' money prizes are different. For example, if the high prize is $20 for one player and $5 for the other, and if low prizes are zero, an equal division of lottery tickets will give expected earnings of $10 for one and only $2.50 for the other.

The apparent unfairness of unequal earnings in the Nash solution may matter more if players know each other's money prize amounts. This observation suggests an interesting experimental treatment, since the binary lottery method of inducing risk neutrality does not depend on whether subjects know one another's money prize amounts. Roth and Malouf (1979) report an experiment in which they induced risk-neutral behavior under alternative, theoretically neutral information conditions: In one treatment, participants knew only their own money prize amounts. In the other treatment, they knew both their own and the other's money prizes. To preserve anonymity, participants sent messages via visually isolated computer terminals. The subject's expected value of money payments was automatically calculated for proposed divisions of lottery tickets. When the subject knew the other bargainer's money prize, the other's expected money payment was also displayed. The authors observed a clear information effect: There was a high proportion of equal splits of the lottery tickets when subjects only knew their own prize values. But when subjects knew both their own and the other's money prizes, there was a strong tendency to deviate from an equal split toward a division of lottery tickets that equalized expected earnings. The authors conclude that the Nash solution may predict well under some information conditions, but that it may not predict accurately under conditions of complete information.[14]

An experiment by Roth and Murnighan (1982) further clarified the effects of informational conditions, by considering intermediate cases in which one player has more information regarding payoffs than the other. Procedures were similar to the earlier Roth and Malouf experiment; bargaining was over 100 lottery tickets, with a money prize of $20 for one player and a money prize of $5 for the other. This game is represented in figure 5.1, with the payoff for the $20 player shown on the vertical axis, as indicated by the parenthetical remarks. A division of 20 tickets for the $20 player and 80 tickets for the $5 player will result in equal expected earnings of $4 each, as shown by the "equal expected earnings" point in figure 5.1. Results of this experiment are summarized in table 5.1. The left-hand column of numbers is the average number of lottery tickets obtained by the $20 player in cases where an agreement was reached, and the right-hand column shows the percentage of bargaining encounters that resulted in disagreement. When it was common knowledge that each player only knew his or her own money prize, the agreement outcomes were approximately at the 50/50 split of the lottery tickets implied by the Nash solution, as shown in row 1 of the table. In contrast, when it was common knowledge that each player knew both money prizes, the agreement outcomes provided the $20 player with 33 percent of the tickets, on average (summarized in row 4). This represents a movement in the direction of the equal-expected-earnings point in figure 5.1. Two additional treatments, summarized in rows 2 and 3, involved situations in which both players knew that only one of them knew both money prize amounts. When the $20 player knew both prizes, results did not deviate too much from the 50/50 split; the average number of lottery tickets obtained by the $20 player is 44. But a comparison of rows 2 and 3 indicates that the $20 player fares much worse in the bargaining when the $5 player is the one who knows both prizes.

These results confirmed the earlier findings of Roth and Malouf: outcomes are dramatically affected by information conditions that do not alter the utility representation of the bargaining game, and hence that do not alter the theoretical Nash solution. Should these results be interpreted as a rejection of the Nash solution? The answer is not as obvious as it might seem, since Nash assumed that the bargainers are highly rational maximizers of their own payoffs, which implies no concern for others' payoffs. The provision of information about others' monetary payoffs in an experimental context may create interpersonal payoff considerations

---

[14] It is natural to suspect that the equal expected money value outcomes observed under complete information were driven by the provision of expected money values for each proposal on participants' computer screens. This suspicion is not confirmed in a follow-up experiment, where expected payoffs were presented on the screen in terms of an intermediate medium (poker chips). See Roth, Malouf, and Murnighan (1981).

Table 5.1 The Effects of Information on Bargaining Outcomes

Treatment Common Knowledge that:	Agreements: avg. # tickets for $20 player	Disagreement percentage
(1) neither player knows the other's prize	49	14
(2) only the $20 player knows both prizes	44	20
(3) only the $5 player knows both prizes	34	19
(4) both players know both prizes	33	17

Source: Roth and Murnighan (1982).

ruled out by this rationality assumption. The sensitivity of outcomes to changes in payoff information may thus indicate a limit to the range of application for the Nash solution, rather than an out-and-out rejection of the theory. From a practical perspective, however, we have unambiguously learned something: Information has a clear, systematic effect on bargaining outcomes in the laboratory. New theory is needed to account for behavior when subjects know each other's payoffs.

Another interesting aspect of the Roth and Murnighan experiment regards disagreement outcomes. The Nash solution is inconsistent with a significant level of disagreements. However, the right side of table 5.1 shows a fairly high and stable percentage of encounters resulting in disagreement (between 14 and 20 percent).[15] The relatively stable level of disagreements suggests that changes in information alter bargainers' expectations about what others will accept, and hence about what should be demanded.[16]

In addition, the agreements that do occur tend to be struck near the end of the bargaining period. A significant fraction (35 percent) of all agreements in table 5.1 involved settlements in the final thirty seconds of the twelve-minute bargaining periods. About half of these occurred in the last five seconds.[17] This pattern, which is observed in other experiments and in union-management negotiations, has been termed the "deadline effect." Any factor that increases the tendency for

---

[15] These patterns were also observed in a parallel series of four treatments without common knowledge about the information condition; for example, both might know both prizes, but neither would know that the other knew both prizes. One difference was that there were more disagreements when the low-prize player knew the other's prize and this was not common knowledge.

[16] For a more careful discussion of this point, see Roth and Schoumaker (1983).

[17] Roth, Murnighan, and Schoumaker (1988, table 2).

subjects to wait until the final seconds to bargain seriously would also be likely to increase the frequency of disagreements. We are not aware of a bargaining theory that explains both the time pattern of agreements and the level of disagreements.[18]

Forsythe, Kennan, and Sopher (1991), however, have shown that the level of disagreements can be affected by underlying economic incentives. Their experiment was motivated by an analysis of strikes, or breakdowns in labor-management negotiations. The authors begin with the observation that labor and management typically negotiate under conditions of asymmetric information: Management is likely to have a better estimate of corporate revenues, and hence of the available wage pool. The issue is how much of this pool is transferred to the workers in the form of wages. It is convenient to explain their design using labor-management terminology, even though the experiment was conducted in a neutral context. Like the previous studies, the design involves unstructured bargaining among subjects who participated in a series of games with different partners. The subjects were in different rooms and could communicate with their partners via written message. Only one of the subjects in each bargaining pair (management) knew with certainty the amount of money available to be divided (a large or a small "pie"). Bargaining was over how much the informed party would transfer to the uninformed party (labor). Although labor did not know which pie was available, labor did know the probability that the pie would be large.

The authors construct a model in which the incidence of strikes is affected by both the size of the pies and the probability that the pie is large: When the payoffs and probabilities are such that making a high demand is attractive (e.g., the pie is likely to be quite large), then the incidence of high demands is predicted to increase. But high demands by labor increase the incidence of strikes, since high demands will be rejected when the pie turns out to be small. Laboratory data supported these predictions. The authors observed a high incidence of disagreements ("rational" strikes) in a treatment that provided labor with an incentive to make high demands. Fewer disagreements were observed in a second treatment where the incentive to make high demands was diminished.

Summary

The Nash solution generates precise predictions about bargaining outcomes, even in the absence of any specification of the strategies available to the bargainers. Experimental investigation of unstructured bargaining games indicates that the Nash solution organizes behavior quite well, under some circumstances. In at least one context, the Nash solution performs better than a commonly used alternative bargaining theory, the Raiffa (Kalai/Smorodinsky) solution. The axioms underlying

---

[18] See Roth, Murnighan, and Schoumaker (1988) for more data on the deadline effect and for a discussion of alternative explanations.

the Nash solution, however, are too sparse to explain a wide range of bargaining results, particularly when there are asymmetries in payoffs and information. Moreover, and inconsistent with the theory, disagreements are frequently observed. Bargaining experiments have also produced a rich source of data regarding behavioral tendencies that are not adequately explained by existing theory. These findings should stimulate new theoretical work.

In any bargaining situation, the most focal outcome is an equal split of monetary payoffs. Experimental results reviewed in this section indicate that equal division is more likely when earnings opportunities are symmetric. There is a large literature on bargaining experiments that was not covered in this section. This literature (surveyed in Hoffman and Spitzer, 1982) documents a number of important empirical tendencies useful for interpreting and evaluating experimental designs discussed in subsequent sections. In particular, the incidence of equal splits can be affected by procedural considerations that seem to highlight fairness issues. Examples include (1) symmetric procedures for assigning roles (e.g., flipping a coin); (2) repeated interaction between the same pair of subjects in a series of bargaining games; and (3) face-to-face bargaining, as opposed to anonymous communications. The sensitivity of bargaining outcomes to design and procedural considerations is a theme that is elaborated in the following sections.

5.3 Bargaining Over an Externality: The Coase Theorem

An unusual feature of the bargaining game shown in figure 5.2 is that the Nash solution is not the efficient, joint-payoff-maximizing outcome. Given the full-efficiency predictions of competitive market models presented in earlier chapters, the potential inefficiency of the Nash solution is notable. It is not always the case, however, that even seemingly competitive markets allocate resources efficiently. In particular, a market can fail to perform well in the presence of an externality.

Many inefficiencies in both market and bargaining contexts are the consequence of a common incentive problem: The agents who stand to receive the extra surplus are not those who generate the efficiency gains. Consider, for example, the problem of a cement manufacturer whose production process emits dust that reduces the earnings of nearby farmers. These farmers would be the principal beneficiaries of a reduction in dust emissions, but it is the firm that determines the emission level. Figure 5.2 illustrates this conflict in an abstract bargaining context. Not only does player 2 fail to enjoy any of the benefits of moving from the Nash solution to the efficient, joint-payoff-maximizing outcome in the lower right-hand corner, but player 2's earnings are decreased from 30 cents to 0 in the process.

Importantly, this incentive problem could be remedied if player 1 could transfer some of the extra surplus to player 2. For example, both players would be better off in the efficient, joint-maximizing outcome than in the Nash solution if player 1 could commit to transfer at least 30 cents to player 2 *ex post*. The possibility of such *ex post* transfers has an important policy application. In one of the most widely cited papers in the economics literature, Ronald Coase (1960) offered the possibility of bargaining over the benefits received outside of market transactions as a rationale for limited judicial intervention in the workings of a competitive economy, even in the presence of significant externalities. Coase's insight, which was a major factor in his obtaining the 1991 Nobel Prize in economics, was that the efficient resolution of a dispute about externalities can be determined in a decentralized manner via bilateral bargaining, under appropriate conditions (e.g., two informed, maximizing parties who will consummate mutually beneficial agreements).[19]

Coase reasoned that efficiency requires a clear determination of property rights, that is, a determination of which party has the right to stipulate the level of the externality-producing activity, and a well-functioning legal system that permits the costless enforcement of contracts that specify compensatory payments. In this setting, Coase reasoned that the person without the property right (to determine the externality) would offer side payments to induce the person with the property right to agree to a jointly efficient outcome. Moreover, this outcome would be realized independently of who is assigned the property right. In the cement plant example given above, the efficient level of production could be determined by bargaining between the plant owner and the nearby farmer, regardless of whether (1) the farmer has no legal right to block the plant's operation and must offer bribes to limit production, or (2) the plant has no legal right to emit dust, and must offer damage payments to obtain permission from the farmer.

The implication of the Coase theorem can be illustrated in the context of a two-person, numerical example in table 5.2, where the earnings for two subjects, A and B, are determined by the level of an "activity." The activity could be a production process for one firm that generates pollution (such as a dust-emitting cement firm), which in turn interferes with the production process of another firm (say, crops for a farmer). As shown in the top row of the table, the activity level can range from 0 to 6. The earnings for subject A increase from 0 to 11 dollars as the activity is increased from 0 to 6. But this increase in the activity reduces the earnings of B from 12 dollars to 0. Notice from the bottom row of the table that combined earnings are maximized at an activity level of 1.

If bargaining were not permitted, the owner of the right to choose the activity level would individually maximize payoffs at a socially inefficient level. For

---

[19] As noted by Hoffman and Spitzer (1982), Coase cautiously ruled out a number of imperfections; he assumed individual maximization, perfectly competitive markets, a costless court system, the absence of wealth effects and transactions costs, and that the two parties to a dispute have perfect knowledge about one another's payoffs. On a somewhat different level, Coase assumed that agents will not forgo a mutually advantageous deal, which implies Pareto optimality, and therefore lends a flavor of cooperative game theory to the Coase theorem.

Table 5.2 Dollar Payoffs for a Coase Bargaining Game

	Activity level						
	0	1	2	3	4	5	6
$ payoff for A	0	4	6	8	9	10	11
$ payoff for B	12	10	6	4	2	1	0
Total payoff	12	14	12	12	11	11	11

Source: Hoffman and Spitzer (1982), Two-Person, Decision 1 Payoffs.

example, if subject A had control over the activity, level 6 would be preferred, generating an 11-dollar return to A. Subject B would earn nothing in this case. Conversely, if B controlled the activity, this subject would prefer to select level 0 and earn 12 dollars, leaving zero earnings for A. Fourteen dollars are earned at the joint-payoff-maximizing outcome level of 1. The Coase theorem asserts that bargaining between A and B results in the efficient activity level 1 (generating a social surplus of 14 dollars), provided that one of the parties has control over the activity level (e.g., a "property right") and that side payments can be used to compensate the property-right holder for deviating from the best choice from a private point of view. For example, if B controlled the activity decision, then A could induce the choice of activity level 1 by offering a side-payment that would raise net earnings for B to something greater than 12 dollars.

The Data: Pareto Optimality

Hoffman and Spitzer (1982) used the payoffs in table 5.2 (and a number of other payoff tables with a very similar structure) to examine the capacity of agents to strike efficient bargains. Each pair of subjects was placed in a room with a monitor, and a random device was used to assign the roles of A and B. The payoff structure was explained without showing the sum of the money earnings (without the bottom row of table 5.2).

Bilateral bargaining outcomes can be very sensitive to variations in procedures, so it is important to consider them carefully. In this context, the establishment of property rights was explained in the instructions:

Two of you will participate together on each decision. One of you will be designated the "controller." The controller may, if he or she wishes, choose the number by himself or herself and inform the monitor, who will stop the experiment and pay both participants. The other participant may attempt to influence the controller to reach a mutually acceptable joint decision; the other participant may offer to pay part or all of his or her earnings to the controller . . . . If a joint agreement is reached, *both* parties must sign the attached agreement form, stating both what the chosen number will be and how much money will be transferred from one participant's earnings to the other's. *No physical threats are allowed.* If a joint agreement is made and the form is signed, the monitor will terminate the experiment and pay each participant according to the terms set forth in the agreement. Are there any questions? (Hoffman and Spitzer, 1982, pp. 83–84)

After the instructions, subjects were asked to answer three questions to test their understanding of the payoff table and procedures. Then the experimenter flipped a coin to determine which person would be the controller. Bargaining was face to face, and payments were made in public.

Payoff possibilities for the game summarized in table 5.2 are shown as asterisks in figure 5.3. For example, the activity level of 0 yields the vertical intercept: $0 for subject A and $12 for subject B, and so forth. The activity level of 1, shown at the point (4, 10), yields a maximum payoff sum of $14. With side payments, the joint payoff maximum of $14 can be continuously divided between the players, as indicated by the straight dashed line. The equal split of this joint maximum is shown at the point that yields $7 for each.

Despite the "focalness" of the (7, 7) equal-split outcome, the controller can unilaterally obtain more. For example, if player B wins the toss and becomes controller, this person can unilaterally choose any asterisked outcome, including the vertical intercept that yields $12. In this sense, the point (0, 12) is the disagreement point, and the set of Pareto-optimal improvements over this point is the boldfaced extension of the dashed line in the upper left corner of figure 5.3. Under risk neutrality, the money payoffs can be interpreted as utilities, and symmetry implies that the Nash solution is at the midpoint of this boldfaced segment, at $1 for A and $13 for B, as shown in the upper-left corner of figure 5.3. Similarly, player A as controller can unilaterally select the horizontal intercept of (11, 0), which is the disagreement point that determines a Nash solution of (12.5, 1.5), located at the midpoint of the boldfaced line segment at the lower right-hand corner of figure 5.3.

To summarize, under risk neutrality the Nash solution is located on the outer face of the payoff frontier (with side payments), at the midpoint of one of the boldfaced segments. The location of the Nash solution depends on which player is the controller, that is, on the disagreement point. Since the Nash solution maximizes the product of utility gains over the disagreement level, it follows that neither player will receive less than the disagreement utility payoff (which would result in a negative value of the objective to be maximized). This result is called (weak)

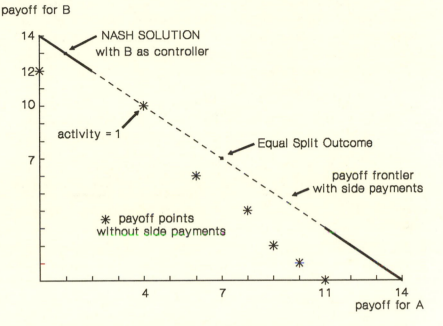

Figure 5.3 Payoff Frontier for a Hoffman and Spitzer (1982) Bargaining Game

individual rationality. The intuition is that it would not be individually rational for a player to agree to an outcome that is worse than the disagreement outcome. This property is relatively noncontroversial, among theorists anyway. Although the Pareto-optimality assumption (of both the Nash bargaining solution and the Coase theorem) only implies that the outcome will be somewhere on the straight-line locus of joint-maximum payoffs, the individual rationality implication of the Nash solution implies that the controller will exploit his or her advantage to obtain a payoff that is considerably above that of the equal-split outcome.

Summary data for two of the Hoffman and Spitzer (1982) treatments are shown in table 5.3. The top row pertains to the cell in which twelve pairs of subjects were given complete information about their partner's payoffs. Moving across this row, we see that eleven of the twelve subject pairs agreed on the joint-maximum, Pareto-optimal activity level of 1, but in five cases the joint payoff was split equally, giving the controller either $4 or $5 less than the disagreement outcome (depending on the controller's type, A or B). In the other seven cases, the controller obtained at least the individually rational amount, and in four of these seven cases the controller did not obtain more than the disagreement payoff. The data shown in the second row of table 5.3 pertain to a parallel series of trials in which neither party knew the other's payoffs; that is, each only saw the part of the payoff table that determined his or her own earnings. Interestingly, the incidence of Pareto-optimal outcomes was not reduced in the partial information treatment.[20] Hoffman and Spitzer interpret the high incidence of Pareto optimality (irrespective of the identity of the controller) as supportive of the main implication of the Coase theorem. But the results are inconsistent with the individual rationality property of the Nash solution, at least if money payments are interpreted as utilities.

Table 5.3 Data for Single-Period, Two-Person Coase Bargaining Games

	Number of pairs	Joint maximum, Pareto optimal	Equal splits (or within $1 of equality)	Controller individually rational
Complete information	12	11	5	7
Partial information	12	11	6	4

Source: Hoffman and Spitzer (1982), table 2.

The drawing power of the joint-maximum, equal-split outcome was even stronger when subject pairs were told that they would be paired twice with the same partner, with a coin flip used at the beginning of each of the two bargaining periods to determine the controller. This "sequential" design creates an additional uncertainty, since the first-stage bargaining occurs before the subjects know who will be controller in the final stage. In this treatment (not shown in the table), all twelve pairs chose the joint-maximum, equal-split outcome. The resiliency of the equal-split outcome in this two-stage treatment is quite surprising (for economists). Hoffman and Spitzer (1985, p. 289) report 100 percent equal-split outcomes when the same two-stage procedures are modified by multiplying all payoffs by 4, in which case the controller would have to give up about $20 to accept an equal split.

Efforts to Find Individual Rationality

Since the basis of the Coase theorem is that individuals, bargaining in their own self-interest, will come to an efficient solution, the failure to observe individual

---

[20] In retrospect, it is not surprising that the results are similar in the complete and partial information treatments. Subjects in the partial information treatment were allowed to discuss their own payoffs with their bargaining partner, and presumably they did so. Although misrepresentation was not ruled out, we would guess that misrepresentation would be more skillfully used by subjects with more experience in laboratory bargaining environments (and with more confidence that misrepresentation would not be revealed by public payment procedures).

rationality on the part of the controllers is disturbing, despite the efficiency of the outcomes. Two questions arise: (1) Is the efficient joint-maximum outcome so pervasive that it will be observed even without the assignment of a unilateral property right? (2) Is the controllers' failure to exploit their advantage due to low incentives or to some artificial symmetry introduced in the laboratory?

The first question, which can be rephrased as whether an externality problem exists in the first place, was addressed by Harrison and McKee (1985). They implemented a "no-property-rights" treatment, with no controller and no contractual mechanism for enforcing agreements about side payments. Payoffs and procedures were similar to those of Hoffman and Spitzer (1982), except that in the event of a disagreement, zero payoffs were assigned to both players, rather than having an outcome determined by a controller.[21] In the absence of side payments, any of the activity levels in table 5.2 would satisfy Pareto optimality, including activity level 2 that gives equal earnings of $6 to each subject. Harrison and McKee used a similar payoff structure in which the set of Pareto-optimal outcomes included one that maximized the sum of payoffs and a different one that yielded equal payoffs, but with a lower total earnings level. All six pairings of subjects in this treatment agreed to the equal-split outcome that did not maximize total earnings.

Having established that there is an externality problem in this context (i.e., that the joint-maximum outcome is not pervasive), Harrison and McKee also addressed the question of why controllers failed to exploit their bargaining positions in previous experiments. The authors approached this second issue by increasing the incentives:[22] They doubled the difference between combined payoffs at the socially efficient activity level (level 1 in table 5.2) and combined payoffs at the equal-split activity level (level 3 in table 5.2). This difference in combined payoffs is $2 in table 5.2, and it can be doubled by increasing both payoffs by $1 for activity level 1.[23] This change would be illustrated in figure 5.3 by moving the "activity = 1" asterisk point to the right by $1.00 and up by $1.00. This change in the original payoff structure reduced the incidence of equal splits from 60 percent to 11 percent.

---

[21] There were some procedural differences, which seem to have been minor in the sense that Harrison and McKee were able to replicate the results of Hoffman and Spitzer when the payoff structure was similar and a controller was used. Harrison and McKee also implemented an alternative, no-property-rights treatment in which a disagreement was resolved by the random choice of one of the activity levels (with equal probability), and this method resulted in a very high incidence of disagreement outcomes.

[22] As discussed above, Hoffman and Spitzer (1985) showed that increases in incentives alone will not eliminate equal-split outcomes in the symmetric, two-stage treatment (with role reversals after the first stage). Repetition with role reversal probably produces equal division because it restores a symmetry to the single-stage bargaining situation with asymmetric property rights. Harrison and McKee evaluate the effects of increased incentives in the context of the asymmetric single-stage game.

[23] Harrison and McKee used different parameters from those shown in table 5.2, but the effect of the transformation of payoffs was essentially the same as described here.

With the higher joint-maximum payoff level, the controller obtained at least an individually rational payoff in eight of nine instances.

Hoffman and Spitzer (1985) also addressed the individual rationality issue, but from a different perspective. They reasoned that the controller in a laboratory may fail to exploit his or her advantage if this advantage is not perceived as being earned. One treatment involved the previously used procedure: a coin flip to determine which subject "is designated to be the controller." A second treatment involved a simple preliminary game of skill (similar to tic-tac-toe) to determine the designated controller. Finally, two additional treatments were constructed by using either the coin flip or the game of skill, but replacing the phrase "is designated to be" with "earns the right to be." The results of this 2 × 2 treatment structure are shown in table 5.4, where the entries are the difference between the average controller payoff and the equal-split payoff. Notice that the use of the "earns the right" terminology increases the controller's payoffs for both controller choice mechanisms. The game of skill results in considerably higher controller earnings when the "earns the right terminology" is used. Interestingly, the change in the wording of the instructions seems to have a more significant effect on behavior than the change in the controller selection procedure.[24] The reader should be alerted; this is a clear example of a case in which "economically irrelevant" changes in procedures have a dramatic effect on the behavior of financially motivated subjects.

Summary

As implied by the Coase theorem, the presence of property rights and costlessly enforced contracts enables participants in experiments to negotiate side payments in a way that usually results in Pareto-optimal allocations. But the controller does not always exploit the property right fully if it is granted by the flip of a coin. This

Table 5.4 The Effect of Controller-Choice Mechanisms on Controller Earnings

	"is designated" terminology	"earns the right" terminology
controller selected by coin flip	1.0	2.6
controller selected by game of skill	1.2	4.5

Source: Hoffman and Spitzer (1985 p. 278).
Note: earnings = average controller payoff − equal-split payoff

---

[24] This conclusion is supported by the authors' statistical analysis of the data; the controller-selection mechanism effect was only marginally significant.

failure to exploit the property right does not violate the efficiency prediction of the Coase theorem, but it does violate the individual rationality property of the Nash solution. The incidence of violations of individual rationality in the laboratory has been reduced by manipulating payoffs and by changing the way that the controller role is explained and awarded. Bilateral bargaining outcomes can be surprisingly sensitive to factors that are not relevant to axiomatic bargaining theory; so experimentalists should be meticulous in selecting, following, and reporting procedural details.

5.4 Structured Bargaining: Ultimatum Game Experiments

Cooperative game theory approaches the theoretical "indeterminacy" of bilateral bargaining by giving up on modeling the strategic bargaining process and instead specifying assumptions about the outcomes. The experiments reviewed in the previous sections, however, reveal data patterns that conflict with one or more axioms of the commonly used Nash solution. In this section, we consider the alternative approach of noncooperative game theory. As mentioned earlier, unstructured bargaining games in real time are so rich and complex in terms of possible bargaining strategies that the only way to make any headway on characterizing the equilibria is to place restrictions on the strategies that can be used.[25] The most commonly used restrictions involve having bargainers take turns in making proposals at fixed points in time (Stahl, 1972, and Rubinstein, 1982). The simplest case, to be discussed here, involves a single round in which one person proposes a split of a pie, which is an ultimatum that the other must accept or reject. Bargaining games with more than one round are considered in the subsequent section.

Ultimatum and Dictator Games: Are Equal Splits Due to Altruism?

An ultimatum game arises naturally as a special case of a market. Consider the negotiation for a single unit, offered to a single buyer by a posted-offer

---

[25] Harrison and McCabe (1988, p. 6) note that it is impossible to write down the extensive form for the bargaining games used in Roth and Malouf (1979), and Roth and Murnighan (1982). Harrison and McCabe are able to specify the extensive form for a two-stage noncooperative bargaining game implemented in the Roth and Schoumaker (1983). This latter game consisted of a stage in which two subjects could independently make demands for shares of a payoff pie, followed by a stage in which subjects could independently repeat their own demands or accept the other's first-stage demand. Harrison and McCabe show that any Pareto-optimal outcome in this two-stage game is a noncooperative equilibrium. They conclude that the observed "misbehavior" of subjects who do not select the Nash bargaining solution is nevertheless perfectly consistent with noncooperative behavior (a conclusion similar to that reached in Wilson, 1985).

monopolist. The monopolist's posted price determines a split of the surplus between the buyer's value and the seller's cost. The buyer may then either accept the proposal (purchase) or not. Despite the direct nature of this analogy, market terminology is typically not used in these experiments. Rather, one subject proposes a division of a fixed amount of money, and the other then accepts the proposed division or rejects. A rejection results in a default payment (usually zero) for each subject. Due to the extreme asymmetry in available actions, the equilibrium for this game involves very asymmetric payoffs: Subgame perfection requires that the recipient of the offer accept any positive payoff (in excess of the default level), no matter how small. It follows that the equilibrium offer is the one that provides the smallest positive payoff to the recipient. Such offers are viewed as being very unfair, and it is not surprising that extreme offers are frequently rejected. This section explores the sensitivity of offer and rejection behavior to experimental treatment conditions: experience, incentives, and so forth.

The first ultimatum-game experiment to be discussed is that of Güth, Schmittberger, and Schwartz (1982), hereafter Güth et al. All subjects were placed in the same room where they could see each other, but no subject knew the person with whom he or she was paired. Initial demands and the accept/reject responses were made by written message, and all earnings were paid in cash. Given the theoretical prediction that the player making the demand will ask for essentially all of the payoff pie, it was surprising that the modal demand was for half of the pie. Although a majority of demands were for more than half of the pie, very few subjects demanded anything near 100 percent of the surplus. This procedure was repeated one week later, and demands were somewhat more aggressive, but again nowhere near the theoretical prediction. Rejections were uncommon, but aggressive demands were more likely to be rejected. Recall that any rejection is irrational in the sense of reducing the payoff of the respondent.

The tendency for the proposer to give away a significant fraction of the pie in ultimatum games was also observed by Kahneman, Knetsch, and Thaler (1986). They speculate that a major reason for the generosity of initial offers in ultimatum games is a concern for the respondent's well-being. This concern for fairness would be a type of altruism that, although not inconsistent with the formal structure of economic theory, would be inconsistent with the assumption of nonaltruistic self-interest that is commonly used by economists. As a result, economists have suggested alternative explanations that are less problematic for the assumption of self-motivated agents in economic markets.

Güth et al. (1982) conjecture that the failure of the proposer to exploit fully a first-mover advantage in their ultimatum games was attributable to procedural characteristics that raised concerns among the participants regarding "fairness." For example, they suggest that proposers would have been more aggressive if market terminology had been used or if subjects had been visually separated.[26] Forsythe, et al. (1988) further note that the subject-pool selection process may have generated concerns for fairness. Participants in the Güth et al. experiment were not volunteers but students whose participation was required as part of a course. The prospect of continued interaction of participants outside of the laboratory setting may contaminate incentives, as subjects may see themselves as being involved in a larger, multi-stage game with the others. (In fact, the subjects did interact again in the same game a week later.)

To evaluate the effects of anonymity on "fairness" in ultimatum games, Forsythe et al. conducted an experiment where volunteer participants, recruited from the student body at large, made strictly anonymous decisions. Participants had no information about the identities of those in the pool with whom they could possibly be matched, either before, during, or after the laboratory session. The bargaining was over the split of a fixed dollar amount. Each subject only participated in a single bargaining game, and earnings from this game were paid in cash.[27] Even with these precautions, the 50/50 split was still the modal proposal. The frequency distribution of proposed splits of the $10 pie is represented by the white ribbon with the dark shadow at the back of figure 5.4. (At present, please ignore the textured ribbons in the front part of the figure.) Here, the horizontal axis represents the dollar amount offered to the respondent, so $5 is the equal-split offer and $.01 is the subgame-perfect equilibrium offer. The vertical dimension shows the percentage of offers at each dollar amount. The dark spike at $5 indicates the preponderance of equal-split offers. To summarize, the procedural safeguards taken to prevent a contamination of the incentive structure do not eliminate the tendency for proposers to give away a significant fraction of the pie in ultimatum games.

On the other hand, evidence from an experiment by Hoffman, et al. (1991) indicates the importance of other procedural details. In particular, these authors examine the effects of presenting the experiment in a market context, and the effects of having the bargainers "earn the right" to be the proposer. A market interpretation of the game was developed by converting the Fouraker and Siegel bilateral monopoly design into an ultimatum game by only giving the seller a single unit: The seller made a price proposal, and the buyer responded by either purchasing or not. Participants earned the right to be the proposer (seller) by getting more correct

---

[26] There is some earlier evidence to support the conjecture that market terminology may matter. Fouraker and Siegel (1963) observed nearly complete exploitation of a first-mover position in a closely related posted-offer bilateral-monopoly experiment. Note, however, that the structure of Fouraker and Siegel's bilateral-monopoly design deviates from the ultimatum game in that the buyer may vary the purchase quantity, rather than make an all-or-nothing response.

[27] The authors also conducted a parallel series of sessions under which subjects received only a fixed payment, and their earnings were unaffected by the bargaining outcomes.

answers than their bargaining partner in a trivia quiz. In each case, subjects participated in one ultimatum game and were then paid and released.

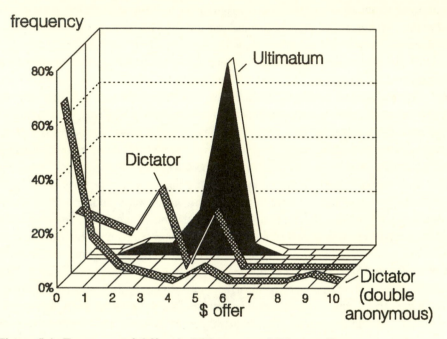

Figure 5.4 Frequency of Offers in Ultimatum and Dictator Games
(Source: Forsythe et al., 1988, for ultimatum and dictator game data;
Hoffman et al., 1991, for double-blind, dictator-game data)

For purposes of comparison, our discussion of results focuses on a series of treatments with the same incentive structure used by Forsythe et al. (e.g., participants received a $3 fee for showing up, and bargained over a $10 pie).[28] In a baseline treatment, where buyer/seller terminology was not used, and where the identity of the proposer was determined by a random device, results were very similar to those reported by Forsythe et al.; the median offer was (the equal-split) $5. However, with the addition of buyer/seller terminology, the median offer dropped to $4. When half of the subjects earned the right to be sellers, the median offer dropped even more, to $3. The combined effect of these two treatments was dramatic: more than half of the offers were for 50/50 splits using neutral, nonmarket terminology and a random assignment of the seller roles. But only about a tenth of the offers were for an equal split when market terminology was used and the seller role was earned.

---

[28] Offers, however, were restricted to integer dollar amounts in Hoffman et al.

These results confirm the earlier findings for unstructured bargaining games (with side payments), that is, that economically irrelevant procedural details can have a significant effect on bargaining behavior, especially when such details alter the perceived symmetry of the situation. Although the Hoffman et al. (1991) procedures have the effect of increasing the aggressiveness of proposers, it is important to notice that these proposers persist in giving away a nonnegligible fraction of the pie.[29]

It may be the case that the apparent generosity of proposers in these ultimatum games has little to do with fairness or altruism. Rather, the nearly equal splits of the pie may be a rational "strategic" response to the spiteful tendency of respondents to reject unequal offers. Forsythe et al. investigate this possibility by examining performance in a game that is even starker than the ultimatum game; the "dictator" game. In this game, the decider simply makes an allocational decision regarding the distribution of a $10 pie, and the pie is split in accordance with this decision. The fear of rejection is thus eliminated in dictator games, and the optimal response for the decider is to take all $10, independent of any beliefs regarding the rationality of the other participant. Presumably, only considerations of fairness would motivate more equitable divisions in such games.

Aside from the lack of recourse on the part of receivers, procedures were essentially identical to those of the ultimatum game by Forsythe et al. described above. Results of this session are illustrated as the frequency distribution of dictators' offers, shown as the textured ribbon in the middle part of figure 5.4. About 21 percent of the dictators took the whole pie (offered $0), but other dictators left varying amounts to the other player. About 21 percent of the dictators even went so far as to divide the pie equally. A comparison of the dark spike for the ultimatum game data with the textured ribbon for the dictator game data yields two conclusions: (1) strategic responses to the possibility of rejection are important, as dictators are significantly more aggressive in making lower offers when there is no chance of rejection, and (2) strategic considerations are not the whole story, as most subjects are reluctant to take full advantage of their roles as dictators.

---

[29] While market-based terminology is nonneutral relative to abstract bargaining terminology, it may represent a relatively neutral way to compare behavior across cultures. Roth et al. (1991) used market terminology in this manner to compare the bargaining behavior in four cities: Jerusalem, Ljubljana (Yugoslavia), Pittsburgh, and Tokyo. In each location, paired participants were students who interacted under similar instructions, payoffs, and procedures in a series of ten ultimatum games with different partners. One of the games was chosen at random *ex post* to determine subjects' earnings. In all four countries, the proposer tended to offer the other person a significant fraction of the pie, but the bargainers with the first-mover advantage were less aggressive in the United States and Yugoslavia, where the modal proposal involved a 50/50 split of the gains from trade. In contrast, the modal proposal in Japan and Israel provided the proposer (buyer) with 60 percent of the gains from trade. These differences were statistically significant, and the authors tentatively attribute the differences to cultural factors by ruling out other factors (e.g., currency or experimenter effects). Even though the offers were seemingly more aggressive in Japan and Israel, the rate of rejection was no greater. This observation leads the authors to speculate that the main cultural difference across subject pools is in terms of what is considered a division that is fair enough not to be rejected.

A further dictator game reported by Hoffman et al. (1991) suggests that the apparent generosity of laboratory dictators may be largely due to unintended procedural features rather than to fairness considerations. In most of the bargaining experiments discussed in this section, participants are anonymous in the sense that they do not know one anothers' true identities. But the subjects knew that the experimenter could observe who made which decisions, and perhaps participants were influenced by this knowledge. Hoffman et al. investigated the possibility of experimenter-observation effects by conducting a *double-anonymous* dictator game in which nobody, not even the experimenter, ever finds out who made which decisions.[30] This was accomplished by giving each dictator a manila envelope with a combination of paper slips and/or dollar bills. The dictator was instructed to remove one-half of the slips and/or bills, in any desired combination, and then to reseal the envelope. Envelopes were distributed and decisions were collected by a student monitor in a manner that made it impossible for the experimenters ever to figure out what decisions were made by any dictator.[31] This added anonymity served to increase the shares taken by the dictator, and the effect was dramatic. Two-thirds of the dictators claimed the whole pie. The frequency distribution of offers is represented by the textured ribbon at the front of figure 5.4. There were almost no equal-split offers, although one subject was a benevolent despot who gave the other person $9. A comparison of data for dictator games with and without double-anonymous procedures (represented by the textured ribbons in figure 5.4) supports the authors' conclusion that subjects care more about the opinions of third parties (e.g., the experimenters) than they care about the earnings of their partners.[32]

---

[30] Hoffman et al. refer to this treatment as being double-blind. We use slightly different terminology because the term "double-blind" usually refers to a situation in which neither the subject nor the person conducting the experiment is aware of the experiment's purpose. Although the person conducting the experiment in the Hoffman et al. treatment was unable to associate decisions with particular individuals, the experimenter (an author) did know the purpose of the experiment. Double-blind and double-anonymous treatments are similar in that they are intended to reduce "experimenter demand" effects.

[31] More specifically, a session consisted of twenty-nine participants. Of these, fourteen were assigned the dictator role, and another fourteen were placed in a separate room. The remaining participant (a volunteer) was a monitor who distributed and collected envelopes. Dictators were called, one at a time, to the back of the room, and were given one of fourteen unmarked envelopes by the monitor. All envelopes were equally thick: Twelve of the envelopes contained ten one-dollar bills and ten blank paper slips, while the other two envelopes contained twenty blank paper slips. Each dictator was instructed to take a total of ten paper slips and/or dollar bills from their envelope. They did this, in private, and then sealed the envelope, which they returned to the monitor. After all dictators had made decisions, the monitor took the envelopes to a separate room and distributed them to other participants. Neither market (buyer/seller) nor "dictator" terminology was used.

[32] The process of making the procedures completely anonymous may have introduced other subtle biases. For example, the presence of two envelopes containing only blank slips of paper means that two people will receive nothing. This consequence may have suggested to the dictators that they should take $10. Further experimentation could determine whether this procedure did or did not bias behavior.

Summary

Not surprisingly, when the predictions of noncooperative game theory involve sufficiently severe inequities, they tend to break down, even in very simple games. Attitudes about fairness and about what the other party is likely to accept seem to be sensitive to procedures that determine how roles are assigned and whether market terminology is used. But regardless of procedures, respondents in ultimatum games frequently reject disadvantageous offers, even though the rejection reduces their earnings and the situation involves a single encounter under conditions of anonymity. As a result, the proposers commonly offer a significant share of the pie (often half) to the respondent. But even when the fear of rejection is removed by giving the proposer dictatorial powers, most subjects give away a significant share of the pie to their bargaining partners. Recent results with double-anonymous procedures indicate that this apparent generosity is not altruism, but rather seems to arise largely from concerns about opinions of outside observers. These results provide additional evidence of the importance of attention to procedural details in bargaining experiments. An important issue that remains to be investigated is whether procedural adjustments will yield more aggressive demands in ultimatum games.

5.5 Structured Bargaining: Alternating-Offer Experiments

The ultimatum games discussed in the previous section can be thought of as having a single "round" in which one subject proposes and the other responds. One way to increase the relevance of this highly structured game to natural bilateral bargaining situations is to increase the number of rounds. Most bargaining situations involve at least the possibility of a series of rounds, each with a proposal and response. If there is a finite number of rounds, then the last round is simply an ultimatum game. It is also natural to think of bargaining games with no a priori limit on the number of rounds, although the costs of bargaining may reduce incentives to continue haggling. One way in which bargaining can be costly is in terms of lost production during a strike. Another bargaining cost is in terms of delayed payment; a dollar earned in an agreement after a later round is not as valuable as a dollar earned now, since the dollar earned now can be invested. This time preference is implemented in experiments by a discount factor that shrinks the size of the pie being divided. For example, a discount factor of 10 percent would cause a pie of $100 in round 1 to shrink to $90 in round 2, $81 in round 3, and so forth. This discounting gives subjects an incentive to reach an agreement earlier.

The remarkable implication of using the notion of a subgame-perfect Nash equilibrium is that subjects will reach an agreement in the very first period. As noted in chapter 2, subgame perfection implements a type of backward induction that precludes the use of threats that are not credible, for example, the rejection of a "stingy" offer in the final stage of a bargaining game. In a multiround bargaining game, an agreement is possible in the first round because backward induction allows players to think ahead about what would happen if bargaining were to continue into subsequent subgames. This backward-induction argument, which was generalized by Stahl (1972) and Rubinstein (1982), will be explained first in terms of simple games with two rounds.

Two-Round Games: Theory

The two-round game represented in figure 5.5 presents an exaggerated case of a shrinking pie. The vertical axis provides a measure of the pie to be split in each round. As indicated below the horizontal axis, the pie is worth 100 pennies in round 1, in which player 1 makes an offer. If this offer is rejected by player 2, the pie is only worth 25 pennies in round 2, in which player 2 makes an offer. If the round 2 offer is rejected, both players earn nothing (the pie shrinks to 0). Using backward induction, consider first what would happen in the final round. In theory, player 1 prefers any small positive payoff to nothing, so player 2's offer of 1 penny to player 1 in the final round would be accepted, leaving essentially the whole pie (24 cents) for player 2. Player 2's second-round demand of 24 is indicated in the figure by the filled line segment with a height of 24, and the unfilled 1-penny segment is what goes to player 1.

Working backward, we consider the first round, where player 1 makes an offer to split 100 pennies, knowing that player 2 can obtain 24 in the final round. Therefore, if player 1 offers 25 pennies to player 2 in the initial round, player 2 will (in theory) accept. The 75 cents that remain of the first round pie would go to player 1, as represented by the division of the vertical line for round 1 into a 25-cent filled segment and a 75-cent unfilled segment.

This same logic works for any variation of the two-round game. The second player can essentially claim the whole pie that remains in the second round, so player 1 can begin with a first-round offer to player 2 that equals the size of the second-round pie. This offer will, in theory, be accepted, so player 1 earns the difference between the first-round pie and the second-round pie. In other words, player 1 is able to earn the amount by which the pie shrinks. This shrinkage was large (75 percent) in figure 5.5, but it is possible to vary the shrinkage percentage, and thereby vary the fraction of the initial pie that goes to player 1 in equilibrium.

Two-Round Games: Data

In a two-round game, the final round is an ultimatum game. Given the observed failure of subjects to exploit fully the advantage of being a proposer in an ultimatum game, it would be surprising if the theory worked consistently for the

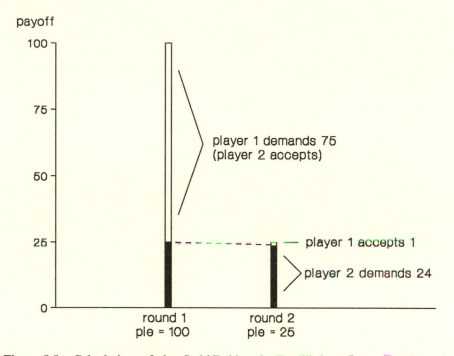

Figure 5.5 Calculation of the Stahl/Rubinstein Equilibrium for a Two-Round, Alternating-Offer Bargaining Game

more complicated two-round games.[33] The results reviewed in this section indicate whether, and to what extent, demands are responsive to changes in strategic considerations.

The first experiment of this type was reported by Binmore, Shaked, and Sutton (1985), who used the two-period structure in figure 5.5, where the payoff numbers on the vertical axis are percentages of 1 pound (UK). The average first-round demand was for a .57 share of the pie, which is considerably below the predicted .75 share for player 1. But when the subjects who had the role of player 2 were given the role of player 1 in a second session, the average demand increased to .67. For purposes of later comparison, it is instructive to illustrate this result in terms of a graph showing the relationship between equilibrium predictions and average first-period demands. In figure 5.6 equilibrium predictions are measured along the horizontal axis. The dashed 45 degree line represents points for which behavior matches the theory. The results of the second Binmore et al. session, with reversed

---

[33] But recall that the proposer's behavior was more rational under some procedural conditions than under others.

roles, are represented by the asterisk in figure 5.6. The points on the dotted lines above and below the asterisk each represent a single standard deviation from the mean. Notice that outcomes in this second session were within one standard deviation of the .75 equilibrium prediction.

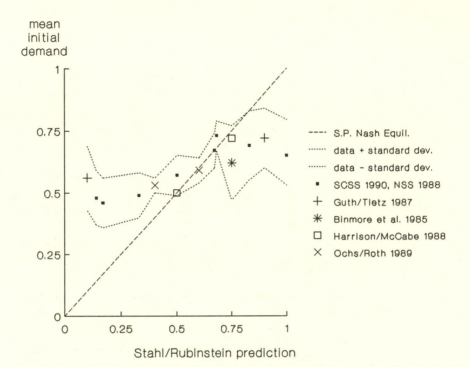

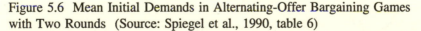

Figure 5.6 Mean Initial Demands in Alternating-Offer Bargaining Games with Two Rounds (Source: Spiegel et al., 1990, table 6)

The same figure 5.5 design was used by Harrison and McCabe (1988), and they find mean initial demands of .72, represented by the unfilled box with a horizontal coordinate of .75 in figure 5.6.[34] Additional supportive results were obtained by Neelin, Sonnenschein, and Spiegel (1988) (NSS in figure 5.6) for a two-round game with a theoretical prediction of .68 for the initial demand, and by Spiegel et al. (1990) (SCSS in figure 5.6) for a game with a theoretical prediction of .67. These data points are represented by dots with horizontal coordinates of .67–.68 in figure 5.6.

---

[34] No standard deviations are provided for the Harrison and McCabe data, although they note that the standard deviations for their various treatments are in the 5 to 10 cent range. Interestingly, Harrison and McCabe obtained essentially the same results in a parallel treatment in which subjects bargained over 100 lottery tickets, as in the binary lottery bargaining experiments discussed in the previous section.

But Neelin et al. obtained results that were inconsistent with the Stahl/Rubinstein theory in games with more rounds. Furthermore, it is apparent from figure 5.6 that systematic deviations from the dashed-line prediction are observed when the predicted first-round demand falls outside of the range from .5 to .75. When the initial demand is predicted to exceed .75, subjects tend to demand less than they "should," as observed by Güth and Tietz (1988) in a treatment with an outcome that is represented by the "+" on the right side of figure 5.6. This result is consistent with behavior in ultimatum games. Indeed, Spiegel et al. (1990) conducted a 2-round experiment in which the value of the pie in the second round was exactly zero, which essentially transforms the two-round game into an ultimatum game. The mean demand was .65, as shown by the dot on the far right side of figure 5.6. Even more interesting are the data points on the left side of the figure, that is, when the proposer is predicted to demand less than .5 in the initial round (because the pie shrinks by less than 50 percent between rounds). In these cases, the proposer in the first round is relatively disadvantaged, but nevertheless tends to demand an equal split, a demand that is often accepted.

To summarize, it is apparent from figure 5.6 that the average initial proposal in two-round games is somewhat responsive to strategic considerations, especially in the range from .5 to .75. But behavior is not as responsive as predicted by the Stahl/Rubinstein theory; the bias is always toward an equal split of the pie. Proposers fail to exploit their advantage fully when it is relatively great, and they try for a 50/50 split when disadvantaged. Notably, the pattern in the figure illustrates these systematic deviations from accepted theory; it does not provide an alternative theory.[35] A general theory of bargaining behavior will have to be responsive to these experimental results. Another task for experimentalists would be to find an environment in which the currently received theory does work well when the equilibrium predicts unequal division.

Multiround, Alternating-Offer Games

The calculation of the subgame perfect equilibrium for games with three rounds is a straightforward extension of the backward-induction arguments given above. The proposer in the first of the three rounds can simply offer the other player a little more than what that player would get in the final two rounds that would follow a rejection. In this manner, the first-round proposal would be accepted. At this point,

---

[35] Bolton (1991) has developed an explanation of these data that is based on an assumption that each agent's utility is a function of both his/her own earnings and the difference between these earnings and the earnings of the other bargainer. This theory can explain why a subject would reject a first-round offer and then make a counteroffer in the second round that yields less than the offer that was just rejected. The intuition is that the "disadvantageous counteroffer" can reduce the difference between the bargainers' earnings.

it is useful to list several reasons for expecting the results of multiround games to differ from this theoretical prediction. First, the predicted behavior in the first round depends on a correct anticipation of equilibrium outcomes in the final two rounds, but we have seen that subjects deviate from the equilibrium in two-round games when the pie shrinkage is either very high or very low. Second, experiments in other contexts (such as the centipede game) have shown that subjects are not very good at backward induction. In two-period asset-market experiments (discussed in chapter 7), subjects actually have to experience the trading situation in the final period before pricing behavior in the initial period can reflect correct expectations. Forsythe, Palfrey, and Plott (1982) have termed this the "swingback hypothesis": adjustment to equilibrium in a repeated sequence of two-period markets will occur first in the final period, and only in later markets will behavior in the first period swing into line with predictions of a theory based on perfect foresight.

Neelin et al. (1988) observed anomalous results in three-round games. What subjects in their experiments seem to do in making an initial proposal is to treat the final two-round subgame as if it were a single round. Harrison and McCabe (1988) observed similar results in initial matchings of bargaining pairs. (Subjects were rematched in an anonymous manner between bargaining games.) Harrison and McCabe, citing the swingback hypothesis, put subjects in a three-round game in even-numbered matchings, and in the final two-round subgame in odd-numbered matchings. In this manner, subjects were given the experience necessary to form correct expectations about what would happen if the initial proposal in the three-round game were to be rejected. With this type of experience, the initial proposals tended to converge to the theoretical prediction.

Less encouraging results of experience with subgames were reported by Spiegel et al. (1990). Importantly, however, the experience treatment they use differed from that used by Harrison and McCabe. Rather than providing subjects with repeated alternating experience with the same subgames, Spiegel et al. had subjects participate in a single series of nested subgames, consisting of the last stage, the last two stages, the last three stages, and so on, telescoping back to a subgame consisting of the (six-stage) game as a whole. It is perhaps not surprising that this sort of experience does not improve performance of the theory in these longer games, since subjects only see each subgame once.

The bewildered reader is probably best advised to use intuition gained from thinking about the results of simpler games in assessing the nature of these results. For example, demands in ultimatum games (without double-anonymous procedures) are much less aggressive than predicted by the theory, and so experience in ultimatum subgames may not do much to increase the incidence of equilibrium outcomes in longer games. One parallel with the results of simpler games is that strategic considerations do seem to matter, even if the effect is not always as strong as predicted by the theory.[36]

Summary Discussion

While perhaps the most primitive of economic arrangements, the rich message space in bilateral bargaining makes it very difficult to analyze. Since cooperative solutions are based on one or more axioms (assumptions about outcomes) that are contradicted in bargaining experiments, there is considerable interest in simplified bargaining models where strategic considerations can be explicitly evaluated. The most common simplification involves an assumption that bargainers make proposals in an alternating sequence. The major conclusion of this section, however, is that the Stahl/Rubinstein theory has some explanatory value, but there are systematic deviations. Behavior does seem sensitive to strategic considerations, and experience in different roles and in subgames can reduce the disparities between theory and data. But seemingly nonstrategic considerations are also relevant. In simple dictator games, for example, behavior that seems to be either altruistic or irrational is diminished by a procedural modification; the introduction of sufficient anonymity. Indeed, bargaining experiments provide the most dramatic cases of "economically irrelevant" procedural details that have major effects on observed behavior.

It is also important to note that the alternating-choice model is somewhat artificial; bargaining environments with exogenously imposed limits on the timing, source, and number of proposals are very uncommon in natural contexts. For structured, alternating-choice models to have any empirical relevance outside of the laboratory, they must be viewed as models of what happens in *unstructured* bargaining situations. Thus the Stahl/Rubinstein theory must further be enriched if it is to explain the disagreements observed in the unstructured bargaining experiments discussed in earlier sections.

5.6 Auctions with Fixed Supply

Bilateral bargaining represents one class of trading institutions that differ from the organized market rules considered in the early chapters. A second class of trading institutions commonly arises when one agent, usually a seller, needs to create

---

[36] Binmore, Shaked, and Sutton (1989) report another situation where strategic considerations appear to be important but do not explain all outcomes. These authors implemented alternating-offer games with no final period, but with either discounting (pie shrinkage) or random termination mechanisms. They used two treatments that they considered to be similar from a fairness/focalness perspective but that had different equilibrium behavior. Observed behavior was sensitive to the change in the strategic situation, and subjects tended to rationalize the outcome *ex post* as being "fair."

a special market to sell a fixed supply of some commodity for which there is no well-developed, ongoing sales outlet. Institutions in this second class are generally referred to as auctions.[37] Auctions are typically arranged for commodities that are sufficiently unusual, for example, unique items ranging from junk furniture to fine works of art. In addition, auctions are used when one person hires someone else to arrange a purchase or sale in a way that reduces opportunities for illegal kickbacks. For this reason, auctions are popular with heirs and government agencies.[38] In contrast with the usual situation in which buyers compete to submit the highest price at auction, a government-sponsored auction often works in reverse, with the public agency acting as a monopsony buyer who invites sellers to compete for a contract to be awarded at the lowest price.

People who use auctions may have a variety of special concerns. In an auction for perishable goods, such as fresh flowers, the speed of transactions is very important. In other instances, for example, government bond sales, there is a great deal of concern about the likelihood of collusion among buyers. A rich diversity of auction forms have evolved in response to this variety of needs. This diversity has motivated a considerable amount of theoretical and experimental work.

The economic analysis of auctions falls into two broad classes of theoretical models, which vary according to the kind of uncertainty participants face when making decisions. The simplest models are those characterized by uncertainty regarding the value of the auctioned item for each bidder. In auctions involving unique, specialized items for which there are no well-developed markets, it is not unreasonable for the value of the item being auctioned to differ from one bidder to another. Each bidder's private prize value is not directly observed by the others. This uncertainty is relevant to the bidding decision, because others' values determine the maximum amount that they are willing to bid. Models in this class are called *private values* models.

In other contexts, the relevant uncertainty regards the ultimate value of the item, which is the same for all bidders. For example, consider an auction for an offshore oil lease site. The value of the site depends on the quantity, quality, and availability of oil; this value is the same for all bidders, assuming equal recovery costs, but it is unknown at the time bids are solicited. If bidders make imperfect estimates of the value before bidding, then their value estimates will be correlated. Models in this second class are called *common-value* models. Most bidding situations have both private- and common-value characteristics, but for the purposes of developing intuition, economists have focused on the polar cases. The remainder

---

[37] From an economist's perspective, just about any type of centralized market trading institution can be considered an auction (e.g., a double auction or a posted-offer auction). In common usage, however, the term "auction" generally is used to define a class of institutions where supply is fixed.

[38] See Cassady (1967) for a colorful and interesting account of a variety of auction markets for items as diverse as fish, tobacco, ships, and brides.

of this section and the next develops the theory of private-value auctions and summarizes the results of laboratory implementations of these auctions. Common-value auctions are considered in a subsequent section.

Private-Value Auctions

The majority of auction experiments implement one of the four institutions listed in table 5.5. Auctions in the top two rows involve the submission of sealed bids, and in this sense, bidding is simultaneous. In the *first-price auction* summarized in the top row, the person making the highest sealed bid will purchase the object for an amount that equals the person's own bid. As indicated by the parenthetical remarks in the top row of the table, the *discriminative auction* just generalizes this to the case of multiple prizes, with each winning bidder paying his or her own bid. This is the sense in which there can be price discrimination (and considerable regret on the part of the highest bidders). The second row summarizes characteristics of the *uniform-price auction*, which avoids price discrimination by selling all prizes to the highest bidders at a common price, the highest rejected bid.[39] The *second-price auction* is just a special case of a uniform-price auction; with only one prize, the highest rejected bid is the second-highest price.

Auctions listed in the bottom two rows of table 5.5 involve sequential bidding rather than the simultaneous bidding that occurs in the first and second price auction mechanisms. A *Dutch auction*, described in the third row, is used to sell bulbs and flowers in Holland. This auction is implemented by having a pointer fall over a range of prices; a sale is enacted when one of the bidders stops the Dutch clock by signaling acceptance of the price indicated by the pointer. Acceptance can be indicated by the press of a button or by a hand signal. The *English auction*, summarized in the fourth row, is a sequential auction where prices are raised sequentially, instead of being lowered. An English auction mechanism is commonly used in the sale of art, wine, and antiques. Multiple-unit versions of these sequential auctions are described in the table.[40]

When bidders have private, known values, there are important parallels between the sequential auctions at the bottom of table 5.5 and the sealed-bid auctions at the top. These parallels will be developed in the remainder of this section, but it is useful to begin with an overview. The English auction and the second-price sealed-bid auction are strategically similar in the sense that, in both cases, bidders have a

---

[39] It is also possible to implement a uniform-price auction where the winning bidders all pay a price that equals the lowest accepted bid instead of the highest accepted bid. This alternative has less desirable incentive properties and for this reason is rather infrequently used.

[40] As noted in section 5.9, it is also possible to implement a multi-unit Dutch auction with a uniform price. The price is lowered sequentially until confirmations have been received. The final confirmation determines the common sale price.

Table 5.5 Standard Auction Institutions for a Single Seller

Auction Institution	Bidding Process	Description
First-price (discriminative)	sealed bids	The high bidder wins and pays his or her own bid price. (With M prizes, the highest M bidders pay their bid prices.)
Second-price (uniform-price)	sealed bids	The high bidder wins and pays the second highest bid price. (With M prizes, the highest M bidders pay the $M+1$st bid.)
Dutch	bids decline	Price is lowered sequentially until a sale is confirmed by the first bidder to indicate acceptance of a price. (With M prizes, price is lowered until M confirmations have been received. Bidders pay their confirmation prices.)
English	bids increase	Price is raised sequentially until the bidding stops, i.e., only one active bidder remains. (With M prizes, price is raised until M bidders remain.)

simple dominant strategy of letting the bidding reveal one's own private value. This strategy is based entirely on the bidder's value for the item, and in particular, it is independent of risk preferences and beliefs about the bidding behavior of others. In a parallel manner, the sequential Dutch auction is strategically similar to the first-price sealed-bid auction. Bidding strategies in these latter two auctions, however, are more complex, as they involve the actual calculation of a bid that is a best response to others' bidding behavior. Therefore, an optimal bid in these auctions will be sensitive to the bidder's risk attitudes and beliefs about others' behavior.

First consider the incentives in an English auction. For simplicity, we restrict attention to the case of a single prize. Any bidder's dominant strategy is simply determined by their value for the item: A bidder should remain in the bidding until the proposed price passes his or her own value. The bidding would stop when the person with the second highest value drops out of the competition, so the bidder with the highest value obtains the prize, as required for efficiency, and pays a price equal to the second highest value.[41] Notice how this strategy is independent of the actions taken by other bidders. Suppose that all of the bidders, except a bidder X,

---

[41] As Ashenfelter (1989) notes, the actual bidding situation in an English auction often involves a little more latitude for strategic behavior, as the seller may have a reservation price that is unknown to the bidders, and the seller's agent can "knock down" the item to the seller in a fictitious sale if the bidding does not go high enough. But in some models, the seller gains nothing by not publicly announcing the optimal reserve price (Riley and Samuelson, 1981).

decided to remain active until the bidding exceeded each of their values by $1.00. Should bidder X respond by bidding higher? No, of course not. Although a higher bid raises the probability of purchasing the item, the bidder would regret purchasing at a bid price that exceeds the value of the prize.

The second-price auction provides analogous incentives to submit a bid based on value. This is clear by considering the optimal bid for a given bidder X, with some arbitrarily chosen value, say $5. Notice first that X cannot increase earnings by submitting a bid below $5, since the price is determined by the second highest bid. Rather, a bid of less than $5 would simply lower X's chances of winning the auction, without changing the price paid in the event of a win. Similarly, although bidder X can increase the probability of winning by submitting a bid above $5, X would never want to win the auction in this manner, as the following example illustrates. Suppose X submitted a bid of $6. If the second highest bid were less than $5, then X would have won the auction with a bid of $5, so the bid increase has no effect on X's earnings. On the other hand, if the second highest bid were $5.50, X would win the auction but lose $.50. Thus, as in the English auction, bidders have a simple dominant strategy to let the bid reveal their private values, regardless of risk attitudes or beliefs about others' values.[42]

Finally, notice that price and efficiency predictions for the second-price auction are identical to those for the English auction. Since optimal bids reveal values in a second-price auction, it follows that the bidder with the highest value submits the highest bid, so the outcome is efficient (in theory). Moreover, the winner pays an amount that is equal to the second highest value, which is approximately the same place where the bidding would stop in an English auction. It follows that the English auction yields the same expected sales revenue and efficiency as the second-price auction, despite the seemingly large differences in the trading rules.

There is an important sense in which the English and second-price auctions differ. In an English auction, no calculation of a strategy is necessary. The bidder need only compare his or her private value with the auctioneer's current price: Purchase of an item remains profitable until the auctioneer's price equals one's value, and it is foolish to continue bidding at higher prices. In this manner, the bidder with the highest value *discovers* that it is not necessary to pay more than the price at which the second highest bidder drops out. In contrast, no such learning takes place during a second-price auction. Rather, an optimal bid may be deduced only with considerable reasoning, since what one pays is not what one bids. Moreover, the consequences of deviations from a value-revealing bid depend on conjectures about the bids of others. Due to this difference in what is learned in the

---

[42] This argument was first made in an auction context by Vickrey (1961), and therefore, a second-price auction is sometimes called a Vickrey auction.

auction process, it would not be surprising to observe differences in bidding behavior between in English and second-price auctions.[43]

Now consider the other two institutions, Dutch and first-price, in which there is one prize and the winning bidder pays his or her own bid price. It is obviously not optimal to bid above one's value, and a bid that equals one's value will ensure a payoff of zero, whether or not one wins. In deciding how much to bid below one's value, the bidder should consider the tradeoff between the increased profitability of winning with a lower bid and the reduced chances of winning. This tradeoff depends on a bidder's beliefs about competitors' bids. Notice that this tradeoff must be considered in both the first-price and Dutch auctions. Moreover, the relevant information is the same in each case, since the bidder's value is known and the sequential reduction of price in a Dutch auction tells the bidder nothing that could not (and should not) be considered in advance.[44]

To summarize, there are four auction institutions that are commonly used in experiments, two with sequential bidding and two with simultaneous bidding. For the case of private values, there is an equivalence between (1) the second-price and English auctions, and (2) the first-price and Dutch auctions. Further comparisons require an analysis of equilibrium bidding for the first-price and Dutch auctions under more restrictive assumptions, which is the next topic.

5.7 First-Price Auctions with Private Values

A first-price auction is easy to implement, and as we shall see, the Nash equilibrium bidding strategies can be quite simple and intuitive. Although the analysis that follows is stated in terms of a first-price auction, the same arguments apply for a Dutch auction.

Equilibrium Bidding Strategies

Consider a first-price sealed-bid auction with N bidders. Each bidder has a private value, which will be denoted by v_i, and is faced with the problem of determining a bid b_i, where $i = 1 \ldots N$. The optimal bid depends on a bidder's own value and on the bidder's beliefs about others' bids, which in turn will depend on their values. Since values are determined by subjective preferences, it is natural to model the situation as one in which no bidder knows any other's value with certainty. We will consider a simple model of this type, in which uncertainty is

---

[43] This point was made to us by Vernon Smith. In the terminology of game theory the point is that English and second-price auctions have the same normal form, but different extensive forms.

[44] As with the English and second-price auctions, the normal forms for the Dutch and first-price auctions are the same, while their extensive forms differ.

symmetric; each bidder has the same subjective probability distribution for any other bidder's value. This symmetry of beliefs is induced in the laboratory by using the same random device to generate each subject's value. Participants do not see each other's values, but they know how these values are generated. For simplicity, assume that the bidders are risk neutral, and that values for each bidder are independent draws from a uniform distribution. If this distribution is on the interval [0, 1], then, as discussed in chapter 2, the density is flat and $f(v_i) = 1$. In experiments, values are usually drawn from an interval between 0 and some upper bound V_{max} that is larger than 1 (typically $10). A uniform distribution on [0, V_{max}] also has a flat density, but $f(v_i) = 1/V_{max}$ instead of 1.

The risk-neutral bidder wants to maximize expected earnings, which is the product of the probability of winning and the earnings from winning, $v_i - b_i$. A higher bid increases the probability of winning but lowers earnings, and thus there is a tradeoff between probability and profitability. The problem for the bidder is to develop a bidding strategy that maximizes expected earnings in terms of this tradeoff. Appendix A5.1 shows that for the case of two risk-neutral bidders, this balance is struck with a bid equal to one-half of a bidder's prize value: Bidding 1/2 of value is shown to be Nash equilibrium strategy (i.e., if one bidder has a strategy of bidding one-half of value, the best response of the other bidder is to bid one-half of value, and vice versa). In the more general case of N bidders, the Nash equilibrium bidding strategy is also linear:

$$(5.1) \qquad b_i = \frac{N - 1}{N} v_i \quad for\ i = 1 \ldots N.$$

The relationship between N and the optimal bid bears emphasis. As the number of bidders increases, optimal bids approach values. With only one bidder, the optimal bid is 0, since any bid will win. With two bidders, $(N-1)/N = 1/2$, and the strategy in (5.1) reduces to bidding half of one's value, as noted previously. As the number of bidders increases, the situation becomes more competitive. In the limit, $[N-1]/N$ approaches 1 as N becomes infinite, and equilibrium bids approach values.

Revenue Equivalence

One implication of the discussion regarding alternative auction forms in the previous section is that the change in institution from an English auction to a first-price auction can have a dramatic effect on bidding behavior. In the English auction, bidders should remain active until the bid price exceeds their values, and in this sense, each losing bidder's final bid is approximately equal to that bidder's value. (For this reason the winning bidder pays an amount that equals the second highest value.) In contrast, each bidder strategically bids below value in a first-price sealed-bid auction: To bid at one's value would ensure a profit of zero, even though it would maximize the probability of winning. Does the fact that bidders bid below value in a first-price auction mean that the seller will obtain a lower selling price on average? The answer is negative, as can be seen by considering the simple case of two bidders.

Let us begin with an example of a first-price auction with two bidders, who happen to draw two very particular values on the range $[0, V_{max}]$: $v_1 = [2/3]V_{max}$ and $v_2 = [1/3]V_{max}$, as shown in figure 5.7. (As explained below, there is a reason to use these particular value draws.) Since $N = 2$, the bidders' bids are at one-half of their values. In particular, bidder 1 wins with a bid of $[1/3]V_{max}$. Notice that the sale price in this first-price auction, b_1, is exactly equal to the second highest value, v_2, in this example. But the second-highest value is where the bidding would have stopped in an English auction. Thus, in this numerical example, the revenue from selling the prize is the same in the first-price and English auctions.

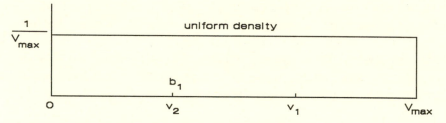

Figure 5.7 Values Drawn from a Uniform Distribution

In fact, the revenue equivalence illustrated in figure 5.7 is rather general. This is because the draws assumed above, $v_1 = [2/3]V_{max}$ and $v_2 = [1/3]V_{max}$, are the expected values of the highest and lowest of two draws from a uniform distribution on $[0, V_{max}]$. The intuition is clear from the uniformity (flatness) of the density. If we know that the highest-value draw is some number v_1, then the second-highest draw is equally likely to be anywhere between 0 and v_1, with a mean halfway between these numbers. Similarly, if we know that the lowest draw is some number v_2, then the highest is equally likely to be anywhere between v_2 and V_{max}, with a mean halfway between. These observations imply that the expected values of the highest and lowest of two draws divide the interval from 0 to V_{max} into thirds, as shown in figure 5.7.

In a first-price auction with $N = 2$, the expected value of the highest draw is $(2/3)V_{max}$, and dividing by 1/2, we obtain the expected value of the winning bid, $(1/3)V_{max}$, which is in turn equal to the expected value of the second highest draw. But the bidding stops at the second-highest value draw in an English auction. Therefore, these two institutions yield the same expected sales revenues in this two-bidder case.

The same revenue equivalence applies to the case of N bidders: Just as we divide the interval $[0, V_{max}]$ into thirds to find the expected values of the highest and lowest of two draws, we can divide the interval into $N+1$ segments to find the expected values of the highest, second-highest, etc. of N draws.[45] When there are N bidders in a first-price auction, the expected value of the winning bidder's draw is $[N/(N+1)]V_{max}$, which converges to the upper limit, V_{max}, as the number of bidders gets large. By replacing v_i in the equilibrium bidding strategy (5.1) with this expected value of the highest draw, we obtain a formula for the expected sales revenue in this auction:

$$(5.2) \qquad expected \ sales \ revenue \ = \ \frac{(N - 1)V_{max}}{N + 1}.$$

Now consider an English auction with N bidders, where the bidding will stop when the bidder with the second-highest value drops out. The right side of (5.2) also represents the expected value of the second-highest of N draws, as can be seen intuitively by dividing the interval $[0, V_{max}]$ up into $N+1$ equal segments. Therefore, the expected sales revenue in an English auction (with values drawn from a uniform distribution) is also given in (5.2), just as is the case for a first-price auction.

The revenue equivalence of English and first-price auctions derived in the preceding paragraph applies to any situation where bidders are risk neutral and the values are independently drawn from a common distribution (which need not be uniform).[46] Together with the equivalence results of the previous section, this implies that all four auction mechanisms are equivalent under risk neutrality (and the maintained assumptions of Nash behavior and private values drawn from the same distribution), as summarized in the bottom row of table 5.6. Therefore, the expected transactions price (or sales revenue) in (5.2) is both (1) the expected value of the winning bid in the first-price, Dutch, and English auctions, and (2) the expected value of the second highest bid in the second-price auction. Finally, the top two rows of table 5.6 summarize the equivalence relationships that were derived in the previous section without an assumption of risk neutrality, but rather with the more general assumption of expected utility maximization.[47]

---

[45] This property of the expected values of rank-ordered draws from a uniform distribution can be verified using the properties of "order statistics."

[46] See Vickrey (1961) for initial insights. For an intuitive introduction to more recent work, see Milgrom (1989) and Riley (1989).

[47] The equivalence of second-price and English auctions in the middle row does not require an assumption of Nash behavior, at least in the sense that the optimal bidding strategy is a dominant strategy that should be used by an expected utility maximizer, regardless of beliefs about others' bids.

Table 5.6 Theoretical Revenue Equivalence Relationships

Auction Equivalence in Revenues and Allocations	Under Assumptions
First-price and Dutch	expected utility maximization, Nash behavior, private values
Second-price and English	expected utility maximization, private values
First-price, second-price, Dutch, and English	risk neutrality, Nash behavior, private values

Experimental Evidence

The first laboratory auctions with independently drawn private values were reported by Coppinger, Smith, and Titus (1980). The authors examined performance in each of the four private-value auction types discussed above. Results of the experiment are summarized in table 5.7, which lists the deviations of average sale prices from the theoretic predictions. Sessions were conducted in a manner that parallels the above theoretical development, except that subjects participated in a series of auctions, each one with new random drawings of the private values. In all sessions, V_{max} = \$10. Under risk neutrality, the theoretical expected sale price is the same for all four institutions and is given in equation (5.2): When $N = 8$, this price is $(7/9)(\$10) = \$7.78$, and when $N = 5$, the expected sales price falls to $(2/3)(\$10)$ = \$6.67. These values are printed in the second column of the table. Each cohort of subjects participated in three sequences of auctions in an ABA or BAB pattern, with each cohort switching between English and Dutch or between first-price and second-price auctions. As indicated by the −28 and −23 cent deviations for the English and second-price auctions, respectively, average prices for these two auctions were slightly, but not significantly, below the theoretical price predictions. Thus, the bidding in both second-price and English auctions was consistent with the use of the dominant strategy of bidding one's value, although considerable learning was required to eliminate the initial tendency to bid below value in the second-price auction.

The anomaly in table 5.7 is that the first-price and Dutch auctions do not seem to be equivalent. The small (−14 cent) and statistically insignificant deviation from the theoretical price prediction in the Dutch auction was very similar to outcomes observed in the English and second-price auctions. Importantly, however, the theoretical predictions for the Dutch and first-price auctions in the table require an added assumption of risk neutrality. Although the Dutch auction results are roughly consistent with an assumption of risk-neutrality, the deviation from the risk-neutral Nash prediction in the first-price auction is large (+39 cents) and statistically significant.

Table 5.7 Average Sale Price for Four Auction Institutions

N	Expected Value of Price Paid $10[N-1]/[N+1]$	Mean Deviations from Expected Value of Price Paid (t statistics for significance of difference from 0)			
		English[a]	Dutch[a]	First-price[b]	Second-price[b]
8	7.78	−.28 ($t = -1.06$)	−.14 ($t = -.83$)		
5	6.67			+.39 ($t = 1.8$)	−.23 ($t = -.86$)

Source: Coppinger, Smith, and Titus (1980).
[a] Data are pooled for sessions 5 and 6.
[b] Data are pooled for sessions 8, 11, and 12.

Subsequent studies have utilized computerized procedures, more refined controls, and more replications, but the general pattern of table 5.7 holds up. In particular, there is a clear tendency for bidding to be close to the prediction for risk neutrality in a Dutch auction and to be above the prediction based on risk neutrality in a first-price auction.[48] The positive deviations in the first-price auction are consistent with risk aversion. It is a well-known theoretical result that a risk-averse bidder tends to raise bids in order to reduce the risk of losing the auction.[49] To the extent that higher prices are observed, risk aversion could provide an explanation. However, the difference in observed prices between first-price and Dutch auctions is something of a puzzle.

In an analysis of individual bidding data in first-price auctions, Cox, Smith, and Walker (1988) classify about 90 percent of the 202 subjects as bidding above the levels predicted in a Nash equilibrium under risk neutrality. For about 70 percent of the subjects, the deviations are statistically significant at conventional levels.

---

[48] Subsequent research provides even stronger evidence that bids significantly exceed risk-neutral Nash levels. See Cox, Roberson, and Smith (1982) and Cox, Smith, and Walker (1988).

[49] See Holt (1980), Riley and Samuelson (1981), and Harris and Raviv (1981).

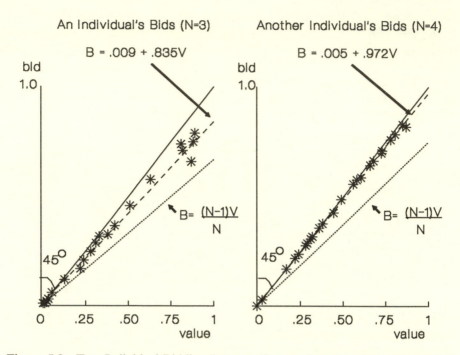

Figure 5.8. Two Individual Bidding Patterns (Source: based on figures 3 and 4 in Cox, Smith and Walker, 1988)

Consider, for example, the participant in a three-bidder auction whose bids are shown on the left side of figure 5.8 (bids, denoted by asterisks, are expressed as proportions of V_{max} so that they lie in the range from 0 to 1). This individual exhibits a typical pattern of bidding in an approximately linear pattern somewhere below the 45 degree line and above the dotted line that represents Nash bidding under risk neutrality. The regression relationship between bids and values is shown at the top of the figure and is drawn as a dashed line. The right side of the figure shows the bidding pattern of a different individual in a different auction with four bidders; this bidder submitted bids that were approximately equal to the value draws. Cox, Smith, and Walker (1988) conclude that individuals' bidding strategies tend to be linear, as implied by equation (5.1), but that the slope of the bidding strategy can differ from individual to individual, as illustrated in figure 5.8.

Adjustments to the Theory

To explain observed variations in the slopes of individuals' bidding strategies, one can introduce asymmetries in risk aversion into the bidding model presented above.[50] Suppose that each bidder has a utility function with constant relative risk aversion (see chapter 2): $U(x) = x^{1-r_i}$, where r_i is the coefficient of relative risk aversion, which is greater than or equal to 0 and less than 1. These risk-aversion parameters can vary across bidders; bidders do not know each others' risk-aversion parameters with certainty. The equilibrium bidding strategy, for any bidder i, turns out to be a simple generalization of (5.1):[51]

$$(5.3) \qquad b_i = \frac{N-1}{N-r_i} v_i \qquad for\ i = 1 \ldots N.$$

Notice that when bidder i is risk neutral ($r_i = 0$), the bidding strategy in equation (5.3) reduces to (5.1). In the other extreme case, as r_i approaches 1, the bidder becomes very risk averse, and the bid determined by (5.3) approaches the bidder's value. Hence, risk aversion raises bids above the levels for a Nash equilibrium with risk-neutral bidders. This is the reason that Cox, Smith, and Walker (1988) and others have argued that bids above the risk-neutral Nash prediction can be explained by risk aversion. And since the slope of the bidding function in (5.3) depends on the bidder's own risk-aversion parameter, it follows that differences in risk aversion can explain differences in the slopes of bidding strategy functions that are observed in experiments.

Harrison (1989) questioned the risk-aversion explanation of bids above the prediction under risk neutrality. He showed that observed deviations from the equilibrium prediction under risk neutrality would only generate very small losses in expected payoffs. The intuition is that the expected money payoff function (derived in appendix A5.1) is quadratic and hence is very flat around the maximum payoff. This "flat-maximum critique" has been a source of considerable controversy. The main counterargument is that the deviations from the risk-neutral prediction are not random, but rather are almost always in an upward direction. There is no generally accepted alternative theory that would explain the one-sided nature of the bias. But perhaps small psychological factors such as the desire to "win" may become important in the presence of a flat maximum.[52]

---

[50] This model was developed in Cox, Roberson, and Smith (1982) and Cox, Smith, and Walker (1982).

[51] See appendix A5.1 for a derivation of this strategy for the case where $N = 2$.

[52] For a more spirited discussion of the causes of deviations from predictions of a Nash equilibrium under risk neutrality, see Kagel (1991), Kagel and Roth (1990), Cox, Smith, and Walker (1990), and the references therein.

5.8 Common-Value Auctions and the Winner's Curse

In the private-value auction models discussed in the previous section, the relevant uncertainty involves differences in the valuations among the various bidders; each bidder harbored a private value for the auctioned item but did not know the others' private values with certainty. Bidding strategies in this case centered about assumptions regarding the value of the item to other bidders. In a wide variety of natural contexts, however, the auctioned item is worth roughly the same amount to each bidder, but no bidder knows this underlying "common" value with any precision prior to making a purchase. Rather, agents bid on the basis of imperfect estimates of value. The uncertainty regarding underlying value presents a critical problem that must be addressed in submitting an optimal bid. Auctions for oil-drilling rights on offshore tracts represent a classic example of a common-value problem of this sort; the value of an oil strike is roughly the same to all bidders. Prior to actually drilling, however, no one knows whether there is oil in a given tract.

Bidders in common-value auctions are susceptible to a "winner's curse." Since bids are based on imperfect estimates of value, the bidder who has the highest estimate of the value is likely to win the auction. The highest estimate is likely to be an overestimate, and therefore the high bidder may be "cursed" by winning the auction and paying more for the item than it is worth. This phenomenon was first identified in the context of bidding for oil leases.[53] Once a well-known economic theorist at the Stanford Business School was called in to consult with officials of a major oil company on a bid for an offshore lease. The company officials presented all of the relevant geological and economic evidence, and they proposed a bid that was less than half of the estimated market value of the lease. When the professor asked them whether they were willing to make a higher bid to increase the probability of winning, they replied that people who submit such bids are no longer in business![54]

To understand better the nature of the winner's curse, consider an auction in which the value of the prize is the same for all bidders, who nevertheless may make different estimates of this common value. The estimates are informative but imperfect indicators or "signals" of value. Since a high estimate tends to indicate a high value, one would expect bidders to submit high bids when they obtain high estimates. As a consequence, the person with the highest bid is often the person with one of the highest estimates. In this sense, the winning bidder's estimate is likely to be biased upward, and if this is not considered in advance, the winner may end up paying an amount that exceeds the common prize value. The problem is not

---

[53] See Capen, Clapp, and Campbell (1971).

[54] This story was related in a conference presentation by the person involved, Robert Wilson.

that the estimates themselves are biased, but rather that the highest of a group of unbiased estimates provides biased information.

Kagel and Levin (1986) devised a simple theoretical model of equilibrium bidding in common-value auctions, with signals that are drawn from a uniform distribution centered on the unobserved value of the prize. The relationship between the common prize value and the individual signals is explained clearly in the instructions that implement a test of this theory:

> The value of the auctioned commodity ($V*$) will be assigned randomly and will lie between $25.00 and $225.00 inclusively. For each auction, *any value* within this interval has an *equally likely chance* of being drawn. . . . The $V*$ values are determined randomly and independently from auction to auction. . . .
>
> Although you do not know the exact value of the item in any particular trading period, you will receive information which will narrow down the range of possible values. This will consist of a private information signal which is selected randomly from an interval whose lower bound is $V*$ minus epsilon (ε), and whose upper bound is $V*$ plus epsilon (ε). Any value within this interval has an *equally likely* chance of being drawn and being assigned to one of you as your private information signal. You will always know what the value of epsilon is.
>
> For example, suppose that the value of the auctioned item is $128.16 and that epsilon is $6.00. Then each of you will receive a private information signal which will consist of a randomly drawn number that will be between $122.16 ($V* - \varepsilon = $128.16 - $6.00) and $134.16 ($V* + \varepsilon = $128.16 + $6.00). [see figure 5.9]

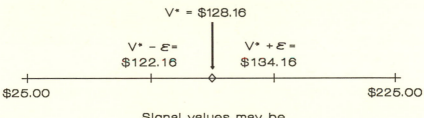

Figure 5.9 A Common-Value Example (Source: Adapted from Kagel and Levin, 1986, Instructions)

In this common-value setup, each person has the same prize value, $V*$, which is known to be drawn from a uniform distribution on the interval from $25 to $225. The value estimates, denoted x_i, are bidder specific, and each value estimate, taken by itself, is an unbiased estimate of V^*, as long as the estimate is greater than $25+\varepsilon$ and less than $225-\varepsilon$. Under an assumption of risk neutrality, everything in the auction setup is symmetric across individuals except for the value estimates. Therefore, the Nash equilibrium bidding strategies will specify a person's bid as a function of the value *estimate* (instead of being a function of the person-specific value, v_i, in the private-values model of the previous section). The equilibrium bidding strategy for the common-values model of this section is more difficult to derive, but it can be shown to be

(5.4) $$b(x_i) = x_i - \varepsilon + Y,$$

where Y is a decreasing function of both x_i and N.[55]

Despite the fact that Y is a decreasing function of x_i, it can be shown that the linear x_i term on the right side of (5.4) dominates, so that the person with the highest value estimate will submit the highest bid in a symmetric Nash equilibrium. Since the N value estimates are each independent estimates of the unknown value V^*, it follows that the highest of these estimates is likely to be an overestimate. In other words, the fact that a bidder turns out to win the auction means that the bidder's estimate is likely to have been above the true value. The calculation of the Nash equilibrium bidding strategy takes this into account; each bid is adjusted downward to reflect the information that is contained in the event that the bid turns out to be highest.[56]

If the bidders do not account for the fact that winning itself is an informative event when making their bids, they will fall prey to the winner's curse and will tend to bid high and lose money. Kagel and Levin (1986) observe that this type of overbidding is more prevalent in auctions with six or seven bidders than with three or four bidders. Even when subjects are experienced, auctions with six or seven bidders produce negative earnings, consistent with the winner's curse. In most of the sessions with large numbers of bidders, more than half of the winning bids were higher than the expected value of the prize, conditional on the information that the winner's value estimate is the highest of the N estimates.

One procedural problem that arises in winner's-curse situations is how to deal with large losses. Kagel and Levin (1986) provided subjects with an initial cash

---

[55] The Y function is: $Y = [2\varepsilon/(N+1)]\exp[-(N/2\varepsilon)(x_i - (\underline{x}+\varepsilon))]$, where $\underline{x}$ is the lower bound of the distribution of V^*. The strategy in equation (5.4) is calculated on the assumption that bidders are risk neutral and that x_i is not within a distance of ε from either endpoint of the distribution of possible values of V^* (see Kagel and Levin, 1986).

[56] The intuition behind Y being a decreasing function of N is that the potential bias in the winner's estimate is more severe if there are many other bidders. For example, if there are 100 other estimates that all turn out to be lower than the remaining bidder's estimate, then it is very likely that estimate will have the maximum possible bias, that is, that it is very close to $V^* + \varepsilon$. Thus, to avoid overbidding, the bid must be adjusted downward to a greater extent when N is large.

balance, and subjects were required to stop bidding and leave if this initial balance was lost. Hansen and Lott (1991) pointed out that the implicit protection from having to pay the experimenter in the event of large negative earnings may cause subjects to make very risky decisions. As noted in chapter 2, such large risks may be attractive even for a risk averter if the losses on the downside would not be paid, but large gains on the upside would be received. If this payoff asymmetry were a significant factor, then we might see some subjects going bankrupt as a result of rational behavior, not because of a winner's-curse misperception. Lind and Plott (1991) deal with this problem in a couple of ways, one of which involves letting bidders simultaneously participate in a second task in which they earn money. Even when bidders are protected from bankruptcy in this manner, bidders tend to bid at unprofitably high levels. Lind and Plott find that the winner's curse may decrease over time, but it does not disappear. Nevertheless, they conclude that the Nash equilibrium concept provides a better overall explanation of the data patterns than models of naïve, suboptimal behavior.

On the other hand, the creation of an outside alternative greatly diminished the winner's-curse outcome in an experiment reported by Cox and Smith (1992). These authors modify the standard common-value auction design by giving bidders a choice between either participating in the auction or obtaining a certain payoff from a "safe haven." The safe-haven payoff is an independent private-value draw from a uniform distribution; each participant learns his or her safe-haven draw before making a participation decision. Participants receive their signal of the common value only if they forgo the safe-haven payoff. Although high bids and winner's-curse behavior were observed when participants were inexperienced, Cox and Smith report that the winner's curse diminishes or vanishes when participants are experienced.

There are two possible explanations for the differential effects of the outside income sources used by Cox and Smith, and by Lind and Plott. First, there may be an experience effect. Lind and Plott used participants who were inexperienced with the common-value auction (although these participants did have experience with other experiments). Cox and Smith observe reductions in winner's curse outcomes only when participants are experienced. The second explanation has to do with the structure of the alternative-income opportunity. Lind and Plott presented subjects with a simultaneous alternative, while the alternative presented by Cox and Smith was exclusive: participants either took the alternative or participated in the common-value auction. Cox and Smith conjecture that the safe haven reduces an experimenter demand effect: Without the safe haven, participants may think that they should be in the auction and should try to win. With a safe haven, subjects can avoid a bidding activity when it generates persistent losses.

A Second Example of the Winner's Curse: Corporate Takeovers

It is important to recognize that the existence of multiple bidders is not a necessary prerequisite for an auction winner to be "cursed" in a common-value context. To the contrary, it is possible for a even single bidder to fall victim to a type of winner's curse, given sufficient informational asymmetries. For example, it is sometimes alleged that losses have resulted from excessive bidding for corporate takeovers. The basic idea is that the seller is the target of a takeover attempt. The seller, who currently owns the firm, knows its basic profit possibilities. The buyer does not know the target's profitability with certainty, but the buyer is a better manager who would increase the value of the firm, whatever this value turns out to be. The buyer makes a takeover bid, which the target either accepts or rejects.[57] If the buyer bids too high, losses can occur.

This problem may be more clearly understood in the context of a specific experimental design. Consider an experiment that involves a single buyer and a single seller of a commodity unit, whose value to the seller is a random variable, V, drawn from a uniform distribution on $[0, 100]$. The seller, but not the buyer, observes the draw. Regardless of the outcome, however, the unit is worth 1.5 times more to the buyer than the seller; for example, the prospective buyer knows how to operate the firm more efficiently than the current management. Thus, the buyer's *ex ante* subjective beliefs are that the firm's value is uniform on $[0, 150]$. The buyer is allowed to make a single, take-it-or-leave-it price offer, which the seller must accept or reject. Then the earnings are calculated, and the buyer and seller are rematched with different people.

If the experimental procedures effectively induce a single-period game, it follows that the optimal decision for the seller is to sell if the price offer exceeds the seller value, V. The buyer's problem is to choose the optimal price offer, which will be denoted by p. At this point the reader should pause and decide what he or she would offer in such an experiment; your price offer should be a dollar amount no less than 0 and no greater than 100, because 100 is the maximum possible value to the seller, and hence a bid of 100 should always be accepted.

Most subjects in this situation reason as follows. Value to the seller ranges between 0 and 100, with an average of 50. Value to the buyer ranges between 0 and 150, with an average of 75. Therefore the buyer "should" bid below 75. If the buyer bids something just over 50, it is more likely to be accepted than not, and the buyer should have average earnings of just under 25. For example, consider figure 5.10, which shows the behavior of a bidder who made a sequence of independent bidding decisions, facing a simulated seller who was programmed to sell whenever

---

[57] An auction of this type is a variant of an ultimatum game with asymmetric information. For a careful theoretical discussion of these games, see Samuelson (1984).

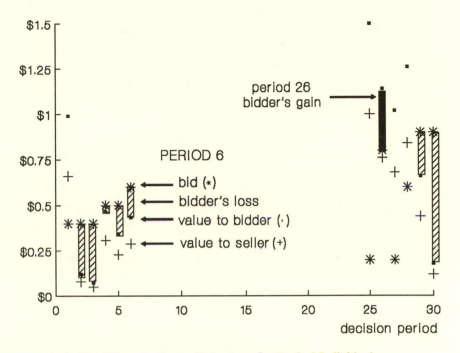

Figure 5.10 The Winner's Curse: Behavior of a Typical Individual
(Source: experiment run by the authors at the University of Virginia)

the bid exceeded the randomly determined seller value V for that period.[58] The bids, represented by asterisks in the figure, are between 40 and 60 cents in the first six periods, which is roughly consistent with the argument given at the start of this paragraph. In the first period, the bidder earns nothing since the seller value, represented by the "+", is above the bid. A purchase is made in periods 2–6, since bid (*) is above the seller value (+). But the bid also exceeds the buyer value (·) in each of these periods, and the buyer suffers a loss, shown by the striped bar. Outcomes of intermediate periods have been removed to simplify the figure, but the bidder continued with average bids of about 50 cents. This bidder made losses in twelve of the thirty periods and made gains in five periods (with rejected bids in the other thirteen periods). The largest gain was 33 cents, as shown by the dark solid

---

[58] Since the seller is relatively passive, as in a posted-bid auction, it is natural to consider an experimental setup in which the decision of the seller is simulated. Instructions for such an experiment are provided in appendix A5.2. On the other hand, ultimatum-game experiments indicate that nonsimulated agents may affect outcomes, even when they are given an essentially passive role: offers may be tempered by the possibility of irrational rejections.

bar in period 26. The subject's cumulative earnings fell from an initial balance of $9.00 to a level of $7.77 in period 30.[59]

The problem, of course, is complicated by the fact that the buyer's acceptance is contingent on the realized seller value. For example, a bid of 60 cents will be accepted only if the seller's value is below 60. Since seller values are uniformly distributed, the average seller value for the case when an offer of 60 is accepted is 30 (e.g., halfway between 0 and 60). But this implies that the average value to the buyer of an accepted offer is only $(1.5)30 = 45$ cents. In period 6, for example, the buyer bid 60. The actual seller value was 29 cents, yielding a buyer value of only $(1.5)(29) = 44$ cents, generating a loss indicated by the striped bar for period 6 in the figure.

This propensity to earn losses occurs for any bid of p between 0 and 100; such a bid will be accepted if $V < p$, so the expected value of the commodity, conditional on the bid being accepted, is $p/2$ for the seller, and therefore is $1.5[p/2]$ for the buyer. But the buyer must pay a price p, and $1.5[p/2] - p$ is negative, so *any* positive bid will yield negative profits on average. Therefore, a risk-neutral buyer would not want to make a positive bid. In fact, this result holds for any non-risk-preferring buyer, as shown in appendix A5.3. The reader should be embarrassed if the suggested bid was not zero. Ball, Bazerman, and Carroll (1990) report an experiment with this structure, but with human rather than simulated sellers. Very few of the buyers bid zero the first time, and most of them never reduced their bids to zero.[60]

Subjects in an experiment generally expect positive earnings, and it is very unlikely that they would ever suspect that the optimal decision involves essentially giving up all hope of obtaining the unit, by submitting a bid of zero. Holt and Sherman (1991) report data for a bidding situation that is similar to that discussed here, except that the lower bound of the range of seller values is nonzero. The effect is to move the optimal buyer's bid away from the lower bound of seller values; that is, optimal bidding involves a positive probability of obtaining the

---

[59] This session was conducted at the University of Virginia, using a computer program written by Lisa Anderson and Charles Holt. The instructions were quite similar to those in appendix A5.2, except that the instructions were presented on the monitor, and all random numbers were generated by the computer.

[60] Samuelson and Bazerman (1985) ran the first laboratory experiment with this basic structure. They used procedures that were similar to those of Ball, Bazerman, and Carroll (1990), but seller values were drawn from a discrete uniform distribution with only five values: 0, 20, 40, 60, 80, or 100. Procedures by Samuelson and Bazerman also differed in that, before seller values were drawn, sellers were asked to specify the lowest acceptable selling price for each possible realization of the seller value. Despite these and other procedural differences, the data also show buyers falling victim to the winner's curse, with the modal bid being in the 50–55 range.

object. A consistent pattern of bidding too high is also observed for some parameterizations; subjects still fall prey to the winner's curse.[61]

5.9 Design of New Auction Institutions

The third class of institutions to be considered in this chapter consists of generalizations of single-sided auction markets that have been customized to meet the requirements of a specific trading situation. Issues in institutional design can arise when there is interest in creating a market for a good that has previously been allocated only through centralized regulation or decentralized bilateral negotiations. The Federal Energy Regulatory Commission, for example, recently considered the problem of creating a unified market for transportation rights over natural gas pipelines. Similarly, NASA has considered using a market mechanism to allocate access to a space laboratory. New markets of this type often present special problems that invite the use of new, and as yet untried, institutional rules. The value of transportation rights over a particular pipeline, for example, is likely to be determined in part by the availability of related goods, such as contemporaneous transportation rights over connecting pipelines. An efficient market would have to resolve the potential allocational problems arising from such interrelatedness. The laboratory represents a natural place to start examining the behavioral characteristics of such "synthetic" institutions.

The experimental literature on institutional design is fairly diverse, and for specificity we confine our discussion in this section to a particular application: electronic trading of financial assets. Competition is forcing many financial exchanges to allow (or at least consider) off-hours trading through electronic messages. This development raises the issue of how to institute new trading mechanisms made possible by advances in computer and communications technologies. A second issue is whether it is possible to devise institutions that are less likely to generate volatile price bubbles.

The double auction, which approximates the trading process on the floor of centralized stock exchanges in the United States, has a variety of desirable characteristics. As indicated in chapter 3, this institution is an extremely efficient mechanism for coordinating trades among numerous buyers and sellers. The double

---

[61] Holt and Sherman further explore the effects of this type of informational asymmetry, over a variety of seller value ranges. In addition to the winner's-curse situation discussed in the text, they identify cases where naïve behavior (ignoring the information contained in the event that a bid is accepted) will cause bidders to bid too low, that is, below the level that maximizes the expected earnings, correctly calculated. They refer to this behavior as the "loser's curse." Holt and Sherman observe that the same subjects who fell prey to the winner's curse will consistently bid too low when the range of seller values is such that naïve behavior generates a loser's curse. Irrational underbidding in loser's-curse situations was also observed by Horkan (1990).

auction also has a valuable *feedback* feature; that is, it provides considerable information to traders about underlying market conditions. The feedback provided by the double auction allows for the possibility that privately held "insider information" can be disseminated through the act of trading (see the discussion in chapter 7).

The double auction is not flawless, however, and the relative performance of alternative institutions may be evaluated in terms of other criteria. The real-time trading process of a double auction generates a high volume of messages that can degrade performance of a large electronic exchange. Thus, the *feasibility* of implementing a proposed institution in very thick electronic markets is important. An additional drawback of the double auction is that price volatility makes it necessary for traders to pay close attention to market movements, which may be costly in off-hours trading. As a consequence, there is considerable interest in institutions for which all units trade at the same price at a pre-announced time; this uniformity property will be called *fairness*. A related characteristic absent from the double auction is that of *forgiveness*; in a double auction, bids and offers are potentially binding commitments. Since valuations and expectations can change over time, it might be desirable in some circumstances for traders to be able to modify or withdraw buy/sell orders continuously, as new information arrives.

While desirable in an abstract sense, there is no guarantee that operating characteristics such as feasibility, fairness, and forgiveness are consistent with efficient performance. Traders may try to take advantage of forgiveness options and feedback information to modify orders in an effort to manipulate the final price in their favor. Laboratory experiments can provide some information about relative efficiencies, and attention can be restricted to stress testing and fine tuning institutions that perform well in initial tests.

Some Alternative Market Institutions

In some sense the double auction may be viewed as a multi-unit, multi-seller generalization of the English auction. Although the buyer side of a double auction involves upward bidding as in an English auction, the bidding process is reversed on the seller side, with sellers bidding downward.[62] A natural place to begin exploring alternative market institutions is with generalizations of the other single-seller, single-unit auction mechanisms discussed in the preceding sections. Due to concerns about fairness and forgiveness, generalizations of the uniform-price sealed-

---

[62] Our comparison of English and double auctions is a little imprecise. McCabe, Rassenti, and Smith (1990) discuss a more direct generalization of the English auction. Like the one-sided English auction, their "Double English" auction uses a third-party auctioneer (e.g., a mechanical price clock) that raises the price for buyers in response to excess demand and lowers the price for sellers in response to excess supply. This process stops when the buyers' and sellers' prices cross (at zero excess demand).

bid auction as well as uniform price variants of the Dutch and English auctions are of particular interest. Collectively, these generalizations are called "call markets," since in each case bids and offers are first collected, and then all transactions are simultaneously effected at a uniform price. Call-market procedures have long been used in financial markets in Europe and to determine daily opening prices on the New York, American, and Tokyo stock exchanges. A call-market procedure has also been implemented in at least one electronic "off-floor" trading mechanism in the United States, to be discussed below.

Table 5.8 shows key similarities among some uniform-price mechanisms.[63] Institutions are categorized on the left as being either single-sided (one seller and multiple buyers) or double-sided (multiple buyers and sellers). For financial market applications, the two-sided auctions in the bottom row are of primary interest. It aids our presentation, however, to include the single-sided auctions in the top row.

Table 5.8   Uniform-Price Auctions

	nonsequential	Sequential, No-Backtracking	Sequential, with Backtracking
Single-sided	Uniform Price Sealed Bid	Dutch	Continuous Bid
Double-sided	Sealed Bid\Offer	Double Dutch	Continuous Bid\Offer (UPDA and Walrasian)

Institutions are categorized across columns in terms of whether the decisions are made independently or sequentially in real time, and whether or not price sequences are monotonic (i.e., whether or not "backtracking" is allowed). For example, the Dutch auction is a single-seller procedure with sequential decisions. There is no backtracking in the sense that price is lowered sequentially with no reversals, and purchases, once indicated, are locked in and cannot be canceled in a Dutch auction. The far-right column contains sequential auctions with continuous feedback and the possibility of price backtracking. But first we will discuss the simpler nonsequential institutions in the left column of the table.

Sealed Tender, Uniform-Price Auctions

Consider the single-seller case in which buyers independently submit bids that are arrayed from high to low, and a fixed number of units are sold at the highest

---

[63] The categories in this table are loosely based on the layout of table 1 in McCabe, Rassenti, and Smith (1991).

rejected bid price. This is called a *uniform-price, sealed-bid auction,* to distinguish it from the discriminative auction. In figure 5.11, for example, the seller offers three units, and there are two buyers with unit valuations indicated above the corresponding steps of the solid-line demand function. Each buyer is permitted to submit distinct bids for each unit, and the bids in this example are shown on the dotted-line step function. The top three bids are accepted and sold at the same uniform price that is determined by the highest rejected bid, which is buyer 2's lower bid in the example. Since bids are made independently, neither buyer would be likely to know exactly what the other is going to bid. If buyer 2 had known buyer 1's bids, then buyer 2 could have manipulated the price by bidding lower on the second unit, which would have lowered the uniform market price determined by the highest rejected bid. This would have increased earnings on buyer 2's first unit. As indicated earlier, when each bidder has a single unit, it is a dominant strategy to submit a bid that exactly equals ("reveals") the unit value. The presence of multiple units for one or more buyers can provide the marginal buyer with market power.

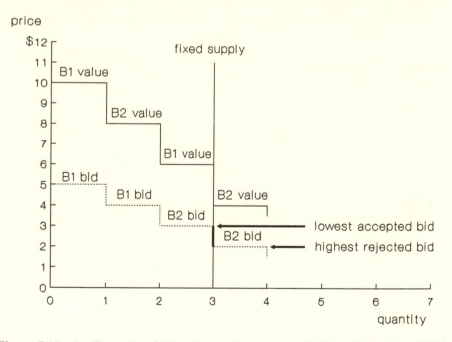

Figure 5.11   An Example of Price Determination in a Uniform Price Sealed-Bid Auction (with Multiple Bids)

The uniform-price sealed-bid institution did not evolve naturally, but rather was proposed by Friedman (1960), who argued that its adoption would increase revenues from the sale of a fixed supply of Treasury securities.[64] Smith's (1967) experimental comparison of uniform-price and discriminative auctions provided some support for Friedman's argument. The Treasury ran a subsequent field experiment by conducting six uniform-price sealed-bid auctions for securities on a trial basis in the early 1970s, but the idea never caught on. An executive for Exxon, who had previously worked at the Treasury, implemented a uniform-price sealed-bid procedure for auctioning off Exxon bonds. This procedure is now frequently used to set dividends on preferred stock issues (McCabe, Rassenti, and Smith, 1991, pp. 1–2).

The double-sided generalization of this nonsequential institution, referred to as a *sealed bid/offer auction* in table 5.8, allows buyers to submit bids and sellers to submit offers. The bids are arrayed from high to low as a demand function, and the offers are arrayed from low to high as a supply function. The intersection of the bid-and-offer arrays determines the price and quantity. If the bid-and-offer arrays overlap vertically, as shown by the boldfaced line segment on the left side of figure 5.12, the price is determined to be the average price in the region of overlap. Individuals in this institution may have an incentive to bid below value (and ask above cost), which can create inefficiencies. The intuition behind this result is consistent with the incentive for B2 in figure 5.11 to manipulate price by lowering the bid on a marginal unit.

Smith et al. (1982) report a comparison of the double auction and uniform-price sealed-bid/offer auction.[65] The design that they used most frequently involved four inexperienced buyers, four inexperienced sellers, and a buyers' surplus that was twice the level of sellers' surplus. Recall that the latter feature causes prices to converge to the competitive equilibrium from above in a double auction. By period 7, the average price in ten double-auction sessions was about 5 cents above the competitive equilibrium, as compared with an average price deviation of 7 cents in five parallel sealed bid/offer sessions. Efficiency averaged 94 percent in period 7 of the double auctions, compared with 92 percent for the sealed bid/offer sessions.[66]

---

[64] Friedman referred to this as a competitive auction, and he suggested that the uniform price be the lowest accepted bid (e.g., B2's high bid in figure 5.11). Also, in light of the scandal involving the Salomon Brothers and the market for Treasury bonds, Friedman recently reiterated his opinion that the competitive auction would be more resilient to conspiracy than a discriminative auction (*Wall Street Journal*, August 28, 1991).

[65] Smith et al. refer to the uniform price sealed bid-offer auction being discussed here as the $P(Q)$ mechanism, since bidders can submit different price bids or offers on different units, and in this sense, bid price P is a function of quantity Q.

[66] A simple variation of the sealed bid/offer procedure seemed to improve efficiencies; this modification involved letting each trader with an accepted bid or offer vote "yes" or "no" on whether to accept the allocation as final. Agents with no accepted bids or offers could not vote. A unanimity rule was used; any "no" votes resulted in a new submission of bids and offers as before. Efficiencies exceeded double-auction levels when an agreement was reached, but no agreement was reached in some

These results, while not decisive, indicate the possibility of designing a simple and attractive alternative to the double auction.

Dutch Auctions

One way to improve the efficiency of the sealed bid/offer auction is to provide bidders with real-time information about others' trading activities. Although less informative than the double auction, the Dutch auction transmits some information as the clock price falls continuously. In the multi-unit, uniform-price version of a Dutch auction, a single seller offers a fixed number of units for sale. Trading is a sequential, real-time process in the sense that buyers indicate a willingness to purchase one or more units as the price is lowered continuously. The price falls until there is no excess supply, and all units are sold at the final, zero-excess-supply price.

For example, suppose that three units are offered for sale, and that the two buyers' values are as shown in figure 5.11 discussed earlier. When the price falls below $10, buyer B1 can earn a profit. Even if a bid were made at the unit's value of $10, this would not necessarily earn a zero return, since a bid indicates a willingness to buy at that price or below. The price in the figure 5.11 example falls to $5 before B1 bids for a unit. The clock continues to fall to $4, at which point B1 bids on a second unit. When the clock reaches $3, B2 takes the third and final unit, which stops the clock, regardless of whether B2 had intended to bid again at $2. All three units are sold at $3, which is the lowest accepted bid.[67] The Dutch auctions are indicated as having "no backtracking" in the column heading of table 5.8, since the price movements are unidirectional, and agents cannot withdraw their willingness to buy or sell once it is indicated.

A double-sided *Double Dutch* version of this procedure has separate clocks for buyers and sellers. When there is excess supply, one clock lowers the buyers' price, and buyers indicate a willingness to purchase one or more units as in the single-sided version. But when enough intended purchases are signaled to make excess demand positive, the buyers' clock stops falling and the sellers' clock starts rising. As the sellers' price rises in this manner, sellers can indicate a willingness to sell one or more units. If excess supply becomes positive again, the sellers' clock stops and the buyers' clock starts to fall. This alternating process continues until the buyers' and the sellers' clock prices meet, and the meeting price is a uniform price at which all previously indicated purchases and sales are effected. In figure 5.12, for example, the price falls from $10 to $8 before a buyer locks in a unit at point *a*, creating excess demand. As can be seen from the right side of the figure, the

---

of the unanimity-rule auctions with inexperienced subjects.

[67] The reader should verify that, with a single unit, this procedure implements the Dutch auction discussed previously.

seller clock starts to rise from zero, until sellers have locked in two units at point *b*, creating excess supply. Then the buyer clock starts to fall, and it continues until buyers bid on the second and third units, point *c*. Finally, the seller clock starts rising from its previous level of $2. Excess demand is reduced to zero when a third unit is offered as the seller clock passes $3, but the clock continues to rise to a level of $6, point *d*, where it crosses the buyer clock price. All units that had been locked in are then bought or sold at $6. Notice that traders can watch the clock prices converge, and in a static sense they have an incentive to put marginally profitable units into play as the end nears.

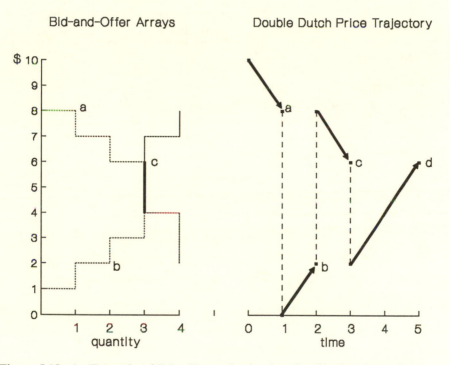

Figure 5.12 An Example of Price Determination in a Double Dutch Auction

McCabe, Rassenti, and Smith (1992) report that the Double Dutch auction yields higher efficiencies than the double auction in two designs, one with stationary, asymmetric demand and supply used by Smith et al. (1982), and a second design with random shifts.[68] Table 5.9 summarizes data for the random-shifts design. As

---

[68] The random-shift design is clever in that subjects' values and costs were juggled in a way that made it very difficult for a subject to use his/her own private value or cost to infer the market equilibrium price from period to period. Market demand consisted of five steps at deviations from the competitive price of 40, 30, 20, 10, and −10 cents, and each of five buyers was assigned randomly to one of the

shown in the left column of the table, the efficiency was 95.2 percent for five double-auction sessions with inexperienced traders, as compared with 96.9 percent efficiency for comparable Double-Dutch sessions. These findings were suggested in the paper title: "Designing Auctions: Is Double Dutch the Best?"

Table 5.9 A Comparison of Mean Efficiencies in a Design with Random Shifts

	Mean Efficiency (all sessions, periods 4–12)	
	Inexperienced (5 sessions)	Experienced (3 sessions)
Double Auction	95.2	96.6[a]
Double Dutch	96.9[b]	—
Continuous Bid/Offer	88.4	89.5
Continuous Bid/Offer (closed book, other side rule)	92.0	94.2

Source: McCabe, Rassenti, and Smith (1991 and 1992).

[a] There were only 2 sessions in this cell.

[b] There were only 4 sessions in this cell.

More Interactive Call Markets: The Continuous Bid/Offer Institution

The Double-Dutch auction does not allow backtracking in prices or cancellation of bids and offers once they are locked in. This lack of forgiveness may be desirable in the sense of discouraging attempts to manipulate the market with "false" signals that are withdrawn at the last instant. But in some field situations, changes in information and clients' orders may make it necessary to modify, change, or withdraw orders. Continuous versions of the bid/offer auction discussed previously can provide this flexibility. For example, Jarecki (1976) described a procedure used for over fifty years to "fix" the London gold bullion price. This process involves five dealers who meet twice daily in a type of verbal *tatonnement* auction; the

---

demand steps. Similarly, each of five sellers was assigned randomly to each of five cost steps: –40, -30, –20, –10, and 10. In each period, a parameter-disguising constant is added to all values and costs, so subjects could not distinguish the separate effects of the shift parameter from their own reassignment on the demand or supply curve. Yet in all periods there was an equilibrium price "tunnel" of 20 cents and an equilibrium quantity of 4.

chairman first proposes trial prices until at least one dealer is willing to buy and at least one is willing to sell. Then the chairman asks for purchase and sales quantity intentions, and the price is further adjusted in response to excess demand or supply. During this process, dealers are in phone contact with their own offices, so that new orders can be transmitted instantaneously. Each dealer has a small British flag on the table, and the flag is placed upright when the dealer still wishes to make additional buy or sell orders at the current proposed price. When a dealer's flag is placed on its side, all orders are satisfied at the current price, and the chairman can tell at a glance when all flags go down, that is, when supply equals demand. In this manner all dealers must approve before the price is fixed and all units are transacted.

The London bullion meeting seems to operate effectively, but electronic trading opens possibilities for the inclusion of large numbers of traders, who can bypass dealers. In the United States, Wunsch Auction Systems Inc. operates the Arizona Stock exchange, an electronic auction for securities listed on the NYSE and other major exchanges. For each security, traders can send in bids or offers, which are arrayed in supply-and-demand arrays that are provided continuously to all prospective traders in an "open book" arrangement. These arrays are continuously intersected, and agents can observe: (1) the bid price that a seller has to meet to be sure of making an additional sale, and (2) the ask price that a buyer has to meet to be sure of making an additional purchase. The market is "called" at a prespecified time, after the close the NYSE. All accepted units are transacted at the uniform, market-clearing price at that time. The inflow of bids and offers can cause the tentative price to fluctuate, and in this sense there is backtracking. Commissions on a per share basis are about one-tenth of standard commissions on other exchanges. The initial success of the Wunsch procedure, in terms of both attracting business and obtaining an SEC exemption from being regulated as an exchange, makes this institution a prime candidate for laboratory studies. Since the current terms of trade fluctuate continuously up to the call time, we have called this type of market a *continuous bid/offer auction* in table 5.8. When supply is fixed, the single-sided version of this auction will be called a *continuous bid auction*.

McCabe, Rassenti, and Smith (1991) have implemented several variations of continuous bid/offer auctions.[69] Under an open book arrangement, all traders' messages are presented and explained as in table 5.10, which should be read at this time.

In one variation of the continuous bid/offer auction, any new order or improvement of an existing order is acceptable, and a trader may enter the queue of tentatively accepted orders by either bettering the terms of a provisionally accepted order from his own side or by accepting the terms of a currently rejected order from

---

[69] They call these variations "uniform price double auctions" (UPDA).

Table 5.10 A Continuous Bid/Offer Auction with an Open Book

id	BID		ASK	id
3	406	1	351	2
>1	400	2	369	3
4	400	3	378	2
>1	400	4	385	5
3	398	5	386	3
>1	388	6	397	4
2	387	7		
		8		

This auction is based on the following principle: the CDC [computer] must determine one price at which all units are traded at the end of the auction. To achieve this goal the CDC makes sure that all acceptable BIDs are always greater than or equal to all acceptable ASKs. . . . The table on the left is a sample of what is known as the logbook. . . . The columns labelled id show you who submitted the BIDs and ASKs, while the inner columns show you exactly what prices were submitted. Notice that all BIDs which belong to you have been pointed out by an >. . . . As the clock counts down, the CDC continuously updates its division of BIDs and ASKs into two categories: those acceptable, which appear above the separating line, and those unacceptable, which appear below the line. . . . Notice that both above and below the separating line, BIDs are sorted from highest to lowest, while ASKs are sorted from lowest to highest. The BID and ASK immediately above the separating line are called the last acceptable BID and ASK. . . .

Source: McCabe, Rassenti, and Smith (1991).

the other side.[70]   For example, buyer 2 would not have to beat the lowest acceptable bid of 398 to make a purchase, since this buyer could take the currently unaccepted offer of 397. Under these rules, the efficiency for the five-seller/five-buyer random shift design averaged 88.4 percent with inexperienced subjects, and 89.5 percent with experienced subjects, as shown in the "continuous bid/offer" row of table 5.9. The bottom row of the table shows comparable efficiencies for a modification of this auction that involves using a closed book in which agents only see the bid/ask spread, not the whole array of bids and offers. This design also used an "other-side acceptance rule"; to gain acceptance of a currently unacceptable unit, the trader was required to accept the terms of a trader on the other side of the market. This prevents inefficiently slow haggling when traders on the same side of the market repeatedly better each other's terms by minimal amounts. These modifications raised efficiency to levels that are comparable to those of the double-auction baseline in table 5.9. These results are quite promising. The next step is to evaluate some of the design alternatives in different environments, including situations in which price bubbles have been observed with double auctions.

---

[70] The Wunsch auction permits any new order or an improvement on any existing order, but such changes are penalized at a rate that gets more severe as the call time nears. The purpose of such penalties is to reduce end-game effects prior to the closing time.

5.10 Conclusions

From discussions in earlier chapters of this book, it is evident that the selection of trading rules can importantly affect allocative outcomes. This chapter has presented a sampling from the diverse set of alternative institutional forms that can define the way exchange is conducted in a market. Our discussion was divided into three parts: bilateral bargains, single-seller auctions, and two-sided, uniform-price auctions. An overview of the behavioral results from each section allows us to draw several broad conclusions. From the analysis of bilateral bargaining games we learned that, with the exception of very symmetric environments, cooperative (axiomatic) bargaining theories do not organize outcomes particularly well. Further analysis of performance in highly structured bilateral bargaining games indicates that attention to strategies may not alone be sufficient to explain bargaining outcomes. Nonstrategic factors, such as concerns for fairness, may affect outcomes, although the importance of nonstrategic factors is strongly affected by procedural details. In particular "double-anonymous" procedures increase the predictive power of theory in simple dictator games. Richer versions of noncooperative game theory, for example, those which incorporate concerns for altruism or fairness, may turn out to be useful in other, more complex games.

Results of single-seller auction experiments break down along the basic dimensions of the models. In experiments with private values, where the relevant uncertainty regards other bidders' values, noncooperative Nash equilibrium predictions generally explain outcomes quite well. In one such auction, the first-price sealed-bid auction, it appears that participants harbor heterogenous risk attitudes, and that risk attitudes affect outcomes (although this is the topic of some controversy). On the other hand, in common-value auctions, where the relevant uncertainty regards the underlying value of the auctioned good, participants suffer a persistent and sizable "winners curse" in the form an *ex post* loss. The winner's curse appears remarkably resilient to experience with the institution but may be alleviated by the presence of an alternative market activity.

Finally, our summary of multiseller synthetic institutions indicates that, with the development of automated and computer-assisted trading devices, it may be possible to construct new, flexible trading arrangements. Some of these institutions are not only efficient but also exhibit the properties of "fairness" and "forgiveness" that are valuable for after-hours electronic trading.

APPENDIX A5

A5.1 Equilibrium Bidding Strategies[*]

This appendix develops the equilibrium bidding strategy in a first-price sealed-bid auction (or a Dutch auction), for the case of two bidders. First we consider an equilibrium strategy for the case of risk-neutral bidders who receive private values that are randomly generated from a uniform distribution. Subsequently, an equilibrium strategy for the case of bidders with heterogenous risk preferences is considered.

Risk-Neutral Bidders

Denote bidder values by v_1 and v_2, and bids by b_1 and b_2. Values for each bidder are independent draws from a uniform distribution defined over the range [0,1]. Moreover, values are private: although the bidders know how values are generated, they see only their own value realization.

It is natural to expect bidders with higher values to submit higher bids. A Nash equilibrium strategy for each bidder specifies the equilibrium bid as an increasing function of the bidder's value. We will show that the equilibrium bidding strategy is linear, of the form

(5.5) $$b_i = zv_i \quad for \quad i = 1, 2,$$

where z is a constant fraction. A bidder would never want to pay more than the value of the object, so $z < 1$, and it is assumed that only positive bids will be accepted, so $z > 0$.

In a Nash equilibrium, each bidder's strategy is a best response to the other's. We will show that when one bidder uses the linear strategy in (5.5), the best response of the other is to bid exactly one-half of his/her own value, which is a special case of (5.5). Therefore, if both bidders choose bids that are half of their values, neither would have any incentive to bid otherwise, and this would be a Nash equilibrium.

To determine z, the equilibrium ratio of bids to values, assume that bidder 2 is using a linear strategy of the type given in (5.5) and consider the optimal response of bidder 1, that is, the strategy that maximizes this bidder's expected payoff. This expected payoff is the product of the profit of winning, $v_1 - b_1$, and the probability of winning, which must be determined next. Since bidder 2 is using (5.5), the event

---

[*] The material in this section is somewhat more advanced.

that bidder 1 wins the prize with a bid of b_1 is the event that $b_1 > zv_2$. By dividing both sides of this inequality by z, we see that bidder 1 wins if $v_2 < b_1/z$. Since the distribution function of v_2 is uniform on $[0,1]$, the probability that $v_2 < b_1/z$ is just b_1/z. To summarize, the probability that bidder 1 wins with a bid of b_1 is:[71]

$$(5.6) \qquad \begin{aligned} prob[b_2 < b_1] &= prob[v_2 < b_1/z] \\ &= b_1/z, \qquad\qquad for \ b_1 \leq z. \end{aligned}$$

The product of this probability and the earnings from winning determine the expected profit for bidder 1:

$$(5.7) \qquad\qquad [v_1 - b_1][b_1/z], \quad for \ b_1 \leq z.$$

Bidder 1's optimal bid is obtained by equating the derivative of expected profit to zero. The expected payoff in (5.7) is a simple quadratic function of the bid, so the derivative with respect to b_1 is linear $[v_1 - 2b_1][1/z]$. When this derivative is equated to zero, the resulting equation yields $b_1 = v_1/2$. Therefore, the best response to the linear bidding strategy in (5.5) is to bid one half of one's value. Since bidding one half of one's value is just a special case of (5.5), it follows that the best response to bidding one-half of one's value is to do the same, and therefore this is a symmetric Nash equilibrium.

The analysis of the Nash equilibrium for the case of N bidders is a little more complicated, but the method is the same, and results in equation (5.1) in the text.

Asymmetric Risk Preferences

Consider now the equilibrium bidding strategy for 2 bidders, given heterogenous coefficients of constant relative risk aversion. Suppose that each bidder i has a utility function $U(x) = x^{1-r_i}$, where r_i is the coefficient of relative risk aversion, which is greater than or equal to 0 and less than 1. Then the utility of winning with a bid of b_1 is $(v_1 - b_1)^{1-r_1}$. The probability of winning depends on bidder 2's strategy, and as before, assume that bidder 2 is using the linear strategy with slope z, which in the present asymmetric model will turn out to depend on bidder 2's coefficient of risk aversion. Bidder 1 does not observe r_2, but suppose that bidder 1 has some beliefs about this coefficient and, on this basis, forms an expected value of z. For each possible value of z, the probability of winning is b_1/z

---

[71] The qualification that b_1 not exceed z ensures that the probability does not exceed 1. Since all values are below 1, the highest possible rival bid as determined by (5.5) is z, so it is never optimal to bid above z, and the probability of winning, b_1/z, will be less than 1. Also, note that the possibility of a tie has been ignored in these calculations. Ties occur with probability zero when bids and values are real numbers, but ties can and do occur when bids are restricted to be penny increments in the laboratory.

as calculated in equation (5.6), and the bidder's payoff is the product of this probability and the utility of winning. Since z is unknown to bidder 1, the expected utility is

(5.8)
$$E\{[v_1 - b_1]^{1-r_1}[b_1/z]\}$$

where the expected value E is calculated over bidder 1's subjective distribution for z. This expected utility can be expressed as the product of a non-random component $[v_1 - b_1]^{1-r_1}[b_1]$ and an expected value $E\{1/z\}$. This product is maximized by choosing the bid b_1 for which the derivative of expected payoff is zero:

(5.9)
$$0 = [-(1 - r_1)(v_1 - b_1)^{-r_1}b_1 + (v_1 - b_1)^{1-r_1}]E\{1/z\}.$$

Dividing both sides of (5.9) by $E\{1/z\}(v_1 - b_1)^{-r_1}$, we obtain an equation that is linear in b_1 and is solved

(5.10)
$$b_1 = \frac{v_1}{2 - r_1}.$$

Equation (5.10) provides the best response of bidder 1 when bidder 2 is using a linear strategy. Since equation (5.10) is linear itself, the best response of bidder 2 to (5.10) is to use the function that is analogous to (5.10), with b_1, v_1, and r_1 replaced by b_2, v_2, and r_2. The equilibrium strategy for the N-person case, shown in equation (5.3), is derived analogously.

A5.2 Instructions for a Bargaining Game with Asymmetries

This experiment deals with the economics of decision making under uncertainty.[72] Various agencies have provided funds for the experiment. If you follow the instructions and make good decisions, you can earn a significant amount of money, which you will receive in cash, privately, after the experiment.

You are a potential buyer in this experiment. In each of a series of periods, you will be asked to decide on an amount to bid for a product without knowing its precise value. The current owner of the product, who is the potential seller, knows

---

[72] This is a slight revision of the instructions used in the noncomputerized sessions reported in Holt and Sherman (1991). Parameters have been changed to match those of Ball, Bazerman, and Carroll (1990). Note that the initial earnings balance has been set high enough to preclude the possibility that a subject will go bankrupt in a five-period session.

more about the product's current value than you know as the potential buyer. On the other hand, the object will be worth more to you than it is to the current owner. The potential transactions can be described in the following way.

During each period, you may bid on a product. The *product's value to its current owner* will lie in a range between $0.00 and $0.99. All penny values within this range ($0.00, 0.01, . . . 0.99) will be equally likely. The *product's value to you*, should you acquire it, will be 1.5 times the value to its current owner.

Please turn to the Decision Sheet on the last page of this packet. Note that there are eight numbered columns, with column 1 indicating the period. The lower limit of the range of values to the current owner is $0.00 for each period, as recorded in column 2. The upper limit of the range of values to the current owner is $0.99, as recorded in column 3. There is space on the sheet for five decision periods, and in each one you must decide what you wish to bid. Once you have decided on a bid, write the bid in column 4, labeled "your bid," and turn the Decision Sheet face down on your desk.

After all participants have recorded their bids for a period, dice will be rolled to determine the product's value *to its current owner*. This value will be a number between 0.00 and .99 determined by the throw of two ten-sided dice. The first die to be thrown determines the first ("tens") digit, and the second die to be thrown determines the second ("ones") digit. The dice will be rolled separately for each current owner.

Please look at the Decision Sheet again. After you make a bid and the dice have been rolled, return the sheet to the face up position and write the number indicated by the dice in column 5, labeled "value to current owner." Multiply this number by 1.5 and write the resulting figure in column 6, labeled "value to you." (If necessary, round your answer upward so that it is in integer pennies.) This "value to you" figure is, of course, the product's value to you if you acquire it.

If your bid is greater than or equal to the product's value to its current owner, you will acquire the product. In this case, your gain or loss will be the product's value to you, which is 1.5 times the value to its current owner, minus your bid. If your bid is less than the product's value to its current owner (col. (4) < col. (5)), you will not acquire the product and will neither gain nor lose anything (earnings will equal 0). The following statements summarize the calculation of *your* earnings during each period:

VALUE to current owner = number indicated by dice

(1)   If BID ≥ VALUE to current owner,
                EARNINGS = (1.5 x VALUE to current owner) – BID

(2)   If BID < VALUE to current owner,
                EARNINGS = 0.

At the end of each period, record your gain or loss for that period in column 7, labeled "your gain or loss" on the Decision Sheet. By adding this period's earnings to previous earnings, maintain a cumulative earnings total in column (8).

You will begin the experiment with an initial earnings balance of $9.00. If you gain money during a period, your earnings will increase by the amount that you gain. If you lose money during a period, your earnings will decrease by the amount that you lose. At the beginning of the experiment, your cumulative earnings are $9.00, as shown at the top of column 8. You will be paid privately in cash immediately after the experiment. Are there any questions at this point?

We now begin the bidding periods that will affect your earnings. There will be five periods. Please do not talk to each other during the experiment; raise your hand if you have any questions.

At this time, please write your bid for period 1 in column 4 (and for period 1 only). After everyone has recorded their bid, we will come around to your desk and throw the dice.

Decision Sheet

(1)	(2)	(3)	(4)	(5)	(6)	(7)	(8)
Period	Lower Limit	Upper Limit	Your Bid	Value to Current Owner	Value to You 1.5 × (5)	Your Gain or Loss	Cumulative Earnings $9.00
(1)	0.00	.99					
(2)	0.00	.99					
(3)	0.00	.99					
(4)	0.00	.99					
(5)	0.00	.99					

A5.3 Derivation of the Optimal Bid in an Ultimatum Game with Value and Information Asymmetries[*]

A risk-averse, expected-utility maximizer would choose the price offer, p, to maximize the expression in (5.11), which will be explained subsequently:

$$(5.11) \qquad \int_0^p \frac{U(1.5V - p)}{100} \, dV.$$

Notice that the variable of integration is the unknown value, V, which has a uniform density of $[1/100]$ on the range $[0,100]$. Next, consider the limits of integration. There is no purchase, and nothing is earned unless the value V is less than the bid p, so the integration is over values of V between 0 and p. The absence of a second integral for the case of no purchase is appropriate if we use the normalization that $U(0) = 0$. Finally, consider the expression $U(1.5V - p)$ in the integrand; this is the utility of the difference between the buyer's value and the price paid.

To determine the optimal bid, we calculate the derivative of the expected utility expression in (5.11) with respect to the decision variable, p. Since p appears twice in (5.11), this derivative has two parts, one of which is the probability-of-purchase effect determined by the range of integration, and the other is the payment effect determined by the " $-p$ " term in the integrand. An optimal bid involves the appropriate tradeoff between increasing the probability of winning and reducing the amount paid. A necessary condition for an interior solution is that the derivative of (5.11) be equated to zero:

$$(5.12) \qquad \frac{U(1.5p - p)}{100} - \int_0^p \frac{U'(1.5V - p)}{100} \, dV = 0.$$

Since $U(0)$ is normalized to zero, the first term on the left side of (5.12) is zero at $p = 0$, and the second term is also zero at $p = 0$, so a bid of zero is a natural candidate for an optimal bid. The second derivative of the expected utility expression, obtained by differentiating the left side of (5.12), is the sum of $-U'(.5p)/100$ and the integral from 0 to p of $U''(1.5V - p)/100$, which is negative for a risk-averse person. It follows that expected utility is concave and is maximized at $p = 0$. Notice that this setup has the unusual (and very desirable) property that the predictions of the relevant theories apply for a broad class of utility functions, that is, for all risk averters.

---

[*] The material in this section is somewhat more advanced.

REFERENCES

Ashenfelter, Orley (1989) "How Auctions Work for Wine and Art," *Journal of Economic Perspectives*, *3*(3), 23–36.

Ball, Sheryl B., Max H. Bazerman, and John S. Carroll (1990) "An Evaluation of Learning in the Bilateral Winner's Curse," *Organizational Behavior and Human Decision Processes*, *48*, 1–22.

Binmore, Kenneth, Avner Shaked, and John Sutton (1985) "Testing Noncooperative Bargaining Theory: A Preliminary Study," *American Economic Review*, *75*, 1178–1180.

——— (1988) "A Further Test of Noncooperative Bargaining Theory: Reply," *American Economic Review*, *78*, 837–839.

——— (1989) "An Outside Option Experiment," *Quarterly Journal of Economics*, *104*, 753–770.

Bolton, Gary E. (1991) "A Comparative Model of Bargaining: Theory and Evidence," *American Economic Review*, *81*, 1096–1136.

Cassady, Ralph (1967) *Auctions and Auctioneering*. Berkeley: University of California Press.

Capen, E. C., R. V. Clapp, and W. M. Campbell (1971) "Competitive Bidding in High-Risk Situations," *Journal of Petroleum Technology*, *23*, 641–53.

Coase, Ronald H. (1960) "The Problem of Social Cost," *Journal of Law and Economics*, *3*, 1–31.

Coppinger, Vicki M., Vernon L. Smith, and Jon A. Titus (1980) "Incentives and Behavior in English, Dutch and Sealed-Bid Auctions," *Economic Inquiry*, *18*, 1–22.

Cox, James C., Bruce Roberson, and Vernon L. Smith (1982) "Theory and Behavior of Single Object Auctions," in V. L. Smith, ed., *Research in Experimental Economics*, vol. 2. Greenwich, Conn.: JAI Press, 1–43.

Cox, James C., and Vernon L. Smith (1992) "Common Value Auctions with Endogenous Entry and Exit," working paper, University of Arizona.

Cox, James C., Vernon L. Smith, and James M. Walker (1982) "Auction Market Theory of Heterogeneous Bidders," *Economics Letters*, *9*, 319–325.

——— (1988) "Theory and Individual Behavior of First-Price Auctions," *Journal of Risk and Uncertainty*, *1*, 61–99.

——— (1990) "Theory and Misbehavior in First Price Auctions: Comment," working paper, University of Arizona.

Forsythe, Robert, Joel L. Horowitz, N. E. Savin, and Martin Sefton (1988) "Replicability, Fairness and Pay in Experiments with Simple Bargaining Games," Working Paper 88–30, Department of Economics, University of Iowa, forthcoming in *Games and Economic Behavior*.

Forsythe, Robert, John Kennan, and Barry Sopher (1991) "An Experimental Analysis of Strikes in Bargaining Games with One-Sided Private Information," *American Economic Review, 81*, 253–278.

Forsythe, Robert, Thomas R. Palfrey, and Charles R. Plott (1982) "Asset Valuation in an Experimental Market," *Econometrica, 50*, 537–567.

Fouraker, Lawrence E., and Sidney Siegel (1963) *Bargaining Behavior*, New York: McGraw-Hill.

Friedman, Milton (1960) *A Program for Monetary Stability*. New York: Fordham University Press, 63–65.

Güth, Werner, and Reinhard Tietz (1988) "Ultimatum Bargaining for a Shrinking Cake: An Experimental Analysis," in R. Tietz, W. Albers, and R. Selten, eds., *Bounded Rational Behavior in Experimental Games and Markets*. Berlin: Springer.

Güth, Werner, Rolf Schmittberger, and Bernd Schwarze (1982) "An Experimental Analysis of Ultimatum Bargaining," *Journal of Economic Behavior and Organization, 3*, 367–388.

Hansen, Robert G., and John R. Lott (1991) "The Winner's Curse and Public Information in Common Value Auctions: Comment," *American Economic Review, 81*, 347–361.

Harris, Milton and Artur Raviv (1981) "Allocation Mechanisms and the Design of Auctions," *Econometrica, 49*, 1477–1499.

Harrison, Glenn W. (1989) "Theory and Misbehavior of First-Price Auctions," *American Economic Review, 79*, 749–762.

Harrison, Glenn W., and Kevin A. McCabe (1988) "Testing Bargaining Theory in Experiments," Department of Economics, University of Arizona, Discussion Paper No. 88–10, forthcoming in M. Isaac, ed., *Research in Experimental Economics*, vol. 5. Greenwich Conn.: JAI Press.

Harrison, Glenn W., and Michael McKee (1985) "Experimental Evaluation of the Coase Theorem," *Journal of Law and Economics, 28*, 653–670.

Hoffman, Elizabeth, and Matthew L. Spitzer (1982) "The Coase Theorem: Some Experimental Tests," *Journal of Law and Economics, 25*, 73–98.

———— (1985) "Entitlements, Rights and Fairness: An Experimental Examination of Subjects' Concepts of Distributive Justice," *Journal of Legal Studies, 14*, 259–297.

Hoffman, Elizabeth, Kevin McCabe, Keith Shachat, and Vernon Smith (1991) "Preferences, Property Rights, and Anonymity in Bargaining Games," draft, Department of Economics, University of Arizona.

Holt, Charles A. (1980) "Competitive Bidding for Contracts under Alternative Auction Procedures," *Journal of Political Economy, 88*, 433–445.

Holt, Charles A., and Roger Sherman (1991) "The Loser's Curse," working paper, University of Virginia.

Horkan, Edward R. (1990) "On Rationality and the Winner's Curse," senior thesis, University of Virginia.

Jarecki, Henry G. (1976) "Bullion Dealing, Commodity Exchange Trading and the London Gold Fixing: Three Forms of Commodity Auctions," in Y. Amihud, ed., *Bidding and Auctioning For Procurement and Allocation*. New York: New York University Press, 173–186.

Kagel, John H. (1991) "Auctions: A Survey of Experimental Research," forthcoming in J. Kagel and A. Roth, eds., *Handbook of Experimental Economics*, Princeton: Princeton University Press.

Kagel, John H., and Dan Levin (1986) "The Winner's Curse and Public Information in Common Value Auctions," *American Economic Review*, 76, 894-920.

Kagel, John H., and Alvin E. Roth (1990) "Comment on Harrison versus Cox, Smith and Walker: 'Theory and Misbehavior in First-Price Auctions'," draft, Department of Economics, University of Pittsburgh.

Kahneman, Daniel, Jack L. Knetsch, and Richard Thaler (1986) "Fairness and the Assumptions of Economics," *Journal of Business*, 59, S285–S300.

Kalai, E., and M. Smorodinsky (1975) "Other Solutions to Nash's Bargaining Problem," *Econometrica*, 45, 513-518.

Lind, Barry, and Charles R. Plott (1991) "The Winner's Curse: Experiments with Buyers and with Sellers," *American Economic Review*, 81, 335–346.

McCabe, Kevin A., Stephen J. Rassenti, and Vernon L. Smith (1990) "Auction Institution Design: Theory and Behavior of Simultaneous Multiple Unit Generalizations of the Dutch and English Auction," *American Economic Review*, 80, 1276-1283.

——— (1991) "Designing a Uniform Price Double Auction: An Experimental Evaluation," working paper, Economic Science Laboratory, University of Arizona.

——— (1992) "Designing Auction Institutions: Is Double Dutch the Best?" *Economic Journal*, 102, 4-23.

Milgrom, Paul (1989) "Auctions and Bidding: A Primer," *Journal of Economic Perspectives*, 3(3), 3–22.

Nash, John F. (1950) "The Bargaining Problem," *Econometrica*, 18, 155–162.

Neelin, Janet, Hugo Sonnenschein, and Matthew Spiegel (1988) "A Further Test of Noncooperative Bargaining Theory: Comment" *American Economic Review*, 78, 824–836.

Nydegger, Rudy V., and Houston G. Owen (1975) "Two-Person Bargaining: An Experimental Test of the Nash Axioms," *International Journal of Game Theory*, 3, 239–249.

Ochs, Jack, and Alvin E. Roth (1989) "An Experimental Study of Sequential Bargaining," *American Economic Review*, 79, 355–384.

Raiffa, Howard (1953) "Arbitration Schemes for Generalized Two-person Games," in H. W. Kuhn and A. W. Tucker, eds., *Contributions to the Theory of Games*. Princeton: Princeton University Press, 361–387.

Rapoport, Anatol, Oded Frenkel, and Josef Perner (1977) "Experiments with Cooperative 2X2 Games," *Theory and Decision*, *8*, 67–92.

Riley, John G. (1989) "Expected Revenue from Open and Sealed Bid Auctions," *Journal of Economic Perspectives*, *3*, 41–50.

Riley, John G., and William F. Samuelson (1981) "Optimal Auctions," *American Economic Review*, *71*, 381–392.

Roth, Alvin E., and Michael W. K. Malouf (1979) "Game-Theoretic Models and the Role of Information in Bargaining," *Psychological Review*, *86*, 574–594.

Roth, Alvin E., Michael W. K. Malouf, and J. Keith Murnighan (1981) "Sociological versus Strategic Factors in Bargaining," *Journal of Economic Behavior and Organization*, *2*, 153–177.

Roth, Alvin E., and J. Keith Murnighan (1982) "The Role of Information in Bargaining: An Experimental Study," *Econometrica*, *50*, 1123–1143.

Roth, Alvin E., J. Keith Murnighan, and Francoise Schoumaker (1988) "The Deadline Effect in Bargaining: Some Experimental Evidence," *American Economic Review*, *78*, 806–823.

Roth, Alvin E., Vesna Prasnikar, Masahiro Okuno-Fujiwara, and Shmuel Zamir (1991) "Bargaining and Market Behavior in Jerusalem, Ljubljana, Pittsburgh, and Tokyo: An Experimental Study," *American Economic Review*, *81*, 1068–1095.

Roth, Alvin E., and Francoise Schoumaker (1983) "Expectations and Reputations in Bargaining: An Experimental Study," *American Economic Review*, *73*, 362–372.

Rubinstein, Ariel (1982) "Perfect Equilibrium in a Bargaining Model," *Econometrica*, *50*, 97–109.

Samuelson, William (1984) "Bargaining under Asymmetric Information," *Econometrica*, *52*(4), 995-1005.

Samuelson, William, and Max H. Bazerman (1985) "The Winner's Curse in Bilateral Negotiations," in V. L. Smith, ed., *Research in Experimental Economics*, vol. 3. Greenwich, Conn.: JAI Press, 105-137.

Smith, Vernon L. (1967) "Experimental Studies of Discrimination Versus Competition in Sealed-Bid Auction Markets," *Journal of Business*, *40*, 56–84.

Smith, Vernon L., Arlington W. Williams, W. Kenneth Bratton, and Michael G. Vannoni (1982) "Competitive Market Institutions: Double Auctions versus Sealed Bid-Offer Auctions," *American Economic Review*, *72*, 58–77.

Spiegel, Matthew, Janet Currie, Hugo Sonnenschein, and Arunava Sen (1990) "First-Mover Advantage and the Division of Surplus in Two-Person Alternating-Offer Games: Results from Bargaining Experiments," working paper, Columbia Business School.

Stahl, Ingolf (1972) *Bargaining Theory*.   Stockholm: Stockholm School of
    Economics.
Vickrey, William (1961) "Counterspeculation, Auctions, and Competitive Sealed
    Tenders," *Journal of Finance*, *16*, 8–37.
Wilson, Robert (1985) "Reputations in Games and Markets," in A. E. Roth, ed.,
    Game-theoretic Models of Bargaining.   Cambridge: Cambridge University
    Press.

Chapter 6

PUBLIC GOODS, EXTERNALITIES, AND VOTING

6.1 Introduction

The preceding chapters pertain to allocational issues regarding *private* goods, or goods for which it is the case that a producer of the good unilaterally bears all costs of production, and a single consumer of the good enjoys all benefits of consumption. Not all goods are private, however, and markets can generate inefficient allocations or fail altogether as a result. In the absence of environmental regulation, for example, air pollution may be excessive since producers do not bear the full social cost of pollution and individual consumers do not enjoy the full benefits of decentralized cleanup activities.

This chapter examines the behavioral effects of variations in the assumption of privacy. To understand how the chapter is organized, it is instructive to consider two essential components of privacy: *rivalry* and *excludability*. Rivalry refers to the effects of one person consuming a unit of the good on another's capacity to consume the same unit of the good, at the same time. A good is said to exhibit nonrivalry in consumption if multiple consumers can simultaneously consume the same unit of the good. Thus, nonrivalry in consumption is a characteristic of a television broadcast and not a characteristic of a hamburger. Excludability means that it is feasible to prevent consumption by those who fail to pay. Most standard consumer goods are easily excludable; even nonrivaled goods such as satellite television can be made excludable with scrambling devices. Nonexcludability often becomes an issue when property rights are ill-defined, for example, fishing rights in international waters.

Products in natural contexts are scattered about rivalry/excludability space, but for purposes of analysis it is convenient to focus on the extreme cases, or "corners" of this space. *Pure private goods*, or goods that are both completely rivaled and excludable, have been induced by the incentive structure of experiments discussed in the preceding chapters. The next several sections of this chapter assess the opposite case of *pure public goods*, which are both nonrivaled and nonexcludable. In subsequent sections we will consider goods characterized by either nonrivalry or nonexcludability, but not both.

Pure public goods are susceptible to underprovision for reasons similar to those presented by the prisoners' dilemma discussed in chapter 2: Even though provision of a group good (say, national defense) may be in everyone's joint interest, any individual has an incentive to take a "free-ride" off others' contributions and spend potential contributions in other, higher-valued uses. Of course, if everyone follows such individual incentives, the good is produced at an inefficiently low level, or not at all. In terms of the chapter 2 discussion, an inefficient production level is a Nash equilibrium that is Pareto dominated by the nonequilibrium outcome where everyone contributes to the group good.

The incentive to free-ride has generated a standard presumption among economists that decentralized allocation mechanisms cannot be relied upon to provide public goods efficiently (e.g., Samuelson, 1954). The vast resources devoted to the government provision of goods and services in developed economies supports a general public perception that the free-rider problem is pervasive. This presumption, however, is not without its critics. Noting the billions of dollars voluntarily contributed annually to a wide variety of charitable causes, these critics argue that emphasis on free-rider incentives is misplaced. Consumers, it is argued, will honestly reveal their preferences for any good through their contributions, regardless of the capacity to free-ride. For example, Johansen (1977, p. 147) concludes, "I do not know of many historical records or other empirical evidence which show convincingly that the problem of correct revelation of preferences has any practical significance."

To address this question of the behavioral significance of the free-rider hypothesis, the first three sections of this chapter review experimental investigations designed to assess the extent of the public-goods problem, as well as the effects of various schemes designed to alleviate free-riding behavior. Section 6.2 describes a basic "voluntary contributions mechanism" that has been used for the bulk of laboratory research in public goods issues, and it relates the free-rider predictions to noncooperative game theory. Experimental evidence regarding the extent of public goods underprovision is summarized in section 6.3. Finally, given the presence of a free-rider problem, section 6.4 describes alterations to the voluntary-contributions mechanism intended to increase provision of the public good.

Sections 6.5 and 6.6 consider the application of experimental techniques to provision problems arising from goods that are not pure public goods but exhibit *either* rivalry or excludability: Section 6.5 reviews experiments designed to evaluate incentive-compatible mechanisms for the provision of nonrivaled but excludable goods, such as public parks. Section 6.6 then evaluates externalities, and in particular, the problem of common pool resources such as fisheries, where goods are rivaled in consumption but not excludable. Finally, provision levels for many public goods are decided by voting rather than via a decentralized market. Although we do not review in detail the extensive literature on voting experiments, we illustrate in section 6.7 a basic laboratory result, that the institution (in this case the voting agenda) can affect a voting outcome. Section 6.8 contains a brief summary.

6.2 The Voluntary-Contributions Mechanism

The free-rider hypothesis has been examined in a variety of laboratory contexts, and, as might be expected, both institutional and environmental alterations can affect the incidence of free-riding. To provide a frame of reference, we describe here a basic version of the *voluntary-contributions mechanism*, the institutional framework that has been most commonly used to examine public goods provision. The subsequent discussion of results may then be characterized in terms of deviations from this baseline environment.[1]

The voluntary-contributions mechanism is a simple repeated game. Instructions for a noncomputerized version of this game are provided in appendix A6.2. A standard implementation proceeds in the following manner.[2] A group of participants are seated at visually isolated locations (typically computer terminals) and are told that they are about to participate in a decision-making experiment involving alternative investments. In each decision period, the participants are endowed with a number of "tokens," which may be allocated either to a private exchange or to a group exchange. Tokens invested in the private exchange will be converted to cash at a constant rate (typically one penny per token). Tokens invested in the group exchange yield a lower return to the individual, but these tokens yield an additional return that accrues to each participant in the group, including the contributor.

For simplicity, the returns to the group investment are typically proportional to their investment. To facilitate the calculation of benefits from investing in the group exchange, the payoffs associated with various group investment levels are

---

[1] It is important to emphasize that provision problems have been investigated in alternative, equally legitimate environments. One particularly interesting alternative, designed by Palfrey and Rosenthal (1991, 1992), is discussed in appendix A6.1

[2] Variations of this mechanism have been studied since public goods allocation problems were first addressed in the laboratory (see, e.g., Smith, 1979, 1980). The description in the text follows the mechanism used by Isaac, Walker, and Thomas (1984), which has become a standard for research in this area.

320   CHAPTER 6

presented to participants in a table, similar to table 6.1. In this table, contributions
are listed in ten-token increments, ranging from 0 to 120; intermediate contribution
and payoff possibilities are omitted for brevity. Standard implementations of the
voluntary-contributions mechanism provide payoffs for every possible aggregate
contribution. Note also in table 6.1 that each ten-token allocation by an individual
to the group exchange yields a 7-cent return to *every* participant in the group.
Therefore, the *marginal per capita return* (MPCR) of a contribution to the group
exchange is 7/10 of a cent.[3]

Table 6.1 Returns for Contributing to the Group Exchange in a Voluntary-
Contributions Mechanism Decision Period

Aggregate Contributions to Group Exchange (tokens)	0	10	20	30	40	50	60	70	80	90	100	110	120
Payoff to Each Individual (cents)	0	7	14	21	28	35	42	49	56	63	70	77	84

Participants make allocation decisions privately, but once all members of the
group have completed their decisions, the aggregate investment in the group
exchange is announced and private earnings are calculated. Then the payoff from
the group exchange can be added to each individual's earnings from the private
exchange to obtain that individual's total earnings for the period. Following a
determination of earnings, participants are reendowed with tokens and a new
decision period begins. This process is repeated a preannounced number of times
(usually ten). Following the terminal period, either a second treatment is conducted,
or the session ends.

For example, consider the case of two participants, player 1 and player 2, each
with an endowment of 60 tokens. Assume that the MPCR is .7, as in table 6.1.
Table 6.2 illustrates the decision problem for player 1, along with sample responses
for the first decision period. The sequence of actions in the table is denoted by the
column headings (a), (b), and (c). First, player 1 allocates resources between the
group and private exchanges. Suppose that player 1 contributes 20 tokens to the
group exchange and invests the remaining 40 tokens in the private exchange. This
decision, highlighted by the numbers under heading (a) in the table, is made without

---

[3] A less important, but still notable characteristic of table 6.1 is that its format is invariant to the
number of participants in a session. Although participants may certainly evaluate contributions to the
group exchange in light of the number of other possible contributors, changes in the number of
participants alter only the maximum possible contributions in the table. Due to this characteristic, design
alterations in this type of experiment are procedurally very simple.

information regarding player 2's choices. Suppose player 2 allocates 50 tokens to the group exchange and 10 tokens to the private exchange. After each player submits a decision, total contributions to the group exchange are calculated and announced. In this case, total contributions to the group exchange by players 1 and 2 sum to 70, as indicated under heading (b) in table 6.2. Finally, player 1 calculates earnings as the sum of the returns from the individual allocation of tokens to the private exchange and the aggregate allocation of tokens to the group exchange. The appropriate total is 89, printed under heading (c). Not shown, player 2 would earn $10 + .7(70) = 59$ cents this period. Following the calculation of earnings, a second decision period begins.

Table 6.2 A Sample Decision Sheet in a Voluntary-Contributions Mechanism Experiment

Period	Endowment	(a) Allocation Decision		(b) Total Contributions to Group Exchange	(c) Earnings
		Private Exchange	Group Exchange		
1	60	40	20	70	$40 + .7(70) = 89$
2	60				
3	60				
.	.				
.	.				

Note that the "group exchange" in this context is an abstract, pure-public good. It is abstract in the sense that it has no value except in exchange. The good is a pure-public good since everyone fully enjoys the benefits of any contribution to it; that is, returns are both nonexcludable and nonrivaled. These characteristics offer a great deal of experimental control. In particular, the abstract nature of group exchange avoids confounding effects regarding individual attitudes toward contributing to public works or charities. Moreover, since the good is valued purely in monetary terms, it can be easily and identifiably manipulated.

The Voluntary-Contributions Mechanism and the Prisoner's Dilemma

Consider the parallels between the public-goods problem in tables 6.1 and 6.2 and the prisoner's dilemma. Denoting x_1 and x_2 as contributions by players 1 and 2 to the group exchange, earnings are calculated:

(6.1)
$$60 - x_1 + .7(x_1 + x_2) \quad \textit{for participant 1,}$$

$$60 - x_2 + .7(x_1 + x_2) \quad \textit{for participant 2.}$$

This voluntary-contribution mechanism may be reduced to a standard prisoner's dilemma by restricting participant choices to allocations involving either all or none of their token endowment to the group exchange. If both players contribute their entire endowment to the public good, then each earns $.7(60 + 60) = 84$ cents, as shown in the upper left-hand box of figure 6.1. If player 1 contributes all tokens to the group exchange, but player 2 contributes nothing, then player 1 earns $.7(60) = 42$ cents, while player 2 earns $60 + .7(60) = 102$ cents, as shown in the upper right-hand box, where the lower left entry pertains to player 1. Earnings are reversed if participant 2 alone contributes to the group exchange. Finally, if neither contributes anything to the group exchange, they each earn 60 cents.

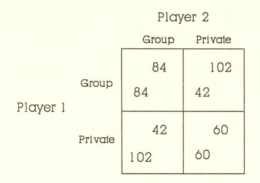

Figure 6.1 A Two-Person, Two-Choice Public-Goods Problem

The prisoner's dilemma nature of this game is evident from inspection of the payoffs in figure 6.1: Joint income is maximized if both players contribute to the group exchange. Each player also has an individual incentive, however, to place tokens in the private exchange. For example, given that player 2 contributes to the group exchange, player 1 can unilaterally increase earnings from 84 to 102 cents by free-riding off player 2 and investing exclusively in the private exchange. Contributions to the private exchange also minimize player 1's vulnerability to the decisions of player 2, since by contributing to the private exchange, player 1 avoids the possibility of earning only 42 cents in the event that player 2 chooses to free-ride. Due to the symmetry of the game, player 2 faces similar incentives. Thus, contributions to the private exchange represent a unique Nash equilibrium for the game. Each player has a dominant incentive to free-ride off the other, and as a consequence, neither contributes to the group exchange.

Free-riding remains a dominant strategy in this example when the number of players is increased. Consider the case of three players, illustrated in figure 6.2. The matrix on the left side of the figure illustrates the consequences of choices by players 1 and 2, when player 3 contributes all tokens to the group exchange, while the matrix on the right illustrates the consequences of choices for players 1 and 2 when player 3 contributes all tokens to the private exchange. Payoffs for (player 1, player 2, player 3) are printed in each payoff box. Payoffs for player 3 are circled for emphasis.

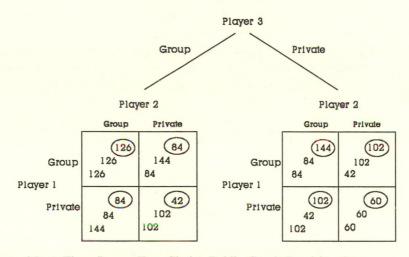

Figure 6.2 A Three-Person Two-Choice Public-Goods Provision Game

From pair-wise comparison of (uncircled) player 1 and player 2 payoffs across payoff matrices in figure 6.2, it is immediately clear that the addition of a third player does not change the incentives for players 1 and 2 to contribute only to the private exchange. Within each matrix, players 1 and 2 face a prisoner's dilemma. For example, it is clear from inspection of the matrix on the right side of the panel that players 1 and 2 face exactly the same set of outcomes available in the two-person prisoner's dilemma in figure 6.1 in the event player 3 contributes only to the private exchange. Inspection of the circled payoffs reveals that player 3 shares incentives to contribute only to the private exchange, regardless of what players 1 and 2 do: The circled numbers on the right side of the figure are greater than the corresponding numbers on the left side.

The Pareto-dominant, welfare-maximizing solution in figure 6.2 occurs when all players contribute to the group exchange, generating earnings of (126, 126, 126), shown in the upper left corner of the matrix on the left. But it is a dominant strategy for each player to contribute to private exchange, and so in the unique Nash equilibrium, earnings are reduced to (60, 60, 60), shown in the lower right corner of the matrix on the right. It is worth noting that the difference between the cooperative and Nash equilibrium outcomes increases across the two- and three-person games shown in figures 6.1 and 6.2. Holding the MPCR constant, the gains from cooperation increase with the number of players, since more participants are able to make contributions that are collectively enjoyed by all.

Illustration of the problem quickly becomes intractable with the addition of more players, but this three-person prisoner's dilemma can readily be generalized to any arbitrary number of players N: If everyone contributes to the group exchange, each player earns $.7(60)N$. The dilemma arises because each player has an incentive to contribute to the private good and earn $.7(60)(N-1) + 60$. In the unique Nash equilibrium for the game, each player contributes only to the private good and earns 60 cents.

It is useful to present the public-goods problem in the context of more nearly continuous contributions options. This can be seen from the following general characterization of the voluntary-contributions mechanism. Denote endowments and decisions for each participant with a subscript i: $i = 1 \ldots N$. Each participant has an initial endowment, E_i, of which some amount x_i is contributed to the group exchange, and the remainder $E_i - x_i$ is invested in a private exchange and converted to cash. The individual return from contributions to the group exchange is a function of the sum of contributions by all participants, $V(\Sigma x_j)$. Thus, the problem for each participant is to choose x_i to maximize return on investment R_i, where

$$(6.2) \qquad\qquad R_i = E_i - x_i + V(\Sigma_j x_j).$$

A public-goods problem arises when contributions to the private exchange are individually optimal, but not optimal for the group. The individual optimality condition requires evaluating the marginal effects of contributions to the public and private exchanges. These conditions can be compared by taking the derivative of (6.2) with respect to individual contributions x_i. This derivative is $-1 + V'(\Sigma x_j)$. In this context, the MPCR is V', and the marginal return of a contribution to the private exchange is 1. Contributions to the private exchange are individually optimal if the MPCR is less than 1, or if $V'(\Sigma x_j) < 1$. Total group income is the sum of all individual returns from the group exchange. If individuals are identical, this may be expressed as the product $N \cdot V(\Sigma x_j)$. Contributions to the group exchange increase aggregate income more than contributions to the private exchange as long as $N \cdot V'(\Sigma x_j) > 1$. Combined, these conditions characterize the free-rider problem:

$$(6.3) \qquad\qquad \frac{1}{N} < V'(\Sigma x_j) < 1.$$

Notice that a free-rider problem can arise even with a very small group. For example, if the MPCR is between 1/2 and 1, free-riding is predicted for a group of two.

Although neither the number of participants nor the continuity of choices affects the unique, pure-strategy equilibrium in a single-stage implementation of the voluntary contributions mechanism, it is important to observe that other components of the implementation can affect equilibrium predictions. As was the case for collusion in the repeated oligopolies discussed in chapter 4, cooperation can be supported in an infinitely (or indefinitely) repeated game through the use of threats. That is, contributions to the public good can be an equilibrium, if they are supported by a threat to "punish" cheaters with zero contributions to the public good. To avoid the possibility of these "cooperative" equilibria, standard implementations of the voluntary-contributions mechanism typically include an announcement regarding the number periods.

6.3 The Voluntary-Contributions Mechanism: Results

Initial laboratory examinations of the free-rider problem generated widely divergent results. On the one hand, Marwell and Ames (1979, 1980, 1981) and Schneider and Pommerhene (1981) found far less free-riding than predicted by economists. In a wide variety of treatment conditions, participants rather persistently contributed 40 to 60 percent of their token endowments to the group exchange, far in excess of the 0 percent contributions rate consistent with a Nash equilibrium. The only treatment unquestionably to induce free-riding by Marwell and Ames (1981) was the use of a cohort of thirty-two first-year graduate students in economics (who contributed only 20 percent of their endowments to the group project), leading the authors to entitle their paper "Economists Free-Ride, Does Anyone Else?"[4] On the other hand, nearly complete free-riding has been generated in other laboratory contexts (e.g., Kim and Walker, 1984, and Isaac, McCue, and Plott, 1985), particularly in the terminal periods of multiperiod sessions.

Figure 6.3 provides a sense of the variety of outcomes observed in initial investigations. The figure summarizes mean contribution rates for eight sessions reported by Isaac, Walker, and Thomas (1984). Period numbers are listed along the horizontal axis, while mean contribution rates are printed on the vertical axis. Each line represents mean contribution rates for a single ten-period session.

Isaac, Walker, and Thomas were interested in identifying reasons for the differences in contribution rates reported in initial experiments. Consequently, their experiment included a variety of the design features that were varied across earlier

---

[4] Subsequent investigations have not corroborated this finding of a subject-pool effect. In a different public-goods context, Isaac, McCue, and Plott (1985), for example, report near-zero contributions to a group exchange by a cohort of sociology undergraduates, as well as by several cohorts of economics undergraduates. Similarly, a cohort of presumably "cooperative" human ecologists and anthropologists also engaged in substantial free-riding in the laboratory (Mestelman and Feeny, 1988).

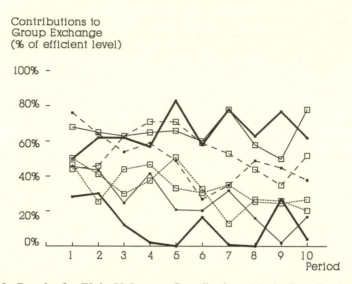

Contributions to
Group Exchange
(% of efficient level)

Figure 6.3 Results for Eight Voluntary Contributions Mechanism Sessions, under Various Treatment Conditions (Source: Isaac, Walker, and Thomas, 1984)

experiments, including the size of the group (four and ten), experience levels (inexperienced and experienced) and the MPCR (.30 and .75). Nevertheless, all sessions shared the characteristic that complete free-riding, or a contribution rate of 0, is the unique Nash equilibrium, and that joint income is maximized when all participants contribute all tokens to the group exchange. The primary conclusion that may be drawn from figure 6.3 is that, despite this common prediction, virtually every kind of behavior was observed. Contribution rates ranged from nearly 0 percent (illustrated by the bold line near the horizontal axis of the chart) to roughly 75 percent (as illustrated by the bold line near the top of figure).

Given the diversity of results, some identification of consistent sources of variation is warranted, both as a means of identifying when standard theory works well and as a means of suggesting modifications to the theory when it fails. In the remainder of this section, we consider a variety of potentially important determinants of free-riding, including experience, repetition, and the MPCR.

Repetition

The most obvious difference across the early studies was the number of periods. The 40 to 60 percent contributions rates reported by Schneider and Pommerhene (1981) and Marwell and Ames (1979, 1980, 1981) were for single-period games. Similar contribution rates were observed in initial decision-periods by Isaac, McCue, and Plott (1985) and Kim and Walker (1984). However, contribution rates decayed substantially when the decision sequence was repeated. For example, in five sessions reported by Isaac, McCue, and Plott (1985), average contribution rates decayed from 38 percent of the efficient contributions level in the initial period to 9 percent in the terminal period.[5]

It is an oversimplification to conclude that contribution rates uniformly diminish with repetition: Some of the series in figure 6.3 decay rather regularly, while others do not. Although an aggregation of contribution rates in figure 6.3 would generate a negative slope, such an aggregation misstates the prominent effect of repetition in certain environments.

For those environments where contribution rates generally diminish with repetition, it is useful to consider reasons for the decay. First, there is a learning effect. Many participants may learn that contributing to the private exchange dominates contributing to the group exchange only after observing several instances of free-riding by other participants. Second, the decay may be a consequence of strategic play. Although participants know that not contributing is a dominant strategy, they may nevertheless contribute in early periods and reserve a noncontribution option as a punishment for the failure of others to contribute.[6]

Andreoni (1988) reports an experiment designed to evaluate these learning and strategic-play explanations. The design turns on the observation that strategic punish/reward play is only potentially useful if participants remain paired in the same group for consecutive periods. A pure-learning effect could be isolated by shuffling the composition of participant groups after each trial. Consequently, Andreoni conducted the following two-treatment experiment. A first "partners" treatment consisted of three sessions with the standard voluntary-contributions mechanism. A second "strangers" treatment was identical, except that instead of leaving the same group intact for ten consecutive periods, participants in a cohort of twenty were randomly and anonymously regrouped after each decision period. Design features common to both treatments included an MPCR of .5, decision groups consisting of five inexperienced participants, and complete information about group size, session length, and the results of each decision period.

Results of this experiment are summarized by the mean contributions rates for the "partners" and "strangers" treatments, shown in figure 6.4. Obviously, contribution rates declined with repetition in each treatment. Contrary to

---

[5]   Mean contribution rates understate efficiency, or the proportion of possible gains from contributing to the group exchange in the Isaac, McCue, and Plott design since these authors induced a diminishing marginal value schedule for contributions to the group exchange. Efficiency extraction rates decayed from 53 percent to 16 percent for the five sessions mentioned in the text. Also, these authors conducted a total seven sessions in their experiment but report summary results on the basis of five sessions. Two sessions were excluded on the basis of aberrant, "irrational" participant decisions.

[6]   In a game with a commonly known and finite number of periods, this is not a subgame-perfect Nash equilibrium strategy. However, it is part of a Nash equilibrium strategy, and it may have some behavioral appeal.

expectation, however, significantly higher contribution rates were generated in the "strangers" treatment.[7] Andreoni concludes that the contributions pattern is not attributable to strategic motivations (this hypothesis would be supported by significantly higher contributions in the partners treatment). The similar rate of decay in each treatment supports a learning explanation. The difference in contributions rates is provocative. To the extent that strangers do in fact tend to persistently contribute more than partners, a richer set of behavioral motivations (such as altruism, revenge, social norms, and regret theory) merits consideration.

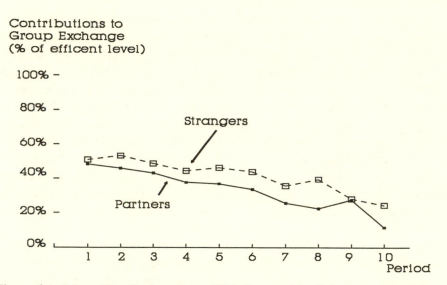

Figure 6.4   Mean Contributions Rates With Regrouping (Strangers) and Without Regrouping (Partners) (Source: Andreoni, 1988)

Experience

Given the well-documented effects of experience in market experiments, one would be surprised if experience did not also affect contributions rates in the voluntary-contributions mechanism. As suggested by the two pairs of sessions illustrated in figure 6.5, contributions to the group exchange do in fact tend to diminish consistently when participants are experienced with the mechanism. Results in figure 6.5 are taken from the Isaac, Walker, and Thomas experiment

---

[7]   Andreoni reports that these results are statistically significant. Specifically, the author reports a chi-squared test of the null hypotheses that observations in each treatment are drawn from the same distribution. This hypothesis can be rejected at $\alpha > .01$.

summarized in figure 6.3. The two panels in the figure represent different parameterizations (both of which satisfy equation 6.3). The left panel illustrates two sessions conducted with groups of four participants and an MPCR = .3. The right panel summarizes two sessions with groups of size ten and an MPCR = .75. Notice that in each case, experienced participants generally contributed less than inexperienced participants. This experience effect was general: Overall, mean contribution rates were 10 percent lower in the four sessions using experienced participants than in the four comparable sessions using inexperienced subjects. Similar experience effects have been observed elsewhere. Perhaps for this reason, the majority of reported experiments use an experienced participant pool.

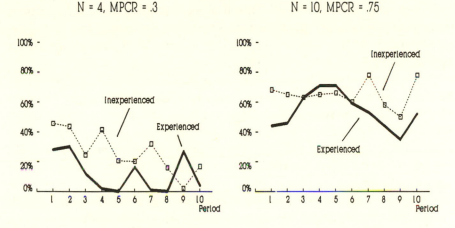

Figure 6.5 Contribution Rates for Two Pairs of Sessions (Source: Isaac, Walker, and Thomas, 1984)

Marginal Per Capita Return versus Group Size Effects

Consider next the effects of group size on contributions to a group exchange. A common conjecture is that incentives to free-ride are magnified as the size of the group increases.[8] One would, for example, expect provision of a pure public good on a national scale, such as defense, to be much more susceptible to free-riding than, say, a voluntary arrangement to clean the bathroom in a shared apartment. One might expect contributions to diminish with increases in the group size, since both efforts to coordinate contributions and attempts to punish free-riding become more

---

[8] For example, Browning and Browning (1989, p. 586) write "As the group size increases, it is more likely that everyone will behave like a free-rider, and the public good will not be provided."

difficult in larger groups. (But note that as the number of people increases, the public good that comes from making an individual contribution to the group exchange is more widely distributed. Therefore, given any particular MPCR, the social benefits of contributing to the group exchange increases with the group size.)

Next consider the possible effects of changes in the MPCR on contributions. Underprovision is always predicted whenever the individual return to a group investment is even slightly less than that available in an alternate private investment. Nevertheless, the decision to allocate resources to the group exchange may be determined in large part by quantitative differences in the costs of contributing. A higher MPCR reduces the cost of contributing to the group exchange and as a result may increase contributions.

Although stark differences in both the group size and the MPCR may occur in natural contexts, these effects are difficult if not impossible to isolate. Instances where two different-sized groups fund the same project are hard to find. Even more problematic is $V'(\Sigma x_j)$, which is difficult to observe as it depends on private preferences.

The relative effect of these alternative motivations for free-riding, however, can be directly observed in the laboratory. Isaac and Walker (1988a) report the results of a particularly well-designed experiment conducted to distinguish group size and MPCR effects for relatively small groups (sizes four and ten), and for large changes in the MPCR (rates of .30 and .75). The design consisted of four treatment cells, one for each of the group size/MPCR combinations. The authors conducted twelve sessions, six sessions using four-person groups, and an additional six using ten-person groups. Each session consisted of two ten-period decision sequences under standard procedures. One of the sequences in each session was conducted under the high MPCR (.75) condition, and the other under the low MPCR (.30) condition. To control for possible sequencing effects, the order of the high and low MPCR treatments was varied across sessions, in a balanced manner.

The left panel of figure 6.6 summarizes the results of this experiment. Labels in the panel identify treatments by group size and the MPCR rate. The label *10L*, for example, represents mean contributions for the six sequences in the ten-person, low-MPCR condition. The MPCR effect clearly dominates the group-size effect: the *10L* and *4L* lines uniformly lie below the *10H* and *4H* lines, indicating that mean contribution rates in the low-MPCR condition are consistently below those in the high MPCR condition, independent of group size. In fact, if there is any group effect at all, it is opposite to that expected by the conventional wisdom. While there is little difference in contribution rates for the small and large groups in the high-MPCR condition, the *4L* line lies considerably below the *10L* line, suggesting that underprovision of the public good may be a more significant problem for small groups than for large groups.

The relationship among MPCR, group size, and contributions to a group exchange was further explored by Isaac, Walker, and Williams (1991), who examined contribution rates for much larger groups. The results of three forty-person sessions in the MPCR =.3 treatment are illustrated by the line on the right side of figure 6.6. As is clear from comparison of the left and right panels of figure 6.6, very different performance is observed in larger sessions. The mean contribution rate for the three sessions in the *40L* design are much higher than either the *4L* or the *10L* sessions shown on the left of figure 6.6. Moreover, there is virtually no decay in contributions in the *40L* treatment.[9]

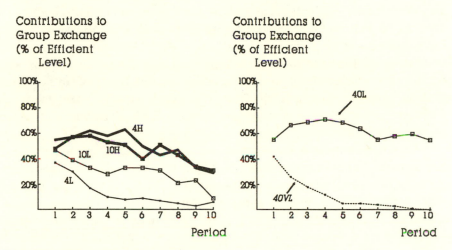

Figure 6.6   Mean Contribution Rates for Four-, Ten-, and Forty-Person Sessions (Sources: Isaac and Walker, 1988a; Isaac, Walker, and Williams, 1991)

One can only conjecture as to why the contributions increase when the size of the group increases, but such conjectures are useful because they can suggest a subsequent experiment. Clearly, it is the case that, other things constant, contributions to the group exchange have a larger effect as the size of the group increases. Recall again that MPCR = V', and that the marginal social benefits of contributions to the group are $N \cdot V'$. Thus, the benefits of concerted action increase linearly with increases in the group size. This is clearly shown in the fourth column of table 6.3, which lists the marginal social benefit of a contribution to the group exchange for $N = \{4, 10, 40\}$.

---

[9] These authors generate very similar results in a series of large-group sessions conducted in a "multisession" variant of the voluntary contributions mechanism, where participants make allocational decisions in sequences lasting a week, and where participants are rewarded in terms of extra-credit points rather than cash. Treatments included changes in the group size (40 and 100 people) and in the MPCR (.3 and .75). For these parameters, both mean contribution rates and the rate of decay in contributions appear invariant. Performance was virtually identical in all cells and closely resembles the results for the forty-person sessions illustrated in the text.

Alternatively, Isaac, Walker, and Williams suggest that the primary explanation of contributions to the group exchange may be the proportion of the group necessary for a *minimal profitable coalition*, that is, the smallest collection of participants for whom the return from contributions to the group exchange exceed the return from investing in the private exchange. Of course, the likelihood of a global coalition probably diminishes with increases in the size of the group. Given an MPCR of .3, a minimum of four people must contribute to the group exchange in order for the return from their collective contributions to exceed the return from investments in the private exchange. (This is because 4 is the smallest integer N for which $.3N > 1$.) Thus, the proportion of participants that must invest in the group exchange in order for contributions to the group exchange to remain profitable diminishes as the group size increases. This observation is summarized in the right-most column of table 6.3, which lists the minimum percent of a group necessary for a profitable coalition of four. Notice that with a group of four, everyone must contribute to the group exchange. But with a group of forty, contributions of only 10 percent of the group are needed for a profitable coalition.

This conjecture is consistent with the results summarized in figure 6.6. Regardless of the treatment, individuals initially contribute about half of their tokens to the group exchange. But decay rates vary with the group size. For example, when MPCR = .3, contribution rates decay rapidly in the *4L* treatment, where profitable coalitions require unanimity. The rate of decay is somewhat slower in groups of size ten, where 40 percent of group members are necessary for a profitable coalition. Decay rates for the large groups are still slower and less distinguishable for the forty-person sessions shown in the right side of the figure, where a minimum successful coalition requires contributions from only 10 percent of the group.

Evidence from an additional forty-person session further supports the hypothesis that contributions rates are affected by the minimal profitable coalition. Consider the bottom row of table 6.3. In this row, it is seen that decreasing the MPCR by a factor of 10, to .03, increases the minimal profitable coalition for a large, forty-person group. With the MPCR the minimal profitable coalition is 85 percent of the group (since 34 is the smallest integer N for which $.03N > 1$). Results of a single session, illustrated by the dotted *40VL* line on the right side of figure 6.6, show dramatic decay in contributions. Results parallel data for the *4L* treatment. Of course, these results are also consistent with an explanation based on the "marginal social benefit" column in table 6.3. These two alternatives could be distinguished with additional experimentation.

Summary

Despite a common and unique game-theoretic prediction, contributions rates in laboratory investigations of the voluntary contributions mechanism vary widely. A variety of determinants affect contributions, in spite of the fact that they are

Table 6.3 Group Size and Minimum Profitable Coalitions

Incentive	MPCR (V')	N	Marginal Social Benefit ($N * V'$)	Minimum Profitable Coalition (percent of group)
L	.3	4	1.2	100%
L	.3	10	3.0	40%
L	.3	40	12.0	10%
VL	.03	40	1.2	85%

theoretically irrelevant in the sense that they to not affect the Nash equilibrium. Such factors include repetition, experience, and the decreases in the MPCR; all of which increase free-riding.

Upon further examination, however, the determinants of contribution rates appear less settled, and some interaction effects may be present. For example, it is clear from early studies that both repetition and experience exert a larger effect on performance in smaller groups with low MPCRs. Also, and perhaps somewhat surprisingly, contributions appear to increase as the group size expands, at least for some particular MPCRs.

6.4 Factors That May Alleviate Free-Riding

Despite the variety of environmental factors that affect free-riding, it is clear that the underprovision of public goods presents a significant problem in a fairly wide variety of contexts. A natural line of related inquiry involves consideration of variations in the institutional rules of the voluntary-contributions mechanism that might mitigate the observed underprovision rates. This section discusses two such institutional manipulations: communications and provision points.

The unsettled nature of the experimental literature assessing the various environmental determinants of contributions rates provides a rather unstable backdrop against which the effects of these institutional variations might be evaluated. Nevertheless, experimental analysis can identify factors that increase contribution rates relative to performance in a particular baseline environment where free-riding is predominant. Given the diversity of baseline results, however, the generality of such institutional adjustments remains an open question.

Communications

Alterations in the flow of information among participants represent one obvious modification of the voluntary-contributions mechanism that may affect contributions rates. In the extreme, participants could meet and negotiate a contract that specified contributions rates for all individuals, as well as a set of penalties for failures to contribute at the contractual rate. Government budget allocations represent the most standard examples of binding communications of this sort. The illegality of free-riding in this context implies that the underprovision problem can be avoided.

A variety of interesting issues arise when free-riding is illegal, such as determining the appropriate level of public-goods provision, creating optimal schemes for collecting necessary revenues, and determining penalties for not contributing. Some of these issues are addressed in section 6.7 on voting. Our interest in this section, however, is on modifications of a *voluntary* contributions mechanism. For this reason, we will restrict our attention to nonbinding, preplay communications.

Importantly, since contracts and formal agreements are explicitly barred, it is natural to conjecture that nonbinding communications are theoretically innocuous. But this is generally *not* the case. Communications can take a variety of forms, ranging from a single binary message communicated over a computer network (for example, are contributions intended?) to face-to-face, unstructured discussions. In stark public-goods environments with highly structured communications opportunities, it has been shown that communications can improve efficiency by helping to coordinate participants' efforts on one of a variety of possible outcomes (see, e.g., Palfrey and Rosenthal, 1991). Although it is much easier to model the effects of limited, highly structured communications, the following discussion focuses on free-form, face-to-face negotiations, which probably give communications a "best shot" at affecting contributions.

An experiment by Isaac and Walker (1988b) identifies a baseline case where unstructured communications clearly increase public-goods provision rates. This experiment consisted of ten sessions in a variation of the four-person design with MPCR = .3 used by Isaac and Walker (1988a), discussed above. In particular, participants were experienced and had identical endowments. In the efficient solution, all participants should contribute all tokens to the group exchange.

Communications were introduced in the following manner: Prior to each period, the four participants were gathered together. They were allowed to discuss anything of interest, subject to the restrictions that they (a) reveal no private information about their endowments or their payoffs, and (b) neither make physical threats nor arrange for side payments. Participants could talk for a maximum of four minutes prior to making each decision. Following each discussion, participants returned to their terminals and privately made the usual group-exchange/private-exchange investment decisions.

In a first treatment, designated C/NC, communications were allowed in ten initial periods, followed by ten periods without communications. Three sessions were conducted with this treatment. Three sessions were also conducted with a second NC/C treatment, in which communications were not allowed at the outset but were permitted in the final ten periods.[10]

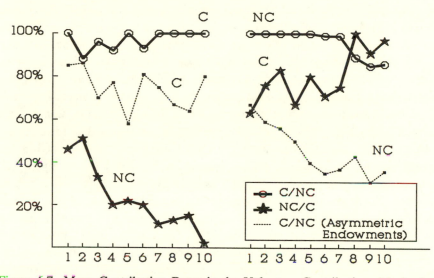

Figure 6.7 Mean Contribution Rates in the Voluntary Contributions Mechanism, With and Without Communications (Source: Isaac and Walker, 1988b)

Average contributions rates for the C/NC and the NC/C treatments are illustrated in figure 6.7 by the bold lines with circled and starred period markers, respectively. (Ignore the dotted line for now.) In either treatment, communications clearly affect outcomes: mean contributions are much higher in the sequences where communications were allowed.[11] But a sequencing effect is also apparent. Contributions decay slowly after communications are suspended in the NC portion of the C/NC treatment. Conversely, contributions increase slowly after communications are introduced in the C portion of the NC/C treatment. These

---

[10] The authors calibrated these sessions with an NC/NC treatment, which consisted of four sessions where communications were never allowed.

[11] In subsequent investigation, Isaac and Walker (1991) find that the effects of communications are resilient to the introduction of meeting costs. Positive meeting costs have considerable relevance to many natural contexts. For example, residents in a neighborhood will not respond to an unpopular zoning change, unless the costs of organizing and attending a neighborhood meeting are overcome. The obvious incentives to shirk on efforts to organize a neighborhood meeting creates an additional free-riding problem.

results suggest a "history" effect: A history of cooperation tends to discourage free-riding, while a history of free-riding tends to discourage cooperation.

In many respects, the introduction of nonbinding communications in the public-goods situation parallels explicit conspiracy in oligopolies.[12]   In both cases communications allow participants to implement a successful cooperative arrangement. This parallel suggests an obvious line of inquiry: How do the factors that frustrate explicit conspiracies affect contributions in a public-goods context where communications are allowed?

Consider, for example, the effects of asymmetries in token endowments. Asymmetric endowments are similar to the cost asymmetry condition thought to frustrate the implementation and maintenance of high, cooperative prices in an oligopoly. Isaac and Walker (1988b) explore the effect of endowment asymmetries in a second experiment using a minor variant of the C/NC design, where token endowments for two of the participants were 28 percent higher than for the other two participants. Average contributions rates for three sessions conducted in this asymmetric-endowment design are represented by the dotted line in figure 6.7. Communications clearly represent a much less effective coordinating device in these sessions.   Although contributions rates in the first ten communications periods substantially exceed contributions rates in the no-communications treatment, they are considerably below those observed in the C/NC treatment where participants shared symmetric endowments. Moreover, communications have little residual effect in the (dotted line) no-communication sequences, as evidenced by the marked decay in contributions to the group exchange in these sessions.[13]

Nonbinding communications were also an ineffective coordinating device in a third experiment by Isaac and Walker (1988b). This experiment consisted of twelve sessions conducted in somewhat more complex design. Although participants had symmetric endowments, G' was not constant, and $G'' < 0$ (thus inducing a diminishing marginal utility for additional units of the public good). As a result, in the optimal solution participants contributed only 50 percent of their endowments to the group exchange.   Also, the group size was expanded from four to six participants, and each session consisted of a single ten-period sequence. Six of the sessions were conducted under the communications condition, while the remaining six sessions were conducted under the no-communications conditions. As is readily

---

[12]   In fact, both of the results illustrated in figure 6.7 have been independently observed in oligopoly experiments. See, e.g., Daughety and Forsythe (1985).

[13]   The authors also conducted a series of sessions where participants had complete information regarding token endowments in this experiment. The information treatment was strongly affected by the endowment condition: Given complete information and symmetric endowments, communications generated high and lasting effects. But when participants had asymmetric endowments, complete information failed to improve the effects of communications over the incomplete information treatment. Moreover, contributions to the group exchange virtually collapsed in the no-communication sequences of these sessions.

apparent from inspection of mean contributions rates for these sessions in figure 6.8, communications are less effective in this environment. Although contributions rates are higher in the communications treatment than in the no-communications treatment, participants do not, on average, manage to establish a stable pattern of contributions to the group exchange in this design, even with communications. Rather, mean contributions rates in the communications condition exhibit a pattern of decay similar to that observed in the no-communications condition.[14]

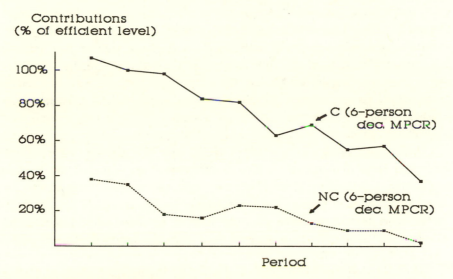

Figure 6.8 Mean Contributions Rates with and without Communications (Source: Isaac and Walker, 1988b)

In summary, nonbinding communications can powerfully increase contributions to the group exchange in sufficiently simple environments, with a small number of participants. The results, however, are not particularly robust. Even in very small groups, the effects of communications are sensitive to asymmetries in endowments. In larger groups, under more general conditions, communications appear only to attenuate the rate of decay in contributions to the public good.

In closing, we note that even the most favorable findings regarding the effects of communications would not suggest a particular general remedy for public-goods allocations problems. There do exist a variety of small-group contexts where discussions are not impractical, such as the provision or use of common goods by

---

[14] Isaac, McCue, and Plott (1985) report even more modest effects of communication in a complex ten-person design with asymmetric and diminishing MPCRs. In their experiment, the authors allowed participants a single opportunity to meet and discuss contributions. Following the discussion, contributions to the group exchange increased by only 2 percent.

members of trade and neighborhood-residence associations. But meetings, particularly those that are unstructured, become difficult in a group of any significant size, and practically impossible when the group is dispersed.

Provision Points

In a variety of natural contexts, fund drives are frequently conducted for a specific public good, under the condition that the good will only be provided in the event that a certain minimum level of funding is surpassed. The Association of Oregon Faculties, for example, successfully funded the salary for a lobbyist by soliciting contributions from all faculty in the state, under the condition that the lobbyist would be retained only if the salary ($30,000) was collected by a specified date.[15] Similarly, Bagnoli and McKee (1991) report that Canada's New Democratic party enjoyed success in a pair of fund-raising campaigns, each administered under a targeted minimum-aggregate-contributions condition.[16] The minimum-aggregate-contribution requirement will be called a *provision point*.

Unlike nonbinding communications, the addition of a provision point changes the set of Nash equilibria in a fairly straightforward way. Recall that a Nash equilibrium is evaluated in terms of whether unilateral deviations from a particular allocation would be profitable. The free-rider equilibrium emerges in the voluntary-contributions mechanism because, for any level of aggregate contributions, every individual can unilaterally increase earnings by reducing contributions to the public good, as long as the MPCR < 1.

A provision point creates additional equilibria by breaking the continuity of rewards for unilateral reductions in contributions. The effect of a provision point on incentives is easily seen in the payoffs for a single participant in a simple public-goods game. Suppose there are two participants, a player X and a player Y, each of whom has an endowment of ten tokens. As usual, tokens may be either kept (and converted to dollars at a 1-to-1 rate) or contributed to the group exchange, where the MPCR = .75.

Table 6.4 presents payoffs for player X, given various contributions levels by player X (columns) and player Y (rows). For brevity, contributions listed in the table are restricted to $2 increments. In the efficient solution, players X and Y each contribute ten tokens to the group exchange, and player X earns $15 (as does player Y). For convenience, we will refer to contributions combinations in terms of ordered pairs. The efficient solution, for example, is the (10, 10) allocation that yields the bolded $15.00 payoff in the table.

---

[15]   See Dawes et al. (1986).

[16]   Both of the examples cited in the text differ from the designs to be discussed initially in that funds were collected under a "give-back" option, where contributions were returned in the event the provision point was not met. The effects of a give-back option are discussed below.

Table 6.4 Payoffs for Player X in a Two-Person Public-Goods Game
(Key: *Nash Payoff*; **Payoff in the Efficient Allocation**)

		Contributions by Player X (tokens)					
		0	2	4	6	8	10
	0	*$10.0*	$ 9.5	$ 9.0	$ 8.5	$ 8.0	$ 7.5
	2	$11.5	$11.0	$10.5	$10.0	$ 9.5	$ 9.0
	4	$13.0	$12.5	$12.0	$11.5	$11.0	$10.5
Contributions by Player Y (tokens)	6	$14.5	$14.0	$13.5	$13.0	$12.5	$12.0
	8	$16.0	$15.5	$15.0	$14.5	$14.0	$13.5
	10	$17.5	$17.0	$16.5	$16.0	$15.5	**$15.0**

Player X's incentive to free ride is readily apparent: In the bottom row of the table, for example, player X could increase earnings from $15.00 in the efficient solution to $15.50, by reducing contributions to eight tokens. This incentive to reduce contributions unilaterally is pervasive: player X can increase earnings by shading on any level of contributions to the group exchange. By the symmetry of the situation, player Y has identical incentives, and so the (0, 0) allocation with the italicized $10 payoff is the unique Nash equilibrium.

Consider now the effects of imposing a provision point. For simplicity, suppose that the provision point is set at the efficient level. In this case, any contribution to the group exchange will yield a return of 0, unless both players contribute their entire token endowments. The relevant incentives for player X are illustrated in table 6.5. The simplicity of payoffs in the table bears emphasis. Except for the (10, 10) allocation, contributions to the group exchange are worthless: every $2 contribution reduces earnings for player X by $2. The degenerate (0, 0) contributions level remains a Nash equilibrium, since any unilateral deviation from this allocation will reduce player X's earnings (and similarly for player Y).

The provision point, however, creates a second Nash equilibrium. Player X (and player Y) may earn $15.00 if both players contribute all ten of their tokens to the group exchange. This allocation is a Nash equilibrium, since any unilateral deviation is extremely unprofitable. For example, if Y reduces contributions by two tokens, X's earnings fall to 0. (Not shown, player Y's earnings drop to $2.00.) This "full-contributions" equilibrium has the added characteristic of Pareto dominance, since payoffs for both players exceed those in the alternative free-rider equilibrium.

Table 6.5 The Effects of a Provision-Point on Payoffs for Player X
(Key: *Nash Payoff*; **Payoff in the Efficient Allocation**)

		Contributions by Player X (tokens)					
		0	2	4	6	8	10
	0	*$10.0*	$ 8.0	$ 6.0	$ 4.0	$ 2.0	$ 0.0
	2	$10.0	$ 8.0	$ 6.0	$ 4.0	$ 2.0	$ 0.0
	4	$10.0	$ 8.0	$ 6.0	$ 4.0	$ 2.0	$ 0.0
Contributions by Player Y (tokens)	6	$10.0	$ 8.0	$ 6.0	$ 4.0	$ 2.0	$ 0.0
	8	$10.0	$ 8.0	$ 6.0	$ 4.0	$ 2.0	$ 0.0
	10	$10.0	$ 8.0	$ 6.0	$ 4.0	$ 2.0	***$15.0***

The payoff in this allocation is both italicized and bolded, to indicate that it is a Pareto-dominant Nash equilibrium.

Despite these characteristics, the full-contributions equilibrium is extremely unstable. Player X, for example, would be very reluctant to contribute ten tokens to the public good, if there was any significant probability that player Y would "tremble" and contribute something less than ten units. Trembling of this type might be caused by a failure of player Y to understand fully the incentives, or by uncertainty on the part of player Y regarding player X's understanding of the incentives. This instability becomes even more pronounced if the provision point depends on the contributions of more than two players. Isaac, Schmidtz, and Walker (1989) conducted a series of six sessions using the all-or-nothing provision-point condition illustrated in table 6.5. The authors used variants of a four-person, MPCR = .3 baseline design discussed above (e.g, Isaac and Walker, 1988a, 1988b) where free-riding was shown to be significant. Each session consisted of ten periods, and all participants were experienced.

The left panel of figure 6.9 presents mean contribution rates for these six sessions. As is clear from this panel, the provision point did little to damp the decay in contributions. A comparison with data for comparable no-provision-point sessions (e.g., the *4L* treatment in left panel of figure 6.6) reveals virtually no treatment effect. Given the instability of the provision-point equilibrium, this result is not surprising.[17]

---

[17] Another instance where Pareto dominance is not a useful device for selecting among multiple Nash equilibria is the coordination game discussed in section 2.5 of chapter 2.

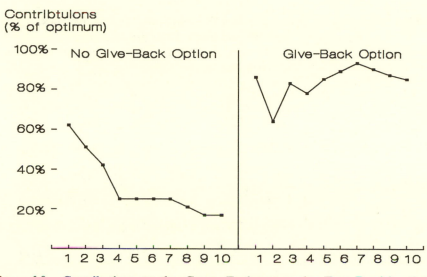

Figure 6.9   Contributions to the Group Exchange under Two Provision-Point Regimes (Source: Isaac, Schmidtz, and Walker, 1989)

The risk of contributing to the group exchange may be mitigated by refunding contributions if the provision point is not met. A *give-back* option of this type is characteristic of most natural applications of the provision-point mechanism. For example, both of the fund-drives using a provision point cited above used a give-back option.

The give-back option decreases the risk of contributions by creating a "safety net" below the provision point. The safety-net feature of the give-back option is illustrated in table 6.6 for the two-person voluntary-contributions design: For any allocation except for full contributions, player X earns $10. Due to the "flatness" of the payoff table, there is no particular incentive to free-ride. Player X will earn $10.00 not only by contributing 0 to the group exchange, but for *any* allocation other than (10, 10). As a consequence, with a give-back option, every allocation where both players contribute less than ten tokens is a (weak) Nash equilibrium, as indicated by the italicized payoff entries in the table.[18] Notice also that earnings jump to $15 at the (10, 10) allocation, indicating that, as in table 6.5, the provision point is a Pareto-dominant Nash equilibrium. This equilibrium is dynamically much more stable, however, because participants are no longer concerned about the

---

[18]   When one player contributes ten, the best response of the other is to increase contributions to ten. For this reason, some of the payoffs in the bottom row and along the right-hand column of table 6.6 are not italicized.

Table 6.6 Earnings for Player X with a Provision-Point and a Give-Back Option
(Key: *Nash Payoff*, **Payoff in the Efficient Allocation**)

| | | \multicolumn{6}{c}{Contributions by Player X (tokens)} | | | | | |
		0	2	4	6	8	10
	0	*$10.0*	*$10.0*	*$10.0*	*$10.0*	*$10.0*	$10.0
	2	*$10.0*	*$10.0*	*$10.0*	*$10.0*	*$10.0*	$10.0
	4	*$10.0*	*$10.0*	*$10.0*	*$10.0*	*$10.0*	$10.0
Contributions by Player Y	6	*$10.0*	*$10.0*	*$10.0*	*$10.0*	*$10.0*	$10.0
(tokens)	8	*$10.0*	*$10.0*	*$10.0*	*$10.0*	*$10.0*	$10.0
	10	$10.0	$10.0	$10.0	$10.0	$10.0	***$15.0***

"tremblings" of others. For example, although player X's earnings will fall from $15 to $10 in the event that player Y deviates from the (10, 10) allocation, player X has no incentive to reduce contributions, since $10 is guaranteed regardless of the choice of player Y.[19]

The give-back option improves observed contribution rates. The right side of figure 6.9 shows the average contribution levels for six additional sessions with both a provision-point and a give-back option. In the sessions with the give-back option, average contributions to the group exchange were slightly below the provision point, indicating that the public good was not always provided. But average contribution rates for these sessions were more than four times higher than for comparable sessions without the give-back option. Moreover, the provision point was consistently met in the last half of most sessions. Bagnoli and McKee (1991) report very similar results in a somewhat different design.

The provision-point/give-back combination does not always perform as impressively as in figure 6.9. In particular, both theoretic and behavioral complications arise if the provision point does not require full contributions by all participants. For example, suppose that a provision-point requires only 50 percent of the aggregate token endowment. In many instances, each combination of contributions that satisfy the provision-point will be a Nash equilibrium. These multiple equilibria create formidable coordination problems, because players will

---

[19] In game-theoretic terminology, the give-back option causes any contribution level below ten to be weakly dominated by contributing ten tokens.

generally have differing preferences for the equilibrium selected. For example, suppose the provision-point is twelve in the two-person game just discussed, and that any combination of contributions that totals twelve units is a Nash equilibrium. Player X would prefer the equilibrium where Y contributed ten units to the public exchange and X contributed two units. Player Y would prefer just the reverse. Isaac, Schmidtz, and Walker refer to the incentives to coordinate on a more favorable provision-point equilibrium as "cheap-rider" incentives. These authors report additional sessions in the design just reviewed that suggest that cheap-rider incentives can frustrate cooperation, even in environments with a give-back option.

In summary, it appears that the combination of a provision-point and a give-back option can substantially increase contributions to a public good. Each of these institutional modifications adds a theoretically attractive property to the public-goods contribution mechanism. The provision point creates Pareto-dominant Nash equilibria that involve nonzero contributions to the public good. The give-back option adds an element of stability to the provision-point equilibria, although cooperation can be frustrated by cheap-rider incentives in some contexts.

6.5 Incentive-Compatible Mechanisms

In theory, underprovision remains a problem for impure public goods, such as goods characterized *either* by nonrivalry or by nonexcludability. However, when goods are impure in the sense that they are nonrivaled but excludable, more elaborate mechanisms for facilitating the provision of the good are possible. For example, broadcast rights to public television programs are nonrivaled but excludable goods: The marginal cost of allowing an extra public television station to broadcast a program is very nearly zero. Licensing restrictions, however, make it easy to exclude any stations from broadcasting a program, if desired. If excludability is not exercised, an inefficiently low number of programs would be produced, as all stations would have incentives to free-ride off the production efforts of others. Excludability may increase the number of programs offered. Nevertheless, the *diversity* of programming may remain suboptimal. It may be the case, for example, that production decisions are determined by the large stations who can unilaterally fund new programs (and sell them to smaller stations with specialized audiences, such as agricultural concerns in the Midwest). Large stations might produce specialized programs for the small stations, if profitable. But the small stations would be reluctant to reveal their demands to the large stations truthfully, out of a fear that they will simply raise the license fee.

The problem is to devise a mechanism that induces revelation of the value of a public good. For example, programming diversity could be increased by constructing an auction to allow participant stations to submit preference-revealing "bids" for various entries on a menu of program possibilities. If the mechanism were constructed in an iterative fashion, so as to allow stations to update bids on the basis of cost shares generated by the bids of others, a more efficient equilibrium might be elicited. As reviewed later in this section, such a mechanism was introduced for public television programs in 1974.

It is possible to design alternative mechanisms with the desirable characteristic of *incentive compatibility* — that is, not only is the efficient provision level a Nash equilibrium, but participants are provided with incentives to reveal honestly their preferences for a public good.[20] A variety of these incentive-compatible mechanisms have been formulated, with the intellectual origins attributable to Vickrey (1961), Clarke (1971), and Groves (1969, 1973). Perhaps the most frequently cited process is a quadratic tax mechanism proposed by Groves and Ledyard (1977).

This section reviews experiments designed to evaluate the performance of incentive-compatible mechanisms. We proceed by developing the underlying intuition, and then by discussing some experimental results. These institutions are theoretically quite general, in the sense that efficient outcomes are part of the equilibrium set for a diversity of marginal valuation arrays. To facilitate the evaluation of these institutions, it is instructive to review a more general notion of efficient contributions levels.

Efficient Contributions and the Lindahl Optimum

In most of the voluntary contributions mechanism experiments discussed above, marginal valuations were of a very straightforward type: They were a constant for each participant and symmetric across participants. The simplicity of these valuation structures is an important shortcoming of the experiments designed to evaluate factors that may alleviate free-riding. Even though significant free-riding behavior has been observed in starkly simple environments with few participants, results reported by Isaac, McCue, and Plott (1985) and by Isaac and Walker (1988b) suggest that free-riding may be both more pervasive and more difficult to correct in designs where marginal valuations are nonconstant and asymmetric.

Incentive-compatible mechanisms have largely been evaluated in light of their capacity to elicit efficient contributions in these more complex environments. For

---

[20] Ideally, these mechanisms would be incentive compatible in the sense that honest preference revelation is a dominant strategy, for example, all participants are motivated to reveal their preferences for the public good, regardless of the decisions submitted by others. The impossibility of such equilibria, however, is well established (see, e.g., Hurwicz, 1972, for the case of private goods, and Green and Laffont, 1977, for public goods). But full revelation may be a dominant strategy in these mechanisms under a restricted set of strategic responses. In particular, the Groves–Ledyard mechanism described below has the property that full-revelation is a dominant strategy, if the strategy set is restricted to Nash–Cournot responses.

this reason it is instructive to discuss briefly the concept of efficiency in a more general public goods context, which is defined as a *Lindahl optimum.*

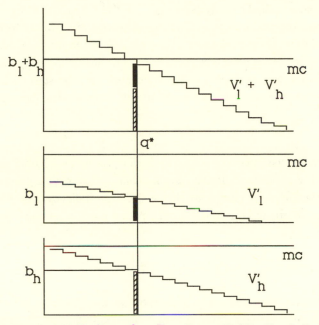

Figure 6.10 The Lindahl Optimum in a Two-Person Public-Goods Problem

Figure 6.10 illustrates the notion of Lindahl optimum for a variant of the experimental design used by Isaac, McCue, and Plott (1985). The illustrated environment consists of two agents with asymmetric and diminishing marginal valuations.[21] The marginal valuations are just the MPCR's discussed in earlier sections. Marginal valuation schedules for the two agents are illustrated by the two arrays at the bottom of figure 6.10. The "high" marginal valuation schedule is denoted with a V'_h, while the low valuation schedule is denoted V'_l. Units of the public good may be provided in varying amounts at a constant marginal cost per unit, *mc*, illustrated by the dashed lines in each of the three panels of the figure. Notice from the bottom two panels that neither agent would privately purchase any units of the public good, since the marginal cost exceeds the vertical intercept for both marginal valuation schedules.

Given nonrivalry in consumption, however, the marginal social benefit of any unit of the public good is the sum of marginal private benefits. Thus, as illustrated

---

[21] The design used by Isaac, McCue, and Plott deviates from figure 6.10 in that it involved twice the number of demand steps, and there were five participants of each type.

by the demand array in the upper panel of figure 6.10, the marginal social benefit schedule is the vertical sum of the marginal private valuation schedules. Notice that *mc* intersects the marginal social benefit array at q^*. In a Lindahl optimum the socially efficient quantity q^* is produced. If the individual marginal valuation schedules were known, one way to fund the production of q^* would be to charge the individuals different prices, b_l and b_h, for each unit of the public good. As can be seen from figure 6.10, the sum of these prices just equals the marginal production cost, *mc*. At the optimal level of the public good, q^*, the sum of the individual marginal valuations just equals the marginal cost of producing the public good:

(6.4)
$$\Sigma V_i' = mc.$$

Importantly, the usual incentives to free-ride prevent the Lindahl optimum from being a Nash equilibrium. Rather, the Lindahl optimum is a general efficiency criterion for public goods provision. Notice also that efficiency does not require that agents either contribute all resources to the public good, or all contribute the same amount.

Incentive Compatibility in Public-Goods Provision

The root of the public-goods problem is that there is no incentive for individuals to submit bids equal to their marginal valuations for a public good. Rather, there is an incentive to underbid when the amount contributed depends only on one's own bid. Incentive-compatible mechanisms deal with this problem via a system of marginal taxes (which depend on all bids) that penalize individuals for deviating from honest revelation. A variety of these mechanisms exist. To develop some appreciation for the way they work, we illustrate a simple quadratic tax mechanism by Groves and Ledyard (1977).

The Groves–Ledyard (G–L) mechanism is organized as follows. Let n participants, identified by the subscript i ($i = 1 \ldots n$) collectively determine the quantity of a public good to produce, X. Each agent privately submits a quantity increment x_i to a "center" (presumably some government agency). The increment may be either positive or negative. The aggregate quantity, X, is the sum of individual increments: $\Sigma x_i = X$. Also, let S_i denote the aggregate quantity proposal less the contribution submitted by agent i, so $X = x_i + S_i$. The good is produced under conditions of a constant marginal cost, *mc*. Therefore, the total production cost for a quantity X is $mc[x_i + S_i]$. After all participants have made quantity increment submissions, the agency returns a cost proposal to each agent i on the basis of the quadratic cost function:

(6.5) $$C(x_i|S_i) = \frac{mc}{n}(x_i + S_i) - nS_i(x_i + S_i) + \frac{n-1}{2}(x_i + S_i)^2.$$

This tax function is the sum of the per capita share $(1/n)$ of production costs (the first term to the right of the equality), adjusted by a linear term (the second term on the right) and a quadratic term (the third term on the right). The adjustment terms modify the average cost share by the product of the aggregate proposal, and factors related to the number of respondents and the sum of others' proposals, S_i. It is rather difficult to develop an intuitive feel for the reason that this tax function elicits honest preference revelation. But it should at least be clear from (6.5) that the adjustment terms exert countervailing effects; costs decrease with one's own contribution via the linear term, but increase via the quadratic term. It is shown in appendix A6.3 that these countervailing effects exactly balance; optimal responses to the cost assignment scheme in (6.5) satisfy both conditions in (6.4) for a Lindahl optimum.[22]

Although the incentive compatibility of the G–L mechanism is attractive, the mechanism may nevertheless fail to allocate goods efficiently. The incentive structure in (6.5) is complex, and it is doubtful that the desirability of honest revelation would be apparent to participants, especially in a one-shot version of the game. To surmount this difficulty, laboratory implementations iterate the above process: Participants submit proposed allocations to the center. The center aggregates the information and returns to participants a proposed tax scheme. This process is repeated until either (a) all participants repeat their quantity proposal twice (indicating that the tax is acceptable) or (b) a preannounced number of iterations passes without agreement.

As will be seen, iterated variants of the G–L mechanism work quite well in some respects. Iteration, however, introduces the important theoretical deficiency that many (inefficient) allocations can be equilibrium outcomes. This may be seen by recognizing that any agent has the option of forcing the game to the final iteration by continually altering the quantity proposal. But consider incentives in the final iteration. An affirmative vote (repeated quantity proposal) generates the proposed allocation. A change in the proposed quantity generates payoffs of zero. Since something is preferred to nothing, it easily follows that any allocation with a positive payoff to all participants is a Nash equilibrium.

---

[22] This particular formulation does not balance the budget. Although the mechanism elicits the optimal quantity by balancing marginal costs and benefits, lump-sum transfers may occur in such a manner that total contributions do not equal total costs. For this reason, formulations of this type are sometimes referred to as "deficit" mechanisms. Deficit mechanisms can be modified by an additive term to ensure a balanced budget for every positive allocation. This term is excluded from the presentation for ease of exposition.

The iterative process is also problematic because the performance of the mechanism is largely determined by the dynamic response of participants to the proposals submitted by participants. No generally accepted theory explains how people "learn" the optimal bid from the messages returned from the center.

Results of Experiments Involving Incentive-Compatible Processes

Laboratory investigations indicate that incentive-compatible mechanisms quite successfully increase contributions to a public good. Smith (1979), for example, found that collectives of sizes four, five, and eight are generally able to agree on an efficient outcome in a G–L mechanism.[23] Moreover, these efficient outcomes were generated in a design characterized by nearly complete free-riding in baseline sessions.[24] Smith's initial results further suggest that these mechanisms may actually elicit Lindahl-optimal individual bids. However, subsequent investigations in richer environments and under more complicated (balanced-budget) variants of these mechanisms indicate that Lindahl-optimal individual bids are not elicited in more general cases. Smith (1980) and Harstad and Marrese (1982) find that despite highly efficient aggregate outcomes, individual bids frequently deviate substantially from Lindahl-efficient levels.

A Field Experiment: The Station Program Cooperative

One clearly desirable feature of public-goods provision mechanisms is that decisions are not made by a central authority. At least one iterated auction of this type has been implemented in a natural context. Starting in 1974, the Station Program Cooperative (SPC), a collection of public television stations, began to use an iterated auction to determine a program menu. The problem is that a large number of programs are proposed each year, many more than can be funded. The purpose of the SPC auction is to determine which programs are produced and how the fixed production cost is allocated.

In essence, the auction proceeds as a series of "yes" or "no" votes to proposed cost allocations. More precisely, consider a situation where all stations are the same size and have the same operating budget. In an initial vote, stations bid by voting "yes" or "no" for each proposed program. The "center" then totals the votes and

---

[23]   Smith also considers an auction-type mechanism, which resembles a Vickrey auction. Participants iteratively submit price/quantity bids to the center, which returns to each participant a proposed price/quantity allocational proposal consisting of (i) a price equal to the difference between marginal costs and the sum of bids submitted by others, and (ii) a quantity that equals the average of all quantity submissions. In practice, the auction and G–L mechanisms are roughly similar. The auction process, however, typically requires a larger number of iterations to establish an agreement, and the frequency of disagreement outcomes is somewhat higher.

[24]   Harstad and Marrese (1981) report similar results.

returns to each station a set of proposed cost allocations for various programs. A station is allocated a cost share for a program if it voted for the program. The proposed allocation is simply the program's cost, divided by the number of affirmative votes. In subsequent iterations, the stations again vote "yes" or "no" for programs, this time based on the proposed cost allocations. The process is repeated until everyone repeats their votes.[25]

Early implementations of the auction seemed to work quite well; unanimous programming decisions were generated rather quickly, and participating member stations were quite pleased with the process. Examination of the theoretic properties of the institution, however, reveals a number of deficiencies that make the apparently satisfactory performance rather surprising. In particular, there is little reason to expect the program menu that is selected to be the most efficient outcome, since the stations have a limited capacity to reflect intensity of preferences. Suppose, for example, that a public station in Bozeman, Montana, is very interested in producing a program on advances in agriculture in the northern plains states. Clearly there is a limited market for the program. Under the SPC auction, where messages are restricted to yes/no signals, the allocation of costs is proportional to the number of "yes" votes. Therefore allocation possibilities are restricted to symmetric outcomes: A station can fund the entire program, split the cost with one other station, split the cost with two other stations, and so on. A variety of potentially efficient asymmetric allocations are prohibited, such as an allocation where Bozeman pays for three-fourths of the program cost and another station funds the remaining one-fourth.

Inefficient allocations may also arise because final allocations are extremely sensitive to the initial set of votes (which could turn out a number of ways, depending on the assumed preferences of other stations). In fact, there is no assurance that the mechanism will ever stabilize on *any* allocation. It is quite possible, for example, for stations to cycle between funding and not funding some subset of programs, with votes changing each iteration, after new cost allocations are announced.

Ferejohn, Forsythe, and Noll (1979) construct an alternative auction that corrected these theoretical deficiencies and was incentive compatible. In an experiment, however, their theoretically more attractive institution performed no better than the simplified SPC mechanism. To the contrary, although final efficiencies were similar across institutions, SPC auction rules tended to generate a solution in a smaller number of periods than the alternative, "strongly individual-incentive-compatible" mechanism.

---

[25] In practice, of course, the SPC auction is considerably more complicated. The cost-allocation scheme allows for different budgets of various stations. Moreover, rules are adapted to parse out proposed programs, particularly in early rounds. Details of the first two auctions are detailed by Ferejohn and Noll (1979).

In summary, the benefits of an efficient, decentralized mechanism for producing public goods are both large and obvious. Moreover, laboratory testing has been encouraging in the sense that the mechanisms tend to increase public-goods provision dramatically. Results are troubling, however, in that Lindahl-efficient contributions are typically not elicited at the individual level. Also, while it is clear that participants do not use Nash strategies, no one has successfully identified what strategies participants actually do employ. Perhaps due to the lack of a theoretical explanation regarding the dynamic (learning) properties of these markets, experimental investigations of these mechanisms largely ceased in the early 1980.[26]

6.6 Externalities

Goods that are rivaled in consumption but are nonexcludable suffer from potential overuse. As a general class, such problems of negative externalities are caused by the incomplete assignment of property rights. Inefficient amounts of air and water pollution arise, for example, because no one fully owns the atmosphere and water. This section reviews experiments designed to investigate externality problems. We first present a "common-pool-resource" environment that has been used as the basis for a number of laboratory studies. Other experiments designed to evaluate externalities, along with some remedial policy options, are discussed in a second subsection.

The Common-Pool-Resource Mechanism

One important class of externality problems regards use of *common-pool resources*, or renewable resources such as fisheries, forests, and aquifers. The potential for common-pool-resource misallocation is typified by the classic "problem of the commons." Suppose a village sets aside a common area for villagers to graze their cattle. All villagers have the incentive to purchase cattle, which can be fed "free" on the commons. But given a sufficiently small common area, private optimizing responses will result in overgrazing, in an extreme case killing both the grass and the herd.

Gordon (1954) analyzes the common-pool-resource problem more formally. Since any member of a group uses only a fraction of the resource, they tend to ignore the fact that their own use reduces the productivity of the resource at the margin. Therefore, individuals tend to make allocative decisions on the basis of the average productivity of the resource rather than its marginal productivity. If anyone who wants to can use the resource without paying a fee (e.g., it is an *open-access*

---

[26] Banks, Plott, and Porter (1988) and Binger, Hoffman, and Williams (1985) are notable exceptions.

resource), then individuals will increase their usage until the average productivity of the resource is reduced to zero.[27]

To examine the misallocative consequences of problems of this type, Gardner, Ostrom, and Walker (1990) developed a *common-pool-resource mechanism*. The mechanism proceeds through series of periods (between twenty and thirty). In each period, participants are given a token endowment to divide between investment in two markets. After all decisions are made, total allocations are announced and earnings are calculated. Participants are given a new token endowment in each subsequent period.

An example is instructive.[28] Suppose that each member in a group of eight participants is endowed with ten tokens to divide between market 1 and market 2. Each token invested in market 1 yields a 5-cent return. The return is potentially higher in market 2, but it decreases with the total number of tokens invested by the group, denoted by Σx_i. The individual return to market 2 may be motivated as follows. Suppose all eight participants devote one token to market 2 (e.g., they each fish for one hour). Then it would be reasonable to assume that they obtain equal returns (one-eighth of the catch). In general, the assumption is that each person's return (catch) in this market is proportional to the ratio of their investment to total investment, $x_j / \Sigma x_i$. Thus, an individual's return in market 2 is the product of $x_j / \Sigma x_i$ and the total return from investing in market 2, which is specified to be $23 \Sigma x_i - .25(\Sigma x_i)^2$. For this reason, R_j, the total return to a participant j who invests x_j in market 2 and $10 - x_j$ in market 1, is

(6.6)
$$R_j = [\frac{x_j}{\Sigma x_i}] [23 \Sigma x_i - .25(\Sigma x_i)^2] + 5[10 - x_j].$$

Equation (6.6) can be alternatively expressed as

(6.7)
$$R_j = x_j[23 - .25(\Sigma x_i)] - [5x_j - 50].$$

From (6.7) the reader may recognize that this is simply a Cournot problem where x_j is the individual's output, $23 - .25\Sigma x_i$ is a linear demand function, and $5x_j - 50$ is a total cost function.

The optimal investment (production) decision for participant j is determined by taking the derivative of (6.7) with respect to x_j and setting it equal to 0. This process equates the marginal returns to investment in each market:

---

[27] But when the private opportunity cost of using the resource is greater than 0, then free entry will drive the average productivity of the resource only down to opportunity cost of using the resource.

[28] This example is from Walker, Gardner, and Ostrom (1990).

(6.8) $23 - .25\Sigma x_i - .25 \; x_j \; = \; 5.$

The source of the externality problem is evident from the left side of (6.8). Investing x_j tokens in market 2 not only decreases marginal productivity for that participant, but also diminishes marginal productivity for all other agents as well (since all participants are affected by a change in Σx_i). Thus, given the externality, the optimal x_j is a function of the choices made by all agents.

Consider a symmetric outcome where each participant invests eight tokens in market 2. In this case aggregate resource use $\Sigma x_i = 64$. This outcome has the property of being a (unique) Nash equilibrium, as can be verified by assuming that seven of the eight participants pick 8. If the others' outputs in (6.8) are replaced by $x_i = 8$, then the best response for participant j, as determined by this equation, is also 8, so no unilateral deviation from 8 is profitable. Aggregate income in this case is 528 cents.

This outcome may be compared to several alternatives. First, the efficient outcome may be generated by assuming that a single agent controls the group's entire token endowment and unilaterally selects the aggregate level of investment in market 2. In this case $x_j = \Sigma x_i$. Maximizing (6.7) in light of this simplification yields

(6.9) $23 - .5x \; = \; 5.$

In this case, $\Sigma x_i = 36$, and aggregate income is 724 cents.

A second outcome useful for purposes of comparison is the solution proposed by Gordon (1954). In this case, agents ignore the marginal effects of their token investments on aggregate output and treat the average return in market 2 as a constant. In terms of (6.7), this amounts to treating the bracketed term as a constant (just as a competitive firm would treat price as a constant). Equating the average return to the opportunity cost of investing in market 1 yields

(6.10) $23 - .25\Sigma x_j \; = \; 5.$

Therefore, $\Sigma x_i = 72$. In a symmetric solution, each of the eight participants would invest nine units in market 2. In this "zero-rent" solution, the average return on investment in either market is 5, so each participant earns 50 cents ($= 5 \times 10$ tokens). Aggregate income is thus 400 cents ($= 8 \times 50$).

The relationship between these three outcomes is illustrated in figure 6.11, where, marginal and average productivity are represented by *MRP* and *ARP*, respectively. Due to the crowding effect, both lines are downward sloping. The opportunity cost of investing in market 2 (i.e., the 5-cent return in market 1) is labeled *MC*. In the rent-maximizing solution, *MRP* = *MC*, which occurs at an investment level of 36 tokens. The zero-rent solution occurs where *ARP* = *MC*, at an investment of 72 tokens. The Cournot-Nash equilibrium, which involves an aggregate investment of 64 tokens, is intermediate between the rent-maximizing and zero-rent outcomes.

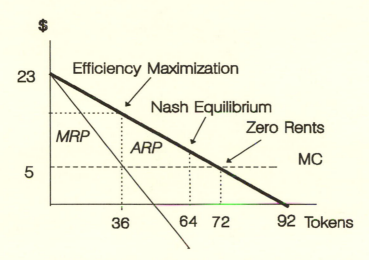

Figure 6.11 Theoretic Predictions in the Common Pool Resource Problem

Gardner, Ostrom, and Walker (1990) examined the drawing power of these alternative solutions, in an eight-person design similar to that presented above, except that the market 2 return parameters differed very slightly, resulting in multiple Nash equilibria that are very near the symmetric equilibrium discussed above.[29] Results are evaluated in terms of the portion of aggregate rents extracted from market 2 (i.e., the portion of the triangle to the left of the *ARP* line, and above the *MC* in figure 6.11). Rent extraction rates are bounded between 100 percent in the efficient solution and 0 percent when *ARP* is reduced to 5. In the Nash equilibrium, 41 percent of possible rents are extracted. Summary results for the experiment are illustrated in the left panel of figure 6.12, where the horizontal dotted line indicates the predicted rent level in the Nash equilibrium. Average token investments for ten inexperienced sessions and eight experienced sessions are illustrated by unbolded and bolded lines, respectively.

The persistent overinvestment of tokens in market 2 caused rents to be far below the efficient level. Averaging across all eighteen sessions, only 36 percent of possible rents were extracted. Moreover, the resource overuse appears to worsen with experience. The mean rent extraction rate dropped from 41.5 percent in the

---

[29] These multiple equilibria were caused by rounding off the numbers that were presented in the payoff tables. Allocations differed very little across equilibria but involved slightly asymmetric contributions by the agents.

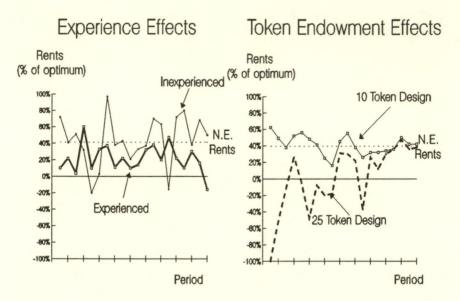

Figure 6.12   Mean Efficiencies in Two Common-Pool-Resource Experiments
(Source: Gardner, Ostrom, and Walker, 1990; and Walker, Gardner, and Ostrom,
1990)

sessions using inexperienced participants to 30.55 percent with experience. It is
worth emphasizing that rents in the experienced treatment cell are below the Nash
equilibrium prediction. This is true in all but two of the twenty periods, and it
indicates that the common resource was dissipated even more than would be
predicted by noncooperative behavior.[30]

A second experiment by these authors was designed in part to assess the effects
of variations in the token endowment. Although theoretic predictions regarding use
of a common-pool-resource are invariant to marginal changes in endowments, the
authors suspected that endowment variations may affect allocations, particularly in
early periods of a session, because the magnitude of possible aggregate errors
increases with endowment sizes. The experiment consisted of six sessions and used
experienced participants. Parameters are those given in equation (6.6), which yields
a unique Nash equilibrium. Endowment effects were evaluated by giving
participants ten tokens per decision period in three sessions, and giving them twenty-

---

[30]   Recall the interpretation of (6.7) as the profit for a firm in a Cournot oligopoly. The observed
overusage of the common pool resource relative to the noncooperative equilibrium is analogous to
industry output above the noncooperative (Cournot) level in a Cournot oligopoly. Parallel to the results
reported in this section, high industry-output levels are commonly observed in Cournot experiments with
more than two sellers (Holt, 1992, p. 22, and references therein).

five tokens each in the remaining three sessions. Each line on the right panel of figure 6.12 represents the results of three sessions. Although performance improved, on average, toward the end of the sessions, low and even negative rent extraction rates were again observed, especially in the twenty-five-token design. Resource overuse was so pervasive in initial periods of this treatment that the overall average extraction rate was negative (–3 percent), indicating that, on average, the return from investing in market 2 was slightly below the constant return available in market 1. Thus, as the authors conjectured, increasing the token endowment appears to complicate the learning problem for participants.

In summary, the common-pool-resource mechanism appears to generate the predicted resource misallocations. Moreover, although outcomes generally conform to theoretical predictions, it is again clear that there are persistent deviations from Nash behavior, especially in early periods. In particular, a theoretically innocuous change in the endowment level tends to increase overuse of the common-pool resource.

Other Experiments Involving Externalities

Experimental studies assessing of externalities have been conducted in other environments.[31] Plott (1983), for example, reports a double-auction experiment where an externality was introduced in the form of a "damage schedule," in which per unit earnings fell with the *total* number of contracts completed in a trading period. For example, each of the first ten contracts completed by buyer/seller pairs reduced everyone's earnings by two cents.[32] This damage schedule may be viewed as driving a wedge between private and social production costs.

The left panel of figure 6.13 presents the supply and demand arrays for this externality design. In the figure, aggregate marginal valuations are represented by the market demand curve, D, and private production costs determine the market supply curve, S. Total social costs, which include the loss in aggregate earnings due to the damage schedule, as well as private production costs, are illustrated by the curve labeled "Social Cost." Standard price theory suggests that in an unregulated market, buyers and sellers will be attentive only to private valuations and private production costs, respectively. Thus, the price/quantity combination (P_e, Q_e) is predicted. The inefficiency of this combination is evident from comparison of the demand and social cost at the competitive quantity prediction Q_e. The competitive

---

[31] Some of the bargaining experiments discussed in chapter 5 may also be given an externality interpretation (e.g., Hoffman and Spitzer, 1982). In these environments, a "disagreement" constitutes a resource overuse problem, and agents have the opportunity to negotiate contracts to resolve the externality.

[32] The damage schedule was "progressive." For contracts 11 to 20, individual loses increased to $.03 per contract. Losses increased to $.04 for each subsequent contract.

price prediction P_e vastly understates the social cost of production. The total loss in social efficiency is represented in figure 6.13 by the thatched area to the left of the competitive price/quantity prediction. The intersection of the social cost curve and the demand function generates a socially efficient price/quantity pair (Q_o, P_o).

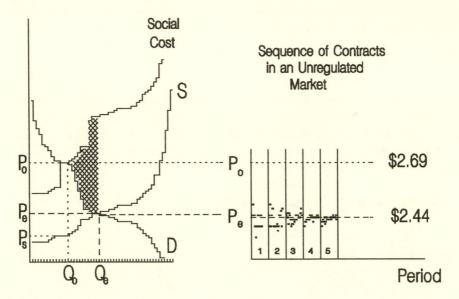

Figure 6.13   Supply-and-Demand Arrays and Contract Prices for an Externality Design   (Source: Plott, 1983)

The externality in this design resulted in overuse and inefficiencies, as was the case in the common-pool-resource experiments. Consider, for example, the sequence of contracts for the double-auction market shown on the right side of figure 6.13: Participants seemed to ignore the effects of the damage schedule in making their trading decisions, and market prices converged to $P_e = \$2.44$. This "competitive" behavior was very costly to the group. Average market efficiency for two baseline sessions conducted in this design was –44.5 percent. (Efficiency can be negative if the losses from the damage schedule exceed any realized gains from trade.)[33]

Corrective Policies

It is natural to suspect that externality problems might be alleviated by the same factors that diminish free-riding in a public goods context. In some cases this

---

[33]   Very similar results were observed by Harrison et al. (1987) in the initial periods of six double auctions conducted in essentially the same design.

is clearly true. Ostrom and Walker (1991), for example, report that nonbinding communications clearly diminish resource overuse in the common-pool-resource mechanism discussed above. Similarly, Kunreuther, Kleindorfer, and Knez (1987) design an iterative auction mechanism for siting noxious facilities and report impressive results in pilot sessions.

Nevertheless, some policy options available in the public-goods context may not be adapted to an externality problem. There is no natural analogue, for example, to the provision-point modifications of the public-goods environment in a common-pool-resource problem.[34] Other remedial options may uniquely resolve externality problems. In particular, since misallocations due to externalities arise from an incomplete assignment of property rights to a common resource, an obvious class of remedies are mechanisms for assigning property rights.

Plott (1983) investigated two schemes for resolving externality problems in the double-auction design of figure 6.13. The first policy is the analogue of a crude emissions control standard. Under this "quantity restriction" scheme, participants were individually allowed to negotiate contracts as usual, but in aggregate, they were only allowed to consummate the socially efficient number of contracts, Q_o, after which the market was automatically closed. Aggregate output was also restricted to Q_o in a second "pollution license" regime. However, rather than simply restricting aggregate sales, licenses to sell output units were distributed to sellers. Sellers could then buy and sell these rights in a double-auction license market. This pollution-license regime is one way of fully assigning property rights: with the licenses, owners have an asset that can be bought and sold, which in turn provides incentives for efficient use.

Plott conducted only two markets under each scheme. In each case, total efficiency improved relative to the baseline. The license-option treatment, however, was far more efficient: After the first two periods, average per period efficiency in the license-option treatment was 98.3 percent, compared to 34.4 percent in the quantity-restriction treatment. The two panels of figure 6.14 illustrate the sequence of contracts for sessions in the quantity restriction and license-policy treatments. The source of the performance difference is readily apparent. Simple quantity restriction, shown in the upper panel, creates the wide equilibrium price range, between P_o and the intersection of the supply curve at the quantity restriction, P_s. The wide latitude of potentially acceptable contract prices, combined with intense pressure among participants to strike contracts before the quantity limit was reached, created the tremendous price volatility shown in the upper panel of figure 6.14.[35]

---

[34] Walker and Gardner (1990), however, do discuss a probabilistic environment where a common-pool resource has a "destruction point." Their observation of persistent resource exhaustion in these environments offers little in the way of a policy remedy.

[35] There were so many takers for each contract proposal that Plott was forced to adopt a random process for resolving contract ties in the quantity-restriction regime.

Efficiency losses arose in this regime as there was no means of distinguishing between high- and low-surplus traders.

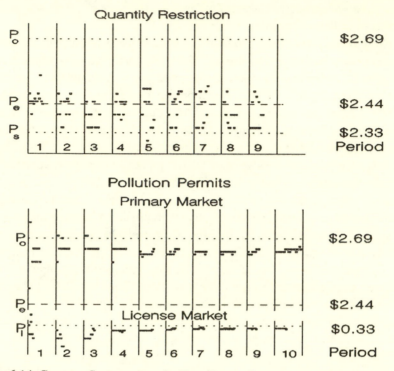

Figure 6.14 Contract Sequences under Two Externality Correction Policies (Source: Plott, 1983)

Higher efficiencies and much more stable prices were created in the license-option regime. The distribution of tradable pollution licenses created opportunities for efficient exchange among the sellers: High-cost sellers with production permits would find selling the license to a low-cost seller more profitable than selling the unit to consumers. Low-cost sellers could enjoy gains from purchasing production permits, and from subsequently selling units of output. The sales opportunities for high- and low-cost sellers in the output market generate derived supply-and-demand curves in the market for licenses, as well as an equilibrium price, P_l, for the permits. A typical buyer in the license market is a low-cost seller, and the "value" of a permit is the difference between the final output price and the seller's cost. A seller in the license market is a high-cost seller. Given the distribution of licenses and the seller cost schedules in Plott's design, the competitive equilibrium-price prediction in this secondary license market is $0.33.

It is clear from the bottom panel of figure 6.14 that the license market removed both the pressure to strike contracts and the incentive for inefficient sellers to produce units of output. Prices in both the output market (shown in the upper part of the panel) as well as in the license market (shown in the bottom portion of the panel) were stable, and near the efficient levels.

In some market contexts, resource misallocations due to externalities may also be resolved by unstructured bargaining. Using a minor deviation of the Plott design in figure 6.13, Harrison et al. (1987) report the results of six double-auction markets where all twelve buyers and sellers gathered prior to the beginning of each trading period and were given the opportunity to strike binding agreements regarding purchase and sales restrictions, including the use of side-payments, if desired. The meetings did substantially increase efficiency extraction rates. In six markets, an overall mean efficiency of 78 percent was observed in the periods where pretrade bargaining was allowed, compared to average efficiency extraction rates of 8 percent in baseline periods. However, we believe that unstructured bargaining of this type does not present a particularly appealing policy option: Market performance was both more volatile and less efficient than in Plott's license markets, due to the occasional failure of groups to reach an agreement. Moreover, allowing unstructured bargaining among buyers and sellers increases transactions costs and may create serious antitrust problems.

Summary

Sizable efficiency losses are caused by the overuse of a nonexcludable resource in a variety of laboratory contexts. Further research regarding the extent of the problem, as well as the efficacy of solutions, is clearly warranted. One particularly promising research avenue involves the investigation of practical mechanisms for the assignment of property rights. The creation of a market for pollution rights shows some promise as a corrective measure in a double-auction context. It bears emphasizing, however, that the competitive characteristics of these ancillary markets should be considered very carefully, for they are potentially vulnerable to abuse. Kruse and Elliott (1990), for example, report results of a double-auction market with an ancillary pollution-permit market, where large sellers successfully accumulated market power by buying up permits and excluding small sellers from the primary market.

A second important dimension of this literature regards the dynamic nature of externality problems, particularly those involving common-pool resources: Producers receive signals that a resource stock is being depleted each period. The capacity of individuals to perceive and respond to these signals may affect outcomes both in baseline environments, and in modified environments designed to remedy observed misallocations.[36]

6.7 Voting

Voting mechanisms represent the standard means of dealing with misallocations due to public-goods and externality problems. Both the level and means of funding public goods are decided via votes in forums ranging from civic councils to legislatures and general elections. Originating with the work of Fiorina and Plott (1978), economists and political scientists have used laboratory methods to investigate a variety of issues in voting theory. In this short section, we introduce this literature by demonstrating the effect of institutional manipulations on voting decisions.

Agendas and Outcomes

Consider the problem of a civic council that must decide on the level of funding for public schools. For simplicity, suppose that just three funding levels are possible: high, medium, and low. The council consists of nine members, who are divided into equal-sized, three-member factions representing high-, medium-, and low-income groups, respectively. These factions have conflicting preferences. Members of the upper-income faction realize that their constituents will send their children to private schools regardless of the funding level. Therefore, their constituents prefer less funding to more; that is, their preference ranking is low, medium, and high. Middle-income constituents find private schooling a considerable financial burden and will send children to the public schools if they are adequately funded. Otherwise, members of the middle-income group would send their children to private schools and seek to minimize their tax burden. Thus, the rank order of funding preferences for the middle-income faction is high, low, and medium, respectively. Finally, constituents of the low-income faction also desire good public schools but consider the tax burden associated with funding public schools at a high level rather oppressive. The low-income faction, therefore, prefers medium to high funding, but high to low funding.

These relationships can be succinctly represented as a set of preference orderings. Denote the high, medium, and low funding levels by H, M, and L, and denote the high-, medium-, and low-income factions by h, m, and l. Using the

---

[36] Walker and Gardner (1990) consider some of these dynamic issues.

notation $X \succ_i Y$ to indicate that a member of faction i prefers option X to option Y, preferences for each group are represented:

(6.11)

$$\text{Voter type } h: \quad L \succ_h M \succ_h H$$

$$\text{Voter type } m: \quad H \succ_m L \succ_m M$$

$$\text{Voter type } l: \quad M \succ_l H \succ_l L$$

Notice that the type index (h, m, or l) corresponds to the *least-preferred* option (H, M, or L).

It follows from (6.11) that no funding option represents the "will" of the group. A simple vote among the three funding levels would result in a three-way tie. Moreover, there is no clear preference in two-way contests: two-thirds of the voters prefer L to M, two-thirds prefer M to H, and two-thirds prefer H to L. This creates a cycle, as can be seen by working backward through the two-way comparisons in the previous sentence: L would lose to H in a two-way contest, and H would lose to M. But M would lose to the option L, where the cycle began.

A natural way to resolve this stalemate is to follow an *agenda*, or set of voting rules. For example, one common agenda identifies 1 of the 3 options as the status quo, perhaps because it is the option that was selected in a previous meeting. The first stage of this agenda involves a contest between the other two alternatives, the winner of which is matched against the status quo in the second stage. This agenda, for the case where option M is the status quo, is illustrated in the left panel of figure 6.15. The first box encountered on the left contains all three options, and the initial decision is between the pairs (M, H) and (M, L). This is a choice between eliminating H or L; the presence of M in both boxes indicates that neither choice eliminates M. The winner in the first stage is matched against M in the second stage, as indicated by the four vertically stacked boxes in the left-hand panel of the figure.

Given an agenda, the option chosen depends on the way committee members vote. For simplicity, we initially suppose that participants engage in *sincere voting*, that is, participants are nonstrategic and simply vote for the alternative (box) that contains their most-preferred option. For example, a voter of type h in (6.11) prefers L and would vote for ML over MH. In the case of a tie (where both alternatives contain the most-preferred option), or in the case where the most-preferred option is unavailable, sincere voters pick the alternative that contains their second-best option. With sincere voting, the status-quo option M will be selected from the agenda illustrated in the left panel of figure 6.15. The path of decisions is highlighted by the dotted arrows: Option set MH defeats set ML by a vote of 6 to 3, since middle-income representatives prefer MH (with their preferred choice H) and low-income representatives prefer MH (with their first and second preferences) to ML (with their first and third preferences). Then M wins a pair-wise contest

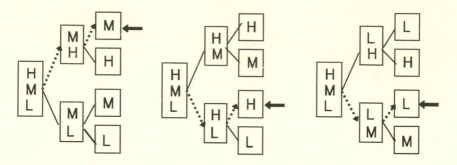

Figure 6.15 A Series of Two-Stage Agendas for Choosing Among Funding Options *H*, *M*, and *L*

between *M* and *H*, since both high- and low-income types prefer *M* to *H*.

The three agendas in figure 6.15 differ in terms of the status quo; *M* in the left-hand panel, *H* in the middle panel, and *L* in the right-hand panel. As indicated by the dotted arrows, the outcome of sincere voting leads the committee to choose the status quo in each case. In the middle panel, for example, *HL* beats *HM* by a vote of 6 to 3, since the high-income members prefer the option *HL* that contains their preferred outcome *L*, and the middle-income members prefer funding level *L* to level *M*. Option *H* then defeats option *L* in a pair-wise contest.[37]

The previous analysis indicates that the outcome of committee voting can be manipulated by altering the option identified as the status quo in the agenda, but the analysis depends on the assumption that voting is sincere. Behavioral assumptions of this type can be evaluated experimentally by inducing preference orderings; a preference of *H* over *M* can be induced by telling the subject that he/she will earn $10 if the committee chooses *H* and $5 if the committee decision is *M*, for example. Other subjects could be given different payoffs, and hence, different preferences. Plott and Levine (1978) first used this method to evaluate agenda effects. Prior to each vote, participants were allowed to discuss qualitative (but not quantitative) information regarding preferences. Discussion was face-to-face and persisted until participants called for a vote. Following a decision, participants were paid the monetary value that corresponded to the outcome selected by the group.

Plott and Levine employed a design somewhat more complicated than that represented above. The design used twenty-one participants per session, who were

---

[37] The outcomes for the agendas shown in figure 6.15 are invariant to several other nonstrategic decision rules. For example, the same outcomes indicated by the dotted lines in the figure would result from all committee members employing an *avoid-the-worst* rule, where members voted against the option set with their least desired outcome in any contest. This invariance is a convenient feature of the agendas used in the figure, but it does not generally hold for other agendas. See Eckel and Holt (1989).

divided into five different preference types. Moreover, preferences were structured so that there was a clear *Condorcet winner*; that is, there existed an option that would best all others in a two-way comparison. By manipulation of the agenda, the authors generated three of the five possible options in four trials.[38]

Even though Plott and Levine were able to manipulate outcomes in a predictable way, economists are uneasy with myopic behavioral assumptions (such as sincere voting), when there are potential gains from more sophisticated behavior. For example, in the analysis of the agendas in figure 6.15, voters decide in the first stage without knowing or thinking ahead about what is likely to happen in the final stage. A *strategic* voter, in contrast, may vote against the option set with his/her most-preferred option in the first stage if this option is going to lose to the voter's least-preferred option in the final stage. Eckel and Holt (1989) conducted an experiment in which the committee decision depends on whether voters are strategic or sincere. Each session consisted of a committee with nine members, who were given earnings tables that induced the preferences in (6.11). Procedures were similar to those used by Plott and Levine, except that committee members participated in a repeated series of committee meetings, using the agenda in the left panel of figure 6.15. Recall that with sincere voting, the type l and type m participants vote for MH in the first stage, and option M is then selected in the second stage. Ironically, option M is the least-preferred outcome for the type m participants who voted with the majority in the first stage. These participants can improve the final outcome through the following reasoning: Noting that their least preferred outcome, M, will always be selected over H in a final round, type m representatives could induce the selection of L by voting for ML in the first round, despite the fact that ML does not contain their most-preferred outcome, H. When type m voters switch to ML in this manner, ML wins in the first stage and L wins in the second stage. This reasoning indicates that L is the strategic outcome when voters think ahead about what is likely to happen in the second stage of this agenda.

Eckel and Holt observed some strategic behavior of this type. Strategic outcomes were frequent after participants made two or three consecutive decisions, under stationary preference conditions. Nevertheless, nonstrategic voting was more common than strategic voting, even under the stationary preference condition. In

---

[38] The agenda manipulation was based on the authors' observation that stable fractions of subjects seemed to use various myopic voting rules such as the sincere voting rule, or the avoid-the-worst rule discussed in the previous footnote. In three of these four trials, selected outcomes were consistent with those predicted by the mix of myopic voting rules. But even the fourth instance provides evidence of the importance of the agenda in selecting outcomes. Participants deviated from the agenda specified in the instructions by conducting an initial straw poll to determine preferences for each option. This poll revealed that one option was least preferred by all committee members. The observed outcome was consistent myopic behavior, given the altered agenda obtained by deleting this least-preferred option. Straw polls were prohibited in subsequent trials.

initial meetings, sincere voting was predominant, and there were no strategic votes in the first meeting of any session.[39]

Summary

Clearly, agenda manipulations can be successful in the laboratory. But do these effects extend to the natural world? In committee meetings outside the laboratory, agenda effects are difficult to document because voters' preferences are rarely observable, and the agenda itself is sometimes not fully specified. One fascinating case of agenda manipulation in the field, however, was reported by Levine and Plott (1977). The authors were responsible for constructing an agenda to organize the process of selecting a fleet of new airplanes for a large flying club to which the authors belonged. With the aid of a questionnaire about members' preferences, the authors attempted to manipulate the outcome by establishing the order of decisions regarding fleet size, composition, and equipment options. The authors preferred a larger (seven-plane) fleet, with at least one large (six-seat) plane. To circumvent the preferences of many club members who preferred an unmixed fleet of only small (four-seat) planes, for example, the authors pitted this group against a coalition of smaller groups with other preferences. Similarly, to enhance the likelihood of purchasing the larger, more expensive fleet, the authors deferred to last the issue regarding costly avionics equipment. The voting followed the agenda, despite repeated attempts by the frustrated chairman to deviate. The outcome was a large fleet that contained two six-seat planes. Results of a follow-up poll indicated that the fleet selected was not the Condorcet winner.[40] The sensitivity of outcomes to the choice of a political process casts doubt on the notions of legislative intent and suggests that the establishment of decision rules and procedures for generating outcomes should be given more than passing attention.

6.8 Summary

Misallocations, in the direction predicted by theory, are observed in a wide variety of experiments when goods are either nonrivaled and/or nonexcludable. Common-pool resources tend to be overused, and free-riding is common, although not as pervasive as most economists would have expected a priori. Experimental results, however, provide far from complete support for theory; misallocations are

---

[39] The preponderance of outcomes reported by Herzberg and Wilson (1988) are also consistent with sincere voting.

[40] The authors note that objections of an ethical nature have been raised to their field experiment. They point out, however, that their agenda manipulation is no more questionable than political acumen or rhetorical skill.

sensitive to a number of environmental factors that are not addressed in standard theoretical models. These factors are so important that much of the experimental literature in this area has been devoted to distinguishing among them. Most public goods experiments, for example, have been devoted to separating the effects of a variety of factors that do not alter the Nash equilibrium, such as repetition, group size, and the marginal per capita return of contributions to the public good. Free-riding is more pronounced in small groups, when the decision process is repeated, when participants are experienced, and when the MPCR is low. The reduced tendency to free-ride in large groups remains a puzzle.

As with market experiments, institutional details appear to affect the extent of the misallocations caused by violations of the conditions of privacy in consumption. The rate of free-riding in a public-goods context, for example, is often significantly reduced by the combination of a minimum aggregate provision point and a give-back option, where funds are returned in the event the provision point is not met. Similarly, activities that cause externalities are curtailed by a complete assignment of property rights.

More complicated "incentive compatible" mechanisms can be used to reduce the underprovision of public goods that are nonrivaled but excludable. These mechanisms have the very concrete advantage of allowing decentralized decision making. Experimental and theoretical research in this area remains incomplete, however, in two respects. First, implementations of these mechanisms are very difficult for participants to understand on an intuitive level. Second, as a practical matter, a single-stage version of such a game does not give participants enough information about others' behavior to produce an equilibrium outcome. But although iterating the game improves laboratory performance, it destroys the theoretical optimality properties of the mechanism, by creating numerous inefficient equilibria.

APPENDIX A6

A6.1 A Public-Goods Problem with Private Information

An alternative class of public goods problems arises when the value of resources contributed to the public exchange varies across potential contributors, and where information regarding these values is private. For example, consider an academic committee that must meet on a monthly basis to consider some routine matter, such as student admissions. The committee members are in substantial agreement regarding admissions policies, but decisions cannot be made unless a quorum consisting of two-thirds of the members attend. The absence of a quorum results in a costly delay. Finally, assume that the meetings are not a particularly pleasant way to spend an afternoon; they tend to be a bit tedious, and they detract from other valuable uses of committee members' time.

Attendance at a monthly meeting has the characteristics of a typical public good: Although everyone is better off if a quorum shows up, given a quorum, any particular committee member is better off not attending. Thus, to hold a meeting, the free-rider problem must be surmounted.

But other interesting issues arise in this context, since it allows for a more precise notion of efficiency. In particular, given that there is no benefit of having more than a quorum, an efficient meeting would consist of the attendance of exactly two-thirds of the committee members. Moreover, an efficient outcome would dictate *who* attends the meeting. From month to month, various committee-members have more or less important alternative uses of their time. In an efficient outcome, only the members with the least valuable alternative activities that month should attend. A (decentralized) attendance policy that achieves an efficient solution relies on the development of a *cut point*: each month each committee member must view his or her cost of attending the meeting in terms of alternative uses of time that month. They should attend the meeting if their attendance costs fall below some critical level. A noncooperative equilibrium is also characterized by a cut point that determines whether or not people will attend.

A version of this problem has been analyzed by Palfrey and Rosenthal (1991, 1992). In their implementation, private (attendance) costs for each member are random draws from a common uniform distribution. For this reason the efficient solution is defined by a common cut point. Below, we outline Palfrey and Rosenthal's experimental design for this problem. Subsequently, we examine laboratory evidence collected by these authors. The treatment to be discussed involves three participants, who are each given a single token that they can either keep or contribute to the public exchange. The private value of a token to each participant is determined as a random draw from a uniform distribution. The good is produced if at least two of the three participants contribute tokens to the public exchange. In terms of the above example, the public good may be thought of as a meeting, and tokens represent the allocation of time. An efficient allocation involves a contribution by the two subjects with the lowest value draws (i.e., a quorum formed by the two members with the lowest valued alternative uses of their time).

Given a specific parameterization, it is relatively straightforward to identify a symmetric equilibrium in which only participants with value draws below some cut point will contribute. Suppose the public good is worth 100 cents to each subject, whether or not they contribute, and that token values are drawn from a uniform distribution between 0 and 150 pennies. Each (risk-neutral) player knows that all values are drawn from this distribution but observes only his or her own value. It should be obvious that the equilibrium cut point lies somewhere between 0 and 100 cents: A private value draw in excess of 100 cents implies that the private good is more valuable than the public good. No participant would want to contribute in this case. On the other hand, if a private value of 0 is drawn, contribution to the public good is costless and would help generate a positive return (if one other participant contributes). The opportunity cost of contributing to the public good increases as the value draw increases. Incentives for this situation are summarized in terms of the uniform density function for value draws, shown below: the equilibrium cut point is a value $C*$ which lies between 0 and 100, for which a player is exactly indifferent between contributing or not.

The indifference point $C*$ determines a symmetric equilibrium for the game. Its value is determined by computing player i's expected profits for contributing and for not contributing, given an arbitrary value draw c_i and the knowledge that the others are using a cut point $C*$. Then $C*$ is identified as the particular c_i draw where the profits for contributing and not contributing are equal.

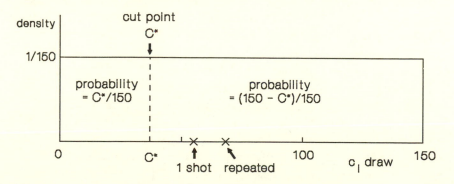

Figure 6.16 Uniform Density of Value Draws, with Cut Point $C*$

Consider first the case where a player does not contribute. Then the player earns his or her private value, c_i, plus the expected value of the public good, which is only provided if both of the others contribute. Given that others use the same cut point, the probability that one of the others will contribute is equal to the area to the left of the dashed-line cut point in figure 6.16, which is $C^*/150$. Since the others' value draws are independent, this probability must be squared to obtain the probability that both of the others contribute. Therefore, the expected payoff for not contributing is

$$\begin{aligned} \text{expected payoff for} &= c_i + 100(\text{prob. that both contribute}) \\ (6.12) \quad \text{not contributing} & \\ &= c_i + 100(C^*/150)^2. \end{aligned}$$

Next consider the payoff for making a contribution. This payoff will be zero if neither of the other players contributes. The probability that one of the other players does not contribute is the area to the right of the vertical dashed line at C^*; this area is $(150 - C^*)/150$, as shown in figure 6.16. Since the others' values are drawn independently, this probability must be squared to obtain the probability that neither contributes $[(150 - C^*)/150]^2$. This is the probability that a player who contributes will earn nothing; otherwise the contributing player will earn 100, so the expected payoff for contributing is

$$\begin{aligned} (6.13) \quad \text{expected payoff for} &= 0(\text{prob. of no other contribution}) \\ \text{contributing} &\quad + 100(1 - \text{prob. of no other contribution}) \\ &= 100(1 - [(150 - C^*)/150]^2). \end{aligned}$$

Player i is indifferent between contributing or not when the expected-payoff expression in (6.12) equals that in (6.13). By definition, this indifference occurs at the cut point: $c_i = C^*$. To find C^*, we replace c_i in (6.12) with C^* and then equate the right sides of (6.12) and (6.13). From simple algebra it follows that in this case $C^* = 37.5$. Therefore, subjects will contribute if their own value draw is 37 cents or below, and they will not contribute if their draw is 38 cents of above.

Although this solution is a noncooperative equilibrium, it does not maximize efficiency. To the contrary, if participants contribute only when their value draws lie roughly in the lower third of possible values, the provision point will not be met in a great number of instances. Both the frequency with which the public good is provided, as well as aggregate efficiency, could be increased through a series of cooperative arrangements. For this reason, it is useful to evaluate noncooperative performance in light of a more cooperative benchmark.

The most obvious benchmark is the *ex post* efficient solution. As mentioned above, this occurs when the two players with the lowest value draws contribute.

This represents a fairly unrealistic benchmark, however, since in the absence of full information regarding values, it could not be attained even by cooperative players. A more plausible benchmark is the cooperative solution that maximizes *ex ante* efficiency, or efficiency in the absence of public value information. In this design, the *ex ante* efficient solution turns out to involve a cut point of 113 cents. Notice that this cut point exceeds the private value of the public good. Intuitively, this occurs because the expected social benefits of contributing to the public exchange exceed the private losses that arise from making the contribution.

As with the oligopoly models discussed in chapter 4, a number of factors might increase efficiency over the noncooperative level. For example, if the game were repeated (e.g., meetings were in fact held every month instead of only once), participants might be able to improve efficiency, via the use of trigger strategies; for example, if one person contributes (attends) insufficiently often, the other players could punish the noncontributor by playing a noncooperative attendance policy.

This analysis raises a number of behavioral questions. Do participants behave as though they adopt a cut point in a problem of this type? Do factors such as repetition permit an improvement over the noncooperative equilibrium outcome? Palfrey and Rosenthal (1991, 1992) conducted a series of laboratory sessions to assess these and other questions. The laboratory sessions involved cohorts of nine to twelve subjects, who where seated at computer terminals and were divided into groups of three but were not told the identities of the others in their group. In a "one-shot" treatment, subjects were randomly reassigned to a new group after each game, and this process was repeated for a preannounced number of games. The groupings in the "repeated-play" treatment were maintained for at least twenty periods, with a ten-sided die thrown to determine whether to continue after the twentieth and each subsequent period. The process was terminated if the die yielded a 4, that is, with a probability .1, which corresponds to a discount factor of .9. The authors show that this discount rate is high enough to support an optimal rotation in which players take turns contributing in pairs, which is supported by a threat to revert to the one-shot Nash outcome (with $C^* = 37.5$) if anyone ever deviates.

Overall, it appears that the notion of a cut point organizes observed decisions quite well: Over 90 percent of individuals' contribution decisions may be correctly classified, by finding the cut points that minimize the classification errors on a subject-by-subject basis. The average of these individual cut points is 44 cents, which is only slightly above the theoretical prediction of 37.5, and the difference is not statistically significant.

It does not appear, however, that repetition solves the coordination problem. In the repeated trials, the average cut point rose to 68 cents. Although the authors were able to reject the null hypothesis that the cut point in the repeated trials equals the theoretical noncooperative prediction, the observed mean is still considerably closer to the noncooperative equilibrium (37.5) than to the *ex ante* efficient outcome (113) cents. This can be seen in figure 6.16, where average cut points for the one-stage and the repeated trials are represented by "×" marks on the horizontal axis. Moreover, there is little evidence that participants attempted other mechanisms to increase efficiency (such as rotating contributions).

To summarize, the notion of a cut point appears to organize behavior well in this context, and the data from one-shot games are quite close to the prediction of a symmetric Nash equilibrium. Moreover, the low rate of contributions consistent with the Nash equilibrium indicates that, as in experiments with the voluntary contributions mechanism, the free-rider problem is pervasive in this environment.

The failure of repetition to raise contribution rates by a large amount was of some concern to Palfrey and Rosenthal, who conclude that the absence of cooperation is "not encouraging news for those who might wish to interpret as gospel the oftspoken suggestion that repeated play with discount rates close to 1 leads to more cooperative behavior" (Palfrey and Rosenthal, 1992, p. 4). However, we do not find the absence of cooperation either particularly troublesome or surprising in this context. Given the privacy of value draws, it is difficult to distinguish free-riding from a high-value draw. Thus, it is hard to assess when a punishment should be administered. In terms of the meeting example used to motivate this problem, one can never tell if you skipped the meeting because your daughter was in the hospital or because you wanted to go fishing!

A6.2 Instructions: The Voluntary Contributions Mechanism

This is an experiment in the economics of group decision-making.[41] You have already earned $3.00 for showing up at the appointed time. If you follow the instructions closely and make decisions carefully, you can substantially add to this total.

There will be ten decision-making periods in this experiment. In each period, you are given an endowment of tokens. Your problem is to decide how to divide these tokens into either or both of two accounts: a private account and a group account. Each token you place in the private account generates a cash return to you (and to you alone) of one cent. Tokens placed in the group account yield a lower return. However, every member of the group also receives that same return for each token you place in the group account. Similarly, you receive a return for every token that other members of the group place in the group account. Thus, earnings in a decision period are the number of tokens you place in your private account, plus the return from all tokens you and other members of the group place in the group account.

---

[41] Brock (1991) contains an alternative set of instructions tailored for classroom use, along with some suggestions for associated classroom exercises.

Returns to the group account are listed in table entitled Return from the Group Account. The table is divided into four columns. In each row of a column, the left entry denotes a total number of tokens that the group may place in the group account. The right entry lists your earnings for that total.[42]

Decision Periods

Your token endowment information for each period, as well as your decisions and earnings, will be recorded on the Decision and Earnings Sheet. As indicated by the numbers in the left column of this sheet, each row represents a single decision period. Endowment information is presented in the second column from the left.

Each period proceeds as follows:

First, decide on the number of tokens to place in the private and in the group accounts by entering numbers in column (a) and/or in column (b) of the Decision Sheet. Your entries in columns (a) and (b) must sum to your endowment. While you make your decision, the ___ other members in your group will also divide their token endowments between private and group accounts.

Second, after everyone has made a decision, one of us will come around and total the number of tokens placed in the group account by all participants. We will write this total (but not the individual decisions) on the blackboard. Write this number in column (c).

Third, your earnings in a decision period are the sum of the tokens you placed in your private account, and the return from the total of tokens placed in the group account. To determine your earnings in the group account, find the earnings number listed opposite the appropriate entry on the Returns for the Group Account table. Write this number in column (d). Your earnings in a period are the sum of your entries in columns (a) and (d). Write this total in column (e).

In each subsequent period, move down to the next row on the Decision Sheet. Note your endowment for that period, make a decision, and record entries in columns (a) and/or (b).

After calculating your earnings for the last period, calculate your total earnings for the session by summing all entries in column (e). Write this sum next to the Total Earnings entry at the bottom of column (e) on your Decision Sheet.

Are there any questions?

---

[42] The Return from Group Account table presents the relationship between group contributions and earnings for the simple case where the MPCR is constant (.3) and the same for all participants. Note that for brevity the table includes only aggregate contributions up to 100. An implementation of this environment for groups larger than five (or endowments larger than twenty tokens) should include payoff options for all contingencies. Use of the table format allows for a general variety of treatments. With appropriate modifications, it is possible to implement treatments with diminishing and/or asymmetric returns from the group account. The effects of asymmetric token endowments can be evaluated even more simply, with no changes in the table.

Starting the Experiment

At this time, we begin the experiment. Notice your endowment for period 1 in the second column of your Decision Sheet. Please divide this endowment between the group and private accounts by writing entries in column (a) and/or in column (b). The sum of the two amounts that you write in columns (a) and (b) should equal your endowment for the period. Write *only* in the first row at this time. Also, please do not look at others' Decision Sheets, and please do not talk.

Now, one of us will come around and record your decisions, and check to see that the amounts in columns (a) and (b) sum to your endowment. Then we will sum the individual contributions to the group account and write this total on the blackboard.

After the First Period

_____ tokens were placed in the group account this period. Please write this number in column (c) on the first row of your Decision Sheet at this time. Now convert this total into earnings by referring to the Returns to Group Account table. Write this number in column (d). Finally, sum (c) and (d) to determine your total earnings. Write this total in column (e).

We will now begin period 2. Notice your token endowment for period 2, on the second row of your Decision and Earnings Sheet. At this time, divide this endowment between the private account and/or the group account by writing entries in column (a) and/or in column (b). (An analogous statement should be read prior to each subsequent period.)

After the Last Period

The experiment is ended. To determine your payment for the experiment, please sum your earnings from each period, in column (e) of your Decision Sheet. Add to this total your initial $3.00 payment and record the sum in the Total Earnings entry at the bottom of column (e). Round this total up to the nearest quarter to determine you payment (e.g,. $3.56 becomes $3.75). Record this sum in the Payment entry.

Please write this total, as you would a check on the receipt form at the bottom of the Earnings and Decision Sheet. Also, please sign and date the receipt form, and record your social security number on it. In a moment, one of us verify your calculations and pay you. You will then be free to go, but please leave all experiment materials in this room. Finally, please remain silent, and do not look on others' Decision Sheets. Thank you for your participation.

Returns from the Group Account

Tokens in Group Account	Your Earnings	Tokens in Group Account	Your Earnings	Tokens in Group Account	Your Earnings	Tokens in Group Account	Your Earnings
1	0	26	8	51	15	76	23
2	1	27	8	52	16	77	23
3	1	28	8	53	16	78	23
4	1	29	9	54	16	79	24
5	2	30	9	55	17	80	24
6	2	31	9	56	17	81	24
7	2	32	10	57	17	82	25
8	2	33	10	58	17	83	25
9	3	34	10	59	18	84	25
10	3	35	11	60	18	85	26
11	3	36	11	61	18	86	26
12	4	37	11	62	19	87	26
13	4	38	11	63	19	88	26
14	4	39	12	64	19	89	27
15	5	40	12	65	20	90	27
16	5	41	12	66	20	91	27
17	5	42	13	67	20	92	28
18	5	43	13	68	20	93	28
19	6	44	13	69	21	94	28
20	6	45	14	70	21	95	29
21	6	46	14	71	21	96	29
22	7	47	14	72	22	97	29
23	7	48	14	73	22	98	29
24	7	49	15	74	22	99	30
25	8	50	15	75	23	100	30

Decision and Earnings Sheet

Pd.	Endow-ment	Your Decision		(c) Total Tokens in Group Account	(d) Value of Tokens in Group Account	(e) Earnings (a) + (d) ($3.00)
		(a) Private Account	(b) Group Account			
1	20					
2	20					
3	20					
4	20					
5	20					
6	20					
7	20					
8	20					
9	20					
10	20					

Total Earnings:
($3.00 + earnings)

Payment:
(Earnings Rounded up
to nearest $.25)

Receipt Form

Received: _____dollars and _____ cents

Signature: _____

SSN: _____

Date: _____

A6.3 Incentive Compatibility in the Groves–Ledyard Mechanism*

Although not particularly intuitive, it is relatively straightforward to show that the Groves–Ledyard mechanism results in an optimal level of the public good, where the sum of the individual marginal valuations equals the marginal cost, mc, of producing the public good. Each person will choose a quantity increment, x_i, to maximize the difference between the individual's value of the public good and the cost determined by the Groves–Ledyard mechanism. Individual i should increase the quantity increment until the marginal individual valuation is equal to the individual marginal cost, that is, until $V_i' = C'(x_i|S_i)$, where S_i is the sum of the quantity increments of the other individuals. As before, let X denote the sum of the quantity increments for all n individuals. It is straightforward to show that the derivative of the cost function in equation (6.5) with respect to x_i is the term on the far right side of (6.14):

$$(6.14) \qquad V_i'(x_i|S_i) \;=\; C_i'(x_i|S_i) \;=\; \frac{mc}{n} - nS_i + (n-1)(x_i + S_i),$$

for $i = 1, \ldots n$. Since equation (6.14) determines the optimal quality increment for each individual, we can sum these conditions to obtain

$$(6.15) \qquad \begin{aligned} \sum_i V_i' \;=\; \sum C'(x_i|S_i) \;&=\; mc - n\sum S_i + n(n-1)X \\ &=\; mc - n[\sum S_i - (n-1)X] \\ &=\; mc, \end{aligned}$$

where the final step follows from the fact that $\Sigma S_i = (n-1)X$. But equation (6.15) is equivalent to the optimality condition in (6.4), that the marginal cost of producing the public good equal the sum of the individual marginal valuations.

---

* The material in this section is somewhat more advanced.

References

Andreoni, James (1988) "Why Free Ride?: Strategies and Learning in Public Goods Experiments," *Journal of Public Economics*, *37*, 291–304.

Bagnoli, Mark, and Michael McKee (1991) "Voluntary Contribution Games: Efficient Private Provision of Public Goods," *Economic Inquiry*, *29*, 351–366.

Banks, Jeffrey S., Charles R. Plott, and David P. Porter (1988) "An Experimental Analysis of Unanimity in Public Goods Provision Mechanisms," *Review of Economic Studies*, *55*, 301–322.

Binger, Brian R., Elizabeth Hoffman, and Arlington W. Williams (1985) "Implementing a Lindahl Equilibrium with a Modified Tatonnement Mechanism: Some Preliminary Experimental Results," working paper, Indiana University.

Brock, John R. (1991) "Teaching Tools: A Public Goods Experiment for the Classroom," *Economic Inquiry*, *29*, 395–401.

Browning, Edgar M., and Jacquelene M. Browning (1989) *Microeconomic Theory and Applications*, 3d ed. Glenview: Scott, Foresman.

Clarke, Edward H. (1971) "Multipart Pricing of Public Goods," *Public Choice*, *2*, 17–33.

Daughety, A. F., and R. Forsythe (1985) "Regulation and the Formation of Expectations: A Laboratory Analysis," working paper, University of Iowa.

Dawes, Robyn M., J. M. Orbell, R. T. Simmons, and A. J. C. van de Kragt (1986) "Organizing Groups for Collective Action," *American Political Science Review*, *80*, 1171–1185.

Eckel, Catherine, and Charles A. Holt (1989) "Strategic Voting in Agenda-Controlled Committee Experiments," *American Economic Review*, *79*, 763–773.

Ferejohn, John A., and Roger G. Noll (1976) "An Experimental Market for Public Goods: The PBS Station Program Cooperative," *American Economic Review: Papers and Proceedings*, *66*, 267–273.

Ferejohn, John A., Robert Forsythe, and Roger Noll (1979) "An Experimental Analysis of Decision Making Procedures for Discrete Public Goods: A Case Study in a Problem in Institutional Design," in V. L. Smith, ed., *Research in Experimental Economics,* vol. 1. Greenwich, Conn.: JAI Press, 1–58.

Fiorina, Morris P., and Charles R. Plott (1978) "Committee Decisions under Majority Rule: An Experimental Study," *American Political Science Review*, *72*, 575–598.

Gardner, Roy, Elinor Ostrom, and James M. Walker (1990) "The Nature of Common Pool Resource Problems," *Rationality and Society*, *2*, 335–358.

Gordon, Scott (1954) "The Economic Theory of a Common Property Resource: The Fishery," *Journal of Political Economy, 62*, 124–142.

Green, Jerry, and Jean-Jacques Laffont (1977) "Characterization of Satisfactory Mechanisms for the Revelation of Preferences for Public Goods," *Econometrica*, *45*, 427–438.

Groves, Theodore (1969) "The Allocation of Resources Under Uncertainty: The Informational and Incentive Roles of Prices and Demands in a Team," Technical Report, no. 1, Center Research in Management Science, University of California at Berkeley.

————— (1973) "Incentives and Teams," *Econometrica*, *41*, 617–631.

Groves, Theodore, and John Ledyard (1977) "Optimal Allocation of Public Goods: A Solution to the 'Free Rider' Problem," *Econometrica*, *45*, 783–809.

Harrison, Glenn W., Elizabeth Hoffman, E. E. Rutstrom, and Matthew L. Spitzer (1987) "Coasian Solutions to the Externality Problem in Experimental Markets," *Economic Journal*, *97*, 388–402.

Harstad, Ronald M., and Michael Marrese (1981) "Implementation of Mechanisms by Processes: Public Good Allocation Experiments," *Journal of Economic Behavior and Organization*, *2*, 129–151.

————— (1982) "Behavioral Explanations of Efficient Public Good Allocations," *Journal of Public Economics, 19,* 367–383.

Herzberg, Roberta Q., and Rick K. Wilson (1988) "Results on Sophisticated Voting in an Experimental Setting," *Journal of Politics, 50,* 471–486.

Hoffman, Elizabeth, and Matthew L. Spitzer (1982) "The Coase Theorem: Some Experimental Tests," *Journal of Law and Economics*, 25, 73–98.

Holt, Charles A. (1992) "Industrial Organization: A Survey of Laboratory Research," forthcoming in A. Roth and J. Kagel, eds., *Handbook of Experimental Economics*. Princeton: Princeton University Press.

Hurwicz, Leonid (1972) "On Informationally Decentralized Systems," in R. Radner and C. McGuire, eds., *Decision and Organization*. Amsterdam: North Holland.

Isaac, R. Mark, Kenneth F. McCue, and Charles R. Plott (1985) "Public Goods Provision in an Experimental Environment," *Journal of Public Economics, 26,* 51–74.

Isaac, R. Mark, David Schmidtz, and James M. Walker (1989) "The Assurance Problem in a Laboratory Market," *Public Choice,* 62, 217–236.

Isaac, R. Mark, and James M. Walker (1988a) "Group Size Effects in Public Goods Provision: The Voluntary Contributions Mechanism," *Quarterly Journal of Economics, 103,* 179–200.

————— (1988b) "Communication and Free-Riding Behavior: The Voluntary Contributions Mechanism," *Economic Inquiry,* 26, 585–608.

————— (1991) "Costly Communication: An Experiment in a Nested Public Goods Problem," in T. Palfrey, ed., *Contemporary Laboratory Research in Political Economy.* Ann Arbor: University of Michigan Press.

Isaac, R. Mark, James M. Walker, and Susan H. Thomas (1984) "Divergent Evidence on Free Riding: An Experimental Examination of Possible Explanations," *Public Choice*, *43*, 113–149.

Isaac, R. Mark, James M. Walker, and Arlington Williams (1991) "Group Size and the Voluntary Provision of Public Goods: Experimental Evidence Utilizing Large Groups," working paper, Indiana University.

Johansen, Lief (1977) "The Theory of Public Goods: Misplaced Emphasis?" *Journal of Public Economics*, *7*, 147–152.

Kim, Oliver, and Mark Walker (1984) "The Free Rider Problem: Experimental Evidence," *Public Choice*, *43*, 3–24.

Kruse, Jamie L., and Steven R. Elliott (1990) "Strategic Manipulation of Pollution Permit Markets: An Experimental Approach," working paper, University of Colorado.

Kunreuther, Howard, Paul Kleindorfer, and Peter J. Knez (1987) "A Compensation Mechanism for Siting Noxious Facilities: Theory and Experimental Design," *Journal of Environmental Economics and Management*, *14*, 371–383.

Levine, Michael E., and Charles R. Plott (1977) "Agenda Influence and its Implications," *Virginia Law Review*, *63*, 561–604.

Marwell, Gerald, and Ruth E. Ames (1979) "Experiments on the Provision of Public Goods I: Resources, Interest, Group Size, and the Free Rider Problem," *American Journal of Sociology*, *84*, 1335–1360.

———— (1980) "Experiments on the Provision of Public Goods II: Provision Points, Stakes, Experience and the Free Rider Problem," *American Journal of Sociology*, *85*, 926–937.

———— (1981) "Economists Free Ride, Does Anyone Else?" *Journal of Public Economics*, *15*, 295–310.

Mestelman, Stuart, and David Feeny (1988) "Does Ideology Matter?: Anecdotal Experimental Evidence on the Voluntary Provision of Public Goods," *Public Choice*, *57*, 281–286.

Orbell, John M., Robyn M. Dawes, and Alphons J. C. van de Kragt (1988) "Explaining Discussion Induced Cooperation," *Journal of Personality and Social Psychology*, *54*, 811–819.

Ostrom, Elinor, and James K. Walker (1991) "Communications in a Common: Cooperation without External Enforcement," in T. Palfrey, ed., *Contemporary Laboratory Research in Political Economy*. Ann Arbor: University of Michigan Press.

Palfrey, Thomas R., and Howard Rosenthal (1991) "Testing for Effects of Cheap Talk in a Public Goods Game with Private Information," *Games and Economic Behavior*, *3*, 183–220.

———— (1992) "Repeated Play, Cooperation and Coordination: An Experimental Study," working paper, California Institute of Technology.

Plott, Charles R. (1983) "Externalities and Corrective Policies in Experimental Markets," *Economic Journal*, *93*, 106–127.

Plott, Charles R., and Michael Levine (1978) "A Model of Agenda Influence on Committee Decisions" *American Economic Review*, 68, 146–160.

Samuelson, Paul A. (1954) "The Pure Theory of Public Expenditures," *Review of Economics and Statistics, 36,* 387–389.

Schneider, Friedrich, and Werner W. Pommerhene (1981) "Free Riding and Collective Action: An Experiment in Public Microeconomics," *Quarterly Journal of Economics, 96,* 689–704.

Smith, Vernon L. (1979) "Incentive Compatible Experimental Processes for the Provision of Public Goods," in V. L. Smith, ed., *Research in Experimental Economics*, vol. 1. Greenwich, Conn.: JAI Press, 59–168.

——— (1980) "Experiments with a Decentralized Mechanism for Public Good Decisions," *American Economic Review, 70,* 584–599.

Vickrey, William (1961) "Counterspeculation, Auctions and Competitive Sealed Tenders," *Journal of Finance, 16,* 8–37.

Walker, James M., Roy Gardner, and Elinor Ostrom (1990) "Rent Dissipation in a Limited-Access Common-Pool Resource: Experimental Evidence," *Journal of Environmental Economics and Management, 19,* 203–211.

Walker, James M., and Roy Gardner (1990) "Rent Dissipation and Probabilistic Destruction of Common Pool Resources: Experimental Evidence," working paper, Indiana University.

Chapter 7

ASYMMETRIC INFORMATION

7.1 Introduction

Students of economics have long been interested in the contrast between the simple equilibrium predictions of neoclassical price theory and the seemingly quirky patterns of economic activity. Nowhere is this contrast greater than in markets with imperfect and dispersed information, such as securities markets and markets for professional services. For example, Akerlof (1970) begins with the observation that many people are surprised by the significant difference between the price of a new car and one offered for resale a short time after purchase. Akerlof's explanation is that the owner has acquired "insider" information about the quality of the car, information that cannot be observed in the showroom. Since the owner would be likely to keep a recently purchased car with no unexpected maintenance and performance problems, the prospective buyers will assume that the car is a "lemon" and will be reluctant to purchase. In this manner, asymmetric information may cause markets for some high-quality used items not to exist. Moreover, producers may select inefficiently low quality standards when quality cannot be observed prior to purchase. There is considerable interest in the extent of such market failures, as well as the corrective capacity of factors such as sellers' reputations for delivering high quality (Nelson, 1970, 1974), warranties or other costly "signals" of quality (Spence, 1974; Stiglitz, 1975), and contracts that allocate risk efficiently (Cheung, 1969).

Somewhat different informational problems arise in finance, where some traders may have insider information about the underlying value of an asset. In particular, does the process of trading on the basis of inside information somehow reveal this information to the market? A theoretical answer to this question is provided by the *rational expectations hypothesis*, which implies that agents process all available information rationally, including information leaked by insiders' actions. In this manner, the market can serve as an information-disseminating mechanism.

The laboratory represents a natural place to investigate the effects of information asymmetries. Private information regarding either product quality or asset value is difficult to observe in natural markets. Such information is itself a valuable commodity that is not freely revealed to observers. Moreover, inside information about future earnings and dividends is usually imperfect, transitory, and difficult to measure. For these reasons, many auxiliary assumptions are required for empirical tests of theories of asymmetric information based on data from natural markets. For example, if one wants to use the change in stock prices in an organized securities market to measure the cost of a new regulation, it is necessary to identify the precise date that traders first became aware of the regulation. But if some information about the regulation and its likelihood of adoption leaks out of early legislative or regulatory proceedings, then the true impact of the regulation will exceed the decline in stock prices observed on the date of the initial press coverage. In contrast, the precision, timing, and initial distribution of information can be controlled in a laboratory setting.

The purpose of this chapter is to introduce a series of laboratory situations in which informational asymmetries can result in resource misallocations. The reader will soon realize that our understanding of informational imperfections is somewhat preliminary. Most of the experiments presented here identify simple "baseline" conditions under which an informational asymmetry degrades efficiency, or under which a remedy has the predicted effect. With a couple of exceptions, the resiliency of these results remains to be explored. The value of identifying simple environments in which the theories do work should not be understated, however, as the identification of tractable baseline environments provides a foundation for further investigation. Moreover, many of these designs are remarkably clever. Informational issues are often complex and subtle, and designing appropriate laboratory procedures is by no means a trivial task. Finally, the novelty of these designs also provides us the opportunity to discuss a number of procedural issues that must be confronted when introducing informational asymmetries into a laboratory market context.

The chapter is organized as follows. The first half focuses on misallocations arising in markets where product quality is known to sellers but unknown to buyers prior to purchase. Section 7.2 presents the results of experiments that address the possibility of a "lemons-market" outcome, in which inefficiently low-quality goods drive out high-quality goods. The experiments reviewed in section 7.3 pertain to the capacity of reputations to ensure the delivery of high-quality goods. Another way that sellers can increase the credibility of claims about unobserved product quality is to make commitments (e.g., warranties) that are more costly if the product turns out to be of low quality. The possibility that such commitments can signal product quality in the laboratory is the topic of section 7.4.

The second half of the chapter pertains to asset markets. Section 7.5 introduces an experiment designed to assess the efficiency of market allocations for a two-period asset where the value of the asset is known, but private in the sense that traders do not know each others' values. Section 7.6 then turns to situations where the underlying value of the asset is unknown, and where value varies both across traders and across states of nature. The primary issue in these two sections is to determine the extent to which the act of trading resolves informational asymmetries or uncertainty, by either disseminating or aggregating disparate bits of partial information held by different groups of traders. An unusual application of the informational efficiency of asset markets, a "presidential stock exchange," is introduced in section 7.7. In such a market, participants trade stock shares during an election campaign, with the knowledge that the *ex post* payout for a share of a particular candidate's stock will be proportional to the percentage of votes received by that candidate on election day. Although traders in such a market do not represent a random sample of voters, they are nevertheless financially motivated to find and incorporate information about candidates' strengths into their own trading strategies. As will be seen, the available evidence suggests that markets of this type may provide both continuous and remarkably accurate polling information. A summary and some concluding comments are contained in section 7.8.

7.2 Quality Uncertainty and "Lemons" Market Outcomes

Consider a product with a quality attribute that cannot be ascertained prior to purchase. The current owner (seller) is likely to have superior quality information, and as indicated in the introduction, this asymmetry can produce a market failure. It is useful to consider here a sequence of events that can lead to such a failure. Suppose that there are just two quality levels, high and low. Then the price that buyers would be willing to pay will presumably not exceed the average value of a unit offered for sale. Owners of high-quality items may not wish to sell at a price that only depends on the *average* quality level. But when these prospective sellers of high-quality items withdraw, the proportion of low-quality items for sale increases, which lowers the average quality and hence the price that buyers are willing to pay. This in turn causes more owners of high-quality items to withdraw. In this manner, the market can unravel from above, leaving only low-quality "lemons" for sale. The market falls apart altogether if consumers find low-quality items to be sufficiently distasteful, or if aggregate demand for lemons is insufficient to intersect market supply at a positive price.[1]

Akerlof (1970) uses this unraveling argument to explain why it is difficult for elderly people to buy health insurance at reasonable rates; the premium depends on the average medical costs of those being insured, but the most healthy may not be willing to pay a premium that depends on average health levels. As the most healthy people opt to self-insure, the average health level falls, and the insurance companies may end up charging very high premiums to a relatively unhealthy pool of customers. This problem is one of *adverse selection*: from the insurance company's perspective, it is the least desirable customers who buy the insurance. The adverse selection problem depends critically on the asymmetry of information, that is, that the elderly know more about their basic health than the insurance company. Physical exams, which reduce or eliminate the informational asymmetry, can enable the company to establish different premiums for customers with different health risks.

Laboratory experimentation can be used to show that market inefficiencies actually do arise in simple situations with asymmetric quality information. A purpose of experimentation in this context is to identify the pervasiveness of such inefficiencies, and to evaluate the effectiveness of corrective measures. We discuss double-auction experiments of this type in the following subsection. Experiments involving other institutions are discussed subsequently.

A Double Auction with Quality Uncertainty

Lynch et al. (1986) modified the standard double auction by requiring each seller to choose a product quality level before the beginning of the trading process. One procedural problem that must be faced in designing a market with quality gradations is how to refer to the alternative qualities. A neutral approach would consist of terminology such as commodities x and y. The danger here is that subjects might become confused about which commodity is more desirable. A slightly less neutral approach is to refer to commodities as grade 1, grade 2, and so on, which is convenient when there are many quality variations, but which does suggest a quality ranking. A more colorful alternative is to use clearly suggestive language, such as high and low quality. This approach has the advantage of removing any confusion regarding the quality of the good, but has a potential disadvantage of distorting the financially induced preferences for quality. There is a trade-off here, and either choice can potentially invite criticism. In making a

---

[1] Appendix A7.1 provides instructions for a market with the general characteristics just described. These instructions can be used in a classroom demonstration. In any event, the reader may find it useful to review them at this time, to consider what price and quality transactions might be expected in an experimental session of this type, both early on and after several market periods.

choice, the researcher should rely on intuition, related research, pilot sessions, and the purpose of the experiment.

Lynch et al. used the more suggestive approach: the two goods were labeled Regulars and Supers. Supers cost more to produce, but they are more valuable to buyers. All units offered by a seller had to be of the same quality. The market, represented in figure 7.1, consists of six sellers and eight buyers. Sellers may each offer up to two units for sale; the cost is 120 for each unit that is a Super, but the cost is only 20 for each unit that is a Regular. With six sellers and two units each, there are at most twelve units supplied. If Supers are produced, the supply function is horizontal at a price of 120 up to a quantity of twelve, as shown by the solid line S_S in the figure. Similarly, the supply function for Regulars is horizontal at a price of 20, as shown by the dashed line, S_R. Each of the eight buyers has redemption values of 330, 300, and 270 for the first, second and third Super, respectively. The

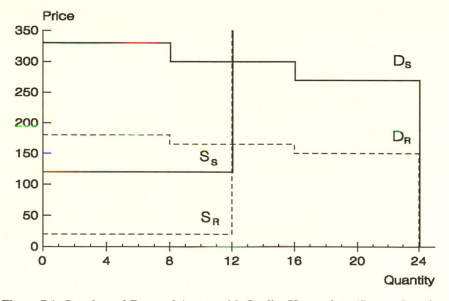

Figure 7.1 Supply-and-Demand Arrays with Quality Uncertainty (Source: Lynch et al., 1986)

marginal values for Regulars are 180, 165, and 150 for the 1st, 2nd, and 3rd units. Therefore, the solid-line market demand curve for Supers, denoted D_S, is located above the dashed-line market demand for Regulars, D_R, as shown in figure 7.1. The solid-line demand-and-supply curves for Supers intersect at a price of 300, and the aggregate trading surplus, determined as the area between the supply and demand curves, is 2,400 francs. But if only Regulars are produced, the competitive price would be 165, determined by the intersection of the dashed-line demand-and-supply curves, and the trading surplus would be reduced to 1,860.

The equilibrium for Regulars is relatively inefficient; it yields only 78 percent (1,860/2,400) of the maximum surplus available in a competitive market for Supers. But if buyers cannot observe the quality level prior to purchase, sellers have a strong incentive offer Regulars, which cost 100 less per unit to produce. Many economists believe that a variety of market characteristics may prevent the "lemons" outcome. The inefficient equilibrium may be avoided, for example, if sellers can advertise, offer warranties, or develop reputations on the basis of previous deliveries. Lynch et al. evaluated the relative effects of some of these variables in a series of twenty-one double-auction markets, conducted in variants of the design discussed above.

Each market lasted from seven to fourteen periods. After the sellers made quality choices, standard oral double-auction procedures were employed, with three exceptions. First, payoffs were denominated in laboratory "francs" rather than dollars. Francs were converted to U.S. dollars at a rate of 1 franc = 2 cents for buyers, and 1 franc = 1 cent for sellers.[2] Second, to prevent uncontrolled leakage of information about product quality, buyers and sellers were placed in separate rooms. After sellers made their quality decisions, bids and offers were transmitted from room to room over a CB radio, with the bid/offer "T" charts being maintained simultaneously in each room. Third, buyers were given both a bonus of 50 francs each period and an unexpected one-time endowment of 200 francs at the end of the first period. The bonuses and the endowment were introduced to offset the initial losses suffered by buyers, who tended to purchase Regulars at a Supers price in the first trading period. Even with the per-period bonuses, many buyers would have had no prospect of realizing a positive balance until many trading periods had passed, without the additional first-period endowment. Buyers were (truthfully) told to expect no further endowments after period 1.[3]

The authors investigated a number of different treatment conditions, and behavior varied substantially from session to session. Nevertheless, some persistent findings were observed. In particular, the authors were able to identify conditions under which inefficient lemons-market outcomes are consistently generated. In portions of seven sessions, seller identities were not disclosed to buyers (thus

---

[2] Since conversion rates are private information, the use of a franc filter may reduce interpersonal payoff comparisons. This device would be ineffective, however, if subjects assumed that all conversion rates are identical. Nevertheless, the use of laboratory francs is common in these asymmetric-information experiments. As indicated in chapter 1, the danger of using a franc filter is that induced financial incentives may be distorted by a money illusion associated with using high payoff numbers.

[3] The use of unannounced payments presents something of a dilemma. On the one hand, such payments may help to maintain incentives (and morale) within a session. On the other hand, their use risks a loss of credibility: the subjects may suspect that bold decisions leading to large losses in subsequent periods might be forgiven. It seems that this issue could have been avoided by simply giving buyers a 200 franc balance at the start of the session.

preventing the development of reputations), and sellers were prohibited from making quality disclosures. In the periods conducted under this treatment, 96 percent of all units sold were Regulars, and average prices were within 5 francs of the equilibrium price for Regulars. Average efficiency for these periods was even less than the lemons-market equilibrium prediction of 78 percent.

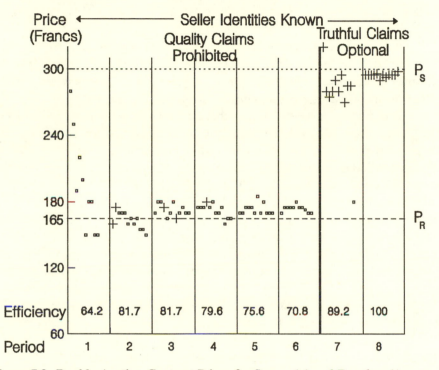

Figure 7.2 Double-Auction Contract Prices for Supers (+) and Regulars (·) (Source: Lynch et al., 1986)

The presentation of seller identities was not enough to avoid an inefficient outcome. This result is illustrated by the sequence of contract prices for the market session illustrated in figure 7.2. The figure is formatted in the usual manner, with data for each trading period separated by vertical lines. Dots represent contract prices at which Regulars were transacted. Crosses represent contract prices for Supers. The dashed horizontal line at 165 represents the Regulars equilibrium market price, while the dotted horizontal line at 300 represents the equilibrium market price for Supers. In the first six periods of this session, sellers' identities were known, but advertising, truthful or otherwise, was prohibited. Buyers purchased some units in the first period at prices above the Regulars equilibrium price. However, competition among sellers drove prices down. At the end of the period, each buyer discovered that the purchased units were Regulars. In periods 2, 3, and 4, buyers paid only for the delivery of Regulars, despite the occasional efforts of sellers to offer Supers, as indicated by crosses. Sellers stopped offering Supers altogether in periods 5 and 6. Average trading efficiency for periods 5 and 6 was 73 percent, even below the lemons market equilibrium prediction of 78 percent. This pattern of low prices and quality is fairly representative of other sessions where advertising was not permitted (but the data in figure 7.3 below represent an exception).

On the other hand, truthful advertising, either voluntary or mandatory, appears to resolve the quality uncertainty. The final two trading periods in figure 7.2 illustrate an instance where this occurred. In these periods, sellers were given the option to make claims regarding quality when offering contracts for sale. The experiment monitor, however, required that the claims be truthful. As evidenced by the cluster of crosses about the competitive price prediction for Supers, optional truthful advertising claims almost immediately moved this market to the efficient Supers equilibrium. The efficiencies, shown at the bottom of the chart, increase from 70.8 percent in period 6 to 100 percent in period 8.

The effect of truthful advertising claims illustrated in figure 7.2 is representative of results in other sessions. In parts of six sessions, truthful advertising was not only possible, it was required. In these periods, nearly 90 percent of the units sold were Supers, and efficiency always exceeded 90 percent. Moreover, by the second period in each session, all contracts were within 10 francs of the Supers equilibrium price. Nearly identical performance was observed in portions of four other sessions where advertising was optional, but where claims that were made were required to be truthful.

Quality Uncertainty in Other Environments

A problem with using the double auction in the sessions discussed above is that this institution is designed to parallel the structure of financial markets. It is more natural to think of inefficient, low-quality outcomes as being characteristic of other trading institutions, such as markets with posted prices, or markets with nonpublic contract terms. A posted-offer market with endogenous quality was examined by Holt and Sherman (1990). They modified posted-offer procedures by letting sellers choose both price and quality independently before buyers shopped. The quality selection was made from one of either six or eighteen possible quality gradations, labeled grade 1, grade 2, and so on. The multiplicity of quality gradations provided sellers the opportunity to engage in rather subtle shading on quality deliveries. Also, unlike Lynch et. al, Holt and Sherman located sellers in the same room as buyers. *Ex post*, this was probably a poor design decision. It was apparent to the experimenters that a few sellers felt embarrassed after charging high prices for low-quality products. Sellers were paid and released before buyers to minimize post-experiment interactions.

Since both costs and valuations depended on the grade, it is possible to calculate the trading surplus that would result if all units were of a particular grade and were sold at the competitive price for that grade. The grade that yielded the maximum trading surplus in the Holt and Sherman design was not the highest available grade, which opens the possibility of having an inefficiently high level of quality as well as an inefficiently low level of quality. Each of the eight posted-offer sessions began and ended with a number of full-information periods in which both price and quality selections were revealed to buyers prior to shopping. In these periods, the average-quality grade was near the surplus-maximizing grade level, and 84 percent of the maximum possible gains from trade were realized. In contrast, average quality was lower, and only 46 percent of gains from trade were realized in periods for which prices, but not quality grades, were posted.[4]

Yet another context where asymmetric quality information may affect performance arises in markets for professional services, where the buyer is *never* able to observe the product quality decision made by the seller. Consider, for example, a market for accounting services. A firm owner might retain an external auditor to reduce the likelihood of losses due to mismanagement or fraud on the part of managers with no ownership interest. Although there is some possibility that the external auditor will fail to detect fraud even if the auditor conducts a very careful audit, the possibility of a loss diminishes with increases in auditor effort. Situations of this type, where the informational asymmetry is due to the buyer's inability to observe the actions taken by a hired agent, are referred to as *principal-agent* problems. The agent's incentive to take advantage of this situation, for example, to reduce service quality, is called *moral hazard*.[5]

DeJong, Forsythe, and Lundholm (1985) conducted a series of four sealed-offer auctions designed to evaluate moral hazard problems in a principal-agent context. In these markets, sellers could again offer multiple quality gradations, and the efficient solution was not the highest grade. Unlike the posted offer just discussed, however, sellers made buyer-specific price and quality representations privately (e.g.,

---

[4] Holt and Sherman designed their experiment to assess the possibility that price claims can signal quality. The authors found that in the absence of quality information, price advertising did nothing to improve performance. In periods in which price (but not quality) was advertised, mean efficiency was 46 percent, somewhat below the 53 percent mean efficiency in periods with no advertising. (The no-advertising treatment involved letting each buyer, in turn, choose a seller without seeing prices or qualities and then decide whether to purchase or not in that period on the basis of the selected seller's price. Quality was only revealed to a buyer who made a purchase.)

[5] Inefficient performance can arise in a principal-agent context even if there is no problem of moral hazard, but moral hazard tends to magnify inefficiencies. For this reason, we confine attention here to circumstances where sellers can misrepresent product quality. DeJong, Forsythe, and Uecker (1985) and Berg et al. (1985) report experiments investigating agency problems in the absence of moral hazard.

seller 1 might offer a unit of quality grade 3 to buyer 2 for a price of 30 francs). Increases in quality were known to diminish the likelihood that a random event at the end of the period would cause a loss to buyers. Sellers were bound to their offer price, but not to their quality representations. After all offers had been posted, buyers made purchases. Once a purchase was made, sellers chose the quality level to deliver. Buyers were never told the service quality that was actually delivered. Rather, after all buyers made purchase decisions, the random state of nature was determined, and buyers observed either a loss or no loss. Thus, the setup has the feature that buyers received only stochastic *ex post* information regarding the quality that the seller provided. Similar to the lemons market environments, inefficiently low quality was frequently delivered in these markets (about half of the time).

Inefficiently low-quality deliveries are readily eliminated by costly auditing mechanisms. In a subsequent experiment, DeJong et al. (1985) report that low quality deliveries diminished from 60 percent in two sessions where quality cannot be observed to 4 percent in two other sessions conducted with both costly investigation and a "negligence liability rule." In this latter treatment, buyers could pay a fee to determine what quality was delivered in the event of a loss. If sellers were determined to have delivered a sufficiently low quality, they were deemed "negligent," and had to pay for the loss. Due to the complexity of the treatment, the reason for the quality increase is unclear: it could be due to the additional information provided by auditing, and/or to the deterrent effect of the penalty that follows a negligence ruling. Despite the improvement in delivered quality, however, the treatment did not improve overall market performance. The gains in efficiency brought about by the improved quality delivery were almost entirely consumed in auditing expenses. The authors note that this result was anticipated by Akerlof (1970), who argued that although institutional modifications may evolve that eliminate informational asymmetries, these modifications may not improve market efficiency because of their cost.

Closer inspection of the data, however, suggests that auditing may have a more promising effect: In the latter periods of these sessions, surplus extraction rates improved rather dramatically, from about 55 percent to about 75 percent of the maximum gains from exchange. The efficiency improvements are attributable to the buyers who cut down on their investigation rates in the final periods of each session, without suffering a degradation in the quality of delivered services. One interpretation of these results is that the high rate of investigations by buyers in the early periods of the session was inefficient only from a static perspective. The buyers overinvestigated in early periods to establish reputations as agents who would actively investigate losses that are correlated with low quality. Excessive investigations ceased once it was clear to sellers that the buyers would prosecute apparent quality misrepresentations.

Given the prominence of the principal-agent paradigm in the theoretical accounting literature, more work in this area can be expected. One particularly interesting adaptation of the principal-agent framework might involve identifying baseline circumstances where inefficiently *high* quality tends to be provided, for example, if sellers must bear a portion of the investigation costs. Parallels to natural contexts are immediate, particularly in the medical services industry, where the threat of litigation often leads to excessive expenditures on diagnosis.

In addition to informational asymmetries regarding the quality of services received, the market for medical services suggests other interesting issues. In particular, medical care providers have the unusual characteristic of both prescribing and selling the service, and in this sense these agents simultaneously influence the supply and demand for their services. Plott and Wilde (1982) report an experiment in which the buyer of a service could request a diagnosis from one or more sellers. The seller could observe information about the buyer's condition that made such a diagnosis possible, but the correct diagnosis was not necessarily the same as the diagnosis that would maximize the seller's earnings. In the experiment, buyers would tend to shy away from a seller who provided a diagnosis that deviated from the diagnoses given by other sellers, and this behavior helped buyers to avoid being misled.

Summary

Although lemons market outcomes are not universal, asymmetric information regarding the quality of a good or service has been observed to generate substantial inefficiencies in a fairly robust set of circumstances. When seller identities are revealed, but buyers cannot discern product quality before purchasing, quality levels often fall to inefficiently low levels. Service quality, and to some extent market performance, can be improved by buyers if they have an opportunity to audit. And in at least one environment, buyers can often avoid being the victim of an opportunistic diagnosis of the buyer's condition by seeking diagnoses from a number of sellers. We now turn to the issue of whether seller reputations can resolve some of the inefficiencies discussed above.

7.3 Reputation Effects

Although the inefficiencies discussed in the previous section could be alleviated by auditing and regulation, direct interventions of this type often have undesirable political and economic consequences. Prior to advocating regulatory solutions it is desirable to enquire whether the marketplace can naturally resolve these informational problems through the development of reputations. As discussed above, the delivery of low quality often represents a dominant strategy for sellers in a nonrepeated transaction, when quality cannot be assessed prior to purchase. In many markets, however, buyers and sellers engage in ongoing relations that can change the

incentive structure. In particular, over time sellers may invest in a reputation for
high quality, which they would be reluctant to risk for short-term gains from selling
low-quality products at high prices.

The incidence of quality misrepresentations in the multiperiod markets
discussed in the preceding section indicates that reputation development is not a
wonder drug: the delivery of low quality was often far from complete in many of
the these sessions. For example, DeJong, Forsythe, and Lundholm (1985) report that
high quality was delivered about one-half of the time, despite the sellers' short-term
incentives to reduce quality. These authors suggest that at least some of the
deviations from low-quality delivery might be due to concerns about reputations.

Moreover, reputations are sometimes strong enough to support efficient, high-
quality outcomes in the double-auction markets reported by Lynch et al. (1986).
This is illustrated in figure 7.3, which is formatted in the same manner as figure 7.2,
with the dotted line at 300 representing the equilibrium price for Supers, and the
dashed line at 165 representing the equilibrium price for Regulars. Crosses indicate

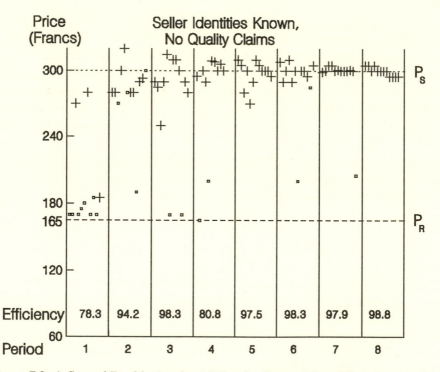

Figure 7.3 A Second Double-Auction Market for Supers (+) and Regulars (·) with
Informational Asymmetries (Source: Lynch et al., 1986)

prices at which Supers were delivered, and dots indicate prices at which Regulars were delivered. The market illustrated in figure 7.3 was conducted under conditions very similar to those used in the first six periods of figure 7.2; although buyers knew the identities of sellers, sellers could not make quality claims when prices were posted. But buyers could, of course, keep track of which sellers had delivered Supers to them in previous periods. Notice the predominance of Supers clustered about the dotted-line competitive price prediction for high quality goods. The efficiencies shown at the bottom of the figure are quite high for all periods other than 1 and 4. These outcomes stand in stark contrast to the performance generated in the first six periods of the market illustrated in figure 7.2.

Although figure 7.3 indicates that reputations for delivering high quality sometimes develop and dominate lemons market incentives, the similarity of conditions underlying the markets in figures 7.2 and 7.3 suggests that the evolution of reputations is difficult to predict. The variability of outcomes under essentially identical conditions presents a problem for the experimenter. It may be the case that the variability is due to some unintended but potentially controllable factor. In the present case, for example, there is a possible subject-pool effect: Participants in the figure 7.2 market were inexperienced students from Pasedena Community College, while participants in the figure 7.3 market were Cal Tech undergraduates, with relevant market experience.[6]

But it may also be the case that the variability is caused by essentially uncontrollable characteristics, such as individual propensities to cooperate. For example, Lynch et al. (1986) observe that the efforts of individual sellers to develop reputations are often affected by "reputational externalities"; that is, that quality-shading by some sellers impedes the efforts of others to develop or maintain reputations. While a diversity of outcomes can be interesting in itself, this diversity reminds us that each market session is in some sense a single independent observation, and that additional observations may be necessary.

An alternative means of dealing with outcome variability in complex markets is to consider streamlined environments that isolate key elements of the incentive structure. For example, Davis and Holt (1990) examined a type of reputational development in a three-person game where the notion of a punishment was salient to the subjects: a single buyer faced two sellers and could switch away from a seller who delivered low quality. This unstable "triangular" situation makes it natural to interpret a buyer's decision to switch as a punishment.

Although Davis and Holt did not present the incentives to subjects in market terms (e.g., "buyers," "sellers," and "qualities"), these terms will be used here for expositional purposes. In figure 7.4, the buyer must choose between seller S1 and

---

[6] Differences of this type are frustrating, but to ignore them by essentially confining attention to a narrow, "qualified" subject pool is not always the best approach. To the extent subject-pool effects are important, restrictions in the subject-selection process limit the generality of results.

seller S2. Payoffs for the buyer are in the lower-left part of each box, and payoffs for sellers S1 and S2 respectively are in middle and upper-right parts of each box. In this game, each seller can be thought of as making a choice between high quality, H, and low quality, L. The buyer's purchase decisions are labeled by the seller chosen, S1 or S2. All choices are made simultaneously, so quality delivery is unknown prior to purchase.

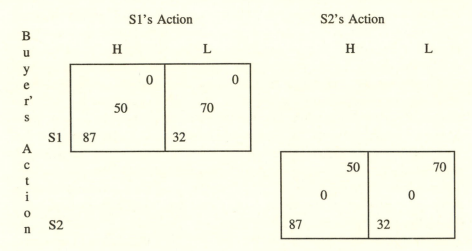

Figure 7.4 A Three-Person Stage Game That Is Repeated (Source: Davis and Holt, 1990)

This interpretation is more easily understood by considering one possible set of outcomes. Suppose that the buyer decides to purchase from seller 1 by selecting action S1, and this seller delivers low quality by picking action L. Then seller S1 receives 70 cents for having picked L, and the buyer receives 32 cents as a consequence of this low quality. Notice that seller S1 gains 20 cents by choosing L rather than H, but this quality reduction reduces the buyer's earnings by 55 cents. In the meantime, the seller not selected, in this case S2, earns nothing. It is apparent from the lower box on the right side of figure 7.4 that seller S2 has the same incentive to reduce quality as seller S1.

In a one-stage version of this game, the delivery of low quality (decision L) is a dominant strategy for each seller, and the buyer should be indifferent between S1 and S2. If, however, the game is repeated even once, a "cooperative" play of H in the first stage can be part of an equilibrium strategy: suppose the buyer (arbitrarily) chooses to deal with S1 in the first stage and only switches in the second stage if low quality is delivered. The strategies for both S1 and S2 are to choose H in the first stage and L in the second. In this case, the gain of 20 that seller S1 could realize by defecting and providing low quality in the first stage is more than offset by the cost, 70, of not being selected in the final stage.[7] Recall that both sellers provide low quality in the final stage in this subgame-perfect equilibrium. It follows that the equilibrium is weak since the buyer's second-stage payoff of 32 would not be any lower if the threat to switch following a defection were not carried out.

A switch-to-punish and stay-to-reward strategy can be communicated more effectively when the stage game is repeated more than once. In a three-stage game, for example, suppose seller S1 uses a strategy of choosing L in all stages. Then a switch from S1 to S2 would increase the buyer's expected payoff if seller S2 offers high quality in the second-stage with any positive probability. Multiple-stage variants of this game have the advantage that the buyer can see whether sellers provide low quality in early stages, and the sellers can see whether the buyer will punish such behavior. In this way, cooperative outcomes might develop as a result of the buyer's reputation for punishing and rewarding.

Davis and Holt conducted nine sessions with variants of this design. Each session involved nine inexperienced participants, who made decisions in a series of games, using the parameters in figure 7.4. All sessions were presented in a computerized environment, and only payoff relevant information was provided. In particular, the quality choice of the seller selected was never displayed to the other seller in a given stage. Following each game, participants were anonymously rearranged into new groups of three participants. The treatment variable was the number of stages in the game, that is, the number of times that the same participants go through the stage game in figure 7.4 in the same role. Three baseline sessions consisted of a series of single-stage games, where participants were rematched into a new three-person group after each game. In addition, there were three sessions with two-stage games and three sessions with ten-stage games.

A variety of buyer responses are conceivably consistent with punish/reward behavior by buyers, particularly in the ten-stage games (where buyers could deliver a variety of punishments ranging from switching away for a single period to switching away for all of the remaining periods.) Perhaps the most straightforward punishment/reward strategy, however, is for buyers to punish sellers by switching away in the event that low quality is delivered, and to reward sellers who deliver high quality by remaining with them in each period subsequent to a high-quality delivery choice. Data from sessions involving two-stage and ten-stage games indicate that this simple strategy is very natural for most buyers, as shown in the middle column of table 7.1. Roughly 70 percent of buyer choices were consistent with this simple switch/stay strategy in each session of either treatment. However, as is apparent from the third column of the table, this strategy improved quality

---

[7] Obviously, the punishment strategy could be similarly used to induce the other seller, S2, to provide high quality if selected in the first stage. There are other, more asymmetric equilibria with the same cooperative outcome but in which the seller not selected offers low quality in both stages, and the seller selected cooperates in the first stage.

Table 7.1   Use of Switch/Stay Strategies and Mean Cooperation Rates in a
Three-Person, Choice-of-Partner Game

Treatment	Incidence of Switch/Stay Punishments and Rewards	Incidence of High-Quality Delivery
One-Stage Games	–	23%
Two-Stage Games	69%	26%
Ten-Stage Games	70%	72%

Source: Davis and Holt (1990).
Note: The data represent the percentage of times that the indicated decision was made in the final third of the games in all sessions using a given treatment. The incidence of high-quality delivery is calculated for the nonterminal stages of the two-stage and ten-stage games.

delivery only in the ten-stage games: In the last third of games, cooperation rates (measured by the proportion of the time that a seller chose to deliver high quality in periods other than the final period) were 72 percent in the sessions with the ten-stage treatments, and 26 percent in sessions conducted in the two-stage treatments. The 26 percent cooperation rate in the two-stage games was virtually the same as the incidence of high quality delivery in the one-stage games (23 percent), where punishment was impossible.

To summarize, punishment in the form of shopping elsewhere appears to be a very natural strategy for buyers in this context. However, punishing and rewarding in this way improves quality only when buyers and sellers interact a sufficient number of times for buyers to develop a reputation for not tolerating the delivery of low quality. This conclusion was anticipated by Nelson (1970), who argued that the incidence of low-quality delivery in an asymmetric environment is a function of the amount of interaction between buyers and sellers.

The Davis and Holt study is only an initial investigation of the importance of reputations as a means of avoiding lemons market outcomes. Moreover, comparison of the Davis and Holt results with the evidence of reputation development in the market designs discussed in the preceding section suggests that factors affecting reputation development may be context specific. Nevertheless, there clearly exist situations in which agents can avoid undesirable outcomes without external regulations, through the development of reputations.

7.4 Signaling

Even when buyers cannot observe product quality directly, they may be able to infer quality from the behavior of sellers. For example, if it is less expensive to attach observable "extra" features to a basically high-quality unit than it is to attach these features to a low-quality unit, then firms desiring to sell high quality might "signal" the underlying quality of their products by including extra features. In this manner, problems associated with informational asymmetries may be resolved without direct regulation of quality levels.

Product warranties may serve as a quality signal in a market context. Consider once again the market for used automobiles, and for simplicity, suppose that there are two types of firms selling used automobiles; one firm type sells "lemons" and the other sells high-quality "cherries." Each firm knows the quality of automobile that it offers, but consumers are unable to distinguish lemons from cherries until some time well after purchase. In the absence of seller reputations for quality, lemons are likely to drive out the cherries, and only inefficiently low quality would be produced. Suppose, however, that the sellers start competing on the basis of months of full warranty coverage. The expected cost of a month of warranty coverage is likely to be much lower for a cherry than for a lemon. If the cost difference is sufficient, and if buyers appreciate the informative value of the warranty signal, sellers of the high-quality cherries could distinguish themselves from sellers of lemons by offering enough months of warranty coverage that the sellers of lemons would lose money on a sale with the same warranty, even in the event they successfully misrepresented their lemon as a cherry to a purchaser.

Warranties can serve other purposes besides signaling. For example, a warranty on a failure-prone product transfers some of the risk from the consumer to the producer. This may be why the most reliable brands do not necessarily have the most comprehensive warranties. These alternative rationales for warranties can be purged from the laboratory environment. In this way, the informative role of warranties and other signals can be more directly studied. One issue to be considered is whether signaling arises in a market environment that is favorable for quality discrimination. A second issue arises because theoretical analysis indicates that there are often many signaling equilibria. Laboratory methods can be used, in very sparse environments, to evaluate the devices that theorists have suggested for selecting among the alternative equilibria.

Market Experiments with Signaling

Miller and Plott (1985) examine the capacity of signals of this sort to separate high- and low-quality products in double-auction markets. Their experiment consists of eleven sessions, with a wide variety of market structures. With one exception, the markets had six sellers and four to six buyers. In each market, all sellers faced identical cost conditions: sellers were free to determine the basic quality or "grade" of the unit (either a low-cost Regular or a higher-cost Super). In addition, sellers could choose the offer price and the number of quality increments to be added to each unit. Buyers could not distinguish between Supers and Regulars prior to purchase, but sellers did communicate their quality increment choice as part of their offer. The cost of adding quality increments to Supers was less than the cost of adding quality increments to Regulars in a way that potentially allowed the sellers of Supers to signal information regarding grade via the quality increments. The demand side of the market consisted of a number of identical buyers. Each buyer received a redemption value that depended on both the grade (Regular or Super) and the number of added quality increments.

The markets were organized as oral double auctions, with buyers and sellers in the same room. Bids and offers were made in the usual way, except that messages specified both a price and quality increment. For example, an offer would be of the form "S1 offers a 50 for 320," indicating that seller S1 is willing to sell a unit with 50 quality increments (but of unspecified grade) for 320 francs. At the end of each trading period, the grade of each unit sold was publicly announced. In later periods, grade deliveries were further distinguished *ex post* by circling them with colored chalk. If there is a correlation between the quality increment signal and the delivered grade, then these procedures would highlight this correlation.

In a *separating equilibrium*, there is a systematic relationship between the number of observable quality increments added to a unit and the unobserved grade. In this case, buyers would be willing to pay more for a product with a high number of quality increments. Sellers offering Supers would distinguish themselves by adding more quality increments than a seller of Regulars could profitably offer, even if the Regular sold for a Super price. If sellers offering Supers do not distinguish themselves by offering enough quality increments, then the sellers of Regulars would have an incentive to add quality increments and sell the product at the going price for Supers. If Regulars and Supers with the same observed signal are mixed in this way, the result would be a *pooling equilibrium*.

Significant quality separation via signaling occurred in about half of the Miller and Plott sessions. A typical adjustment pattern was for signaling to occur first in excessive (inefficient) amounts, that is, more than was needed for separation. Expenditures on quality increments would subsequently decline toward the efficient level that just deters the sale of Regulars with comparable quality increments. Efficient signaling outcomes occurred more frequently when the difference in signaling costs for Supers and Regulars was large. This experiment indicates that signaling is possible in a rich environment with endogenous price and quality choice.

Results are characterized by a high degree of variability, however, and both pooling and quality-separating outcomes were observed under the same treatment conditions. The variability of results across sessions may have been increased by the *ex post* provision of public information about all grade decisions, and by the possibility of additional signals between market participants in the same room (e.g., tone of voice, body language). In any event, these factors make it very difficult to analyze the market situation as a game. Many issues of interest to theorists should be investigated in more stark environments for which the predictions of game theory can be derived explicitly.

Signaling Games

Consider a simple two-person game, where players select (or try to interpret) a single binary signal choice, which we will interpret as the acquisition of a specific education credential. The two participants can be thought of as a worker, who makes the education decision, and an employer, who makes a job-assignment decision. The worker has an ability level that is either low or high; this ability is assumed to be known by the worker, but it cannot be observed directly by the employer. The worker chooses whether or not to obtain the education credential, and the employer responds with a job-assignment decision. Education is the potential signal in this context; it will be informative in the case that only high-ability workers obtain education.

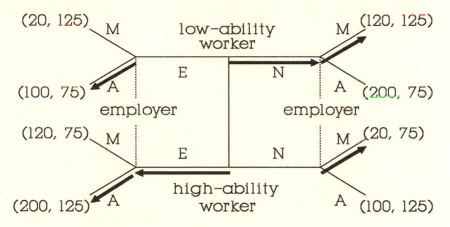

Figure 7.5 A Labor-Market Signaling Game with a Separating Equilibrium
Key: (worker payoff, employer payoff)

The extensive form of the game to be considered is shown in figure 7.5. The game proceeds in two steps; first the worker chooses to obtain the education credential (E) or not (N). The employer observes the education decision, but not the ability level, and chooses a job assignment: mechanical (M) or administrative (A). In terms of the figure, the play starts in the center, either at the top or at the bottom, depending on the worker's ability. The employer knows that the worker is randomly selected from a population where some fraction (say 1/2) of its members are of high ability and the rest are of low ability. The worker's education decision corresponds to a move to the right (N) or the left (E). If the worker chooses N, the employer knows that the right side of the figure is relevant but still does not know whether the relevant part is the upper right or the lower right. The assumption that the employer does not observe the worker's ability *ex ante* is represented by the dotted lines that connect the "employer" label with the two possible decision nodes on each side of the figure. Recall that these dotted lines are the information sets discussed in chapter 2.

Given the worker's ability, each combination of decisions leads to an outcome and an associated pair of payoffs, with the worker's payoff listed first. For example, if a low-ability worker chooses N and the employer responds with M, then this sequence can be represented by the dark, linked arrows leading to the upper right-hand part of the game in figure 7.5. The resulting payoffs are 120 for the worker and 125 for the employer. Notice that the employer payoff, listed second in each pair, is always 125 when the low-ability worker is assigned the mechanical job or the high-ability worker is assigned to the administrative job; otherwise the employer payoff is only 75. (In this sense, "high" ability represents administrative, not mechanical skill.) The employer's problem is to match the worker with a job that is appropriate for the worker's abilities. In particular, notice that education is not productive in this example; the employer payoffs on the left (education) side of the game are identical to the employer payoffs on the right (no-education) side.

The intuition behind the assumed payoffs for the worker are a little more involved. Both types of workers prefer the A job, but the high-ability worker enjoys education, whereas the low-ability worker does not (education involves nonmechanical topics). Consider a low-ability worker, for whom the worst outcome would be to suffer through education and still end up in the mechanical job; this yields a payoff of 20, as shown in the upper-left corner of the figure. If the administrative job had been obtained after education, this worker's payoff would have been 100 instead of 20, so the marginal value of the administrative job assignment to the worker is 80. For any given job assignment, the low-ability worker's payoff increases by 100 if the education can be avoided; for example, the payoff increases from 20 to 120 if education can be avoided before ending up in the M job. In contrast, the high-ability worker enjoys the education, so the worst outcome is to miss the education and end up in the less-preferred M job, which yields a payoff of 20. The other payoffs for this high-ability worker can be calculated: For a given job assignment, the additional value of the education is 100, and for a given education level, the additional value of the preferred (A) job is 80.

The essential prerequisite for signaling to occur is for the education signal to be more costly for the low-ability workers, as is the case in the example under consideration. Suppose that a low-ability worker's strategy is N and that a high-ability worker's strategy is E, as indicated by the dark arrow to the right at the top of the figure and the dark arrow to the left at the bottom. In this case, education is perfectly correlated with ability, and the employer's best response is to assign job A if education is observed, as indicated by the downward sloping arrows on the left side of the figure, and to assign job M otherwise, as indicated by the upward-sloping arrows on the right side of the figure. Notice that neither worker type has an incentive to deviate from this separating equilibrium: The high-ability worker obtains the maximum payoff of 200. The low ability worker obtains 120, and a deviation to get an education would result in the preferred A job, but the cost of the education (100) is more than the additional value of the preferred job, so the deviation is not attractive.

In retrospect, the game in figure 7.5 is easy to analyze. The worker types have such strong preferences about education that N is a dominant strategy for the low-ability worker and E is a dominant strategy for the high-ability worker. Now let us see what happens if we reduce the marginal value of the preferred education level from 100 to 40. Look at the extensive form on the left side of figure 7.6, and start with the low-ability worker's worst payoff of 20 in the upper left-hand corner. If the worker could keep the M job without suffering through the education, the payoff increases to 60, as can be seen by moving horizontally from the upper-left to the upper-right corners of the extensive form. Similarly, all of the other horizontal differences in worker payoffs are 40, but the high-ability worker prefers the education, as before. The first question to be considered is whether the reduction in the low-ability worker's cost of education will change things. Suppose that the worker types separate as before, with high-ability workers choosing E and getting the A job, and with low-ability workers choosing N and getting a payoff of 60 in the M job. The low-ability worker can increase payoff from 60 to 100 by deviating and getting an education, since the employer observes the education decision, not the ability. This unilateral deviation leads to a payoff increase, so separation is not a Nash equilibrium.

To continue the story, suppose that the employer expects that low-ability workers will choose E in order to be pooled with the high-ability workers in the preferred A job. When both worker types choose education, the employer cannot use the signal to infer ability, and the employer has to rely on prior information. It is assumed that the employer knows that the worker is randomly drawn from a population that consists of 2/3 high-ability workers, as indicated by the [2/3] notation at the bottom of the extensive form. Since the employer's objective is to match the job assignment to the worker's ability, the employer's best response to pooling is to put the worker in the A job as long as the probability of encountering a high-ability worker is greater than 1/2.[8] The equilibrium path of decisions is shown by the solid lines on the left side of the left part of figure 7.6. The worker has no incentive to deviate from this pooling equilibrium as long as the worker believes that a deviant choosing no education (N) will be assigned to the less preferred job, M. This employer response to deviation is appropriate if the employer believes that the deviant is more likely to be of low ability. These beliefs and the employer response

---

[8] This statement can be verified by calculating the expected employer payoff for each decision.

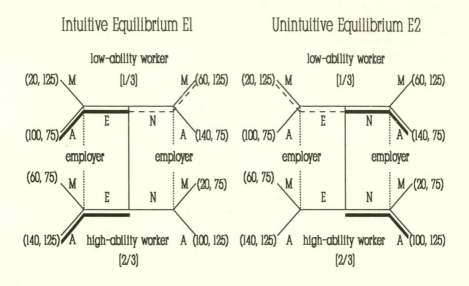

Figure 7.6 A Signaling Game with Two Pooling Equilibria

are indicated by the dashed line that follows the N/M path. To summarize, in pooling equilibrium E1, both types choose an education, and the employer's strategy specifies an A job for educated worker and an M job otherwise.

But this game has another pooling equilibrium, which is represented on the right side of the figure. As indicated by the solid lines, both worker types choose no education, and the employer responds with the A job because this is the appropriate job for the high-ability workers, who are more likely to be encountered. The low-ability worker receives the maximum payoff of 140, so this worker type would never consider deviating. The high-ability worker obtains 100 in this equilibrium, and a deviation is deterred if the employer responds to a deviant E signal with the less preferred M job assignment, which would yield only 60 for the high-ability worker. The M assignment is appropriate if the employer thinks that the deviant is more likely to be of low ability. The unreasonableness of this second pooling equilibrium is suggested by the labels of the decisions: neither worker type obtains an education for fear that a deviant who obtains the education will be thought to be of low ability and will be assigned to the less preferred, mechanical job![9]

---

[9]   Despite this counterintuitive property, this second pooling equilibrium is a sequential Nash equilibrium. Recall from the appendix to chapter 2 that we must specify both players' strategies and their beliefs at each information set. In particular, beliefs must be consistent with decisions made in equilibrium. The N signal that is chosen by both types has no information in this pooling equilibrium,

To summarize, there are two pooling equilibria represented in figure 7.6, both of which meet the requirements of a sequential equilibrium (involving consistency of beliefs and best responses). The "intuitive criterion" proposed by Cho and Kreps (1987) discriminates among equilibria on the basis of the plausibility of beliefs off the equilibrium path. To apply this criterion, we focus on a particular equilibrium, say E2, and on the payoffs that each worker type obtains: 100 for the high-ability worker and 140 for the low-ability worker. The low-ability worker could never earn more than this equilibrium payoff by deviating, since a deviation to E will either yield a 20 or a 100, depending on the employer's response. In contrast, the high-ability worker could possibly increase the payoff to 140 by a deviation to E. Therefore, it is unreasonable for the employer to interpret a deviation as being more likely to come from a worker of low ability, and the M response is unreasonable. But if the employer responds to an E deviation with an A assignment, then the high-ability worker would want to deviate, and this breaks the equilibrium. In this manner, the intuitive criterion rules out the pooling equilibrium E2.[10] The basic motivation for the intuitive criterion (and related refinements) is that the sequential equilibrium concept, which requires that beliefs be consistent with equilibrium decisions, does not place enough restrictions on beliefs in parts of the extensive form that are not reached via the equilibrium decisions.

As this example illustrates, even simple signaling games may have multiple sequential equilibria, some of which are thought to be unreasonable. Theorists have been quite interested in identifying general criteria (such as the intuitive criterion) that can be used to determine which equilibrium is "selected." Specific examples, such as the game in figure 7.6, are essentially the data points that have guided the literature on strengthening ("refining") the notion of a Nash equilibrium to rule out unwanted equilibria. The role of experiments here is to provide real, not hypothetical, data points.

---

and therefore the employer's beliefs after observing N must match the prior probability that there is a 2/3 chance of meeting a high-ability worker. In contrast, the E signal is not observed on the equilibrium path, so the worker decisions place no restrictions on the employer beliefs for the information set on the left side of the extensive form. If we specify that the employer believes that the E signal came from a low-ability worker, then the employer's best response, the M job assignment, will deter deviations of both worker types. In this sense, the beliefs are consistent with decisions and prior probabilities, and the decisions are optimal best responses given the beliefs. Similarly, it is straightforward to verify that the other pooling equilibrium, in which both types send the E signal and the employer responds to a deviation with M, is also a sequential equilibrium.

[10]   This argument cannot be used to rule out the other pooling equilibrium, E1, for which the employer's beliefs are that a deviant N signal is more likely to come from a worker of low ability. These beliefs (off the equilibrium path) are not unreasonable, since the low-ability worker could possibly increase his/her payoff (to 140) from such a deviation.

Brandts and Holt (1991) report an experiment using the payoff structure of figure 7.6.[11]   The experiment consisted of a number of sessions, in which anonymously paired worker-type and employer-type participants made a series of decisions. (The "worker," "employer," and "ability" terminology was replaced with more neutral terms.) In each session a cohort of eight participants was divided into equal-sized groups, and the groups were placed in separate rooms. Within each room, all participants had the same role, and they were paired once with each of the participants in the other room. Then roles were reversed and the pattern was repeated. Types (worker ability levels) were determined prior to each decision by a throw of dice in the room containing the worker participants. Decisions observed in this setup closely corresponded to the intuitive equilibria E1. Of 112 signaling games conducted in the last two-thirds of the matchings in each session, 101 yielded the equilibrium outcome for E1, and only 7 corresponded to E2.[12]

Although each subject is only matched with any other subject once in the same role, the process of adjustment from matching to matching is revealing. In early matchings, separation was common: the subjects with low-ability worker roles tended to choose the preferred no-education signal, and the subjects with the high-ability worker roles tended to choose the education signal. This separation is not an equilibrium, since employers tended to assign jobs exclusively on the basis of the education signal, causing low-ability workers to switch to the education signal in order to obtain the preferred (administrative) job assignment. This is the intuitive pooling equilibrium in which both worker types obtain the education signal, and the employer responds with the administrative job. Notice that the out-of-equilibrium beliefs, that a deviant, no-education signal comes from a low-ability worker, are consistent with what was actually observed in early matchings. This suggests that the *process of out-of-equilibrium adjustment* affects beliefs off of the equilibrium path.

After observing the adjustment patterns in the initial signaling experiment, Brandts and Holt changed the payoff parameters in an effort to induce an adjustment pattern that would reinforce the beliefs of the unintuitive equilibrium. To better study the adjustment process, the number of subjects per session was increased from eight to twelve, to permit six matchings with different partners before roles are reversed.[13] The parameters of the game were transformed by making the relative

---

[11]   Brandts and Holt changed the N/A payoff for the high-ability worker from 100 to 120 in order to equalize expected payoffs in the two pooling equilibria. This change does not alter any of the equilibrium calculations.

[12]   Experiments supporting this and even more subtle equilibrium refinements have reported been by others, e.g., Camerer and Weigelt (1988) and Banks, Camerer, and Porter (1990).

[13]   An alternative would have been to match subjects with each other more than a single time, but to do so would complicate the extensive form of the game in a way that can add equilibria and change the nature of the refinements arguments. Adjustments might also be affected by providing information

values of the two job assignments depend on the worker's education level. Although the transformation preserved the configuration of the intuitive and unintuitive pooling equilibria, it was done to induce decisions in early matchings to correspond to the case where low-ability people do get an education, and high-ability people do not. This "reverse separation" was observed to some extent, and it corresponds to the out-of-equilibrium beliefs of the unintuitive equilibrium. In later matchings, the low-ability workers tended to switch to the no-education signal, as predicted by the unintuitive equilibrium, which is supported by employers' beliefs that seemed to have been affected by the results of initial matchings. The lesson to be learned is that out-of-equilibrium beliefs are formed during the adjustment process to equilibrium. For this reason, the refinements literature may need to consider the process of adjustment more carefully.

Summary

The investigation of signaling behavior in the laboratory indicates that differentially costly signals can serve as a mechanism by which agents can distinguish quality, when it is not directly observable prior to purchase. The variability of results in rich double-auction environments calls for the investigation of simpler game and market structures to allow identification of conditions under which separating equilibria will and will not occur, as well as insight into the type of pooling equilibrium that will be selected when separation does not occur. Investigation of pooling equilibrium selection is particularly interesting in light of the theoretical "refinements" literature, which generates predictions that turn on relatively subtle assumptions regarding beliefs off the equilibrium path. Initial investigations of these refinements in the laboratory suggest that surprisingly subtle refinements may have considerable behavioral appeal. However, these game-theoretic experiments represent only a starting point for analysis. For example, while the "intuitive" refinement criterion organizes data well in the design discussed above in figure 7.6, Brandts and Holt (1991) also report other parameterizations where most of the decisions correspond to the strategies of the unintuitive equilibrium.[14] Since theoretical concepts that work in some conditions may fail in others, experiments can provide the critical data points to guide refinements of theory. These data are important, since nature rarely replicates the exact conditions of even simple games. Before these experiments, the only available "data" were

---

about others' decisions *ex post*. These approaches have serious disadvantages. For example, announcing the results of each matching publicly transforms the entire session with eight participants into a single, multistage, eight-person game. In experiments designed to test subtle game theoretic concepts, it is important to keep the design simple.

[14] Cadsby, Frank, and Maksimovic (1992) also report a signalling experiment in which the data corresponds to an unintuitive equilibrium for some parameterizations.

theorists' intuitions about what outcomes were and were not reasonable in particular games.

7.5 Informational Asymmetries in Asset Markets

Securities, or assets, differ from other commodities in that they derive their value over time, from a stream of dividends and capital gains, rather than from directly induced costs and valuations. The temporal dimension of assets creates several sources of uncertainty: asset values may vary due to exogenous factors, such as states of nature, as well as with endogenous factors, such as traders' expectations regarding capital gains and losses. An important advantage of laboratory methods is that they allow us to control exogenous sources of uncertainty so that endogenous behavior can be more directly examined.

It is useful to distinguish two types of exogenous uncertainty in an asset market context.[15] First, the dividend payoff of the asset may depend on the outcome of a randomly determined state of nature, for example, the popularity of a firm's product or the results of research and development. This creates *state uncertainty*, as in the common-value auction model of the previous chapter. Second, although each trader knows his own value for the asset's payoff in each state, traders may be uncertain about the asset's payoff to other traders. For example, different traders can have different tax positions that cause a given dividend change to yield different levels of after-tax earnings. This creates *type uncertainty*, as in the private-values auction models of the previous chapter.

The notions of type and state uncertainty should be distinguished from endogenous *behavioral uncertainty* about how others form expectations and trade on the basis of these expectations. Whereas variables creating state and type uncertainty have been objects of experimental control, no attempt is made to control behavioral uncertainty. To do so would entail manipulating traders' expectation formation process, for example. But the process of expectation formation is precisely what distinguishes competing asset pricing models. Consequently, the expectation formation process is itself the object of investigation, not control.

The most commonly considered behavioral assumption in asset market experiments is the notion that expectations are *rational* in the sense that they are based on the best information available regarding the underlying value of the asset. In economic models, the rationality of expectations is like an equilibrium or consistency condition. Expectations affect behavior, which in turn affects the time series of prices and other variables. Loosely speaking, expectations are rational if they are consistent with the outcomes generated by behavior that is optimal for those

---

[15] We are indebted to Robert Forsythe for suggesting this distinction. We deviate somewhat from his suggested terminology, and bear the responsibility for any resulting confusions or imprecision.

expectations. It helps to imagine a circle of arrows that connect expectations with behavior, behavior with market outcomes, and market outcomes with the same expectations that began the chain. The popularity of rational expectations models is certainly attributable in part to the fact that they often yield the efficient outcomes that would be generated in environments with less uncertainty.

One implication of rational expectations pertains to the way traders respond to state uncertainty regarding dividends. If traders are risk neutral, for example, there should be no speculative bubbles that cause prices to diverge from the intrinsic expected value of an asset, since a bubble arises when prices are expected to continue rising, which is inconsistent with the downturn that follows. In the introduction to double-auction asset markets at the end of chapter 3, we saw that this implication frequently did not hold in markets for relatively long-lived (fifteen-period) assets, when participants were inexperienced laboratory traders. Surprisingly large speculative price bubbles can grow and collapse under these conditions. However, speculative behavior usually diminishes as participants become experienced.

The rational-expectations assumption also has implications for resource allocations in markets characterized by asymmetries, either in valuations across traders (type uncertainty) or in information regarding valuations (state uncertainty). Suppose, for example, that the value of an asset dividend stream is generally unknown to traders, but is revealed to a few informed "insiders." Given the existence of insider information, a fully efficient allocation of resources is based on this information. In this context, the assumption of rational expectations implies that the market serves as an information-transmission mechanism. That is, the course of trading resolves uncertainty by "leaking" inside information to uniformed traders in the market.

In this section and the next, we introduce the experimental literature that addresses the capacity of securities markets to transmit asymmetric information. As will be seen, the role of the market as an information-transmission mechanism can be examined in environments that are, in some respects, much simpler than the markets for the relatively long-lived assets discussed in chapter 3. We proceed through a series of progressively more complicated circumstances. The remainder of this section pertains to a relatively simple case of type uncertainty, in which the private values of dividends differ from trader to trader. The next section reviews experiments with state uncertainty, which assess the capacity of markets to transmit and aggregate insider information.

Type Uncertainty in a Simple Asset Market

Although type uncertainty can arise in markets for financial assets, it is perhaps most natural to consider this problem in the context of a piece of physical capital that has different values for different investors. The highest valued use of a wheat combine, for example, may change from Minnesota to Arkansas over the months from August to October. In a financial market setting, the value of a particular dividend payment can vary from investor to investor, for tax or risk reasons, and the difference in such private values is generally not public information. But if the market is efficient, trading should transmit this information, and assets should be diverted to the highest-valued investor in each time period.

Forsythe, Palfrey, and Plott (1982) first investigated the capacity of markets to transmit information regarding asymmetric valuations. The experiment involved a series of five sessions where participants traded a two-period *compound* asset, or an asset whose value differed across traders and over time. The market design consists of nine traders, who trade asset units over a series of market "years." The sequence of negotiations and dividends for a trading year is summarized in table 7.2. Starting at the left side of the table, each trader is given an initial endowment consisting of two asset units and a "working capital" loan of 10,000 laboratory francs. Moving right, trading years consist of two seven-minute trading periods, designated A and B. Following the termination of each period, traders holding assets receive a dividend for each unit they hold. At the end of the second period (following

Table 7.2 The Sequence of Events in a Two-Period Asset Market

Period A	Period B
Trade	Trade
Endowment: Asset Units and Working Capital Dividend Payment	Dividend Payment Repayment of Working Capital

payment of the period B dividend listed on the right side of table 7.2), asset units are worthless, and the working capital loan must be returned in its entirety to the experimenter. Thus, participants earn money from two sources: from dividends on asset units held at the end of each period, and from capital gains realized from the sale of units during periods.

Traders are subdivided into three equal-sized groups: types I, II, and III. Dividend payoffs for each trader are summarized in the right-most two columns of table 7.3. Note that dividends vary both across trader types and between trading periods. Type I traders, for example, receive a dividend of 300 francs for assets held at the end of period A, and a dividend of 50 francs for assets held at the end of period B. This time pattern of payoffs is reversed for type II traders. No trader was given any information about the dividend profile of any other trader.

Table 7.3 A Two-Period Asset Market with Type Uncertainty

Investor Type (# of Traders)	Initial Portfolio		Dividend Value	
	Cash	Asset Units	Period A	Period B
Type I (3 traders)	10,000	2	300	50
Type II (3 traders)	10,000	2	50	300
Type III (3 traders)	10,000	2	150	250

Source: Forsythe, Palfrey, and Plott (1982).

The differences in dividend payoffs provide an efficiency motivation for trading. In a "naïve" equilibrium, traders would value the asset only in light of their own dividend values, and not on the possibility of gains from the purchase and subsequent resale of assets. The most that a naïve trader would be willing to pay in the first period is the sum of his/her own dividend values for the two periods. This sum of dividend values is greatest for type III traders, at 400 francs. Notice that *any one* of these traders has enough working capital (10,000) to buy up all 16 units from the other eight traders at any price below 625 (= 10,000/16).[16] Since there are three type III traders, there would be considerable excess demand from them at any price below 400, and the price would be driven up to 400 in the first period. These traders would purchase all units in the first period, earn a first-period dividend of 150 francs per unit, and then sell them to type II traders (who value the units at 300 francs) in the second period. Total dividend payments are thus 450 francs. The price and allocation predictions of the naïve equilibrium are summarized in the top row of table 7.4.

But this naïve equilibrium involves expectations that are not rational: Consider the assumption that each trader in the first period is willing to pay an amount that equals the two-period sum of his/her own dividend values. This assumption is incorrect if the asset can be resold in the second period for more than one's dividend value, as was the case for type II traders in the naïve equilibrium. Suppose instead that traders have perfect foresight in the sense that they realize that the asset can be sold for 300 to type II traders in the second period. Then type I traders, who get a

---

[16] This maximum price at which a single trader could corner the market could be different in the second period for a trader who had bought or sold units in the first period.

Table 7.4 Equilibrium Predictions for a Two-Period Asset Market with Type
Uncertainty

Equilibrium	Price		Allocation: Trader Type (# units)		Trading Efficiency
	Period A	Period B	Period A	Period B	
Naïve	400	300	III (18)	II (18)	35.7%
Perfect-Foresight	600	300	I (18)	II (18)	100.0%

Source: Forsythe, Palfrey, and Plott (1982).

dividend of 300 in the first period, would be willing to pay up to 600 for the asset units in the first period. Total dividend payments on each unit are increased to 600 when the units are owned by type I traders in the first period and by type II traders in the second. This social gain (from 450 per unit in the naïve equilibrium to 600) is fairly obvious from the complete information in table 7.3. The efficient transfer of assets (to type I traders in period A and to type II traders in period B) results in a rational, perfect-foresight equilibrium, as summarized in the bottom row of table 7.4.

The trading efficiencies for the two equilibria are provided in the right-most column of table 7.4. The standard measure of market efficiency (e.g., the percentage of total possible surplus extracted) tends to overstate performance, as participants realize a sizable portion of the total possible surplus if they engage in no trades and simply take their dividend payments. In an effort to correct for this efficiency inflation, it is standard to use *trading efficiency*, defined as the increase in dividend payments over payments generated in the absence of trade, expressed as a percentage of the maximum possible increase. Consider the naïve equilibrium, for example. If all traders simply held their asset endowments, aggregate dividend earnings would be 6,600 francs per period (calculated as the sum of the two-period dividend total for each of the 18 units). In the full-information equilibrium, each of the 18 units generates a return of 600 francs, for a total surplus of 10,800 francs. In the naïve equilibrium, each of the 18 units generates a return of 450 francs, so the total surplus is 8,100 francs. Thus, trading efficiency in the naïve equilibrium is $(8,100 - 6,600)/(10,800 - 6,600) = .357$.[17]

---

[17] This calculation differs slightly from the 33.2 percent efficiency prediction reported by the authors.

Obviously, trading efficiency equals 0 if all agents hold their assets throughout the year, and it equals 100 percent in the full-information equilibrium, as all possible gains from trade are extracted. Notably, trading efficiency measures can be quite low, even in a double auction where most of the available surplus is extracted. In fact, negative efficiencies arise if asset units are channeled to traders who earn lower dividends than would be earned if the asset units were not traded at all.

It is worth emphasizing that attainment of the full-information equilibrium is far from a trivial task in this market, as traders enjoy considerably less than full information. They know only their own portfolio, and the return on the assets. To achieve a full-information equilibrium, traders must learn from the market the relative valuations placed on the asset by others. Particularly troublesome is the problem for type I traders, whose equilibrium price of 600 francs in period A is contingent on the understanding that assets have a trading value of 300 francs in period B. This information could only be communicated through prior experience with the two-stage structure. For this reason, sessions in this design were conducted as a series of *repeated stationary* two-period market years. At the end of each year (prior to the last), participants were reendowed with the same trader-type identities and incentives, for a subsequent year. If type I traders learn the value of assets in period B and adjust their period A valuations for the asset upward, one would expect them to do so only after several years. This conjecture, which Forsythe, Palfrey, and Plott (1982) call the "swing-back hypothesis," is that equilibrium prices will emerge first in period B, leading to the subsequent establishment of equilibrium prices in period A.

Four sessions reported by Forsythe, Palfrey, and Plott were conducted in variants of the design summarized in tables 7.3 and 7.4. Each session consisted of at least six two-period "years." Two of the sessions used exactly the design discussed above, and relatively minor variants were considered in two other sessions.[18] Results were very homogeneous across sessions, and provide fairly strong support for the perfect-foresight, full-information equilibrium in this simple environment. The sequence of contracts for a representative session are illustrated in figure 7.7. The market, which used inexperienced participants, consisted of eight two-period years and used the parameters listed in table 7.3. Years are separated by thick vertical bars in the figure, and periods within years are separated by thinner vertical bars. Equilibrium price predictions for each period are illustrated as horizontal lines. The solid horizontal lines, at 600 in period A and at 300 in period B, represent the full-information price prediction. The dashed horizontal line in period A of each year at a price of 400 reflects the naïve equilibrium price prediction. The series of dots within each pair of vertical bars represents the

---

[18] Inexperienced subjects were used in the first two sessions. Participants in the remaining sessions were drawn from the eighteen participants in sessions 1 and 2. The double-auction markets were conducted orally.

sequence of contracts in a trading period. Mean contract prices (for each period) and efficiencies (for each year) are listed across the bottom of the chart.

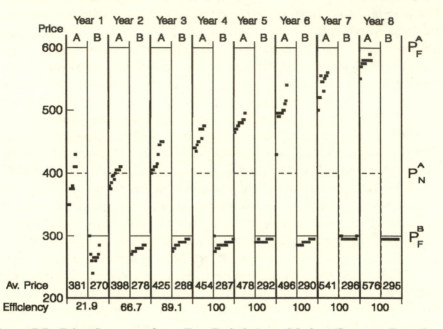

Figure 7.7 Price Sequence for a Two-Period Asset Market (Source: Forsythe, Palfrey, and Plott, 1982)

Two conclusions are apparent. First, and perhaps not surprising, the value of the asset in period B is evident to participants at the outset. Mean period B prices for the first two years are 270 and 278, respectively, and remain close to, but just below, 300 throughout the session. Second, although the naïve equilibrium has some appeal in period A of the early years, by the end of the session transactions prices tend to cluster about the perfect-foresight price prediction: In year 8, the mean trading price is within 25 francs of the full-information equilibrium prediction. This transition of prices from the naïve to the perfect-foresight price prediction is consistent with the pattern predicted under the swing-back hypothesis. The relatively slow climb in period A prices throughout the session indicates a gradual recognition by the market of the value of the asset.

Trading efficiency measures, printed along the bottom of figure 7.7, follow price performance. The trading efficiency of 21.9 percent in the first year is close to the prediction in the naïve equilibrium. But trading efficiency quickly increases in subsequent years, reaching 100 percent by year 4 and remaining at 100 percent throughout the remainder of the session. Very similar performance was observed in the other sessions. Aggregating over the four sessions, 46.5 percent of the total possible gains from trade were extracted in the first period, while mean trading efficiency for all years after the second was 98.9 percent.

The authors also conducted a fifth session that included a *futures* market, or a second market in period A, where participants were allowed to make agreements regarding the purchase and sale of asset units in period B. The futures market was introduced to evaluate the hypothesis that futures markets facilitate the attainment of a full-information equilibrium. Results of this single session support the notion that futures markets enhance the formation of the full-information predictions: a trading efficiency of 77 percent was generated in the first year, and the market was 100 percent efficient in every following year. This finding remains tentative, however, as the authors did not replicate this session. Moreover, participants in this final session were more experienced with the authors' asset-market design than were participants in other sessions.

In summary, Forsythe, Palfrey, and Plott established a simple environment where market trading transmits enough information for individuals (who possess only private information regarding individual payoffs) to generate full-information equilibrium predictions. The next section summarizes the results of experiments with asymmetries in information that provide more stringent tests of assumptions about rationality and market efficiency, assumptions that are common in the theoretical finance literature.

7.6 State Uncertainty and Insider Information

A second sort of informational problem in asset markets arises when there is state uncertainty that affects dividend payments. In the simplest case, only a single period is needed to investigate problems of this sort. Consider an asset that yields different returns to different participants at the end of a single trading period, as in the previous section's example. The highest-valued use of the asset, however, depends on an unknown state of nature (e.g., a random natural event that affects the relative demands for various products). Information regarding the state of nature is revealed only after asset trading is completed.

It is natural for some traders to have better information than others, perhaps as a result of research or of a chance discovery. Consider the extreme case in which some of the traders know precisely which state of nature will occur, and other traders do not know the state with certainty. Armed with this information, an insider would generally wish either to buy from or to sell to the uninformed traders. If the insider knows that the underlying state of nature, and if this state determines a dividend for him that exceeds the expected dividend of other traders, then the insider can profitably buy assets. If a market is an efficient mechanism for providing information, however, the purchases or sales of the informed traders should "leak" information to the uniformed traders. If this information is transmitted efficiently, the state uncertainty will be resolved, and full-information equilibrium predictions should be observed.

Plott and Sunder (1982) report an experiment in which market trading can reveal insider information. The experiment consisted of five sessions, each conducted under a slightly different parameterization. One of these parameterizations is summarized in table 7.5. In many respects, this single-period setup parallels the two-period, type-uncertainty design discussed above. The market consists of a series of seven-minute trading periods. In each period, traders are given the opportunity to alter the composition of their initial portfolio by either buying or selling assets. As indicated in the left column of the table, there are three types of traders, and four traders of each type, for a total of twelve traders. As before, each trader's initial portfolio consists of two asset units and 10,000 francs of working capital, which must be repaid at the end of the trading period.

Table 7.5 An Asset Market with State Uncertainty and Insider Information

Investor Type (# of traders)	Initial Portfolio		Dividend Value		Prior Probability		Expected Dividend
	Cash	Asset Units	State		State		
			X	Y	X	Y	
Type I (4)	10,000	2	400	100	.4	.6	220
Type II (4)	10,000	2	300	150	.4	.6	210
Type III (4)	10,000	2	125	175	.4	.6	155

Source: Plott and Sunder (1982).

The novelty of the Plott and Sunder design is that the dividend stream varies across two states of nature, X and Y, rather than over time. The structure of dividends, and the state probabilities are summarized under the columns labeled "dividend value" and "prior probability" in table 7.5. Type I traders earn the highest return (of 400 francs) if the state X occurs, while type III traders earn the highest return (of 175 francs) if state Y occurs. In the absence of prior information regarding the state of nature, the best that a market with risk-neutral agents could do is allocate asset units to the traders with the highest expected returns, which are calculated for each trader as the dividend in a given state of nature multiplied by the probability of the state, summed over all possible states. The expected return to type I traders, for example, is $(.4)(400) + (.6)(100) = 220$ francs. Expected returns for each trader type are printed in the right-most column of table 7.5. In the absence of inside information, type I traders have the highest expected valuation.

Insider information was provided in this design by passing out cards to all participants at the beginning of each trading period. On one-half of the cards, X or Y was revealed to be the underlying state. The remaining six cards were blank. Two traders of each type received marked cards, and the other two received blank cards. The insiders did not know which other traders were insiders, and the uniformed did not know either the state or the identities of the insiders.

Equilibrium predictions vary with the extent to which the information provided to the insiders leaks out to the rest of the market. Full-information equilibrium predictions are summarized in the first row of table 7.6. These predictions also vary with the state of nature, as is clear from reexamination of table 7.5. For example, if the state is X, then type I traders are the highest valued asset holders, and should purchase any assets available for prices below 400 francs. The equilibrium price prediction is 400 francs, since working capital endowments for each of the four type I traders create substantial excess demand at any price below 400. By identical reasoning, excess demand among the type III traders creates an equilibrium price prediction of 175 in the case of state Y. Trading efficiency is again defined in terms of the ratio of the observed gain in surplus over the no-trade condition to the maximum possible gain in surplus over the no-trade condition. As before, maximum trading efficiency is, by definition, 100 percent in each state.

The bottom row of table 7.6 provides predictions for a *private-information equilibrium*, where no information leakage occurs. These predictions vary with the state of nature. If the state is X, type I traders have the highest valuation for the units, and price and trading efficiency predictions are the same as in the full information equilibrium. The only difference between the full and private

Table 7.6 Equilibrium Predictions for an Asset Market with State Uncertainty

State	Price		Trader Type Holding Units		Trading Efficiency	
	X	Y	X	Y	X	Y
Full Information	400	175	type I (all)	type III (all)	100%	100%
Private Information	400	220	type I (insiders)	type I (outsiders)	100%	−125%

Source: Plott and Sunder (1982, Design III).

information equilibrium predictions in this case is in the allocation of units: In the private information equilibrium, only the two type I traders with inside information should purchase all units. The other two type I traders are uninformed and would not be willing to pay more than the expected dividend value of the asset, which is 220 (assuming risk neutrality). Predictions differ more substantially if the state of nature is Y. In this case the expected value of the asset for the uninformed type I traders, at 220 francs, exceeds the highest value to any informed trader, which is 175 francs for type III traders. In the private information equilibrium, informed traders should profit by dumping their units on the uniformed type I traders, who should pay up to 220 francs per unit. Losses for the uninformed type I traders are substantial in this equilibrium, as they pay 220 francs for units that prove to have a private value of only 100 francs.[19] The inefficiency that results from having units held by uninformed type I traders instead of type III traders amounts to 75 francs per unit. It can be shown that trading efficiency in this case is −125 percent, indicating that more social surplus would have been earned had no trading taken place at all.

Some idea of the relative drawing power of the alternative equilibria can be garnered from inspection of the sequence of contracts shown in figure 7.8, where trading periods are separated by vertical lines. The state is indicated by an (X) or (Y) after the period number at the bottom of the figure. This session was conducted with the parameters in table 7.5, and the horizontal lines represent rival equilibrium price predictions: The solid-line segments indicate the rational expectations price prediction. The dashed horizontal lines represent the private-information price prediction, when it differs from the full-information prediction.

In the middle eight periods of this session, conditions for the private-information treatment were in effect. Information leakage in the private-information periods is almost complete: prices in these periods are drawn to the full-information predictions in state Y, when the private- and full-information predictions diverge. Both price and trading efficiency allocations were closer to the full-information than to the private-information predictions in each of the five private-information periods characterized by state Y. Performance was particularly impressive in the final two periods with state Y, periods 8 and 10. Mean prices were within 10 francs of the full-information prediction in each case, and at least 98 percent of the trading efficiency was extracted. Performance of the full-information predictions under the inside-information treatment compares favorably with performance under common information conditions, as can be seen by examining the sequence of contracts in the first two periods (where all participants were uninformed) and the last two periods (where all participants were provided full information).

Examination of the earnings of insiders relative to the uninformed traders provides additional evidence regarding the extent of information leakage. Insiders have an incentive to exploit their information by striking profitable contracts with the uninformed side of the market. To the extent leakage occurs, uninformed traders

---

[19]   Thus, every unit purchased by a type I trader for 220 francs results in a loss of 120 francs. As a result, losses and even bankruptcies are quite likely for the uninformed type I traders.

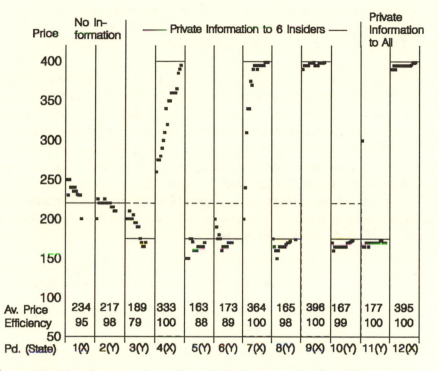

Figure 7.8 Price Sequence for a Single-Period Asset under State Uncertainty (Source: Plott and Sunder, 1982)

learn about the underlying state of nature from the market, and profits for informed and uninformed traders will be similar. In the market illustrated in figure 7.8, insider earnings were more than twice those of the outsiders in the first period in which insider information was provided. However, this ratio declined quickly. In the remaining seven periods, the ratio exceeded 1.3 only once and was less that 1.05 in four instances.

The market illustrated in figure 7.8 is representative of performance in the other sessions reported by Plott and Sunder. Aggregating across four sessions, trading efficiency was 45.5 percent in the periods where full and private information predictions differ.[20] (Bear in mind that trading efficiency predictions are 100 percent in the full-information equilibrium and vary between −112 percent and −133 percent in the private-information equilibrium, depending on the

---

[20] The authors exclude session 1 from their aggregate calculations because evaluation of performance is complicated by the presentation of probabilistic sample information.

parameterization.[21]) Excluding the first period of the inside information treatment in each session, the earnings of insiders relative to "outsiders" averaged 1.23.

State Uncertainty and Information Aggregation

The environment discussed in the preceding subsection constitutes a specific case in which the market *disseminates* information regarding an uncertain state of nature. Some economists have argued that a market can have a more remarkable effect as an *aggregator* of disparate information. The idea is that individual traders may have only bits of information regarding the unknown state of nature. Although no single individual has enough inside information to determine the true state, collectively there is enough information to resolve the uncertainty. If the act of trading in the market effectively aggregates this disparate information, then uncertainty would be resolved via trading, and contracts, allocations, and efficiencies would best be predicted by a full-information equilibrium.

Table 7.7 An Asset Market with State Uncertainty and Incomplete Information

	Initial Portfolio				
	Cash	Units	Dividend by State		
State (probabilities)			X (.35)	Y (.20)	Z (.45)
Type I, 6 traders	10,000	2	70	160	300
Type II, 6 traders	10,000	2	230	90	60

Source: Forsythe and Lundholm (1990).

A variant of the design discussed above provides a simple setting for evaluating information aggregation. Consider the twelve-person market for a single-period asset of the type summarized in table 7.7. Each trader is given two asset units and a working capital endowment of 10,000 francs, which must be repaid in its entirety at the end of the period. As can be seen in the table, there are two trader types and three states of nature. The states of nature, denoted X, Y, and Z, occur with probabilities .35, .20, and .45, respectively.

---

[21] In these periods, market efficiency (as opposed to trading efficiency) was 88.3 percent on average.

Information was provided by passing a slip of paper to each participant at the beginning of a period, informing them of one state that will not occur. For example, if six participants are told "not Y," and if six other participants are told "not X," then enough information exists in the market to determine that the state is Z. Full- and private-information equilibrium predictions are calculated as before, and are state contingent. If the state of nature is Z, for example, then under the full-information prediction, the six type I traders should hold all asset units at the end of the period, and competition among these traders for the available units should drive the price up to 300 francs. Similarly, in a full-information equilibrium, type II traders will purchase assets for 230 francs if the underlying state is X.

Private-information predictions are also state dependent. The calculation of these predictions, however, is complicated by the addition of the third possible state. Although a partially informative message does not remove uncertainty, it does allow each trader-type to refine or update their expectation regarding asset value. If a type I trader is given the message "not Z," for example, then the asset value will be determined either by state X or state Y. Given the information that Z is not possible, the prior probabilities of X and Y (.35 and .20, respectively) should be scaled up proportionally to sum to 1. Therefore, the postmessage *posterior probability* of X is .35/(.35+.20) = .64, and the posterior probability of Y is .20/(.35+.20) = .36.[22] The expected asset value is the sum of the products of these posterior probabilities and the associated dividends, that is, .64(70) + .36(160) = 103 francs. Expected valuation updates for other trader/message combinations are determined similarly and are listed in table 7.8.

For each state there are two possible messages; for example, when the state is X, the messages are "not Y" and "not Z." The combination of two trader types and two messages creates four expected valuations for the asset under each of the

Table 7.8 Expected Dividends in an Asset Market with State Uncertainty and Incomplete Information

	Expected Dividends			
	No Information	Not X	Not Y	Not Z
Type I, 6 traders	191.5	257	199	103
Type II, 6 traders	125.5	69	134	179

Source: Forsythe and Lundholm (1990).

---

[22] This scaling up of prior probabilities to account for new information is an example of Bayes' rule, which is further discussed in chapter 8.

possible states. In a private-information equilibrium, the asset will go to the trader-type/message combination with the highest expected value, at the price equal to the highest expected value. If X is the state of nature, for example, then each type I and II trader will receive either a "not Y" or a "not Z" message. The four trader-type/message combinations generate the updated expected dividends summarized in the right-most two columns of table 7.8. The highest of these four numbers, 199, is the expected dividend for trader I types with a "not Y" message. Bidding by trader I types with the "not Y" message generates the equilibrium price prediction of 199. Other private-information predictions are generated in a similar fashion. For brevity, we do not enumerate these predictions. However, as before, the rational-expectations hypothesis can be evaluated by comparing observed prices, efficiencies, and allocations in instances where partial- and full-information predictions differ.[23]

The reader should consider for a moment the informative task that the rational expectations hypothesis imposes on the market. Participants know neither the dividend profiles nor the messages received by others. Further, they may communicate in the market only via bids, offers, and acceptances. The underlying state of nature could be inferred by participants only in the event that sufficiently high or low prices allow them to rule out one of two possible remaining states. Plott and Sunder (1988) failed to observe information aggregation in variants of the design summarized in table 7.7.[24] In a subsequent investigation, however, Forsythe and Lundholm (1990) determined that the added conditions of experience with the environment (though not necessarily with the same cohort, or the same payoff parameters) and complete information about the structure of payoffs were jointly sufficient to generate full-information equilibrium predictions. The full-information condition seems plausible in this context, since information regarding possible payoffs is necessary for participants to rule out particular states of nature from market price observations. Copeland and Friedman (1987) also find considerable aggregation of private information in a somewhat different environment, where bits

---

[23] Plott and Sunder (1988) and Forsythe and Lundholm (1990) also evaluate market performance in light of the predictions of a third, "maximin" equilibrium concept, in which all traders base valuations on the largest minimum payoff in each state. Maximin predictions had very little drawing power in either experiment.

[24] Plott and Sunder (1988) did, however, identify some simpler environments where information aggregation occurred. For example, full-information equilibrium predictions were generated in a design where there were three states of nature, but only a single trader type. These authors also observed full-information predictions in series of markets in a multiple-asset design, where agents negotiated over assets that generated a positive return only in a given state of nature (e.g., a Y-asset was worth 70 francs if the state of nature was Y, and worth 0 otherwise). Intuitively, one might expect traders to transmit considerably more information regarding the state of nature when trading such "state-contingent" assets. In this design, a "not-Y" message, for example, informs half the market that type-Y assets are worthless. Efforts to sell off this asset to the uninformed side of the market may reduce its price enough to inform the entire market that Y is not the underlying state.

of information are sequentially revealed to different trader types throughout the course of a trading period.[25]

Copeland and Friedman (1991) further exploit the sequential-information character of their environment to construct and test a model of the way that private information is disseminated to the market. The basic idea is that participants transmit signals of "good" or "bad" news (e.g., high or low dividends) by either raising bids or lowering asks. The very clever feature of the authors' model is that they are able to predict distinct bid- and ask-changing responses or signals for each possible bit of private information. In an experiment consisting of sixteen market sessions, Copeland and Friedman report behavior that conforms more closely to the predictions of their signaling model than to predictions of a "strong form" of the rational expectations hypothesis. The authors note, however, that some refinement of their signaling or partial revelation model remains necessary, since it does not outperform strong-form rational expectations predictions in all respects. Most importantly, pricing behavior more nearly conformed to the strong-form rational expectations predictions.

Summary

The asset-market studies summarized here are significant, both because they provide simple frameworks for evaluating subtle rationality predictions and because they isolate baseline conditions in which the market successfully serves the informative role predicted under rational expectations. But most of the designs represent highly stylized "best-case" scenarios. It is unclear how the informative role of markets will work in even slightly more complicated contexts. Friedman, Harrison, and Salmon (1984) examined a series of designs with type and state uncertainty, but generalized to three periods. The data reported by these authors were remarkably supportive of the theoretical predictions in each case. However, Anderson et al. (1992) encountered a great deal of difficulty in replicating the simplest of the Friedman, Harrison, and Salmon's oral-auction results in the computerized NovaNet environment. Anderson et al. did observe prices "swinging back" to the full-information prediction in a three-period asset market with no state uncertainty, but only with participants who had participated twice in previous sessions using a similar design, and who had previous experience with the computerized double action.[26] In further contrast to Friedman, Harrison, and

---

[25] To be more precise, Copeland and Friedman distinguish private information predictions from both "strong" and "weak" versions of the rational expectations hypothesis (see their paper for definitions). In their design, information aggregation is predicted to occur only under strong-form rational expectations. Results reported by the authors are most consistent with strong-form rational expectations predictions.

[26] Subjects in the Friedman, Harrison, and Salmon study were apparently inexperienced (there is no reference to experience level in the paper). The subjects were MBA students at UCLA.

Salmon, and to the other papers in this literature, the three-period markets conducted by Anderson et al. exhibited significant speculative pricing behavior in the early parts of sessions.[27]

Similarly, in a first experiment regarding information aggregation, Plott and Sunder (1988) were unable to generate full-information equilibrium outcomes in the baseline design described above, but in an environment where participants did not have complete information about other traders' dividend profiles.

Other aspects of the baseline designs described above are highly restrictive, and the resilience of full-information predictions to these alterations deserves close attention. In all of the above experiments, for example, each trader has enough working capital to purchase all others' asset units at the full-information price. This budget flexibility allows informed traders the opportunity to control outcomes inordinately. It might be instructive to evaluate the capacity of informed traders to manipulate markets when they have a more limited capacity to leak information.

7.7 The Iowa Presidential Stock Market

In November 1988, Douglas Wilder was running for the governorship of Virginia, and if elected, he would become the first elected black governor of any state since Reconstruction. Just prior to the election, opinion polls showed Wilder to have a comfortable margin over his Republican opponent from the suburbs of northern Virginia. Although race was not an overt issue and there were no dramatic developments in the final days of the campaign, Wilder won by a only very narrow margin. The conventional wisdom was that some voters, who were wary of appearing to be racist, were reluctant to admit to pollsters that they were voting against Wilder. Another situation in which polls can be biased occurs in countries where governments restrict pollsters in an effort to cover up voting fraud. For example, Daniel Ortega led in the polls in Nicaragua, only to lose overwhelmingly to Mrs. Chamorro. Even in "normal" elections in the United States, polls are notoriously inaccurate. The Gallup poll forecast that is released on the weekend prior to the presidential election has failed to fall inside of the 95 percent confidence interval (determined by sample size of the poll) in four of the last nine elections.[28]

---

[27] Given Williams' initial work on the effects of computerization discussed in chapter 3, it is perhaps not surprising that computerized asset markets take longer to converge to the rational expectations outcome. One possible conjecture is that computerized trading leads to different behavior than oral trading, at least initially. In any case, traders clearly have different information sets in these two environments.

[28] Even when the Gallup organization adjusted the responses, using a rule to allocate undecided voters, the adjusted predictions fell outside of the 95 percent confidence interval in six of the last nine presidential elections (Forsythe et al., 1992). Exit polls taken on election day are much more accurate.

Economists are often skeptical of the results of surveys, since the respondents have no financial incentive to be truthful about how and whether they are going to vote. Pollsters try to identify respondents who are not likely to vote, but this is a very difficult task, especially in the United States, where voter participation rates are relatively low. Indeed, a person who does not plan to vote but who has a strong preference for a particular candidate (e.g., a protest candidate) may have some incentive to misrepresent the likelihood of voting. One interesting question is whether laboratory market institutions, which are efficient aggregators of information in asset market experiments, would be useful in obtaining an continuous indicator of public opinion in the field.

Although there are various anecdotes about election stock markets that are conducted at various graduate economics and business schools, these operations have been informal and have generated low trading volume. One problem is that the common setup is for an asset that represents a candidate to pay a dividend only in the event that the candidate wins. Therefore, an asset that corresponds to a weak candidate would have almost no value for any participant, and trading volume would be very low due to the low dispersion of individual valuations.

Forsythe et al. (1992) devised a mechanism that avoids this winner-take-all property. This market pertained to the 1988 presidential election, and participants could purchase a number of units, each of which would provide a share of Bush, a share of Dukakis, a share of Jackson, and a share of "rest of field." Each unit cost $2.50, and each share paid a dividend that equaled the product of the unit price ($2.50) and the proportion of the popular vote received by the candidate. Since the candidates' vote proportions sum to 1, a subject who bought a unit and held all shares without trading would simply recover the initial investment.

Consider how participants would value such shares. Since each share pays the vote percentage times the unit price ($2.50), a person who is sure that Bush will obtain 50 percent of the vote would be willing to pay up to $1.25 for a share of Bush. Normally, a participant is somewhat uncertain about the percentage that any candidate will obtain, and a risk-neutral person would be willing to pay the expected dividend, that is, $2.50 times the person's expected value of the vote proportion for the candidate in question. Moreover, these beliefs could be affected by the market activity. For example, a person who is very sure that Dukakis will win 60 percent of the vote may have second thoughts if the highest outstanding bid is only $1.00, corresponding to a 40 percent vote for Dukakis (since $1.00/2.50 = .40$).

The 1988 presidential stock market was open to all University of Iowa students and employees, and 191 people participated. A mail survey taken in September revealed that participants in the Iowa market were slightly more likely to be Republicans and less likely to be independents, in comparison with the United States population in general, as indicated by a New York Times/CBS survey taken in the same week. Bush enjoyed a three-point lead over Dukakis in the Iowa mail survey, as compared with a six-point edge in the NYT/CBS survey.

Trading was done in a double auction, using computer terminals that were attached to a central mainframe. Traders could enter bids and offers, with quantity limits and expiration times specified by the trader. Short sales were not allowed. Only the lowest offer and highest bid were displayed. Except for a brief shutdown for daily computer maintenance, the market was open continuously from June 1 until the opening of the polls on election day. Since the dividend payments exactly equaled the initial stakes, aggregate net earnings were 0, as in any betting pool. Individuals earned money through dividends, and earnings and losses were incurred through purchases and sales of shares. The largest profit for any trader was a gain of $13.54, on a total initial investment of 100 units ($250.00), and the largest loss was $22.48, on a total investment of $95.00.

The market opened on June 1, 1988, and despite the initial publicity, relatively few shares were traded in the first 3 weeks. The daily closing prices (prior to the computer maintenance) can be divided by $2.50 to obtain the implied vote proportions for each candidate. The time series of Bush's lead in percentage points is shown in figure 7.9. Notice that Bush is generally trailing by several points in June and July, with one notable exception being in early July just after the announcement of Bentsen as Dukakis's running mate (see "Bentsen" marked on time series). The Gallup poll results are indicated by an asterisk plotted on the final day of the polling period.[29] The Gallup poll showed Bush to be trailing by twelve percentage points in early June, and leading by five points in July. These and subsequent swings in the poll results appear to be much more volatile than the stock market price movements, and the poll does not seem to lead or "cause" movements in the presidential stock market. Forsythe et al. note that other national polls also show more volatility than is indicated in the stock price time series.

The Gallup poll and the stock market percentages shift at about the same time in late August when Bush takes the lead, just after the Republican convention.[30] The first debate seems to have had no impact, which is not surprising since the conventional wisdom was that there was no clear winner. Quayle was widely viewed as the loser in the second (vice-presidential) debate, but the stock prices do not change much, presumably because expectations about Quayle's performance were so low that the debate produced little new information. The third debate, which Dukakis is widely thought to have lost, seems to have contained new information, and the Bush lead jumped, both in the market and in the Gallup poll. There was a very high volume of trade just before and just after this debate. A survey of the participants revealed that buyers (sellers) of Bush shares generally thought that he had won (lost) the debate, and that the latter opinions were correlated

---

[29] The poll would be reported several days later.

[30] There was very little trading early and mid August, while most students and faculty were on vacation, and consequently, the stock prices during this period do not contain much information.

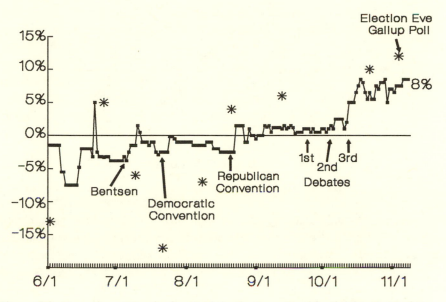

Figure 7.9 Percentage Margin for Bush in the Iowa Presidential Stock Market (connected line) and in the Gallup Poll (*) (Source: Forsythe et al., 1992)

with political preferences. The Bush lead, as implied by market prices, leveled off in the final weeks and ended up at 8 percent prior to the voting. Bush's lead in the Gallup poll continued to climb and finished at 12 percent. The final margin of victory for Bush in the popular vote was 7.8 percent, and the poll outcomes flanked this, as shown in figure 7.10.

One episode with Jackson shares illustrates the importance of financial motivation. After Jackson's convention speech in which he vowed to support the Democratic candidate, trading in Jackson shares was thin, presumably because of the low variance in individual valuations. As a consequence, it was possible for dedicated supporters to "send a message to Jesse" by trading shares of Jackson stock at prices of several pennies. But if the price rose to a level above a nickel, other traders would notice, and the flood of sell offers would increase the cost of sending a message and drive the price down.

Although it is dangerous to generalize on the basis of one experiment, the results are promising. The market outperformed the polls, and by providing a continuous time series of expected vote percentages, it was able to gauge the effects of major events, relative to prior expectations. The authors have subsequently implemented stock markets for elections in Germany, the United States, and Turkey,

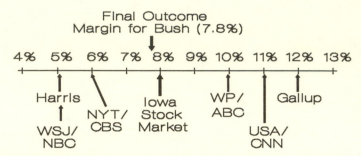

Figure 7.10 Percentage Margin for Bush on Election Eve, 1988 (Source: Forsythe, et al., 1992)

with similar results.[31]   Although the political stock markets have been highly accurate in European elections, they have not done consistently better or worse than election-eve polls. This may be because the European polls are often more accurate, perhaps due to higher voter turnout rates. Even in this context, however, political stock markets have the advantage of providing a continuous data series.

7.8 Conclusion

In this chapter we have considered a variety of clever experimental designs for dealing with asymmetric information. Three main conclusions emerge. First, informational asymmetries can seriously degrade laboratory market performance; when buyers cannot observe product quality in advance, inefficiently low quality can result.   Second, these inefficient outcomes can sometimes be averted, without external regulation of quality, through the development of seller reputations or through seller choices of observable signals. Third, in some instances the market trading process itself can play an important efficiency-enhancing role by disseminating privately held insider information or by aggregating disparate bits of information. Additional experimental research remains to be done, however, as the robustness of each of these conclusions has not been established. Moreover, there is a large theoretical literature identifying circumstances when each of these conclusions either will or will not hold, which provides a rich source of laboratory research topics.

---

[31]   These authors obtained clearance from the Securities and Exchange Commission to conduct an expanded, interstate version of the presidential stock market for the 1992 presidential election, using participants from several universities.

APPENDIX A7

A7.1 Instructions: A Market Experiment with Information Asymmetries

Today we are going to set up a market in which half of you will be buyers and the other half will be sellers. The decisions that you make will determine your earnings, in dollars and cents. You will keep track of these earnings on the form provided. All money that you earn during the trading will be yours to keep and will be paid to you, privately, in cash at the end of the session today.[32]

On your desk, you will find a sheet labeled "Buyer Decision Sheet" or "Seller Decision Sheet," which will be used to calculate your earnings. The information that you record on this sheet is private, please do not reveal it to anyone. You should now look at your decision sheet to see whether you are a buyer or a seller. Has everyone done this?

First, I will read instructions as to how buyers and sellers will compute their earnings, then I will explain how buyers and sellers arrange sales and purchases in the market. Trading will occur in a sequence of market periods, each of which will last for about five to ten minutes. After reading the instructions, I will give you a chance to ask questions. Then we will move the sellers into a nearby room before the first trading period begins, and each person will be given identification numbers at that time, for sellers these will be S1, S2, . . . , and for buyers these will be B1, B2, ...

Specific Instructions for Sellers

The Seller Decision Sheet attached to these instructions will be used to record your decisions and earnings. As can be seen from the top of the decision sheet, there will be a number of market periods, and there is a column for each. In each period, you will have a single unit of the commodity, which you may either keep or sell to a buyer. If you keep the unit, you will earn the amount to be listed in row 1 of your Seller Decision Sheet, marked *value of unit to you*. The unit value in row 1 will be determined by the throw of a six-sided die at the start of each period, as explained below. After this value is determined, you will be asked to post a price at which the unit is offered for sale; this price is then recorded in row 2. You may write "no sale" in row 2 if you do not wish to offer the unit for sale. If your unit sells, you receive the sale price in row 2. If your unit does not sell, you receive the unit value in row 1. Row 3 will be used to inform you of whether or not your unit

---

[32] If this experiment is done for classroom demonstration and cash earnings are not to be paid, substitute: These earnings are hypothetical; nobody will make or receive actual cash payments.

sold. Your earnings for the period are recorded in row 4. To summarize, in each market period, you earn either the unit value or the sale price, not both. After recording your earnings for the period in row 4, you can calculate your cumulative earnings and record the amount in row 5. Earnings for subsequent periods will be calculated in subsequent columns in the same manner. Notice that you begin period 1 with a cumulative earnings balance of $6.00, as shown on the left side of row 5.

The value of the unit to you will be determined at the beginning of each period by the throw of a six-sided die. The result of the die is multiplied by 10 cents to determine your unit value. Therefore, the unit values of $0.10, $0.20, $0.30, $0.40, $0.50, and $0.60 will be equally likely.

Specific Instructions for Buyers

The Buyer Decision Sheet attached to these instructions should be used to record your decisions and earnings. As can be seen from the top of your decision sheet, there will be a number of market periods, and there is a column for each. In each period, you will have the opportunity to buy a single unit of the commodity, without knowing its precise value. The current owner of the product, who is the potential seller, knows more about the unit's current value than you know as the potential buyer. On the other hand, the unit will be worth 1.5 times more to you than it is to the current owner. Specifically, the relationship between possible buyer and seller values is listed below:

throw of die	1	2	3	4	5	6
value to seller	$0.10	$0.20	$0.30	$0.40	$0.50	$0.60
value to buyer	$0.15	$0.30	$0.45	$0.60	$0.75	$0.90

The value of each seller's unit is determined by the throw of a fair six-sided die to be either $0.10, $0.20, $0.30, $0.40, $0.50, or $0.60. Each of these outcomes is equally likely. The bottom row of the table shows that the value to you is 1.5 times the value to the seller. At the time that you decide whether or not to make a purchase, you will not know the value to the seller (and hence you will not know the value to you). If you purchase a unit, your earnings will be equal to the difference between the value to you and the purchase price.

If you buy a unit, you should enter the purchase price in row 2 of the Buyer Decision Sheet at the time of purchase. You will subsequently be told the *value of the unit to you*, which is to be entered in row 1. If you purchase a unit, your earnings are the difference between the value to you in row 1 and the purchase price in row 2. This difference is recorded in row 3, labeled *earnings on purchase*. If the value of the unit to you turns out to be less than the purchase price, your earnings from purchase will be negative and should be entered in row 3 with a minus sign.

If you do not purchase a unit, you should enter $0 in row 3. Regardless of whether or not you make a purchase, you will receive $0.35 in each period for participating, as indicated in row 4. Your earnings for the period, to be recorded in row 5, are the sum of the *earnings from purchase* in row 3 and the $0.35 participation payment in row 4. To summarize, in each market period, you will receive $0.35 plus any earnings (minus any losses) from purchasing a unit. After recording your earnings or loss for a period in row 5, you can calculate your cumulative earnings and record the amount in row 6. If your earnings are positive, your cumulative earnings go up by that amount; if your earnings for the period are negative, your cumulative earnings go down by that amount. Earnings for subsequent periods will be calculated in subsequent columns in the same manner. Notice that you begin period 1 with a cumulative earnings balance of $6.00, as shown on the left side of row 6.

Market Organization

At the beginning of each market period, one of us will go to the desk of each of the sellers and throw the six-sided die to determine that particular seller's unit value for the period. Unit values can differ from seller to seller and from period to period. After seeing his/her own value, each seller is given two minutes to write a price offer in row 2 of the Seller Decision Sheet (in the column for that period). After all sellers have chosen their prices for the period, the Seller decision sheets will be collected and the prices of units offered for sale (but *not* the seller values) will be written on the blackboard in the room with the buyers. For each unit offered, the seller's price will be recorded below the seller's identification number.

Once sellers' prices are posted below their identification numbers, buyers will be given the chance to make purchases if they wish to do so. A buyer will be chosen using a random device and will be given the chance to purchase a unit from one of the sellers or to decline to purchase. If the buyer makes a purchase, the buyer's identification number will be written below the seller's price. For example, if buyer 1 makes a purchase from seller 2, the blackboard will appear:

Seller	S1	S2	S3
Price	$x.xx	$x.xx	$x.xx
Buyer		B1	

At this point, S2 has sold his/her unit for the period and is out of stock.

When the first buyer selected has made this decision and has recorded the purchase price (if a purchase was made), another buyer will be selected at random and will make a decision similarly, choosing among the seller(s) who have not previously sold a unit. The process will be continued until all buyers have had a chance to make purchases. Then the decision sheets of buyers who made purchases will be collected and matched with the corresponding sellers. The value to the buyer (1.5 times the value to the seller) will be recorded in row 1 of the Buyer Decision Sheet. For each unit that sells, a "yes" will be recorded in "unit sold" row 3 of the Seller Decision Sheet, otherwise a "no" is recorded. Then the decision sheets are returned and earnings are calculated. This completes the trading period. Buyers and sellers are not to discuss any aspect of the trading process during or between periods. We will reopen the subsequent trading period by throwing the die to give each seller a new value before sellers select their prices.

Summary of Procedures

1. Throw dice to determine the unit value for each seller.
2. Each seller chooses a price and records it.
3. Collect Seller Decision Sheets and take them to the buyers' room.
4. Write sellers' prices (along with their ID numbers) on the blackboard.
5. Select buyers randomly in sequence, and let them make purchases.
6. Collect Buyer Decision Sheets and record buyer values in row 1.
7. Record units sold (yes or no) in row 3 of each Seller Decision Sheet.
8. Return Buyer and Seller Decision Sheets.
9. Calculate earnings for the period, and update cumulative earnings.

Final Observations

A seller receives a unit in each period, with a value between $.10 and $.60. A seller earns money by keeping the unit, or selling it to a buyer. A buyer receives $.35 in each period. A buyer may earn additional money by purchasing a unit from a seller.

Each of you will begin the experiment with an initial earnings balance of $6.00. You should keep track of your cumulative earnings after each period. You will be paid privately in cash immediately after the experiment. If your cumulative earnings fall below $3.00, then you will be paid the $3.00 and excused from the remainder of the experiment.

Are there any questions at this point? We now begin the periods that will affect your earnings. There will be five periods. Please do not talk to each other during the experiment; raise your hand if you have any questions. One of us will be present in each room at all times. Now we will take the sellers to a nearby room and give identification numbers to all buyers and sellers.[33]

---

[33] In a classroom demonstration, buyers and sellers may remain in the same room. In this case replace the final two sentences with: "Sellers should now move to a seat in the back of the room and face the back wall. Buyers should remain in the front of the room, facing the blackboard. Now we will

Seller Decision Sheet
identification #: S__

Period Number

	1	2	3	4	5
(1) Value of unit to you					
(2) Offer price					
(3) Unit sold (yes or no)					
(4) Earnings for period from (1) or (2)					
(5) Cumulative earnings (start with $6.00)					

Buyer Decision Sheet
identification #: B__

Period Number

	1	2	3	4	5
(1) Value of unit to you					
(2) Purchase price					
(3) Earnings on purchase					
(4) Participation payment	$0.35	$0.35	$0.35	$0.35	$0.35
(5) Earnings for period (3) + (4)					
(6) Cumulative earnings (start with $6.00)					

privately give identification numbers to buyers and sellers."

REFERENCES

Akerlof, George A. (1970) "The Market for 'Lemons': Qualitative Uncertainty and the Market Mechanism," *Quarterly Journal of Economics*, *84*, 488–500.

Anderson, Scott, David Johnston, James Walker, and Arlington Williams (1992) "The Efficiency of Experimental Asset Markets: Empirical Robustness and Subject Sophistication," forthcoming in R. Mark Isaac, ed., *Research in Experimental Economics*, vol. 4. Greenwich, Conn.: JAI Press.

Banks, Jeffrey S., Colin F. Camerer, and David Porter (1990) "An Experimental Analysis of Nash Refinements in Signaling Games," forthcoming in *Journal of Games and Economic Behavior*.

Berg, Joyce E., L. Daley, John Dickhaut, and J. O'Brien (1985) "Tests of the Principal-Agent Theory in An Experimental Setting," working paper, University of Minnesota.

Brandts, Jordi, and Charles A. Holt (1991) "An Experimental Test of Equilibrium Dominance in Signaling Games," forthcoming in *American Economic Review*.

Cadsby, Charles B., Murray Frank, and Vojislav Maksimovic (1992) "Equilibrium Dominance in Experimental Financial Markets," working paper, University of Guelph.

Camerer, Colin, and Keith Weigelt (1988) "Experimental Tests of a Sequential Equilibrium Reputation Model," *Econometrica*, *56*, 1–36.

Cheung, Steven N. S. (1969) "Transaction Costs, Risk Aversion and the Choice of Contractual Arrangements," *Journal of Law and Economics*, *12*, 23–42.

Cho, In-Koo, and David M. Kreps (1987) "Signaling Games and Stable Equilibria," *Quarterly Journal of Economics*, *102*, 179–221.

Copeland, Thomas E., and Daniel Friedman (1987) "The Effect of Sequential Information Arrival on Asset Prices: An Experimental Study," *Journal of Finance*, *42*, 763–797.

——— (1991) "Partial Revelation of Information in Experimental Asset Markets," *Journal of Finance*, *46*, 265–295.

Davis, Douglas, and Charles A. Holt (1990) "Equilibrium Cooperation in Three-Person Choice-of-Partner Games," working paper, Virginia Commonwealth University.

DeJong, D. V., Robert Forsythe, and Russell Lundholm (1985) "Ripoffs, Lemons, and Reputation Formation in Agency Relationships: A Laboratory Market Study," *Journal of Finance*, *40*, 809–820.

DeJong, D. V., Robert Forsythe, and Wilfred C. Uecker (1985) "The Methodology of Laboratory Markets and Its Implications for Agency Research in Accounting and Auditing," *Journal of Accounting Research*, *23*, 753–793.

DeJong, D. V., Robert Forsythe, Russell Lundholm, and Wilfred C. Uecker (1985) "A Laboratory Investigation of the Moral Hazard Problem in an Agency Relationship," *Journal of Accounting Research, 23* (supp.), 81–123.

Forsythe, Robert, Forrest Nelson, George Neumann, and Jack Wright (1992) "Forecasting the 1988 Presidential Election: A Field Experiment," working paper, University of Iowa, forthcoming in M. Isaac, ed., *Research in Experimental Economics*, vol. 4. Greenwich, Conn.: JAI Press.

Forsythe, Robert, Thomas R. Palfrey, and Charles R. Plott (1982) "Asset Valuation in an Experimental Market," *Econometrica, 50,* 537–582.

———— (1984) "Futures Markets and Informational Efficiency: A Laboratory Examination," *Journal of Finance, 39,* 955–981.

Forsythe, Robert, and Russell Lundholm (1990) "Information Aggregation in an Experimental Market," *Econometrica, 58,* 309–347.

Friedman, Daniel, Glenn Harrison, and Jon Salmon (1984) "The Informational Efficiency of Experimental Asset Markets," *Journal of Political Economy, 92,* 349–408.

Holt, Charles A., and Roger Sherman (1990) "Advertising and Product Quality in Posted-Offer Experiments," *Economic Inquiry, 28,* 39–56.

Lynch, Michael, Ross M. Miller, Charles R. Plott, and Russell Porter (1986) "Product Quality, Consumer Information and 'Lemons' in Experimental Markets," in P. M. Ippolito and D. T. Scheffman, eds., *Empirical Approaches to Consumer Protection Economics.* Washington, D.C.: Federal Trade Commission, Bureau of Economics, 251–306.

Miller, Ross M., and Charles R. Plott (1985) "Product Quality Signaling in Experimental Markets," *Econometrica, 53,* 837–872.

Nelson, Phillip (1970) "Information and Consumer Behavior," *Journal of Political Economy, 78,* 311–329.

———— (1974) "Advertising as Information," *Journal of Political Economy, 82,* 729–754.

Plott, Charles R., and Louis Wilde (1982) "Professional Diagnosis vs. Self-Diagnosis: An Experimental Examination of Some Special Features of Markets with Uncertainty," in V. L. Smith, ed., *Research in Experimental Economics*, vol. 2. Greenwich, Conn.: JAI Press, 63–112.

Plott, Charles R., and Shyam Sunder (1982) "Efficiency of Experimental Security Markets with Insider Information: An Application of Rational-Expectations Models," *Journal of Political Economy, 90,* 663–698.

———— (1988) "Rational Expectations and the Aggregation of Diverse Information in Laboratory Security Markets," *Econometrica, 56,* 1085–1118.

Spence, A. Michael (1974) *Market Signaling: Informational Transfer in Hiring and Related Screening Processes.* Cambridge: Harvard University Press.

Stiglitz, Joseph E. (1975) "The Theory of 'Screening,' Education, and the Distribution of Income," *American Economic Review, 65,* 283–300.

CHAPTER 8

INDIVIDUAL DECISIONS IN RISKY SITUATIONS

8.1 Introduction

At the very foundation of neoclassical economics stands an assumption regarding individual behavior: Economic agents, either firms or households, are presumed to behave in a rational, self-interested manner. In simple situations this basic assumption seems almost trivial. It places little strain on the imagination, for example, to presume that firms prefer more profits to less. In more complex circumstances, however, individual optimization implies that agents behave in a manner that is consistent with solutions of rather complicated calculations under conditions of stochastic and even imperfect information. The relevance of these theories turns on whether agents behave as if they make such calculations. Of particular interest has been the economists' standard approach to modeling decisions in uncertain environments: the expected utility theory of Savage (1954) and von Neumann and Morgenstern (1947).

Laboratory evaluations of expected utility theory have typically been conducted in the context of questions that cleanly isolate particular assumptions. Often the questions involve choices between paired lotteries. Consider, for example, the following two questions. First, make a choice between lotteries *S1* and *R1*:

S1 $3,000 with certainty   or   *R1* $4,000   with probability .8
                                                           $0   with probability .2

Now make a choice between the lotteries *R2* and *S2*:

S2 $3,000 with probability .25 or   *R2* $4,000   with probability .2
       $0   with probability .75 $0   with probability .8

Regardless of whether people are asked to make these decisions under hypothetical conditions, as you have been asked to do, or under real payoff conditions (in scaled-down versions of the above lotteries), there is a predominant response pattern: Participants tend to select "safe" lottery *S1* in the top pair of lotteries, for a certain payoff of $3,000, and then to select "risky" lottery *R2*, which gives a .2 chance of $4,000, in the bottom pair. Although typical, such a choice pattern is inconsistent in the following sense: Each bottom lottery, left or right, is generated by taking a 3/4 chance of zero and a 1/4 chance of the lottery directly above it. In the right-hand lotteries, for example, a 3/4 chance of 0 and a 1/4 chance of ($4,000 with probability .8) is just $4,000 with probability .2, since .2 equals 1/4 of .8.

If you are convinced that the choice between the first pair of lotteries should be independent of the incorporation of a 3/4 chance that either lottery will pay nothing, then the typical choice pattern is a puzzle. This choice pattern is an anomaly in the sense that any person whose behavior corresponds to the maximization of the expected value of a utility function would either prefer the left-hand lottery in each pair or the right-hand lottery in each pair. This particular anomaly is an example of the "common-ratio problem," where the term is due to the fact that the probability of the positive outcome in the first pair is reduced by the same proportion to obtain the second lottery pair.

An anomaly of this nature may not trouble a statistical decision theorist, who views expected utility theory as a prescription for how decisions should be made. Decision theorists consider it their job to assist people in calculating the relevant conditional probabilities, determining their (von Neumann-Morgenstern) utility function, and using this information to generate an optimal decision. Under hypothetical payoff conditions, such an anomaly may not even trouble an economist. But, given significant individual or market incentives, these anomalies are indeed troublesome for economists, who typically *assume* that individuals behave as if maximizing expected utility. The value of expected utility theory for an economist depends on its predictive power. This predictive power has been questioned from the beginning; at about the time that Savage (1954) completed his classic work on decision theory, Allais (1953) described an anomaly that is similar to common-ratio problem discussed above. Even Savage is reported to have answered lottery-choice questions in a manner that violates a basic axiom of expected utility theory.

Psychologists and economists have found a variety of anomalies in which a majority of subjects make decisions that appear to contradict basic properties of expected utility theory.[1] In some instances to be discussed below, for example, different presentations of the same decision problem have resulted in different patterns of behavior. Such "framing effects" not only pose obvious design problems for an experimentalist, who must decide how a problem is to be presented through the instructions, but they also pose a challenge to theorists interested in modeling human behavior. This chapter introduces a variety of experiments conducted to evaluate the correspondence between predictions of individual optimization and actual behavior. Our aim is both to identify when behavioral "paradoxes" arise and to shed light on which axioms appear to be most consistently violated. Despite considerable evidence of behavioral inconsistencies, expected utility theory is far from dead: the pervasiveness and interpretation of observed violations are hotly debated, and no widely accepted alternative theory has arisen.

The discussion is organized as follows. The first half of the chapter focuses on violations of expected utility maximization revealed in paired lottery choices. Section 8.2 begins this discussion with a review of expected utility theory in the context of a *probability triangle*, a particularly useful representation for the present purpose. Section 8.3 then introduces experimental evidence regarding inconsistencies in choices among lottery pairs. Most of the experiments discussed in this section involve decisions made under hypothetical incentives. Some lottery choices with real financial incentives are discussed in section 8.4. Although financial incentives increase the saliency of decisions, they may also create problems since wealth changes (with earnings) over the course of a session. Section 8.4 also introduces some methods of controlling for these wealth effects.

The second half of the chapter pertains to assorted topics in individual decision making. Many individual decision-making experiments differ from those discussed in earlier chapters in that the experimenter is interested in *eliciting* information about underlying preferences rather than *inducing* behavior via incentives. Section 8.5 considers three contexts where economists are interested in eliciting preferences: value elicitation, forecasting, and probability elicitation. We return to the lottery choice framework in section 8.6 to consider a curious pattern of "preference reversals" that arises with the use of alternative methods for eliciting preferences between a pair of lotteries. Not all individual decision problems involve problems of elicitation. For example, it would be useful in many contexts if specific risk postures, as well as values, could be imposed on participants. Efforts to induce risk attitudes are considered in section 8.7. Just as expected utility has been questioned, many psychologists argue that subjects do not process new information in the

---

[1] In fact, the *Journal of Economic Perspectives* has a regular column called "Anomalies," which is devoted to this topic.

manner dictated by statisticians, that is, using Bayes' rule. Section 8.8 discusses Bayes' rule and related experimental work. Section 8.9 contains a summary.

8.2 Probability-Triangle Representations

For reasons that will become evident later in this section, most of the lottery-choice situations that seem to violate expected utility theory involve choices between pairs of lotteries that are related via some multiplicative and/or linear transformation. When all lotteries involve no more than three "prizes" or outcomes, the relationship between actual and theoretically consistent behavior can be neatly illustrated in a probability triangle created by Marschak (1950), and later used by Machina (1982).

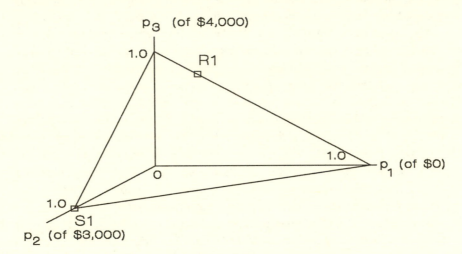

Figure 8.1   A Three-Dimensional Representation of Lotteries

The probability triangle is perhaps best developed in the context of a specific series of lotteries. Consider, for example, the lotteries *S1*, *S2*, *R1*, and *R2* presented above. These involve prizes of either $0, $3,000, or $4,000. As shown in figure 8.1, these lotteries can be represented in three dimensions, by letting the probability of each prize define a dimension. In the figure, the probability of the most preferred prize, $4,000, is represented as p_3 on the vertical axis. The probability of the $3000 intermediate prize is represented as p_2, and the probability of the least preferred prize of $0 is represented as p_1 on the horizontal axis. Thus, for example, since "safe" lottery *S1* generates $3,000 with certainty, it is represented by point $p_1 = 0$, $p_2 = 1$, and $p_3 = 0$ in figure 8.1. Similarly, "risky" lottery *R1* involves $4,000 with probability .8 and $0 with probability .2, and is represented by the point $p_1 = .2$, $p_2 = 0$, and $p_3 = 0.8$.

Notice, however, that a lottery is not completely defined unless the sum of probabilities equals 1. It is impossible, for example, to evaluate a lottery involving a prize of $3,000 with probability .4 and a prize of $0 with probability .3, unless you are told what happens with the probability .3 that remains! This constraint on the sum of the probabilities requires the points representing lotteries to be on the outer face of the simplex in figure 8.1. This outer face, which is outlined with the dashed lines, can be collapsed into two dimensions by viewing it from the perspective of a point such as $S1$ on the p_2 axis in figure 8.1. It is this two-dimensional perspective, illustrated in figure 8.2, that forms a probability triangle, with p_3 on the vertical axis and p_1 on the horizontal axis. To see more clearly the nature of this graphical device, consider the locations of lotteries $S1$ and $R1$ in figure 8.2 relative to figure 8.1. The $S1$ lottery provides $3,000 with certainty, so both $p_1 = 0$ and $p_3 = 0$. Thus, this lottery is located at the origin in figure 8.2. Lottery $R1$ provides $4,000 with probability .8 and $0 with probability .2. Consequently, $R1$ appears along the boundary for which $p_3 + p_1 = 1$.

Recall that the lotteries $R2$ and $S2$ are generated by a 3/4 chance of $R1$ or $S1$, respectively, and a 1/4 chance of 0. Since the $0 payoff corresponds to the lower right-hand corner in figure 8.2, point $R2$ is 3/4 of the distance from $R1$ to this corner. Similarly, $S2$ is 3/4 of the distance from $S1$ to the lower right-hand corner. Notice that a straight line connecting $R1$ and $S1$ would be parallel to a line

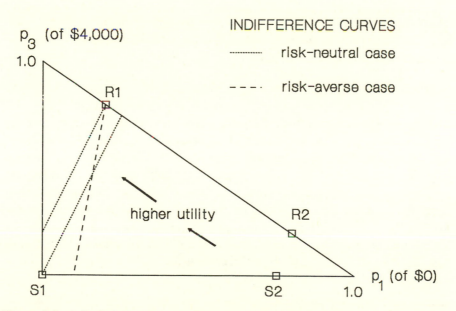

Figure 8.2 A Probability-Triangle Representation of Lotteries

connecting $R2$ and $S2$. As will be seen, this geometric relationship will be very important in tests of expected utility theory.

Risk Neutrality

Since each point in the probability triangle corresponds to a lottery, a subject's preferences over a family of such lotteries can be represented as indifference curves in the triangle.[2] This is most easily seen in the case of a risk-neutral person, who by definition is indifferent between all lotteries with equal expected values. The indifference curve passing through the origin contains all points that correspond to lotteries with an expected payoff that equals \$3,000, which is the expected payoff of the lottery $S1$ at the origin. This locus is constructed

$$(8.1) \qquad \$3,000 \;=\; p_3(\$4,000) + p_2(\$3,000) + p_1(\$0).$$

Eliminating p_2 by using the fact that the probabilities sum to 1, this equation can be expressed

$$(8.2) \qquad \$3,000 \;=\; p_3(\$4,000) + [1 - p_3 - p_1](\$3,000) + p_1(\$0).$$

Finally, solving for p_3 yields

$$(8.3) \qquad p_3 \;=\; 3p_1,$$

which is represented in figure 8.2 as the dotted line through the origin with a slope of 3. By identical reasoning, it follows that the locus of lottery points with an expected value of X is determined by

$$(8.4) \qquad p_3 \;=\; [X - 3] + 3p_1.$$

All such indifference curves are parallel straight lines, since the slopes of these curves are always 3. The two dotted lines passing through points $S1$ and $R1$ are representative indifference curves (please ignore the dashed line through $R1$ for the moment). The case where $p_3 = 1$ generates the most preferred prize (of \$4,000 with certainty), so the direction of preference is toward the upper left-hand corner of figure 8.2, as indicated by the arrows in the figure. Thus, for example, the dotted-line indifference curve passing through point $R1$ lies above and to the left of the indifference curve passing through $S1$, because the expected value of $R1$ is \$3,200 (calculated as .8[\$4,000] + .2[\$0]), which exceeds the expected value of $S1$, \$3,000.

---

[2] Violations of basic axioms of rationality, such as intransitivities, would preclude such a representation.

The effect of risk aversion on the slopes of indifference curves in the probability triangle is discussed in the next subsection. For purposes of reference, it is useful to develop a more general expression for the slope of risk-neutral indifference curves. Consider a family of lotteries with three prizes, ranked $x_1 < x_2 < x_3$, for which the associated probabilities are p_1, p_2 and p_3:

(8.5)
$$p_1 x_1 + p_2 x_2 + p_3 x_3$$

represents the preferences of a risk-neutral subject in the sense that more preferred lotteries have higher values in (8.5). From the linearity of probabilities in (8.5) it follows that the indifference curves will be straight lines in the (p_1, p_3) space used for the probability triangle. Using the fact that $p_2 = 1 - p_1 - p_3$, it follows that the slopes for the risk-neutrality case are:[3]

(8.6)
$$\frac{x_2 - x_1}{x_3 - x_2}.$$

Notice that the formula in (8.6) yields a slope of 3 for the example given above with $x_1 = 0$, $x_2 = 3,000$, and $x_3 = 4,000$.

Risk Aversion

Kahneman and Tversky (1979) conducted a series of experiments involving choices of the type presented at the outset of this chapter. As with many of the initial experiments regarding expected utility theory, decisions were not motivated by real financial rewards, so indicated preferences are suspect. Nevertheless, these authors observed that 80 percent of their subjects were risk averse in the sense that they selected the safe lottery, *S1*, over the more risky lottery, *R1*, despite the fact that the latter has a higher expected value.[4] When *S1* is preferred to *R1*, the indifference curve passing through *R1* must cross the horizontal axis to the right of point *S1* at the origin, as shown by the *dashed* line through *R1* in figure 8.2. In this way, aversion to risk makes the indifference curves steeper in the triangle.

More formally, a risk-averse expected utility maximizer will choose the lottery that maximizes the expected utility of earnings, rather than expected earnings

---

[3] The calculation is performed by setting (8.5) equal to a constant K, using $p_2 = 1 - p_1 - p_3$, and solving for p_3 as a function p_1. The coefficient of the p_1 term is the slope in (8.6).

[4] This pattern of risk-averse behavior shows up in many experiments with real financial incentives. Historically, economists have discussed lottery choices in terms of large hypothetical payoffs, and the initial experiments did not involve financial incentives. We reference the Kahneman and Tversky results because they shaped much of the subsequent debate.

directly. Representing the utility of outcome x_i as $U(x_i)$, a risk-averse agent will select the lottery that maximizes:

(8.7)
$$p_1 U(x_1) + p_2 U(x_2) + p_3 U(x_3).$$

Indifference curves for utility functions are obtained by equating (8.7) to a constant (again using $p_2 = 1 - p_1 - p_3$), and solving for p_3 as a linear function of p_1. The linearity of (8.7) in the probabilities will again cause these indifference curves to be linear in the (p_1, p_3) space, and the common slope will be

(8.8)
$$\frac{U(x_2) - U(x_1)}{U(x_3) - U(x_2)},$$

which is the obvious generalization of (8.6).

To see the effect of risk aversion on the slope of indifference curves algebraically, let outcomes $x_1 = 0$, $x_2 = 1/2$, and $x_3 = 1$. Without loss of generality, extreme points of the utility function may be normalized at 0 and 1, so $U(x_1) = 0$ and $U(x_3) = 1$. Now if an agent is risk neutral, there is a linear relationship between and x_i and $U(x_i)$, so, given the utility normalization, $U(x_2) = 1/2$. Inserting these numbers into (8.8), the slope of the indifference curves is 1. Risk aversion implies that an agent's utility function is concave, or equivalently that $U(x_2)$ is closer to $U(x_3)$ than to $U(x_1)$. Suppose, for example, that $U(x_2) = .75$. Then, by equation (8.8), the slope of indifference curves is 3. In this way, risk aversion increases the slope of the indifference curves in the probability triangle.

8.3 Lottery-Choice Experiments

A lottery is nothing more than a list of prizes and associated probabilities. For example, the choices discussed in the introduction are lotteries. It is convenient to represent lotteries of this type in the following manner:

S1	($3,000, 1; $0, 0)	*R1*	($4,000, .8; $0, .2)
S2	($3,000, .25; $0, .75)	*R2*	($4,000, .2; $0, .8),

The notation ($3,000, 1; $0, 0) indicates that lottery *S1* consists of $3,000 with certainty. Similarly, the notation ($4,000, .8; $0, .2) indicates that lottery *R1* consists of $4,000 with probability .8, and $0 with probability .2. In what follows, we will also continue with the convention of labeling lottery pairs with the notation *S1, R1, S2, R2,* and so on, where the "*S*" indicates a safer option and the "*R*" indicates a riskier option.

The methodological convenience of presenting participants with the rather complex problem of two paired lottery choices follows from the discussion of probability triangles. We have shown in the previous section that indifference "curves" in the triangle should be parallel lines, with a common slope that depends on the degree of risk aversion. Two paired lottery choices are needed at a minimum to examine whether indifference curves are in fact parallel: By placing paired lottery choices on parallel lines in the triangle, violations of expected utility theory can be detected via inconsistent choices in different probability regions. In figure 8.2, for example, participants first select between *R1* and *S1*, and then between *R2* and *S2*. Since indifference curves are parallel, an expected utility maximizer would choose either the *R* lottery in each pair, or the *S* lottery in each pair. A violation is indicated by the choice of an *R* lottery in one region and an *S* lottery in another.

Recall that lotteries *R2* and *S2* are simple transformations *R1* and *S1*: Lottery *R2* is constructed from *R1* by reducing the likelihood of *R1* to .25, and increasing the likelihood of $0 by .75. Lottery *S2* is similarly related to *S1*. Scaling down the probability of a positive payoff by the same ratio, .75, moves the initial lotteries to *R2* and *S2*, which are three-fourths the distance from *R1* and *S1* to the lower right corner of the triangle. This transformation is a standard method of obtaining lottery choices that are parallel in the triangle, known as the "common-ratio" effect. The common ratio (in this case .75) ensures that the transformed lotteries are on a line parallel to the line connecting the original pair.

Humans rather frequently make inconsistent choices in this common-ratio context. Kahneman and Tversky (1979), for example, conducted an experiment with the parameters discussed above, using hypothetical payoffs (denominated in Israeli pounds instead of dollars used in the text). They found that although 80 percent of the subjects preferred *S1* over *R1*, a majority of subjects (65 percent) also preferred *R2* to *S2*. Despite the use of hypothetical payoffs, this response pattern is typically interpreted to be a direct violation of the independence axiom of expected utility theory: the choice between *S1* and *R1* should be independent of the common, and hence "irrelevant," prospect of a 75 percent chance of zero. The importance of such a violation bears emphasis. The computational simplicity of expected utility theory is due to the fact that probabilities appear linearly in expected utility expressions. This advantage is impaired to the extent the independence axiom is violated.

A second method for constructing lotteries that are parallel in the probability triangle is known as a "common-consequence" transformation. In this case, the lottery pairs are constructed by an additive rather than a multiplicative transformation. Consider, for example, choices between lotteries *S3* and *R3*, which have $5 million, $1 million, and $0 as possible outcomes:

S3 = ($5 million, 0; $1 million, 1.0; $0, 0)   or

R3 = ($5 million, .1; $1 million, .89; $0, .01).

Notice that both of these lotteries offer a $1 million payoff with a probability of .89 or above. These lotteries could be transformed replacing this common consequence with ($0, .89) in each lottery. This generates the lotteries

$S4$ = ($5 million, 0; $1 million, .11; $0, .89)   or

$R4$ = ($5 million, .1; $1 million,   0; $0, .90).

Lottery pairs ($S3$, $R3$) and ($S4$, $R4$) are illustrated in figure 8.3. By adding an .89 probability of 0, and keeping the probability of $5 million constant, the points $R3$ and $S3$ move to the right by .89, in a parallel manner. Therefore, as with the common-ratio problem, transforming lottery choices $S3$ and $R3$ by a common consequence generates a pair of lotteries, $S4$ and $R4$, that appear along parallel lines in the triangle. (Please ignore the third parallel line in the upper left corner.) But notice that, in this case, one of the lotteries ($R3$) does not fall along a border, as all three outcomes occur with a positive probability.

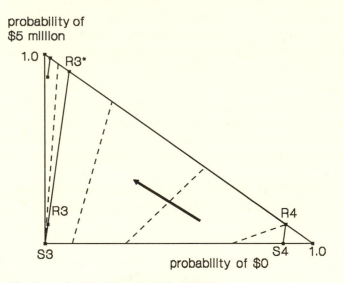

Figure 8.3 The Lotteries Used by Conlisk (1989)

In any event, a common-consequence problem allows for the same choice inconsistency as presented in the common-ratio problem: Since the slopes of the indifference curves remain fixed throughout the probability triangle, participants violate expected utility theory if they switch between an "S" lottery in one choice and an "R" lottery in the other. Presented in terms of the common-consequence problem, this inconsistency is termed the Allais paradox. Again, "paradoxical" behavior is very commonly observed. Conlisk (1989), for example, gave 236 subjects the choices stated above as (*S3*, *R3*) and (*S4*, *R4*) with hypothetical payments. Sixty percent of the participants switched between an "*S*" and an "*R*" lottery choice.

Thus, the common-ratio and common-consequence problems appear to generate a violation of at least one axiom of expected utility theory in experiments conducted under hypothetical payoff conditions. It is natural for an economist to inquire whether the violations disappear when participants face real payoffs.[5] We will discuss the effects of real payoffs on human subjects in the next section, but first we consider an alternative approach.

Animal Experiments

One rather novel way to induce highly salient rewards involves the use of animals, who make choices that prominently affect their daily caloric intake. Battalio, Kagel, and MacDonald (1985) report an experiment in which rats were given the choice between two levers, each of which yielded a randomly determined number of food pellets.

The experiment involved four rats and proceeded over a series of several months. Each day the rats were taught the underlying distribution of pellet payoffs via a series of "forced trials" in which only one of the levers was available. To facilitate learning, the distribution of pellet payoffs was programmed to match the theoretical random distribution in these initial trials. Following the forced trials, each rat faced a fixed number of "free trials" in which both levers were available and the payoffs for each lever were generated from the appropriate underlying distribution in a truly random manner. This procedure was repeated daily for a period of two to three weeks. The levers corresponding to the safe and risky prospects were rotated, however, since it is known that rats sometimes exhibit a preference for a specific lever. The treatment conditions (payoffs and probabilities) were changed after observing no trend in choices over a five-day period.

Each rat was presented with the following three lottery choices in sequence:

---

[5] Conlisk (1989) does report a pilot experiment where Allais inconsistencies disappear. The experiment involved lotteries (*S3*, *R3*) and (*S4*, *R4*), but with $5 million, $1 million, and $0 replaced by $25, $5, and $0, respectively. Each of the fifty-three subjects made decisions for both lottery pairs under hypothetical incentives, and then made a decision for one of the two lottery pairs under real financial incentives. In each case, participants virtually always chose the lottery with the highest expected value (i.e., the risky lottery), both with and without financial incentives. Thus, the transformation (not the financial incentives) virtually eliminated the inconsistent choice pattern. This discussion is relegated to a footnote because of the large differences in the expected values of these transformed lotteries. Expected values are $5 for *S3* versus $6.95 for *R3*; and $.55 for *S4* versus $2.50 for *R4*. One obvious question is whether the Allais paradox would reappear if the two highest prize values were closer (for example, $6 and $5 instead of $25 and $5). We think this is important because most subjects may not perceive much of a difference between $5 million and $1 million in the untransformed payoffs but may perceive a sizable difference between $25 and $5.

$S5$ = (8 pellets, 1.0 ; 1 pellet, 0.0) $R5$ = (13 pellets, .75 ; 1 pellet, .25)

$S6$ = (8 pellets, 0.5 ; 1 pellet, 0.5) $R6$ = (13 pellets, .375; 1 pellet, .625)

$S7$ = (8 pellets, 0.33; 1 pellet, 0.67) $R7$ = (13 pellets, .25 ; 1 pellet, .75).

As should be clear, these lotteries present a common-ratio problem: The second pair of lotteries is derived from the first pair by reducing the probability of the higher payoff by a common ratio of .5. The third pair of lotteries is related to the first via a common ratio of .33. For purposes of calibration, the baseline ($S5$, $R5$) choice was repeated after the ($S7$, $R7$) treatment.

Results are reported as the average proportion of choices of the less-risky prospect over the final five days of the treatment condition. For example, rat subject 304 selected the lever corresponding to lottery $S5$ over the lever corresponding to lottery $R5$ in 57 percent of the choice opportunities. This indicates risk aversion, since the $R5$ lottery has a higher expected payoff. Rat 304 was representative of the other rats in this regard. Risk preferences among the rats also appeared invariant to changes in initial wealth, which were implemented by altering the number of forced-choice trials at the beginning of each session.

The four rats were homogeneous in exhibiting a "common-ratio" inconsistency. Each rat tended to chose the safe prospect less frequently in the higher-numbered lottery pairs. Averaging across rats, $S5$ was chosen over $R5$ 58 percent of the time; $S6$ was chosen over $R6$ in 49 percent of instances, and $S7$ was chosen over $R7$ only 43 percent of the time. After a return to the baseline, $S5$ was chosen over $R5$ 63 percent of the time.

One drawback of this experiment's design is that there is no control for wealth effects. The common-ratio effect violates expected utility theory if the decisions for each lottery pair are made from the same initial situation, that is, for the same utility function at the same initial wealth. Although risk preferences did not appear to be affected by changes in wealth, expected caloric intake was clearly higher in the baseline ($S5$, $R5$) treatment than in the ($S6$, $R6$) or the ($S7$, $R7$) treatments. Kagel, MacDonald, and Battalio (1990) alleviate this problem in a subsequent experiment by having rats chose between lotteries with prizes that are all a single pellet, but with a randomly determined delay in the delivery time. The highest prize, then, is the one that corresponds to the shortest delay. Since the time between trials is fixed and the final offering is always a single pellet, a rat will have always consumed the same number of pellets at about the same time into each session, regardless of the random outcomes of the lotteries chosen. In this sense, a rat's wealth position is approximately the same for any two daily sessions with different treatments. Despite the controls for wealth, common-ratio inconsistencies persisted in this context. These authors also observed a common-ratio effect in a parallel series of sessions conducted with people, using real money payoffs in dollars.[6] It is very interesting that the same qualitative pattern of violations of expected utility theory is observed in both rats and humans.

Alternative Theories of Choice under Uncertainty

In both the common-ratio and common-consequence problems, the typical pattern of inconsistent choices involves selection of the relatively safe "S" lottery when its outcome is certain, and switching to the riskier "R" lottery when neither lottery offers a certain payoff. In terms of figure 8.3, for example, participants typically choose the certain outcome in lottery $S3$ over lottery $R3*$ (in the common-ratio problem) or over lottery $R3$ (in the common-consequence problem), but then choose $R4$ over $S4$. This choice is inconsistent, as it implies that indifference curves are not parallel throughout the probability choice space: A preference for lottery $S3$ over $R3$ reflects a relatively risk-averse indifference mapping, reflected by the steep dashed line passing through $S3$ and above $R3$. On the other hand, a preference for $R4$ over $S4$ implies risk-preferring behavior, reflected by the relatively flat dashed line through $R4$. Although inconsistent with standard expected utility maximization, the choice pattern of $S3$ over $R3$, and $R4$ over $S4$, would be consistent with a preference mapping where the indifference curves "fanned out" from a common point below the origin, as suggested by the dashed lines in figure 8.3.

Machina (1982) commented on this pattern, as well as on several other violations of expected utility theory, and proposed a generalization of the independence axiom that permitted such fanning out. In order for indifference curves to fan out, they must be steeper in the upper left corner of the probability triangle, that is, the corner with more preferred lotteries. Since steeper indifference curves indicate more risk aversion, a pattern of fanning out would mean that a subject violates expected utility in a manner that exhibits more risk aversion in the region of more preferred lotteries. A number of experimental tests of the fanning-out predictions have been conducted, for example, Chew and Waller (1986), Conlisk (1989), and Camerer (1989).[7] Although the standard common-ratio and common-consequence inconsistencies were replicated in these studies, there was little support for the fanning-out hypothesis. Using financial incentives, Camerer (1989) found

---

[6] Wealth effects were controlled in human subjects by asking them to indicate all choices between lottery pairs, under the condition that only one choice, selected *ex post* at random, would yield the lottery that would actually be played out to determine the subject's monetary earnings. In this manner, no wealth is being accumulated during the experiment. This "random-selection" method is discussed in section 8.4 below.

[7] Many of the studies involved hypothetical choices. Notably, Camerer (1989) used financial incentives with a random-selection method of controlling for wealth effects. This method will be discussed in the next section.

little evidence of fanning out in the northwest corner of the probability triangle, and under hypothetical incentive conditions, both Chew and Waller (1986) and Conlisk (1989) report a pattern of choices in this corner that suggest *fanning in.*[8]   For example, Conlisk used the lotteries (with hypothetical payoffs) indicated by the unlabeled dots in the northwest corner of figure 8.3. Fanning out would suggest that subjects who prefer *S1* to *R1* near the origin would not prefer the unmarked risky lottery on the outer face in the upper left corner of the figure. But 45 percent of the subjects made paired choices that violate expected utility (by choosing a mix of safe and risky lotteries), and of these, 83 percent choose a mix of *S1* and the unmarked risky lottery in the upper-left corner.

There are a variety of alterations of expected utility theory that might account for Allais paradoxes in addition to Machina's generalized expected utility theory. These include the "prospect theory" of Kahneman and Tversky (1979), the "weighted utility theory" of Chew and MacCrimmon (1979), the "regret theory" of Bell (1982), Fishburn (1982), and Loomes and Sugden (1982), and the "rank-dependent utility theory" of Quiggin (1982).[9] For a variety of reasons, none of these alternatives has become widely accepted. First, the pattern of violations of expected utility theory is not as clear as was once believed, and no rival theory persuasively organizes the somewhat mixed data. Second, their application involves complicated specifications of utility functions, which theorists find rather cumbersome. The third reason, which is the subject of the next subsection, is that more recent experimental work casts some doubt on the need for a more general expected utility theory. It may be the case that observed inconsistencies are a consequence of violations of the less problematic reduction-of-compound-lotteries axiom, rather than independence.

Is Independence Really Violated?

Some experimental evidence suggests that the inconsistency may be due the complexity of the problem, rather than to a violation of independence. For example, along with the common-ratio questions involving lottery choices (*S1*, *R1*) and (*S2*, *R2*), Kahneman and Tversky (1979) also presented their common-ratio lottery choice decision in a manner that makes the relationship between the lotteries much more transparent. In this second series of lottery choices (also with hypothetical payoffs), participants again made a first choice between *R1* and *S1*, but then made a second choice between modified but mathematically equivalent representations of

---

[8] In particular, see the discussion of Chew and Waller (1986) in appendix III of Conlisk (1989).

[9] Hey (1991) does a nice job presenting a number of variants to standard expected utility theory, and he summarizes experiments designed to assess these alternatives. He further argues that the inconsistencies may be attributable to consistent errors or mistakes made by participants, and he calls for the development of a "theory of errors."

R2 and *S2*, which we denote *R2** and *S2**, where *R2** = (*R1*, .25; $0, .75) and *S2** = (*S1*, .25; $0, .75).[10] The equivalence of the starred and unstarred lotteries can easily be seen by expressing the compound representations in terms of outcomes. For example, lotteries *S2* and *S2** each yield $3,000 with a probability of .25, and $0 with a probability of .75.   Framed in compound-lottery form, the choice inconsistency disappeared: 78 percent of the subjects preferred *S2** to *R2**, virtually identical to the 80 percent who choose *S1* over *R1*.

This result has been replicated. Conlisk (1989), for example, gave 212 subjects the paired choices in the common-consequence problem given above as (*S3*, *R3*) and (*S4*, *R4*), but stated outcomes as compound lotteries (again with hypothetical payoffs). When stated in compound-lottery form, only 28 percent of the outcomes involved inconsistent choices (compared to a 60 percent incidence of inconsistent choices when the lotteries were presented in reduced form). Camerer and Ho (1990) replicated both the Kahneman and Tversky (1979) and the Conlisk (1989) results.[11] Camerer (1991) also reports results indicating that violations of expected utility theory are rare when all lottery choices are in the interior of the probability triangle. Taken together, these results suggest that in many applications, modification of expected utility theory may be unnecessary. Rather than a general violation of the independence axiom, it appears that people have some difficulty evaluating compound lotteries, particularly when some of the lotteries involve outcomes with near-zero probabilities.

8.4 Financial Incentives and Controls for Wealth Effects

Most of the results described in the preceding section involved hypothetical payoffs. If financial incentives did not matter in lottery-choice situations, then monetary payments would be unnecessary, keeping both the cost and complexity level of this research fairly low. Experimental evidence, however, suggests that financial incentives do matter here. Battalio, Kagel, and Jiranyakul (1990), for

---

[10] Kahneman and Tversky presented this choice between compound lotteries to the subjects in the following manner: "Consider the following two-stage game. In the first stage, there is a probability of .75 to end the game without winning anything, and a probability of .25 to move into the second stage. If you reach the second stage you have a choice between

($4,000, .80; $0, .2)   and   ($3,000, 1).

Your choice must be made before the game starts, i.e., before the outcome of the first stage is known."

[11] Unlike Conlisk, Camerer and Ho (1990) had the same subjects make the choices in both the compound lottery and reduced-form lottery paired choice situations. Keller (1985) has also shown that the frequency of anomalous behavior in Allais paradox problems is affected by the way in which the choice problem is presented.

example, found that subjects tend to be more risk averse when the choices involve real payoffs. Similarly, as noted below, Starmer and Sugden (1991) report that monetary incentives affect the quantitative (although not the qualitative) nature of lottery-choice inconsistencies.

The upshot of these observations is no different from the conclusion drawn regarding the use of money payments in chapter 1: It is usually (if not always) advisable to use monetary incentives, since financial incentives can affect performance, and since economists are primarily interested in decisions that are not hypothetical. Harrison (1990a) presents this view with a particular passion:

> Why attempt to verify or falsify models of motivated behavior on the altar of experiments that do not motivate subjects.... The renowned and enjoyable intellectual imperialism of economists aside, we arguably have no useful business fussing around in an attempt to make sense of unmotivated behavioral entrails.

Further, it is important to emphasize that it is not sufficient simply to provide *some* financial incentive. Rather, the sensitivity of money earnings to decisions must be high enough to dominate participants' decision-making costs. Results of many individual decision-making experiments, even with financial incentives, have been questioned for the lack of "payoff dominance" (e.g., Harrison, 1989, 1990a, 1990b).

The use of monetary payoffs generates some special methodological concerns in the context of lottery choices. In particular, since risk attitudes may be theoretically affected by wealth, participant choices can be affected by the stream of payments (either expected or actual) that accrue in the course of a session. Very little research has been conducted to assess the effects of wealth changes on the decisions of financially motivated participants in a lottery situation, and the research that has been done is inconclusive.[12] On the one hand, Cox and Epstein (1989) find little evidence that wealth changes affect lottery decisions. These authors placed subjects in a sequence of lottery-choice situations, and each lottery selected was played immediately, with the earnings being added to the subject's cumulative total. When they ran regressions with cumulative earnings as an independent variable, the coefficient on this variable was generally insignificant. On the other hand, in a lottery-like asset-market context with randomly determined dividends, Ang and Schwarz (1985) appear to conclude that observed risk premiums are influenced by

---

[12] In fact, there is some theoretical controversy over whether subjects exhibit wealth effects. One of the primary tenets of Kahneman and Tversky's (1979) prospect theory, for example, is that risk attitudes are determined in relation to current wealth, and that a person is risk-preferring for losses and risk averse for gains, *regardless of the current level of wealth*. The evidence cited to support this claim typically involves hypothetical gains and losses.

the effect of wealth changes on investor risk attitudes, although other possible explanations are mentioned.

A serious experimental effort to document wealth effects would be useful. Even in the absence of strong evidence suggesting the presence of wealth effects, however, it remains desirable to control for them, since significant wealth effects could complicate or invalidate the interpretation of the data for experiments conducted under conditions of uncertainty. For this reason, we digress in this section into a methodological discussion of four ways to control for wealth effects. This description is followed by the review of an experiment by Starmer and Sugden (1991) designed to evaluate the effectiveness of the most popular of these techniques, the random-selection method. An additional feature of the Starmer and Sugden experiment is that it allows for a general test of the reduction-of-compound-lotteries axiom. The final portion of this section contains a summary of what has been learned from lottery-choice experiments.

Methods of Controlling for Wealth Effects

Four methods of controlling for wealth effects have appeared in the literature: *ex post* analysis, induced preferences, between-group design, and random selection. Consider them in turn.

1. *Ex Post Analysis.* A researcher can analyze subjects' decisions to see whether there is any apparent relationship between earnings and behavior in risky situations. This is the approach taken by Cox and Epstein (1989), discussed above. Although this approach both is simple and requires relatively little forethought, it has an important theoretical deficiency: When participants face a series of lottery choices, their perceived wealth position may either change with the stream of realized earnings or remain roughly constant (if they enter the experiment with a strong prior perception regarding likely expected earnings for the entire session). The interaction between changes in accumulated wealth and changes in expected future earnings makes it difficult to isolate wealth effects via this approach.

2. *Induced Preferences.* In theory, wealth changes do not affect lottery choices if people are risk neutral or if their utility function exhibits risk aversion in a manner that is not affected by wealth. Thus, a second way to control for wealth effects is to adopt a method of paying subjects in a manner that is designed to *induce* wealth-independent preferences. The principal shortcoming of this approach is that the standard method of inducing risk neutrality, to be discussed in section 8.7 below, does not seem to work very well, at least in some contexts.

3. *Between-Group Design.* A third method involves separating the subject pool into two groups, and having subjects in one group make a decision in one lottery-choice problem while the subjects in the other group make a parallel decision in another problem. This is the approach taken by Conlisk (1989). A between-

group design avoids the potential problems of *ex post* analysis, since there is only a single financial payment, and hence both expected and actual wealth are constant at the time a decision is made. This technique has less statistical power, however, in the sense that no single subject ever makes an inconsistent pair of decisions. Rather, the researcher must make statistical inferences on the basis of an assumption that subjects in each group are drawn from the same population.

4. *Random-Selection Method.* Under this method, a subject is given a sequence of choices. One of these choices is randomly selected, *ex post*, and is used to determine the subject's financial earnings. To see why this method controls for wealth effects, suppose that there are two decisions that are equally likely to be selected. Then the subject's expected utility equals 1/2 times the expected utility resulting from the first decision, plus 1/2 times the expected utility resulting from the second decision. Since the two decisions enter overall expected utility as addictively separable components, the optimal decisions involve maximizing each expected utility component separately. Consequently, the potential earnings due to one decision should have no effect on the other decision.

This fourth method both is easy to administer and economizes on data collection efforts (since each participant can make multiple independent decisions). For these reasons, this method is probably the most standard means of controlling for wealth effects. It is worth emphasizing, however, that the appropriate application of this method does not economize on subject payments. Even though subjects are paid for only one of their decisions, the money payoff for each of the components that could have been selected must be high enough so that all decisions are salient. Thus, for example, if there are ten decisions, only one of which is to be selected to determine earnings, then each decision is 1/10 as important as it would be with straight money payments. Therefore, the potential payoff for each decision should be ten times higher than the case where the subject receives payments for all decisions. Moreover, the method relies heavily on assumption that expected utility expressions are linear in the probabilities, so violations of the axioms of expected utility theory may invalidate this approach. The next subsection discusses a direct test of this approach.

A Test of the Random-Selection Method

Starmer and Sugden (1991) report a common-consequence experiment that allows evaluation of the random-selection method of controlling for wealth effects. Their idea was to compare the decisions of financially motivated subjects in a single-choice setting with the decisions of other subjects who make multiple choices, with a random-selection control for wealth effects. If the control works, the decisions made in the single-choice setting will not differ significantly from the decisions made in the multichoice setting.

Starmer and Sudgen created the following lotteries *S8*, *R8*, *S9*, *R9*, with prizes in British pounds.

S8 = (£10, 0.00; £7, 1.00; £0, 0.00) or   *R8* = (£10, 0.20; £7, 0.75; £0, 0.05)

S9 = (£10, 0.00; £7, 0.25; £0, 0.75) or   *R9* = (£10, 0.20; £7, 0.00; £0, 0.80)

The paired choices (*S8*, *R8*) and (*S9*, *R9*) form the familiar parallelogram pattern shown in figure 8.4, which is an Allais paradox problem that is almost identical to the problem in figure 8.3.

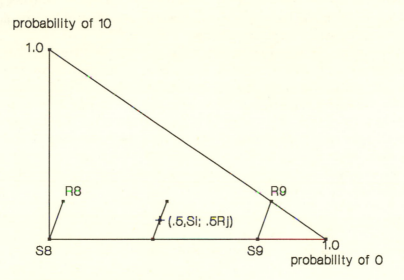

Figure 8.4 The Starmer and Sugden Design

Lotteries were presented visually in a manner that highlighted the common consequence. For example, lotteries *S8* and *R8* were represented in a table similar to figure 8.5. The top row of the figure contains numbers from 1 to 100 that would be determined randomly, and the next two rows show the paired lotteries and their prizes in pounds. A random number between 6 and 80 yields a payoff of £7 for either lottery, which is the result of a common consequence that is visually highlighted by the structure of the table. Lotteries *S9* and *R9* are formed by replacing this common consequence with a .75 chance of getting £0.

Following a sequence of decisions in which payments were hypothetical, subjects were divided into three groups, A, B and C, consisting, respectively, of 40, 40, and 80 participants. Group A participants each made a single real-payoff choice between lotteries *S8* and *R8*, and then a choice between lotteries *S9* and *R9* with hypothetical payoffs. Group B participants each made a single real-payoff choice

	1–5	6--80	81----------100
S8	£7	£7	£7
R8	£0	£7	£10

Figure 8.5 Visual Presentation of Two Lotteries with a Common Consequence

between lotteries S9 and R9, preceded by a choice between lotteries S8 and R8 with hypothetical payoffs. Finally, group C members made choices for both lottery pairs, with the understanding that only one of the choices, to be determined randomly *ex post*, would be used to determine earnings.

Results of this experiment are summarized in table 8.1. The data in the first two rows reveal the standard pattern of inconsistent responses across control groups A and B: Certain alternative S8 is preferred to R8 by 68 percent of the subjects (in the top row), while relatively safe S9 is preferred to R9 by only 42 percent of the subjects in the other single-choice group (the second row). The effectiveness of the Random-selection method as a means of controlling for wealth effects is evaluated by comparing the numbers in the top two rows with the bottom row. To the extent the method works, each entry in the bottom row should be identical to its counterpart in one of the top two rows.

Table 8.1 Data on the Random-Selection Procedure

	Percent of Subjects Choosing	
	S8 over R8	S9 over R9
40 subjects with single financially motivated choice	68%	~
40 subjects with single financially motivated choice	~	42%
80 subjects with Random-Selection Procedure	49%	31%

Source: Starmer and Sugden (1991).
Key: ~ = no monetary incentives.

Such a comparison casts some doubt on the effectiveness of the random-selection method: Behavior does not appear to be the same across groups. In each case, group C participants choose the relatively "safe" lottery less frequently.

Starmer and Sugden report that the bias is significant only for the case of the (*S8, R8*) pair. Since the bias is not uniformly away from the standard Allais paradox choice pattern (*S8* over *R8*, and *R9* over *S9*), Starmer and Sugden conclude with guarded support for the random-selection procedure. But our reading of the data is somewhat more qualified. We urge the reader to look down the columns in table 8.1 and decide whether entries are sufficiently close to allow use of the random-selection method as a control for wealth effects. Our own view is that, at least for the purposes of theory rejection, the entries are too different.

The problem with the random-selection procedure as implemented here may be nothing more than that incentives for each choice are diluted in a way that makes subjects more willing to take a risk.[13] Since only one of the two decisions made by group C participants is relevant, expected payoffs per decision fell by one-half. If this conjecture is correct, more consistent behavior would be generated by doubling the group C payoffs for each lottery.

The random-selection method may work as well as it does because, as Camerer and Ho (1990) and Starmer and Sugden (1990) have noted, there may be a psychological benefit for subjects to consider each lottery choice separately, instead of viewing the random-selection procedure as a choice between compound lotteries composed of the component choices in each individual choice problem. This is an example of what Kahneman and Tversky (1979) have called the "isolation effect."

A Test for Violations of the Reduction-of-Compound Lotteries Axiom

An additional, clever feature of the Starmer and Sugden design is that it allows for a specific test of the reduction-of-compound lotteries axiom which does not require the assumption of independence. The idea is the following: Two lottery choices are made by a subject, and one is selected at random by the experimenter to determine the payoffs. If parameters are chosen so that the choice patterns precluded by the independence axiom (e.g., *R8, S9*; or *S8, R9*) generate the same (reduced) probabilities and payoffs, then they are equivalent under the reduction-of-compound-lotteries axiom. For this reason, participants should be indifferent between the inconsistent lottery choice patterns, if they are able to reduce the compound lotteries. On the other hand, the reduction-of-compound-lotteries axiom may fail if one inconsistent choice pattern is persistently selected over the other.

The overlap of inconsistent choice pairs in the Starmer and Sugden design can be seen in figure 8.4. With the random-selection mechanism, a subject does not know which of the lotteries selected will be relevant, so the subject effectively chooses between the following four compound lotteries:

---

[13] Recall that Battalio, Kagel, and Jiranyakul (1990) observed less risk-averse behavior in a lottery choice context when real payoffs were replaced with hypothetical payoffs.

$$(S8, .5; \quad S9, .5), \quad (R8, .5; \quad R9, .5),$$

$$(S8, .5; \quad R9, .5), \quad (R8, .5; \quad S9, .5).$$

As mentioned, the latter two compound lotteries represent combinations of S and R lotteries that indicate violations of expected utility theory. Now note the location of these lotteries in figure 8.4. Lottery $(S8, .5; \quad R9, .5)$ is located exactly halfway between points $S8$ and $R9$ in the probability triangle. Similarly, lottery $(R8, .5; \quad S9, .5)$ is located halfway between points $R8$ and $S9$. Thus, both of these "mixed" lotteries are represented by a common point in figure 8.4, labeled $(Si, .5; \quad Rj, .5)$. As shown in the figure, this point is geometrically identified by the intersection of the lines connecting $S8$ and $R9$, and $R8$ and $S9$. Participants who reduce the compound lotteries appropriately should be indifferent between these two choices.[14]

The actual choice patterns for the relevant group (the one that made two paired choices) are shown in the two-right hand columns of table 8.2. It is evident that the compound lottery involving $S8$ and $R9$ is selected more than twice as often as the lottery involving $R8$ and $S9$, which the authors interpret to be a violation of the reduction-of-compound-lotteries axiom.[15]

Table 8.2 Pattern of Choice Between Compound Lotteries
Determined by the Random-Selection Method

Lottery Choice Pattern	S8, S9	R8, R9	S8, R9	R8, S9
Choice (percent)	16%	36%	33%	15%

Source: Starmer and Sugden (1991).

Summary of Lottery-Choice Experiments

Systematic violations of expected utility theory are observed in Allais paradox situations. Despite considerable effort, the meaning and importance of this regularity is not clear. Research has been impeded by a variety of procedural concerns.

---

[14] This argument does not use the independence axiom, since both of the compound lotteries map to the same point. For this reason, indifference between the lotteries has nothing to do with the independence (or other axioms) that determine the linearity of indifference curves in the probability triangle. Notice that, to the extent participants make consistent choices (choose $R8$ and $R9$; or $S8$ and $S9$), the test says less about the reduction-of-compound-lotteries axiom.

[15] The null hypotheses that the frequencies of $(S8, R9)$ and $(R8, S9)$ are the same can be rejected in a one-tailed test based on the binomial distribution ($p = .017$).

Particularly troublesome is the absence of a persuasive method of controlling for wealth effects. These problems aside, however, experimentation has generated a number of important insights. First, there is no clear pattern of fanning out of indifference curves in most parts of the probability triangle. Second, paradoxical behavior can persist when financial incentives are present in standard common-consequence situations. Third, violations may yet prove to be somewhat less serious than previously thought. Expected utility theory organizes the choice patterns in the center of the triangle better than known alternatives. Moreover, where violations occur, the existing evidence points to a failure of the reduction-of-compound-lotteries axiom, at least in several specific contexts, rather than to a failure of the more essential independence axiom.

8.5 Preference Elicitation: Problems and Applications

Value inducement represents one of the most useful tools available to the experimental economist. Laboratory tests of efficient market allocations, for example, hinge on the ability of researchers to induce specific cost and preference conditions for sellers and buyers. In some instances, however, researchers are interested in eliciting rather than inducing preferences. Assessing the value of a nonmarketed public good, such as clean water or a clear view, for example, is a matter of preference elicitation. Preference elicitation presents a series of procedural issues not yet considered. In some contexts, stated preferences turn out to be very sensitive to the way in which questions are asked. One important issue, then, regards determining the method of asking a question that comes closest to eliciting an individual's true monetary value.

This section considers a series of elicitation issues. We proceed by considering the above-mentioned problem of value elicitation; first in a nonstochastic context, and then in a stochastic context. A subsequent subsection considers the problem of eliciting price forecasts. The section concludes with a discussion of the somewhat more complicated problem of eliciting subjective probability perceptions.

Value Elicitation, Willingness to Accept, and Willingness to Pay

Due to inexpensive land and local access to fuel, many coal-burning electrical plants are located in the rural western part of Virginia. The emission of pollutants by these plants reduces visibility from the mountains overlooking the Shenandoah Valley. Suppose that emissions could be reduced (and visibility improved) through the installation of expensive filtration systems. To determine whether the installation of these systems would increase social welfare, a policy maker needs to know the monetary value Virginia residents place on high visibility over the Shenandoah valley.

A typical survey might consist of questions asked in light of "before" and "after" photographs. Respondents could be asked to state valuations in one of two obvious ways. On the one hand, they might be asked to state the least amount that they would be willing to accept as compensation for the depicted visibility reduction. Denote the response to this "willingness-to-accept" question as W_{WTA}. Alternatively, they might be asked to state the most that they would be willing to pay to avoid the illustrated visibility reduction. We denote the "willingness-to-pay" response to this latter question as W_{WTP}.[16]

Consider how the alternative framing of this question may affect valuations. The framings differ only by a wealth factor, for example, the willingness-to-accept question presumes ownership in the asset (e.g., of a clean environment) and thus assumes a higher level of initial wealth than willingness-to-pay question. Most economists think that the effects of the wealth change on responses should be relatively small.[17]

Perhaps surprisingly, there is a sizable disparity, with a consistent direction: answers to willingness-to-accept questions are typically much larger than answers to willingness-to-pay questions. Hammack and Brown (1974), for example, discuss the results of a survey in which hunters required an average compensation of $1,044 for destruction of a duck-hunting habitat but were only willing to pay $247 to prevent the habitat's destruction. This disparity presents an obvious dilemma to policy makers who are searching for measures of the economic costs and benefits of alternative policies.

One explanation for the difference in stated valuations is that respondents behave strategically: By one framing of the question they may think that they may be compensated for an increase in air pollution, and therefore they should state a high minimum willingness to accept. By the alternate framing they may think that they may be taxed to pay for a decrease in air pollution, and they should thus state a low minimum willingness to pay, to avoid imposition of the tax. Another explanation, favored by some psychologists, is that there is a basic fallacy in the way economists model the valuation of commodities, and that ownership itself makes a commodity more valuable, resulting in a high selling price. This has been called the "endowment effect"; see Knetsch (1989), for example. The presence of an endowment effect would be unsettling for many areas of economic analysis. In the analysis of legal institutions, for example, the classic Coase theorem asserts that,

---

[16]   This literature is discussed in Cummings, Brookshire, and Schulze (1986) and Hoffman and Spitzer (1990, especially note 13).

[17]   But this is not a theoretical result; it depends on the relevant elasticities. In particular, Hanemann (1991) argues that there is a theoretical explanation for the divergence between willingness-to-accept and willingness-to-pay responses for the case of a public good. He shows that the divergence in responses should be greater if there is imperfect substitutability between the public good and each available private good.

under frictionless conditions, the initial assignment of property rights is irrelevant to economic efficiency; for example, it does not matter whether the owner of a factory is required to compensate neighbors for pollution or whether the neighbors must pay the factory owner not to pollute.

Coursey, Hovis, and Schulze (1987) devised a simple experiment to measure the difference between willingness-to-pay and willingness-to-accept responses, under conditions of both hypothetical and real incentives. The experiment consisted of a brief but unpleasant initial sensation (tasting a drop of an extremely bitter but harmless liquid, sucrose octa-actuate, "SOA"), followed by a question designed to elicit the cost a participant would incur from a longer, more intense sensation of the same type (holding 1 ounce of SOA in their mouths for twenty seconds). Treatments differed by the type of question and by the nature of incentives. Subjects were asked to state either the most that they would be willing to pay to avoid this taste experience or the least that they would accept in compensation for tasting the SOA. Questions were asked under two incentive schemes: a survey with no financial incentive to answer truthfully, and a variation of a second-price auction to elicit money values with financial incentives. Crossing question-type and incentive-type dimensions, there are four treatment cells.

To see how value information could be elicited via a competitive auction, consider the willingness-to-pay response elicitation. The auction consisted of eight subjects who were each given a $10 credit. Subjects submitted bids with the understanding that the top four bidders would avoid the tasting, but that the winning bidders would have to pay amount that equals the highest rejected (fifth) bid. As discussed in chapter 5, the dominant strategy in a one-shot "competitive" auction of this type is to bid one's true willingness to pay, because one's bid does not affect the price but only whether or not one tastes the SOA. A bid below one's value, for example, introduces the possibility of (inefficiently) tasting the SOA when there is a price one would rather pay to avoid the sensation. Similarly, a bid above one's value introduces the possibility of avoiding the tasting at a price that exceeds the disutility associated with the tasting.

Willingness-to-accept information was similarly elicited via an inverse competitive auction. In this case, participants are to state selling prices for the obligation to taste the SOA, with the understanding that the four lowest bidders would be able to unload the obligation for a compensation that equals the lowest rejected (fifth lowest) bid. Unlike the treatment described above, subjects in this auction received no initial cash credit. It is again straightforward to show that the optimal bid is the subject's true willingness to accept in a one-shot binding auction.

As was reported earlier in nonlaboratory surveys without financial incentives, the willingness to pay was less than half of the willingness to accept in the survey treatment: $3.00 – $4.50 versus $7.00 – $15.00. Similarly, in early rounds of the auction-elicitation treatments, willingness to accept was much higher than willingness to pay. In later rounds, however, the willingness to accept fell to about $4.00, which was only slightly above the willingness to pay. Coursey, Hovis, and Schulze note that the difference is not statistically significant. Gregory and Furby (1987) reanalyzed these data, eliminating extreme outliers, and found that willingness to accept exceeded willingness to pay by a statistically significant amount, about $1.00 on average. Nevertheless, even with this correction, financial incentives and experience appear to reduce the extent of the difference in this context, to a level that is not so disconcerting to an economist who does not believe in overwhelming wealth effects.

Despite the novelty of this design, a number of procedural details noted by Knetsch and Sinden (1987) complicate the interpretation of the results. Two bear mention here. First, recall that subjects were given a $10 credit in the willingness-to-pay auctions, but not in the willingness-to-accept auctions. Although it would have been more expensive to give all subjects a cash credit, doing so would have eliminated an income effect that potentially interacts with the primary treatment of interest. Second, incentives to reveal preferences honestly were complicated in the auctions conducted by these authors, because participants were given the opportunity to veto any outcome that they considered unacceptable. This veto possibility eliminates the disincentive to bid above one's true willingness to pay. For example, a subject with a $5 willingness to pay suffers no penalty from bidding $50, since the subject can veto the auction if the going price turns out to exceed $5. Similarly, the veto option eliminates the disincentive to bid below one's true willingness to accept. These factors together may account for some or all of the reduced difference between measured willingness to accept and willingness to pay in the auction treatments.

As a consequence, the reason for the difference between elicitation methods remains unresolved. Despite the ambiguity of experimental results, the policy maker is not left rudderless. The relevant method of elicitation is generally determined by the context of the policy issue, for example, are we going to build a park (willingness to pay) or take one away (willingness to accept)? But a number of important issues warrant further investigation. In particular, do willingness to pay and willingness to accept in fact differ, or are the measured differences an artifact of the experimental procedures (e.g., is the strategic situation misunderstood by subjects)? This question could be examined by careful attention to the structure of financial incentives. Further, if willingness to pay and willingness to accept do differ, is it because of standard income and substitution effects (e.g., Hanemann, 1991), or is it a violation of preference theory (e.g., the "endowment effect" discussed in Kahneman, Knetsch, and Thaler, 1990)? On the other hand, if willingness to pay and willingness to accept do not differ, it would be useful to know which, if either, of the two ways of asking the valuation question is more likely to elicit true preferences in surveys used in field studies.

Valuation of Stochastic Events

Economists are also sometimes interested in eliciting information regarding uncertain events. An agent's risk posture, for example, could be determined by the cash equivalents placed by subjects on a series of lotteries. Becker, DeGroot, and Marschak (1964) present a simple method of eliciting the cash equivalent of a lottery.[18] The subject is given a ticket that constitutes a right to play a lottery and receive the resulting monetary payoff. The subject is then asked to name the smallest price for which he/she would be willing to sell the lottery, with the understanding that the experimenter will randomly generate a bid, and sell the lottery for the subject if the bid exceeds the subject's selling price. In other words, the experimenter gives the lottery to the subject, asks for a selling price, and then plays the mechanical role of an (honest) sales agent for the subject. If there is no sale, that is, if the randomly generated bid is below the subject's selling price, then the subject keeps the lottery and plays it. If there is a sale, the subject earns a certain money amount that equals the bid (and the lottery becomes irrelevant to the subject).

Under these conditions, it is in the subjects' own best interest to report their true (willingness to accept) cash equivalent for the lottery. Intuitively, a truthful report is optimal because the price reported by the subject affects only the probability of selling the lottery, but not the distribution from which bids are drawn (or the sales price). Thus, the subject should report a price that maximizes the likelihood of selling at a profit. But the reported price that maximizes the probability of selling at a profit is the lottery's cash equivalent: Any price below the cash equivalent increases the chance of selling the lottery but does so only under unfavorable conditions, that is, at prices below the subject's cash equivalent. Any price above the cash equivalent only diminishes the likelihood of a profitable sale.[19]

An iterated application of the Becker, DeGroot, and Marschak method allows estimation of subject's von Neumann-Morgenstern utility function. The trick is to start by eliciting a cash equivalent in a simple, two-prize lottery for which the utilities of the payoffs have been normalized to 0 and 1 (without loss of generality). The subject's stated cash equivalent generates a third point in (income, utility of income) space. Consider, for example, the lottery $S10 = (\$0, .5; \$20, .5)$. Letting $U(\$0) = 0$ and $U(\$20) = 1$, the utility of lottery $S10$ is calculated $.5[0] + .5[1] = .5$. Suppose a subject reports a cash equivalent of $5 for lottery $S10$. Thus $U(\$5) = .5$

---

[18]   Appendix A8.1 presents instructions for one implementation of the Becker, DeGroot, and Marschak procedure.

[19]   The technical argument for this result parallels the argument for submitting bids equal to values in a second-price auction. See the discussion in chapter 5. In applying the Becker, DeGroot, and Marschak procedure, it is important for participants to appreciate that honest revelation is in their own best interests. The reader may wish to review the section entitled "specific instructions for the elicitation of a selling price" in appendix A8.1, which represents one attempt to present this argument to participants in a simple form.

becomes a third point on the utility function. Additional points on the utility function could be identified by constructing new lotteries consisting of prizes with known utilities, and finding the certainty equivalents of these lotteries. This method, also due to Becker, DeGroot, and Marschak (1964), is explained in more detail in appendix A8.3.

Becker, DeGroot, and Marschak propose a specific sequential procedure that allows a check on the consistency of responses. In this procedure, the cash equivalents elicited in later stages are generated from responses in earlier stages in such a way that the same point on the utility function is measured twice. The authors report a limited experimental evaluation of this procedure: A pair of subjects participated in a series of three, twenty-four-stage sessions. A random-selection procedure was used to prevent wealth effects from altering risk attitudes during the elicitation process. The method appeared to produce sensible utility numbers, and the frequency of inconsistencies was reduced in the later sessions.

This sequential procedure has the disadvantage, however, that a subject's answers to selling-price questions will affect the structure of the lotteries for which selling prices are subsequently elicited. Becker, DeGroot, and Marschak attempted to minimize the possibility of strategic responses to this situation by not using the subject's answers at one stage until several stages later. But in a second application of this sequential procedure, Harrison and Rutström (1985) observed that some experienced subjects strategically inflated selling prices in early stages in order to obtain more favorable wagers in later stages. To eliminate incentives for strategic misrepresentation, Harrison (1986) suggests a correction in which the sequence of wagers is determined randomly. As Harrison notes, this correction incurs the cost of forgoing a check on the consistency of responses.

Forecasting

One especially interesting type of value-elicitation problem regards obtaining a forecast of the future value of some random variable. Forecasting behavior has been studied in a wide variety of contexts. In this subsection, we introduce some of the relevant issues by focusing on price forecasting in a market context.

Consider a double auction with stationary demand-and-supply conditions, and let P_t denote the mean transactions price in period t. Suppose subjects are asked to forecast the mean transactions price one period in advance. If the empirical distribution of prices remains unchanged from period to period, then the best forecast is the mean of that distribution. In a market setting, individual forecasts will vary from person to person. We will say that forecasts are rational if there is no systematic, correctable difference between forecasts and actual prices. In the stationary environment being considered, this means that the forecasts must be unbiased, or

(8.9)
$$F_{it} = P_t + e_{it},$$

where F_{it} is the forecast of trader i and the e_{it} are independent random errors with mean 0.

The most commonly discussed alternative to the specification in (8.9) is the *adaptive expectations* model:

(8.10) $$F_{it} = F_{i,t-1} + B(P_{t-1} - F_{i,t-1}) + e_{it}, \qquad 0 < B < 1.$$

This forecasting rule has the intuitive property that the current forecast, on the left side of (8.10), equals the previous forecast plus a correction factor for the previous forecast error $(P_{t-1} - F_{t-1})$. This is a model of partial adjustment since it is assumed that the correction factor, B, is greater than zero but less than one.

The most extensive studies of forecasting behavior have involved surveys of experts' predictions about the consumer price index. Finglewski and Wachtel (1981) analyze the well-known Livingston survey data and conclude that forecasts are not rational, but rather that the data are best explained with variations of adaptive expectations models. Schmalensee (1976) took a different, more experimental approach. He showed twenty-three subjects the historical realizations of prices in the nineteenth-century British wheat market and asked them for forecasts of subsequent five-year price averages. An adaptive-expectations model provided a better fit than a naïve model in which the subjects simply extrapolated past price changes. Schmalensee did not consider rational expectations. Indeed, rational and adaptive forecasts are not necessarily different in this context, since the environment is not stationary. It is well known that for some nonstationary processes, the rational forecasting rule is adaptive.[20]

For the case of stationary market conditions discussed above, however, rational forecasting is characterized by (8.9), which clearly differs from the adaptive rule in (8.10). In particular, (8.9) implies that forecast errors in previous periods should have no effect on current forecasts, that is, that $B = 0$ in (8.10).

Williams (1987) conducted a series of double auctions under stationary conditions, and subjects were asked to forecast the average price for each trading period at the beginning of that period. In addition to their earnings during the trading process and the $3.00 participation fee, a $1.00 award was paid at the end of the experiment to the subject with the smallest cumulative forecast error for all periods. Then Williams estimated a variation of (8.11):

---

[20]   In particular, if the variable being forecast is the sum of "permanent" and "transitory" components that cannot be observed separately, and if all distributions are normal (including the prior distribution of the unobserved component), then the application of Bayes' rule (discussed in section 8.8) yields an adaptive formula.

(8.11) $(F_{it} - F_{i,t-1}) = A + B(P_{t-1} - F_{i,t-1}) + e_{it}.$

A comparison with (8.10) shows that adaptive expectations implies that $A = 0$ and $0 < B < 1$. Similarly, comparison of (8.11) with (8.9) indicates that, in this stationary environment, rational expectations implies that both $A = 0$ and $B = 0$. (since in a stationary environment with rational traders, the expected values of $F_{i,t-1}$, P_{t-1}, and P_t are equal). For the final three periods, the parameter estimates are

(8.12) $(F_{it} - F_{i,t-1}) = -.0058 + .8607(P_{t-1} - F_{i,t-1}) + e_{it},$

where both the constant and the slope parameters are significantly different from zero (t-values of –2.83 and 34.72, respectively). Williams concludes that the data are fairly consistent with the adaptive forecasting model.

Williams's result that expectations tend to follow an adaptive process has been replicated in a multiperiod asset market context (Smith, Suchanek, and Williams, 1988). In this context, it can be shown that adaptive forecasts are not rational, i.e. they generate persistent, correctable errors. However, Smith, Suchanek, and Williams observe that prices eventually tend to the rational, perfect foresight level (e.g., speculative bubbles are eventually eliminated). This suggests that, with sufficient experience, expectations also become rational. This point is made explicitly by Peterson (1991). Analyzing results of very long (forty-five-period) laboratory asset markets with an adaptive expectations specification that has time-variant parameters, Peterson shows that expectations converge to rationality.

An important advantage of the "forecasting prize" approach, used by Williams and others, is that the market participants are the agents making the price forecasts. A potential problem with this approach, however, is that the prize may bias the trading process. Williams attempts to avoid this problem by selecting a forecast prize amount that was large enough to be salient, but not so large as to cause subjects to try to manipulate the average price in the direction of their forecast.[21] One can never be assured, however, that the appropriate forecast prize has been selected: any payment high enough to be salient in forecasting may be salient in the trading process. Other approaches are possible. For example, one alternative is to have traders rotate in and out of the market in alternate periods, making financially motivated forecasts when sitting out.[22] As a second alternative, subjects could be

[21] In fact, Williams reports a pilot study with a higher forecasting reward where efforts were clearly made to manipulate the trading process in order to win the forecasting prize.

[22] This approach is very naturally applied in the case of an overlapping generations model, with generations of "young," "old," and "forecasters" (waiting to be reborn). See Lim, Prescott, and Sunder (1988) and Marimon and Sunder (1988).

asked to forecast outcomes of an exogenously determined price series.[23] Yet a third approach, applicable in a Cournot quantity-choice context, is to have subjects make price forecasts and to pay a cash reward only for a correct price prediction.[24]

Probability Elicitation

Special problems can arise when a researcher is interested in eliciting information regarding a value that is not denominated in monetary terms. Consider, for example, the problem of eliciting subjective probability information. On a very practical level, a lack of experience with probability information may cloud probability reports. Few people regularly assess events in terms of probabilities (weather forecasters and professional gamblers being notable exceptions). Moreover, probability distributions are never directly observed. Rather, only sample information is seen; for example, some of the possible outcomes in a lottery are realized, and the others are not.

Despite these practical problems, mechanisms exist that theoretically elicit a subject's subjective probability, p, of a particular event. Such mechanisms are called *scoring rules*. A scoring rule is administered as a two-step process. In the simplest laboratory example, an experimenter first asks a subject for a probability report, r. Following this report, both the experimenter and the subject observe whether the random event occurs, and the subject receives a payoff. Of course, there is no way to ensure that a subject is reporting his or her true subjective probability, since this information is unknown to the experimenter. However, by making the subject's payoff a preannounced function of both the report and the observed outcome, incentives can be structured so that the subject's expected money payoff is maximized when $r = p$. A scoring rule that provides such incentives is said to be *proper*; see Savage (1971) for a seminal theoretical analysis of proper scoring rules.

The most commonly used scoring rule is the quadratic rule, sometimes called the Brier rule. (Instructions for a laboratory implementation of a quadratic scoring rule are presented in appendix A8.2.) It is instructive to develop the quadratic scoring rule in the context of a simple weather-forecasting game. Consider the problem of the supervisor of a meteorologist, who would like to impose a reward scheme that generates accurate snow forecasts. Let p denote the forecaster's (subjective) perception of the probability of snow on a given day. This probability is not directly observable, but the meteorologist does submit a report, r, that is

---

[23]   See Dwyer et al. (1988).

[24]   Participants have no incentive to manipulate price with variations in their quantity choice in this context. The optimal quantity decision is to maximize expected profit (given the expected quantities chosen by the others) and to adjust the price prediction accordingly. Holt and Villamil (1986) report a session with a stable counterclockwise cobweb adjustment pattern.

between 0 and 1. Following the report, it either snows or does not. This outcome is summarized by a binary indicator variable, I. If it snows, $I = 1$, otherwise $I = 0$.

The scoring rule specifies a payoff in terms of r and I:

(8.13) $payoff = 1 - (r - I)^2 = \begin{cases} 1 - r^2 & if\ I = 0, \\ 2r - r^2 & if\ I = 1. \end{cases}$

The payoff in (8.13) is bounded by 0 and 1. The maximum payoff (of 1) is generated when an event is predicted with certainty, and the event occurs. The meteorologist, for example, receives a maximum payoff by predicting a 0 percent chance of snow, and it does not snow ($r = 0$ and $I = 0$), or by predicting snow with certainty, and it snows ($r = 1$ and $I = 1$). Symmetrically, the minimum payoff (of 0) occurs when the weather forecaster is completely wrong, for example, predicting snow with certainty, when it doesn't snow ($r = 1$ and $I = 0$). For the intermediate cases, the term $- (r - I)^2$ can be thought of as a quadratic loss that allows the forecaster to hedge his/her bets by receiving some positive payoff for a given report r, whether or not it snows ($I = 0$ or $I = 1$). It is this incentive to hedge bets via the quadratic loss function that theoretically elicits honest revelation of an agent's subjective probability, p.

Given this subjective probability, a risk-neutral forecaster's expected payoff is the probability-weighted average of the payoff in (8.13), for the cases when $I = 0$ and $I = 1$, or

(8.14) $expected\ payoff = p(2r - r^2) + (1 - p)(1 - r^2).$

Suppose, for example, that $p = .33$. In selecting a report r, a subject must balance the earnings ($2r - r^2$) from the .33 chance that the event occurs, and earnings ($1 - r^2$) available from .67 chance that the event does not occur. This expected payoff can be calculated for each value of r in the range from 0 to 1. These calculations are plotted in figure 8.6 as the bold line. Notice that expected payoff is maximized at a report of $r = .33$, which equals p. The other three solid lines in the figure represent expected payoff functions for the cases of $p = 0$, $p = .66$, and $p = 1.0$; these three lines are maximized at the "x" marks above $r = 0$, $r = .66$, and $r = 1.0$, respectively. As a general matter, properness requires that for any subjective probability, p, the optimal report be $r = p$. The properness of the quadratic scoring rule can be shown by taking the derivative of (8.14) with respect to r, and equating this derivative to zero. It is easy to show that the result of this exercise is $r = p$ for all values of p.

Although a quadratic scoring rule has been used to elicit subjective probability information in experimental contexts (e.g., Grether, 1992; McKelvey and Page, 1990), to our knowledge there has been no direct examination of the procedure itself. There is, however, reason to suspect its behavioral usefulness. As suggested by the

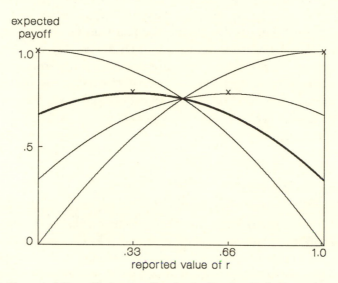

Figure 8.6 Expected Payoffs for the Quadratic Scoring Rule Procedure

very flat slope of the payoff lines in figure 8.6, experimental implementations of a quadratic scoring rule are susceptible to Harrison's (1989, 1990) "flat maximum" critique. For some values of p, expected earnings are insensitive to deviations from the optimal response. When $p = .33$, the optimal report is $r = .33$. However, at least 90 percent of expected earnings are generated for deviations from the optimal report that span more than half the possible range (e.g., reports between .05 and .61). It may be very difficult for a participant to determine the optimality of a response $r = .33$ under these circumstances. The "flatness" of incentives becomes somewhat less pronounced for more extreme values of p, but incentives do not become very peaked even for the limiting values of $p = 0$ and $p = 1$. Although the quadratic scoring rule has the advantage of being fairly easy to explain, other scoring rules may ultimately prove to be more useful in the laboratory.[25]

Summary

In a number of instances, the experimenter is interested in eliciting rather than inducing preferences. Rather elegant devices have been developed that, in theory, provide incentives for individuals to honestly reveal underlying preferences, risk

---

[25] Holt (1986b) discusses a number of scoring rules that are useful, even though they are not proper. It turns out that "properness" is not a decisive advantage in the laboratory, as long as the relationship between the subjective probability and the optimal report is known.

attitudes, and even subjective probability perceptions. However, the examination of elicitation techniques in the simplest contexts, (e.g., value elicitations for nonstochastic goods) suggests that these procedures must be applied with caution. In particular, elicited responses can be very sensitive to the way a question is framed. As seen in the next section, the effects of framing on responses extends to the case of lottery-choice experiments. Interestingly, participant experience in a market environment appears to be one factor that mitigates such "framing" effects. This finding suggests that the market not only is important as an allocative device but also facilitates learning.

8.6 Preference Reversals

One of the most interesting and perplexing patterns of behavior observed in the laboratory involves eliciting values in the context of a lottery choice. This problem arises from inconsistencies between alternative methods of eliciting preferences between two lotteries with roughly equal expected values: a relatively "safe" lottery with a high probability of a moderate payoff, and a relatively "risky" lottery with a lower probability of a very high payoff. For example, suppose you were given a choice between the following two lotteries:

$S12$ ($4, 35/36; –$1, 1/36)   and $R12$ ($16, 11/36; –$1.50, 25/36)

Which would you choose? Now, suppose you were given lottery $S12$. What is the minimum price you must receive in exchange for the chance to play $S12$? Finally, suppose you were given lottery $R12$. What is the minimum price you must receive in exchange for the chance to play $R12$?

Given an opportunity to choose one of the two lotteries, rational participants should select the one that they value the most. This preference should also be reflected in the last two questions, regarding the pattern of minimum sales prices for each lottery: The most valued lottery should have the highest sales price.[26] Curiously, however, this pattern of responses is frequently violated. The most common pattern of reversal is for participants to choose a safe lottery like $S12$ over the riskier option $R12$, but then to reverse this preference pattern by placing a higher minimum selling price on $R12$ than on $S12$. Such reversals were first reported by Lindman (1971) and Lichtenstein and Slovic (1971), and were the subject of considerable attention in the 1970s among psychologists.

---

[26] Instructions for a preference-reversal problem are presented in appendix A8.1. The problem uses the parameters discussed in the text, except that for presentational purposes the lotteries $S12$ and $R12$ are presented to participants in terms of pies and are denoted as bet A and bet B.

Perhaps the classic study on preference reversals is by Grether and Plott (1979). This study was motivated by the fact that earlier papers either had not used financial incentives at all or had used financial incentives without an effort to control for wealth effects. Grether and Plott designed a preference-reversal experiment with a control, no-payoff treatment, and second treatment where decisions were motivated by financial incentives. In each treatment subjects were given a series of six choices between lottery pairs consisting of a "P bet" with a high probability of a positive payoff (similar to *S12*) and a "$ bet" with a relatively high maximum payoff (similar to *R12*). In addition to the lottery selections, subjects responded to a series of questions in which a minimum selling price was elicited for each of the twelve bets, via the Becker, DeGroot, and Marschak procedure. Thus, each subject made a total of eighteen decisions (six lottery choices and twelve selling prices). When money payments were made, the author controlled for wealth effects by randomly selecting one of the eighteen decisions to determine the subject's payoff. Additionally, to ensure positive net earnings, subjects in the money payoff treatment started each session with a $7 endowment (subjects were vulnerable to a maximum loss of $2 in the lotteries). In the control, hypothetical-payoff treatment, subjects were paid a fixed fee for responding to the eighteen questions.

Experiment results are summarized in table 8.3. Two observations are relevant. First, independent of the incentive conditions, the incidence of reversals varies substantially with the bet choice. Those who choose the P bet are much more likely to reverse (by placing a higher selling price on the other bet) than those who choose the $ bet. Second, and perhaps more important, real financial incentives do not

Table 8.3 Preference-reversal Data

	Percent of subjects choosing P bet	Percent reversals for P bet choosers	Percent reversals for $ bet choosers
No Incentives	49%	56%	11%
$ Incentives	36%	70%	13%

Source: Grether and Plott (1979).

eliminate the preference-reversal problem. To the contrary, the number of reversals increased with the introduction of financial incentives. This effect is particularly pronounced for subjects who initially selected the P bet: With the introduction of monetary incentives, the incidence of their reversals increased from 56 percent to 70 percent. These results have been replicated by other economists; although results vary from study to study, the frequency of reversals typically exceeds 40 percent.[27]

Which Axiom Is Violated?

By choosing a lottery with the lower elicited value, a subject would seem to be making choices that are not consistent with transitivity; for example, lottery $R12$ is preferred to some amount of money, X, but X is preferred to lottery $S12$, which in turn is preferred to $R12$. Grether and Plott (1979, p. 623) conclude their study on an even more pessimistic note: "The inconsistency is deeper than mere lack of transitivity or even stochastic transitivity. It suggests that no optimization principles of any sort lie behind even the simplest of human choices."

But it is not necessarily the case that preference reversals violate transitivity, or even more basic axioms of expected utility theory. From a theoretic perspective, Holt (1986a) and Karni and Safra (1987) show that the reversals may be caused by violations of the independence axiom.[28] Alternatively, Segal (1988) argues that preference reversals may be caused by violations of the reduction-of-compound-lotteries axiom.[29]

A more behavioral motivation for the inconsistencies has been suggested in recent experimental work by Berg and Dickhaut (1990). These authors suggest that the problem may be due to insufficient financial incentives, and they show that the rate of reversals varies inversely with the level of financial incentives. Berg and Dickhaut consequently suggest a simple explanation that is based on the presence of random, independent errors that are sensitive to the opportunity cost of making mistakes. The idea is this: Participants may be very nearly indifferent between gambles with nearly identical expected values. In such cases inconsistencies, even persistent ones, may be observed. The inconsistencies diminish, however, when the relative expected values of the options differ more significantly.[30]

---

[27] See Pommerehne, Schneider, and Zweifel (1982) and Reilly (1982), for example.

[28] If the independence axiom is violated, for example, the Becker, DeGroot, and Marschak method of eliciting preferences may not elicit true certainty equivalents, and the random-selection method may not control for wealth effects.

[29] A number of other explanations have been offered; these include regret theory (Loomes and Sugden, 1983), and anchor-and-adjust models (Lichtenstein and Slovic, 1971). Wilcox (1989) discusses how preference reversals may be explained by costs of various components of making a complex decision.

[30] Harrison (1990b) makes a similar point (illustrated by a figure labeled R.I.P. Preference Reversals). But experiments with extreme differences in expected values should be interpreted with care. If the difference in expected values is large enough, people will almost always both select and place a higher selling price on the $ bet (with higher expected value). In this way the overall incidence of preference reversals can be made arbitrarily low. More interesting is the incidence of preference reversals among people who choose the (P bet) with the lower expected value.

Importantly, neither the theoretic nor the behavioral explanations mentioned here have been received uncritically, and the issue is far from settled. To the extent a problem exists, preference reversals represent an important contradiction, since they imply that some axiom of expected utility theory is violated.

Framing Effects that Generate Choice Reversals

It is not necessarily the case that observed reversals are a consequence of alternative elicitation techniques. Cox and Epstein (1989), for example, observed reversals in a lottery-choice experiment of the type discussed in sections 8.3 and 8.4, where a single elicitation technique was used, and where participants made choices first from an initial pair of lotteries, and then from a second pair of lotteries that were a transformation of the initial pair. The novelty of the Cox and Epstein design is that the transformation was particularly simple: Essentially, the transformed lottery was formed from the initial lottery by giving the subject 25 cents, and then subtracting 25 cents from all prizes. Since the subject would be choosing between the same final wealth positions in each lottery choice, the transformation should have no effect on the subject's preference between the two lotteries. In terms of the probability triangle, the initial and transformed lotteries are represented by the same point, and the transformation only affects the frame of reference in terms of monetary payoffs, that is, the way in which the choice is "framed."

More specifically, the Cox and Epstein experiment consisted of choices under two treatment conditions: In a first "direct-choice" treatment, subjects made choices between the 6 pairs of lotteries used by Grether and Plott (1979). After each decision, the selected lottery was played for a cash prize that was added to cumulative earnings.[31] The second treatment was similar to the first, except that the lotteries were transformed by the offsetting changes in fixed payments and prize amounts, described above. The authors report that about a third of the paired decisions were reversals. These reversals are very similar to preference reversals. However, we will call them "choice reversals," to emphasize that they are prompted by a (transparent) lottery transformation rather than by a change in elicitation techniques. But in each case, the different ways of presenting the problem yielded different response patterns.

---

[31] Doubtful of the effectiveness of the random-selection method as a means of eliciting preferences, Cox and Epstein elected to elicit responses under conditions of actual payoffs in each of the six paired-lottery decisions. To keep the level of total payoffs manageable, these authors reduced all prize amounts to a level that is one-fourth of the amount used by Grether and Plott. Notably, this experiment design is subject to the insufficient incentive criticism offered by Berg and Dickhaut (1990): Since the expected monetary values differed across each paired lotteries by only approximately one cent, a risk-neutral subject would lose very little by making random decisions. Expected values were also nearly identical across lotteries in the Grether and Plott design.

In summary, as with the Allais paradox discussed above, the preference and choice reversals represent another instance where expected utility theory appears to be violated. In Allais paradox situations, we learned that in some circumstances subjects quite regularly make inconsistent choices among "irrelevant" transformations of lottery pairs. The reversals discussed in this section further indicate that individuals can make inconsistent choices even among lottery pairs that are identical in probabilities and final payoffs, depending on the way the choice problem is presented. Also, as with the Allais paradox behavior, neither the underlying reason nor the scope of the reversals is fully understood. On the one hand, the reversals indicate that conditions exist under which people are very sensitive to the way a problem is presented. On the other hand, most of the reversals are observed in circumstances where the expected values of the lotteries are very similar. It may be the case that "framing effects" are important primarily in circumstances where participants are nearly indifferent between the available choices.

There may be three directions for subsequent research: One approach is to revise expected utility theory by relaxing one of the axioms. Preference-reversal experiments may not be an ideal vehicle for evaluating these theoretical alternatives, since, as noted above, the preference-reversal design may be too complicated to isolate failures of a particular axiom. A second approach is to develop a theory of error rates based on the costs of deviating from optimal decisions predicted by accepted theory.[32] A third approach is a theory of errors based on psychological rules of thumb.[33] Notably, the evaluation of error theories, based either on decision-making costs or on rules of thumb, would likely be sensitive to increases in incentives.[34]

8.7 Inducing Risk Preferences

Although many economics models are quite general, the predictions of these models often depend critically on assumptions about agents' risk preferences. Typically, agents are assumed to be risk neutral, or at the least to harbor homogeneous risk attitudes. Absent controls for risk preferences, laboratory tests of such models are really tests of the joint hypothesis that risk attitudes are as assumed, and that the model is a good one.

A good experiment cleanly isolates the theoretical issue of interest from auxiliary assumptions about risk preferences. There are a number of ways of dealing with this issue. In some cases it is possible to construct a design where the

---

[32] Some progress along these lines has been made by Dickhaut and Berg (1990) and Wilcox (1989).

[33] See, for example, Tversky and Kahneman (1981).

[34] See Harrison (1990a, 1990b).

predictions do not depend on risk attitudes.[35]   Although this option is methodologically cleanest, it is rarely available. Alternatively, one can attempt to measure underlying risk attitudes in a preliminary stage, and then sort subjects on the basis of revealed risk attitudes.[36] As indicated in previous sections, it is not always easy to elicit detailed information regarding preferences. Moreover, although subjects can be divided into more and less risk-averse groupings via this second approach, this categorical method is imprecise, and risk attitudes can change during a session (for example, as a consequence of changes in wealth). Finally, one can try to manipulate participants' risk postures directly. This approach is widely applicable, and if it works, it allows precise control. This short section describes two methods commonly used to induce, or at least alter, the risk preferences of laboratory participants. The results of experiments designed to evaluate each procedure are evaluated subsequently.

The Lottery-Ticket Payoff Procedure

The standard method for inducing risk preferences in the laboratory is a two-stage lottery procedure suggested by Smith (1961) and used by Roth and Malouf (1979), Berg et. al (1986), and others. In this method, payoffs to a primary research problem are denominated in terms of "tickets" or "points," which affect the probability of winning a prize in a lottery that is played in the second stage.

To understand how this procedure works, it is instructive to describe its operation in a particular application. Consider, for example, the problem of conducting a first-price sealed-bid auction experiment under conditions of induced risk neutrality.[37] Each iteration or "trial" consists of two stages. The first stage proceeds as any first-price sealed-bid auction: Participants privately submit sealed bids for an item, then the bids are collected and opened, and the participant submitting the highest bid is identified as the auction winner. The only difference between this first stage and conditions described in chapter 5 is that both private valuations and the bids are denominated in terms of tickets to a lottery to be conducted in the second stage. These tickets determine the portion of the total range on a uniform distribution under which the auction winner gets the prize in the second-stage lottery. For example, a person with a value of 400 might win an auction with a bid of 250, and earn 150 of 1,000 available lottery tickets. These tickets determine the proportion of stops on a roulette wheel that generates a win. The trial ends after the experimenter makes a random draw from the uniform

---

[35] The probability-matching experiment, discussed in chapter 2, is an example of this approach.

[36] This is the approach used by Murnighan, Roth, and Shoumaker (1988), and Millner and Pratt (1990, 1991).

[37] Appendix A8.2 contains instructions for a different application of this procedure.

distribution (e.g., spins the roulette wheel) and determines whether or not the auction winner gets the money prize.

The reason this procedure theoretically induces risk neutrality is simple, and it follows directly from the assumption in expected utility theory that a utility function is linear in probabilities, regardless of any concavities or convexities the function might exhibit with respect to monetary earnings. More formally, suppose a participant (as a result of first-stage decisions) obtains n of N total tickets to a second-stage lottery with a money prize of W. Then the expected utility of winning the lottery is

$$(8.15) \qquad\qquad [\ \frac{n}{N}\ ]\ U(W),$$

where, without loss of generality, the utility of not winning the lottery has been normalized to 0. Regardless of the concavity of the utility function, expected utility is linear in the proportion of lottery tickets earned, n/N. Therefore, subjects should submit risk-neutral responses for a first-stage problem denominated in lottery tickets, as explained in chapter 2.

Prior to reviewing experimental evidence evaluating the effectiveness of this procedure, we offer three comments. First, independent of its effectiveness, the lottery-ticket-payoff procedure is both theoretically elegant and fairly easy to administer. For these reasons, it has been frequently used and, for some experimenters, represents a standard operating procedure. Second, in theory, the procedure is quite general and may be used to induce not only risk neutrality, but *any* desired risk posture. A given degree of risk aversion could be induced, for example, by the use of a concave filter function that converts lottery ticket "earnings" into increments in the likelihood of winning the lottery at a decreasing rate. Varying degrees of risk aversion have been induced in the laboratory via modifications of this type. We focus on the effectiveness of the comparatively simple problem of inducing risk neutrality, as there is little reason to investigate the more complicated context if the procedure fails in the simple case. Third, notice that in order for this lottery ticket procedure to induce risk neutrality successfully, subjects must reduce the compound lottery presented in the first and second stages. Evidence from the lottery-choice experiments discussed in sections 8.3 and 8.4 suggests that many subjects may be incapable of such a reduction. Thus, we have some reason to suspect that this procedure may fail. Despite initially encouraging results reported by Berg et al. (1986), further experimentation suggests that the lottery-ticket procedure may not work, at least in some contexts.

A Test of the Lottery-Ticket Payoff Procedure

A clever experiment by Millner and Pratt (1990) allows some insight into the capacity of the lottery-ticket payoff procedure to induce risk neutrality. The experiment was conducted in the context of a rent-seeking game considered by Tullock (1980). This game is patterned after situations like lobbying for a law: Lobbying efforts can diminish the social benefits of a new law, since all interested parties who attempt to influence the outcome incur real costs, but only the efforts of the party who obtains a favorable outcome are rewarded. The question is the extent to which the economic rents generated by the law are dissipated by lobbying expenditures.

In Millner and Pratt's rent-seeking game, participant pairs are given several minutes to make series of sequential, nonrefundable commitments to obtain a fixed prize (say $1.00). For each participant, the probability of winning the prize equals his/her proportion of the total commitments made by both participants; the participant making the highest commitment has the greatest chance of winning. However, since all bids are nonrefundable, rent dissipation occurs as the sum of commitments made by both participants increases. The theoretical effect of risk aversion on rent seeking depends on the specific form of the utility function. Nevertheless, as a general matter, the level of rent dissipation should be affected by changes in risk preferences.[38]

The idea underlying the Millner and Pratt design is straightforward: First segregate participants into groups of more and less risk-averse subjects. Then have participants play a series of rent-seeking games with others in their own risk group, under conditions of both monetary and lottery-ticket payoffs. If the lottery-ticket procedure effectively induces risk neutrality, any differences in behavior between groups observed under direct monetary payoffs should disappear when payoffs are denominated in terms of lottery tickets.

Millner and Pratt successfully segregated participants into more and less risk-averse groups by using a lottery-choice pretest. The groups behaved differently in the rent-seeking game under standard monetary payoffs: Members of the more risk-averse group consistently dissipated a smaller portion of the rents than did members of the less risk-averse group. But the lottery-ticket payoff procedure did not cause behavior differences across these groups to diminish. In fact, Millner and Pratt were

---

[38] Higher commitments in the rent-seeking game simultaneously imply an increased chance of winning, and an increased expected loss. The relative weights of these arguments depend on the form of a particular participant's utility function.

unable to reject the hypothesis that the lottery-ticket payoff procedure was neutral (e.g., had no effect on performance) in this context.[39]

Payoff Transformations

Given the difficulty of inducing specific risk preferences, the question naturally arises regarding whether any alteration of the payoff function can affect participants' risk postures. Although it would be nice to impose a set of preferences directly, in some situations it is only necessary to evaluate the effect of changes in risk aversion from some current but unknown level. One simple way to alter the risk aversion of an expected-utility maximizer is to transform the money payoff function by making it more or less concave. Consider, for example, a transformation in which a subject who earns M dollars in a decision-making situation is actually paid a dollar amount $(M)^q$. If the von Neumann utility function is denoted by $U(M)$, the subject will maximize the expected value of $U(M^q)$ after the transformation. If $q < 1$, utility *as a function of M* becomes more concave, which increases risk aversion for decisions that determine M. Conversely, if $q > 1$, then utility *as a function of M* becomes more convex, which reduces risk aversion.

Evidence regarding the effects of this simpler scheme is not encouraging. In the context of a first-price sealed-bid auction, Cox, Smith, and Walker (1988) transformed the payoff functions using exponents of .5 (to increase risk aversion) and 2 (to increase risk preference). The results are mixed; there is no clear indication from the bidding data that the payoff manipulations are altering risk attitudes in the anticipated direction. Use of the first-price auction complicates the interpretation. The failure of the transformation clearly to affect bidding could be due to problems with the Nash equilibrium bidding model. Although the Nash equilibrium model works fairly well in the first-price auction context, a test that does not rely on auxiliary game-theoretic assumptions would be even more convincing.

In summary, it is theoretically possible to alter the degree of risk aversion of subjects by transforming the payoff function. In fact, it is theoretically possible to induce any desired specific degree of risk aversion via such a transformation. Although these possibilities would greatly facilitate the capacity of economists to evaluate theories in the laboratory, initial experimental work along these lines is not encouraging. Risk-inducement procedures may fail for the same reasons that Allais paradox inconsistencies arise: many subjects do not appear able to reduce compound lotteries.

---

[39] Cooper et al. (1989, p. 573) also note that the payment in lottery tickets seems to have no effect on behavior in simple battle-of-the-sexes games; that is, they observe no apparent difference when subjects are paid in dollars directly.

8.8 Information Processing: Bayes' Rule and Biases

Economists frequently model uncertainty under the presumption that agents know the probability distributions of unknown variables, such as prices and dividends. Workers, for example, are assumed to know the underlying job-offer distribution in the sequential search models described in chapter 2. But in many contexts, information regarding the distribution of job offers may be much more limited. In these circumstances, an agent uses the process of looking for jobs to learn simultaneously about the underlying wage distribution, and to decide when to stop searching (take a job). Solutions to models of this sort require some specification of the way new information is processed. This section describes and evaluates the most standard approach to incorporating new information regarding an uncertain event, *Bayes' rule*. Experimental evidence suggests that Bayes' rule has some drawing power. However, participants also appear to rely on psychological rules of thumb that can yield systematic biases in beliefs. We conclude this section with a brief discussion of a second sort of information-processing bias, called "hindsight bias." An example of this bias is the tendency for new information to cause participants to overestimate the precision of information available at the time an earlier decision was made.

Bayes' Rule

In situations where new information is acquired, it is useful to distinguish among the initial (prior) beliefs, new information, and the subsequent (posterior) beliefs. In statistical terminology, the initial beliefs are represented by a *prior distribution* over the unknown parameter(s), new information arrives in the form of a random sample from a population of possible information indicators, and the subsequent beliefs are represented by a *posterior distribution*. Bayes' rule is an optimal procedure for forming posterior beliefs on the basis of prior and sample information.

For purposes of presentation, it is useful to consider a specific problem. Suppose two bingo cages, labeled A and B, are located behind a screen. Each cage contains a number of white and/or black balls: In cage A, half of the balls are white, and rest are black. In cage B, all of the balls are black. From behind the screen, an experiment monitor flips a fair coin. Given a "heads," the monitor draws a ball from cage A, otherwise a ball is drawn from cage B. The monitor then announces the color of the drawn ball and places it back into the cage. The task for participants is to determine, from the ball's color, the probability that the ball was taken from cage A.

If the sample is white, the problem is simple, since the only white balls are in cage A. In this case, the posterior probability that the sample came from cage A is 1, or equivalently $P(A \mid white) = 1$. More interesting is the case where the sample is black. According to Bayes' rule, the posterior probability P(A | black) is optimally formed by "updating" prior probability P(A), or multiplying it by an update factor that measures the relative likelihood that a black ball came from cage A. The update factor is just a ratio consisting of the chance of drawing a black ball from cage A to the overall chance of drawing a black ball (from either cage):

$$\textit{the posterior} \quad = \quad [\textit{the update factor}] \quad x \quad [\textit{the prior}]$$

(8.16)

$$P(A|\textit{black}) \quad = \quad \frac{\textit{Prob. of black from cage A}}{\textit{Prob. of black from either cage}} \quad x \quad P(A).$$

The structure of the update factor in (8.16) is quite intuitive. The more likely a black ball is to be drawn from cage A relative to cage B, the larger the numerator relative to the denominator in (8.16) and hence, the larger the posterior.

In the example being considered, the probability of drawing a black ball from cage A is 1/2, which forms the numerator of (8.16). Since each cage has a .5 chance of being used, the probability of drawing a black ball from either cage is 3/4 (= .5[1/2] + .5[1]), which forms the denominator of (8.16). Thus, the update factor is 2/3 = [1/2]/[3/4]. Finally, to obtain the posterior probability, the update factor is multiplied by the prior probability, also 1/2 in this case, or P(A | black) = [2/3][1/2] = 1/3.

Now consider a more general statement of Bayes' rule. Denote the probability that a sample S would be observed when the cage is A as P(S|A), and similarly for P(S|B). As before, the update factor is a ratio consisting of the chances of drawing sample S from cage A, P(S|A), in the numerator, and the overall changes of drawing a sample of S from either cage, in the denominator:

$$(8.17) \quad \frac{P(S|A)}{P(S|A)P(A) \;+\; P(S|B)P(B)}.$$

The denominator is just the chance of drawing S from cage A, times the probability of using cage A, plus the chance of drawing S from cage B, times the probability of using cage B. According to Bayes' rule, the posterior probability given the sample S is formed by multiplying the prior probability P(A) by (8.17), or

$$(8.18) \quad P(A|S) \quad = \quad \frac{P(S|A)\,P(A)}{P(S|A)\,P(A) \;+\; P(S|B)\,P(B)} \quad \textit{(Bayes rule)}.$$

Bayes' rule allows for the sequential updating of probabilities. For example, the probability that the monitor was drawing from cage A could be further refined with a second sample from the same cage. In this case, the posterior probability generated from the first observation becomes the new prior. A new posterior is formed by observing the color of a second draw, and again updating P(A), by considering the chances of observing that draw. If, for example, a black ball is drawn again, then the update factor in (8.17) becomes 3/5 (= (1/2) / [(1/2)(1/3) + (1)(2/3)]. Thus, the new posterior probability for cage A is the product of 3/5 and the prior (after the initial draw):

$$(8.19) \qquad P(A \mid Black, \ 2nd \ sample) \ = \ \frac{3}{5} \ x \ \frac{1}{3} \ = \ \frac{1}{5}.$$

Notice that not only can the subject's posterior beliefs change in response to sample information, but the update factor itself can change. This follows from the effects of P(A) and P(B) in the denominator of (8.17). This is intuitive, since the perceived chance of observing a particular sample (say, a black ball) is affected by the subject's beliefs about the cage from which the monitor is making draws.

Experimental Evidence Regarding Bayes' Rule

Kahneman and Tversky (1973) report an initial experiment designed to compare Bayes' rule with a simple rule-of-thumb device that they term the "representativeness heuristic." Under this heuristic, posterior beliefs are overwhelmingly affected by the similarity or representativeness of a sample to a given population. In the context of the previous example, the draw of a black ball is representative of cage B, since cage B contains only black balls. Thus, a subject seeing a black draw will consider cage B to be more likely, regardless of the prior probability.

The experiment consisted of probabilistic responses elicited from subjects regarding the likely occupation of professionals described in a series of hypothetical personality profiles. The subject pool was divided into roughly equal sized groups. The groups differed in the initial instructions. The first group was told:

> A panel of psychologists have interviewed and administered personality tests to 30 engineers and 70 lawyers, all successful in their fields. On the basis of this information, thumbnail descriptions of the 30 engineers and 70 lawyers have been written. You will find on your forms five descriptions chosen at random from the 100 available. For each description, please indicate your probability that the person described is an engineer on a scale of 0 to 100. (Kahneman and Tversky, 1973, p. 241)

The other group was given the same message, except that they were told that the population consisted of 70 engineers and 30 lawyers.

If the participants reason according to Bayes' rule, the probabilities reported by subjects in each group should be colored by the underlying proportion of engineers and lawyers in the sample. For example, given any personality profile, the reported likelihood that a person is a lawyer should be higher in the group where participants were told that 70 percent of the profiled persons were lawyers than in the group where participants were told that only 30 percent of the profiled persons were lawyers.

Subject responses provided little behavioral support for Bayes' rule. Rather, for any profile, subjects in the first group tended to submit about the same probability (that the profile was an engineer) as subjects in the second group. The oversight is particularly striking in the case of one of the descriptions, which was written with the intention of providing no useful information:

> Dick is a thirty-year old man. He is married with no children. A man
> of high ability and high motivation, he promises to be quite successful in
> his field. He is well liked by his colleagues. (Kahneman and Tversky,
> 1973, p. 242)

For each of the two groups, the median probability of an engineer was about .5, indicating that although the subjects seemed to regard the profile as uninformative, the prior probabilities were ignored. Similarly, both groups reported uniformly high probabilities of an engineer for the description that was intended to sound like an engineer, and vice versa for a lawyer-like description. The results naturally suggest the representativeness heuristic as an explainer of behavior: subjects appear to place a high posterior probability on an event if the sample information is representative of the parent population that corresponds to that event.

Although the results of the Kahneman and Tversky experiment are suggestive, a number of procedural problems may leave an experimental economist unconvinced. In particular, the subjects did not face very well-defined financial incentives to provide careful answers. They were told that the "same task has been performed by a panel of experts, who are highly accurate in assigning probability to various descriptions. . . . you will be paid a bonus to the extent that your estimates come close to those of the expert panel" (Kahneman and Tversky, 1973, p. 241). Subjects were not told exactly how the experts processed information, nor were they given a precise way to interpret the word "probability," which may mean different things to different people.

Moreover, the whole decision situation seems a little contrived; subjects were told that the thumbnail descriptions were randomly sampled from a larger population, which was not the case. As Grether (1980, p. 540) notes, "subject's responses would agree with Bayes' rule only if they either 'played the game' or believed the experimental instructions and thereby badly misperceived what was going on."

These procedural problems were addressed by Grether (1980), who designed an experiment to evaluate the use of Bayes' rule in guessing the cage from which a sample of balls had been drawn. Subjects observed a sample of six balls drawn with replacement from one of two cages. Cage A contained four black and two white balls, while cage B contained three balls of each color.[40] Before the sample was drawn, the cage to be used was selected randomly (by a draw from a third cage) in a manner that yielded a well-defined prior probability for cage A, which was either 2/3, 1/2, or 1/3. To ensure the credibility of these procedures in the eyes of the subjects, the subjects elected one of themselves to serve as a monitor to observe the draws from cages that were not visible to the other subjects.

In this design, Bayes' rule and the representativeness heuristic can be distinguished in circumstances where the rules generate conflicting responses, for example, when a particular sample "represents" one of cages, but where the prior probabilities make it more likely that the balls were drawn from the other cage. For instance, although a sample of four black and two white balls is "representative" of cage A, Bayes' rule indicates that the sample was more likely drawn from cage B, if the prior probability of a draw from cage A is only 1/3.

Table 8.4 Posterior Probabilities for Cage A

Prior Probability for Cage A	4 black / 2 white sample (representative of Cage A)	3 black / 3 white sample (representative of Cage B)
1/3	.41*	.26
1/2	.58	.41
2/3	.74	.58*

Source: Grether (1980).
* indicates a case where the sample is representative of one cage, but the other has a higher posterior probability.

Table 8.4 lists Bayesian posterior probabilities for the cases where "representative" samples are drawn, such as samples consisting of four black and two white balls (resembling cage A), or three black and three white balls (resembling cage B). Prior probabilities are listed in the left-most column of the table. Instances where Bayes' rule and the representativeness heuristic generate different predictions are highlighted by an asterisk. The .41* entry at the top of the

---

[40] We present the experimental design in terms of black and white balls for expositional purposes. Actually, the balls were not colored but were marked with the letters N and G.

middle column, for example, is the posterior probability that a sample of four black and two white balls was drawn from cage A when the prior probability is 1/3. As just discussed, although this sample is representative of cage A, this cage is less likely since its prior is so low. Similarly, another asterisk appears at the bottom of the column on the right. In this case the sample is representative of cage B, but the prior on cage A is sufficiently high (2/3) that cage A has a higher posterior probability (.58).

The experiment consisted of a sequence of "rounds" in which subjects were told the prior in operational terms, without the use of the word probability (e.g., they were told the population of balls dictating selection of cage A and cage B). In each round the experimenter drew a ball to determine which cage to sample from, and then drew a sample of six balls. The results of the sample were shown to the subjects, who then indicated the cage that they believed to be the more likely source of the sample. For one group of subjects, financial incentives were used, and wealth effects were controlled via the random-selection method: One of the decisions made by each participant was randomly selected *ex post* to determine earnings. The participant received $15 if the cage that they indicated was more likely had actually been used in that round. Otherwise, the subject earned $5. To evaluate the effect of salient incentives, a second group of participants made decisions under identical conditions, except they were only paid a fixed fee, independent of their decisions. Sessions were conducted at six colleges and universities.

In contrast to Kahneman and Tversky, results of this experiment suggest that participants do not entirely ignore their priors. Consider, for example, the sessions conducted under salient incentives. When Bayes' rule and representativeness suggested differing responses, the proportion of cage choices that were consistent with Bayes' rule ranged from 55 percent to 69 percent (compared to a range of 69 percent to 95 percent when representativeness coincided with the implication of Bayes' rule). Participants made similar decisions in sessions conducted under nonsalient incentives, except there was a greater incidence of obvious nonsense responses. Grether concludes that the experiment provides guarded support for Bayes' rule. Although subjects may give too little weight to prior information in this context, the prior information does have a significant effect. Nevertheless, participant behavior appears to be affected by representativeness. Participants generally made more wrong choices when representativeness conflicted with Bayes' rule than when these criteria coincided. Grether (1992) emphasizes this point in subsequent experimental work: Participants appear to pay attention to priors when representativeness is not available. However, a large number of choices are more consistent with representativeness, when it is available.

Hindsight Bias and the Curse of Knowledge

A very different sort of biased response to imperfect information is investigated by Camerer, Loewenstein, and Weber (1989). These authors observe that when subjects are presented with additional information regarding an uncertain event, it is easy to overestimate the level of information that was previously available to themselves or to others. This difficulty in reconstructing one's earlier perspective can lead to a "hindsight bias" that exaggerates what was known before an event occurred. It is psychologically rather difficult for people to appreciate that an *ex ante* decision may have been optimal, if the decision led to a loss. In other words, new information can bias beliefs about what was actually known earlier, and incorrect decisions can result from this bias.

For example, consider again the problem of drawing colored balls from the two urns discussed above: Urn A contains three black balls and three white balls, and urn B contains six black balls. It may be difficult for a participant to appreciate that it was optimal to guess that the draw of a black ball was more likely to come from urn B, given the observation of a white ball on a later draw (which rules out urn B).

Camerer, Loewenstein, and Weber refer to these incorrect decisions as "the curse of knowledge." There are a variety of natural instances where such biases might arise. On a very practical level, any teacher unable to communicate with a class may suffer from the curse of knowledge: Once one has mastered a subject, it may be difficult to remember what it was like to not understand the material.

To assess the effects of hindsight bias, the authors conducted the following two-stage experiment. In the first stage, a group of fifty-one Wharton students were asked to predict 1980 earnings for eight actual (but little known) companies.[41] Subjects made these estimates on the basis of information about the companies provided by the experimenters, which included a description of each firm's business, earnings history, and a 1980 earnings projection.[42] Participants in this group were paid $1.00 for each forecast that was within 10 percent of actual 1980 earnings. We refer to these participants as *uninformed*, since they had to submit an estimate in the absence of information about realized earnings.

The second stage, conducted two months later, was designed to determine the extent of hindsight biases, as well as the capacity of a market to resolve these problems. Participants in the second stage were *informed*, in the sense that they were told the *actual* earnings for the firm in 1980, in addition to the information

---

[41] It is not standard to use actual company data, rather than more precisely defined laboratory commodities. The authors judged that real company data were necessary for credibility, and for increased parallelism with the uncertainty that arises in real markets. As far as they could tell, none of the participants knew anything about the companies used.

[42] This information was provided in the form of a 1980 Value Line report. Value Line issues reports used by investors to assess the earnings potential of firms.

given to the uninformed participants. To elicit the extent of hindsight biases, the informed participants were asked to guess the average earnings estimates submitted by the uniformed participants in the first stage.[43] To assess the bias-reducing effect of market trading, the informed participants also participated in a series of eight double-auction asset markets, one for each the eight companies.[44] In each market participants were endowed with two assets, and $50 in working capital that had to be returned after trading. The participants were allowed to trade cash for assets, and vice versa. At the end of the market, each asset unit paid a dividend equal to the average return *previously predicted* by the uninformed group. After dividends were paid, the asset was worthless.

The authors observed a significant bias in probability assessments. In nearly every instance, estimates submitted by the informed group were biased toward the company's actual 1980 earnings level. Moreover, trading the assets tended to reduce (but not eliminate) the bias. Contract prices were closer to the forecasts submitted by the uninformed group. The effects of the market in this context are similar to those observed in the value elicitation experiments discussed above, and they suggest the same conclusions: (a) systematic deviations from "rational" behavior are sometimes observed, and (b) the market can serve as a mechanism for reducing these biases.

In conducting an experiment of this type, the researcher has to decide whether to present the problem in a realistic marketlike setting, or in a more Spartan setting, for example, with simple randomizing devices such as dice or bingo cages. The authors considered this issue and chose the realistic approach in order to generate differences in subjective beliefs of the type found in a market. One problem with this approach is that the complexity of the information processing task may make it difficult to determine the exact source of the error. Although it is clear that the earnings estimates of the informed participants were biased in the direction of subsequent actual earnings, this bias might be attributable either to a hindsight bias or to other cognitive effects. For example, actual earnings information may highlight certain features of the *ex ante* descriptions that an uninformed person may simply fail to notice. If two individuals who look at the same accounting data tend to receive different, noisy signals, then knowing the actual *ex post* earnings level may help one individual infer something about the signal that the other obtained. In any event, if hindsight bias is significant, it should also appear in a more Spartan environment.

---

[43] Actually, the design was slightly more complicated. The informed participants made three separate estimates of the earnings forecasts submitted by the uninformed, at different points in the markets described below. Informed participants were rewarded with 25 cents for each estimate that was within 10 percent of the mean prediction of the uninformed group.

[44] The authors conducted two nine-person markets. In each market, participants had previous experience in a double auction.

8.9 Summary

Individual decision-making experiments allow clean evaluation of the assumptions underpinning complex behavioral theories. The axioms of expected utility theory have received particular scrutiny because of Allais paradox inconsistencies; for example, subjects frequently reverse their preferences between a pair of lotteries when the lotteries are altered by the "irrelevant" transformation of a common consequence. The inconsistency is troublesome in that it suggests that the independence axiom may be violated.

The absence of financial motivations in early experiments presented an obvious explanation for such inconsistencies. However, in a number of subsequent studies, the same pattern of "paradoxical" behavior is commonly observed with and without financial incentives; for example, in Allais paradox situations (Battalio, Kagel and Jiranyakul, 1990; Camerer, 1989); in preference-reversal situations (Grether and Plott, 1979); and in non-Bayesian information processing (Grether, 1992). Critics of these latter experiments argue that the persistence of inconsistencies is due to inexperience or nonsaliency; for example, on a per-decision basis, the losses due to irrational behavior are often a matter of pennies (Harrison, 1989, 1990a, 1990b). Whether or not this criticism is valid, it is clear that monetary incentives do affect the nature of responses. For example, with financial incentives, subjects are more risk averse in lottery-choice situations (Battalio, Kagel and Jiranyakul, 1990) and make fewer nonsense decisions in processing sample information (Grether, 1992). Given our interest in responses to real rather than hypothetical incentives, the use of salient financial incentives is essential.

The use of monetary payoffs does present an additional methodological issue, however, because inconsistent behavior must be distinguished from preference changes caused by changes in wealth during a session. Neither the behavioral importance nor the usefulness of procedures for controlling for wealth effects is well understood at this time, and this remains an area of continuing investigation.

Problems with wealth effects aside, the subsequent investigation of lottery-choice behavior has generated a number of insights regarding both the scope and the likely source of Allais paradox inconsistencies. First, the scope of the problem may be narrower than first believed. Most of the inconsistences are observed around the border of the probability triangle, such as when one of the lottery outcomes occurs with a near-zero probability. Second, rather than the independence axiom, the source of the inconsistencies appears to be a violation of the reduction-of-compound-lotteries axiom. In other words, since many subjects do not reduce compound lotteries correctly, responses are sensitive to the way the lottery-choice question is posed or framed.

"Framing effects" have been observed in a variety of other contexts. Apparent reversals in preferences for a single lottery pair have been generated when the values for the lotteries are elicited in different ways. Similarly, the stated value placed on a nonmarketed good (such as clean air) is very importantly affected by whether the valuation issue is posed in terms of the most one must pay to avoid having the good taken away, or the least one would accept as compensation for not having the good.

The sensitivity of responses to the framing of a question does not imply that people have no coherent preferences. In some instances, inconsistencies may be a consequence of confusion, and some techniques do appear to reduce confusion. For example, it is probably the case that subjects make better decisions when problems are presented visually rather than orally. Framing effects may also be alleviated by placing a problem in a more familiar context; for example, the differences between "willingness to pay" and "willingness to accept" valuation techniques are significantly reduced when participants are forced to value goods in a market. Neither does sensitivity to framing imply that humans are fooled into selecting a less preferred alternative in a wide variety of contexts. Preference reversals, for example, could be a consequence errors made under conditions of near indifference for two lotteries, and the reversals appear to arise largely when the expected value of two lotteries is nearly identical.

It is important to keep in mind that an explanation for the inconsistencies observed in individual-choice experiments remains an area of continuing controversy and investigation. Our conclusions on these issues should be viewed as personal rather than as the consensus of the field. Some thoughtful economists and psychologists are so convinced of the pervasiveness of observed inconsistencies that they see the research agenda as one of developing an acceptable alternative to expected utility theory. Others remain skeptical of the importance of the observed violations and view the most pressing task as one of incorporating the effects of low-cost decision errors into a theory that explains the patterns of violations. Still others doubt the existence of the problem altogether and seek laboratory/incentive situations where the inconsistencies disappear.

Even if consensus emerges regarding either the existence or source of observed inconsistencies, major procedural as well as theoretical consequences remain unresolved. For example, controlling risk postures represents a critical impediment for evaluating some theories. An alternative to (or modification of) the standard method of controlling risk preferences, the lottery-ticket payment procedure, must be developed if participants cannot reduce compound lotteries. The challenge to both theorists and experimentalists is clear.

APPENDIX A8

The first two sections of this appendix contain several components of instructions that are useful in individual-decision experiments. Section A8.1, adapted from Grether and Plott (1979), presents instructions for a lottery-choice experiment and for the Becker, DeGroot, and Marschak (BDM) procedure for eliciting the certainty equivalent of a lottery. These two procedures can be combined to conduct a preference-reversal experiment. For a simple classroom demonstration, subjects could be asked the lottery choice decision, and the two selling-price decisions given in the instructions. Additionally, the bracketed inserts to these instructions explain the random selection method of controlling for wealth effects. Section A8.2 contains instructions for a quadratic scoring-rule procedure to elicit a subjective probability from a subject.[45] These instructions also induce risk neutrality by letting the first (elicitation) stage determine a fractional number of lottery tickets that are used to determine a subject's monetary earnings in the second (lottery) stage. Section A8.3 expands on the discussion in the text regarding the way that iterated application of the BDM procedure can be used to elicit a subject's von Neumann-Morgenstern utility function.

A8.1 Instructions for Lottery Experiments [*bracketed material is for the random-selection method of controlling wealth effects*]

This is an experiment in the economics of individual decision making. You will be paid for your participation. Your earnings will depend partly on your decisions and partly on chance. If you are careful and make good decisions, you have a good chance of earning a considerable amount of money, which will be paid to you privately, in cash, at the end of the experiment today.[46]

The experimenters are trying to determine how people make choices among alternatives with uncertain outcomes. We have designed a simple choice experiment in which we shall ask you to make choices in a sequence of *items*, or decision-making situations. Each item contains one or more lotteries or *bets*, which are represented as pie charts. Item 1 on the following page, for example, illustrates an item consisting of two bets.

A bet is *played* by drawing a numbered ball from a bingo cage. The cage contains 36 balls, numbered 1, 2, . . . , 36. Winnings or losses depend on whether

---

[45] Parts of these instructions are adapted from McKelvey and Page (1990).

[46] Of course, it should be emphasized that earnings are hypothetical if the experiment is conducted as a classroom demonstration.

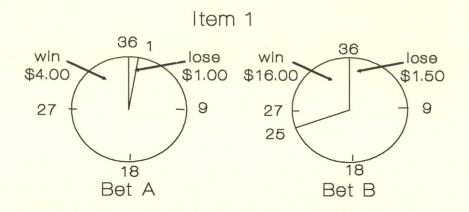

Item 1

Bet A   Bet B

the number drawn is greater or less than the *loss cutoff* specified in the bet. Consider, for example, the bets in item 1. The loss cutoff specified by bet A is 1. If bet A is played, you lose $1.00 if the number 1 is drawn, and you win $4.00 if any number greater than 1 (from 2 to 36) is drawn. Similarly, the loss cutoff in bet B is 25. If bet B is played, you lose $1.50 if a number less than or equal to 25 is drawn, and you win $16.00 if a number greater than 25 is drawn.

Your earnings are determined in the following manner. We first give you a $7 credit. Then you will consider a sequence of items. The bet determined by your decision for each item will then be played, and you will win or lose the amount indicated by the outcome of the bet. [*Each item is identified by its number in sequence. After you have made a decision on all items, **one** of them will be randomly chosen for play by drawing a numbered ball from a bingo cage. Notice that it is equally likely that any item will be selected to determine your earnings. Thus, even though your earnings are determined by only one item, it is in your best interest to think carefully about each decision.*] Winnings and losses will be added to or subtracted from the $7. Notably, parameters are chosen so that the most that you can lose on a bet is $1.50.[47] Immediately after the experiment, your earnings will be paid to you in private, and in cash.

Specific Instructions for a Lottery-Choice Decision

Lottery-choice decisions are like item 1. Your problem is to choose a bet, A or B, or to indicate your indifference between the two by writing DC ("Don't Care").

---

[47] This sentence would have to be modified if more than one bet were to be used to determine payoffs.

Decisions and earnings are to be recorded on the *Record Sheet for Lottery-Choice Problems* in the row that corresponds to the item listed on the left. You will write your choice A, B, or DC under the "Bet Choice" column (1). Decisions for additional items of this type will be similarly recorded in subsequent rows. Write the cutoff value for the bet specified by your choice under the "Loss Cutoff" column (2). If you selected DC, a coin will be tossed to select the bet that determines your earnings: You will play bet A if the result of the coin toss is a head. Otherwise you will play bet B. To record the result of the coin toss, write /A or /B to the right of your DC response, as appropriate, and record the cutoff value for that bet in column (2).

Record Sheet for Lottery-Choice Problems

Item	(1) Bet Choice (A, B or Don't Care)	(2) Loss Cutoff (1 to 36)	(3) Lottery Outcome (1 to 36)	(4) Win $((3) > (2))$ or Lose $((3) \leq (2))$	(5) Earnings $7.00 +
Item 1					
.					
.					

Following your decision, a ball numbered between 1 and 36 will be drawn from a bingo cage. Write this number under the "Lottery Outcome" column (3) on the record sheet. If the lottery outcome exceeds the loss cutoff, you win the bet and write W under column (4) and record your earnings under column (5). Otherwise, you lose the bet and write L under column (4) and record your losses (with a minus sign) under column (5).

Are there any questions?

Now consider the two bets in item 1 and indicate your choice by writing the letter for one of the bets (or by writing DC) in column (1) of the row for item 1. Now we will come around and flip a coin for anyone who recorded DC.

Next write the appropriate loss cutoff in column (2). Please raise your hand if you have a question about this.

At this time, we will draw one of the thirty-six numbered balls from the urn. The draw is ____. Please record this number in column (3). Compare the number of the draw in column (3) with the loss cutoff that you wrote in column (2), and determine whether you won or lost the bet. Then write W or L as appropriate in column (4). Finally, look at the payoffs for the bet in item 1 *that you chose* (or was chosen for you) to determine the monetary amount of your earnings. Write your earnings in column (5), using a minus sign in the event of a loss. We will be coming around to answer any questions.

(The pairs of bets for subsequent items can be distributed, one at a time, and the payoffs can be determined in an analogous manner.)

[*At the end of the session, the experimenter will randomly determine which of these items will determine your earnings. You will mark the row corresponding to the selected item with an asterisk.*]

Specific Instructions for the Elicitation of a Selling Price

Items 2 and 3 illustrate selling-price problems. In each of these items, you are given a ticket for a bet, and you must select a *minimum sales price*, or the smallest amount of money you must be paid in order to sell your ticket to play the bet. Decisions and earnings for selling-price items are recorded on the *Record Sheet for Sales-Price Elicitation*. Your minimum price is to be entered under the "Minimum Sales Price," column (1) in the row that corresponds to the item listed on the left. Decisions for additional items of this type will be similarly recorded in subsequent rows.

Following your selection of a minimum sales price, the experimenter randomly determines an *offer price*, by drawing three balls from a bingo cage containing ten balls numbered 0, 1, 2 . . . , 9. The balls are drawn with replacement; each drawn ball is replaced in the urn prior to a subsequent draw. The numbers on these three balls will determine the digits of an offer price between $0.00 and $9.99, with the first number being the dollar (left) digit, the second number the dime (middle) digit, and the third number the penny (right) digit. Write this number under column (2) of the Record Sheet. If this offer price is greater than or equal to the minimum sales price you entered in column (1), you sell the bet and receive the offer price. Otherwise, you play the bet listed on the ticket.

Notice that it is in your best interest to be accurate in listing a minimum sales price. If the price you state is too high or too low, then you are passing up opportunities that you prefer. For example, suppose you would be willing to sell a bet for $4 but instead you say that the lowest price you will sell it for is $6. If the offer price drawn at random is between the two (for example, $5) you would be forced to play the bet even though you would rather have sold it for $5. Suppose again that you would sell it for $4 but not for less, and that you state that you would sell it for $2. If the offer price drawn at random is between the two (for example $3) you would be forced to sell the bet even though at that price you would prefer

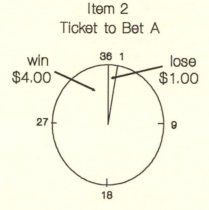

Item 2
Ticket to Bet A

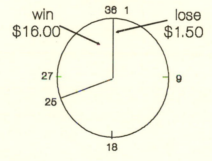

Item 3
Ticket to Bet B

to play it.[48]

Playing the Bet

If not sold, a bet is *played*, in the following manner. First, observe that the lottery "pie" for each bet in items 2 or 3 is divided into thirty-six segments. Define the *loss cutoff* as the largest number that generates a loss. The loss cutoff for bet A

---

[48] We are a bit concerned about using a specific numeric example in instructions. Payoff numbers in the specified range may potentially bias responses, while numbers outside the specified range can confuse participants. On the other hand, a specific example certainly clarifies incentives and presents no concerns for purposes of classroom demonstration. Our example corresponds to the one used by Grether and Plott (1979). These authors also include a practice item in which the experimenter elicits a minimum selling price for one of the example bets.

in item 2, for example, is 1, and the loss cutoff for bet B in item 3 is 25. You will write the appropriate loss cutoff in column (3) of the record sheet. Next, a numbered ball will be randomly drawn from a bingo cage containing thirty-six balls, numbered 1, 2, ... , 36. You will write this number under the "Lottery Outcome" column (4). If the lottery outcome exceeds the loss cutoff, you win the bet; write W under column (5) and record your earnings under column (6). Otherwise, you lose the bet; write L under column (5) and record your losses (with a minus sign) under column (6).

Record Sheet for Sales-Price Elicitation

	Price Elicitation		Lottery (if (1) > (2))			Earnings
	(1)	(2)	(3)	(4)	(5)	(6)
Item	Minimum Sales Price	Random Offer Price	Loss Cutoff Value	Lottery Outcome	Win (4) > (3) or Lose (4) ≤(3) ?	(2) or result of (5) $7.00 +
Item 2						
Item 3						
. .						

Starting the Experiment

Before beginning the experiment, we need to choose one of you to assist us as a monitor. As mentioned above, the monitor will draw balls from the bingo cage and ensure that the procedures are followed precisely, as explained above. For his/her efforts, the monitor will be paid a fixed amount of $____. Each of you will now be assigned a number, and a monitor will be randomly selected by drawing a numbered ball from the bingo cage.

[*At the end of the session, the experimenter will randomly determine which of these items will be used to determine your earnings. You will mark the row corresponding to the selected item with an asterisk.*]

Are there any questions?

At this time choose a minimum sales price for the bet in item ____ and enter it in column (1) of the row for item ____ .

Has everyone recorded their minimum sales price? Now we will draw three balls in sequence to determine the random offer price. The dollar digit is ____ . The dimes digit is ____ . The pennies digit is ____ . Enter the random offer price in column (2). If this offer price is greater than or equal to your minimum sales price in column (1), then you have sold the bet, and the offer price should be entered in the earnings column (6). If the offer price is less than your sales price, then you keep the bet and we will play out the bet, following the "specific instructions for a lottery-choice decision." In particular, the earnings for the bet are determined by comparing the loss cutoff for the bet with the outcome of the draw of a numbered ball from the urn. If you did not sell the bet, enter the loss cutoff for this bet in column (3). Has everyone (who did not sell the bet) done this? The draw from the urn is ____ . Please determine whether you won or lost the bet, and enter your earnings for this bet in column (6), using a minus sign for losses.

Selling prices for other bets will be obtained subsequently.

[*After decisions have been made and earnings calculated for all items, one of the items is selected randomly, and the earnings for that item are added to (or subtracted from) the initial $7 credit, and the resulting amount is to be entered on each person's receipt form.*]

A8.2 Instructions for Scoring-Rule Probability Elicitation [*with Lottery-Ticket Payoff Procedure for Inducing Risk Neutrality*]

This is an experiment in the economics of individual decision making. You will be paid for your participation. Your payments will depend partly on your decisions and partly on chance. If you are careful and make good decisions, you have a good chance of earning a considerable amount of money, which will be paid to you privately, in cash, at the end of the experiment today.

The experimenters are trying to determine how people make decisions with uncertain consequences. We have designed a simple choice experiment, in which we shall ask you to make choices in a series of *rounds*. Each round consists of two stages. Your decisions, lottery outcomes, and earnings are to be recorded on the record sheet provided on the next page. Although the choices you make in the first stage affect outcomes in the second stage, it is easiest to start by explaining the second stage, adding only the comment that earnings in the first stage are denominated in terms of a three-digit fraction between 0 and 1. This number can be thought of as the proportion of 1,000 available tickets you earn for a lottery that is played in the second stage. For example, the .708 written under the Lottery-Ticket Earnings column (3) on the record sheet indicates that in the sample round you earned 708 of the 1,000 available tickets.

Record Sheet

	First Stage			Second Stage	
	(1)	(2)	(3)	(4)	(5)
Round	Your Report	Urn Used (A or B)	Lottery-Ticket Earnings	Cutoff Fraction	Earnings $1.00 if (3) ≥ (4) $0.10 if (3) < (4)
Sample			.708	.506	$1.00
1					
2					
3					
4					
5					

Second-Stage Lottery

The second stage consists of a simple lottery in which you win a $1.00 prize if the proportion of lottery tickets earned in the first stage is greater than or equal to a randomly determined *cutoff fraction*. The three-digit cutoff fraction is determined by three throws of a ten-sided die: The first throw determines the value of the first digit to the right of the decimal, the second throw determines the value of the middle digit, and the third throw determines the value of the right-most digit. Once the cutoff fraction is determined, it should be written in the "Cutoff Fraction" column (4) of your Record Sheet, and compared with Lottery-Ticket Earnings from the first stage in column (3). If lottery-ticket earnings are greater than or equal to the cutoff, you win $1.00; otherwise you win $0.10. In the sample round, for example, the cutoff fraction of .506 is less than lottery ticket earnings of .708, so you would earn $1.00, as written in column (5). Notice that your chances of winning the $1.00 amount are directly related to the fraction (of lottery tickets) that you earn in the first stage.

The First Stage

Notice in the front of the room that there are two urns, labeled A and B. As you can see, urn A contains three white balls and three blue balls, and urn B contains six blue balls. Also, notice that this information has been recorded on the blackboard. In the experiment, these urns will be hidden from view. At the start of the first stage, a fair coin will be flipped: Heads determines urn A and tails determines urn B. Then a ball is drawn from the urn selected and displayed to you. You will not see the outcome of the coin flip, so you will not know in advance which urn was being used. Your problem in the first stage is to use this information to make a *report* that will affect your (lottery ticket) earnings. You will record this number in column (1) of the record sheet. After making your report, you will be told which urn was used, A or B. You will record this letter in column (2) of the record sheet.

The number of lottery tickets you win in the first stage is determined by the relationship between your report and the urn from which the ball was in fact drawn. This relationship between reports and lottery ticket earnings is shown in the Payoff Table. The table contains a row for each possible report: If urn A was used, you earn the fraction of lottery tickets listed under column II in the Payoff table. If urn B was used, you earn the fraction of lottery tickets listed under column III. This fraction will be written under the "Lottery-Ticket Earnings" column (3) in the Record Sheet. This number will be used in the second stage to determine your cash earnings for the round, as explained above.

In examining the Payoff Table, notice that high reports (closer to 1) yield higher proportions of lottery tickets if urn A was used. Low reports (closer to 0) yield higher proportions of lottery tickets if urn B was used. Intermediate reports yield lottery ticket earnings that are less sensitive to whether urn A or urn B was used. In this sense, a higher report will increase your ticket earnings to the extent you think that urn A was used, and a lower report will increase your ticket earnings to the extent you think that urn B was used.[49]

Summary

Each round consists of two stages. In the first stage, a coin is tossed to determine which urn will be used. You do not see the urn that is used, but you do see a ball drawn from the urn selected. After seeing the ball, you submit a report, which is a number between 0 and 1. Then you will be told which urn was actually used. The proportion of lottery tickets that you earn is determined in the Payoff Table by the combination of your report and the urn used.

Lottery tickets are converted into cash earnings via a second-stage lottery. A cutoff fraction is determined by three throws of a ten-sided die. If the proportion of lottery tickets earned in the first stage is greater than or equal to the cutoff fraction, you earn $1.00. Otherwise you earn $0.10.

---

[49] Some researchers have been very careful to avoid this type of linkage between the report and the likelihood of some event. The issue is whether the added clarity of procedures and incentives is worth the risk of introducing the potential biases of such a linkage.

After earnings are recorded, either a subsequent round begins or the experiment ends. At the end of the experiment, you will be paid the sum of your earnings from each round. Are there any questions?

Starting the Experiment

Before beginning the experiment, we need to choose one of you to assist us as a monitor. The monitor will draw balls, roll dice, and ensure that the procedures are followed precisely, as explained above. For his/her efforts, the monitor will be paid a fixed amount of $____. Each of you will now be assigned a number, and monitor will be randomly selected by drawing a numbered ball from the bingo cage.

To begin, the monitor will now examine the balls in each urn and verify that the contents of each earn match the summary information that is written on the blackboard.

Are there any questions before we begin?

Now we will begin round 1 by flipping a coin to determine the urn from which to draw. Heads will determine urn A, and tails will determine urn B. The monitor will observe the coin flip quietly. The urns have been placed behind a screen, but the monitor will ensure that the draw is taken from the urn determined by the coin flip.

The urn has been determined, and now the ball is drawn from the designated urn. The color of the ball drawn is _____ . Now look at the payoff table and consider your report. Write your report in column (1) of the row for round 1. Has everyone written a report?

Monitor, please tell us the urn that was used in this round. Write the letter for the urn used in column (2), and use the payoff table to determine your fractional lottery ticket earnings, which should be recorded in column (3). Please raise your hand if you have a question, and one of us will come to your desk to answer it.

Now we will use the ten-sided die to determine the cutoff fraction. This fraction is ____, which should be entered in column (4). If your lottery ticket earnings are greater than or equal to this cutoff fraction, you earn $1.00, otherwise you earn $.10. Please enter your earnings for round 1 in column (5). Please raise your hand if you have a question, and one of us will come around to answer it.

Subsequent rounds will be conducted in the same manner. At the end of the session, add up your earnings in column (5) to determine your total earnings, which will be paid to you privately in cash, immediately after the session today.

Payoff Table (for the Quadratic Scoring Rule Procedure)

I	II	III		I	II	III
Your Report	Fraction of Lottery Tickets			Your Report	Fraction of Lottery Tickets	
	If Urn A	If Urn B			If Urn A	If Urn B
0.00	0.000	1.000		0.50	0.750	0.750
0.02	0.040	1.000		0.52	0.770	0.730
0.04	0.078	0.998		0.54	0.788	0.708
0.06	0.116	0.996		0.56	0.806	0.686
0.08	0.154	0.994		0.58	0.824	0.664
0.10	0.190	0.990		0.60	0.840	0.640
0.12	0.226	0.986		0.62	0.856	0.616
0.14	0.260	0.980		0.64	0.870	0.590
0.16	0.294	0.974		0.66	0.884	0.564
0.18	0.328	0.968		0.68	0.898	0.538
0.20	0.360	0.960		0.70	0.910	0.510
0.22	0.392	0.952		0.72	0.922	0.482
0.24	0.422	0.942		0.74	0.932	0.452
0.26	0.452	0.932		0.76	0.942	0.422
0.28	0.482	0.922		0.78	0.952	0.392
0.30	0.510	0.910		0.80	0.960	0.360
0.32	0.538	0.898		0.82	0.968	0.328
0.34	0.564	0.884		0.84	0.974	0.294
0.36	0.590	0.870		0.86	0.980	0.260
0.38	0.616	0.856		0.88	0.986	0.226
0.40	0.640	0.840		0.90	0.990	0.190
0.42	0.664	0.824		0.92	0.994	0.154
0.44	0.686	0.806		0.94	0.996	0.116
0.46	0.708	0.788		0.96	0.998	0.078
0.48	0.730	0.770		0.98	1.000	0.040
0.50	0.750	0.750		1.00	1.000	0.000

Source: McKelvey and Page (1990).

A8.3 Utility Elicitation[*]

A von Neumann-Morgenstern utility function may be estimated through iterated use of the Becker, DeGroot, and Marschak (BDM) method for eliciting the cash equivalent of a lottery. Consider a lottery that pays a money amount A with probability p and pays a higher amount, B, with probability $1-p$. The cash equivalent for this lottery is x_1:

(8.20)
$$U(x_1) = pU(A) + (1-p)U(B).$$

The researcher, who specifies the lottery, knows p, A, and B. The cash equivalent x_1, for this lottery can be elicited using the BDM method (see A8.1). The next question to be considered is what x_1 tells us about the agent's utility function. Recall that the utility function is unique only up to a linear transformation, so we can arbitrarily assign utility numbers at two points. Without loss of generality, we can let

(8.21)
$$U(A) = 0, \qquad U(B) = 1,$$

so that equation (8.20) provides the utility of x_1:

(8.22)
$$U(x_1) = 1 - p.$$

Given the cash equivalent x_1, equation 8.22 provides a third point on the utility function.

A fourth point may be elicited by reversing the probabilities of the high and low prizes, for example, by considering the lottery $(1 - p, A; p, B)$. Let x_2 denote the cash equivalent for this lottery, which is obtained from the BDM procedure. Again using the normalization in (8.21), the utility of x_2 is

(8.23)
$$U(x_2) = (1-p)U(A) + pU(B) = p,$$

which is the fourth point.

Additional points on the utility function may be subsequently elicited by using the cash equivalents x_1 and x_2 to construct new lotteries for which the expected utility can be calculated from equations (8.20) – (8.23). For example, the lottery that yields A with probability p and x_1 with probability $1 - p$ has an expected utility:

---

[*] The material in this section is somewhat more advanced.

(8.24) *expected utility of* $(p, x_1 ; 1-p, A)$ $= p U(x_1) + (1-p) U(A)$
$$= p(1-p),$$

where the final equality follows from the normalization in (8.21) and the formula for the utility of x_1 in (8.22). Let x_3 denote the cash equivalent of the lottery in (8.24), so

(8.25)
$$U(x_3) = p(1-p),$$

which provides another point on the utility function once x_3 has been elicited using the BDM procedure. Other points on the utility function can be determined in a similar manner, using lotteries with prizes that are taken from the set $\{A, B, x_1, x_2, x_3\}$ of prizes with known utilities.

To summarize, the procedure consists of the following steps:

1.   Use the BDM selling-price elicitation procedure to elicit the cash equivalents, x_1 and x_2, of two lotteries involving only A and B.

2. Use these two cash equivalents to construct more lotteries, for which the cash equivalents can be elicited, such as x_3.

3. Use normalization (8.21) and theoretical calculations such as (8.22), (8.23), and (8.25) to obtain other points on the utility function. More points can be obtained by repeating the process outlined in steps (2) and (3).

One desirable feature of this utility-elicitation mechanism is the ability to check responses for internal consistency. For example, it follows from the normalization in (8.21) and from the formula for $U(x_2)$ in (8.23) that the lottery $(A, p; x_2, 1-p)$ has an expected utility of $pU(A) + (1-p)U(x_2) = (1-p)p$, which is the same as the utility of the lottery shown in (8.24). Two lotteries with the same expected utilities should have the same cash equivalents, which provides the consistency check alluded to earlier.

REFERENCES

Allais, Maurice (1953) "Le Comportement de l'homme Rationnel devant le Risque, Critique des Postulates et Axiomes de l'Ecole Americaine," *Econometrica, 21*, 503–546.

Ang, James S., and Thomas Schwarz (1985) "Risk Aversion and Information Structure: An Experimental Study of Price Variability in the Securities Markets," *The Journal of Finance, 40*, 825–844.

Battalio, Raymond C., John Kagel, and Don N. MacDonald (1985) "Animals' Choices over Uncertain Outcomes: Some Initial Experimental Results," *American Economic Review, 75*, 597–613.

Battalio, Raymond C., John Kagel, and Komain Jiranyakul (1990) "Testing Between Alternative Models of Choice under Uncertainty: Some Initial Results," *Journal of Risk and Uncertainty, 3*, 25–50.

Becker, Gordon M., Morris H. DeGroot, and Jacob Marschak (1964) "Measuring Utility by a Single-Response Sequential Method," *Behavioral Science, 9*, 226–232.

Bell, David E. (1982) "Regret in Decision Making under Uncertainty," *Operations Research, 30*, 961-981.

Berg, Joyce E., and John W. Dickhaut (1990) "Preference Reversals: Incentives Do Matter," draft, Graduate School of Business, University of Chicago.

Berg, Joyce E., L. Daley, John W. Dickhaut, and John R. O'Brien (1986) "Controlling Preferences for Lotteries on Units of Experimental Exchange," *Quarterly Journal of Economics*, 101, 281–306.

Camerer, Colin F. (1989) "An Experimental Test of Several Generalized Utility Theories," *Journal of Risk and Uncertainty, 2*, 61–104.

——— (1991) "Individual Decision Making," forthcoming in J. Kagel and A. Roth, eds., *Handbook of Experimental Economics*. Princeton: Princeton University Press.

Camerer, Colin F., and Teck-Hua Ho (1990) "Isolation Effects in Reduction of Compound Lotteries," draft, Decision Sciences, University of Pennsylvania.

Camerer, Colin F., George Loewenstein, and Martin Weber (1989) "The Curse of Knowledge in Economic Settings: An Experimental Analysis," *Journal of Political Economy, 97*, 1232–1254.

Chew, Soo Hong, and Kenneth R. MacCrimmon (1979) "Alpha-nu Choice Theory: An Axiomatization of Expected Utility," University of British Columbia, Faculty of Commerce, Working Paper 669.

Chew, Soo Hong, and W. Waller (1986) "Empirical Tests of Weighted Utility Theory," *Journal of Mathematical Psychology, 30*, 55–72.

Conlisk, John (1989) "Three Variants on the Allais Example," *American Economic Review*, 79, 392–407.

Cooper, Russell W., Douglas V. DeJong, Robert Forsythe, and Thomas W. Ross (1989) "Communication in Battle-of-the-Sexes Games: Some Experimental Results," *Rand Journal of Economics*, 20, 568–587.

Coursey, Don L., John L. Hovis, and William D. Schulze (1987) "On the Supposed Disparity between Willingness to Accept and Willingness to Pay Measures of Value," *Quarterly Journal of Economics*, 102, 679–690.

Cox, James C., and Seth Epstein (1989) "Preference Reversals without the Independence Axiom," *American Economic Review*, 79, 408–426.

Cox, James C., Vernon L. Smith, and James M. Walker (1988) "Theory and Individual Behavior of First-Price Auctions," *Journal of Risk and Uncertainty*, 1, 61–99.

Cummings, Ronald G., David S. Brookshire, and William D. Schulze (1986) *Valuing Environmental Goods: An Assessment of the Contingent Valuation Method.* Totowa, N.J.: Rowman and Allanheld.

Dwyer, Gerald, Arlington Williams, Raymond Battalio, and Timothy Mason (1988) "Are Expectations Rational in a Stark Environment?" working paper, Texas A&M University.

Finglewski, Stephen, and Paul Wachtel (1981) "The Formation of Inflationary Expectations," *Review of Economics and Statistics*, 63, 1–10.

Fishburn, Peter C. (1982) "Nontransitive Measurable Utility," *Journal of Mathematical Psychology*, 26, 31–67.

Gregory, R., and L. Furby (1987) "Auctions, Experiments, and Contingent Valuation," *Public Choice*, 55, 273–289.

Grether, David M. (1980) "Bayes' Rule as a Descriptive Model: The Representativeness Heuristic," *Quarterly Journal of Economics*, 95, 537–557.

——— (1992) "Testing Bayes Rule and the Representativeness Heuristic: Some Experimental Evidence," *Journal of Economic Behavior and Organization*, 17, 31–57.

Grether, David M., and Charles R. Plott (1979) "Economic Theory of Choice and the Preference Reversal Phenomenon," *American Economic Review*, 69, 623–638.

Hammack, Judd, and Gardner Brown (1974) *Waterfowl and Wetlands: Toward Bioeconomic Analysis.* Baltimore: Johns Hopkins Press.

Hanemann, W. Michael (1991) "Willingness to Pay and Willingness to Accept: How Much Can They Differ?" *American Economic Review*, 81, 635–647.

Harrison, Glenn W. (1986) "An Experimental Test for Risk Aversion," *Economics Letters*, 21, 7–11.

——— (1989) "Theory and Misbehavior of First-Price Auctions," *American Economic Review*, 79, 749–762.

————— (1990a) "The Payoff Dominance Critique of Experimental Economics," manuscript, University of South Carolina, Department of Economics.

————— (1990b) "Expected Utility Theory and the Experimentalists" working paper, University of South Carolina.

Harrison, Glenn W., and E. E. Rutström (1985) "Experimental Measurement of Utility by a Sequential Method," working paper, University of New Mexico.

Hey, John D. (1991) *Experiments in Economics*. Oxford: Basil Blackwell.

Hoffman, Elizabeth, and Matthew Spitzer (1990) "The Divergence Between Willingness-to-Pay and Willingness-to-Accept Measures of Value," California Institute of Technology, Social Science Working Paper 755.

Holt, Charles A. (1986a) "Preference Reversals and the Independence Axiom," *American Economic Review*, 76, 508–514.

————— (1986b) "Scoring-Rule Procedures for Eliciting Subjective Probability and Utility Functions," in P. K. Goel and A. Zellner, eds., *Bayesian Inference and Decision Techniques: Essays in Honor of Bruno de Finetti*. Amsterdam: North-Holland, 279–290.

Holt, Charles A., and Anne P. Villamil (1986) "A Laboratory Experiment with a Single Person Cobweb," *Atlantic Economic Journal*, 14, 51–54.

Kagel, John H., Don N. MacDonald, and Raymond C. Battalio (1990) "Tests of 'Fanning Out' of Indifference Curves: Results from Animal and Human Experiments," *American Economic Review*, 80, 912–921.

Kahneman, Daniel, Jack L. Knetsch, and Richard H. Thaler (1990) "Experimental Tests of the Endowment Effect and the Coase Theorem," *Journal of Political Economy*, 98, 1325–1348.

Kahneman, Daniel, and Amos Tversky (1973) "On the Psychology of Prediction," *Psychological Review*, 80, 237–251.

————— (1979) "Prospect Theory: An Analysis of Decision Under Risk," *Econometrica*, 47, 263–291.

Karni, Edi, and Zvi Safra (1987) "'Preference Reversal' and the Observability of Preferences by Experimental Methods," *Econometrica*, 55, 675–685.

Keller, L. Robin (1985) "The Effects of Problem Representation on the Sure-Thing and Substitution Principles," *Management Science*, 31, 738–751.

Knetsch, Jack L. (1989) "The Endowment Effect and Evidence of Non-Reversible Indifference Curves," *American Economic Review*, 79, 1277–1284.

Knetsch, Jack L., and J. A. Sinden (1984) "Willingness to Pay and Compensation Demanded: Experimental Evidence of an Unexpected Disparity in Measures of Value," *Quarterly Journal of Economics*, 99, 507–521.

————— (1987) "The Persistence of Evaluation Disparities," *Quarterly Journal of Economics*, 102, 691–695.

Lichtenstein, Sarah, and Paul Slovic (1971) "Reversals of Preference between Bids and Choices in Gambling Decisions," *Journal of Experimental Psychology*, 89, 46–55.

Lim, Suk S., Edward C. Prescott, and Shyam Sunder (1988) "Stationary Solution to the Overlapping Generations Model of Fiat Money: Experimental Evidence," working paper, University of Minnesota.

Lindman, Harold R. (1971) "Inconsistent Preferences Among Gambles," *Journal of Experimental Psychology*, *89*, 390–397.

Loomes, Graham, and Robert Sugden (1982) "Regret Theory: An Alternative Theory of Rational Choice under Uncertainty," *Economic Journal*, *92*, 805–824.

———— (1983) "A Rationale for Preference Reversal," *American Economic Review*, *73*, 428–432.

Machina, Mark J. (1982) "'Expected Utility' Analysis without the Independence Axiom," *Econometrica*, *50*, 277–323.

McKelvey, Richard D., and Talbot Page (1990) "Public and Private Information: An Experimental Study of Information Pooling," *Econometrica*, *58*, 1321–1339.

Marimon, Ramon, and Shyam Sunder (1988) "Rational Expectations vs. Adaptive Behavior in a Hyperinflationary World: Experimental Evidence," working paper, University of Minnesota.

Marschak, J. (1950) "Rational Behavior, Uncertain Prospects, and Measurable Utility," *Econometrica*, *18*, 111–141, and (1950) "Errata," *Econometrica*, *18*, 312.

Millner, Edward L., and Michael D. Pratt (1989) "An Experimental Investigation of Efficient Rent Seeking," *Public Choice*, *62*, 139–151.

———— (1990) "A Test of Risk Inducement: Is the Inducement of Risk Neutrality Neutral?" draft, Department of Economics, Virginia Commonwealth University.

———— (1991) "Risk Aversion and Rent Seeking: An Extension and Some Experimental Evidence," *Public Choice*, *69*, 81–92.

Murnighan, J. Keith, Alvin E. Roth, and Franciose Shoumaker (1988) "Risk Aversion in Bargaining, an Experimental Study," *Journal of Risk and Uncertainty*, *1*, 101–124.

Peterson, Steven (1991) "Forecasting Dynamics and Convergence to Market Fundamentals: Evidence from Experimental Asset Markets," working paper, Virginia Commonwealth University, forthcoming in *Journal of Economic Behavior and Organization*.

Pommerehne, Werner W., Friedreich Schneider, and Peter Zweifel (1982) "Economic Theory of Choice and the Preference Reversal Phenomenon: A Reexamination," *American Economic Review*, *72*, 569–574.

Quiggin, John (1982) "A Theory of Anticipated Utility," *Journal of Economic Behavior and Organization*, *3*, 323–343.

Reilly, Robert J. (1982) "Preference Reversal: Further Evidence and Some Suggested Modifications in Experimental Design," *American Economic Review*, *72*, 576–584.

Roth, Alvin E., and Michael W. K. Malouf (1979) "Game-Theoretic Models and the Role of Information in Bargaining," *Psychological Review*, *86*, 574–594.

Savage, Leonard, J. (1954) *The Foundations of Statistics*, New York: Wiley.

———— (1971) "Elicitation of Personal Probabilities and Expectations," *Journal of the American Statistical Association*, *66*, 783–801.

Schmalensee, Richard (1976) "An Experimental Study of Expectation Formation," *Econometrica*, *44*, 17–41.

Segal, Uzi (1988) "Does the Preference Reversal Phenomenon Necessarily Contradict the Independence Axiom?" *American Economic Review*, *78*, 233–236.

Smith, Cedric A.B. (1961) "Consistency in Statistical Inference and Decision," *Journal of the Royal Statistical Society*, Series B, *23*, 1–25.

Smith, Vernon L., Gerry L. Suchanek, and Arlington W. Williams (1988) "Bubbles, Crashes and Endogenous Expectations in Experimental Spot Asset Markets," *Econometrica*, *56*, 1119–1152.

Starmer, Chris, and Robert Sugden (1991) "Does the Random-Lottery Incentive System Elicit True Preferences? An Experimental Investigation," *American Economic Review*, *81*, 971-978.

Tullock, Gordon (1980) "Efficient Rent-Seeking," in J. Buchanan, R. D. Tollison, and G. Tullock, eds., *Toward a Theory of the Rent Seeking Society*. College Station: Texas A&M Press, 97–112.

Tversky, Amos, and Daniel Kahneman (1981) "The Framing of Decisions and the Psychology of Choice," *Science*, *211*, 453–458.

von Neumann, J., and O. Morgenstern (1944) *Theory of Games and Economic Behavior*. Princeton: Princeton University Press.

Wilcox, Nathaniel T. (1989) "Decision Anomalies and Decision Costs," working paper, University of Houston.

Williams, Arlington W. (1987) "The Formation of Price Forecasts in Experimental Markets," *Journal of Money, Credit, and Banking*, *19*, 1–16.

CHAPTER 9

Economic Behavior and Experimental Methods: Summary and Extensions

9.1 Introduction

In three decades of experimental research we have learned much, both about economic behavior and about laboratory methods. The body of experimental research is growing so quickly, and is being applied in so many areas of economics, that completing this book forces us to resist a constant temptation to incorporate new findings that are produced each month. Nevertheless, several major themes have emerged. Identifying these themes can provide insight into general directions for new research. Also, laboratory procedures are improving, and seminal papers do not always set appropriate procedural standards for current research. Thus, it is useful to articulate some of the lessons that have been learned about experimental technique.[1]

A review of experimental technique is also instructive in light of standard criticisms of the use of experimental methods in economics. Some critics would argue that experiments do too little, since the environments are too simple to allow meaningful statements about either theory or the natural world. Others would contend that experimentalists try to do too much. Particularly in complicated environments (such as market experiments), too few independent observations are

---

[1] We would like to acknowledge that much of the impetus for the discussion of design and statistics in this chapter came from suggestions made by Catherine Eckel, Robert Forsythe, and Roger Sherman. The usual disclaimer applies.

typically generated, and too many variables are changed across observations. Although we do not believe that either of these criticisms is condemning, neither do we believe that they are groundless. Attention to these objections forces the experimenter to qualify the claims that are made, and to improve the way that experiments are designed and analyzed.

Some of the objectives of this chapter are similar to those of chapter 1: to explain what economics experiments are, how they are conducted, and what has been learned from them. The difference is that these topics can now be discussed in light of broad themes, comparisons, and specific examples taken from earlier chapters. The information presented in earlier chapters also allows us to discuss some methodological issues in very concrete terms. The chapter is organized as follows: Section 9.2 contains a summary of the major patterns of experimental results. Section 9.3 reconsiders the process of testing in light of the relationship among theory, experiments, and natural economic environments. Some aspects of experimental design are considered in section 9.4, and section 9.5 discusses the relationship between experimental design and appropriate statistical analysis. Sections 9.6 and 9.7 discuss the application of some specific nonparametric statistical tests. Concluding comments are offered in section 9.8.

9.2 Major Results of Experiments to Date

One useful perspective on the diverse areas of experimental research is provided by a list that relates results to major areas of economic theory.

1. *In many situations, neoclassical price theory explains observed behavior quite well.* Competitive market predictions have been observed in a rich variety of circumstances and in literally hundreds of instances. In double auctions, competitive outcomes occur under more general conditions than traditionally have been considered necessary. For example, the reliability of competitive predictions does not require the "limiting case" assumptions of either large numbers of traders or complete information about cost and value parameters (chapter 3).

Moreover, there are important behavioral consequences of violations of standard assumptions that underlie competitive market predictions: Market power persistently generates supracompetitive prices in posted-offer markets (chapter 4). Very small numbers (bilateral bargaining) can lead to inefficient disagreements (chapter 5). Free-riding and inefficient levels of externality-causing activities are often observed when goods are not private (chapter 6). Deviations from full information regarding either the quality or the quantity of goods can cause inefficient, "lemons-market" outcomes (chapter 7).

2. *Institutions matter.* It is a mistake to conclude that experimental analysis has merely confirmed what economists have suspected about the world for two centuries. Standard market predictions do not always work, and they do not work equally well in all contexts. Perhaps the most important confounding variables are those that determine the nature of the trading institution.[2] The best-known example of the effects of the trading institution is documented in chapters 3 and 4: Otherwise comparable markets tend to competitive predictions more quickly in double-auction trading than in posted-offer trading. Even within the double auction, prices converge more quickly under some rules (a bid-ask spread improvement rule with a rank-ordered queue) than under others. The insights gleaned from laboratory studies are starting to be used in the design of new trading institutions that take advantage of advances in computer and communications technologies (chapter 5).

3. *Some predictions of game theory describe behavior well.* The importance of specifying institutional details parallels the development of game theory, which provides a systematic way of analyzing the theoretical effects of both institutional and structural variations. These new models are more "institution-specific" than neoclassical models that depend only on structural conditions. Behavior in experimental games is affected by strategic factors, at least as a first approximation. In particular, a unique noncooperative Nash equilibrium has considerable drawing power in simple one-stage matrix games, after some repetition with different partners.[3] A unique Nash equilibrium for the stage game may also predict well in some more complicated repeated games, such as the voluntary-contributions mechanism or the private-values, first-price auction. In the latter case, bids are linearly related to private values, as predicted, with deviations being in an upward direction that is consistent with risk aversion. Individual differences observed in the laboratory have stimulated new theoretical work on auctions with asymmetries in risk attitudes.

4. *Other game-theoretic predictions have a more restricted range of application.* For example, laboratory bidders do not learn to revise their bids so as to avoid the winner's curse, except in auctions involving a relatively small number of bidders or with an alternative (safe-haven) market activity. Similarly, when multiple equilibria exist in a game, the theoretic "refinements" used to discriminate among them have had mixed success in the laboratory. Pareto dominance, for example, has been shown to be a poor criterion for selecting the equilibrium with

---

[2] This observation was first made by Fouraker and Siegel (1963) in an oligopoly context, and by both Williams (1973) and Plott and Smith (1978) in an auction-market context.

[3] See Holt (1985), and to a lesser extent Cooper et al. (1991).

the most predictive power, both in matrix games,[4] and in some public-goods experiments.[5]

Another important refinement with a limited range of application involves the backward-induction reasoning used in repeated games. As the number of decision stages in a game increases, the number of Nash equilibria can explode. The most basic criterion for reducing the set of equilibria (subgame perfection) requires backward-induction reasoning and common expectations regarding the actions of others. But backward induction is not something that subjects do naturally: "irrational" phenomena such as speculative pricing bubbles in relatively long, asset-market experiments are common.

Behavior often becomes more "rational" when the whole game is repeated. Repetition, both within a session and across sessions, allows subjects to learn (through experience) what to expect in later game stages. Experience, for example, appears to eliminate speculative pricing bubbles in asset markets and promotes efficient trading in shorter asset markets with uncertainty about other traders' preference types. But learning does not resolve all problems. There are very spartan environments, such as the centipede game, where a substantial proportion of responses are inconsistent with theoretic equilibrium predictions, even after subjects play the game many times with different partners (chapter 2).

Other equilibrium refinements, which are more subtle than subgame perfection, appear to predict well in some contexts.[6] But some of the most popular of these subtle equilibrium selection criteria are based on behavior that is rarely observed in the laboratory. In repeated games, for example, "collusive" equilibrium outcomes can (in theory) be supported by trigger strategies involving punishments for defections. Trigger strategies are rarely employed in many laboratory contexts where such equilibria are conventionally considered quite appealing, such as oligopoly experiments. When a game involves more than two players it can be difficult to determine when a defection occurs, to identify who defected, and to direct a punishment toward the defector without appearing to be defecting yourself.[7]

---

[4] See Van Huyck, Battalio, and Beil (1990).

[5] Specifically, Pareto dominance is not a good selection method in public-goods games with a provision point but without a give-back option (Isaac, Schmidtz, and Walker, 1989).

[6] See Camerer and Weigelt (1988) for tests of the sequential equilibrium concept, and Banks, Camerer, and Porter (1990) for tests of more subtle refinements. The range of application for these concepts, however, also appears limited, e.g., Brandts and Holt (1991).

[7] See the discussion of the three-person public goods game in appendix A6.1. But punishment strategies are more common in other contexts, when defections can be observed and punishments can be directed to specific defectors. For example, buyers frequently punished sellers who delivered low quality in the Davis and Holt (1990) seller-selection experiment.

5. *Even apart from the institutional specification, many results are characterized by a "gray" area where variables irrelevant to the theory affect outcomes.* In voluntary contributions experiments with identical Nash equilibria, for example, the incidence of free-riding can be prominently affected by repetition, experience, and differences in the return from contributing to the public good (chapter 6). Similarly, outcomes in sequential bargaining games are sometimes drawn away from the subgame perfect equilibrium toward an equal split of the pie. As indicated in chapter 5, laboratory procedures can affect behavior in ways that have important implications for the interpretation of anomalies. For example, the puzzling hesitancy of subjects to demand the whole pie in dictator games is greatly diminished under double-anonymous conditions, when aggressive demands cannot be linked directly to the dictator, either by other subjects or by the experimenter. In addition, bargaining outcomes may be sensitive to the subject pool (different nationalities), the wording of instructions ("market" versus "pie-splitting" terminology), or the procedures for assigning the role with a strategic advantage (game-of-skill versus random assignment). The behavioral importance of these "irrelevant" variables suggests a need for richer theories that incorporate psychological motivations, learning, and decision errors.

6. *Our understanding of individual behavior is incomplete; some recurrent anomalies are fundamental challenges to rational models of behavior.* Individuals frequently make decisions that seem to be irrational, especially in choices among lotteries (chapter 8). Inconsistencies such as the Allais paradox and the preference-reversal phenomenon indicate that we are able to identify conditions where participants regularly violate one or more of the axioms of expected utility theory. In some contexts, choices are sensitive merely to the way a question is framed. There is an ongoing controversy over whether this behavior is a matter of insufficient financial incentives, or whether expected utility theory must be modified, by altering the axioms or modeling the nature of decision "errors."

Depending on where you start on the above list, the results provide quite different views of the state of economics. The first three items on the list imply that experimentation has accompanied game theoretic analysis along an ordered progression from neoclassical models to institution-specific analysis. The last three items offer almost the opposite conclusion: on a fundamental level, we are unable to explain some of the most basic decisions that people make.

We take an intermediate view that both accommodates and qualifies each of these conclusions. On the one hand, standard economic theory has been shown to perform well in some instances, particularly in markets. Our understanding of markets, however, is far from complete. Much remains to be learned about the range in which standard theories apply, as well as about the process by which equilibrium outcomes are "learned" and selected. We do know that markets can serve as a learning device; participant responses given in nonmarket or bilateral bargaining contexts may reflect perceptions of fairness that remain unaltered until confronted with competitive incentives in a full market setting, such as a double auction.

On the other hand, we recognize that in some instances behavior may be inconsistent with the predictions of expected utility theory and game theory. Although troublesome, anomalies are not necessarily fatal for a behavioral theory, particularly if there is no alternative theory that explains both the anomalies and standard patterns of behavior. It is interesting to note that anomalies are characteristic of many sciences. Perhaps these inconsistencies are regarded as being more serious by economists than by scientists in other disciplines, because economists are trained almost entirely in the realm of logic. Graduate microeconomics texts contain only the briefest allusions to data, and graduate econometrics courses stress proofs of the theoretical properties of estimators. Although a *logical* inconsistency is a condemning (and usually correctable) error, it is unrealistic to expect perfect conformity between theory and behavior. Behavioral inconsistencies should not be viewed as errors; rather, they provide the impetus for further investigation, both theoretical and experimental. The discipline of subjecting theoretical work on adjustment, learning, and decision making to experimental tests can prevent wasteful discussion of irrelevant propositions and conjectures, and can raise additional questions regarding issues not yet addressed by theory.

9.3 The Relationship among Theoretical, Experimental, and Natural Economic Environments

Most economic processes are complex, both in the trading institution and in the structure of preferences, technology, and information. To a greater or lesser degree, theoretical models of these processes are abstractions. For example, almost all natural bargaining situations place no restrictions on which party can make the next offer or counteroffer, but such unstructured situations are difficult to analyze as noncooperative games. The most tractable model of noncooperative bargaining is the highly structured alternating-offer model discussed in chapter 5. Similarly, prices in many markets can be revised at any time, but standard oligopoly models assume that price choices are made simultaneously at discrete time intervals.

Experimentation can provide evidence relevant to the evaluation of both theory and economic processes in a number of ways, and in reviewing the experimental literature (or in designing experiments of your own) it is important to consider the relationship between the setup in a particular experiment and the structure of economic interactions outside of the laboratory. In this section, we describe several types of experiments, ranging from stark abstract settings to complex designs that closely parallel naturally occurring markets.

Types of Experiments

The divergence between the restrictive assumptions underlying a theoretical model and the complexity of the economic activity for which the model is intended to apply presents the experimentalist with a dilemma: should the laboratory setup correspond more closely to the theoretical model or to the relevant parts of the economy? This dilemma has become more severe as computerization has increased the numbers of subjects and simultaneous markets that can be coordinated in a standard two-hour session.[8] The appropriate degree of complexity depends on the purpose of the experiment: it is not very productive to evaluate industrial policy issues in a 2-by-2 prisoner's dilemma experiment, and a complicated, multimarket environment is not the best place to begin testing a simple game theoretic concept.

Experiments can be categorized by plotting the relationship between the domain of a theoretical model and the domain of the natural economic process being studied. Since many of the important results of experimental economics involve specification of the trading institution, we distinguish institutional elements from environmental variables such as the number of periods, redemption and cost values, and information conditions. These two broad classes of variables, institutional and environmental, are represented in different dimensions in figure 9.1. In each dimension complexity increases as you move out along the axis. For example, the institution labeled $I1$ on the institutional axis is less complex than the institution labeled $I2$: Institution $I1$ could represent a standard posted-offer auction, and $I2$ could represent a posted-offer auction modified to allow for private discounts. Similarly, the simpler structural environment $E1$ on the horizontal axis could represent a box-shaped, single-step supply-and-demand design, and the environment $E2$ label could represent a more complex, multistep design.

Economic processes tend to be complex in both dimensions, as suggested by the location of the "natural economic process" region bounded by the curved, dashed line in the figure. This region contains the points that correspond to the class of processes being studied, for example, retail consumer-goods markets. The boundaries of this region are rarely known with precision.

A good theory is based on simplifying assumptions that discard the relatively inessential complexities and maintain the environmental and institutional elements that critically affect economic outcomes. A salient feature of most retail markets is that sellers are not price takers, as assumed in neoclassical theory, but rather that they post prices on a take-it-or-leave-it basis. The standard Bertrand model incorporates this feature but restricts sellers to choose prices independently at fixed

---

[8] For example, Plott's (1991a) multiple-unit double auction (MUDA) program can coordinate up to twenty double auctions simultaneously. Moreover, satellite communications have made it possible to conduct NovaNet double auctions with participants at multiple locations (e.g., Indiana University and the University of Arizona).

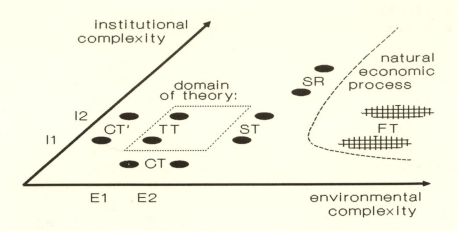

Figure 9.1 Types of Experiments (Key: CT – component test, TT – theory test, ST – stress test, SR – search for empirical regularities, FT – field test)

intervals, as opposed to the possibility of more-or-less continuous price changes in retail markets. This simplicity makes it possible to derive specific predictions about the effects of changes in environmental or institutional variables on economic outcomes such as price. The region in figure 9.1 that is labeled "domain of theory" represents the region over which the key predictions of the theory can be determined. Note that the areas shown in the figure are illustrative; neither the rectangular shape of the domain of the theory, nor the distance between this domain and a natural economic process are of any particular significance.

The most direct *theory test* is an experiment that is conducted on the domain for which the theory provides predictions, for example, the pair of dark points that bracket the TT label in the figure. Each dot represents a particular configuration of institutional and environmental variables and, hence, represents a treatment. An experimental design usually stipulates a comparison of two or more dots that are related in a specific manner. For example, the dots with coordinates (*E1*, *I1*) and (*E1*, *I2*) could correspond to a comparison of posted-offer and double auctions in the same structural environment, *E1*. There are more and less sophisticated theories, and as a general matter, a separate domain would exist for each. In some instances, experiments involve evaluating two points within the domain of a single theory (e.g., evaluating the predictions of neoclassical price theory across posted-offer and double-auction institutions). Other experiments identify a region for which the domains of two competing theories overlap and yield different predictions. For example, both competitive and collusive price predictions might overlap in a posted-offer oligopoly experiment.

Notice that environment *E1* is one of the simplest structural environments that is covered by the dotted-line domain of theory, and in this sense it is a special case. This raises one of the common objections to laboratory experiments, that is, that they are "too simple." But a rejection of the theory in a simple environment on its domain indicates a critical flaw, assuming that the result is not an artifact of faulty procedures or motivation.

Two related types of experiments follow from theory tests. If the predictions of the theory are borne out in a simple setting, it is natural to consider *stress tests*, which examine performance of the theory in more complex cases. For example, a test of *I1* in environment *E2* (dot not shown) would represent a stress test still within the domain of the theory. But as Smith (1989, p. 152) notes: "Testing theories on the domain of their assumptions is sterile unless it is part of a research program concerned with extending the domain of applications of theory to field environments." Ultimately, the investigator will examine performance in environments that are off the domain of the theory, as illustrated by the points labeled ST in the figure.

The relation between theory tests and stress tests is not always unidirectional. Experimentation may actually begin off the domain of theory, at points such as ST. For example, all of the common-value auction experiments discussed in chapter 5 involved subjects whose attitudes toward risk were not controlled, either by a pretest for risk neutrality or by a lottery-ticket inducement procedure. Therefore, the tests were conducted off the domain of the theory for risk-neutral bidders that was used to generate the behavioral predictions. Such tests are incapable of falsifying a theory, since an apparent failure of the theory could be traced to violations of auxiliary assumptions. Failures of this type are often easier to condemn *ex post* than to anticipate *ex ante*, since assumptions that turn out to be critical may have been overlooked or considered unimportant initially. Regardless of results, a follow-up test on the domain of the theory is usually warranted.

When a theory clearly fails on its domain, a *component test* is appropriate. Experiments of this type are designed to identify the cause of a theory failure by isolating some component or assumption of the theory. For example, the dots labeled CT in figure 9.1 involve an environmental comparison (*E1* versus *E2*), but for an institution that is simpler than *I1* or *I2*. This is approximately the sequence of treatments that was used in the structured bargaining experiments: the failure of subjects to demand all of the pie in ultimatum games motivated use of the simpler, dictator-game institution that eliminated the risk of having an offer rejected. Alternatively, one may consider component tests such as CT′, with the same institutions as the theory test TT, but with a simpler environment (e.g., the single-period, "strangers" public-goods experiments that followed the failure to observe quick and complete free-riding behavior in ten-period sequences). The value of a component test hinges on its ability to identify elements of the theory in question that do or do not perform well.[9] The results of such tests can stimulate the development of a modified theory.

Not all experiments are conducted with strict reference to a particular theory. For example, subjects in the Miller and Plott (1985) signaling market experiments knew less about others' preferences and costs than is assumed in most theories of signaling behavior. Another example comes from the Plott and Wilde (1982, p. 76) study of professional versus self diagnosis: "While the experiments were designed with some hypotheses in clear focus, other aspects of the design were intended to 'cast a net' since . . . the theory for the situations we are investigating has not been fully worked out." The observation of empirical regularities can suggest the effects of alternative policies or parameter changes off the domain of any specific theory, and experiments are sometimes conducted to evaluate hypotheses based on observation or intuition. As indicated in chapter 1, this process is sometimes called "searching for empirical regularities." Such a test is represented by the points labeled SR in figure 9.1. Good evaluations of this type are not just "shots in the dark." Even though the experiment does not implement the institution/environment specification of any particular theory, the researcher must have a clear preconception of the expected pattern of data. Although controversial, this type of experiment can lead to new theoretical work, or it can help us understand dynamic adjustment processes that often elude the reach of equilibrium theories. A good example of this type of experiment is the double auction; the competitive tendencies of this institution have stimulated a major theoretical effort to devise models of the price adjustment process, as indicated in chapter 3.

A final type of experiment is a *field test*, where some variable is directly manipulated in an otherwise naturally occurring process. One well-known field test (mentioned in chapter 5) was the use of a competitive, uniform-price auction to sell U.S. Treasury bills in six auctions in the early 1970s. A field experiment is represented by the cross-hatched areas labeled FT in the "natural economic process" region of figure 9.1. The added realism of the field environment has several costs, however. First, field experiments tend to be extremely expensive, both in terms of administration and planning costs and in terms of the real costs of disrupting normal economic activity. Second, many of the key environmental variables may not be well controlled, and these elements may change from the time or location at which one treatment is conducted to the time or location of the other(s). A comparison of the revenues raised in alternate weeks in uniform-price and discriminative Treasury bill auctions, for example, would require an analysis of weekly changes in economic factors that affect interest rates.   To indicate this relatively uncontrolled

---

[9] As a general matter, component tests are often tests within the domain of another (simpler) theory. For example, there is a unique Nash equilibrium prediction for a dictator game.

environmental range, the two treatments labeled FT are represented by elongated, cross-hatched areas.

The Relationship between Experimental and Nonexperimental Methods

Theorists tend to question the usefulness of experiments with designs at ST or FT, but these pairs of points should be thought of as falling in the shadow of the theory.[10] If a theory predicts that prices will be higher with institution *I2* than with *I1* in the (dotted box) theory domain, a contradictory pattern of prices at ST or FT does not contradict the behavioral assumptions of the theory. But such contradictory evidence does indicate that the theory has omitted a critical environmental variable. *Ex post*, such stress tests may be viewed as part of the process of identifying theoretical errors of omission and abstraction.

Some theorists question the interpretation of contradictory experimental evidence obtained even at points in the domain of the theory. This criticism can be paraphrased: "If you had correctly induced all of the elements of the theory, then the evidence would not have been contradictory, since the theory is logically true." This reaction misses the point of a theory test; the points at TT do induce the *structural* (institutional and environmental) assumptions of the theory, but not the *behavioral* assumptions such as noncooperative behavior, and Bayesian information processing. If all behavioral assumptions are "hard-wired" into the experiment, then subjects are forced to make specific decisions.[11] Even though human subjects would be present, the result is a *simulation*, not an experiment. A simulation is essentially a numerical calculation of economic outcomes for specific parameter values. This technique is useful for generating results in models that are too complex to solve analytically.[12] A simulation can provide no information, however, about the accuracy of behavioral assumptions.

Finally, consider the relationship between experiments and econometric studies. In traditional econometric analysis, institutional elements are frequently ignored because natural experiments with institutions are rare, so analysis is collapsed along the dimension of environmental complexity. In addition, econometric analyses require a number of auxiliary assumptions, and many key variables may be measured with error, which can create a situation that is even less controlled than that

---

[10]   The relationship between a test and the domain of a theory is sometimes less clear than suggested by figure 9.1. Theory is often ambiguous as to its domain. For example, the classification of a particular experiment as a stress test or a theory test depends on whether the theory is viewed as encompassing any changes in variables about which it is silent.

[11]   Sometimes it is useful to induce some aspect of behavior (e.g., simulated buyers) in order to get a clearer picture of other aspects of behavior.

[12]   Hoffman, Marsden, and Whinston (1986, 1990) discuss procedures for linking experimental, simulation, and econometric techniques.

indicated by cross-hatched FT points. For this reason, it is rare that a theory is convincingly rejected on the basis of econometric analysis. Another difference when natural data are used is that the observations are not at points matched to control for some factors while allowing others to change; that is, key variables cannot be varied orthogonally. Indeed, econometric techniques were developed to a large extent because, until recently, economists have not thought about doing controlled experiments. There are very sophisticated techniques for dealing with the control and measurement problems that arise in econometric analysis, and the usefulness of standard econometric methods is reflected in the preponderance of empirical studies based on nonlaboratory data. Econometric analysis can also be useful in studying laboratory data, for example, when there are random decision errors. The complementarities between experimental and standard econometric methods bear emphasis, and the researcher should select the method or combination of methods that is best for the particular problem at hand.

In summary, there are a number of distinct types of experiments: Theory tests evaluate performance strictly within the domain of a theory. If the predictions of theory are borne out in simple environments, stress tests can be used to examine the limits of the theory's application. But if the theory fails, simpler component tests can help detect precisely where the breakdowns occur. Experiments also can be conducted to verify expected behavioral regularities, even absent the conditions of a specific theory. This type of search for empirical regularities can assist in the formulation of new theories. In some instances, field tests are conducted within the domain of the natural process. Such tests may be expensive and may involve considerable loss of control, but these disadvantages are sometimes outweighed by the usefulness of making direct observations in the natural environment. Finally, the econometric methods that were developed to interpret observations from rich but uncontrolled natural experiments can also be used in the analysis of laboratory data.

9.4 Experimental Design

The *design* of an experiment specifies the treatment structure (i.e., the relationships between the locations of points in figure 9.1) as well as other factors, such as the order of treatments and the numbers of observations. Design issues become increasingly important as the field matures. Many papers (including our own) have relied on relatively simplistic design and statistical techniques. These procedures have usually been tolerated, perhaps because the major controversies in the experimental literature to date have not revolved around issues of statistical design and data analysis. Instead, many of the methodological controversies have erupted over informational and incentive issues (saliency, inducement of risk attitudes, privacy, anonymity, etc.), and a number of the early experiments involved counterexamples (e.g., a lemons-market outcome is possible). Broader claims, which go beyond establishing the possibility of certain phenomena, require that careful attention be paid to design and data analysis. In addition, some prior attention to design decisions can strengthen claims made on the basis of data generated. Experimental design is discussed in this section, and some issues regarding specific statistical tests are deferred to the sections that follow. In keeping with our general approach to this important (but rather dry) topic, we frame the discussion in terms of particular examples.

Experimental Design and Statistical Models

The optimal design of an experiment depends critically on how the data will be analyzed. As anyone who has had an elementary statistics course will recall, data analysis typically proceeds by constructing a statistical model, consisting of a research hypothesis, a null hypothesis, and a decision rule that determine when the null hypothesis will be rejected. The *research hypothesis* is a specific claim of interest. It is evaluated in light of a *null hypothesis*, that the claim is not observed. The null hypothesis is rejected in favor of the research hypothesis if outcomes fall in a *region of rejection*, or deviate sufficiently from those outcomes expected under the null hypothesis. The statistical model must be precise enough to identify a region of rejection in probabilistic terms, and to allow calculation of the probability that the observed data could have been generated if the null hypothesis were true.

To see the relationship between statistical analysis and experiment design, an example is instructive. Consider a research hypothesis that communications will increase voluntary contributions for the provision of a public good. The null hypothesis is that communications have no effect. Sufficiently high contribution rates will warrant rejection of the null hypothesis. The design of the experiment requires identifying a point of reference for the null hypothesis, behavior under the treatment (communications) condition, and specification of enough observations to reach a conclusion with some confidence. In this case, suppose that each data point is an aggregate contribution level for a different cohort of subjects. One obvious design involves two treatments: a control or *baseline,* where contribution decisions are made in the absence of communications, and a communications treatment where contribution decisions are made following a (nonbinding) discussion of intended contributions. In this design, the research hypothesis can be evaluated by comparing contribution rates with and without communications.

Most experiments should involve control and research treatments. Even "counterexample" experiments, conducted to demonstrate only the possibility of a certain phenomenon, are more appealing if conducted in light of baseline sessions where the phenomenon fails to occur. In this case, the comparison with a relevant baseline can indicate that the phenomenon is a consequence of economically relevant variables, rather than of some peculiar procedural characteristic. For example, a demonstration that it is *possible* to observe cooperation rather than free-riding if there are communications is more convincing if only free-riding has been observed in the absence of communication.

More convincing demonstrations require the observation of a communications effect in multiple, independent trials with different groups of subjects. With multiple observations, a statistical problem arises from the variability that is anticipated in the data. One would expect some differences in contribution levels across cohorts, even if the treatment had no effect, so the average contribution levels would not be equal for the two treatments, except by chance. The problem is to infer whether observed variations in contribution levels are different enough to allow the researcher to conclude that the null hypothesis is false. The nature of this statistical inference problem will be discussed in the following section, with particular emphasis on nonparametric statistics, that is, on statistical models that do not involve specific parametric assumptions about the distribution of observations (such as normality). The point to be made here is that a good design is usually one that provides a clear null hypothesis that contradicts the primary research hypothesis of the experiment. Although pairing of treatments is often desirable, not all experiments must involve a baseline and a single research treatment. We discuss three distinct types of designs in the subsections that follow.

Single-Treatment Designs

The simplest design corresponds to a single point in figure 9.1, that is, there is a single configuration of treatment variables. This single-point design may be appropriate if the only objective is to compare observed behavior with the predictions of a theory. For example, the treatment may be the two-seller posted-offer institution with a market-power design discussed in the appendix to chapter 4. In the mixed-strategy equilibrium, prices are determined randomly, and hence they will vary from period to period. The statistical problem is to infer when the observed prices are so extreme that it is unlikely that they were generated by the theoretical distribution. In a single-point design of this type, the null hypothesis is often the basis of a *goodness-of-fit* test to determine whether the observed data match a theoretical distribution. In the present case, the null hypothesis is that the observed prices are drawn from the theoretical mixed distribution. The alternative (research) hypothesis is diffuse and includes *any* pricing distribution other than that specified under the null hypothesis.

A second example of a single-point design allows some insights into the intuition underlying a goodness-of-fit test, as well as the number of observations necessary to make statistical claims in an experiment. Consider a variant of the symmetric, two-person, battle-of-the-sexes game described in chapter 2, where the mixed-strategy equilibrium involves choosing each decision with probability 1/2 (instead of 1/3 and 2/3). The obvious null hypothesis is that participants randomize with a probability of 1/2 (i.e., observations come from a binomial distribution with a mean of 1/2). The alternative hypothesis is diffuse, that the probability is anything other than 1/2.

Suppose that the experiment consists of only four subjects, each of whom makes a single decision, H or T. To determine payoffs, subjects' decisions are anonymously paired. Under the null hypothesis, each of the four decisions is equally likely to be an H or a T. By numbering the subjects from 1 to 4 and listing their decisions in order, it is seen that there are sixteen possible sample outcomes:

1 way of getting 4 Hs: *HHHH,*

4 ways of getting 3 Hs: *HHHT, HHTH, HTHH, THHH,*

6 ways of getting 2 Hs: *HHTT, HTTH, TTHH, THHT, THTH, HTHT,*

4 ways of getting 1 H: *TTTH, TTHT, THTT, HTTT,*

1 way of getting 0 Hs: *TTTT.*

Each of the sixteen outcomes is equally likely under the null hypothesis and has a probability of 1/16 (=.0625). The null hypothesis is rejected if an outcome deviates sufficiently from an even mix of H and T choices. It is worth emphasizing that there is no sample that would *prove* the null hypothesis to be false: even an extreme sample consisting of four H observations could occur with probability 1/16 when the null is true. Moreover, there are definite limits regarding what may be learned from a given amount of data. For example, suppose that a 95 percent significance level is considered appropriate (e.g., the region of rejection consists of observations that would occur only 5 percent of the time if the null hypothesis were true). Given just four observations, it is impossible to reject a null hypothesis, since even a most extreme observation (such as a 4 H sample) could be observed with a probability of .0625. Both more extreme observations and more intermediate possibilities can be obtained by increasing the sample size.

The result of a goodness-of-fit test should be interpreted carefully. First, notice that a rejection of the null hypothesis only justifies the conclusion that participants do *not* randomize according to the theoretic mixing distribution. This is a fairly weak claim, since a wide variety of alternative distributions may be possible. Stronger claims about the mixed distribution actually used by participants could be made if one were simultaneously unable to reject the hypothesis that subjects were using some specific alternative distribution of interest. Second, a failure to reject the null should not lure the researcher into an acceptance of the randomization hypothesis in this context. For example, it could be that subjects mix with equal probabilities in any symmetric battle-of-the-sexes game, even though theoretical predictions vary with the parameterization. This conjecture would be evaluated with a second design, for example, a symmetric game for which the mixed equilibrium is asymmetric and involves probabilities of 1/3 and 2/3.

In general, single-point designs leave too many unanswered questions. For example, was the failure to reject a theory due to the presence of an unintended nuisance factor (symmetry) that biased behavior toward the theoretical prediction? Or alternatively, was a rejection the result of some procedural bias, i.e., an effect that would show up in a second, diagnostic treatment? These are calibration issues that were discussed in chapter 1. Calibration requires a two-point design of the type to be discussed next.

Paired-Treatment Designs

The use of a matched pair of treatments allows more flexibility. Experiments of this type can be used to evaluate the comparative-statics properties of a theory, or the effect of changing a policy variable. In figure 9.1, for example, the matched pair CT holds the institution constant and varies the environment (e.g., reallocating capacity to create market power in a posted-offer market). Another design that has been encountered repeatedly is one such as pair TT, which holds the environment constant and changes the institution (e.g., a comparison of double and posted-offer auctions in the same asymmetric-rent design). Here the null hypothesis would be that the change in the treatment variable has no effect; that is, the observations obtained under each treatment are independent draws from the same distribution.

Choosing a control treatment to serve as a basis of comparison is an essential and often neglected element in a good design. In a prisoner's-dilemma game, for example, even a high incidence of cooperative behavior after preplay communications would be relatively uninteresting if the incentives to defect were not high enough to generate Nash equilibrium outcomes in baseline sessions without communications. A baseline treatment provides a better basis of comparison if it generates stable behavior.

A simple two-point design allows one to isolate the effect of a single treatment variable, and for this reason it is often most useful. As discussed below, more complicated, multiple-treatment designs are also sometimes warranted. But as a general rule, parsimony is preferred. The temptation is to try to look at the problem from many angles, by changing too many variables in too many ways. This temptation is particularly strong when initial experiments are yielding unanticipated data. The important thing to remember is that only a limited amount can possibly be learned from any given data set, and that nothing very precise is learned if too many things are changed at once.

For example, suppose that the two treatments used in figure 9.1 were $(E1, I1)$ and $(E2, I2)$. In other words, both the institution and the environment were changed at the same time. This design is *incomplete*, since any observed difference in behavior could be attributed either to the institutional or to the environmental alteration. A complete design would isolate the effects of both variables (by investigating behavior in all four combinations of the treatment variables). Although the disadvantages of incomplete designs are obvious, one finds many examples in the literature where an experiment treatment differs from the baseline in more than one dimension. Often the researcher believes that one of the variables changed was inessential, for example, the payment of a $10 fixed fee in one treatment (where large losses were possible) but not in another (where such losses were not possible). The problem is that other researchers may not agree that the secondary change is neutral. A common reaction of statisticians who specialize in experimental design issues is that too many things are changed from one treatment to another in economics experiments.[13] A related criticism is that the changes in supposedly neutral, "nuisance" variables create a large number of distinct treatments, with small numbers of observations per treatment.

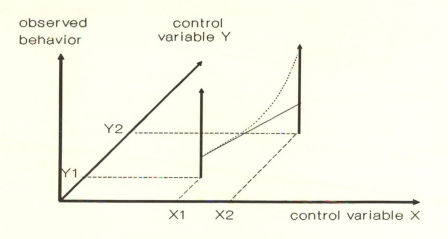

Figure 9.2   A Design to Test H_0 (Solid-Line Prediction) against H_1 (Dotted-Line Prediction)

One cannot, however, mechanically adhere to the rule that an experiment must involve the alteration of only a single variable. In some instances, a change in a theoretical prediction requires the simultaneous manipulation of several variables. Consider a case where there are two variables, X and Y, under the control of the experimenter. The values of these variables determine a point on the floor of figure 9.2. These could be any two variables, environmental and/or institutional. Suppose that there are two alternative theories of interest, and the predicted behavior of these theories is graphed in the vertical dimension. For example, the vertical dimension

---

[13]   See the examples cited in Hinkelmann (1990).

may represent the average price prediction. Then a natural design is to start with a baseline, such as (*X1*, *Y1*), and to change *both* X and Y so that the prediction of one of the theories is unchanged, but the prediction of the other theory is clearly different. This type of design is represented in figure 9.2 by the flat (solid-line) prediction of one theory and the increasing (dotted-line) prediction of the other.

For example, suppose we wish to evaluate the effects of introducing market power when the market supply and demand (and hence the competitive price) remain unchanged. In a posted-offer design used by the authors, this could occur if the capacities of large and small sellers are simultaneously adjusted.[14] In this case, the solid line of uniform height in figure 9.2 represents the competitive price prediction, which does not change, and the dotted line represents the predicted increase in prices that would result from the noncooperative exercise of market power. By finding a treatment where the prediction of one theory is unchanged, we have a natural null hypothesis, and an alternative hypothesis (change in the direction predicted by the second theory).

Complex Designs and Blocking

Finally, multiple-treatment designs are also useful in some instances. One application arises if the treatment variable of interest ranges over a large number of possible values. For example, suppose you suspect that the size of an initial appearance fee affects individual choices in a lottery experiment, and that this variable has ten possible values ($1 to $10). If the theoretical effect of this treatment variable is not known with any precision, then it may be desirable to examine lottery choices under a range of initial payment conditions, and to use standard regression methods to test for a significant relationship.

A multiple-treatment design may also establish the robustness of a particular treatment effect, since a given effect is more persuasive if it appears as expected in two or more different settings. This can be accomplished by using a 2×2 (or higher-order) factorial design. An example from chapter 5 is the wording and selection method used to determine the "controller" in the Coase bargaining experiments. Here, the two wording conditions were the "earns the right" and "is designated" terminology in the instructions, and the two selection conditions were the random-selection and game-of-skill methods. A multicell design provides information about the generality of a treatment-variable effect and can also indicate interaction effects.[15] Under the null hypothesis of no treatment effect, the observations for all treatment cells (four in the 2×2 design) are assumed to be independent draws from

---

[14]   This design is summarized in appendix A4.2.

[15]   In contrast, a simpler design that omits some of the treatment combinations allows one either to lower cost or to obtain more observations per cell.

the same distribution. Analysis of data in light of the null hypothesis allows the simultaneous investigation of multiple research hypotheses; for example, that either the wording of instructions, the selection method, or that some combination of the treatments affects behavior.

The capacity to investigate multiple research questions with a single experiment is alluring. Note, however, that when treatment variables can be changed orthogonally (as in the bargaining game example) the number of treatment cells explodes with increases in the number of treatment dimensions. Consider, for example, a duopoly experiment. If the researcher wishes to evaluate the effects of changing the trading institution from posted-offer to double auction, only two treatment cells are necessary. Expanding the scope of the investigation to include an evaluation of the effects of nonbinding communications requires four ($= 2^2$) cells, one for each possible trading institution/communication combination. A third independent treatment variable, for example, the presence or absence of market power, increases the number of treatment cells to eight ($= 2^3$). For a given research budget, an overly ambitious researcher can quickly reduce the number of observations per treatment cell to the point where nothing of interest can be learned from an experiment.

The problem is compounded by the presence of *nuisance* variables, which may affect behavior but are nevertheless not the primary focus of research. A common example arises when joint research is conducted by authors at two universities. If there is any suspected difference in participants from the two institutions, then it would be a serious mistake to subject all cohorts from one university to one treatment and to subject all cohorts at another to a different treatment. The most straightforward solution to this problem is to use a complete, balanced *block*; that is, to replicate each treatment an equal number of times at each location.[16] Blocking is also useful when experience and/or sequencing effects are possible. As mentioned in chapter 1, it is not possible to block for every nuisance variable, and randomization can be used in such cases. For example, it might be a good idea to select one participant at random to be the monopolist in a double-auction monopoly session, since other arbitrary role-assignment rules (e.g., arrival time at the session or willingness to volunteer) might be correlated with the ability to negotiate high contract prices. The best rule to follow is to block wherever it can be done without great difficulty, and to randomize other possible nuisance variables. The researcher may find this rule to have been a useful one *ex post*, even if it is not clear *ex ante* whether a given nuisance variable would have any effect. The researcher should

---

[16] The term "blocking" arose in the context of agricultural experiments, where the main interest is on a primary treatment variable, such as the type of fertilizer, but many nuisance variables such as soil, exposure, and moisture can affect crop yields. If there are two primary treatment conditions, the solution is to divide the land into pairs of adjacent blocks and randomly to assign one of the treatment conditions to each block.

also be careful to consider possible nuisance variables when designing the structure of treatment variables, since in a complete factorial design, each binary block increases the number of treatment cells by a factor of 2.

When there are a large number of nuisance variables, it is possible to economize on the number of observations per cell by using partial blocking designs, such as Latin square and/or lattice procedures.[17] Such procedures reduce the number of necessary treatment cells, which is particularly useful if the number of nuisance-variable/treatment combinations is large relative to the feasible number of observations. This situation often arises in agricultural economics. For example, suppose that there are four seed treatments of interest, and that there are four locations and four harvesting machines, the effects of which are of secondary interest. Together, there are sixty-four combinations. The nuisance variables (harvesting machine and location) yield a 4×4 table, and a Latin square design specifies a way in which each of the four seed treatments will be used exactly once in each row (machine) and in each column (location). This is a partial block, since only sixteen of the sixty-four combinations are used, but the procedure provides balance in the process of omitting cells. These types of partial blocks have rarely been used in economics experiments, perhaps because few variables are generally recognized as being nuisances. Partial block designs may become more popular, however, if further investigation identifies an increased number of nuisance effects.

Some variables that are ignored by (and hence are irrelevant to) a theory may be regarded as something other than nuisance variables. The noncooperative equilibrium conditions for a particular game (e.g., a single, Pareto-dominated Nash equilibrium in a prisoner's dilemma game) often place relatively few restrictions on the magnitude of payoff variations. Although payoff variations clearly must surpass some perceptual threshold in order for the equilibrium to have any drawing power, the parameter space is often immense, and it is impractical to consider all (or even a wide variety of) possible parameter combinations. As a practical matter, researchers often conduct *pilot* sessions in an effort to identify a baseline combination of parameters that generates the behavior predicted by theory. Subsequently, the effect of a treatment variable (e.g., communications) can be examined relative to performance in the baseline that was established initially. It is important to recognize that the process of conducting this type of pilot session sharply limits the generality of the claims made from a particular experiment: The generality of a treatment effect becomes increasingly suspect as the researcher has to search longer and harder to find an appropriate combination of baseline parameters.[18] Roth (1990) argues persuasively that authors should discuss pilot

---

[17] See Box, Hunter, and Hunter (1978) for a more complete description of Latin square and other partial blocking designs.

[18] A less controversial use of pilot sessions involves conducting preliminary sessions to ensure that there are no unintended procedural problems with a design. This process was discussed in chapter 1.

sessions (perhaps in a footnote) to give the reader some feel for the specificity of the results, and to help develop some intuition regarding what factors affect data patterns. We concur with this observation but add that the search for an appropriate baseline is often an interesting and important research problem in its own right.

In summary, we have considered three broad types of designs: those involving a single treatment, those involving two treatments, and those involving multiple treatments. Single-treatment designs are usually to be avoided, unless previous experiments with similar designs can be used to provide the appropriate calibration. In a great many instances, two-treatment designs are most desirable: these are the most parsimonious designs that allow isolation of the effect of a treatment variable. Richer, multiple-treatment designs allow the examination of the effects of several variables, or of gradations of a single variable. The proliferation of treatments, however, can quickly place too great a strain on a given data set, making it difficult to conclude anything from the experiment.[19]

If multiple treatments are used, it is generally a good idea to design the experiment so that the effects of each treatment can be investigated independently (i.e., to use a complete design). When deciding on the total number of trials to conduct in an experiment, it is important to plan the same number of observations in each cell. When small samples are used, the efficiency of statistical tests involving two or more samples is prominently affected by the number of observations per sample. The appropriate design is often determined in part by the availability of funding. If it appears that research funds will allow generation of only a few observations per cell, then the researcher may want to opt for a simpler design. On the other hand, relatively few observations are necessary to make strong statistical claims if the treatments are expected to exhibit dramatic effects.

9.5 Statistical Analysis of Data from Economics Experiments

Satisfactory design of an experiment calls for identifying the sorts of outcomes that would either support or fail to support the hypotheses of interest. But designs can be further improved by considering the structure of statistical tests that will be used to evaluate the data. Many tests are commonly used in the analysis of experimental results. The appropriate test in each situation depends on (1) the data type (binary, discrete, or continuous); (2) the nature of the sample (matched or independent observations); and (3) the structure of the statistical hypothesis (regarding a single parameter, multiple parameters, or an entire distribution). Good descriptions of these tests are available in a number of standard references, and the reader is strongly encouraged to consult these sources, both when designing

---

[19] Eckel and Johnson (1990) list a number of relevant examples.

experiments and when analyzing results.[20] Some general discussion of statistical tests is useful here as a means of improving experimental design. Since the way an experiment is designed prominently affects the claims that can be made from results, some prior consideration of statistical analysis can dramatically increase what may be learned from an experiment.

Any statistical test is based on specific assumptions about the nature of the data. First, virtually all tests require that the observations be independent draws from a probability distribution. *Parametric* tests also make more restrictive assumptions about the specific functional form of the underlying distributions. For example, a *t* test of the equality of two sample means is based on an assumption that the observations are independent draws from normal distributions. In contrast, *nonparametric* tests are usually based on weaker assumptions, for example, that the observations are independent draws from some (unknown) distribution that generates the assumed data type, for example, realizations of a continuous random variable.

Both parametric and nonparametric tests may be applied to experimental data. For a number of reasons, however, it is useful to focus on nonparametric methods. First, the absence of auxiliary parametric assumptions makes nonparametric methods appealing to experimental researchers, who avoid making other auxiliary assumptions, by directly inducing the parametric structure of the relevant process (e.g., by inducing specific demand and supply functions). It can be risky to presume that errors are normally distributed, particularly when experimental data often appear to be highly nonnormal.[21] A second advantage of nonparametric methods is that they are particularly useful for analyzing *categorical* data that arise when subjects are faced with a finite and limited number of choices, as is often the case with lottery-choice and game experiments. Differences in such outcomes can lack any cardinal meaning, which also makes nonparametric methods appropriate. Finally, most students of economics are already familiar with standard parametric tests but are not as well acquainted with nonparametric tests. The following discussion of nonparametric tests can serve as an introduction to some nonparametric empirical techniques commonly used by experimentalists.[22]

We discuss specific statistical tests in the sections that follow; tests involving single-treatment designs are considered in section 9.6, while tests for designs using two or more treatments are the subject of section 9.7. The remainder of this short

---

[20] See, for example, Box, Hunter, and Hunter (1978), Conover (1980), DeGroot (1975), Siegel (1956), and Siegel and Castellan (1988).

[21] See Friedman (1988). Nonnormality is a common characteristic of data from game and individual-decision experiments as well as from market experiments.

[22] Much of the material in this section is based on the insightful discussion in Siegel (1956), which is updated in Siegel and Castellan (1988). This is the same Siegel who was involved in the classic probability matching and oligopoly experiments discussed in earlier chapters.

section considers issues pertaining to the independence assumption that is common to all statistical tests.

Independence of Observations

Although experimentation in economics is inexpensive relative to the costs of other forms of primary data collection, both the time and financial costs of experimental research can appear quite burdensome to an economist, particularly one more accustomed to theoretical work. Sessions involving a relatively large group of participants have fairly high fixed organization costs (a room must be reserved, participants contacted, a design finalized, etc.) For this reason, experimentalists have every incentive to create as many independent observations per session as possible.

One should be careful, however, not to overstate the number of independent observations obtained from an experiment. As noted in earlier chapters, this is a persistent temptation in complex, multistage experiments. In double auctions, for example, the closing prices in one period can affect prices in the next. Extreme cases of such temporal interdependencies in observations, or autocorrelation, occur in double auctions with overlapping supply-and-demand box designs. As seen in chapter 3, prices tend to stabilize in this design, but at levels that vary a lot from cohort to cohort. In this sense, each multiperiod market provides only a single independent observation, unless appropriate econometric techniques for panel data sets are used. Problems of interdependent observations extend to individual choice experiments. An uncontrolled wealth effect, for example, might influence a sequence of decisions made by a single subject.

One common attempt to resolve this problem involves reporting statistical tests for observations that are not likely to be independent, but then qualifying results with a cautionary footnote. Even this rather straightforward approach is unsatisfactory, however, since the reader must adjust the published probability statements solely on the basis of unguided intuition. A popular alternative is to present results graphically. Although an illustration is no substitute for statistical analysis, a tremendous amount of information can be convincingly communicated in a graph, and for this reason graphical presentations are a powerful tool for the experimentalist. A well-conceived and carefully constructed illustration of results can simultaneously convey relationships between predicted and observed patterns, and troublesome interdependencies among observations. Nevertheless, graphical analysis is generally a fairly imprecise way to deal with problems of nonindependent observations.

It is possible to control for interdependencies among observations through the use of more sophisticated methods of data analysis. For example, valid hypothesis tests involving interdependent observations can be constructed through a careful econometric specification of the interdependencies. Use of estimation techniques for panel data sets would often be appropriate when a cohort of subjects interact over a sequence of time periods. Although this approach may ultimately prove to be very useful, it has the disadvantage of reintroducing auxiliary assumptions (regarding the structure of error terms in a variance-covariance matrix) into analysis of results.

Finally, interdependencies among observations may be avoided altogether by use of an appropriate design. Gaining this advantage becomes difficult, however, if the researcher finds it necessary to generate multiple observations from each participant in a cohort, for example, to facilitate learning. Nevertheless, it is sometimes possible for a researcher to generate multiple observations with a single cohort, while simultaneously maintaining the independence of these observations. In some two-person games, for example, a rather elaborate mechanism for rotating participant pairs after each decision can be used: the idea is to rotate participants in such a manner that each person in a cohort meets each of the others only once, and never meets anyone who has any direct or indirect contact with a previous partner. This procedure has the property of "no contagion," since it is impossible for subjects to engage in any kind of signaling across games.[23] If understood and believed by subjects, it will induce a series of single-period games. But even this procedure cannot guarantee independence. For example, suppose that the behavior of one subject is so unusual and bizarre that it affects the subsequent behavior of all partners (e.g., rejecting equal splits in an ultimatum game). Even though the aberrant subject cannot hope to gain from his or her behavior, the subject will be paired with many (perhaps all) of the others and can color the decisions of every other subject in the cohort. In this case, it may not be appropriate to treat latter-period observations as being independent; in the final periods, most or all of the observations may be biased by the deviant subject.

To summarize, in many experiments the number of independent observations may be smaller than it first seems. This problem can be pervasive, and it potentially applies to individual-choice and game experiments as well as to market experiments. We are not advocating "throwing data away"; much of the data from period to period might be used with an appropriate econometric analysis of the error structure. We are only warning about the potential biases of using more data than really exist (at least in the sense of independent observations being used to make precise statements about the probability that the data could have been generated if the null hypothesis were true). Without trivializing the costs of experimentation, its bears repeating that a methodologically pure (but costly) solution is always available; one can merely increase the planned number of observations.

---

[23] This no-contagion scheme was first used by Cooper et al. (1991).

9.6 Statistical Tests: Single-Treatment Designs

Let us now put the problems of independence aside and consider the kinds of tests one would use in different types of experimental designs. Many of the standard nonparametric tests are easiest to explain in a one-sample context, but these same tests can be adapted to multiple-treatment designs. For this reason, it is useful to begin by introducing several one-sample tests that are appropriate for the investigation of single-treatment designs. In such instances, the issue is whether the data are consistent with some point prediction or distribution that is specified by a theory.

The Binomial Test

When the underlying process generates binary outcomes (falling into one of two possible categories) a *binomial test* is appropriate. For example, the discussion of the frequency of H and L decisions in the battle-of-the-sexes game described in the last section was an informal presentation of a binomial test. The null hypothesis was that H and L outcomes were equally likely, as implied by the mixed-strategy equilibrium. The test described was essentially one of deciding how likely it is that the observed number of "heads" could have come from four flips of a fair coin. If this probability is less than some prespecified level of significance, the null hypothesis (of equal probabilities) is rejected. Such a test may be applied to any binary process. In particular, the probabilities need not be 1/2. For example, binomial tests could be used to analyze the mixed equilibrium for the battle-of-the-sexes game in chapter 2, which involved probabilities of 1/3 and 2/3.

In general, let the probability of one of the outcomes, say H, be denoted by p, so the probability of the other outcome is $1 - p$. If N independent outcomes are obtained, the probability of observing exactly X of the H outcomes is

(9.1)   *Probability of X successes in N trials* $= \dfrac{N!}{X!(N-X)!} \, p^X(1-p)^{N-X},$

where the "!" notation denotes a factorial calculation: $N! = (N)(N–1)(N–2) \ldots 1$, and by definition, $0! = 1$. For example, if the probability of an H is .5, then (9.1) implies that the probability of observing four of the H decisions in four trials is 1/16, calculated as $(4!/4!0!)(1/2)^4(1/2)^0 = (1/2)^4 = 1/16$. This calculation based on (9.1) is consistent with the previous section's observation that $HHHH$ is one of sixteen outcomes that are equally likely under the null hypothesis.

In statistical analysis, the null hypothesis is evaluated by calculating the value of a *test statistic*, or a summary measure of the observed data. The actual value of the test statistic is compared with the (sampling) distribution of possible values that applies if the null hypothesis were true. The null hypothesis is rejected if the test statistic falls outside a range of "reasonable" outcomes, or falls in a *region of rejection*. The region of rejection is defined by a predetermined *significance level*, α, which is the probability of observing a particular outcome (or something more extreme) when the null hypothesis is true. Smaller values of α imply more conservative tests, as they correspond to a smaller chance of incorrectly rejecting the null hypothesis. For the binomial test, the null hypothesis is that observations are taken from a binary process where one of the outcomes (a "success") occurs with underlying probability p. The test statistic is the number of successes (X) out of total trials, N. The null hypothesis is rejected if the probability of X (or something even more extreme) when the null is true is below the significance level.

The attentive reader may have wondered about the parenthetical "or something more extreme" phrase in the last sentence; an example will clarify its meaning. Suppose that we observe six individuals who make independent, lottery-choice decisions, between a relatively safe lottery, S, and a riskier lottery, R. Each lottery has the same expected value, and the null hypothesis is one of indifference, that is, that the probability of S being chosen is 1/2. Suppose, for purposes of discussion, that the alternative hypothesis is that the probability that S is chosen is not equal to 1/2, that is, this probability is either greater or less than 1/2. Before observing the data, the researcher would specify a significance level, say $\alpha = .05$, which identifies how unlikely an observed test statistic must be in order to reject the null hypothesis. Given this significance level and the sample size, $N = 6$, we can determine the region of rejection. To do this we use (9.1) and the probability of 1/2 specified by the null hypothesis to calculate the probabilities of observing exactly zero S choices, one S choice, . . . six S choices. These probabilities are shown in figure 9.3. For example, the probability of observing no S choice (no "heads" in six tosses of a fair coin) is 1/64, but an outcome that is just as extreme as this in the other direction is to observe six S choices, which also has a probability of 1/64. Therefore, the probability of observing an outcome as extreme as zero or six S choices is 2/64 (approximately .03) when the direction of the alternative hypothesis is unspecified. In other words, about 3 percent of the density is contained in the shaded "tails" of the distribution in figure 9.3, far from the number, 3, that is the expected value under the null hypothesis. An observed outcome of six S choices would allow the null hypothesis to be rejected at a 5 percent level of significance, but not at a 1 percent level. Since the alternative hypothesis does not specify the direction of the deviation from the null hypothesis, the region of rejection has two shaded tails in figure 9.3, and therefore this is called a *two-tailed test*.

Suppose instead that the null hypothesis is that the probability of S being chosen is less than 1/2, and the alternative hypothesis is that the safe lottery S is more likely to be chosen, that is, $p \geq 1/2$. And suppose further that we observe six S choices. Since the alternative hypothesis specifies a direction, a *one-tailed test* is appropriate. For a predetermined significance level of $\alpha = .05$, the region of rejection would be the shaded, right-hand tail of figure 9.3, and the observation of

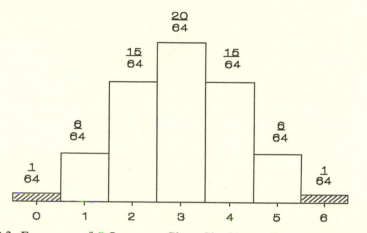

Figure 9.3 Frequency of S Outcomes Given Six Observations, and $p_S = 1/2$

six S choices would enable us to reject the null hypothesis.[24] If only five S choices had been observed, the null hypothesis could not be rejected, since the probability of obtaining an outcome at least as extreme as five S choices is 7/64 (calculated as the probability of six S choices, 1/64, plus the probability of five S choices, 6/64). Notice that a one-tailed test allows rejection of a given null hypothesis at an increased level of confidence relative to a two-tailed test. For example, given six S choices and a significance level of $\alpha = .02$, the null hypothesis that S and R choices were equally likely could be rejected with a one-tailed test, but not with a two-tailed test. Importantly, however, the researcher does *not* have the freedom to choose among tests merely for the purpose of affecting confidence levels. Rather, the appropriate test is dictated a priori by the kind of question being investigated.

The χ^2 Test

In many experiments there are more than two types of outcomes, and in such cases the binomial test does not apply. This subsection considers goodness-of-fit tests when data are categorical (as would be the case in a game involving a limited number of decisions). One useful test for this situation is the χ^2 (*chi-square*) test. It is instructive to motivate this test in the context of a particular experiment. Consider the coordination game experiment reported by Van Huyck, Battalio, and Beil (1990), discussed in chapter 2.[25] The game involves fourteen to sixteen

---

[24] Given the discreteness of outcomes in this example, the same shaded region of rejection would apply for any significance level between $\alpha = .015$ (1/64) and $\alpha = .085$ (7/64).

[25] The reader may wish to review the discussion of table 2.7 and figure 2.5.

subjects and is organized as follows: In each stage, the subjects independently choose a numbered decision, from 1 to 7. After all decisions are made, the minimum of the decisions is announced. Payoffs for each player are determined by his or her own decision, and the announced minimum.

As mentioned in chapter 2, there are seven Nash equilibria in the stage game, one for every common decision (everyone chooses decision 1, everyone chooses decision 2, etc.). These Nash equilibria are Pareto ranked, with each higher-numbered equilibrium yielding a higher payoff. A minimum equilibrium payoff of 70 per player is generated for a common decision of 1, and payoffs increase as the common decision increases, up to a maximum of 130 per player, for a decision of 7. But payoffs are also structured so that risks increase with the decision numbers: the payoff corresponding to equilibrium decision 1 is riskless, since it is realized regardless of what the others do. Each higher-numbered equilibrium is riskier in the sense that a participant is exposed to a progressively lower minimum payoff in the event that someone deviates and selects a lower-numbered decision. Thus, this design pits two equilibrium-selection criteria against each other: Pareto dominance and risk avoidance.

Van Huyck, Battalio, and Beil generated a sizable data set in this design. Their experiment consisted of seven sessions. In each session a cohort of fourteen to sixteen participants made a sequence of decisions in ten stage games. Given that each cohort made a sequence of decisions, however, individual observations are clearly not independent. For simplicity, let us confine our attention to the data for the first stage of each session, since there is no reason to believe that these decisions are not independent. The aggregate data for the first-stage choices are tabulated in the top row of table 9.1. As should be clear from the table, aggregating across the seven sessions, a total of 107 participants made a decision in the first stage.

A one-treatment version of this experiment could be administered to evaluate the distribution of observed responses relative to responses predicted under either the Pareto-dominance or risk-avoidance equilibrium-selection criterion, or in light of the hypothesis that neither criterion organizes behavior. For purposes of illustration, let us evaluate performance using the latter hypothesis, that is, the null hypothesis that all seven noncooperative equilibrium decisions are equally likely.

The χ^2 test is based on a comparison of the difference between the observed number of outcomes in each category i, O_i, and the number expected under the null hypothesis, E_i. The intuition underlying the test is that if the distribution of responses differs enough from that posited by the null, then the null hypothesis must be rejected. In this case the 107 decisions are equally divided among the seven decision categories under the null hypothesis, so there would be $107/7 = 15.3$ observations in each category, as shown in the second row of the table. It is apparent that the observed numbers of decisions in the top row are quite different from the expected numbers of decisions in the second row. The test statistic, denoted χ^2, is calculated by squaring each difference, dividing by the expected

Table 9.1 A χ^2 Test with Data from a Coordination Game

	Decision							
	1	2	3	4	5	6	7	Total
Observed # of observations (O_i)	2	5	5	18	34	10	33	107
Expected # of observations ($E_i = 107/7$)	15.3	15.3	15.3	15.3	15.3	15.3	15.3	
$(O_i - E_i)^2/E_i$	11.6	6.9	6.9	.5	22.9	1.8	20.5	71.1

Source: Van Huyck, Battalio, and Beil (1990).

number of observations in each category, E_i, and summing over categories:

$$(9.2) \qquad \chi^2 = \sum_i \frac{(O_i - E_i)^2}{E_i}.$$

This test statistic has an approximate chi-square distribution with a number of degrees of freedom that equals the number of categories minus one.[26] The null hypothesis will be rejected if there are large differences between the observed and predicted numbers of observations in each cell: for example, if the value of the test statistic is sufficiently large. Notice also that the sum of squared differences tends to increase with the number of observations, so to maintain a constant significance level, α, the critical value of the test statistic (that defines the region of rejection) will increase as the sample size increases.

Once the test statistic has been calculated, statistical tables available in standard references can be used to determine the region of rejection for any desired level of significance. In our example, there are seven categories, so there are six degrees of freedom. Using a significance level of 0.01, the entry turns out to be 16.81. For the data in table 9.1, the bottom row shows the terms that, when summed, yield a χ^2 statistic of 71.1. Since the chi-square table entry of 16.81 is less than the calculated test statistic of 71.1, the hypothesis of equal probabilities can be rejected.

---

[26] This value for degrees of freedom follows because knowing the total number of observations and the number in all but one of the cells uniquely determines the number in the remaining cell.

The χ^2 test is quite popular, as it is simple to calculate and can be used to analyze data in any number of categories. The test does have some limitations, however. In particular, it should not be used with small sample sizes and with small expected numbers of observations per cell.[27] One way to increase the number of observations per cell is to combine cells, but doing this ignores some of the structure of the data, which makes the test less sensitive. For example, suppose that sixty of the observations had been decision 1 and that forty-seven of the observations had been decision 7. As would be expected, this extreme pattern would yield a much larger χ^2 test statistic, so the null hypothesis would be rejected again. But suppose the researcher had divided decisions into two categories: decisions 1–4 and decisions 5–7. Under the null hypothesis that each of the seven decisions is equally likely, one would expect $(4/7)107 = 61.1$ observations in the low-decision category and $(3/7)107 = 45.9$ observations in the high-decision category. These expected numbers of observations are about the same as the observed numbers of observations (60 and 47), and it is straightforward to show that the null hypothesis would not be rejected at any conventional level of significance. This hypothetical example illustrates the danger of combining cells; a null hypothesis that would be clearly rejected before the combination of cells is not rejected after the combination.

The χ^2 test can also be used to analyze numerical data (such as pricing decisions in a market experiment) by dividing observations into a predetermined number of categories. For the reasons just explained, however, condensing outcomes that occur along a fine grid into a coarser grid necessarily fails to exploit some of the available information. We consider next a one-sample test for numerical data that uses all of the available information.

The Kolmogorov-Smirnov Test

When data are numerical, an alternative approach is to compare observed and predicted values of the cumulative distribution function. The *Kolmogorov-Smirnov one-sample test* is a powerful goodness-of-fit test that takes this approach. This test has been used, for example, to compare the observed distribution of prices with the theoretical distribution that results from a mixed-strategy equilibrium created by the exercise of market power.[28] In this context, the χ^2 test would lose information, since there are many more possible prices than actual price observations, and working with broad classes of prices ($0.00–$0.50, $0.50–$1.00, etc.) will make the test less sensitive.

---

[27] In particular, it is usually recommended that a sample be large enough so that the expected frequencies are at least five for a high proportion of the cells. For details, see some of the statistics books referenced previously.

[28] See Davis and Holt (1991) or Kruse et al. (1990).

The Kolmogorov-Smirnov test is based on the intuition that, if the observed distribution of experimental outcomes is close to the theoretical distribution, then the cumulative frequency distribution of the observed data (e.g., prices) should be close to the cumulative distribution, $F(X)$, that is specified by the null hypothesis.[29] For example, suppose there are N independent observations, and for each X, let $S(X)$ represent the fraction of observations that are less than or equal to X. Then the distance between the theoretical and observed distributions at any given value of X can be measured by the absolute value of $F(X) - S(X)$. The test statistic is the value D that maximizes this difference:

$$(9.3) \qquad D = maximum \, | \, F(X) - S(X) \, | \, .$$

A high value of D indicates that the observed distribution differs from the theoretical distribution. The null hypothesis is rejected if D exceeds a critical value determined by the sample size, N, and the level of significance, α. One can use a Kolmogorov-Smirnov table for a one-sample test (found in standard statistics books) to determine the region of rejection.

A simple example will illustrate the calculations involved. Let us reconsider the null hypothesis that the data in the top row of table 9.1 were generated by a distribution with equal probabilities for each decision. These data are categorical, but it is appropriate to speak of a cumulative distribution of responses, since the order of decisions makes a difference (e.g., a 1 decision involves a lower payoff than a 2 decision, etc.). Since there are seven decisions, the null implies that 1/7 of the outcomes will be at each level, so the density is about 0.14 at each decision. The discrepancy between the theoretical and observed cumulative frequencies must be calculated at all points, so that the largest discrepancy can be found, as required by the formula in (9.3).

This situation is illustrated in figure 9.4. In the figure, possible choices (denoted X) are enumerated along the horizontal axis, while the cumulative distributions of outcomes are plotted along the vertical axis. The thin horizontal lines represent different values for the distribution function specified by the null hypothesis, $F(X)$, while the thick horizontal lines represent the observed distribution of responses, $S(X)$. The test statistic is derived from inspection of the difference between the observed and predicted distribution functions, illustrated by the vertical dotted lines at each integer value. The null hypothesis is rejected if the maximum of these differences exceeds a critical value.

---

[29] The theoretical distribution is assumed to be continuous, but the test can be applied if it is discrete. In this case, the test is conservative; if the null hypothesis is rejected on the basis of a statistical table that assumes a continuous distribution, then the probability that the null is true is even less than the significance level provided by the table (Siegel, 1956, p. 59; Siegel and Castellan, 1988, pp. 71–72). See Conover (1980, pp. 350–352) for a discussion of the calculation of exact critical levels when the theoretical distribution is discrete and the sample size is small.

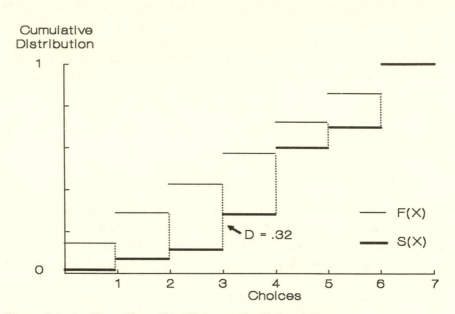

Figure 9.4 An Illustration of the Kolmogorov-Smirnov Test

In this case, the largest difference occurs at decision 3: there are twelve observations that were less than or equal to 3, for an empirical cumulative frequency of 12/107, which is about .11. The theoretical cumulative frequency is that 3/7 (or about .43) of the decisions will be at or below 3, which yields a test statistic $D = .43 - .11 = .32$. For $N = 107$ and a significance level of 0.01, the critical cutoff value turns out to be only .16, so the null hypothesis (that the observed data came from a theoretical distribution having equal probabilities) can be rejected.

Summary

Goodness-of-fit tests may be constructed to compare the relationship between predicted and observed performance for a variety of types of data. The binomial test, which reveals the basic intuition behind many nonparametric tests, is used to compare observed and exogenously specified proportions with binary data. The χ^2 one-sample test is used to compare expected and observed numbers of observations in a discrete number of categories. The Kolmogorov-Smirnov test is used to compare theoretical and observed cumulative frequency distributions. Depending on the application, still other tests may be useful. In particular, the researcher in some instances may wish to determine if data were randomly generated, or if they followed some pattern. For example, consider a posted-offer design where the unique noncooperative equilibrium prediction involved a randomization of pricing decisions by sellers. Suppose that the prices actually selected by sellers followed a saw-tooth pattern of increases followed by decreases. Even if price postings closely matched a predicted distribution, the serial correlation in observations would be inconsistent with the null hypothesis that the prices are independent draws from that distribution. A *runs test* can be used to detect such serial dependence. Runs tests are especially useful in evaluating whether subjects are using mixed strategies or whether forecast errors are random.

9.7   Statistical Tests: Designs Involving Two or More Treatments

When there are two treatments, a natural test is based on the null hypothesis that data from one treatment constitute a sample from the same distribution that produced the data from the other treatment. In this way, it is possible to answer questions such as whether one treatment is *different from* another (two-tailed test), or whether one policy treatment is *better than* another (one-tailed test). These tests are called two-sample tests, with one sample for each treatment. The appropriate statistical test depends on whether the samples are "related" (each subject or cohort is subjected to both treatments in a block design) or are independent (a separate group of subjects or cohorts for each treatment).

Of course, there are many factors other than the specific treatment condition that may cause economic behavior to differ from one sample to another. For example, some groups of people in oligopoly experiments are simply more cooperative than others. A natural way to control for intergroup differences is to use the same people for each treatment, so that each subject or cohort serves as its own control. In some instances, however, other design considerations such as time or wealth effects make it either impractical or unadvisable to present a given cohort with two treatments. Thus, the decision of whether to use related or independent samples depends on the context. We proceed by discussing tests for related samples and independent samples, respectively.

Two Related Samples: Binary or Categorical Data

The simplest tests for two related samples are those for data that are binary in the sense that outcomes fall, or can be regarded as falling, into one of two possible classes. Consider, for example, the coordination game by Van Huyck, Battalio, and Beil (1990), and suppose we are interested in investigating whether or not there is a learning effect. The research hypothesis is that decisions in the final stage differ from those in the initial stage, and the null hypothesis is that there is no difference. We have seven observations in the first stage and seven matched observations in the final stage. Observations will be classified as H if the average decision for all subjects in a given cohort and stage exceeds 3.5, and L otherwise. This yields a "before-and-after" design that is commonly used to evaluate a new treatment in medical experiments. It turns out that each of the seven cohorts is classified as H in the first stage and as L in the final stage, as indicated by the numbers in parentheses in table 9.2.

Table 9.2 A Table for a Matched-Sample, Before-and-After Test

| | | After (stage 10) | |
		L (low)	H (high)
Before	L (low)	LL (0)	LH (0)
(stage 1)	H (high)	HL (7)	HH (0)

The data in this table look decisive, and indeed the authors did not even bother to provide any statistical test to support the conclusion that decision numbers decreased dramatically over time. But for purposes of discussion, consider more formally the decisiveness of the data. Each of the cells in the table is labeled with a pair of italicized letters that represents the pattern of decisions. The number of outcomes in each cell is printed in parentheses to the right of the identification pattern. A natural null hypothesis for a two-tailed test is that, of the observations that did change (from H to L or from L to H), the changes in each direction are equally likely. Thus, $(HL + LH)/2$ is the expected number in both the HL and the LH cells. In testing the null hypothesis expressed in this way, we will ignore the observations with no change, that is, any LL and HH outcome.[30]

One simple procedure is to use a binomial test. The probability that an observed change will be in the downward direction (HL) is .5 under the null hypothesis, as is the probability that an observed change will be in the upward direction (LH). Under this null hypothesis, equation (9.1) can be used to show that the probability of obtaining an outcome *at least as extreme* as that actually observed is the probability of no successes (no LH) in seven trials, plus the probability of seven successes in seven trials, which is $1/2^7 + 1/2^7 = 2/128 = .016$. So the null of equal probabilities can be rejected at a significance level of .02 in a two-tailed test.[31]

An alternative procedure for testing the same null hypothesis is to conduct a χ^2 test for these two cells. For the numbers in parentheses, the expected frequency

---

[30] A different null hypothesis, that the probability of an L is the same, before and after, would require a calculation that uses information from the HH and LL cells.

[31] The binomial test is sometimes called a *sign test* when it is used in this related-samples, before-and-after context. See any standard statistical reference, e.g., DeGroot (1975), for a discussion of procedural details and of using a normal approximation to the binomial when the sample size is large.

for each of these cells is (7+0)/2 = 3.5, so the χ^2 statistic is calculated $(7 - 3.5)^2/3.5 + (0 - 3.5)^2/3.5 = 3.5 + 3.5 = 7$. Since we are ignoring the cells with no change (*HH* and *LL*), there are only two cells, and hence only one degree of freedom. In this case, a χ^2 statistic of 7 turns out to be just significant at the .01 level, so the null hypothesis can be rejected at approximately the same level that was obtained in the binomial test.[32] The use of the χ^2 test here is only illustrative, since the number of observations expected per cell falls below the recommended level (of 5). When the number of observations per cell is sufficiently large, a related-samples χ^2 test with more than two decision categories can be used.

Table 9.3 Choice Patterns for Paired Safe and Risky Lotteries

		Second paired choice	
		S2	R2
First paired choice	S1	7 (expected utility)	15 (fanning in)
	R1	1 (fanning out)	11 (expected utility)

Source: Battalio, Kagel, and Jiranyakul (1990, table 3, set 2.1).

Tests with related samples are particularly valuable when investigating patterns of violations of expected utility theory, since a violation is clearest if it is the same individual who is making the inconsistent choices.[33] Recall from chapter 8 that a standard setup is for subjects to choose between safe and risky lotteries, say *S1* and *R1*, and then choose between a second pair of safe and risky lotteries, *S2* and *R2*. The paired lotteries are structured so that an observed choice of both safe lotteries or both risky lotteries is consistent with expected utility theory, but a choice of a safe lottery in one pair and a risky lottery in the other is not. (Switching implies that the indifference curves in the probability triangle are not parallel.) Table 9.3 shows

---

[32] Actually, the test results are even closer than they appear, since it is advisable to make a small correction for continuity in this particular χ^2 test, which would reduce the level of significance of the test result to 0.02, that is, the null can be rejected at a significance of .02 instead of .01. This variant of the χ^2 test, with matched samples and only two possible outcomes, is sometimes called a *McNemar test*, and a correction for continuity is used since a continuous χ^2 distribution is being used to approximate the sampling distribution of a test statistic derived from discrete, binary data. See Siegel (1956, p. 64) for details and references.

[33] If the samples are not related, the inconsistency must be inferred by comparing the decisions of the two independent groups, on the assumption that they are drawn from the same population. An example of this approach is provided in table 9.4.

data from one experiment of this type. The experiment involved thirty-four subjects who each made two paired lottery choices with financial incentives.[34] About half of the subjects made a pair of decisions that were consistent with expected utility maximization, while the remaining half made inconsistent choices.

Consider first the question of whether there is a pattern in the inconsistent choices. Use as a null hypothesis the claim that if there is a deviation, the probability of $(R1, S2)$ is 1/2, as is the probability of $(R2, S1)$. Notice that only one of sixteen made the $(R1, S2)$ choice pattern (that is consistent with fanning out of indifference curves in the probability triangle). This is equivalent to determining the probability of having a fair coin yield an outcome at least as extreme as one head in sixteen tosses. This probability is less than .01, so the null can be rejected.

A related issue arises if we evaluate the hypothesis that individual decisions conform to expected utility theory. Clearly, the data in table 9.3 do not support this hypothesis, since nearly half of the subjects made inconsistent decisions. The researcher faces a more delicate evaluation problem, however, if only a small number of inconsistencies are observed, since in a strict sense expected utility theory allows no inconsistencies. One approach is to consider the implications of allowing the possibility of decision errors. For example, Conlisk (1989) assumes that a fraction, p, of the population are people who prefer the safe lotteries $S1$ and $S2$, and that the remaining fraction, $1 - p$, prefer the risky lotteries. Each subject, however, errs in making a decision with a probability ε, and therefore the preferred lottery is selected with probability $1 - \varepsilon$. Under these assumptions, the $(S1, R2)$ pattern is observed if either (1) the selected subject prefers safe lotteries and makes one correct choice and one incorrect choice, or (2) the person selected prefers the risky lotteries and makes one incorrect choice and one correct choice. Contingency 1 occurs with probability $(p)(1 - \varepsilon)(\varepsilon)$, and contingency 2 occurs with probability $(1 - p)(\varepsilon)(1 - \varepsilon)$. The sum of these probabilities is $\varepsilon(1 - \varepsilon)$. Similarly, the probability of observing the other mixed-choice outcome, $(R1, S2)$, is calculated as the sum $(1 - p)(1 - \varepsilon)(\varepsilon) + (p)(\varepsilon)(1 - \varepsilon)$, which also equals $\varepsilon(1 - \varepsilon)$. The implication of this decision-error model is that there should be no systematic pattern in deviations. Thus, the research hypothesis that individuals conform to expected utility theory could be evaluated against the null hypothesis that the two mixed patterns, $(R1, S2)$ and $(S1, R2)$, are equally likely. In fact, this is the null hypothesis that was used above.

An additional advantage of modeling the decision-error process is that an estimate of the error rate (ε) could be generated if the theory is not rejected. Such

---

[34] Lottery $S1$ is (−$20, .74; −$14, .2; $0, .06), lottery $R1$ is (−$20, .88; $0, .12), lottery $S2$ is (−$14, .9; $0, .1), and $R2$ is (−$20, .63; $0, .37).

an estimate could be useful, for example, to determine whether estimates of error rates are related to the saliency of incentives.[35]

Two Related Samples: Numerical Data

In many experiments, decisions are not categorical. If observations are measured on a numerical scale so that the *differences* between observations can be ordered, then more powerful tests can be applied. Such tests apply to a wide class of economic data. It is generally meaningful, for example, to talk of differences between the price, quantity, and efficiency outcomes observed in most market experiments.[36]

Table 9.4 Average Prices over the Final Fifteen Periods of Each Treatment

Session	1	2	3	4	5	6	Total
Power treatment	411	468	430	455	397	441 (351)	
No-power treatment	338	307	341	410	310	396	
Difference	+73	+161	+89	+45	+87	+45 (−45)	+500 (+410)
Difference rank	+3	+6	+5	+1.5	+4	+1.5 (−1.5)	+21 (+18)

Source: Davis and Holt (1991).

The topics to be discussed in this subsection are best introduced in the context of an example. Table 9.4 summarizes pricing decisions for a posted-offer experiment designed to assess the effects of market power (see figure 4.11 and related discussion). The experiment consisted of six sessions, as enumerated along the top row of the table. In each session, a group of five sellers made pricing

---

[35] Berg and Dickhaut (1990) make an estimate of this type in the context of a preference-reversal experiment.

[36] But it is not always meaningful to compare differences in measurements. Suppose, for example, a researcher wished to measure the degree of market concentration by calculating the Herfindahl-Hirshman Index (HHI, defined as the sum of squared market shares times 10,000), on the basis of output quantities for a number of laboratory market sessions. While it is possible to say that an HHI of 3,000 is greater than a Herfindahl of 2,500, it is probably not possible to say that the difference between these HHI values is greater than the difference between HHI values of 1,600 and 1,200.

decisions for sixty periods; thirty periods in a market-power treatment, and thirty periods in a no-power treatment. This is a related-samples design, since the same cohorts were exposed to both treatments. The sequence order was blocked, with the no-power treatment coming first in three sessions and last in three sessions. Average price decisions for the last fifteen periods of each thirty-period treatment sequence are used as observations, as shown in the "no-power treatment" and "power treatment" rows in the top part of the table. Each cohort is used to produce only one independent observation for each treatment, since it is unlikely that individual choices within a market would be independent.

A cursory inspection of the data suggests a treatment effect. As indicated by "+" signs in the "difference" row, prices were higher in the market-power treatment in every session. The most intuitive way to analyze the data in the top part of table 9.4 is to apply the binomial test: Consider the research hypothesis that market power increases prices, in light of the null hypothesis that the treatment (power or no power) has no effect. Under the null hypothesis, the probability of a price increase just equals the probability of a price decrease. Thus, the observation of six consecutive price increases is equal to the probability of generating six consecutive heads in a coin toss, or $1/64$ ($= 2^6$), and the null hypothesis could be rejected at a high confidence level, say $\alpha = .05$. (Note that a one-tailed test is appropriate here since the research hypothesis was unidirectional, that market power would raise prices, holding the shapes of supply and demand constant.)

But suppose that the price observations in session 6 had come out differently, with an average price for the power treatment of 351 instead of 441, as shown by the number in parentheses in the session 6 column of table 9.4. In this case power decreases prices by 45 cents. The binomial test would no longer allow rejection of the null hypothesis at $\alpha = .05$, since the probability of observing an outcome as extreme as five price increases and one price decrease rises to $7/64$ (see figure 9.3). Notice, however, that the binomial test ignores information about the magnitude of price changes. The probability that the null hypothesis is true remains $7/64$ regardless of whether the single price decrease was 45 cents or, say, five times as large. Intuitively, the larger of these differences constitutes a more important violation, and a more powerful test would incorporate this information.

One method of including information about magnitudes is the *randomization test*, which is sometimes called the *permutation test*. The underlying intuition for this test is the same as for the binomial test: under the null hypothesis, average prices are no greater in the power design, so each of the six average price pairs came out the way that they did solely because of the random way in which subjects were selected for each particular treatment sequence. A reversed treatment order for the cohort in session 6, for example, would have an average price of 441 for the no-power treatment and only 396 for the power treatment. The null hypothesis is rejected if it is sufficiently unlikely that a particular series of differences is observed. The randomization test incorporates information about the differences by using as a test statistic the *sum* (rather than the signs) of differences. As indicated in the right-most column in table 9.4, the differences sum to 500. The question, then, is the following: Given the six differences observed in table 9.4, what is the likelihood of observing the same or a more extreme sum of differences? In the case of table 9.4, the answer is the same as in the binomial test, since the most extreme observation was generated. The price pairs could randomly fall in one of 2^6 (=64) possible ways, and only one combination yields the total of 500, so the probability is 1/64.

The added power of the randomization test becomes evident if we suppose that a price decrease was observed in one of the sessions. For example, suppose that in session 6 the average price in the power treatment was 351 rather than 441 (as indicated by the number in the power treatment row printed in parenthesis). Then the sum of differences falls to 410. There are three ways to generate a total at least as high as 410: (a) the observed pattern; (b) a reversal of the 351 and 396 in session 6; or (c) a reversal in session 6, combined with a reversal of the 455 and 410 observations in session 4. Thus, under the randomization test, the probability that the null hypothesis is true if a price decrease was observed in session 6 is 3/64 (= .047), so the null can be rejected at a confidence level of α = .05. Compare this to the 7/64 probability generated by applying the binomial test to the identical situation, as described above.

The randomization test is computationally burdensome with large sample sizes, since it is very tedious to consider all of the possible ways in which the paired observations could be interchanged, and how each of these reversals would affect the test statistic (the sum of the differences). A simpler but slightly less powerful test would be to apply the randomization test to the ranked observations.[37] The procedure is to rank the differences, and then to sign the ranks. For example, the smallest difference in absolute value gets a signed rank of 1 if the difference is positive, and a signed rank of –1 if the difference is negative. The second largest rank in absolute value gets an appropriately signed rank of 2, and so on. The ranks of the differences are listed in the bottom row of table 9.4 (please ignore the numbers in parentheses for now). As is clear from the bottom row, ranks are averaged in the case of ties. Since market power generated a price increase in each session, all ranks are positive, and the test statistic is 21. There are sixty-four possible outcomes, and since 21 represents the highest possible sum of ranks, the probability that the null hypothesis is true is 1/64 (as was true for either the binomial or the randomization test).

---

[37] A test based on ranks is also appropriate if the numerical differences for matched pairs of observations can be ranked, but not meaningfully added. This kind of data is rare in economics but common in medical research, when the researcher is making subjective measurements; for example, it is possible to say that one patient improved more than another, but it is not possible to say that the improvement was 1.5 times as great.

The extra precision of a test based on ranks over the binomial test can be demonstrated by once again assuming that in session 6 prices fell to 351 in the power treatment. With a price decrease in session 6, the sum of ranks falls to 18. There are three ways to generate a total at least as high as 18, so as with the randomization test applied to differences, the probability of observing this outcome if the null hypothesis is true is 3/64 (compared to a 7/64 probability generated by application of the binomial test to the same situation).

One very standard test using ranked data is the *Wilcoxon matched-pairs signed-ranks test*, which is essentially the application of the randomization test to ranked differences.[38] The Wilcoxon test is easier to apply than a randomization test on ranks, however, since the critical values are available in standard sources, and it is unnecessary for the researcher to calculate the combinations of difference values. The Wilcoxon test statistic is the smaller of two sums of ranks: the sum of the negative ranks and the sum of the positive ranks. If the treatment has no effect and there is only exogenous noise, one would expect some negative differences and some positive differences, but these should not be too unbalanced, and the two sums should be approximately equal. The null hypothesis is rejected if the differences are sufficiently unbalanced: either the sum of the negative signed ranks or the sum of the positive signed ranks is too small in absolute value.

As an example, use the data in table 9.4 but assume that prices in the power treatment dropped to 351 in session 6. Then the sum of the positive ranks is 19.5, and the sum of negative ranks is –1.5. Thus, the test statistic 1.5. Referring to a standard statistical table, it can be verified that the critical value is 2 for $N = 6$ (the number of observations less the number of treatment differences that equal 0), indicating that the null hypothesis may be rejected at $\alpha = .05$ (one-tailed test).

The Wilcoxon test is less precise than the randomization test based on numerical values, since it ignores absolute magnitudes of differences by implicitly imposing a specific relationship on the differences (e.g., the differences are linearly related, with the greatest difference being six times larger than the smallest). Differences in test results tend to be small, however, and the Wilcoxon test is an efficient alternative.

Two Independent Samples: Classificatory Data

All of the two-sample tests discussed thus far involve related samples. Sometimes, however, it is simply impractical to subject the same participants to two or more treatments. Learning in each treatment condition may require all of the time available in a session, and the researcher may decide not to invite the same subjects back for a second session with a different treatment, either because of the difficulty

---

[38] Siegel (1956, p. 91).

of getting everyone back or because of the risk that subjects will talk to each other about the experiment in the meantime. Another problem with using two treatments on the same subjects is that wealth effects or learning effects from the first treatment may bias behavior in the second. In such cases, it is advisable to use two independent samples, one for each treatment, and to balance the design by making the same number of observations in each case.

When the data from two independent samples fall into discrete outcome categories, a simple χ^2 test can be used. Even if the data are not inherently binary, one can calculate the overall median for both samples and categorize the observations into those that are above and below the median in terms of the observed decision. Then the χ^2 test can be applied to the 2×2 table, where the columns are the two samples and the rows are the above-median and below-median categories.[39]

Table 9.5 A Comparison of Lottery Choices, With and Without the Random-Selection Method

	lottery choice		
	S8	R8	total
subjects with random-selection procedure	39 44	41 36	80
subjects with single financially motivated choice	27 22	13 18	40
total	66	54	120

Source: Starmer and Sugden (1991, table 2).

For concreteness, consider table 9.5.[40] This experiment, which was discussed in section 8.4, involved a comparison of (1) the lottery choices of forty subjects who made a single financially motivated choice between two lotteries, S8 and R8, and (2) the choices of eighty subjects who made two choices, one between lotteries S8 and R8 and another between a second pair of lotteries (S9 and R9), with only one of these choices selected ex post at random to determine cash payoffs. Of the eighty

---

[39] This test, of course, is less precise than a test that uses the full structure of the data. But in some instances, the loss in precision may be small.

[40] This table presents the numbers of decisions that were used to calculate the percentages in the left column of table 8.1. The lotteries used in the experiment are described in section 8.4.

subjects in the random-selection treatment, the numbers who chose each lottery are shown by the boldfaced entries in the top cells of the table, and the corresponding boldfaced numbers for the forty subjects who only made a single choice are shown in the bottom two cells. There was no overlap of participants in the eighty-subject and the forty-subject samples. The issue to be considered here is whether the random-selection method (of controlling for wealth effects) has an effect on individuals' choices. Therefore, the null hypothesis is that there is no difference between the two groups of subjects in terms of the proportion who choose the safe lottery $S8$.

To conduct a χ^2 test, we need to calculate the expected numbers for each cell, that is, the E_i for the formula in equation (9.2). Unlike the single-sample test described above, these expected numbers are not specified by a theoretical distribution. Rather, the question is whether the behavior in one group is like that in another. For this reason, expected responses for each group must be estimated from the aggregate decisions made by the combined group. First consider the upper-left cell. Since 80 of the 120 subjects are in the top row, and 66 of the 120 are in the left column, the predicted *fraction* who are in the top-left cell is the product of 80/120 and 66/120. Multiplying this fraction by the total number, 120, gives the predicted number in the upper-left cell, which is 44, as shown by the italicized entry. The predicted numbers in the other cells are calculated similarly. Thus we have four cells, with four observed numbers (the O_i), and four expected numbers (the E_i). The χ^2 test statistic is calculated as in (9.2): $(39 - 44)^2/44 + (27 - 22)^2/22 + (41 - 36)^2/36 + (13 - 18)^2/18$, which equals about 3.79. Given $\alpha = .05$, this just fails to be significant for a two-tailed test with 1 degree of freedom (= [number of rows − 1][number of columns − 1]).[41]

Other tests may be appropriate, depending on the type of data and the numbers of observations. In particular, when the data are binary, there is a fairly straightforward formula for calculating the exact probabilities for each outcome with two independent samples. This formula parallels use of the binomial formula for calculating exact probabilities for binary data from two related samples. The method, known as the *Fisher Exact Probability test*, is somewhat more complicated than the binomial formula, due to the increased number of outcome combinations possible when samples are independent. The test involves calculating a ratio of factorial expressions for each of the 4 entries in the 2×2 table. Exact probability tests of this type are useful when the sample size is small enough so that the calculations are not too tedious. The exact probability test is especially useful when the sample sizes are so small that the expected frequencies for a χ^2 test are not high

---

[41] Starmer and Sugden (1991) report a significance of .051 for a two-tailed test. This description is admittedly sketchy. In particular, we have not discussed corrections for continuity or the sample sizes needed for the χ^2 test to be advisable.

enough. With small sample sizes, significance levels for the exact probability test can be found in standard statistical tables.[42]

Two Independent Samples: Numerical Data

As was the case for related samples, when the data from independent samples are numerically ordered (e.g., differences between observations are meaningful), more powerful tests are available. The intuition underlying these tests is similar to that for related samples, and the tests can be based on differences in summed observations for each treatment, or on an analysis of ranked data.

The relationship between tests for independent and related samples can be seen by considering again data from the market power experiment in table 9.4. Suppose that the six no-power price averages and the six power price averages listed in the table were drawn from twelve *separate* subject cohorts. A randomization (or permutation) test could once again be used to evaluate the research hypothesis that market power increases prices. As with the test for related samples, the null hypothesis is that any differential effect of the treatments is entirely due to the random assignment treatments of subject cohorts, and the test statistic is the sum of differences (in this case 500). The null hypothesis is rejected if the number of ways that the sum of observed differences (or something more extreme) could be generated when the null is true is sufficiently small.

But the independence of observations increases the computational burden of the randomization test. Rather than calculating the number of ways that the a total at least as high as 500 could be generated from $2^6 = 64$ possible combinations of six price pairs, it is necessary is to count the ways that this total could have been

---

[42] The test proceeds under the null hypothesis that the probability of each decision is the same for each sample. For sample I, let the numbers of observed decisions be A and B for decisions 1 and 2, respectively, and for sample II, let the numbers of observed decisions be C and D:

	Decision 1	Decision 2	Total
Sample I	A	B	$A + B$
Sample II	C	D	$C + D$
Total	$A + C$	$B + D$	N

Therefore, there are $(A + B)$ people in sample I and $(C + D)$ people in sample II. If N denotes the total number in both samples, then the exact probability of this outcome is:

$$p = \frac{(A + B)! \, (C + D)! \, (A + C)! \, (B + D)!}{N! \, A! \, B! \, C! \, D!}.$$

This formula can be used to calculate the sum of probabilities of all of the outcomes that are at least as extreme as the outcome observed.

generated by dividing the twelve price observations into two groups of six. There are $12!/(6!6!) = 924$ possible combinations.

The calculations are straightforward in this case, due to the strength of the treatment effect: only one other combination of the prices yields a difference sum as large as 500, since only one of the prices in the no-power treatment exceeds the lowest price in the power treatment (the 410 observation for the no-power treatment exceeds the 397 observation for the power treatment).[43] Calculations become exceedingly tedious with less extreme outcomes, and it is instructive to illustrate the appropriate calculations in the context of a simpler example. Consider the hypothetical data for a two-treatment market experiment, with three control sessions and three separate treatment sessions listed in the top two rows of table 9.6. Assume that the data were collected in six independent sessions, and that the unit of observation is the average price in each session.

Suppose we are interested in evaluating the research hypothesis that the treatment increases prices, against the null hypothesis that the treatment has no effect. Using the randomization test, the test statistic is the sum of the price differences observed in the treatment condition minus the sum under the control condition $(600 + 400 + 200 - 500 - 300 - 100 = 300)$. There are a total of $6!/(3!3!) = 20$ possible ways that these six independent observations could have been arisen in two sets of three. Seven of these outcomes involve differences at least as extreme as 300: treatment condition results of $(600, 500, 400)$, $(600, 500, 300)$, $(600, 400, 300)$, $(600, 500, 200)$, $(600, 500, 100)$, $(500, 400, 300)$, and the $(600, 400, 200)$ outcome that was observed. Thus, the probability of observing an outcome as extreme as 300 if the null hypothesis is true is $7/20 = .35$, and one would be remiss to reject the null at any conventional confidence level.

The randomization test is attractive when sample sizes are small, since the calculations are not too tedious, and exact probabilities are generated. With larger sample sizes, the most common procedure is to use a *Mann-Whitney test*, which is based on the rank order of the observations. As is evident from the treatment and control rows of table 9.6, data in this example are essentially ranked; data ranks are derived by dividing each price observation by 100. Again, suppose we evaluate the research hypothesis that the treatment increases prices against the null hypothesis of no treatment effect (a one-tailed test). The first step is to rank the observations in order from lowest to highest, and to label each observation as a treatment or control (indicated by the C or T subscripts); 100_C, 200_T, 300_C, 400_T, 500_C, 600_T. The treatment observations have ranks 2, 4, and 6. The test statistic, denoted U, is the

[43] Thus, given independent samples, the probability that the null hypothesis is true is 2/924. Notice that in this case the precision of the randomization test would increase if the observations had been independent. This result occurs (and independent samples are preferable) when the treatment effect is expected to dominate cohort effects.

Table 9.6 Hypothetical Data for a Market Experiment

	Values			Totals
Treatment	200	400	600	
Control	100	300	500	
Differences	100	100	100	300
(Session)	(1)	(2)	(3)	

sum of treatment ranks, so $U = 12$. If the null hypothesis were true, we would expect the sum of the ranks for the treatment observations to be about the same as the sum of the ranks for the control observations. The null hypothesis can be rejected if the sum of treatment ranks is too extreme (e.g., too large for a one-tailed test). Standard tables provide the probability of obtaining a U value as extreme as the one observed, and for the example being considered (with two samples of size 3), this probability is .35 for a one-tailed test, which is the same as that obtained from the randomization test. These results are equivalent because the Mann-Whitney test is essentially a randomization test that uses the rank of each observation instead of the observation itself. When the numerical outcomes are not linearly related to the ranks, the two tests are not equivalent, and the randomization test is more sensitive for additive data, since it takes into account the numerical values of the observations, not just the ranks.

The hypothetical data in table 9.6 can also be used to illustrate the potential importance of using related rather than independent samples (a point that was also made in chapter 1 with reference to figure 1.3). When there is a lot of variation across subjects or cohorts, this variation tends to hide a treatment effect if independent samples are used. Suppose that the data in the three columns of table 9.6 had been generated with three sessions (three cohorts), each of which were subjected to the control and the treatment. The session numbers are shown in parenthesis, in the bottom row. In this related samples case, the most extreme pattern of observations was generated, since the treatment generated a higher price in each session. Using the randomization test for related samples, the test statistic is the sum of the differences generated in each session, or 300. There are $2^3 = 8$ possible ways to generate outcomes via switches of the paired control and treatment values, and of these, the observed outcome is the one that maximizes the sum of the differences. Under the null hypothesis, the probability of getting an outcome this extreme is, therefore, 1/8, which is considerably less than the 7/20 probability calculated under the assumption that the samples were independent. This example illustrates the advantage of using matched samples and blocking when there are large uncontrolled differences between individuals or cohorts. Using related samples becomes less important as the uncontrolled differences between cohorts diminish. For example, the use of related or independent samples would have made less difference if each control outcome was less than the lowest treatment outcome in table 9.6.

Other tests may be used to evaluate independent samples. In particular, one can evaluate the null hypothesis that the two samples came from the same population by comparing the cumulative distributions of observations for the two samples. Recall how the sample cumulative distribution, $S(X)$, was calculated for the one-sample Kolmogorov-Smirnov test, that is, by finding the fraction of sample observations that are less than or equal to each sample outcome, X. By doing this for both independent samples, we obtain two distribution functions, which can be arrayed or plotted as in figure 9.4 to find the maximum difference. For a two-tailed test, the test statistic is the D value calculated in equation (9.3), where $F(X)$ and $S(X)$ represent the cumulative distributions of the two independent samples. This test is sensitive to any difference in the distributions of the two samples.[44] Given the sizes of the two samples, the region of rejection for the desired level of significance can be determined from a table for the *Kolmogorov-Smirnov two-sample* test.[45]

Multiple-Sample Tests

Other tests are needed when the data come from K independent samples ($K > 2$). For example, binary decisions may be collected for a battle-of-the-sexes game in which subjects are paired with a sequence of different partners. The proportion of each decision may vary from session (cohort) to session, and the researcher may wish to pool the data. Pooling would not be appropriate if the data did not come from the same distribution. Hence the null hypothesis is that the K samples all came from the same distribution. With classificatory data, an appropriate nonparametric test is a χ^2 test. The intuition is that the observed proportions of decisions of each type should be the same for each sample, and the test statistic is based on the sum of the squared differences between the observed and predicted numbers of observations in each cell, normalized by dividing by the predicted

---

[44] It is also possible to consider a one-tailed test, for the case in which the alternative hypothesis is that one of the distributions is stochastically greater than another, for example, that prices are higher under one treatment than under another. In this case, D is the maximum difference in the predicted direction.

[45] An alternative to comparing the observed cumulative distributions is to compare other properties of the distributions of sample observations. The Epps-Singleton (1986) test is based on empirical moment generating functions, for example. Forsythe et al. (1988) report that this test has desirable properties in comparing distributions of decisions in simple bargaining experiments.

number in that cell. When these differences are large, the test statistic is large, and standard tables can be used to decide when the null hypothesis can be rejected at any particular level of significance.

As with two-sample tests, there are also multiple-sample tests based on the ranks of observations, and the appropriate test depends on whether the samples are related (e.g., the *Friedman two-way analysis of variance*) or independent (e.g,. the *Kruskal-Wallis one-way analysis of variance*). For example, the Kruskal-Wallis test is appropriate for evaluating the hypothesis that the medians of K independent samples are equal, against the general alternative that they are not equal. Sometimes the researcher is able to specify a specific a priori ordering of the predicted effects of a series of treatments. For example, a series of K market structures might have an increasing sequence of noncooperative equilibrium price predictions. In this case, the null hypothesis is still that the medians for the K independent samples are equal, but the alternative hypothesis specifies a specific ranking of the medians for the K treatments. A useful test for this purpose is the *Jonckheere test for ordered alternatives*.[46]

Summary

The nonparametric tests discussed in this section are summarized in table 9.7, by data type and by design. The K-sample tests are omitted from the table as they were mentioned only briefly. Even for the tests that were discussed, details are admittedly sketchy, and a researcher should consult a statistics text prior to applying any of them. The point, however, is that statistical conclusions can be sensitive both to the kind of data generated and to the way the experiment is designed. As a general rule, it is a good idea to exploit as much of the available information as possible: Power is lost by using arbitrary classes that lose the detail of more continuous data. Designs using related samples can greatly improve the claims that can be made regarding a given hypothesis, particularly when there is a lot of variation across cohorts. In contrast, designs using independent samples are useful when time constraints make it impossible to subject the same cohort to multiple treatments, when the observations from one treatment would be seriously biased by an earlier treatment, or when the treatment effect is expected to dominate cohort effects and biases.

All of above discussion has been framed in terms of nonparametric tests. These tests usefully avoid assumptions regarding the underlying structure of the data. Moreover, they often provide exact probabilities for critical values, even when the sample sizes are very small. There are, however, parametric analogues to the tests described above, and in some instances standard parametric procedures may be more

---

[46] This test is described in Siegel and Castellan (1988, pp. 216–222).

Table 9.7 Some Standard Nonparametric Tests

	Classificatory Data	Numerical Data
One-sample design	binomial, χ^2	Kolmogorov-Smirnov
Two-sample design (related samples)	binomial, χ^2	Randomization, Wilcoxon
Two-sample design (independent samples)	Fisher Exact Probability, χ^2	Randomization, Mann-Whitney, Kolmogorov-Smirnov

useful. Parametric tests are based on stronger assumptions, and these tests are more powerful if the assumptions are reasonable. Parametric tests, particularly regression and analysis of variance, can also be useful for analyzing complex interactions between multiple treatments and/or blocks.

9.8 Conclusion: Toward a More Experimental Science

What have we learned from the application of experimental methods to economic problems? For one thing, experimental research has taught us a lot about how questions should be posed (Plott, 1991b). Most economic theories are general in the sense that they apply to real economic processes with real incentives that are found in the laboratory. The simplest test is to implement the structural assumptions of the theory in the laboratory, and to observe whether the theory's predictions are accurate, that is, whether the behavioral assumptions are good approximations. This approach can usually be improved. Sometimes it is possible to design a critical experiment in which two theories yield identical predictions in a control treatment and yield different predictions in a research treatment. If the theories predict well in the control, calibration has been achieved, and then superior performance by one of the theories in the research treatment is especially convincing. Finding good experimental designs, however, is more difficult than it may first appear. By definition, theories are abstractions from reality, and there will be components of many experimental implementations that are simply not addressed by a theory. Other implications of a behavioral theory may not be observable. Thus, more indirect questions sometimes have to be asked, questions of the sort: Do changes in a variable relevant to a particular theory or proposed policy tend to generate predicted changes in behavior, and do changes in variables omitted from the theoretical model also have significant effects? But theory tests are often suggestive: Affirmative results call for even more extreme tests that stress the theory by going off the assumed domain of the theory or policy proposal. Negative results call for modification, perhaps by incorporating previously ignored variables. "Component tests" can provide evidence that is useful in constructing new theories. In this way, experiments are becoming integrated into an interactive scientific process of modeling and testing. Experiments are also providing the key data needed to evaluate proposed policies and to design and test new trading institutions.

Second, we have learned a lot about how to design and conduct experiments. Much of this knowledge about experimental techniques has been developed in isolation, with little crossover from other experimental sciences.[47] Related disciplines are less concerned with the effects of incentives, and for this reason, a literature on the magnitude and saliency of rewards was (and to some extent, still is) needed in economics. Other variables, such as risk postures, wealth, expectations, altruism, and envy, also need to be considered, and our ability to control or measure these variables has perhaps been oversold. But through practice and error, we have better learned to exploit the control that allows data to be generated from settings that conform to or stress the structural assumptions of theory. This advantage grows more valuable as the institution-specific theories become more complex, especially in terms of message and information structures. Careful laboratory testing may provide the discipline that prevents this new theory from drowning in its own complexity.

To paraphrase Charles Plott (1991b), three decades of laboratory research have provided both the justification and the motivation for converting economics to a more experimental science. The justification is twofold: First, laboratory data indicate that models that attract economists are not outlandish, despite the abstract, mathematical ways in which they are packaged. Neoclassical price theory has a wide range of application in the laboratory, the predictions of game theory are sometimes surprisingly accurate, and individual subjects are often quite "rational" in the economists' definition of the term. Second, these theories are far from complete; there are many surprises in laboratory markets, games, and individual decision problems. If the successes provide economists with a sense of confidence, the failures should temper us with a sense of humility. Economists are a long way from a unified understanding of economic behavior.

In this humility lies the motivation for experimental research. Anomalies exist, and theoretically irrelevant factors matter. Theories must be modified and tested. Tests may be indirect, results may not be definitive, and progress may be slow. This prognosis is troublesome only to the extent that the reader expects the world to

---

[47] One notable exception is the impact of the psychologist, Sidney Siegel, through his classic papers, his books on oligopoly and bargaining (with Fouraker), and his excellent book on nonparametric statistics that stimulated many of our observations in the previous sections.

conform with all the precision of mathematical logic in the models that pervade the journals and textbooks. In short, we believe that economics is well on its way to becoming an experimental science, and we do not anticipate ever finding complete consistency between theory and behavior. Indeed, a willingness to seek out inconsistencies is useful, as Smith (1989, p. 168) notes: "if one wants to gain a greater understanding of economic phenomena, the most productive knowledge-building attitude is to be skeptical of both the theory and the evidence. This is likely to cause you to seek improvements in both the theory and the methods of testing."

REFERENCES

Banks, Jeffrey S., Colin F. Camerer, and David Porter (1990) "An Experimental Analysis of Nash Refinements in Signaling Games," forthcoming in *Journal of Games and Economic Behavior*.

Battalio, Raymond C., John Kagel, and Komain Jiranyakul (1990) "Testing between Alternative Models of Choice under Uncertainty: Some Initial Results," *Journal of Risk and Uncertainty*, 3, 25–50.

Box, George E. P., William G. Hunter, and J. Stuart Hunter (1978) *Statistics for Experimenters*. New York: John Wiley.

Berg, Joyce E., and John W. Dickhaut (1990) "Preference Reversals: Incentives Do Matter," working paper, Graduate School of Business, University of Chicago.

Brandts, Jordi, and Charles A. Holt (1991) "An Experimental Test of Equilibrium Dominance in Signaling Games," forthcoming in *American Economic Review*.

Camerer, Colin F., and Keith Weigelt (1988) "Experimental Tests of a Sequential Equilibrium Reputation Model," *Econometrica*, 56, 1–36.

Conlisk, John (1989) "Three Variants on the Allais Example," *American Economic Review*, 79, 392–407.

Conover, W. J. (1980) *Practical Nonparametric Statistics*, 2d ed. New York: John Wiley.

Cooper, Russell W., Douglas V. DeJong, Robert Forsythe, and Thomas W. Ross (1991) "Cooperation without Reputation," working paper, University of Iowa.

Davis, Douglas, and Charles A. Holt (1990) "Equilibrium Cooperation in Three-Person Choice-of-Partner Games," working paper, Virginia Commonwealth University.

———— (1991) "Capacity Asymmetries, Market Power, and Mergers in Laboratory Markets with Posted Prices," working paper, Virginia Commonwealth University.

DeGroot, Morris H. (1975) *Probability and Statistics*. Reading, Mass.: Addision Wesley.

Eckel, Catherine C., and Cathleen A. Johnson (1990) "Statistical Analysis and the Design of Economics Experiments," working paper, Virginia Polytechnic Institute and State University.

Epps, Thomas W., and Kenneth J. Singleton (1986) "An Omnibus Test for the Two-Sample Problem Using the Empirical Characteristic Function," *Journal of Statistics and Computer Simulation, 26*, 177–203.

Forsythe, Robert, Joel L. Horowitz, N. E. Savin, and Martin Sefton (1988) "Replicability, Fairness, and Pay in Experiments with Simple Bargaining Games," Working Paper 88–30, University of Iowa, forthcoming in *Games and Economic Behavior*.

Fouraker, Lawrence E., and Sidney Siegel (1963) *Bargaining Behavior*. New York: McGraw Hill.

Friedman, Daniel (1988) "Experimental Methods: Points of Consensus and Points of Contention," working paper, University of California, Santa Cruz.

Hinkelmann, Klaus (1990) "Experimental Design: The Perspective of a Statistician," working paper, Virginia Polytechnic Institute and State University.

Hoffman, Elizabeth, J. Marsden, and A. Whinston (1986) "Using Different Economic Data Forms," *Journal of Behavioral Economics, 15*, 67–84.

———— (1990) "Laboratory Experiments and Computer Simulation: An Introduction to the Use of Experimental and Process Model Data in Economic Analysis," in J. Kagel and L. Green, eds., *Advances in Behavioral Economics*, vol. 2. Norwood, N.J.: Ablex Publishing.

Holt, Charles A. (1985) "An Experimental Test of the Consistent-Conjectures Hypothesis," *American Economic Review, 75*, 314–325.

Isaac, R. Mark, David Schmidtz, and James M. Walker (1989) "The Assurance Problem in a Laboratory Market," *Public Choice, 62*, 217–236.

Kruse, Jamie, Steven Rassenti, Stanley S. Reynolds, and Vernon L. Smith (1990) "Bertrand–Edgeworth Competition in Experimental Markets," working paper, University of Arizona.

Mead, R. (1988) *The Design of Experiments*. Cambridge: Cambridge University Press.

Miller, Ross M., and Charles R. Plott (1985) "Product Quality Signaling in Experimental Markets," *Econometrica, 53*, 837–872.

Plott, Charles R. (1991a) "A Computerized Laboratory Market System and Research Support Systems for the Multiple Unit Double Auction," California Institute of Technology, Social Science Working Paper 783.

————— (1991b) "Will Economics Become an Experimental Science?" *Southern Economic Journal*, *57*, 901–919.

Plott, Charles R., and Vernon L. Smith (1978) "An Experimental Examination of Two Exchange Institutions," *Review of Economic Studies*, *45*, 133–153.

Plott, Charles R., and Louis Wilde (1982) "Professional Diagnosis vs. Self-Diagnosis: An Experimental Examination of Some Special Features of Markets with Uncertainty," in V. L. Smith, ed., *Research in Experimental Economics*, vol. 2. Greenwich, Conn.: JAI Press, 63–112.

Roth, Alvin E. (1990) "Lets Keep the Con out of Experimental Econ.: A Methodological Note," working paper, University of Pittsburgh.

Siegel, Sidney (1956) *Nonparametric Statistics for the Behavioral Sciences*. New York: McGraw-Hill.

Siegel, Sidney, and N. John Castellan (1988) *Nonparametric Statistics for the Behavioral Sciences*, 2d ed. New York: McGraw-Hill.

Smith, Vernon L. (1989) "Theory, Experiment and Economics," *Journal of Economic Perspectives*, *3*(1), 151–169.

Starmer, Chris, and Robert Sugden (1991) "Does the Random-Lottery Incentive System Elicit True Preferences? An Experimental Investigation," *American Economic Review*, *81*, 971–978.

Van Huyck, John B., Raymond C. Battalio, and Richard O. Beil (1990) "Tacit Coordination Games, Strategic Uncertainty and Coordination Failure," *American Economic Review*, *80*, 234–248.

Williams, Fred E. (1973) "The Effect of Market Organization on Competitive Equilibrium: The Multi-unit Case," *Review of Economic Studies, 40,* 97–113.

Index

absolute risk aversion, 83
adaptive expectations, 463
adjustment to equilibrium, 404
advance production, in posted-offer
    auctions, 218
adverse selection, 384
advertising, effects of, 387–389
agenda, effects of, 360–363
Akerlof, G., 381, 384, 390, 432
Alger, D., 196, 197, 236
Allais, M., 9, 91, 436, 444–445,
    448–449, 453, 455–456,
    471–472, 476, 485, 500–501,
    509, 554
Allais paradox, 9, 444
alternating-offer games, 269–275
altruism, 92, 263–264, 267, 269,
    305, 328, 553
Ames, R., 325–326, 378
anchor-and-adjust model, 470
Anderson, S., 294, 421–422, 432
Andreoni, J., 327–328, 376
Andrews, J., 89, 123
Ang, J., 450, 500
animal experiments, 445–446
anomalies, 509
Arizona Stock Exchange, 303
Ashenfelter, O., 278, 312
asset markets, 162–167
    as predictor of elections, 422–426
    behavioral uncertainty, 406
    information aggregation, 418–421
    perfect-foresight equilibrium, 410

asset markets (*Cont.*)
    with asymmetric information, 406
    with state uncertainty and insider
        information, 413–421
    with type uncertainty, 406–413
    "naïve" equilibrium, 409
asymmetric information, 381
asymmetries, in voluntary-
        contributions mechanism, 336
auctions
    bid auction, 42
    clearinghouse auction, 39
    competitive auction, 38, 459
    continuous bid\offer auction, 303–304
    discriminative auction, 38, 277
    double Dutch auction, 300–302
    Dutch auction, 42, 277, 280
    English auction, 42, 277–278
    offer auction, 42
    oral double auction, 46, 55
    posted-bid auction, 38, 174
    sealed bid\offer auction, 299
    uniform-price auctions, 277, 298, 303
    types of, 36
    See also common value auction,
        double auction, first-price auction,
        posted-offer auction
axiomatic game theory, 244

backtracking, 297
backward induction, 102–104
Bagnoli, M., 338, 342, 376
Ball, S., 17, 63, 294, 308, 312